Anonymous

Logan's Indianapolis Directory

Anonymous

Logan's Indianapolis Directory

ISBN/EAN: 9783337291433

Printed in Europe, USA, Canada, Australia, Japan

Cover: Foto ©Andreas Hilbeck / pixelio.de

More available books at **www.hansebooks.com**

J. M. LOSIE & CO.,

SOLE MANUFACTURERS OF

KRIEGHOFF'S PATENT

U. S. SPRING BEDS,

—FOR—

THIS CITY AND STATE,

No. 83 East Market St.,

INDIANAPOLIS, INDIANA.

Something New--A Novelty

MUST BE SEEN TO BE APPRECIATED!

A few of the Advantages of this Bed over all others are: Simplicity of Construction, not liable to get out of repair, and if it does can be repaired with less expense and trouble than any other Spring Bed in use. Being made entirely of metal, there is no harbor for VERMIN, and for CLEANLINESS cannot be surpassed. And as a first-class Spring Bed it can be procured at one-third less COST than any other now in use, and can be manufactured to fit any size of bedstead.

Orders From the TRADE

SUPPLIED PROMPTLY AT A HANDSOME DISCOUNT.

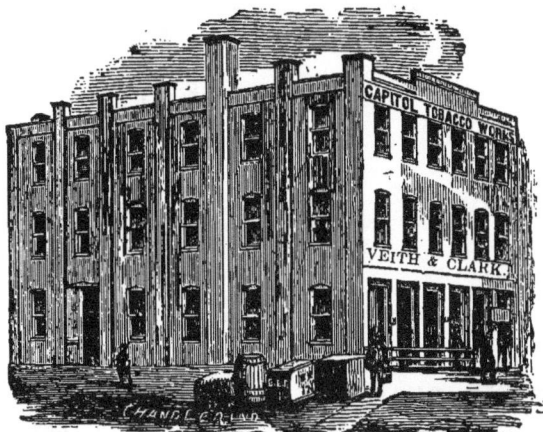

LOGAN'S

INDIANAPOLIS DIRECTORY,

EMBRACING AN

ALPHABETICAL LIST OF CITIZENS NAMES,

GATHERED AND COMPILED EXPRESSLY FOR THIS WORK.

Also, a carefuly written and closely detailed

HISTORY OF INDIANAPOLIS,

FROM 1818 TO 1868,

BY IGNATIUS BROWN,

GIVING A RECORD OF EVENTS OF THE CITY FROM ITS FIRST SETTLEMENT; ITS MERCANTILE, MANUFACTURING, POLITICAL AND SOCIAL PROGRESS, DEVELOPMENT, PRESENT IM-PORTANCE AND FUTURE PROSPECTS. WITH A COMPLETE MUNICIPAL RECORD, GIVING NAMES OF CHURCHES, INSTITUTIONS, COL-LEGES, SOCIETIES AND ASSOCIATIONS, &c., &c.

FOR THE YEAR COMMENCING JULY 1, 1868.

PRICE $3.50.

LOGAN & CO.

COMPILERS, PRINTERS AND PUBLISHERS.

OFFICE,

No. 16½ East Washington Street.

1868.

(A)

A. L. LOGAN,

PUBLISHER

Western Commercial Review and Railroad Journal: also, Directories of
Indianapolis, Columbus, Springfield, Terre Haute,
and other Cities.

INDIANAPOLIS, INDIANA.

CONTENTS.

INDEX TO ADVERTISEMENTS.

CONSTITUTING A MAJORITY OF THE SUBSTANTIAL BUSINESS HOUSES OF INDIANAPOLIS,
"THEY WHO ADVERTISE CONSTANTLY WILL SUCCEED BEST."

INTRODUCTORY.

In presenting this, our second volume of the city directory of Indianapolis to the public, we have, as in the previous volume, suffered great inconvenience from the irregularity in the numbering of houses upon different streets, finding some with two numbers, others with none, while perhaps one-half are correctly numbered; all the result of a neglect in enforcing obedience to an ordinance passed by the city council in 1864, regulating the numbering of houses, which has met with nearly the same success as an ordinance passed to regulate the naming of streets upon the corners, neither of which have been sustained by an appropriation sufficient to secure their completion. But to obviate this difficulty we have made a careful personal canvass of the entire city and suburbs, extending from the Insane Hospital west, to the Blind Asylum east, and from Camp Morton north, to the extreme limits south; covering an area of not less than twelve square miles, at an enormous cost of money and time; sparing no pains or expense to get the names of all heads of families, and all others whose names should properly occur in a work of this kind.

If any have been omitted in our list of citizens, we trust they will pardon the omission as unitentional, and look upon the matter with the mind of a true philosopher, knowing as any one must, that it is absolutely impossible to get the names of all correct, however much we should desire to do so.

In the compilation we have made some changes in this volume, placing an advertising department near the center, where a book naturally opens, and substituting in lieu of classification, a complete chronological, statistical and local history of the city of Indianapolis and vicinity, from the date of the territorial government up to the present time; which is written after careful investigation, by one of Indianapolis' native born citizens, Mr. Ignatius Brown, to whom the citizens are indebted for the production of this impartial history.

POPULATION, STATISTICS, &C.

The following is a brief summary of the statistical importance of the city, as shown by our recent thorough canvass of the entire city and suburbs, covering an area of over twelve square miles. In the following table the figure set opposite the different letters of the alphabet, indicate the number of different individual names of persons occurring in this book of which this is the initial letter of the last or parental name; these exclusive of names of institutions, corporations, buildings, associations or business firms, occurring as follows:

A	390	H	1,116
B	1,271	I	88
C	944	J	343
D	602	K	506
E	231	L	608
F	512	Mc	354
G	565	M	1,061

N	244	U	24
O	214	V	124
P	536	W	880
Q	21	Y	60
R	789	Z	·26
S	1,593		
T	398	Total number of names	14,000

Whole number of population (estimated by the average ratio,) 56,000.

This is proof beyond question that our city and suburbs have in the past year enjoyed a substantial increase in their permanent resident population, of twenty per cent. over that of a year ago, which is as large au increase as any city in the Western States has enjoyed, except St. Louis, Mo., and Omaha, Nebraska.

The number of business men have largely increased, notwithstanding the large number of cases in bankruptcy, occasioned by a failure of crops for the last two years in Indiana, added to an unnecessary closeness in the money market of the West, which are now being materially changed by an immense crop of all kinds, soon to be realized, with a partial if not an entire change in the financial policy of the entire country.

In public and individual improvement there has been something accomplished in the past year, in the completion of two new school buildings of large capacity; three churches at extravagant expense; a fine public building for the use of the State officers, Supreme Court rooms, law library, &c.; a large brick building for the use of county officers; a handsome addition to the Hospital for the Insane, increasing its capacity fully one-third; a convenient addition to the Union Depot buildings, furnishing room for a magnificent dining hall, sleeping parlors, general ticket office, express and telegraph offices; one cotton mill; one iron works, for the manufacture of bar, band and hoop iron, nails, nuts, washers, &c., built by a joint stock association known as the White River Iron Co.; the completion of a new saw manufactory, by Messrs. Farley & Sinker; a very large addition to another saw manufactory, known as Sheffield Saw Works, owned by Messrs. E. C. Atkins & Co.; (there are now more saws manufactured here than in any other city in the west,) a large addition to Messrs. Osgood, Smith & Co.'s wheel, hub and spoke manufactory has been made; several magnificent wholesale houses have been completed and others built, added to numerous fine business blocks, private residences, small stores and shops toward the outer portion of the city. Two new railroads, the Indianapolis & Vincennes and Cincinnati, Connersville & Indianapolis, have been completed to this city, and are now preparing to build their freight depots, shops, &c.; another road, the Indiana & Illinois Central Railroad, is being built, and will be completed between this city and the Illinois State line during this year. There is also another road being pushed to rapid completion, between this city and Terre Haute, there to form a united line with the Terre Haute, Alton & St. Louis Railroad, making one consolidated road between Indianapolis and St. Louis. Those two roads, when completed, will make twelve distinct lines of railroad leading to and from this city, making it the greatest railroad center in the United States of any city of equal or double its population.

We lay the present work before our *patrons* and the *public* with an easy conscience, believing that our efforts to produce it will be appreciated by the enterprising citizens, officials, business men, mechanics, laborers and others, and manifest the same by obtaining a copy at the earliest moment, as by so doing they will be able to secure our history of Indianapolis, which alone is worth the price of the book.

To the advertising patrons of this book we tender our highest regards for their enterprise and liberality, and having done for each as we obligated ourselves to do, feel satisfied that the benefits which will inevitably accrue to each in an increase of business, will richly repay them many times their investments; and as we have shown that we have an honest purpose in the publication of the Directory of this city, we hope to ever receive the liberal and undivided patronage of its citizens, from year to year, as we shall continue to issue a Directory of the city annually, as heretofore.

To the Press, and obliging friends, we return our best wishes for the kindness and patience shown our agents in the canvass, and wishing all success through life, we are, Very respectfully,

LOGAN & CO.,
Compilers, Printers and Publishers.

INDIANAPOLIS, July, 1868.

LOGAN'S ANNUAL
INDIANAPOLIS DIRECTORY.

1868.

ABBREVIATIONS USED IN THIS BOOK.

agt...............agent.	cor...............corner.	n. w.........north-west.	s................south.
asst...........assistant.	Co............Company.	opp...........opposite.	s. e...........south-east.
av................avenue.	e.................east.	p. o.........post-office.	s. s.........south side.
bet.............between.	e. s...........east side.	prest.........president.	s. w.........south-west.
bds............boards.	Ind............Indiana.	propr.........proprietor.	secy.........secretary.
bldg..........building.	lab ....laborer.	rd................road.	supt.....superintendent.
blk............block.	manfs....manufacturers.	res............residence.	treas.........treasurer.
com. mer....commission	n................north.	R. R...........railroad.	w................west.
merchant.	n. e.........north-east.	Ry.........railway.	w. s..........west side.
(col)...........colored.	n. s.........north side.	Rev..........reverend.	(wid)...........widow.

ABASEGRAL F., servant, 40 n. California.

Abbett Charles H., (L. & C. H. A.,) 35 Virginia av., res. same.

Abbett John B., Grand Scribe Sons of Temperance, res. 164 Virginia av.

Abbett John D., photographer, 36½ e. Washington, res. 35 Virginia av.

Abbett John W., (col.,) lab., res. Howard, bet. Second and Third.

ABBETT L. & C. H.,
(Lawson A. & Chas. H. A.,) physicians and surgeons, 35 Virginia av.

Abbett Lawson, (L. & C. H. A.,) 35 Virginia av., res. same.

Abbett Wesley, (col.,) lab., res. 116 Ash.

Abbett William A., (J. W. Adams & Co.,) 49 and 53 w. Washington, bds. 35 Virginia av.

Abbey G. N., (Allen A. & Co.,) 86 s. Meridian, res. Cleveland, O.

Abbott D. H., musician, bds. 263 s. Meridian.

Abbott Miss Eliza, dress-maker, bds. 171 s. Alabama.

Abbott James M., tinner, Munson & Johnson, res. 343 s. East.

Abel Charles, driver Schmidt's beer wagon, res. 401 s. Delaware.

Abishier Arvilla, occupant Deaf and Dumb Asylum.

Abistrier Lodoska A., occupant Deaf and Dumb Asylum.

Abker Henry, Cabinet-Makers' Union, bds. 485 e. Washington.

Abker William, Cabinet-Makers' Union, bds. 485 e. Washington.

Abner John, varnisher, res. 38 Henry.

Aborn Orin, physician, office 68 e. Market, res. 116 Broadway, cor. Cherry.

Abraham Coffin, spoke-maker, Osgoods, res. 389 s. East.

Abrams John, book-keeper, J. George Stiltz, res. 129 n. Noble.

Abrams John, (col.,) lab., res. cor. North and Bright.

Abrams Milton, engineer, Journal Office.

Abrams Wm. J., carpenter, res. 419 n. East.

ABROMET ADOLPH,
agt. Ætna Fire and Life Insurance Cos., of Hartford, Conn., office Ætna bldg., near p. o., res. 21 w. North.

Achas Frederick, lab., res. 130 n. Noble.

Achert Geo. F., clerk, 76 e. Market.

Achey Mrs. Francis, res. 328 w. Washington.

Achey Mrs. Henry, res. 17 Kentucky av.

Achey James, res. 17 Kentucky av.

Achey J., speculator, bds. 17 Kentucky av.

Achey Mrs. Mary, (wid. Henry,) 17 Kentucky av.

Acht John, painter, res. 877 n. Mississippi.

Ackles Mary, waiter, dining room Bicking House, 89 s. Illinois.

Ackleman Andrew, varnisher, res. 285 n. Noble.

Acres Thornton, plasterer.

Adams Alexander, (A. & Minthorn,) 296 e. Ohio, res. 268 e. St. Clair.

Adams Andrew J., clerk, 296 e. Ohio, bds. 268 e. St. Clair.

Adams Armstrong, carpenter., bds. 140 cor. Elm and Grove.

Adams Barney, (col.,) servant, e. Washington, near Arsenal av.

Adams Bertie, lady boarder, 36 s. New Jersey.

Adams B. F., bds. Neiman House.

Adams Charles A., bds. Neiman House.

Adams Charles E., cooper, res. 198 Minerva.

Adams Charles S., tinner, bds. 83 e. McCarty.

Adams Erin, (col.,) lab., res. 182 w. Georgia.

Adams Express Office at Merchants' Union Express Office, 44 e. Washington.

Adams George W., res. 26 Iowa.

Adams G. F., lumber dealer, 169 Bates, res. 175 e Market.

Adams G. H., (Asher A. & Higgins,) 76 c. Market, res. Mineapolis, Minn.

ADAMS HENRY C., deputy sheriff, res. 115 s. New Jersey.

Adams Harriet A., inmate Deaf and Dumb Asylum.

Adams Hubbard S., ex-policeman, res. 149 Winston.

Adam J. G., student, N. W. C. University, bds. 408 n. New Jersey.

Adams John, (col.,) lab., Elizabeth, bet. Blake and Minerva.

Adams John W., (G. W. A & Co.,) 49 and 53 w. Washington, res. 430 n Illinois.

ADAMS J. W. & CO., (J. W. A. & William A. Abbett,) wholesale and retail boots and shoes, 49 and 53 w. Washington.

Adams Levi P., cooper, res. 196 Minerva.

Adams Mrs. Mary, (wid. Reuben,) res. 115 s. New Jersey.

Adams Thomas H., cooper, res. 248 n. Blake.

Adams & Minthorn, (Alexandria A. & John J. M..) grocers, 296 e. Ohio.

Adams Samuel, lawyer, room 3, over 45 c. Washington, res. 297 n. Delaware.

Adams Samuel C., brick-maker, res. 297 n. Delaware.

Adams T. J., book-keeper and cashier, Trade Palace, bds. Bates House.

Adams Wesley M., carpenter, 441 n. Mississippi.

Adam William, lab., res. 465 n. Alabama.

Adams William, plasterer, res. 7 Peru.

Adams William C., farmer, res. National rd., 1¼ miles n. s. river bridge.

Adams William L., (Hume, A. & Co.,) 26 and 28 w. Washington, res. 165 n. Alabama.

Ademyer Frank, clerk, Metzner's drug store, bds. 263 e. Washington.

Adolphus Aaron, salesman, 2 w. Washington, res. 213 n. Pennsylvania.

Adsit C. S., clerk, 40 s. Meridian, bds. Pyle House.

Aeger John, painter, res. 390 n. West.

Aenhorn Godlit, varnisher, res. Court, bet. East and New Jersey.

Æpker Henry, Cabinet-Makers' Union, bds. 520 e. Washington.

Æpker William, Cabinet-Makers' Union, bds. 520 e. Washington.

Affantranger S. G., blacksmith shop, 189 Indiana av., res. 215 w. North.

Afterhyde F., painter, res. 277 Davidson.

Aftong N. D., German book store, 151 e. Washington, res. 270 s. New Jersey.

Afton Henry, res. 277 s. new Jersey.

African M. E. Church, 176 w. Georgia, Enos McIntosh, pastor.

Afunk Andy, res. 277 s. New Jersey.

Ager Samuel, lab., res. 24 Jones.

Ahern Michael, works City Gas Works, res. 48 s. Alabama.

Ahern Michael, lab., res. 264 s. Alabama.

Ahern William, lab., res. on alley, bet. East and Liberty.

Ahlders Ahlrich, saddler, works 224 c. Washington, res. same.

Ahlbrand Ephraim, wagon-maker, 237 s. Delaware.

Ahlbrand William, blacksmith, bds. 240 s. Delaware.

Ahrenz Henry, cabinet-maker, res. 415 e. Washington.

Aikins Edward, brakeman, J. M. & I. R. R., bds. 146 e. McCarty.

Aikman John B., (Roll, Kimble & A.,) 123 s. Meridian, res. 382 n. Tennessee.

Aker Ellis L., carpenter, res. 9 Forest Home av.

Akers John, brakeman, I. C. & L. R. R., bds. 99 Benton.

Akers John C., student, commercial college, bds. 75 Norwood.

Akin Daniel, varnisher, res. 42 Rose.

Akin G. B., patent right dealer, bds. Martin House.

Akin Lewis, clerk, Ludorff & Co., bds. Martin House.

Akin Lewis G., clerk, 42 s. Meridian, bds. 33 w. Maryland.

Akin Margaret, cook, Macy House, bds. same.

Akin Mrs. Martha, (wid.,) res. 280 w. St. Clair.

Akland Miss Abby, servant, 498 n. Pennsylvania.

ALBERSHARDT H. F., boots and shoes, 139 e. Washington, res. same.

Albersmeier Daniel, lab., res. 172 Union.

Albersmeier Miss Mary, bds. 266 s. Pennsylvania.

Albert Ephraim, res. 72 Plum.

Albert John W., carriage trimmer, works Miller, Mitchell & Stough, res. cor. Ash and Vine.

Alberts Lawson, res. 211 n. Missouri.

Albertson A. C, printer, bds. 164 Maryland.

Alberty Miss Frances, res. 2d floor over 162 w. Washington

Alberty Mrs. Matilda, (wid. Frederick,) res. over 162 w. Washington.

Albrecht George, carpenter, res. 332 s. Delaware.

Albright George, varnisher, works Union Factory, res. 182 Davidson.

Albright John, brewer, bds. 94 e. South.

Albro Henry, foreman, Chandler & Taylor, res. 311 s. Delaware.

Alcorn Sarah J., inmate Deaf and Dumb Asylum.

Aldag A., shoe-maker, res. 581 e. Washington.

Aldag Chas., boots and shoes, 175 e. Washington, res. in rear of same.

Alday Louis, shoe-maker, res. 78 n. liberty.

Aldred John, res. 219 e. Washington.

Aldred Mrs. Salina, (wid.,) res. Boyd's blk., Massachusetts av.

Aldridge Aaron, res. 212 w. Ohio.

Aldridge Frank, res. 280 w. Market.

Aldridge P., (col.,) lab., 219 Madison av.

Aldrich Chauncey, carpenter, res. 425 e. St. Clair.

ALDRICH & GAY, (Franklin A. & Alfred G.,) wood yard, cor. Indiana av. and Canal.

Aldrich John, stair-builder, res. 244 Davidson.

Alexander Christina, (wid. John,) res. s. National rd.

Alexander Eli, groceries, n. Illinois, res. 133 w. New York.

Alexander Mrs. Elizabeth, (wid. David,) res. 176 n. East.

Alexander Elvira, (wid. Archibald,) res. 146 e. McCarty.

Alexander Mrs. Emma, (wid. James C.,) res. 287 e. Market.

Alexander Eugene, book-keeper, 24 s. Meridian, bds. Pattison House.

Alexander George W. & Co., real estate agts., 30½ w. Washington, res. 550 n. Tennessee.

Alexander George W., (col.,) barber, 157 w. Washington, res. 181 w. Washington.

Alexander J. D., salesman, Hays, Rosenthal & Co., 64 s. Meridian, bds. Palmer House.

Alexander James T., carpenter, bds. 33 w. Maryland.

Alexander Mary, servant at 104 west Vermont.

Alexander Nort. E., traveling agt. Sentinel office, 16¼ e. Washington, bds. 44 s. Tennessee.

Alexander Theodore T., salesman, Tyler's Bee-Hive, bds. 37 Kentucky av.

Alexander William, farmer, res. 233 Winston.

Alford A. A., trunk-maker, res. 175 n. Alabama.

ALFORD, TALBOT & CO., (Thomas G. A., Richard L. T., William H. Morrison, John P. Patterson & Joseph A. Moore,) wholesale grocers, 2 Morrison's opera blk., s. Meridian.

Alford Thomas G., (A., Talbot & Co.,) 2 Morrison's opera blk., s. Meridian, res. 175 n. Alabama.

Alfred William F., marble-cutter, res. 175 n. Alabama.

Alfrey A., lab., res. 40 Catharine.

Algoe Samuel, shipping clerk, Foster, Wiggins & Co., res. 288 e. South.

Algia John, lab., Commercial Hotel.

Alinger Jacob, lab., res. Kansas, s. city limits.

Allair Andrew, blacksmith, East, near Virginia av., res. Clinton, bet. Ohio and New York.

ALLAIR JAMES P., dealer in lime, coal and cement, 24 Virginia av., res. 95 Jackson.

Alleman Felix, painter, res. 242 s. Mississippi.

Allemong Charles, physician, res. 303 e. Louisiana.

Allen A. C., traveling agt. Wheeler & Wilson's manf. co., res. 448 n. New Jersey.

Allen, Abbey & Co., wholesale stone-ware, brown and yellew-ware, fire-brick, &c., 86 s. Meridian.

Allen Austin W., (Dow & A.,) 18 n. Delaware, res. 107 n. Noble.

Allen Miss Blanche, student, Indiana Female College, 146 n. Meridian, bds. the same.

Allen Charles, (col.,) lab., res. 22 Elm.

Allen Cyrus M., (D. A. Branson & Co.,) bds. Bates House.

Allen D. B., (Abbey & Co.,) 86 s. Meridian, res. 56 s. Pennsylvania.

Allen Edward, (col.,) waiter, Bates House, res. Douglas alley.

Allen Edward G., salesman, 86 s. Meridian, bds. 56 s. Pennsylvania.

Allen Miss Ellen, seamstress, bds. 160 s. Noble.

Allen Firman, traveling agt., Connelly, Wiles & Co., res. 316 n. Illinois.

Allen George, res. 31 w. Georgia.

Allen George, (col.,) lab., res. 490 s. Illinois.

Allen Henry, (H. A. & Co.,) 25 and 27 e. Pearl, res. 130 w. Vermont.

ALLEN, H. & CO.,
(Henry A. & Hugh O'Donell,) livery and sale stable, 25 and 27 e. Pearl, rear Glenns' blk.

Allen Henry S., salesman, Tyler's Bee-Hive, bds, 60 w. Market, cor. Illinois.

Allen Jacob B., brick-mason, res. w. end Morris.

Allen James, lab., res. 218 n. Mississippi.

Allen James R., tin-smith, Bellefontaine shop, res. 173 Winston.

Allen Jerome, (col.,) servant, W. P. Fishback, e. Washington.

Allen J., (col.,) lab., res. Camp Carrington.

Allen Joseph, (col.,) lab., res. 346 w. North.

Allen Miss Laura, lady boarder, 289 e. New York.

Allen Mrs. Mary, (wid. Larew,) res. 271 o. Ohio.

Allen Millia, servant, over 246 e. Washington.

ALLEN MRS. N. M.,
dress and cloak maker and dress-fitter, 36½ e. Washington, over Benham's music store, res. same. See card, page 34.

Allen William, (Sinker & Co.,) res. 134 Virginia av.

Allen William A., clerk, 36½ e. Washington, res. same.

Alley Miss Ruth, student, Indiana Female College, 146 n. Meridian, bds. the same.

Allington John, res. 162 n. Illinois.

Allison Joseph, plasterer, res. 30 Fletcher av.

Allison Robert C., res. 171 s. New Jersey.

Allison Thomas S., plasterer, res. 94 Liberty.

Almon Charles, grocer, 203 Massachusetts av., cor. North, res. Cincinnati R. R., bet. Noble and East.

Alred Garrison W., sexton city cemetary, Kentucky av., res. 215 w. South.

Altag Louis, shoe-maker, res. 78 n. Liberty.

Altenburger Jacob, lab., res. e. side Blake, bet. New York and Washington.

Altland Hiram, constable, res. 173 e. St. Joseph.

Altland Samuel T., carpenter, shop near first ward school, res. 179 Spring.

Altland Miss Sarah, seamstress, 179 Spring, res. same.

Altman Herman, groceries, 185 Bluff rd., res. same.

ALVEY JAMES H.,
(Donaldson & A.,) 54 s. Meridian, res. 10 e. Michigan.

Alvord E. B., res. 334 N. Illinois.

Alvord Elijah S., prest. Citizens' Street Ry, office cor. Tennessee and Louisiana, res. 92 n. Pennsylvania.

Alvord James C., res. 92 n. Pennsylvania, cor. Ohio.

Alward Samuel, salesman, 58. s. Meridian, res. 247 n. East.

Amach Anna, (wid.,) res. 83½ e. Washington.

Amberg Charles, machinist, res. 422 n. New Jersey.

Ambrose Thomas, (col.,) barber, cor. Washington and Kentucky av.

AMERICAN EXPRESS OFFICE,
34 e. Washington, Edward W. Sloan, supt., J. W. Butterfield, agt.

American Horse Insurance Co., office room 13 Vinton's blk., n. Pennsylvania.

Amos A., gas fitter, 77 e. Market.

Amick Miss Jane, cook, Orphan Asylum. res. 711 n. Tennessee.

Amos Aquilla, gas-fitter, Coulter & White, res. 432 e. North.

Amos Ann., (wid.) George, seamstress, res. Stringtown, near river bridge.

Amos Isaac, gas-fitter, res. 497 n. Alabama.

Amos James, spinner, res. 27 n. Blake.

Amos Mr. Nancy, (wid. Aquilla,) res. 432 e. North.

Amberg Charles, shipping clerk, Spiegel Thoms & Co., res. 141 n. New Jersey.

Amos Samuel, works Geisendorff Woolen Factory, bds. n. s. New York, bet. Blake and Minerva.

Amos Thomas D., Bailiff Criminal Court, res. 218 Davidson.

Amos William, brick-mason, res. 124 e. St Joseph.

Ampy Nancy, (col.,) servant, 255 n. East.
Anarcher John, carpenter, res. 124 Hosbrook.
Andany Mrs. Caroline, (wid. Henry,) res. 318 Winston.
Anderegg John, conductor, I. C. & L. R. R., bds. Ray House.
Anderson Miss Ann E., student, N. W. C. University, bds. 297 Winston.
ANDERSON, BULLOCK & SCHOFIELD, (Jas. T. A., Jas. B. B. & Nash M. S.,) wholesale hardware, 62 s. Meridian.
Anderson Charles, carpenter, res. 28 n. New Jersey.
Anderson Charlotte, servant, Palmer House.
Anderson Mrs. Cynthia, (wid. George,) res. 177 e. Market.
Anderson David, carpenter, res. 70 Indiana av.
Anderson Edward, plasterer, res. over 182 e. Washington.
Anderson Miss Fidelia, principal sixth ward school.
Anderson George, carpenter, res. 48 n. New Jersey.
Anderson George P., (A. & Jones,) 19 n. Meridian, res. 279 e. South.
Anderson Harry, moulder, bds. Ray House.
Anderson Harry, (col.,) hod-carrier, res. 163 Cedar.
Anderson Henry, carpenter, bds. 177 e. Market.
Anderson James D., plasterer, res. n. Pennsylvania, beyond city limits.
Anderson James T., (A., Bullock & Schofield,) 62 s. Meridian, res. 367 n. New Jersey.
Anderson Jerome S., (Horn, A. & Co.,) 31 w. Washington, res. 162 n. Tennessee.
Anderson John, clerk, American Express Co., res. 387 s. Illinois.
Anderson John, carpenter, bds. 34 n. New Jersey.
Anderson John, shoe-maker, 22 Virginia av., bds. 364 n. Mississippi.
Anderson John J., plasterer, bds. 519 s. Illinois.
Anderson J. W., agt. American Express Co., Union depot, res. 378 s. Illinois.
ANDERSON & JONES, (George P. A. & Barton D. J.,) real estate and life insurance agts., 19 n. Meridian.
Anderson Martha, (col.,) servant, 85 Massachusetts av.
Anderson Martin, plasterer, res. 315 e. Merrill.
Anderson Randolph W., carpenter, res. 435 e. Georgia.
Anderson Reuben, (col.,) porter. Downey, Brouse, Butler & Co., res. 79 Ann.
Anderson Robert, brick-layer, res. 348 w. Washington.

Anderson Robert, cook, Union depot dining Hall, res. 189 s. Illinois.
Anderson & Ross, grocers and produce dealers, 77 w. Washington.
Anderson Thomas, carpenter, res. 413 n. Mississippi.
Anderson James, lab., bds. 177 e. Market.
Anderson William, 82 e. Washington, res. 177 e. Market.
Anderson William, brakeman, C. C. & I. C. R. R., bds. 58 Benton.
Anderson William R., teamster, res. 139 w. Second.
Anderson W. H., (A. & Ross,) 77 w. Washington, bds. 80 s. Tennessee.
Andra John, saddler and harness-maker, 224 e. Washington, res. 326 e. New York.
Andrews Alfred A., cigar-maker, 141 s. Illinois, bds. 126 n. Mississippi.
Andrews Henry, (col.,) porter, 18 w. Pearl, res. 225 w. Ohio.
Andrew John B., clerk, 10 w. Louisiana, bds. same.
ANDREWS LYMAN N., general freight agt., P. & I. R. R., res 434 n. Tenessee.
Andrews Robert, heater, rolling mill, res. 236 s. Missouri.
Andrews Samuel B., photographer, 94 e. Washington, res. 92 Ft. Wayne av.
Angle A. R., conductor, Bellefontaine Ry., bds. Bates House.
Angus Walter W., teacher, Deaf and Dumb Asylum, bds. e. Washington, beyond city limits.
Anhaus Charles, lab., rolling mill, res. 295 s. Meridian.
Anhorn E., painter, res. 54 Oak.
Anhorn Ibet, painter, res. 99 Ft. Wayne av.
Ankeny Sarah, student, select school, bds. 202 e. Market.
Annoger John, carpenter, res. 124 Hosbrook.
Annan C., book-keeper, 39 s. Meridian, bds. Pyle House.
Annan Otto, res. 244 s. Delaware.
Anspire Frank, lab., res. 226 n. East.
Ante Jacob, res. 299 s. Delaware.
Anthes Jacob, janitor, Metropolitan Theater, res 470 s. New Jersey.
Anthony Alexander, lab., res. e. Georgia, n. s.
Anthony David, carpenter, bds. 240 e. Ohio.
Anthony Frederick, railroader, res. 60 s. Noble.
Anthony Joshua, carpenter, res. 256 n. Blake.
Anthony William, carpenter, res. second floor, 186 w. Washington.
ANTLEES MRS. ESTHER A., res. 373 e. Georgia.
Anton K., second-hand clothing store, 295 e. Washington.

Antonio Early, lab., res. 75 w. South.
Antrim Levi, teamster, res. 58 Cherry.
Antrim William, driver, M. U. Ex. Co., bds. 58 Cherry.
Antrobus John B., cooper, res. Georgia, near Helen.
Apzar Jacob, cooper, res. 34 Helen.
Apsey Elizabeth, servant, C. N. Todd, 228 n. Tennessee.
Apperson Isaac M., bds. 256 Madison av.
Apperson I. H., street car driver, res. 256 Madison av.
Apperson Miss Mary, milliner, over 6 w. Washington, res. 256 Madison av.
Apperson Miss Sarah, bds. 256 Madison av.
Appleby Robert, car-builder, res. 310 w. Washington.
Applegate A. J., clerk, 16 Bates House blk.
Applegate A. W., traveling agt., J. C. Green, res. 175 e. Washington.
Applegate Berg., general com. mer., res. 194 e. Michigan.
Arbuckle Matthew, (Witt & A.,) s. w. cor. Meridian and Washington, res. n. Delaware, out city limits.
Arbuckle S., carpenter, res. 228 w. Ohio.
Arbuthnott Thomas, painter, res. Minerva, bet. New York and Vermont.
Archer William, carpenter, bds. 73 n. Illinois.
Archibald O. A., occupant Deaf and Dumb Asylum.
ARDEN J.,
     boots and shoes, 65 s. Meridian, res. same.
Armbruster Frank E., saloon, 439 w. Washington, res. same.
Armbruster John J., bar-tender, 215 w. Maryland, res. s. West, bet. Georgia and Maryland.
Armentrout Lavina, (wid. David,) res. 313 n. Noble.
Armers Miss Mary, servant, 462 n. Pennsylvania, cor. Pratt.
Armstrong George F., agt., Merchants' Union Express Co., Union depot, res. 331 s. Pennsylvania.

Armstrong James, clerk, New York store, res. 274 n. Alabama.
Armstrong John S., student, N. W. C. University, bds 402 n. New Jersey.
Armstrong Mary, German Sisters, bds. 124 Duncan.
Armstrong Mrs. Mary, (wid.,) seamstress, res. 78 Fayette.
Armstrong Rev. William, pastor, Second Presbyterian Church, res. 197 n. Meridian.
Armstrong William, supt. Young Men's Christian Association, res 497 n. Meridian.
Armstrong William S., (Vinnedge, Jones & Co.,) 66 s. Meridian, bds. 180 n. Illinois.
Arna Sarah, (wid. Presley,) res. Green, bet. McCarty and Stevens.
Arnan Otto, engineer, Sloan's chair factory res. 244 s. Delaware.
Arnault A. H., (A. & Gregoire,) 129 s. Illinois, res. same.
Arnault & Gregoire, French dyers and scourers, 129 s. Illinois.
Arnett Miss Emma, bds. 239 n. New Jersey.
Arnett Mary, (col., wid.,) res. 179 Eddy.
Arnett Samuel N. S., inmate Deaf and Dumb Asylum.
Arnholter Henry, harness-maker, 225 e. Washington, res. 31 s. New Jersey.
Arnholter William, bar-tender, res. 98 Russel.
Arnold John, lab., res. Michigan rd., beyond city limits.
Arnold Martha J., (wid. Willis,) res. Michigan rd., beyond city limits.
Arnold Miss Rhoda, bds. 35 Indiana av.
Arnold Peter, clerk, 210 e. Washington, res. 17 n. New Jersey.
Arnold Peter, moulder, res. s. New Jersey.
Arnot Jacob F., inmate Deaf and Dumb Asylum.
Arnot Jesse R., inmate Deaf and Dumb Asylum.
Arnot Sarah C., inmate Deaf and Dumb Asylum.

Aaron A., salesman, Tyler's Bee-Hive.
Arskin Bridget, servant, 200, cor. West and Washington.
Arthur Thomas, moulder, res. 75 Norwood.
Arthur William, stone-cutter, res. 25 California.
Arthur Wm. A., moulder, bds. 75 Norwood.
Artis William H., (col.,) barber, 197 w. Washington, res. same.
Artby Samuel C., clerk, 151 w. Washington, bds. 9 s. Mississippi.
Asbury Chapel, Rev. J. H. Lozier, pastor, w. side New Jersey, bet. Louisiana and South.
ASHER, ADAMS & HIGGINS, (John R. A., S. H. A. & Charles J. H.) book and map publishers, and dealers in school furniture, 76 c. Market.
Asher, John R., (A., Adams & Higgins,) 76 e. Market, res. 189 c. Ohio.
Ashley George F., res. cor. Michigan and Davidson.
Ashley George F., carpenter, res. 404 c. Michigan.
Ashley Thomas, res. 126 Spring.
Ashmead Jacob N., miller, bds. 350 n. Noble.
Ashmead John S., carpenter, res. 360 n. Noble.
Ashmead Sely W., engineer, Bellefontaine R. R., bds. 360 n. Noble.
Askins Mrs. Bessie, (wid. Patrick,) servant, 257 n. East.
Asmus Christian, res. 15 Lord.
Asmus Louis, saloon, 199 Indiana av.,'bds. 269 n. West.
Asten Joseph, stock-drover, res. 500 n. Illinois.
Atam William, wood-sawyer, res. 465 n. Alabama.
Atherton Fenton, brakeman, C. C. & I. C. R. R., bds. 58 Benton.
Atherton H. F., traveling agt. Miller & Frank, res. Indiana av.
Atherton Samuel, carpenter, res. 28 Center.
Atherton William F., compositor, Journal, res. n. Pennsylvania.
ATHON JAMES S., physician and surgeon, office, room 5, McOuat's blk., Kentucky ave., res. n. e. cor. Meridian and First.
Athon James S., Jr., druggist, room 5, McOuats blk., Kentucky av., bds. cor. First and Meridian.
ATKINS E. C. & CO., (Elias C. A., J. Henry Kappes & H. Knippenberg.) proprs. Sheffield saw work, 215 s. Illinois.
Atkins Elias C., (E. C. A. & Co.,) res. 283 n. Pennsylvania.
Atkins George W., saw-maker, E. C. Atkins & Co., bds. Pyle House.
Atkins Martin, conductor, Bellefontaine R. R., bds. 456 c. Michigan.

Atkinson Benjamin, meat-market, 153 w. Washington, res. 207 w. Washington.
Atkinson Joseph H., engineer, Bellefontaine R. R., res. 237 s. Delaware.
Atkinson Thomas J., house-painter, res. 181 Virginia av.
Attridge Richard, carpenter, Bellefontaine Shop, res. 236 Winston.
AUDITOR OF STATE, office, s. Tennesse, in new State bldg., T. B. McCarty, Auditor.
Aufderhide Gottfried, painter, res. 275 Davidson.
Aufderhide Henry, carpenter, res. 241 Davidson.
Aufderhide John H., wooden shoe-maker, res. 241 Davidson.
Aufderhide Joseph, expressman, res. 432 c. Vermont.
Aufderhide William, turner, works Union factory, res. 235 Davidson.
Aug Adolph, hack-driver, res. 310 c. New York.
Aughinbaugh Charles R., bds 20 w. Michigan.
Aughinbaugh E. S., salesman, Browning & Sloan, bds. 75 n. Illinois.
Aughinbaugh Mrs. Sarah, (wid.,) res. 75 n. Illinois.
Aughinbaugh W. M., clerk, Stewart & Morgan, bds. 75 n. Illinois.
Augstein Charles, varnisher, res., 344 Railroad.
Aukembrock Henry, res. 351 s. Delaware.
Ault. Mrs. Elizabeth, seamstress, res. 150 n. Blake.
Aultnand Louisa, servant, 295 n. East.
Ausbuttle, Louis, gun-smith res. over 174 e. Washington.
Austin Carle, varnisher, res. 344 n. Railroad.
Austin George T., traveling agt., Singer manf. co., res. 424 n. New Jersey.
Austin George F., res. 189 s. Alabama.
Austin John, res. 190 s. East.
Austin John, gardner, res. 287 s. East.
Austin J. S., clerk, Moody & Bro, 180 Indiana av., bds. 148 Indiana av.
Austin Samuel C., cabinet-maker, res. 166 n. Delaware.
Avels George, clerk, 59 s. Illinois, bds. 357 s. Delaware.
Avels Joseph H., flour and feed store, 59 s. Illinois, res. 178 Madison av.
Avels Mrs. Margaret, (wid.) Henry, res. 357 s. Delaware.
Averill Joseph, checkman, T. H. & I. R. R., res. 183 w. South.
Averill (Rev.) M. V., res. with J. O. D. Lilly, n. Tennessee, bet. Second and Third.
Avery Elizabeth, servant, C. G. French, e. Washington, near corporatin line.
Avery Joseph, carpenter, res. 10 w. Pratt.

AVERY JOHN L.,
secy Indianapolis Builders and Manfs.
Association, res. 256 n. Alabama.

Avery John P., physician and surgeon,
office 1 Massachusetts av., res. 250 n.
East, cor. Michigan.

Axen Phœbe, dining room girl, Ray House,

Axley John, teamster, res. w. s. Tennessee,
bet. Fourth and Fifth.

Ayers Mrs. Anna, (wid. Franklin,) res.
Court, bet. Alabama and New Jersey.

Azd Waldo, carpenter, res. McGill.

BAAR B. J., (B. & Markwood,) 20 w.
Maryland, res. 172 e. market.

Baar G. L., scroll sawyer, res, 339 s. Delaware.

Baar & Markwood, tailoring and repairing, 20 w. Maryland.

Baarman & Henry, lab., res. 134 s. McCarty.

Babbitt Samuel, shoe-shop, (B. & Mallihan,) 18 Virginia av., res. 378 e. Michigan,

Bach John, porter, Spencer House, bds. same.

Bacher Conrad, groceries, cor. Illinois and Tinker, res. same.

Bachtel Jacob, lab., res. 247 s. Delaware.

Back Clemens, (B. & Wenkin,) 209 e. Washington, res. same.

Back & Wenkin, (Clemens, B. & Ernest W.,) cigars and tobacco, 209 e. Washington.

Backer Frederick, gardner, res. s. e. cor. Walnut and Illinois.

Backer Henry, blacksmith, res. s. e. cor. Walnut and Illinois.

Backer Mary, servant, 226 e. Ohio.

Backsther Martin, clerk, Weinberger & Co., res. 342 Virginia av.

Backster William, (col.,) lab., res. Howard, bet. Second and Third.

Bacon E. H., physician, office s. w. cor. Meridian and Washington, bds. 299 n. Mississippi.

Bacon E. J. (wid. Elisha,) res. 307 n. Alabama.

Bacon Mrs. Elizabeth, (wife Robert,) dressmaker, 70 e. Ohio, res. same.

Bacon John I., lab.,'res. 61 Dacota.

Bacon John L., blacksmith, res. 307 n. Alabama.

Bacon R. D., clerk, J. E. Fawkner, res. 70 e. Ohio.

Bacon T. L., clerk, U. S. Arsenal, bds. 510 n. Delaware.

Bacon William, clerk, M. U. Ex. Co., 42 and 44 e. Washington, bds. De Ruiter's restaurant.

Bade Anthony, lab., res. 209 s. Alabama.

Bade Charles, clerk, 125 e. Washington, bds. 209 s. Alabama.

Bade William, clerk, C. Frederick, bds. 209 s. Alabama.

Badger John C., drug store, 172 w. Washington, res. same.

Badger Theodore, lab., 163 w. Washington, res. 156 w. Washington.

Bagget Patrick, lab., res. 85 Delaware.

Baggerly C. W., cigars and tobacco, 35 s. Meridian, res. 160 e. Market.

Baggs Frederick, book-keeper, Kennedy, Byram & Co., res. 125 e. Ohio.

Bagley Mrs. Jane, (wid.,) boarding house, 36 w. Maryland.

Bagley Mrs. Sophia, bds. 431 n. Tennessee.

Bagman Mrs. Henrietta, (wid.,) servant, 295 n. East.

Baier Casper, lab., res. over 178 e. Washington.

Bailey George W., painter, res. 307 e. Washington, 2 up-stairs.

Bailey Hamilton, coal-driver, res. 332 w. Washington.

Bailey Julius, carpenter, res. 14 Bates.

Bailey Robert, engineer, res. 332 w. Washington.

Baine Mrs. Jane, (wid.,) seamstress, res. 87 s. Pennsylvania.

Baines James, varnisher, 38 e. Washington, bds. Brady's boarding house.

Bair Leonidas, harness and saddlery, 248 w. Washington, bds. cor. Mississippi and Maryland.

Baird William, cooper, res. 2 Indiana av.

Bakemeir Frederick, lab., res. 148 Bluff rd.

Bakemeir Henry, lab., Union depot, res. 419 Virginia av.

Baker A. H., (B. & Surbey,) res. 228 e. South.

Baker Mrs. Anna, (wid.,) millinery, fancy goods and dress-making, 42 s. Illinois, res. same.

Baker Miss B., millinery, 46 s. Illinois, res. same.

Baker C., varnisher, bds. 174 w. New York.

BAKER CONRAD,
governor State of Indiana, office State house, bet. Washington and Market and Tennessee and Mississippi, res, 149 n. Pennsylvania, cor. New York.

Baker Edgar, painter, bds. 84 Massachusetts av.

Baker Edward, pressman, H. C. Chandler & Co., bds. 48 w. Maryland.

Baker Eugene S., clerk, 48 n. Pennsylvania, res. 373 n. Pennsylvania.

Baker Miss Eveline, dress-maker, 42 s. Illinois, bds. same.

Baker Fred., butcher, bds. 367 e. Washington.

Baker G. J., helper, B. F. Haugh, bds. 307 n. Alabama.

Baker Henry, helper, B. F. Haugh & Co., res. 203 n. Illinois.

Baker Henry, drives coal cart, res. 321 Madison av.

Baker J. M., salesman, 22 e. Washington, res. cor. East and New York.

Baker Elijah, res. 138 Maple.

Baker James, breakman, C. C. & I. C. R. R., bds. 58 Benton.

Baker J., H., carpenter, res. 22 Douglas.

Baker John, machinest, res. 194 e. McCarty.

Baker John H., boot-maker, 63 Massachusetts av.

Baker L. C., harness-maker, 24 n. Delaware, bds. 36 n. Pennsylvania.

Baker Lena, servant, 109 Virginia av.

BAKER N. S., upholster and furniture dealer, 73 e. Washington, res. 75 s. Noble.

Baker S., salesman, New York store, res. 215 n. Mississippi.

Baker S. F., res. 373 n. Pennsylvania.

Baker Sarah A. E., (wid.,) 392 n. Alabama.

Baker & Surbey, (A. H. B. & I. S. S.,) groceries and provisions, 199 Virginia av.

Baker Thomas M. C., tailor, res. 170 c. Michigan.

Baker Thomas W., huckster, res. 281 Indiana av.

Baker Winfield S., bds. 117 e. Michigan.

Baldruff Miss E. A., teacher German in ward schools, bds. 146 n. Meridian.

Baldwick F., restaurant and eating house, 32 w. Louisiana, res. same.

Baldwin ——, Auctioneer, bds. 73 n. Illinois.

Baldwin J. Herman, (J. H. B. & Co.,) 62 e. Washington, res. 396 n. Meridian.

Baldwin J. H. & Co., (J. Herman B. & George S. Warren,) yankee notions, fancy goods, trimmings, toys, etc., 6 e. Washington.

Baldwin M. T., res. 41 Russel.

Babester Charles, (col.,) res. Michigan, bet. West and Indiana av.

Baley Frank, brakeman, C. C. & I. C. R. R., bds. 58 Benton.

Baley Julius M., wheel-tightner, patent right, res. 14 Bates.

Balk Frederick, lab., res. 16 Chadwick.

Balke Charles, saloon, 231 e. Washington, res. same.

Balke Henry, piano-varnisher, 159 and 161 e. Washington, res. 16 Chadwick.

Ball Anton, bakery, 178 s. Illinois, res. same.

Ball Miss Catharine, lady boarder, 169 n. Noble.

Ball G. A., carriage-maker, res. Shelbyville pike, 1 mile s. corporation.

Ball J. A., telegraph operator. W. U. Telegraph office, 135 w. Maryland.

Ball William, carpenter, res. 137 w. Maryland.

BALLARD AUSTIN, seal engraver, 28 Circle, res. same.

Ballard C. E., agt., William P. Wallace, 28 w. Louisiana.

Ballard G. M., dealer in Universal Clothes Wringer and Doty Washer, 14 n. Delaware, res. n. Alabama.

Ballard G. W., works Junction R. R., bds. Wiles House,

Ballard Jesse, painter, bds. 70 e. Market.

Ballard John, lab., res. 232 s. Missouri.

BALLARD SAMUEL, boarding house, 70 e. Market.

Ballard W. L., works Junction R. R., bds. Wiles House.

Ballard William, shoe-maker, 41 e. Washington, res. over 45 s. Illinois.

Ballard William P., special agt. Phœnix Mutual Life Insurance Co., of Hartford, Conn., 3 Talbot & New's blk, n. Pennsylvania, res. 487 n. Mississippi.

Ballersty Charles S., railroader, C. C. & I. C. R. R. bds. 61 s. Noble.

Ballinger Miss Emma, book-keeper, bds. 244 s. Alabama.

Ballinger James, (Greer, Miller & Co.,) bds. 112 s. East.

Ballman Herman, groceries and provisions, 408 Indiana av., res. same.

Ballman Henry, painter and grainer, bds. 23 Kentucky av.

Ballweg A., manf. guns, pistols and rifles, 105 w. Washington, res. same.

Ballweg Fred., eating saloon, 17 n. Illinois, res. 28 Ft. Wayne av.

Bals C. F., saloon-keeper, bds. 110 e. St. Joseph.

Bals Charles H. G., (Hahn & B.,) 25 s. Meridian, res. 110 e. St. Joseph, cor. Delaware.

Balwick Frederick, eating house, 32 w. Louisiana, res. same.

Balz Peter, (B. & Bro.) 427 n. Illinois, res. same.

Balz Philip, (B. & Bro.,) 427 n. Illinois, res. same.

BAMBERGER HERMAN, hats, caps, furs and straw goods, 16 e. Washington, res. 1 Ft. Wayne av.

Bamberger Isaac, clerk, 16 e. Washington, bds. 18 Circle.

Band William H., harness-maker, bds. 80 s. Mississippi.

Banghart Isaac, teamster, res. 779 n. Mississippi.

Baning Wm., teamster, bds. 472 s. West.

Bank Rudolph, painter, res. 5 Elm.

Banke Henry, carpenter, res. e. Georgia, n. side.

Banning Ernest, teamster, res. 472 s. West.

Banningberg James, teamster, res. 175 e. South.

Bannon James, works Gates, Pray & Co., res. 65 s. Meridian.

Bannwarth B., shoe-maker, res. 48 Massachusetts av.

Bansa William, wagon-maker, 379 Virginia av., res. 193 s. East.

Banta John P., (Indianapolis Banking Co.,) 28 e. Washington, res. Franklin, Ind.

Baptist Mission Chapel, cor. Noble and South.

Barbee Albert, moulder, works D. Root & Co., res. 348 s. Delaware.

Barbee Henry, fireman, Bellefontaine R. R., res. 348 s. Delaware.

Barbee Robert B., policeman, first ward, res. 385 n. East.

Barbee Sampson, market-master, res. 348 s. Delaware.

Barber Albert H., life insurance agt., res. 75 Elizabeth.

Barber Andrew, (col.,) servant at 210 n. Meridian.

Barbour Miss Anna, teacher, fourth ward school, bds. 215 n. West.

Barbour Charles, (col.,) farmer, res. Lenox, bet. Eighth and Ninth.

BARBOUR & JACOBS, (Lucian B. & Charles J.,) lawyers and notary public, 14 n. Delaware.

Barbour Lucian, (B. & Jacobs,) 14 n. Delaware, res. n. Meridian, outcity limits.

Barbour S., clerk, P. O., res. 216 n. West.

Barbour Thomas F., saw-maker, bds. Pyle House.

Barbour Thomas O., clerk, Democratic State Central Committee, bds. 216 n. West.

Barclay James, stone-cutter, res. 181 n. Liberty.

Bard J. F., works at 175 w. Cumberland, bds. 26 s. Mississippi.

Barett Patrick, res. 232 w. Maryland.

Barger George W., lab., res. 583 Maple.

Baris Robert, machinest, bds. California House.

Capital Tobacco Works, 19, 21 and 23 n. Tennessee.

Barker Mrs. Jane E., (wid. Byron E.,) res. 227 e. Market.

Barker John, bds. National rd., near White river bridge.

Barker Louis E., traveling agt. capital tobacco works, res. 227 e. Market.

BARKER M. I., wholesale tobacconist, office, Miller's blk., res. 502 n. Illinois.

Barker Mrs. Mary T., (wid. Enoch,) res. 227 e. Market.

Barker S. M., meat market, 210 e. St. Clair, res. same.

Barker W. S., merchant tailor, 10 n. Pennsylvania res. 35 n. East.

Barker William W., teacher penmanship, Bryant & Stratton college, s. e. cor. Washington and Meridian.

Barkley Abram, (col.,) lab., 308 Indiana av.

Barkley James, (col.,) lab., res. 276 Elm.

Barkley Miss Mariah, bds. 76 n. California.

Barkes Mrs. Sarah E., (wid. William,) boarding house, 271 West.

Barksahlte Martin, baker, res. 340 Virginia av.

Barlow Liberty, (col.,) shoe-maker, res. 225 n. Tennessee.

Barlow Thomas J., res. 84 s. Mississippi.

Barmann William, bar-tender, 332 Virginia av., bds. 384 Virginia av.

Barmeier Bernard, clerk, 178 e. Washington, bds. Mozart Hall.

Barnaby Catharine, (wid.,) res. 39 Dacota.

Barnacla Henry, fireman, I. C. & L. R. R., res. 56 Bates.

Barnacla, Mrs. John M., res. 56 Bates.

Barnacla Lorenzo, machinist, Eagle Machine Works, res. 156 s. Noble.

Barnard J., insurance agency, office in Chamber of Commerce.

BARNES A. A., photographer, 30 e. Washington, res. 782 n. Illinois.

Barnes Alexander H., bds. 377 n. Illinois.

Barnes George W., huckster, res. 69 n. Elizabeth.

Barnes H., blacksmith, res. s. Illinois.

Barnes H. F., physician and surgeon, room 6 McOuat's blk., res. 197 n. Alabama.

Barnes Hiram, cooper, res. 209 Union.

Barnes Jerome, cooper, res. 283 e. Georgia.
Barnes John, bar-tender, 48 Virginia av., bds. 173 s. Tennessee.
Barnes Patrick, lab., res. 1 Willard.
BARNES ALISON R., physician and surgeon, 29 s. Delaware, res. same.
Barnes Wesley N., compositor, Sentinel news room, bds. 142 n. Mississippi.
Barnes William, patent right agt., res. 377 n. Illinois.
Barney Buchel, printer, bds. 93 s. Noble.
Barney Chester, supt., Ben. Franklin printing office, No. 13 w. Maryland, res. 93 s, Noble.
Barney Jacob, physician and surgeon, office 81 s. Illinois, res. 245 Davidson.
Barnfiher John L., occupant Deaf and Dumb Asylum.
Barnhamer William, plasterer, res. 284 n. West.
Barnhardt Catharine, servant, 469 n. Illinois.
Barnhardt William, lab., res. 126 Hosbrook.
Barnitz Charles, res. 177 s. Noble.
Barnitt Edward, fireman, res. 268 s. Tennessee.
Barnitt Francis, cooper, res. 11 Massachusetts av.
Barnitt Frank J., clerk, 23 e. Washington, res. cor. Bacon and High.
Barnitt Mrs. Lucy, (wid. Francis,) dress-maker, 11 Massachusetts av., res. same.
Barnitt Sampson, cooper, bds. Washington.
Barnitt Thomas, watchman, city tower, res. 390 n. Mississippi.
Barnitz Charles, real estato agt., res. 177 s. Noble.
Barnitz J. W., real estate agt., res 177 s. Noble.
Barnard Eugene E., clerk, Bee-Hive store, bds. 259 n. Illinois.
Barnard Miss Laura J., bds. 259 n. Illinois.
Barnard Moses R., book agt., Iverson & Finney, N. Y., res. 259 n. Illinois.
Barnard Miss Sarah L., bds. 259 n. Illinois.
Barr Jacob, res. 424 n. Delaware.
Barr L. B., (Lybrand & B.,) grocers, 233 s. Tennessee, res. same.
Barr & Lybrand, grocers, 233 s. Tennessee.
Barr Mrs. Nancy, (wid. George,) res. 89 Ann.
Barr William A., yard-master, I. P. & C. R. R., bds. 53 Bates.
Barrett Adaline, house-keeper, Commercial Hotel.
Barrett Charles E., painter, res. 166 n. Mississippi.
Barrett Edward, lab., res. 277 s. West.
Barrett Edward G., canvasser for the Home Journal, res. 123 Huron.
Barrett Mrs. Elizabeth, boarding house, 224 e. Market.

Barrett Horace H., clerk, 19 n. Meridian, res. n. w. cor. Ohio and Pennsylvania.
Barrett James, lab., res. 126 Stevens.
Barrett John lab., res. n. e. cor. Morris and New Jersey.
Barrett Joseph, (col.,) lab., 257 n. West.
Barrett Mary, servant, R. Browning, 172 n. Illinois.
Barrett Mary, servant, Palmer House.
Barrett Michael, lab., res. 425 s. Tennessee.
Barrett Patrick, lab., res. 174 Meek.
Barribker Levi, lab., res. 42 Rose.
Barry Edward, scroll sawyer, res. 368 s. Delaware.
BARRY E. H., grand secy., Grand Lodge I. O. O. F., 2 Odd Fellows Hall, res. 528 n. Tennessee.
Barry Mrs. Allen, (wid.) Richard, res. 368 s. Delaware.
Barry J., scroll sawyer, bds. 368 Delaware.
Barry Thomas G., (Stewart & Morgan,) 40 e. Washington, res. 197 n. Delaware.
Barse Ernest, lab., Root's foundry, res. 70 s. Liberty.
Bartt Charles, clerk, 29 w. Washington, bds. 387 n. West.
Barth J. W., salesman, 21 w. Washington, bds. 387 n. West.
Barth Louis A., propr. Union depot news stand, res, 104 s. New Jersey.
Barth Rev. Sebastian, minister, M. E. Church, res. 387 n. West.
Barthel Lenhard, (B. & Kaufman,) res. 367 n. East.
Barthel & Kaufman, meat market, 267 n. East.
BARTHOLOMEW C. & BROS., (Charles, S. T. & J. W. B.,) com. mers. and produce dealers, 90 s. Meridian.
Bartholemew Charles, (C. B. & Bros.,) 90 s. Meridian, res. same.
Bartholomew J. W., (C. B. & Bros.,) 90 s. Meridian, res. same.
BARTHOLOMEW P. W., attorney at law, office 20½ n. Delaware, bds. 307 n. East.
Bartholomew S. T., (C. B. & Bros.,) 90 s. Meridian, res. same.
Bartholomew Thomas, cooper, res. Ellen, near Indiana av.
Bartler Richard, (col.,) lab., res. 164 Douglas alley.
Bartlett Harrison, servant, Pattison House.
Bartlett John A., carpenter, res. Eighth, bet. Lenox and Knox.
Bartlett Lydia, (col.,) res. 28 n. Blake.
Bartlett Mrs. Louisa, res. Ninth, near Lafayette R. R.
Bartlett Nancy, servant, Parmer House, bds. same.
Bartley Abraham, (col.,) lab., res. 85 Eddy.
Bartley M. J., occupant Deaf and Dumb Asylum.

Barto Miss Mary, bds. 319 s. Pennsylvania.

Barton Bridget, asst. cook, Commercial Hotel.

Barton Eliza, chamber-maid, Wiles House.

Barton Kate, waits dining room, Commercial Hotel.

Barves Josiah, clerk, bds. 377 n. Illinois.

Bary Mrs. Mary, (wid. Edmond,) res. n. w. cor. Peru and St. Clair.

Basa Mrs. Ellen, (wid. Gottlib,) res. 367 n. Liberty.

Basa Frederick, res. 324 e. Vermont.

Base Christian, carpenter, res. 297 e. Georgia.

Baseg James, propr. Empire Saloon, n. Illinois, bds. 207 w. Maryland.

Basket Mary, (col.) wid. George,) washing and ironing, res. 62 Huron.

Bassett Mrs. N., (wid. Horace,) res. 46 e. Ohio.

Bassett H. H., real estate agt., res. 46 e. Ohio.

Bastly Thornton, (col.) lab., bds. 156 Douglass alley.

Bates Benjamin, cook, res. rear 141 w. Washington.

Bates Charles A., (Rout & B.,) s. e. cor. Illinois and Pratt, res. same.

Bates Harvey, sr., capitalist, res. 190 e. Market.

Bates Harvey, jr., cashier, First National Bank, res. 185 n. Delaware.

BATES HOUSE,
n. w. cor. Washington and Illinois, N. D. Keneaster, propr., E. Hartwell, chief clerk.

Bates John A., cooper, res. 323 w. Market.

Batler Robert, merchant police, bds. 177 s. Illinois.

Battums Nelson G., lab, end Virginia av. beyond city limits.

Batty Edwin, carpenter, res. 124 Broadway.

Batty John H., clerk County Recorder's office, res. 228 e. Louisiana.

Bauch John, lab., res. 289 s. Missouri.

Bauer Gottlieb, tailor, 17 e. Washington, res. 275 n. Noble.

Bauer John J., confectioner, 146 w. Washington, res. same.

Bauer Mrs. Louisa, (wid. Frederick,) res. 318 Winston.

Bauer Mrs. Mary, (wid.,) res. 77 n. Illinois.

Bauer Snider, tailor, res. 275 n. Noble.

Baugher Louis, pastor, English Lutheran Church, cor. Alabama and New York, bds. 79 n. Alabama.

Baughn W., carpenter, res. 9 Elizabeth.

Bauler Mrs. Mary, (wid. Martin,) 331 e. Louisiana.

Bauman Henry, tailor, res. 237 n, Liberty.

Baumhofer Henry, carpenter, res. 236 Madison av.

Baxter Edward, carpenter, res. 187 Davidson.

Baxter & Davis, (Peter D. B. & Abel E. D.,) groceries and produce, 250 w. Washington.

Baxter George, clerk, 250 w. Washington, bds. same.

Baxter John, res. 13 Dacota.

Baxter Mrs. Mollie, (wid.,) res. 119 w. Vermont.

Baxter Peter D., (B. & Davis,) res. 250 w. Washington.

Baxter William A., res. first tolegate Shelbyville pike.

Bayer Jacob, tailor, res. 80 s. Delaware.

Baykel Andrew, drayman, bds. 172 s. Noble.

Baylor Albert E., clerk, 3 Odd Fellows Hall.

Baylor Mrs. Rachel, (wid.,) bds. 512 n. Mississipi.

Baymiller Mrs. Parthenia, (wid. Charles P.,) res. 294 n. Liberty.

Bayr Alexander, shoemaker, 41 e. Washington, res. room 7 McOuits Block.

Bazey Andrew, foundryman, res. 24 Ellen.

Bazey Christian, carpenter, res. 297 e Georgia.

Bazey Henry, carpenter, res. 297 e. Georgia.

Beach Daniel W., printer, Journal office, bds. Commercial Hotel.

Beachley Anna, servant, 426 n. Illinois.

Beachman Henry, bds. 247 e. Washington.

Beal John A., attorney at law, res. 5 Madison av.

Beal John W., butcher, res. 278 s. Missouri.

Beal Joshua, paper hanger, Gall & Rush, res. 77 w. Walnut.

Bealer George, brewer, res. 134 Bluff rd.

Bealer Josaphine, (wid. Benedict,) res. 114 Bluff road.

Beals Jerome, clerk, 30 s. Meridian, res 115 s. Meridian.

Beam David, (Emerson B. & Thompson,) 225 w. Market, res. 187 s. Tennessee.

Beam Edward A. & Co., groceries, 293 e. Washington, res. 187 w. south.

Beam J. M., railroader, bds. 187 w. South.

Beanisite August, machinist, res. 309 s. Pennsylvania.

Beanisite Charles, machinist, res. 309 s. Pennsylvania.

Beansack James, lab., res. 110 Virginia av.

Beard Amos, wagon-maker, res. 256 s. Tennessee.

Beard Benjamin, blacksmith, bds. 157 w. Maryland.

Beard David, blacksmith, bds. 157 w. Maryland.

Beard Soloman, propr. Beard House, cor Maryland and Mississippi.

Bearman William, shoe-maker, bds. Court, between East and New Jersey.

Beasly Thomas, shoe-maker, bds. 144 n. Tennessee.

Beatty Bernard G., tobacconist, bds. Ray House.

Beatty Miss Mary E., teacher, bds. 204 n. Illinois.

Beatty Sarah A., servant, 40 n. New Jersey.

Beaty David S., retired, res. 194 e. Michigan.

Beaty Eliza H., paper-maker, res. 160 Blackford.

Beaty John W., paper-maker, res. 160 Blackford.

Beautica C. S., physician, 63 McCarty, res. 250 Madison av.

Beaver Elisha, teamster, res. 380 n. West.

Beaver George, machinist, res. 244 e. Missouri.

Beaver Leonadus, draughtsman, 1 Brown's Block, bds. Patterson House.

Beaver Thomas F., sawyer, works London, Ind., res. 254 n. East.

Beck Albert, student, bds. 152 n. Mississippi.

Beck Christian, gun-smith, 12 s. Pennsylvania, res. 154 n. New Jersey.

Beck David, tailor, bds. 154 n. New Jersey.

Beck Edward, res. 27 w. Maryland.

Beck Miss Emma, bds. 152 n. Mississippi.

Beck Frederick, butcher, res. 100 Bluff rd.

Beck George, lab., res. 384 e. Market.

Beck Henry, bakery, 88 Ft. Wayne av., res. same.

Beck James A., R. R. conductor, res. 271 w. Washington.

Beck John A., watch-maker, 43 s. Illinois, res. 154 n. New Jersey.

Beck Martin, barber, res. 333 s. Delaware.

Beck S. T., (Porter, Vance & B.,) 85 e. Market, res. cor. New York and Mississippi.

Beck Samuel Jr., jeweler, bds. 152 n. Mississippi.

Beck Samuel, Sen., gun-smith, 63 e. Washington, res. 152 n. Mississippi.

Becker Charles, journeyman barber, works under First National Bank, bds. 28 w. Georgia.

Becker Godfrey, clerk, res. 238 s. New Jersey.

BECKER & HUBER, (Jacob B. & Jacob H.,) mer. tailors, 77 e. Washington.

Becker F. P., (F. P. B. & Bro.,) 17 n. Pennsylvania, res. same.

BECKER F. P. & BRO., (F. P. & Joseph Becker,) bakery, confectionery and ladies restaurant, 17 n. Pennsylvania.

Becker Jacob, (B. & Huber, 77 e. Washington, res. 180 n. New Jersey.

Becker Jacob, cigar-maker, 112 Virginia av.

Becker James, (T. P. B. & Bros.,) 17 n. Pennsylvania, res. same.

Becker John, retired farmer, res. 180 n. New Jersey.

Becket Theophilus M., engineer, C. & I. C. R. R., res. 473 e. Georgia.

Beckley James, (B. & Stephenson,) res. 252 Bluff rd.

Beckley & Stephenson, grocers and produce dealers, 248 Bluff rd.

Beckman Christina, (wid. William,) res. 330 s. Alabama.

Beckman Miss Ellen, tailoress, res. 330 s. Alabama.

Beckman Mrs. H., (wid.,) res. 408 North.

Beckner Samuel H., lawyer, bds. 72 e. Ohio.

Beechner Mrs. Ann, (wid. George,) servant, 134 s. Meridian.

Beechler James J., carpenter, res. 165 Winston.

Beeber George P., carpenter, res. 33 Meek.

Beeler J. L., saddler, res. McCarty, near East.

Beeler John, hostler, 166 n. Meridian.

Beeler S. D., carpenter, res. cor. Cedar and Fletcher av.

Beeman A. J., occupant Deaf and Dumb Asylum.

Beeman Truman, carpenter, res. 171 Jackson.

Beeman Henry, lab., res. 502 s. New Jersey.

Beers F. C., bds. 296 w. New York.

Beever I. R., book-binder, Journal office, bds. 380 n. West.

Bezeman Fred., occupant Deaf and Dumb Asylum.

Behymer Simon, lumber dealer, res. 247 n. New Jersey.

Behrendt A., cigar-maker, works 290 e. Washington, bds. s. Illinois.

Behrent Henry, express driver, bds. 185 Harrison.

Behringer Joseph B., (Marone & B.,) 145 w. Washington, res. same.

Behring William, lab., res. 168 s. Noble.

Beiser August, foreman, City Brewery, res. cor. Madison av. and Tennessee.

Belch Nicholas S., carpenter, cor. Ninth and Michigan rd.

Bell A. R., printer, Journal office, res. w. New York.

Bell Andrew, (col.,) shoe-maker, res. 345 n. Alabama.

Bell Miss Farrie, lady boarder, 27 n. New Jersey.

Bell Henry, boot-black, 143 w. Washington.

Bell M., druggist, 264 Massachusetts av., res. 484 n. East.

Bell Samuel, works in C. C. & I. C. yard, bds. 94 s. Liberty.

Bell Wm. A., principal City High School, bds. Pyle House.

Bell William H., lab., rolling mill, res. 51 Dougherty.

BELLEFONTAINE R. R. CO., general office 538 Alabama, Justice L. Cozad, supt. western division.

Belles Clark, telegraph operator, Bellefontaine office, bds. 325 e. Ohio.

Bellis John R., machinist, Sinker & Co., bds. 221 s. Alabama.

Belshover John, lab., bds. 317 Indiana av.

Beltz Frank, bell-boy, Spencer House, bds. same.

Beltz John A., news dealer, Spencer House, bds same.

Beltz Jacob, plasterer, res. 175 Stevens.

Belzer George, machinist, res. 141 e. St. Mary.

Bence Robert F., physician, res. 86 Ash.

Bendare John, soldier, U. S. Arsenal, res. same.

Bender Tobias, (Bisplinghoff & Co..) 189 e. Washington, res. 293 e. Market.

Bender George W., telegraph operator, I. C. & L. R. R., bds. 272 w. Maryland.

Beneway Almon B., cigar-maker, res. 151 Winston.

Beneway Mrs. Emily, (wid. Egbert B.,) res. 151 Winston.

Benford William B., salesman, 24 w. Washington, res. same.

Benham A. M., (B. Bros. & Co.,) 36 e. Washington, res. 235 e. Vermont.

BENHAM BROTHERS & CO., (H. L. & A. M. Benham & Ebin Sharpe,) music publishers and dealers in pianos, organs, melodeons and musical merchandise, 36 e. Washington.

Benham H. L., (Benham Bros. & Co.,) 36 e. Washington, res. 235 e. Vermont.

Benham John, music dealer, res. 475 n. Meridian.

Benhart John, stone-mason, res. near 350 Railroad.

Benn Willson, expressman, res. 248 Blackford.

Benner Arthur, head porter, 149 s. Meridian, res. s. Illinois.

Bennett Elizabeth, servant, Dr. R. N. Todd, 78 w. Market.

Bennett George W., policeman, first ward, res. 402 n. New Jersey.

Bennett H. W., pattern-maker, Sinker's foundry, res. 138 s. East.

Bennett Miss Harriet, lady boarder, 201 e. Market.

Bennett J. B., student, commercial college, bds. 118 w. Georgia.

Bennett Miss Louisa, res. 56 Bates.

Bennett N. H., brakeman, C. C. & I. C. R. R., bds. 61 s. Noble.

Bennett Robert M., lab., n. s. National rd., w. White river bridge.

Bennet William R., lab., res. 39 Jones.

Benninger 'John, salesman, C. Helwig, res. 576 e. St. Clair.

Benninger Von, image-maker, res. 295 e. New York.

Bensheid Gustave, lithographer, W. & J. Braden, res. cor. Vine and Plum.

Benson David S., second hand clothing and furniture, 206 s. Illinois, res. same.

Benson John A., tolegate keeper, res. end w. Washington.

Benson John S., commission merchant, 89 e. Market, res. 61 Ft. Wayne av.

Benton Allen K., prest. N. W. Christian University, res. n. w. cor. Christian av. and Forest Home av.

Benton Richard, professor N. W. Christian University, res. cor. Christian av. and Plum.

Benton Thos., (col.,) porter Supreme Court rooms, cor. Tennessee and Washington.

Benyman John, machinist, works Chandler & Taylor, res. 424 e. St. Clair.

Bereness Joseph, cabinet-maker, bds. 23 Kentucky av.

Berg Augustus, moulder, bds. 171 e. South.

Berg Frederika, (wid. Charles,) res. 171 e. South.

Berg Henry, (H. B. & Co.,) 193 s. Tennessee, res. same.

Berg Henry & Co., grocers and produce dealers, 193 s. Tennessee.

Berg George, printer, bds. 171 e. South.

Berg William L., hose reel driver No. 3 engine, res. 171 e.|South.

Bergener Gustav, book-keeper Indianapolis Branch Banking Co., bds. 109 w. Washington.

Bergenthal David C., book-keeper, E. Over & Co., 68 s. Meridian, res. 201 n. Liberty.

Berger Fredereke, (wid. Athen,) mid-wife, 78 n. Noble, res. same.

Bergman Francis, soap and candle manufactor, res. s. West, near city limits.

Bergstein Carl, teacher music and voice builder, res. 323 e. Ohio.

Berkhofer George, show-case maker, 5 Virginia av.

BERKSHIRE LIFE INS. CO., office 25 w. Washington, P. W. Bartholomew, State agt.

Berkshire Miss Jane, res. 293 e. New York.

Bernaner Benedict, tailor, s. s. Coburn, between Wright and East.

Bernaner Joseph, teamster, res. 123 Huron.

Berner John, huckster, res. 185 Davidson.

Berner Charles, clerk, Lawrence's grocery, 171 w. Washington, res. 371 w. New York.

Bernhamer N. F. A., law student, Perkins, Jordan & Perkins, bds. 302 n. New Jersey.

Berran Catheny Miss, teacher, German English school, res. cor. Alabama and St. Joseph.

Berry Andrew, plasterer, res. Camp Carrington.

Berry Austin, printer, Journal office, res. 318 e. Market.

Berry C. B., brick-mason, bds. Ray House.

Berry Miss C. C., principal preparatory department Indiana Female College, 146 n. Meridian, bds. same.

Berry Charles A., saw-maker, bds. Concordia House.

Berry Francis, carpenter, res. 93 Benton.

Berry George, lab., res. 318 e. Market.

Berry George W., brick-maker, res. 291 e. New York.

Berry Harriet, (wid.,) servant, Patterson House, 68 n. Alabama.

Berry John, blacksmith, res. 318 e. Market.

Berry John, nurseryman, res. 145 Huron.

Berry John, lab., res. 408 e. Washington.

Berry Mrs. Mary J., (wid.,) bds. 375 n. West.

Berry Michael, stone-cutter, res. 136 Spring.

Berry Patrick, lab., res. 203 w. McCarty.

Bert Henry L., tailor, bds. 124 s. Meridian.

Berryman Henegy, inmate Deaf and Dumb Asylum.

Berryman James, M., machinist, Sinker's Foundry, res. 88 s. Noble.

Berkett John, barber, under Bee-Hive.

Beston Michael, lab., res. 154 s. Noble.

Bess William K:, saloon keeper, 284 w. Washington, res. same.

Bessonies Augustus, pastor St. John's Catholic Church, res. Georgia, adjoining church.

Bettes William H., patent wright for a gaiter boot, res. 112 n. Delaware.

Betz Henry, moulder, bds. 182 Indiana av.

Berans Hiram C., canvassing agt., res. 16 Massachusetts av.

Beyer Frederick, (wid. Adam,) mid-wife, res. 78 n. Noble.

Bez Jacob, shoe-maker, res. and shop over 10 Bates House blk.

Bibb James W. H., (col.,) head waiter, Bates House, bds. same.

Digkel Christian, farmer, res. 406 s. West.

Biddy James M., lab. in Gas Factory, res. 22 between Liberty and East.

Biden Miss Ellen, dress-making, 185 e. Washington, bds. Little Hotel.

Bider Catherine, (wid.,) res. 279 e. Louisiana.

Bider Mathew, cabinet-maker, res. 274 e. Louisiana.

Bidleman Silas G., shoe-maker, bds. 83 n. Pennsylvania.

Biedenmeister C. A., general insurance agt., office 96 e. Washington, res. 149 n. East.

Bicler Jacob L., (Frauer B. & Co.,) 109 e. Washington, res. e. McCarty.

Biennen Mary, servant, M. M. Landis, 506 n. Meridian.

Biepbart Henry, cigar-maker, res. 152 Greer.

Bierman H. H., carver, Spiegle & Thems, res. 38 s. Alabama.

Biglow I. P., plasterer, res. 395 e. Market.

Bigelow J. S., Deputy U. S. Marshal, res. 161 Massachusetts av.

Bigelow James K., physician, 37 Virginia av., res. 323 Virginia av.

Bigelow John S., plasterer, res. Clinton between Ohio and New York.

Biggadike R. C., carriage painter, 123 e. Washington, bds. Union Hall.

Bigger Samuel S., trade palace, res. 211 s. Delaware.

BIGHAM HEYDEN S., flour and feed, 149 e. Washington, res. 203 e. South.

Bilger Joseph, carpenter, works Manny & Sons, res. 332 e. New York.

Billings F. M., traveling agt., Grover & Baker's Sewing Machine Co., 21 e.

Billings William, lab., res. Minerva, between New York and Vermont.

BILLINGSLEY A. D., elmwood fruit farm, w. White river, near Lafayette gravel rd., one half mile n. National rd.

Bills Jared M., (B. & Sipe,) lawyer, 20½ n. Delaware, Hereth's blk., bds. Pyle House.

BILLS & SIPE,
(J. M. B & William A. S.,) lawer and notary public, 20½ n. Delaware.

Billupps Sarah, servant, 119 n. Pennsylvania.

Binegar Peter, stone-cutter, res. 89 Elm.

Bingham J. W., student, bds. 148 w. Washington.

Bingham James, stone-cutter, res. Michigan rd., beyond city limits.

BINGHAM JOSEPH J.,
associate editor Indianapolis Sentinel, res. 148 w. Maryland.

Bingham Wheelock P., (W. P. B. & Co.,) watches, jewelry, diamonds and silver-plated ware, 50 e. Washington, res. 32 n. California.

Bingham William B., traveling agt., 30 s. Meridian, bds. 32 n. California.

Binica Frederick, brick-maker, res. s. w. cor. Coburn and East.

Binkley Benjamin, machinest, bds. 169 s. Tennessee.

BINKLEY S.,
manf. and dealer in trunks, valises and traveling bags, 29 s. Illinois, res. 316 s. Illinois.

Binkley Samuel, res. 116 s. Illinois.

Birch Richard E., (Long & B.,) undertaker, res. 222 n. New Jersey.

Bird Abram, res. 129 n. Illinois.

Bird Frank, bds. Bates House.

Bird George, works Junction R. R., bds. Wiles House.

Bird Mrs. Mary, (wid.,) res. 408 w. North.

Bird Henry, (col.,) res. 75 e. Georgia.

Bird John, carpenter, res. Yeiser, bet. East and New Jersey.

Bird William F., cigar stand, Bates House, bds. 129 n. Illinois.

Birket Charles, tailor 408, Virginia av., res. same.

Bisbing Jacob, marshal Union Depot, res. 212 n. West.

Bishop Caroline, occupant Deaf and Dumb Asylum.

Bishop Emma, (col.) res. n. Missouri.

Bishop George M., fireman, fire engine No. 3, South, res. 221 s. Alabama.

BISHOP J. LEWIS,
soliciting agt., Logan & Co.'s directories and Western Commercial Review and Railroad Journal, 16½ e. Washington, bds. Macy House.

Bishop Jacob, butcher, res. near City Hospital.

Bishop Joseph L., cigars and tobacco, cor. New York and Massachusetts av., res. same.

Bishop Jesse, (col.,) res. 490 s. Illinois.

Bishop Lewis, res. 391 n. New Jersey.

Bishop Louisa, (wid.,) res. near City Hospital.

Bishop Maria, (col.,) res. n. Missouri.

Bishop Sarah A. (wid. John,) res. 393 n. New Jersey.

Bishop Wm. A., brick-layer, res. 77 w. South.

Bisking Christian Herman, lab., res. 140 Huron.

Bisplinghoff Henry, (B. & Co.,) 189 e. Washington, res. same.

Bisplinghoff Isabela, dress-maker, bds. 180 e. Washington.

Bisplinghoff & Co., (Henry B., Joshua Stump & Tobias Bender,) wholesale dealers in wines and liquors, 189 e. Washington.

Biston Victon, bar-tender, 299 e. Washington, bds. in rear.

Bixler David, butcher, res. 424 s. Illinois.

Bixby Mrs. Ellen, (wid. Newman.) res. 166 e Market.

Bixby Frank, student commercial college, res. 166 e. Market.

Black Charles H., blacksmith, works S. W. Drew & Co., res. 206 e. Ohio.

Black George H., stair builder, res. 206 e. Ohio.

Black George W., traveling agt., 42 s. Meridian, bds. Oriental House.

Black J. S., professor, res. 219 e. North.

Black James, (Elliott & B.,) 24½ e. Washington, bds. Oriental House.

Black Mrs. Jenny, (wid. Thomas,) seamstress, bds. 41 Hosbrook.

Black Jerry, (col.,) farmer, res. n. Blake.

Black John, street car driver, res. 164 Indiana av.

Black Joshua, bds. cor. West and Michigan.

Black Mathew H., carpenter, res. 390 n. West.

BLACK PETER,
propr. first national livery, boarding, and sale stables, Court, between Pennsylvania and Delaware, res. 70 n. East.

Black Thomas, employee, Merchants Union Express, bds. 179 s. Tennessee.

Black William, wiper, C. C. & J. C. Round House, res. 327 e. Georgia.

Black William M., supt. Masonic Hall, res. 179 s. Tennessee.

Blackburn G. W., (col.,) barber, 303 e. Washington.

Blackburn Reuben, (col.,) lab., res. 170 Douglass Alley.

Blackwell Henry, res. w. of city limits.

Blackwell Thomas, lab., res. 129 Maple.

Bladen John, saloon, 231 s. Delaware, res. same.

Blades Miss Maria, seamstress, bds. 306 e. North.

Blair Mrs. D. W., (wife John,) ladies bazaar, 172 e. Washington, res. same.

Blair F. M., genl. agt. Brooklyn Life Insurance Co., office Vinton's blk., opp. p. o., res. 152 n. Meridian.

Blair John, pattern-maker, works D. Root & Co., bds. over 172 e. Washington.

Blair John M., saddler, bds. 152 n. Meridian.

Blair Joseph M., printer, bds. 152 n. Meridian.

Blair Mrs. Josephine, bds. 27 w. Ohio.

Blair Mrs. Sarah, (wid. James,) res. rear 342 Railroad.

Blair Thomas M., sen., cupalo tender, res. 185 w. New York.

Blair Thomas M., jr., machinist, res. 175 w. New York.

Blair William, machinist, bds. 175 New York.

Blaisdell S. E., carriage-maker, 26 e. Georgia, bds. 128 s. Illinois.

Blake Albert E., machinist, White River Iron Works, bds. cor. Tennessee and South.

Blake Augustus, moulder, bds. 15 Willard.

Blake James, Sen., retired merchant, res. 308 n. Tennessee.

Blake J. R., (J. R. B. & Co.,) 15 s. Deleware, bds. 308 n. Tennessee.

BLAKE J. R. & CO.,
flour, feed and com. mer., 15 s. Delaware.

Blake John G., delivery clerk, Western Union Telegraph Co., 11 s. Meridian, bds. 308 n. Tennessee.

BLAKE JOHN W.,
attorney at law and collecting agt., over 45 e. Washington, res. 351 n. Tennessee, cor. Walnut.

Blake Miss Mollie, bds. 224 n. Missouri.

Blake Samuel, bds. 308 n. Tennessee.

Blake William M., (J. R. B. & Co.,) 15 s. Delaware, res. 327 n. Tennessee.

Blakemore Jackson, (col.,) lab., res. cor. Second and Lafayette R. R.

Blakely Joseph, (col.,) waiter, Bates House.

Blakeslee John R., works rolling mill, bds. 234 e. Vermont.

Blalock Miss M., dress and cloak-maker, 75 n. Pennsylvania, res. same.

Blame William, lab., I. P. & C. Depot, res. 144 Madison av.

Bland Mrs. M. Cora, associate editress, North-Western Farmer, res. terminus Ft. Wayne av.

Bland F. D., minister, Baptist church, supt. missions, res. 32 n. East.

Bland Miss Mary E., music teacher, res. 32 n. East.

Bland J. G., res. 62 w. South.

BLAND T. A.,
editor and publisher North-Western Farmer, office cor. Meridian and Circle, old Journal bldg., res. n. e. terminus Ft. Wayne av.

Blank Anthony, clerk, 178 e. Washington, res. over 178 e. Washington.

Blankinship Mrs. Mary, dress-maker, res. 300 w. Washington.

Blanvault Charles, wood-hauler, res. Orient, bet. Michigan and National rd., beyond city limits.

Blauvelt D. C., money delivery, M. U. Ex. Co., 42 and 44 e. Washington, res. 142 Blackford.

Blaavelt James, Jr., fireman, I. C. R. R., res. 427 e. Vermont.

Bledan John, carpenter, res. 349 w. Mc-Carty.

Bless Eli, capitalist, res. 346 n. New Jersey.

Bletzinger Z., res. w. White river bridge.

Blettener John, blacksmith, Wash. Ford, res. 284 e. Louisiana.

Blind Asylum, North, bet. Pennsylvania and Meridian.

Block Henry, painter, Bellefontaine shops, bds. 201 Davidson.

Blood Irvine, occupant Deaf and Dumb Asylum.

Bloom Mrs. Julia, res. 27 w. St. Clair.

Bloomer Ellen, servant, e. Washington, near Arsenal av.

Bloomer Isaac L., (Parker & B.,) over 23 e. Washington, res. 155 n. New Jersey.

Bloomer James, brick-maker, res. Shelbyville pike, 1 mile s. corporation.

Bloomerdale Henry A., carpenter, works Sinker & Co., res. 113 Davidson.

Bloomingstock John, hostler, Street R. R. Stables, res. 599 n. Tennessee.

Blotts Amelia, servant, 438 n. Tennessee.

Blotts C., (wid. John,) res. 438 s. Illinois.

Blue Augustus M., gas-fitter, res. 365 n. East.

Blue Benson, carpenter, res. 365 n. East.

Blue C. B., carpenter, res. 365 n. East.

Blue Charles, gas-fitter, 82 w. Washington, res. 365 n. East.

Blue Jared, farmer, res. 498 n. Illinois.

Bledan John, porter, res. 58 McCarty.

Blue Thomas, (col.,) servant, 440 n. Meridian.

Bly George, servant, E. Rammel, bds. end Virginia av.

Bly Jacob, brick-maker, res. 163 Ft. Wayne av.

Bly John, teamster, res. 399 s. East.

Bly O. H. P., lamp-lighter, res. 34 n. New Jersey.

Blybe August, bell boy, Palmer House, bds. same.

Blythe Samuel, lab., res. 187 s. Alabama.

Blythe William M., grocery and produce dealer, 407 n. Alabama, res. 152 e. St. Clair, cor. Alabama.

Boardman Miss Josephine, student, ninth ward school, bds. 306 e. North.

Boardman O. B., policeman, sixth ward, res. 172 Union.

Boaz Charles, bds. 34 w. North.
Boaz Mrs. Noama J., (wid.,) res. 34 w. North.
Boaz Oliver, messenger, Indiana Banking Co., 28 e. Washington, bds. 34 w. North.
Boaz William, res. 319 s. Pennsylvania.
Bobbs Elizabeth, (wid.,) res. 195 n. Pennsylvania.
BOBBS J. S., physician and surgeon, 15 e. Washington, res. near e. Michigan rd., bet. I. & C. and C. C. & I. C. R. Rs.
Bockstaller Martin, clerk, Union depot eating stand.
Bodance Lewis, tailor, res. 229 Union.
Bodenback Christ., street-sprinkler, res. 504 s. East.
Bodenhamer William, printer, Journal office, res. 280 n. Alabama.
Bodemiller Leonard, blacksmith, res. 138 e. St. Mary.
Bœdker Henry, (B. & Neeman,) bds. 272 Winston.
BŒDKER & NEEMAN, carpenters and builders, shop n. s. North, bet. Davidson and Winston. See card, page 46.
Bockhert Frederick, copper-smith, res. 282 e. Washington.
Bœhlan Ernest L., book-binder, Meikels,' res. 56 n. East.
Bœhm Ferdinand, teacher, Zion's school, bds. 27 w. Ohio.
Bœhm Frederick, res. 378 n. West.
Bœrum Joseph S., carpenter, res. 414 n. Delaware.
Bœtticher Otto, printer, works 164 e. Washington, res. 166 e. Washington.
Bœtticher Julius, propr. Volksblatt, 164 e. Washington, res. 166 e. Washington.
Bogardes William, carpenter, res. 199 Harrison.
Bogell Samuel, carpenter, res. 477 n. New Jersey.
Bogemeir Fred., lab., res. 146 Bluff rd.
Bogen Joseph, watch-maker, res. 369 s. Illinois.

Bogert Mrs. Caroline, (wid.,) res. 260 n. Patterson.
Bogert James, trunks, traveling bags, valises, Meridian, under Bee-Hive, res. 490 n. Mississippi.
Boggers Henry H., tobacconist, res. 612 n. Illinois.
Boggs Henry, cooper, res. Canal, near Washington.
BOHLEN DIEDRICH A., architect, room 19 Talbott & New's blk., n. Pennsylvania, res. 71 n. Noble.
Bohn Gustavus, works Hasselman & Vinton, res. 326 s. Delaware.
Bohmie John M., coach-painter, 26 e. Georgia, bds. 67 Madison av.
Bohne Henry, gardner, res. Shelbyville pike, 1 mile s. corporation.
Bohman Peter, bar-tender, Washington Hall saloon, bds. same.
Bokern Joseph, watch-maker, 7 w. Washington, res. 369 s. Illinois.
Bolck Henry, carpenter, bds. 576 e. Washington.
Bolden Henry, lab., res. 260 n. Noble.
Boldsborough John F., engineer, J. M. & I. R. R., res. 138 e. McCarty.
Bolen ——, engineer, C. C. & I. C. R. R., bds. 58 Benton.
Bolen Catharine, servant, 329 e. Market.
Bolen John, stone-cutter, res. 232 s. Missouri.
Bolen Michael, lab., res. 43 Henry.
Bolen William, policeman, fourth ward, res. 386 w. New York.
Bolin Charles, occupant Deaf and Dumb Asylum.
Boller Peter, painter, res. 282 Winston.
Bollman Frederick, propr. Cincinnati Bakery, 107 e. Washington, res. same.
Bollinger James, (Dreher, Miller & Co.,) res. 112 s. East.
Bolser Albert, cooper, res. 38 Helen.
Bolser Andrew, cooper, res. 33 Helen.
Bosler George, painter, res. 125 Bluff rd.
Bolton Thomas, salesman, New York Store, bds. Commercial Hotel.

Bolton James, railroader, res. 289 Winston.

Boman Wm. C., carpenter, res. 418 s. Illinois.

Bomberger David, carpenter, res. 287 Indiana av.

Bome Levi, saloon, 101 s. Illinois, res. 83 w. South.

Bond Alonzo S., engineer, I. C. & L. R. R., res. 56 Bates.

Bond A. V., shoe-maker, works at 32 e. Washington, res. 273 n. Tennessee.

Bond Mrs. Carlin, (wid. Clamson,) res. 457 cor. Huron and Noble.

Bond Edward, carpenter, Bellefontaine shop, res. 270 Railroad.

Bonham B. M., actor, Metropolitan Theater, res. e. Market, between East and New Jersey.

Bonham Thomas A., special agt., North-Western Mutual Life Insurance Co.

Bonnell Miss India, student, Ind. Female College, 146 n. Meridian, bds. same.

Bonsack John R., carpenter, res. 426 and 428 n. Meridian.

Bonso William, wagon-maker, res. 193 s. East.

Booker Miss Margaret, bds. 31 w. Michigan.

Boomer Elizabeth, servant, E. G. English, 48 Circle.

Borgart Anton, lab., res. 342 s. Delaware.

Borger Julia, servant, 124 n. Alabama.

Borgner Charles, clerk, over 35 e. Washington, res. 31 Chatham.

Boriger John, stone-mason, res. 31 Chatham.

Boring Ephraim, plasterer, res. 345 n. West.

Born John, cooper, bds. 259 s. West.

Born Wm. F., rope-maker, res. 259 s. West.

Borodes Homer, student, N. W. C. U., bds. 22 Gregg.

Borst Frederick, meat market, 22 n. Illinois, Bates House, res. on Canal, outside Corporation line.

Bosart Timothy G., clerk, 151 w. Washington, bds. 9 s. Mississippi.

Boss John, drayman, res. 144 Union.

Boss John, carpenter, bds. 84 Massachusetts av.

Bossert John, baker, 112 Bluff rd., res. same.

Bost George, tanner, res. 276 Bluff rd.

Boswell J. K., patentee, Boswell patent fruit dryer and room heater, 16 s. Pennsylvania, bds. 52 s. Pennsylvania.

Botameir William, lab., res. 339 e. McCarty.

Bothwell Henry, groceries and provisions, Mississippi, between First and Second, res. e. side Mississippi, between First and Second.

Bott Gotlieb, baker, works 150 n. East, bds. same.

Bottehest August, saloon keeper, res. 307 e. Washington, No. 5 up-stairs.

Bottam Nelson G., lab., res. 22 Dougherty.

Bonchet Mrs. Sophia, French dye house, 42 Kentucky av., res. same.

Bower Albert, brick-maker, bds. Shelbyville pike, ¾ mile s. Corporation.

Bowen Benjamin, bds. s. w. cor. Mississippi and Sixth.

BOWEN CORNELIUS, engineer, C. C. & I. C. R. R., res. 141 Meek.

Bowen Curts J., res. 141 Meek.

Bowen Gilbert, bar-keeper, 87 s. Illinois, bds. 89 s. Illinois.

BOWEN GEORGE M., general agt., American Life Insurance Co. of Philadelphia, Penn., over 35 e. Washington, bds. 346 n. Meridian.

Bowen John F., teamster, res. cor. Ellen and Indiana av.

Bowen Oliver T., (Tull & B.,) 96 Indiana av., res. s. w. cor. Mississippi and Sixth.

Bowen Silas T., (B., Stewart & Co.,) 18 W. Washington, res. 82 w. Vermont.

BOWEN, STEWART & CO., (Silas T. B., Charles G. and Mrs. Sophia W. Stewart,) book sellers and paper dealers, 18 w. Washington.

Bowen William, painter, res. 22 Fatout's blk., up stairs, w. Washington.

Bower Conrald, lab., res. n. s. National rd., near Insane Asylum.

Bower George, lab., res. s city limits.

Bower J. W. & Co., (J. W. B., J. C. Hoss & W. W. Marshall,) groceries, 67 and 78 Massachusetts av.

Bower J. W., (J. W. B. & Co.,) 67 and 78 Massachusetts av., res. 180 e. Vermont.

Bower Mariette, occupant Deaf and Dumb Asylum.

Bowers Albert A., brick-setter, res. end Virginia av., beyond city limits.

Bowers Frank, teamster, res. 26 Center.

Bowers Frederick, helper, McClane, MacIntire & Hays.

Bowers George, helper, McClane, MacIntire & Hays.

Bowers William, bds. s. s. Douglas, between Washington and New York.

Bowes W. R., special agt. p. o. dept., bds. Palmer House.

Bowker C. B., salesman, 50 Virginia av., bds. 154 s. New Jersey.

Bowker Harrison, grocer and produce dealer, 50 Virginia av., res. 154 s. New Jersey.

Bowles Mary, servant, 98 w. Vermont.

Bowles N. E. D., book agt., office Stewart & Bowen, bds. 169 n. Illinois.

BOWLES THOMAS H., lawyer, res. 493 n. Meridian.

Bowler Wm., salesman, New York Store, bds. 36 w. Maryland.

Bowman Henry, lab., res. 122 s. Noble.
Bowman J. S., mechanic, bds. 211 s. Illinois.
Bowman Jacob, res. one mile w. White river bridge, n. s. National rd.
Bowman Jeremiah, farmer, res. n. s. National rd., w. White river bridge.
Bowsy Abram, tinner, D. Root & Co., res. Forest av.
Bowser Levi C., groceries, 275 Virginia av., res. 277 Virginia av.
Bowser Henry, (col.,) lab., res. cor. Howard and Second.
Boyce Angeline, servant, J. D. Condit, 54 Circle.
Boyd Miss A., 2d floor 172 w. Washington.
Boyd David M., patent wright dealer, res. 177 s. Alabama.
Boyd Mrs. Esther, (wid.,) bds. 94 n. California.
Boyd Frank A., (Wood & B.,) 22 s. Meridian, res. 440 n. Meridian.
Boyd George W., clerk, C. C. C. & R. R., res. 177 s. Alabama.
Boyd James M., fireman, I. C. R. R., res. 200 Bates.
Boyd James T., physician and surgeon oculist, 17 Massachusetts av., res. 117 Massachusetts av.
Boyd Miss Lucy, bds. 60 n. California.
Boyd R. M., res. 182 n. Missouri.
Boyd Wm. H., operator, T. & I. R. R., bds. Bates House.
Boyd Wm. H., of the firm of Edwards & B., that were the heavy directory publishers, now played out, having vanished like the glittering tints of the rainbow.
Boyd W. T., Trade Palace, bds. 440 n. Meridian.
Boyer John, currier, 49 s. Delaware.
Boyles Miss Carrie, book-binder, Journal office, bds. 177 s. New Jersey.
Boyles Catherine, (wid.,) res. 177 s. New Jersey.
Boyles M. W., res 335 n. Alabama.
Boyles Miss Sallie, dress-maker, bds 177 s. New Jersey.
Boyle Barney, peg and last factory, res. 156 High.
Boyle Isabelle, servant, 78 e. Ohio.
Boyle James, (A. Reed & Co.,) bds. 63 w. Maryland.
Brackebush A. C., agricultural warehouse and seeds, 75 w. Washington.
Brackebush C. J., manfs. plows and implements, office 75 w. Washington, res. 220 n. Tennessee.
Brackebush Otto, clerk, Union depot ticket office, bds. same.
Brackebush Mrs. T. L., (wid.,) bds. 204 n. Illinois.
Bracken Susannah, (wid. Jones A.,) cor. California and Georgia.

Bracken Thomas E., (Isgrigg & B.,) 180 w. Market, res. 403 w. New York.
Braddock Joseph, general agt., Donaldson & Co., 57 s. Illinois, bds. Oriental House.
Brademeyer Anthony, switchman, Bellefontaine R. R., res. 279 Davidson.
Brademeyer Charles, lab., res. Clinton, bet. Ohio and New York.
Brademeyer Christian, brakeman, Bellefontaine R. R., res. 279 Davidson.
Brademier, John F., teamster, res. 315 e. New York.
Braden David, assessor sixth district internal revenue, room 15 p. o. bldg., res. 393 n. Pennsylvania.
Braden James, (W. & J. B.,) 24 w. Washington, res. 469 n. Illinois.
Braden Leroy W., clerk, assessor's office internal revenue, bds. 393 n. Pennsylvania.
Braden M., compositor, Downey, Brouse, Butler & Co., res. 269 e. New York.
Braden Patrick, moulder, res. 2 Henry.
BRADEN W. & J., (William & James B.,) blank-book manfs., printers, stationers, paper dealers and lithographers, 24 w. Washington.
Braden William, (W. & J. B.,) 24 w. Washington, res. 473 n. Illinois.
Bradford George, (col.,) lab., res. 86 n. Missouri.
Brafford L. M., tobacconist, bds. Ray House.
Bradford Mrs. Mary, (wid.,) res. 52 Fletcher av.
Bradie George H., pastry-cook, Bates House, bds. same.
Bradley E., clerk, general freight agt., office C. C. & I. C. R. R., bds. Oriental House.
Bradley James S., student, commercial college, bds. 44 s. Tennessee.
Bradley Jeptha W., carpenter, res. 111 Massachusetts av.
Bradley Leland J., second-hand furniture, over 196 w. Washington, res. 231 Massachusetts av.
Bradley William, lab., Smith's brewery, res. bet. East and Noble.
Brado Joseph, salesman, Tyler's Bee-Hive, res. 25 Fletcher av.
Bradshaw George W., cooper, res. 309 Winston.
Bradshaw J. W., teacher, Blind Asylum, res. same.
Bradshaw James M., bds. Bates House. ·
Bradshaw John A., res. 26 e. Vermont.
Bradshaw Miss Mary, teacher, fourth ward school., bds. 264 n. Tennessee.
Bradshaw William A., assignee in bankruptcy, rooms 10 and 11 Talbott & New's blk, n. Pennsylvania, res. Western av., w. of N. W. C. University.

Bradshaw Mrs. Margaret, res. 264 n. Tennessee.

Brady Miss Ellen, dress-maker, bds. 154 w. Market.

Brady John, brick-mason, res. 100 s. East.

Brady Michael, brick-layer, res. 673 n. Illinois.

Brady O. H. P., grocer, 546 e. Washington, res. same.

Braham Otto, (B. & Zink,) barber, Sherman House, res. 18 Willard.

BRAHAM & ZINK, barbers and hair-dressers, under Sherman House.

Brake John S., fireman, C. C. & I. C. R. R., bds. 424 on Central R. R.

Bramble Hamilton G., brick-mason, res. 128 n. East.

Brame Arthur, barber, res. 18 Willard.

Brambaut Henry, lab., res. n. Pennsylvania, beyond city limits.

Brammer William F., carpenter, works Sinker & Co., res. 322 s. Delaware.

Bramon Patrick, porter, Sherman House, bds. same.

Bramwell John M., res. 68 s. Mississippi.

Bramwell Zenas T., res. 124 n. Missouri.

Branch Eighth ward School, basement Asbury Chapel, Miss Sarah Railsbach, teacher.

Brandt Henry, huckster, bds. 518 e. Washington.

Brandt Herman, draftsman, D. A. Bohlen, room 19 Talbott & New's blk., n. Pennsylvania, res. 222 East.

Branham David. C., (D. A. B. & Co.,) bds. Bates House.

Branham D. C. & Co., (David C. B., Cyrus M. Allen & John M. Cravens,) Vincennes R. R. contractors, office, old bank bldg.

Branham Edward, (Mayhew & B.,) 129 s. Meridian, res. 240 n. Tennessee.

Brannel John, lab., res. 71 Maple.

Branson Anna, occupant Deaf and Dumb Asylum.

Branson David A., (D. A. B. & Co.,) room over 23 n. East.

BRANSON D. A. & CO., manfs. and wholesale and retail dealers in inks, writing fluids, shoe-blacking, stove-polish, &c., 23 n. East, (D. A. Branson & J. W. Hosman.)

Brant Augustus, works Washington Foundry, bds. 222 n. East.

Brant John B., minister, Presbyterian church, bds. 331 s. Meridian.

Brantley C. C., occupant Deaf and Dumb Asylum.

Brantley H. H., occupant Deaf and Dumb Asylum.

Brattain J., expressman, res. 362 n. West.

Brattain W. J., huckster, res. 70 n. Delaware.

Bratton Jesse, printer, Sentinel office, bds. 89 s. Illinois.

Brawns Charles E., works Cabinet-Makers' Union, bds. 518 e. Washington.

Bray John S., cabinet-maker, res. 240 n. East.

Bray William H., clerk, res. 240 n. East.

Bray P. L., minister, Roberts Chapel, res. 176 Massachusetts av.

Breedlove Bales, farmer, res. 143 Davidson, cor. New York.

Breedlove Thomas J., real Estate agt., res. 35 s. Bright.

Breen James, division boss, Bellefontaine R. R., res. 339 Winston.

Breening Frederick, carpenter, res. 379 s. Delaware.

Brem Francis J., carpenter, works H. Recker, res. 98 s. Delaware.

Breman Ward, servant, 183 e. Ohio.

Bremerman Benjamin, carriage-maker, 123 e. Washington, bds. 125 e. Washington.

Bremerman Cass, (B. & Renner,) 123 e. Washington, res. n. w. city limits.

Bremerman Frederick, works agricultural works, res. 295 n. Alabama.

Bremerman & Renner, (Cass B. & John B. R.,) carriage manfs., 123 e. Washington.

Breman Daniel, porter, Hume, Adams & Co., res. 27 Thomas.

Brend, Christian, dry goods peddler, res. e. Michigan rd., beyond city limits.

Brener John, cooper, res. 362 w. New York.

Brennin Patrick, lab., res. w. Seventh, near Michigan rd.

Brennan Thomas, painter, 26 e. Georgia, bds. 204 Buchanan.

Brennan William, porter, p. o., res. 204 Buchanan.

Brenton Oliver W., soldier, U. S. Arsenal, res. Arsenal grounds.

Bresnehem Mary, servant, 172 New Jersey.

Brester William, carpenter, bds. 222 e. Washington.

Brestean Hannah, servant, 63 n. Alabama.

Brett Mathew, miller, res. 21 e. Michigan.

Brettin H. J., huckster, res. Buchanan, between Wright and McKernan.

Bretz Adam, dealer in groceries and notions, 44 w. Louisiana, res., 18 s. Illinois.

Brewing George, book-keeper, City Clerk's office, res. cor. Forest Home av. and Jackson.

Brewer A. V., student, commercial college, bds. 44 s. Tennessee.

Brewster John H., supt. Central Transportation Sleeping Cars, Bellefontaine R. R., res. 191 e. Market.

Brickle S., (wid.,) res. 392 n. Alabama.

Brickner Robert, brewer, Schmidt's brewery.

Brickus Jeremiah, lab., res. n. s. National rd., w. White river bridge.

Bridenbaugh Miss Susan, bds. 77 Broadway.

Briddie George H., baker, Bates House, res. cor. Blake and New York.

BRIDGMAN F., paymaster U. S. army, room 14 Talbott and New's blk., n. Pennsylvania, res. cor. Virginia av. and Alabama.

Bridgman Miss Mollie, res. 78 Huron.

Bridihop Richard, expressman, res. 213 Virginia av.

Brien Tedda, lab., bds. 327 Winston.

Brier Charles H., lab., res. 520 e. Washington.

Briggs Alfred, boarding house, 198 s. Illinois, res. same.

Briggs Charles H., conductor, C. C. & I. C. R. R., res. 88 s. Liberty.

Briggs Erastus, carpenter, bds. 36 Cherry.

Briggs Mrs. Elizabeth, res. Geisendorff, near Geisendorff's Woolen Factory.

Briggs James A., carpenter, bds. 638 n. Mississippi.

Briggs Mrs. Olive, res. 88 s. Liberty.

Brigham Charles E., supt. W. & J. Braden's printing office, 24 w. Washington, res. 37 Indiana av.

Bright Charlotte E., seamstress, res. s. e. cor. Tennessee and Third.

Bright David L., teamster, res. on alley, e. Peru and St. Clair.

Bright George A., boiler-maker, Washington foundry, res. 353 s. Delaware·

Bright Mattie, (wid. Jesse,) res. 67 Eddy.

BRIGHT RICHARD J., propr. Daily and Weekly Sentinel, 16½ e. Washington, bds. Bates House, res. Madison, Ind.

Brill John, carpenter, res. 479 s. Illinois.

Brink Christian, clerk, 29 w. Washington, res. 131 n. New Jersey.

Brink William, tailor, res. 393 e. Michigan.

Brinker William, cooper, res. 343 n. New Jersey.

BRINKMAN CHARLES, livery and sale stable, 33 s. Delaware, res. 131 n. New Jersey.

Brinkman Frederick, carpenter, bds. 284 e. Market.

Brinkman William, lab., res. 131 Davidson.

Brinkmeyer Frederick, salesman, 80 s. Meridian, res. 234 n. Davidson.

Brinkmeyer George, (J. C. B. & Co.,) 80 s. Meridian, res. 238 n. Davidson.

Brinkmeyer John C., (J. C. B. & Co.,) 80 s. Meridian, res. 288 n. Liberty.

BRINKMEYER J. C. & CO., (John C. B., Charles Kemker & George Brinkmeyer,) propr's of bonded warehouse No. 1, and wholesale liquor dealers and distillers, 80 s. Meridian. See card, page 50.

Brinning Fred., drayman, res. 141 Bluff rd.

Brison J. D., farmer, bds. 460 s. West.

Brison James Wm., farmer, bds. 460 s. West.

Bristor Anthony J., res. 59 w. Maryland.

Bristor ——, engineer, C. C. & I. C. R. R., bds. 58 Benton.

Bristor Samuel M., retired carriage-maker, res. 135 n. Delaware.

Bristor Wm. A., boots and shoes, 75 e. Washington, res. 135 n. Delaware.

Britt Thomas, lab., alley between West and California and Georgia.

Brittney Mrs. Elizabeth, (wid.,) res. w. s. Douglas, between New York and Washington.

Brittney Eugene, res. w. s. Douglas, between Washington and New York.

Brittney William, clerk, Bellefontaine freight depot, res. w. s. Douglas, between Washington and New York.

Brizins Adolph, inmate Deaf and Dumb Asylum.

Broadhurst, Isaac, piano action and tone regulator, 159 and 161 e. Washington, res. 22 w. St. Clair.

Brock James M., blacksmith, 175 s. Tennessee, bds. Nagle House.

Brock Robert, carpenter, res. 352 Virginia av.
Brock Thomas, brick-maker, bds. 352 Virginia av.
Broden James, moulder, works Sinker & Co., res. 271 e. New York.
Broden John, tinner, works Tutewiler Bros., res. 271 e. New York.
Broden Michael, printer, works Downey & Brouse, res. 269 e. New York.
Brodrick Miss Mary, bds. 142 Indiana av.
Broderick John, machinist, central shop, res. 146 Bates.
Brogen James, lab., Bellefontaine R. R. track, bds. 248 Winston.
Broils Moses, (col.,) res. 227 n. Minerva.
Brooker David, inmate Deaf and Dumb Asylum.
BROKING C. W., supt. Indiana Transfer Co., 403 Maryland, res. 143 Union.
Broking E. H., Indiana Transfer Co.
Broking Frederick, driver, Indiana Transfer Co., res. 71 s. Pennsylvania.
Bromhamp Mrs., (wid.,) res. 281 s. Tennessee.
Bromwell Zeains, engineer, res. 180 n. Missouri.
Bromson Miss Druzzilla, bds. 508 n. Mississippi.
Bronyon Sarah, (wid.,) res. 278 s. Mississippi.
Brooks Bennett, carpenter, res. 178 Massachusetts av.
Brooks Coleman, (col.,) lab., res. Camp Carrington.
Brooks G. C., salesman, 22 e. Washington, res. 160 s. New Jersey.
Brooks Thomas, groceries and provisions, 774 n. Tennessee, res same.
Brooksmith Henry, blacksmith, res. 122 Huron.
Brooksmith Louis, finisher at Washington Foundry, bds. 122 Huron.
Brother Mrs. Elizabeth, (wid. John,) res. 560 e. Washington.
Brough George W., butcher, res. 312 n. Noble.
Brough John W., res. 333 s. Alabama.
Broughton Miss C., principal of primary department, Indiana Female College, 146 n. Meridian, bds. same.
Brouse Andrew, carpenter, 136 e. New York, res. 138 e. New York.
Brouse Charles W., (Downey, Butler & Co.,) cor. Meridian and Circle, res. s. w. cor. n. Meridian and Walnut.
Brouse David W., clerk, Tutewiler Bros., res. 138 e. New York.
Brouse Rev. J. A., (Downey, Brouse, Butler & Co.,) res. 92 e. Market.
Brouse Olin R., attorney at law and notary public, over Bee-Hive, 2 w. Washington, res. 92 e. Market.

Brouse Joseph, student Bryant's commercial college, bds. 444 n. New Jersey.
Brouse Thomas W., Indianapolis Builders' Association, bds. 274 n. Alabama.
Bromer Frederick, painter, res. 570 e. Washington.
Brower George, job printer, Journal office, bds. 39 Ellsworth.
Brower Theodore, printer, W. & J. Bradens', bds. 39 Ellsworth.
Bruner Roman, lab., res. 26 w. McCarty.
Brown A., plasterer, bds. 89 s. Illinois.
Brown Miss Augusta F., asst. fifth ward school, res. 145 n. Meridian.
Brown Albert, grocer, 387 s. Delaware, res. same.
BROWN AUSTIN H., Collector Internal Revenue, sixth district, room 15 p. o. bldg., res. 290 s. Meridian.
BROWN BENJAMIN F., (Logan & B.,) over 4 w. Washington, res. 294 w. St. Clair.
Brown Benjamin F., book-keeper, W. & J. Braden, bds. 204 n. Illinois.
Brown C. H., tailor, works 31 n. Pennsylvania, bds. 58 s. Pennsylvania.
Brown Carrie V., occupant Deaf and Dumb Asylum.
Brown Charles P., lab., bds. W. P. Noble, e. Market, near corporation.
Brown Charles W., occupant Deaf and Dumb Asylum.
Brown Charles H., carpenter, res. Indiana av.
Brown Charles, (col.,) barber, bds. 343 n. Alabama.
Brown Charles L., head cook, Bates House, bds. same.
Brown Christopher, (col.,) lab., bds. 156 Douglas alley.
Brown Daniel R., (Evans & B.,) 75 s. Meridian, res. Noblesville, Ind.
Brown Mrs. Ellen, (wid. Ernest,) res. 286 n. Noble.
Brown Ellison, painter, 25 s. Meridian, res. 564 n. Illinois.
Brown Francis M., groceries and provisions, 59 w. Washington, res. 322 n. Illinois.
Brown George, res. 392 n. Alabama.
Brown G. P. C., (wid. G. P. C.,) res. 383 n. Alabama.
Brown H. C., carpenter, res. 48 w. Market.
Brown Henry P., salesman, Hume, Adams & Co., bds. Pyle House, n. Meridian.
Brown Henry (col.,) minister, Methodist church, res. 311 n. Alabama.
Brown Henry, (col.,) blacksmith, res. 79 s. Missouri.
Brown Henry, (col.,) well-digger, res. Camp Carrington.
Brown Henry, (col.,) dining-room boy, Oriental House.

BROWN IGNATIUS, lawyer, 8½ e. Washington, res. 243 e. South.

Brown Isaac I., plasterer, res. 179 Massachusetts av.

Brown J. C., blacksmith, bds. 213 s. Illinois.

Brown J. W., (Goth, B. & Co.,) 489 n. New Jersey, res. 401 n. New Jersey.

Brown J. H., druggist, with Kiefer & Vinton, 68 s. Meridian, res. 181 Massachusetts av.

Brown John L., policeman, second ward, bds. 54 s. Pennsylvania.

Brown James J., carpenter, res. 274 Madison av.

Brown James B., plasterer, res. 229 Massachusetts av.

Brown James H., clerk, Kiefer & Vinton, res. 181 Massachusetts av.

Brown Jesse B., agt., Pan Handle R. R., res. 106 Broadway.

Brown Miss Jennie, tailoress, bds. 274 Madison av.

Brown Mrs. Julia A., (wid. Phillip,) res. 351 Massachusetts av.

Brown Jerry, (col.,) expressman, res. 349 n. Alabama.

Brown John, plasterer, res. 229 Massachusetts av.

Brown John, shoe-maker, res. 61 Indiana av.

Brown John, janitor, p. o., res. 439 Virginia av.

Brown John, egg-packer, 18 w. Pearl, bds. 92 e. Washington.

Brown John, shoe-maker, res. 148 w. Vermont.

Brown John, salesman, New York Store, bds. Oriental House.

Brown John, lab., res. 567 s. Illinois.

Brown John, works Street Ry., bds. 229 Massachusetts av.

Brown John (col.,) lab., res. rear 343 Massachusetts av.

Brown John G., grocery dealer, 300 n. New Jersey, res. 302 n. New Jersey.

Brown John H. F., tinner, Tutewiler Bros., res. 366 n. Alabama.

BROWN KINSEY, teamster, res. 107 s. Noble.

Brown Lafayette, hds. 157 w. Maryland.

Brown Lizzie, lady boarder, 36 s. New Jersey.

Brown M. L., book-keeper, 147 e. Washington, bds. 80 s. Mississippi.

Brown Mrs. Mary L., (wid. Gardner,) res. 118 s. Mississippi.

Brown Mary, servant, 34 Lockerbie.

Brown Mrs. Mariah J., (wid.,) seamstress. res. 356 w. North.

Brown Miss Mollie, tailoress, works 32 s. Meridian, res. 308 e. Ohio.

Brown Mrs. N. A., boarding house, 54 s. Pennsylvania.

Brown Nathan T., carpenter, bds. 274 Madison av.

Brown Patrick, lab., 341 s. Delaware.

Brown Philip A., sawyer, res. end Virginia av., beyond city limits.

BROWN MRS. R. T., (wid. Richard T.,) dress-maker and milliner, 124 n. East, res. same.

Brown R. F., prof. N. W. C. University, res. Western av., near city limits.

Brown R. H., bds. 54 s. Pennsylvania.

Brown Rabbi, (col.,) plasterer, res. First, bet. Howard and Lafayette R. R.

Brown Richard, blacksmith, bds. n. e. cor. Georgia and Liberty.

Brown Miss Sarah, lady boarder, 281 e. New York.

Brown Miss Sallie A., school teacher, bds. 356 w. North.

Brown Samuel, (col.,) bds. 172 w. Georgia.

Brown T. B., clerk, Sheridan House, bds. same.

Brown Thomas, works C. C. & I. C. shop, bds. n. e. cor. Georgia and Liberty.

Brown Mrs. William, (wid. John,) bds. 170 w. New York.

Brown William H., clerk, M. U. Express Co., 42 and 44 e. Washington, res. Madison rd., outside city limits.

Brown William P., hat manufactory, Miller's blk.

Brown William P., lithographer, W. & J. Braden, bds. California House.

Brown William, Journal office, bds. 204 n. Illinois.

Brown William, (col.,) barber, Dr. Franklin.

Brown W., (col.,) barber, res. 85 Eddy.

Brown William, barber, works 143 w. Washington, bds. same.

Brown William, (col.,) barber, 286 w. Washington.

Brown Willis, (col.,) lab., res. 172 w. Georgia.

Brownlee John Q., law student, bds. 162 n. New Jersey.

Browning Edward, register land office, res. 109 Virginia av.

Browning Frank, clerk, 7 and 9 e. Washington, bds. 172 n. Illinois.

Browning Gordon, hopper clerk, p. o., rooms Yohn's blk., Meridian.

Browning John, conductor sleeping cars, Terre Haute R. R., bds. 229 n. New Jersey.

Browning Robert, (B. & Sloan,) 7 and 9 e. Washington, res. 172 n. Illinois.

BROWNING & SLOAN, (Robert B. & George W. S.,) Druggists' and Apothecaries' Hall, 7 and 9 e. Washington.

Brubaker, Henry W., physician and surgeon, cor. West and Washington, res. 43 Kentucky av.

Bruckner Robert, lab., Schmidt's brewery, res. same.

Brueggemamm William, school teacher, res. 67 n. Noble.

Bruel Edward, prof. of instrumental music, Indiana Female College, 146 n. Meridian, bds. same

Bruening Edward, (E. & J. B.,) 6 e. Washington, res. same.

BRUENING E. & J., (Edward & Joseph B.,) photographers, 6 e. Washington.

Bruening Joseph, (E. & J. B.,) 6 e. Washington, res. same.

Bruening Mary, servant, 238 Davidson.

Brummer Charles, music teacher and organist, res. 25 w. Pratt.

Brundage E. H., livery, boarding and sale stable, 223 e. Washington, res. cor. East and Washington.

Bruner A. (Loucks & B.,) city sealer, res. 402 n. New Jersey.

Bruner Adam, carpenter, res. 129 Massachusetts av.

Bruner Jacob M., carpenter, works Bellefontaine shops, res. 402 e. Michigan.

Brunner Joseph, chair-maker, res. Court, between East and New Jersey.

Bruner Mrs. Margaret J., (wife Adam,) milliner shop and res. 129 Massachusetts av.

Brunner Joan, groceries and provisions, 660 n. Tennessee, res. same.

Brunnemer W. F., policeman, fourth ward, res. 384 w. North.

Bruning Rev. George A., elder, German Methodist, res. Jackson, out city limits.

Bryan A. H., physician, office 126 s. Illinois, res. 420 n. Delaware.

Bryan F. A., dealer in drugs and medicines, cor. Massachusetts av. and Vermont, res. same.

Bryan John M., clerk, J. W. Bryan, bds. 420 n. Delaware.

Bryan J. W., druggist, cor. Illinois and Louisiana, res. 420 n. Delaware.

Bryan Joseph, cooper, res. n. s. New York, between Blake and Minerva.

Bryan Miss Maggie, linen-keeper, Bates House.

Bryan Richard O., varnisher, res. 77 s. East.

Bryant G., book agt., bds. 225 s. New Jersey.

Bryant Theodore, lab., res. 205 e. Market..

Bryant John S. conductor, Bellefontaine R. R., res. 47 n. East.

Brydon R. F., clerk, general tciket office C. C. & I. C. R. R., bds. 73 w. Maryland.

Bryer J. F., actor, Metropolitan Theater, bds. 120 n. Mississippi.

Buell Frederick, lab., res. 563 e. St. Clair.

Buchanan John, lab., res. 298 s. Missouri.

Buchanan Andrew, wagon-maker, opp. Spiegel, Thoms & Co., res. 314 e. Washington.

Buchanan Mrs. Catharine, (wid. Thomas,) res. 314 and 316 e. Washington.

BUCHANAN CYRUS, carpenter, res. s. s. National rd., near Insane Asylum.

Buchanan Frank, (col.,) lab., cor. Brett and Benton.

Buchanan George W., carpenter, res. 131 s. East.

Buchanan James, occupant Deaf and Dumb Asylum, Memphis p. o., Clark county.

Buchanan James, wagon-maker, opp. Spiegel, Thoms & Co., res. 314 e. Washington.

Buchannan John A., carpenter, res. 182 e. McCarty.

Buchanan Oliver, brick-layer, res. 70 Indiana av.

Buchey Fred., boots and shoes, res. 171 Bluff rd.

Buchner Frederick, blacksmith, E. S. Dougherty, first h. s., res. rear.

Buchorn Christian, wagon-maker, works cor. Washington and Benton, res. 98 Davidson.

Buchorn Fred., collar-maker, 20 w. Washington, bds e. Washington.

Buck Christian, carpenter, res. 166 e. Michigan.

Buck Charles, section boss, Cincinnati R. R., res. 30 Biddle.

Buck Mrs. Elizabeth, dress and cloak making, res. 69 w. New York.

Bucheye Fire Insurance Co., of Cleveland, Ohio, J. S. Dunlop & Co., agts., 16 and 18 n. Meridian.

Buckhart A. F., occupant Deaf and Dumb Asylum.

Buckland H., artist, bds. 17½ Virginia av.

Buckley C., servant, 112 n. Meridian.

Buckley John, lab., I. & C. R. R., res. 32 Lord.

Buckley Mrs. Margaret, res. 303 Indiana av.

Buckley Patrick, tobacconist, works J. Cahall & Co., bds. Ray House.

Buckley Timothy, railroader, res. 124 Meek.

Buckner Alexander, (col.,) lab., res. w. Washington, between Canal and Mississippi.

Buckner Lewis, (col,) lab., res. Camp Carrington.

Bucksot J. W., clerk, 9 w. Washington, bds. 482 n. Illinois.

Bucksot Wm., propr. Gem Billiard Room, 9 w. Washington, res. 482 n. Illinois.

Buckstabler Charles, clerk, J. W. Bryan, bds. 72 w. South.

Buckstabler Sarah, (wid.,) res. 72 w. South.

Budd & Hinesley, egg-packers and poultry dealers, 18. w. Pearl.

Budd J. R., (B. & Hinesley, 18 w. Pearl, res. 334 n. Alabama.

Budd Milton, brick-maker, res. 308 Winston.

Budenz Henry, tailor, 266 s. Pennsylvania, res. same.

Budenz Louis, tailor, works over 168 e. Washington, res. 229 Union.

Buddenbaum Henry, (Charles Prange & Co.,) res. n. w. cor. Ohio and Davidson.

Bruddenbaum Henry C., (Charles Prange & Co., res. 396 e. Ohio.

Buegin A. S., works Junction R. R., bds. Wiles House.

Buehler John, lab., Schmidt's brewery, res. 28 Wyoming.

Buehrig Henry E., saloon, 37 e. South, res. same.

BUELL C. H., propr. and manfr. Buell's patent medicines, 75 e. Market, res. cor. Western and Forest Home avs.

Buell J. R., carpenter, res. 15 Madison av.

Buemmele Jas., news store, 153 e. Washington, res. 120 w. Maryland.

Buford William B., clerk, W. & J. Braden, bds. Macy House.

Bugby Mrs. Mary A., (wid. Lyman,) res. 262 n. Noble.

Bugby Miss Metty, dress-maker, res. 262 n. Noble.

Bugby Parker E., engineer, Bellefontaine R. R., res. 262 n. Noble.

Bugg Samuel, (col.,) res. 451 e. Georgia.

Bughter George, grocery, 52 s. California, res. same.

Bughter Theodore, student, bds. 52 s. California.

Buhhoby John, shoe-maker, bds. 17½ Virginia av.

Buist Mrs. M. D., (wid. Thomas,) res. 60 n. California.

Bulach John, bar-tender, Mozart Hall, res. Wabash, bet. Liberty and Noble.

Bulk Louisa, servant, 26 n. Noble.

Bull George W., clerk, White Line freight office, bds. 16 e. Michigan.

Bullard Mrs. Emily, (wid. Charles G.,) res. 62 Greer.

Bullen Mrs. W. S., (wid. William S.,) res. 74 e. Ohio.

Bullock D. D., occupant Deaf and Dumb Asylum.

Bullock James B., (Anderson, B. & Schofield,) 60 s. Meridian, res. 276 n. Tennessee.

Bulsoc John, bar-tender, Mozart Hall, res. e. Market.

Bullock Sarah, servant, 97 n. Delaware.

Bulsterbaum Mrs. E., (wid. John,) groceries, 239 s. Meridian, res. same.

Bunce Alice, occupant Deaf and Dumb Asylum, Lafayette, Tippecanoe Co.

Bunker Alexander, blacksmith, res. 129 e. Walnut.

Bunte John B., (B. & Dickson,) e. Market, res. 114 w. Vermont.

Burbank J. A., (Scott, West & Co.,) 127 s. Meridian, res. Richmond, Ind.

Burch Leonard B., grocer, 50 n. Noble, cor. Market, res. same.

Burch William R., paper-hanger, Hume, Adams & Co., bds. Macy House.

Burchgraf Mrs. Louisa, (wid. Henry,) res. 384 e. Market.

Burchers John F., harness-maker, 425 n. East.

Burchfield Lewis, lab., res. 74 Massachusetts av.

Burcke Herman, currier, 17 s. Delaware, bds. 82 Harrison.

Burestine Asa, pedler, res. 117 w. McCarty.

Burgess Miss Adelade E., student, Indiana Female College, 146 n. Meridian, bds. same.

Burgner Miss Alice, bds. 183 n. Tennessee.

BURGESS C. C., dentist, room 1, Odd Fellows Hall, res. 429 n. Pennsylvania.

Burgess Rev. Otis A., pastor Christian Church, s. w. cor. Delaware and Ohio, res. 324 n. Delaware.

Burgess Cornelius N., compositor, Journal office, res. 98 n. East.

Burgess Rev. Conrad S., minister, Strange Chapel, res. 188 n. Tennessee.

Bnrgess W. G., compositor, Downey, Brouse, Butler & Co., res. 98 n. East.

Burgoinne Stephen, saloon, 139 s. Illinois, bds California House.

Burk A. E., works Junction R. R., bds. Wiles House.

Burk Cook, (col.,) lab., w. side Mississippi, bet. Third and Second.

Burk Catharine, servant, J. D. Condit, 54 Circle.

Burk, Earnshaw & Co., (William C. B., Joseph E. & James H. T.,) manufs. of furniture, 251 s. Pennsylvania.

Burke Henry, shoe-maker, res. 94 n. East.

BURK JOHN, coal dealer, office 23 Virginia av., res. 254 n. Tennessee.

Burk Lemuel, teamster, res. 285 n. Liberty.

Burk Mrs. Mary, (wid. Martin,) res. 70 Railroad.

Burk Martin, soap manfr., s. city limits, res. 112 Dacotah.

Burk Patrick, works Junction R. R., bds. Wiles House.

Burk S. M., carpenter, res. 71 Jackson.

Burk W., railroader, bds. 470 e. Georgia.

Burk Wesley, lab., bds. 94 n. East.

Burk William C., (C. Earnshaw & Co.,) res. 254 n. Tennessee.

Burkart John, chair-maker, bds 146 e. Mc-Carty.

Burke Dennis, porter, Landers, Pee & Co., 58 s. Meridian, bds. Palmer House.

Burke George, saloon, 24 w. Pearl, res. 164 s. New Jersey.

Burke Henry, stone-mason, res. 344 s. Delaware.

Burke Thomas, boarding, 31 s. West.

BURKERT ERASTUS J., secy. American Horse Insurance Co., room 13, Vinton blk., bds. Pyle House.

Burket Milton, baggageman, C. C. & I. C. R. R., bds. 33 Meek.

Burkert W. S., actuary, American Horse Insurance Co., room 13 Vinton blk., bds. Pyle House.

Burkenthaw David, wholesale iron store, res. 201 n. Liberty.

BURKHART ANDREW J., ice merchant, res. 248 n. Mississippi.

Burkhart John, bds. National rd., half mile from river bridge.

Burkhofer George, show case manfr., res. 354 Virginia av.

Burkle J. G., machinest, B. F. Haugh, bds. 62 s. Pennsylvania.

Burkes J. W., sawyer, McCord & Wheatly, bds. Ray House.

Burley George W., traveling agt., res. 22 w. St. Clair.

Burner Charles, clerk. 173 w. Washington, res. w. New York.

Burnett Miss Addie, bds. 235 n. Mississippi.

BURNETT JEROME C., deputy auditor of State, Insurance and Bank department, office, new State bldg., res. 235 n. Mississippi.

BURNHAM A. G., physician and surgeon, homœpathist, 38 w. Market, res. same.

Burnside Henry M., contractor, Indianapolis & Vincennes R. R., res. 280 n. Mississippi.

Burnworth Miss Jennie, book-binder, res. 22 Elm.

Burnworth Mrs. Mary, (wid. George,) res. 22 Elm.

Burnworth Zilid, blacksmith, res. 22 Elm.

Burns Ann, servant, 230 e. Vermont.

Burns Annie, servant, Reinheimers, 175 s. Delaware.

Burns Catharine, servant, 115 n. Illinois.

BURNS & CARTER, (David V. B. & Vinson C.) attorneys at law, 74 e. Washington.

Burns David V., (B. & Carter,) 74 e. Washington, bds. Pattison House.

Burns Edward, brakeman, J., M. & I. R. R., bds. 143 e. McCarty.

Burns Miss Emily C., res. 18 Douglas.

Burns G. H., baggage-master, J., M. & I. R. R., bds. Ray House.

Burns James, dealer in furs, res. 18 Douglas.

Burns James, huckster, res. 61 s. New Jersey.

Burns John, engineer, C., C. & I. C. R. R., bds. 58 Benton.

Burns John, cooper, res. 259 s. West.

Burns John F., clerk, Geisel & Enners, res. 345 n. Noble.

Burns John, Capitol Garden, s. w. cor. Kentucky av. and Tennessee, bds. same.

Burns & Klingensmith, attorneys at law, 115 e. Washington.

Burns Mathew, lab., res. 252 s. West.

Burns Miss Mary J., dress-maker, bds. 317 e. Ohio.

Burns Miss Mary H., res. 18 Douglas.

Burns Michael, lab., T. H. & I. R. R. Freight Depot, res. 252 s. West.

Burns Owen, lab., res. 251 s. Tennessee.

Burns Patrick, lab., res. 13 Henry.

Burns Peter, engineer, Downey, Brouse, Butler & Co., bds. Boston Bakery.

Burney Thomas, puddler, White River Iron Works, bds. California House.

Burns Thomas E., mill-wright, bds. 255 w. Washington.

Burns William, porter, Bates House, res. 218 w. Georgia.

Burns William, works Junction R. R., bds. Wiles House.

Burns William V., (B. & Klingensmith,) 115 e. Washington, res. 18 w. First.

Burris Emily, (col.,) res. cor. Blake and Center.

Burroughs George F., salesman, 6 e. Washington, bds. Pyle House, n. Meridian.

Burrows G. W., traveling agt., Cincinnati House, res. Shelbyville pike, 1½ miles s. corporation.

Burrows Louis, (col.,) white-washer, Wabash, bet. New Jersey and East, res. same.

Burrowes Thompson, porter, Trade Palace, lives 446 w. North.

Burns Patrick, porter, Bates House, bds. same.

Burt Alphonso S., traveling agt., I. & C. R. R., res. 264 e. Ohio.

Burt Frederick, butcher, res. Kansas, s. city limits.

Burt G., (col.,) lab., Terra Cotta Works, res. w. s. Tennessee, bet. Fifth and Sixth.

Burt James C., M. D., trustee, Deaf and Dumb Asylum.

Burt William N., A. B., instructor, Deaf and Dumb Asylum.

Burtlesman Jane, (wid.,) res. 266 Massachusetts av.

Burton Daniel, cooper shop, w. end New York, res. 427 w. New York.

Burton George H., cooper, 138 n. Mississippi, res. same.

Burton Henry, tobacconist, bds. Ray House.

Burton John C. & Co., (John C. B. & William A. Pfaff,) wholesale boot and shoe dealers, 38 s. Meridian.

Burton John C., (J. C. B. & Co.,) 37 s. Meridian, res. 445 n. New Jersey.

Burton Martin, res. 346 n. Illinois.

Burch Michael, blacksmith, 83 Kentucky av., bds. 221 s. Pennsylvania.

Busch Jacob, saloon-keeper, 251 w. Washington, res. same.

Buscher Henry, saloon, 89 e. South, res. same.

Buscher Henry, Jr., brewer, bds. 26 s. Alabama.

Buscher Henry, brewery, Cumberland, res. 26 s. Alabama.

Buscher Mrs. Mary, (wid. Henry,) res. 189 s. Alabama.

Buschman William, (Goth, Brown & Co.,) 489 n. New Jersey, res. 469 n. New Jersey.

Buser George, policeman, fourth ward, bds. 148 Indiana av.

Buser Jacob, night watchman, Union depot, res. 74 w. Louisiana.

Buser J., policeman, bds. 74 w. Lousiana.

Buser Frederick, saloon-keeper, s. Delaware, bds. 293 e. Washington.

Buser Samuel, policeman, fifth ward, res. McOunt's blk.

Bush Adam, carpenter, res. 77 n. Illinois.

Bush David, (col.,) white-washer, res. 112 Benton.

Bush Christian, boots and shoes, 165 w. Washington, res. same.

Bush Jerry, fireman, C. C. & I. C. R. R., bds. 66 s. Benton.

Bush Mrs. Nancy, (col., wid.,) wash-woman, res. Railroad, bet. Ffth and Sixth.

Bush William, bds. 215 n. Mississippi.

Busher Jacob, switch-man, Union R. R. Co., res.432 s. East.

Bushong George L., shoe-shop, 195 Indiana av., res. s. e. cor. Walnut and Fayette.

Bussell Erastus T., patent wright business, res. 258 n. Tennessee.

Bussell Reu., printer, bds. 258 n. Tennessee.

Bussell William M., agt., Evening Commercial, bds. 258 n. Tennessee.

Buswell John, carpenter, res. 24 Wright.

Butler Charles C., printer, Meikels' office, bds. 105 n. Noble.

Butler George, traveling agt., I. & C. R. R., res. 222 s. Noble.

Butler James, fireman, I. C. & L. R. R., bds. 58 Benton.

Butler James O., printer, bds. 105 n. Noble.

Butler Marcus B., occupant Deaf and Dumb Asylum, Lagrange p. o., Lagrange Co.

Butler Mary, servant, 377 n. Illinois.

Butler Mary, nurse, 229 n. New Jersey.

Butler Ovid, Sen., (Downey, Brouse, B. & Co.,) cor. Meridian and Circle, res. Forest Home av.

Butler Ovid D. Jr., (Smith, Harlan & B.,) res. 257 n. East.

Butler Scott, (Downey, Brouse, B. & Co.,) cor. Meridian and Circle, res. Forest Home, n. of city.

Butler Wm., salesman, New York Store, bds. Commercial Hotel.

Butler William, (col.,) lab., res. n. Mississippi, bet. Third and Fourth.

Buts Mrs. D. A., (wid.,) res. 83½ e. Washington.

Butsch Elizabeth, servant, Mrs. M. A. Alvord, 334 n. Illinois.

BUTSCH & DICKSON, (Valentine B. & Jas. D.,) dealers in lime, coal, cement, plasterers' lath and hair, office Georgia, bet. Meridian and Pennsylvania.

Butsch J., ice dealer, res. 68 w. South.

BUTSCH VALENTINE, (V. B. & Co.,) propr. Metropolitan Theater and Academy of Music Hall, office 27 e. Georgia, res. Meridian, bet. First and Second.

BUTTERFIELD C. S. & CO., (Cyrus S. B. & J. F. Thompson,) agts. for Lill's Chicago Brewery Cos. Ales and Porters, 72 w. Washington. See card, page 40.

Butterfield Cyrus S., (C. S. B. & Co.,) 72 w. Washington, res. same, up-stairs.

Butterfield T. H., bill clerk, American and U. S. Express Cos., 34 e. Washington, res. 175 n. Tennessee.

Butterfield J. N., upholster, Hume, Adams & Co., res. 475 n. East.

BUTTERFIELD JEREMIAH, agt. American and U. S. Express Cos., 34 e. Washington, res. n. Pennsylvania, bet. Pratt and St. Joseph.

BUTTERFIELD S. A. & SON, (S. A. & W. Webster B.,) physicians, office 366 n. East.

Butterfield W. Webster, (S. A. B. & Son,) physicians and surgeons, office 366 n. East, res. 382 n. East.

Button Miss Gertie, hair-worker, 50 s. Illinois, res. same.

Button Jessie W., principal fourth ward school, bds. 126 n. Tennessee.

Byers Thomas J., student, N. W. C. University, bds. 40 Christian av.

Byers William C., clerk, Blind Asylum, bds. same.

BYINGTON W. W., State agt., New York Life Insurance Co., of New York City, 11 s. Meridian, res. 78 w. North.

Byrd Frank, engineer, bds. 280 Chestnut.

Byram Norman S., (Kennedy, B. & Co.,) 108 s. Meridian, res. 466 n. Meridian.

Byrd J. A., mechanic, res. 280 Chestnut.

Byrkit Albert, machinist, cor. Tennessee and Georgia, bds. same.

Byrkit D. Y., book-keeper, cor. Tennessee and Georgia, res. same.

Byrkit E. M., (B. & Son,) res. 165 s. Tennessee.

Byrkit Frank, moulder, res. 111 w. South.

Byrkit Hiram, candy-maker, 26 s. Meridian, res. 143 Ft. Wayne av.

Byrkit Hiram, lab., res. 86 e. Pratt.

Byrkit Jacob, carpenter, res. 29 Grant.

Byrkit John W., (Martin B. & Sons,) res. 71 Norwood.

Byrkit Martin, res. cor. Tennessee and Georgia.

BYRKIT M. & SONS, (John W. & Edwin M. B.,) planing mill and sash, door and blind factory, cor. Tennessee and Georgia. See card, p. 2.

Byrkit Socrates, wood engraver, bds. Martin House, 33 w. Maryland.

Byrne Mary, servant, 158 n. Mississippi.

CABEL CHARLES, works Union Starch Factory, res. 224 Winston.

Cady Mrs. Abigal A., (wid.,) res. 24 Circle.

Cady Christie, (col.,) servant, 252 n. Meridian.

Cady D., (D. C. & Co.,) 9. n. Pennsylvania, res. 227 s. New Jersey.

CADY D. & CO., (D. C. & ——) boots and shoes, 9 n. Pennsylvania.

Cady Elmer E., salesman, 25 e. Washington, bds. 227 s. New Jersey.

Cady Nelson W., student, high school, bds. 24 Circle.

CAHALL & CO., tobacco manfs., 175 w. Cumberland.

Cahall James, (Cahall & Co.,) 175 w. Cumberland, res 26 s. Mississippi.

Cahaline Mary, servant, Bates House.

Cahew John S., res. 519 s. Illinois.

Cahill Ellen, servant, 190 o. Market.

Cahill John, policeman, third ward, res. 81 St. Clair.

Cahill John, weaver, res. 247 w. Washington.

Cahill Joseph, spinner, res. 347 w. Washington.

Cahill J. B., pressman, Sentinel Office.

Cahill Mrs. Mary, (wid. Hugh,) res. 347 w. Washington.

Cain Bridget, servant, 473 n. Illinois.

Cain George W., book-binder, bds. 11 n. West.

Cain Hannah, (wid. John,) res 335 n. East.

Cain Henry, servant, J. D. Condit, 54 Circle.

Cain John, occupant Deaf and Dumb Asylum, Osgood p. o., Ripley co.

Cain Oliver J., fireman, I., C. & L. R. R., bds. 99 Benton.

Cain Mrs. Rebecca, (wid. Samuel,) res. over 274 e. Washington.

Cain Rose, servant, bds. 335 n. East.

Cain William A., engineer, I., C. & L. R. R. bds. 99 Benton.

Caldwell & Detrich, dealers in furs, &c., 61 s. Illinois.

Caldwell Edward, lab., bds. 408 w. Washington.

CALDWELL H. W., flour, feed, commission house and grocery, 149 Indiana av., res. 180 w. Michigan.

Caldwell Jesse, salesman, H. Daily & Co., 41 s. Meridian, bds. 378 s. Meridian.

Caldwell John, (Crossland, Maguire & Co.,) 52 s. Meridian, res. 54 n. Mississippi.

Caldwell John M., grader, res. 54, cor. market and Mississippi.

Caldwell J. W., (C. & Detrick,) 61 s. Illinois, bds. Wiles House.

Caldwell Thomas G., tailor, res. 292 e. Michigan.

Caler Frank, lab., res. 135 n. Noble.

Caler Henry, lab., res. 227 n. West.

California House, Adam Kistner, propr., 184 s. Illinois.

Call Joseph, lab., res. 115 Oak.

Callahan Daniel C., lab., bds. 199 Meek.

Callahan David, lab., res. 23 w. Washington.

Callahan James, carpenter, res. 68 Fayette.

Callahan John P., engine driver, engine No. 3, res. 167 e. South.

Callihan Mrs. Margaret, (wid.,) bds. 80 Fayette.

Callihan Michael, lab., res. 202 w. Walnut, cor. Missouri.

Callahan Michael, lab., res. 36 Lord.

Callahan Patrick, lab., res. 130 s. Noble.

Callahan Samuel, lab., I. & C. R. R., bds. end Lord.

Callemeyer Henry, lab., Central Depot, res. 249 s. Alabama.

Callison P. S., occupant Deaf and Dumb Asylum, Union Mills p. o., LaPorte co.

Callon James, reel-driver, No. 2 Engine, res. 44 Massachusetts av.

Callon R. F., paper-hanger, bds. 35 Indiana av.

Calloway Mary E., occupant Deaf and Dumb Asylum, Roosville p. o.

Calloway N. E., inmate Deaf and Dumb Asylum.

Calvert Charles L., farmer, bds. 375 n. West.

Calvert James, farmer, res. 375 n. West.

Calvert R. C., student, commercial college, bds. 375 n. West.

Calvin Miss Mary, servant, n. side e. Georgia, near city limits.

Cambee J. B., clerk, 19 Virginia av., res. 23 Pratt.

Cambren Hattie, (col.,) s. side North, bet. Blackford and Bright.

Cambridge Mrs. Harriet, servant, n. w. cor. New York and Alabama.

Cameron George K., brick-yard, end Virginia av., res. 413 s. East.

Cameron J. J., medical student, 15 e. Washington, bds. beyond city limits.

Cameron William D., printer, bds. 278 n. Alabama.

Cameron William S., steam book and job printer, 8 e. Pearl, res. 278 n. Alabama.

Camlin W. B., pastor Fifth Presbyterian Church, res. 35 n. California.

Campbell Andrew F., tailor, res. 334 w. Washington.

Campbell Charles C., trader, res. 2 w. North.

Campbell Dennis, lab., res. 321 Davidson.

Campbell Dennis, lab., res. 116 Oak.

Campbell Duvaull, butcher, res. 322 e. Market.

Campbell Ezekiel, carpenter, res. 262 s. Delaware.

Campbell George H., law student, 3 Odd Fellows Hall, bds. 2 w. North.

Campbell & Green, (John T. C. & Perry M. G.,) druggists, 149 w. Washington.

Campbell Henry, traveling agt., room 4, Cobern's bldg., w. Washington.

Campbell Rev. J., pastor Christian Church, res. 23 Bright.

Campbell John A., tailor, bds. 334 w. Washington.

Campbell John D., publisher, bds. 346 n. Illinois.

Campbell John T., (C. & Green,) 149 w. Washington, bds. 130 n. Mississippi.

CAMPBELL J. G., passenger agt., Bellefontaine Ry. line, office 53 s. Alabama.

Campbell McCobe, upholsterer, bds. 130 n. Mississippi.

Campbell Miss Margaret, res. 334 w. Washington.

Campbell Miss Martha, teacher A., primary, first ward school, bds. 357 n. East.

Campbell Mary, (wid. George,) washing and ironing, res. 226 Massachusetts av.

Campbell Mrs. Mary, (wid.,) dress-maker, 87 n. Delaware, res. same.

Campbell Miss Mary, res. 334 w. Washington.

Campbell Richard, employe, Vinton blk., res. 34 Union.

Campbell Robert, merchant policeman, bds. 34 Union.

Campbell Samuel L., book-binder, bds. 2 w. North.

Campbell Samuel, messenger, Inndiana-
polis Branch Banking Co., res. cor.
Washington and Pennsylvania.
Campbell Thomas, student, commercial col-
lege, bds. 96 w. Market.
Campbell Thomas S., foreman, Sentinel
bindery, res. 246 n. Illinois.
Campbell Wm., student, commercial college,
bds. 69 w. Market.
Campbell William, blacksmith, res. 243
Mississippi.
Canan J. T., clerk, Spencer House, bds.
same.
Canan Johnson, bar-keeper, Bates House,
bds. same.
CANAN J. W.,
propr. Spencer House, cor. Illinois and
Louisiana.
Canan W. S., clerk, Spencer House, bds.
same.
Cane Mrs. Mary A., (wife Machael,) res.
175 e. Louisiana.
Canfield Bridget, servant, W. H. Hay, 222
n. Tennessee.
Canby John, engineer, B. Line R. R., res.
114 s. East.
Cannell Miss Eliza C., first asst. City High
School, n. w. cor. Christian and Col-
lege av.
Cannon L. G., clerk, freight office I. P. & C.
R. R., bds. Pyle House.
Cannon Mary, servant, 201 n. New Jersey.
Cantana John E., cigar manfr., res. Orient,
bet. Michigan and National rd., beyond
city limits.
Canton Thomas, drayman, res. 94 Fayette.
Cantrell Mrs. Ann, (wid.,) bds. 132 w. Ver-
mont.
Cantrell David M., printer, res. 132 w.
Vermont.
Cantwell Jeremiah, tinner, bds. 128 Win-
ston.
Cantwell Michael, pattern-maker, works
Sinker & Co., res. 132 Winston.
Capen Nathan B., Jr., stone-mason, res.
121 n. Noble.
Capital City Varnish Works, cor. Missis-
sippi and Kentucky av., H. B. Mears,
propr.
Capp A. B., (Franklin & Co.,) 24½ e. Wash-
ington, res. 87 n. Noble.
Carakoff Hamlin, lab., res. foot Michigan,
near National rd.
Card Mrs. Martha, bds. Vermont, bet. Me-
ridian and Illinois.
Cardington Alexander D., groceries, n. s.
National rd., res. s. s. same, near In-
sane Asylum.
Cardder Henry, carpenter, res. n. Douglas.
Carey Albert J., plasterer, bds. 82 e. St.
Clair.
Carey Andrew J., traveling agt., res. 27
Chatham.
Carey B., white-washer, res. 58 Oak.

Carey Anna, inmate Deaf and Dumb Asy-
lum.
Carey Hannah, servant, 260 cor. West and
Washington.
Carey Harvey G., (J. S. C. & Co.,) res. 284
n. Meridian.
Carey James, stove-moulder, res. 151 High.
Carey Jason S., (J. S. C. & Co.,) res. 191
n. Delaware.
Carey J. S. & Co., (Jason S. & Harvey G.
C.,) coopers, foot w. Georgia.
Carey John, lab., res. Michigan rd., beyond
city limits.
Carey Joseph, res. 141 Meek.
Carey Patrick, lab., res. 493 e. Georgia.
Carigg Mary J., inmate Deaf and Dumb
Asylum.
Carigan John, teamster, res. 87 s. West.
Carle Michael, res. 369 s. Missouri.
Carleton George T., clerk, W. & J. Braden,
res. 174 e. New York.
Carleton James M., traveling agt., Fair-
banks' Scales, res. 174 e. New York.
Carleton Phillip J., messenger, American
Express, res. 174 e. New York.
Carley George, miller, res. 52 Bright.
Carlisle Mrs. Ann M., (wid. Daniel,) res.
117 n. Mississippi.
Carlisle Hugh T., printer, Journal office,
bds. Commercial Hotel.
Carlisle H. D., (J. Carlisle & Sons,) res. 77
w. Ohio.
Carlisle John, (J. Carlisle & Sons,) res. 260
w. Washington.
Carlisle J. & Sons, (John H. D. & William
Carlisle,) flouring mill, n. e. cor. Mar-
ket and Canal.
Carlisle William, (John Carlisle & Sons,)
bds. 260 w. Washington.
Carliss Carydon T., Homeopathist, office 72
e. Market, bds. 60 w. Market.
Carlon John, foreman press room, Downey,
Brouse, Butler & Co., bds. 41 Kentucky
av.
Carmichael Jesse D., (Todd, C. & Williams,)
33 e. Washington, res. 456 n. Meridian.
Carnahan McDonell A., student, bds. 410
n. Delaware.
Carman Johnson, bar-tender, Bates House
Saloon, bds. Bates House.
Carney Mrs. Nellie, lady boarder, 131 n.
East.
Caroun J. M., physician, res. 140 Bluff rd.
Carpenter Mrs. Anna, (wid. George,) res.
Court, bet. Alabama and New Jersey.
Carpenter B. O., dealer in tomb stones and
monuments, 36 e. Market, res. 515 n.
Mississippi.
Carpenter Catharine, inmate Home of the
Friendless.
Carpenter Conrad F., painter, bds. 354 s.
Delaware.
Carpenter Edwin, dairyman, res. end Vir-
ginia av.

Carpenter Edwin, (C. & Co.,) res. 357 n. East.
Carpenter E. C., coal dealer, bds. 35 Cherry.
Carpenter Frank, dining-room boy, Oriental House.
Carpenter Hury, lab., Insane Asylum, bds. n. s. National rd., w. White river bridge.
Carpenter John, (Craig, Powell & Co.,) Boyd's blk., Massachusetts av., res. 197 n. Illinois.
Carpenter I. H., book-keeper, 40 s. Meridian, bds. 165 n. Tennessee.
Carpenter Mrs. Mary A., (wid.,) res. 133 n. Mississippi.
Carpenter Nathaniel, supt. Indianapolis Coal and Mining Co., 19 Circle, bds. 440 n. New Jersey.
Carpenters' Union, cor. Meridian and South.
Carr Alexander, bds. 190, second floor, w. Washington.
Carr Christian, teamster, res. 288 e. Market.
Carr E. M., carpenter, res. 423 n. East.
Carr George W., machinist, C. C. & I. C. shop, res. 420 Central R. R.
Carr James, lab., res. 109 Cherry.
Carr James M., (R. S. & J. M.,) 9 Bates House blk., bds. 490 n. Meridian.
Carr John, brick-layer, bds. 82 e. St. Clair.
Carr Mrs. Mary, (wid.,) res. 180, second floor, w. Washington.
Carr Moses, bds. 180, second floor, w. Washington.
Carr Omar B., book-keeper, 9 Bates House blk., bds. 490 n. Meridian.
Carr Patrick, peddler, res. 26 John.
Carr R. S. & J M., (Rolander & James M. C.,) saddle and harness-makers, 9 Bates House blk., w. Washington.
Carr Rolander S, (R. S. & J. M. C.,) 9 Bates House blk., res |490 n. Meridian.
Carr.Richard, street contractor, res. e. McCarty, near Virginia av.
Carr Thomas, groceries, 276 s. Missouri, res. same.
Carr Willis, mason, bds. 82 e. St. Clair.
Carratt Albert, (A. C. & Son,) 257 e. Washington.
Carratt Albert & Son, second-hand clothing, 257 e. Washington.
Carretson S. M., physician, res. 142 n. Mississippi.
Carroll J., plasterer, bds. 404 Virginia av.
Carroll Mary E, inmate Deaf and Dumb Asylum.
Carroll M. E., milliner, 307 e. Washington, res. same.
Carroll Michael, lab., T. H. & I. R. R., res. 369 s. Missouri.
Carroll Thomas, lab., freight depot T. H. & I. R. R., res. on s. Missouri, s. McCarty.
Carron Peter, works J. Cahall & Co., bds. Ray House.

Carson John, engineer, Bates House, bds. same.
Carson Henry L., conductor C. C. & I. C. R. R., res. 183 Meek.
Carson Peter, stone-cutter, res. 199 w. Maryland.
Carter Albert, barber, 229 e. Washington, bds. 225 e. Washington.
Carter A. B., cash boy, 68 e. Washington. bds. 440 n. New Jersey.
Carter Beice M., carpenter, res. 540 n. Mississippi.
Carter C. A., cigar-maker, William Wallace, res. 181 s. Delaware.
Carter Charles A, candy-maker, 40 w. Washington, res. 123 n. West.
Carter David E, physician and surgeon, 51 Indiana av., res. 213 n. Mississippi.
Carter Edward, (Hill & Co.,) 14 Bates House, n. Illinois, bds. 756 n. Tennessee
Carter Miss Emma, seamstress, res. 9 English's blk., e. Washington.
Carter Enoch B., carpenter, res. 198 s. Mississippi.
Carter Frank, clerk, 27 n. Pennsylvania, res. cor. New Jersey and South.
Carter Geo. G. (C. & Haynes,) 40 w. Washington, bds. 169 n. Illinois.
Carter George, (Leathers & C.,) room 3, Odd Fellows' Hall, res. 544 n. Tennessee.
Carter Hannah, (col.,) servant at 210 n. Meridian.
Carter & Haynes, (George H. C. & Philip H.,) wholesale and retail confectioners, 40 w. Washington.
Carter Henry, paper-maker, bds. Nagele House.
Carter James, bds. 236 n. Illinois.
Carter John, (John S. Spann & Co.,) 2 Brown's blk., res. 440 n. New Jersey.
Carter John B., clerk at 25 n. Pennsylvania, bds. cor. New Jersey and South
Carter John W., express messenger Adams Express Co., res. 199 s. New Jersey.
Carter Pleasant, (col.,) servant at 78 w. Market.
Carter Richard, (col.,) white-washer, res. 38 Bates.
Carter Robert, Jr., (col.,) waiter Bates House, res. Howard, bet. Second and Third.
Carter Robert A.,(col.,) works Bates House, res. Geisendorff.
Carter S. A., engineer, bds. 288 Chestnut.
Carter Vinson, (Burns & C.,) 74 e Washington, res. 79 e. St. Joseph.
Carter William, (col.,) lab., res. on Alley rear 115 Davidson.
CARTER WILLIAM E., Palace Saloon, 87 s. Illinois, bds. Commercial Hotel.
Carton Andrew, helper White River Iron Works, res. Sinker.

Cartwright Tom E., bookeeper, 82 w. Washington, res. n. Mississippi.

Carter Chas. P., store-keeper, Bates House.

Carver Mrs. Mary, seamstress, res. e. side Blake, bet. Washington and New York.

Case David H, engineer, res. 252 e. Market.

Case Elon E., (E. E. C. & Co.,) 84 w. Washington, res. 246 n. Meridian.

CASE E. E. & CO., (Elon E. C. & Pennell Sharpless,) agricultural implements, stoves and tinware, 84 w. Washington.

Case Henry C., carpenter, bds. n. e. cor. Mississippi and Michigan.

Case John L., engineer on C. C. & I. C. R. R., res. 128 Bates.

Case John V., engineer, res. 252 e. Market.

Case Lyman, salesman, E. E. Case & Co., res. n. e. cor. Mississippi and Michigan.

Case William O, carpenter, res. 9 Fatout's blk., w. Washington.

Casey Michael, harness-maker, 24 n. Delaware, res. 114 w. Georgia.

Casey Patrick, lab., res. 107 Hosbrook.

Cashen William, lab., 317 w. Market.

Caskey Jacob, watchman, Bellefontaine Shops, bds. 456 e. Michigan.

Caskey James, fireman, Bellefontaine R. R., bds. 456 e. Michigan.

Casman Michael, lab., res. 39 e. McCarty.

Casman Michael, lab., res. 33 Buchanan.

Cass F., hostler, 16 n. Pennsylvania.

Cassebaum Mary, servant, 456 e. Michigan.

Cassels William, works Junction R. R., bds. Wiles House.

Cassidy Miss Frank, clerk, 10 w. Washington, res. cor. New York and Meridian.

Cassidy Mattie, lady boarder, 36 s. New Jersey.

Cassill Harry, printer, bds. 444 n. New Jersey.

Cassing Michael, lab., res. 63 Wyoming.

Cassien William, res. 317 w. Market.

Casson John, engineer, Bates House, res. 218 w. Georgia.

Castell Haman, cigar-maker, res. Blake, bet. New York and Vermont.

Casteele Joshua, last-maker, res. 36 Dougherty.

Casteter Hiram D., druggist, 40 E. Washington, bds. Palmer House.

Castin Henry, teamster, McCord & Wheatley.

Castor Edward A., carpenter, res. Columbia, bet. East and New Jersey.

Cathcart Andrew, engineer, res. 258 s. New Jersey.

Cathcart Robert W., book-keeper, 5 e. Washington, res. 258 s. New Jersey.

Catherwood Joseph, traveling agt., bds. 314 w. New York.

Catlin Mrs. Martha, (wid.,) res. 298 w. Market.

CATLIN MRS. M. J., millinery, straw goods, laces and trimmings, 46 w. Washington, res. 44 n. Mississippi.

Catlin W. W., millinery, w. Washington, res. 44 n. Mississippi.

Cathin William W., 46 w. Washington, res. 44 n. Mississippi.

Cathro David R., salesman, New York Store, bds. Oriental House.

Catterson A. E., policeman, eighth ward, res. 276 e. south.

Catterson H., salesman, 24 w. Louisiana, bds. 276 e. South.

Catterson Robert F., foreman, McOuat's tin shop, bds. 80 s. Tennessee.

Catterson Sarah, (wid.,) res. 57 Maple.

CAVEN JOHN, ex-mayor and attorney at law, over 23 e. Washington, bds. Bates House.

Caven Michael, lab., res. 124 s. Noble.

Cavanaugh Lawrence, works Indiana Central rd. shop, res. near Jeffersonville Round House.

Cavanaugh Mathew, res. 55 Eddy.

Cavanaugh William U., turner, bds. Wiles House.

Caylor Ann, servant, 221 e. Ohio.

Caylor Allen, flour and feed store, 185 Indiana av., bds. 379 n. West.

Caylor Jacob, butcher, res. 321 n. West.

Caylor Otho, expressman, res. 274 Railroad.

Caylor Miss Jane, lady boarder, 281 e. New York.

Cearsy John Sol., res. 24 Kingan.

Cecile Sister, superioress St. Mary's School, Georgia, bet. Tennessee and Illinois.

Ceiter C., cooper, McCarty, bet. Meridian and Union., res. 183 Madison av.

Ceiter Christoph, cooper, bds. California House.

Cemp Margaret, servant, 70 e. Ohio.

Cetinger John, painter, bds. 202 s Illinois.

Chamber of Commerce, Vinton's blk., n. Pennsylvania, J. Burnard, secy.

Chambers Abraham, melter, Root's Foundry, res. 682 n. Illinois.

Chambers Miss Anna, ladies' boarding-house, 201 e. Market.

Chambers Charles, brakesman, J. M. & I. R. R., bds. Globe House.

Chambers Charles S., res. Blake, bet. New York and Vermont.

Chambers Thomas, hostler, W. W. Weaver, 233 n. Illinois.

Chamberlin James, farmer, res. 577 n. Tennessee.

CHAMBERLIN JAMES H., carpenter, Osgood, Smith & Co., res. 225 Virginia av.

Champie Joseph, salesman, Gall & Rush, res. 130 n. Illinois.

Champion William, pressman, Sentinel office, res. 345 s. Meridian.

Chance Harry C., clerk, 7 and 9 e. Washington, res. 43 Bluff rd.

Chandler Mrs. Eliza, (wid.,) bds. 172 w. Michigan.

Chandler F, general ticket-agent, C. C. & I. C. R. W., bds. Bates House.

Chandler & Field, (William C. & Edward S. F.,) wholesale paper dealers, 24 s. Meridian.

Chandler George R., printer, W. & J. Braden's, res. 172 w. Michigan.

Chandler Henry C., (H. C. C. & Co.,) s. e. cor. Meridian and Pearl, res. 278 w. Vermont

Chandler H. C. & Co., (Henry C. C. & George Merritt,) engravers and book and job printers, s. e. cor. Meridian and Pearl.

CHANDLER & TAYLOR, (Thomas E. C. & Franklin T.,) Phœnix Foundry and Machine Works, 370 w. Washington.

Chandler Thomas E., (C. & Taylor,) res. 34 California.

Chandler William, (C. & Field,) 24 s. Meridian, res. 278 w. Vermont.

Chandler W. E., paper-maker, res. 293 w. Vermont.

Chapman Mrs. C. M., (wid. Rufus,) res. over 248 e. Washington.

CHAPMAN D. C., sign and house painter, 20Virginia av., res. 33 Ellsworth, see card page 84.

Chapman George H., judge Marion Criminal Circuit Court, 3 Langsdale's blk., res. e. side n. Meridian, beyond city limits.

Chapman Jane, seamstress, 130 n. Alabama.

Chapman John, wagon-maker, National rd., half mile from river bridge.

Chapman Newman, finisher woolen factory, bds. 75 California

Chapman N. J., inmate Deaf and Dumb Asylum.

Chapman Samuel, res. National rd., w. White river bridge.

Chapman S. E., inmate Deaf and Dumb Asylum.

Chapman Thomas S, carpenter, res. 75 California.

Charles Abraham B., carpenter, res. 311 n. West.

Charles Alexander, (col.,) lab., bds. Mississippi, bet. Second and Third.

Charles Mrs. Emily E., (wid. Daniel B.,) boarding-house, 27 w. Ohio.

Charles Joslyn D., carpenter, res. 128 Meek.

Charles Mathew, teacher city academy, res. 385 n. East.

Charles T., hack-driver, res. 109 s. Noble.

Charter Oak Fire Ins. Co., of Hartford, Conn., Davis & Greene, agts., 27 s. Meridian.

Charter Oak Life Ins. Co., of Hartford, Conn., W. H. Hay, gen'l agt. for Indiana, office 6 Blackford's blk.

Chase A. S., bds. Pyle House.

CHASE DAVID H., boots and shoes, 25 e. Washington, bds. e. Michigan rd., beyond city limits. ●

Chase William, salesman, 25 e. Washington, bds. e. Michigan rd., beyond city limits.

Chasteen Charles, cooper, res. 62 Huron.

Cheatham Washington, (col.,) lab., res. Howard, bet. Third and Fourth.

Cheek Mrs. Elizabeth, (wid. Wm. B.,) res. 40 n. Mississippi.

Cheney G. E., telegraph operator, 11. s. Meridian, bds. Oriental House.

Chenoworth Miss Sarah, tailoress, res. 199 e. Washington, up-stairs.

Chepus Felix, piano-maker, res. 325 e. New York.

Chepus John, stone-cutter, res. 325 e. New York.

Chering Charles, street sprinkler, res. Orient, bet. Michigan and National rd., beyond city limits.

Cherry Andrew, driver, American Express Co., 34 e. Washington, bds. 138 e. New York.

Cheesler Conrad, watchman, Eagle Machine Works, res. 93 n. New Jersey.

Chester Albert A., stair builder, res. 273 Winston.

Chester Charles C., music teacher, res. 749 n. Illinois.

Chessler Ella, servant at 487 n. Illinois.

Chettle M. G., telegraph operator, 11 s. Meridian, res. 176 n. Missouri.

Chevalier Alfonso, painter, 304 e Washington, res. 125 n. Noble.

Chew Mrs. Mary, (wid.,) servant, 269 e. Market.

Chidsey Robert A., brakesman, C. C. & I. C. R. R., bds. 58 Benton.

Child M., Jr., (Jones & C.,) 25 w. Washington, bds. Bates House.

Childers Mrs. E. J., (wid. John,) res. 235 s. Noble.

Childers James, teamster, bds. 235 s. Noble.

Childers Joshua, lab., res. 50 Elm

Childers Levina, (wid.,) res. 3 Vine.

Childers Mary J., (wid. William,) res. 231 s. New Jersey.

Chill Thomas, house carpenter, res. 302 Madison av.

Childson Sarah E., occupant Deaf and Dumb Asylum.

Chittenden Horace N., special agt., Putnam Fire Ins. Co., of Hartford, Conn., office 17 n. Meridian.

Chives E. B., shoe-maker, res. n. side New York, bet. Minerva and Blake.

Chives James A., shoe-maker, bds. New York, bet. Minerva and Blake.

Christ Mrs. Nancy, (wid. William,) bds. 494 Virginia av.

Christ Church, (episcopal,) n. side Circle, cor. Meridian.

Christian Church, s. w. cor. Delaware and Ohio.

Christian Wilmer F., (Shover & C.,) bds. 278 n. Pennsylvania.

Christison David, brick-layer, res. 103 Hosbrook.

Christman Ferdinand, teller, Merchants' National Bank, 48 e. Washington, bds. 27 w. Maryland.

Christopher ———, architect, carver and designer, 141 w. Washington, res. Kentucky av., near Washington.

CHRISTY ALBERT, saloon, 26 Louisiana, res. 13 e. South.

Christy Albert, (col.,) servant, 38 w. Market.

Christy Israel, (col.,) lab., res. 29 n. Harris.

Christy James A., cook, Moffitt's Saloon, res. 281 n. Mississippi.

Christy Sophia, (col.,) res. n. Blake, bet. North and Elizabeth.

Christy William, lab., res. 344 n. Blake.

Church Henry E., employe Journal office, res. 121 n. west.

Church Joseph, saw-maker, res. Sinker, bet. Alabama and New Jersey.

Churchman F. M., (S. A. Fletcher & Co.,) res. 130 n. Alabama.

CHURCHMAN W. H., supt. Institute for the Education of the Blind, res. same.

Cinnick Frank, student, N. W. C. University, bds. 444 n. New Jersey.

Cincinnati Bakery, Fred. Bollman, propr., 107 e. Washington.

CINCINNATI, CONNERSVI'LE & INDIANAPOLIS JUNCTION R. R., office 112 Virginia av., freight depot in rear passenger depot, at Union depot, J. M. Ridenour, vice-prest., J. A. Perkins, general freight and passenger agt.

Cisco Isaac, freight conductor, C. C. & I. C. R. R., res. 605 e. Washington.

Cishm Robert, (col.,) cook, 350 w. North.

City Academy, 13 e. New York.

City Auditor's Office, Glenn's blk., e. Washington.

City Cemetery, Kentucky av., bet. Louisiana and River, G. W. Allred, sexton.

City Clerk's Office, Glenn's blk., e. Washington, D. M. Ransdall, city clerk.

City Council Chamber, Glenn's blk., e. Washington, Daniel Macauley, mayor.

City Judge's Office, Glenn's blk., e. Washington, J. N. Scott, city judge.

City Treasurer's Office, Glenn's blk., e. Washington, R. S. Foster, city treasurer.

CITY DIRECTORY OFFICE, Logan & Co., publishers, 16½ e. Washington, Herald bldg. See introductory in first part of book.

City Hospital, n. w. city limits, terminus Indiana av., G. V. Woolen, supt.

City Flower Garden and Green House, cor. Canal and Kentucky av.

City High School, n. w. cor. Circle and Market.

Citizens' National Bank, 4 e. Washington, I. Mansur, prest., Joseph R. Haugh, cashier.

Citizens' Street Ry. Co., E. S. Alvord, prest., general office, cor. Louisiana and Tennessee.

Claflin Charles C., (Treat & C.,) 30 n. Pennsylvania, res. 489 n. Meridian.

Claffey Christian F., drayman, res. 328 n. Noble.

Claffey Conrad, drayman, res. 69 Huron.

Claffey Frederick, machinist, Central shop, res. 38 Dougherty.

Claffey Mrs. ———, (wid.,) res. 48 Bicking.

Clancey & Holmes, milliners and dressmakers, 30 s. Delaware.

Clancy John, tobacconist, bds. Ray House.
Clancey Mathew, (C. & Webb,) 18 s. Meridian, res. 82 w. Market.
Clancey Mrs. M., (C. & Holmes,) 30 s. Delaware, res. same.
CLANCY & WEBB, (Mathew C. & Ira C. W.,) house, sign and ornamental painters, 18 s. Meridian.
Clark Benjamin, cooper, bds. end Lord, beyond city limits.
Clark Catharine, servant, 222 n. Illinois.
Clark Charles, railroader, 193 w. South.
Clark Chas., works Capital Tobacco Works, bds. 502 n. Illinois.
Clark D. L., operator, Miller & Franks, over 45 e. Washington.
Clark Franklin, (col.,) lab., res. w. Elizabeth, near City Hospital.
Clark George, clerk, W. P. & E. P. Gallup, bds. 78 n. Tennessee.
Clark George A., physician and surgeon, with D. Hole, bds. Macy House.
Clark Hampton, grocer, res. 266 Indiana av.
Clark Henry M., railroader, C. C. & I. C. R. R., bds. 61 s. Noble.
Clark Henry W., soldier, U. S. Arsenal, res. Arsenal grounds.
Clark Hugh, carriage-maker, works 231 w. Washington, res. 213 Massachusetts av.
Clark Isaac brick-moulder, bds. National rd., w. White river bridge.
Clark John, blacksmith, res. Plum, bet. Vine and Cherry.
Clark John, blacksmith, res. 301 s. Pennsylvania.
Clark John, blacksmith, 83 Kentucky av., res. 222 s. Pennsylvania.
Clark John T., miller, res. 222 Bluff rd.
Clark Mrs. Mary, (wid. Jones C.,) res. 2 n. Douglas alley.
Clark Michael J., shoe-maker, 223 w. Washington, res. 272 w. Washington.
Clark Milton L., blacksmith, 175 s. Tennessee, res. 222 Union.
Clark M., fireman, J. M. & I. R. R., bds. Ray House.

Clark Levi, com. broker, bds. s. New Jersey.
Clark Mrs. ——, tailoress, res. 177 w. Vermont.
Clark Orville B., express-messenger, res. 115 e. Ohio.
Clark Reuben O., carpenter, res. 176 w. Michigan.
Clark Richard A., (col.,) lab., res. 183 Douglas alley.
Clark Miss Sarah, milliner, 15 Massachusetts av., res. same.
Clarke Thomas F., traveling agt., Fairbank's Scales, 43 and 45 n. Tennessee, bds. Spencer House.
Clark Timothy, fireman, C. C. & I. C. R. R., bds. 58 Benton.
Clark William, (Veith & C.,) 19 and 21 n. Tennessee, res. 502 n. Illinois.
Clark William, (W. & W. H. C.,) 26 n. Illinois, res: 180 w. Ohio.
Clark William H., (W. & W. H. C.,) 26 n. Illinois, res. 180 w. Ohio.
Clark W. & W. H., merchant tailors, 26 n. Illinois.
Clark William T., 94 Virginia av., res. 27 Lockerbie.
Clary James, lab., res. 127 Maple.
Clary Jasper, lab., res. 61 McCarty.
Clary Jasper, res. 127 Maple.
Clarey Jeremiah, lab., res. 241 s. Tennessee.
Clarry Patrick A., porter, Palmer House, res. 104 n. Blake.
Clary W. J. P., lab., 61 McCarty.
Clay Benjamin, (col.,) res. s. Elizabeth, bet. Blake and Harris.
Clay Henry, (col.,) lab., res. Second, bet. Howard and Lafayette R. R.
Clay Henry, cook, Ray House.
Clay Hilary, (A. Jones & Co.,) 74 and 76 s. Meridian, res. 23 w. Ohio.
Clay John H., (col.,) moulder, bds. 24 w. Georgia.
Clayton B. F., painter, bds. 52 s. Pennsylvania.
Clayton L. W., salesman, D. Root & Co., res. 131 e. New York.

Clem Aaron, (Clem & Bro.,) 143 and 145 n. Delaware, res. 173 Massachusetts av.

Clem & Bro., (Aaron & W. F. C.,) groceries, flour and feed, 143 and 145 n. Delaware.

Clem William F., (Clem & Bro.,) 143 and 145 n. Delaware, res. 266 n. Alabama.

Clements Augustus R., engineer Bellefontaine R. R., res. 138 Davidson.

Clements William A., lab., res. 275 w. Merril.

Clemons Catharine, servant, 121 n. Delaware.

Cleveland J. B., real estate agt., room 5, Odd Fellows Hall, res. Christian av., bet. Broadway and College av.

CLEVELAND, COLUMBUS, CINCINNATI & INDIANAPOLIS RY. CO., general office, 53 s. Alabama, shops, e. end Michigan, freight depot, n. e. cor. Alabama and Virginia av., passenger depot at Union depot, Edward King, vice-prest. and treas.

Clifton C. W., student, commercial college, bds. 289 s. East.

Clifford Betsey, laundress, Bates House.

Clinas Isaac, painter, res. 234 s. Missouri.

Cline Miss Annie, 40 n. Mississippi.

Cline Peter, plainer, Hill's plaining mill, res. 116 s. East.

Cline Miss Sarah, servant at Moore's, e. side Liberty, bet. Meek and Georgia.

Cline William, butcher, res. Helen, bet. Georgia and Maryland.

Clinton Ellen, (col.,) servant, J. M. Maxwell, 330 n. Meridian.

Clinton James, (col.,) waiter, Bates House.

Clinton J. R., deputy city clerk, Glenns' blk., bds. 148 n. Tennessee.

Clippenger George W., physician, 28 n. Delaware, res. 335 n. Pennsylvania.

Clockey Christopher, lab., res. cor. Fourth and Howard.

Cloky Alexander W., pastor United Presbyterian Church, res. 110 n. Delaware.

Close William H., (Robertson & C.,) 10 e. Washington, bds. 335 n. East.

Clover James, brakeman, C. C. & I. C. R. R., bds. 58 Benton.

Cluck Wm., pump-maker, works 57 Massachusetts av., bds. 450 n. Tennessee.

Cluck Wm., well-digger, res. 344 n. Blake.

Clune Michael, groceries, 174 s. Meridian, res. same.

Clune Patrick, grocery, 174 Bluff rd., res. 454 s. Illinois.

Clycket John, shoe-maker, bds. Martin House, 33 n. Maryland.

Coal Albert, engineer, C. C. & I. C. R. R., bds. 33 Meek.

Cobb Mrs. Dilsey, (col.,) res. cor. Mississippi and Fifth.

Cobb Edward A., (Hay & Co.,) 48 w. Washington, bds. 222 n. Tennessee.

Cobert William, lab., res. 443 s. Illinois.

Coble Daniel, produce merchant, res. 99 Hosbrook.

Coble David A., (D. A. & G. C.,) 157 w. Washington, res. 265 n. Mississippi.

Coble D. & G., (David & George,) grocers, 167 w. Washington.

Coble George, carpenter, res. w. side Blake, bet. Washington and New York.

Coble George, (D. & G. C.,) 157 w. Washington, res. 272 n. Blake.

Coble Mrs. Elizabeth, bds. 150 n. Blake.

Coble Jane, servant, H. Griffith, 78 n. Illinois.

Coble Samuel, carpenter, res. n. Douglas.

Coburn Adeline, ladies boarding house, 273 n. Noble.

Coburn Henry, (C. & Jones,) cor. Mississippi and Georgia, res. 125 e. New York.

COBURN & JONES, (Henry C. & William H. J.,) dealers in lumber, lath and shingles, cor. Mississippi and Georgia.

Coburn Hahneman, res. cor. Georgia and West.

Coburn John, lawyer and U. S. representative, office 5 Langsdale blk., res. 126 e. Ohio.

Coburn Mary A., (wid.,) res. cor. Oak and Vine.

Cochran A. J., res. 420 s. Illinois.

Cochrane Miss Emily B., saleswoman, Grover & Baker Sewing Machine Co., 21 e. Washington, bds. 187 e. Ohio.

Cochrane Samuel W., carpenter, res. 424 n. Mississippi.

Cochrane Thomas M., general agt., Grover & Baker Sewing Machine Co., 21 e. Washington, res. 187 e. Ohio.

Cochrom Wm. W., carpenter, res. 420 s. Illinois.

Colclazer Jacob H., watch-maker and jeweler, works 50 e. Washington, bds. 121 n. Delaware.

Coen John, boarding house and paper hanger, 169 s. Tennessee.

Coen Sarah A., inmate Deaf and Dumb Asylum.

Coesby Mrs. Julia, (col., wid.,) wash-woman, res. Missouri, bet. Indiana av. and North.

Coffie Miss Emma, ladies boarding house, 57 n. Douglas alley.

Coffie Miss Jennie, bds. 57 n. Douglas alley.

Coffield Thomas, musician, bds. 235 e. Vermont.

Coffrin Abraham, res. 389 s. East.

Coffin B. S., (Wheat, Fletcher & Co.,) room 1, Vinton blk., res. 410 n. Pennsylvania.

Coffin Charles E., book-keeper, L. R. Martin, bds. 37 Kentucky av.

Coffin David W., (Connelly, W. & Co.,) 149 s. Meridian, res. 26 w. Pratt.

Coffin Miss Eliza T., teacher, public schools, bds. 171 Jackson.

Coffin Julius V., shipping clerk, 149 s. Meridian, bds. Spencer House.

Cofflin George, meat market, 306 w. Washington, res. same.

Coffman Charles W., traveling agt., Vinnedge, Jones & Co., 66 s. Meridian, bds. 188 s. Mississippi.

Coffman George, (C. & Poland,) 306 w. Washington.

Coffman Jacob, carpenter, res. 255 s. New Jersey.

Coffman & Poland, (George C. & John P.,) butchers, 306 w. Washington.

Coffman Samuel, carpenter, res. 305 Virginia av.

Caffey A. E., with Downey, Brouse, Butler & Co., cor. Meridian and Circle, bds. Mrs. Shannon, n. Delaware.

Cogle Mrs. Clarinda, (wid. John,) res. 229 Virginia av.

Cogle Samuel, brakeman, C. I. & C. R. R., bds. 103 s. New Jersey.

Cogle William, res. 223 Virginia av., old No. 186.

Cohick Samuel, porter, California House, bds. same.

Colden J. E., real estate agt., rooms 10 and 11 Talbott & New's blk., n. Pennsylvania, res. 129 Union.

Cole A. B., res. Western av., near city limits.

Cole Miss Augusta T., dress-maker, 15 Massachusetts av., res. Boyd's blk.

Cole B. W., Trade Palace, bds. Oriental House.

Cole Ernest B., clerk, 68 e. Washington, bds. Macy House.

Cole Howard, law student, Porter, Harrison & Fishback, res. 1½ mile east of arsenal.

Cole Miss M. E., teacher D. grade inter. Ninth Ward School, bds. 115 Massachusetts av.

COLE JAMES, carpenter, res. rear 84 n. Alabama.

Cole Oscar F, clerk, T. H. & I. R. R. freight depot, bds. Pyle House.

Coles Miss Susan C., dress-maker, 15 Massachusetts av., res. same.

Cole Wm., (col.,) lab., res. Camp Carrington.

Cole W. B., clerk, Trade Palace, bds. Oriental House.

Coleman Allen M., farmer, bds. 367 n. West.

Coleman Benjamin F., works cemetery, bds. 367 n. West.

Coleman Henry, messenger and porter Governor Baker, res. n. Tennessee, bet. Ohio and New York.

Coleman Henry C., farmer, bds. 367 n. West.

Coleman James, lab., res. 432 s. West.

Coleman John G., book-keeper, L. R. Martin, res. 367 n. West.

Coleman John G., bds. cor. Blake and Elizabeth.

Coleman Louisa, (col.,) servant, 228 e. Market.

Coleman Mary, servant, 51 Madison av.

Coleman Nathan, (col.,) lab., res. 344 w. North.

Coleman Mrs. Ruhamah, (wid.,) res. 367 n. West.

Coleman William, lab., Bellefontaine shop, bds. 382 e. Michigan.

Colestock Ephraim, carpenter, res. 250 n. Illinois.

Colestock George N., book-binder, W. & J. Braden, bds. 250 n. Illinois.

Colestock Wesley A., carpenter, bds. 250 n. Illinois.

Colgan Henrie, principal Fifth Ward School, res. cor. College and Christian av.

Colgan Henry, farmer, res. 77 Christian av.

Colgan Henrietta, teacher 5th Ward School, res. cor. College and Christian av.

Coll Dominick, bar-keeper Bourbon Saloon, bds. s. Illinois.

Colored School, 642 n. Mississippi, J. M. Williams, teacher.

Collard Isaac W., moulder, works Chandler & Taylor, res. 121 e. Ohio.

Collas August, cabinet-maker, bds. Ray House.

Colett Moses M., (John Furnas & Co.,) 68 e. Washington, res. cor. Broadway and Forrest Home av.

Collet Maurice, clerk, 100 e. Washington, bds. Circle Restaurant.

Coller S. A., lawyer, 16½ s. Meridian, res. 338 n. New Jersey.

Collier William S., res. 113 s. New Jersey.

Collins Miss A. E., teacher B. Primary Ninth Ward School, res. St. Joseph.

Collins Miss Anna M., student Ind. Female College, 146 n. Meridian, bds. same.

Collins B., saw-maker, bds. 64 s. East.

Collins Catharine, servant, 83 n. Tennessee.

Collins Cornelius, lab., res. 223 s. West.

Collins Hezekiah, capitalist, res. 134 e. St. Joseph.

Collins Ira F., clerk, 348 e. Washington, bds. 26 n. Noble.

Collins James A., clerk, A. Abromet, Ætna bldg., n. Pennsylvania, bds. 306 n. Delaware.

Collins James Levi, railroader, res. 457 c. Georgia.

Collins Jeremiah, lithographer, W. & J. Bradon, res. 39 s. East.

Collins John, carpenter, 239 Buchanan.

Collins Julia, servant, L. Hills, 208 n. Illinois.

Collins J. G., boarding-house, 52 s. Pennsylvania.

Collins Mrs. Lizzie, bds. 250 Madison av.

Collins Martin, lab., bds. cor. West and Maryland.

Collins Mary, servant, Gen. Love, 81 n. Tennessee.

Collins Norah, servant at n. e. cor. Illinois and Pratt.

Collins Thomas, works Street R. R. Co., res. 20 n. Noble.

Collins William, salesman, 14 n. Delaware, bds. 426 e. North.

Collins William, works U. S. Arsenal, res. 20 n. Noble.

Collopy Hannah, cook, 33 w. Maryland.

Collord Mrs. Elizabeth, (wid. George,) seamstress, 121 e. Ohio, res. same.

Columbus, Chicago & Indiana Central Ry. Company, office s. e. cor. Delaware and Virginia av.

Colter Eliza, servant at 288 n. Tennessee.

Colter John, works Rolling Mill, res. 345 s. Meridian.

Colvin George L., works Junction R. R., bds. Wiles House.

Colvin Scott, (col.,) servant, J. O. D. Lilly, n. Tennessee, bet. Second and Third.

Colton Wm., lab., C. C. C. & I. R. R. shop, bds. 270 Railroad.

Colwell Jesse B., clerk, H. Dailey & Co., bds. 378 n. Meridian.

Collwell Samuel H., fireman, C. C. C. & I. R. R., res. cor. Plum and Vine.

Comber John, heater, White River Iron Works, bds. California House.

Comegys Levy, carpenter and house-mover, res. cor. Sixth and Illinois.

Commercial, (Evening,) 17½ w. Washington, Commercial Co., proprs.

Comingore J. A., (C., Reissner & Co.,) 17 w. Washington, res. 335 n. Liberty.

Comingore John A., physician, res. 335 n. Liberty.

Comingore, Reissner & Co., (J. A. C. M. A. C. & G. A. R.,) dealers in boots and shoes, 17 w. Washington.

Comingore W. H., book-keeper, 17 w. Washington, res. 405 n. New Jersey.

Comly D. J., clerk, Gen'l Ticket Office C. C. & I. C. Ry., res. Michigan rd., e. city limits.

Commercial Hotel, cor. Georgia and Illinois, George McCormick, propr.

Commous John M., private secy. Governor Baker, office State House, res. 80 n. New Jersey.

Compagne Louis, carpenter, res. 118 Huron.

Compton Amanda, inmate Deaf and Dumb Asylum.

Compton Christiana M., inmate Deaf and Dumb Asylum.

Compton Eliza M., clerk, 152 w. Washington, res. cor. Fort Wayne av. and Cherry.

Compton Israel, groceries, 152 w. Washington, res. 167 Fort Wayne av.

Compton A. B., lab., bds. 174 w. Ohio.

Conoly Luke, lab., res. 113 n. West.

Conan Thomas, works Junction R. R., bds. Wiles House.

Conart E. P., fireman, C. C. C. & I. C. R. R., bds. 61 s. Noble.

Conaty James B., millinery, bleaching and manufacturer straw goods, 44 s. Illinois, res. 64 w. Maryland.

Concordia House, cor. Meridian and South, F. Mottery, prop.

Conde Henry T., book-keeper, 47 and 49 n. Tennessee, bds. 74 w. Vermont.

Conte Winfield, printer, Sentinel Office, bds. 89 Indiana av.

Conden Nora, cook, Institute of the Blind, bds. same.

CONDIT ALICE A, inventor of feather cloth, also patentee, res. 36 e. Market.

CONDIT JOHN D., attorney at law, 1 Blackford's blk., s. e. cor. Washington and Meridian, res. 54 Circle.

Condit Amzi B., patent agt., res. 36 e. Market.

Condon J. Frank, special agt. American Life Ins. Co., over 35 e. Washington, bds. Avenue House.

Conduitt Alexander B., (Landers, Pee & Co.,) 58 s. Meridian, bds. Sherman House.

Cone William S., agt. J. M. & I. R. R., bds. 207 w. Maryland.

Cones Charles E., salesman, 129 s. Meridian, bds. Pyle House.

Conger Emanuel H., brick-maker, bds. 281 n. Noble.

Congregational Church, n. w. cor. Meridian and Circle.

Conklin Miss Jane, dress-maker, 36 n. Illinois, bds. 148 Indiana av.

Conklin H. N., (Hogeland, Durfield & C.,) 75 s. Illinois, res. 252 n. Mississippi.

Conkwright Charles, expressman, res. 295 Coburn.

Conlen Michael, bible agt., res. 323 Indiana av.

Connell Thomas, lab., res. 45 s. Benton.

Connell Maurice, bar-tender, res. 45 s. Benton.

Connely Robert, (C., Wiles & Co.,) 149 s. Meridian, res. 296 n. Alabama.

Connely Wiles & Co., (Robert C., William D. & Daniel A. Wiles & David W. Coffin,) wholesale grocers, 149 s. Meridian.

Conner A D., (Witt & Co.,) s. w. cor. Washington and Meridian, bds. 385 n. East.

Conner A. H., (Douglass & C.,) Journal bldg., res. 515 n. Pennsylvania.

Conner Bridget, (wid. Michael,) res. 146 Stevens.

Conner Bridget, (wid.,) res. 384 s. Delaware.

Conner Bridget, servant, Edward King, n. Meridian.

Conner B. F., reg. clerk, p. o., rooms Eden's blk.

Conner Catharine, cook, Indiana Female College, 146 n. Meridian.

Conner Miss Elizabeth, bds. 73 n. Illinois,

Conner Mrs. E. L., (wid. Robert,) res. 229 s. Alabama.

Conner George, shoe-maker, res. end Virginia av.

Conner James, soldier, U. S. Arsenal, res. same.

Conner John, lab., res. 288 s. Delaware.

Conner John, works rolling mill, res. 384 s. Delaware.

Conner John, lab. res. 360 s. Delaware.

Conner John, lab., res. 14 n. Noble.

Connell John S., switchman, Union R. R. Co., res. 103 s. New Jersey.

Conner Miss Lucinda, bds. 73 n. Illinois.

CONNER MRS. MARY, boarding house, 73 n. Illinois.

Conner Michael, lab., bds. 199 Meek.

Conner Morris, works rolling mill, res. 384 s. Delaware.

Conroy Bernard, lab., res. 76 s. West.

Conroy John, coal cart driver, res. 49 s. West.

Conroy Patrick, tailor, 72 s. West, res. same.

Conrad Rufus, (col.,) minister and school teacher, res. 500 n. Mississippi.

Converse Joel, carpenter, res. rear 293 e. Market.

Converse Miss Lou., lady boarder, 27 n. New Jersey.

Conway Margaret, (wife Michael,) Insane Asylum, res. 332 s. Delaware.

Conway Michael, lab., res. 245 s. Tennessee.

Conway Thomas, express-messenger, Union depot, bds. 213 s. Illinois.

Cook Miss Belle, bds. 83 n. Missouri.

Cook Charles, bds. cor. North and Dunlop.

Cook Charles, works Skillen's Mills, bds. 366 w. Washington.

Cook Charlotte, servant, 86, old number, e. Vermont.

Cook Christian, baggageman, Union depot, res. 26 Bicking.

Cook E. S., pastor United Brethren Church, bds. 435 n. East.

Cook & Demmier, (William C. & Charles Demmier,) groceries and dry goods, 249 e. Washington.
Cook Frank, lab., res. 235 w. South.
Cook Frederick, porter, res. 79 s. Liberty.
Cook G. B., traveling agt., Judson & Dodd, bds. Bates House.
Cook George W., painter, res. 376 w. North.
Cook Henry, car inspector, res. 295 e. Georgia.
Cook Henry, lab., res. 22 John.
Cook Ignetz, machinist, res. 278 Bluff rd.
Cook John M., agt., W. & J. Braden, bds. 469 n. Illinois.
Cook John V., wholesale notion peddler, res. 224 n. East.
Cook John W., mill-wright, 132 s. Pennsylvania, res. 115 n. Tennessee.
Cook Mary, servant, e. end Market.
Cook Mary, (wid. John,) res. 38 Chatham.
Cook Rose, servant, 302 n. Delaware.
Cook Samuel M., teamster, Byrkit & Sons, res. 115 n. Tennessee.
Cook Sylvester, carpenter, res. 376 w. North.
Cook Thomas, lab., res. 16 Lockerbie.
Cook Thomas V., house, sign and ornamental painter, 58 n. Pennsylvania, res. s. e. city limits.
Cook William, (Cook & Demmier,) res. 83 s. East.
Cook William G., salesman, A. Wallace, res. 30, old number, n. Delaware.
Cook W. H., hack-driver, res. 376 w. North.
Cook William H., cooper, res. 376 w. North.
Coon Peter, real estate agt., office 88 e. Market, bds. 39 e. Louisiana.
Coons John W., deputy city treasurer, Glenn's blk., res. 274 e. St. Clair.
Cooney Bridget, servant, 81 w. Ohio.
Cooney Dennis, works Sinker & Co., res. 27 n. East.
Cooper Charles, engineer, C. C. & I. C. R. R., res. 185 Meek.
Cooper Edward, pressman, Downey, Brouse, Butler & Co., bds 257 e. McCarty.
Cooper Hamilton, tailor, 2 Bates House blk., res. 260 w. St. Clair.
Cooper Job., gas-fitter, bds. Macy House.
Cooper John J., farmer, res. 422 n. Illinois.
Cooper Joseph, gas-fitter, 77 e. Market. bds. Macy House.
Cooper Joseph, inmate Deaf and Dumb Asylum.
Cooper J. M., (L. Werbe & Co.,) res. 253 n. Illinois.
Cooper Miss Lotta, lady boarder, 201 e. Market.
Cooper Mrs. Rebecca, (wid. John,) res. 257 e. McCarty.
Cooper William H., clerk, W. P. & E. P. Gallup, bds. 257 e. McCarty.
COORS A. F., grocer, 151 w. Washington, res. 9 s. Mississippi.

Copeland Joshua W., straw and millinery goods, 39 s. Meridian and 8 e. Washington, res. 372 n. Meridian.
Copeland W. J., salesman, 78 & 80 e. Market, res. 127 Chatham.
Coffman Henry, saddler, res. 96 Fletcher av.
Corbaley Will H., notary public, cor. Washington and Meridian, res. 15 Fayette.
Corbet Catharine, servant, Institute of the Blind, bds. same.
Cordes Frederick, lab., bds. e. end Virginia av., beyond city limits.
Corden John, porter, Spencer House, bds. same.
Coridan Laurence, res. 354 s. West.
Coridan Mary, servant, Palmer House.
Coridan Thomas, saloon, res. 334 s. West.
Corlon John, pressman, Downey & Brouse, 27½ s. Meridian, res. 164 w. Maryland.
Corn Martin, currier, 49 s. Delaware, res. 249 Davidson.
Cornelius Cassius, plasterer, res. 254 s. Alabama.
Cornelius Edward G., (Kennedy, Byram & Co.,) 108 s. Meridian, res. 398 n. New Jersey.
Cornelius & McElvano, house and sign painters, alley rear of 72 w. Washington.
Cornelius Wilbur F., (C. & McElvano,) rear 72 w. Washington, res. 112 Huron.
Cornwell Carlos, engineer Bellefontaine R. R., res. 312 e. North.
Corney William, hack-driver, res. 315 n. Blake.
Cort Anthony, asst. carpenter Metropolitan Theater, bds. 144 n. Tennessee.
Cortland Anna, servant, W. P. Fishback, e. Washington.
Corran Peter, tobacconist, J. Cahall & Co., bds. Ray House.
Corwell Mrs. Nancy E., res. 350 Indiana av.
Corwin W. R., occupant Deaf and Dumb Asylum.
Corrydon Bridget, servant, 172 e. Ohio.
Cosly R. M., carpenter, res. 138 Christian av.
Cosler David W., carpenter, works Eden & Co.'s Planing Mill, res. 195 Davidson.
Costello Louisa, servant, 76 n. Noble.
Costigan Frank, propr. Oriental House, Illinois, two squares n. Union depot.
Cottingham Sidney D., horse dealer, res. 336 n. Noble.
Costigan Theodore G., clerk, Oriental House.
Costelo John, finisher, Sinker's Foundry, res. 276 w. Maryland.
Costelo John A., boiler-maker, bds. 114 Meek.
Costom Sarah, servant, 419 n. East.

Coston Henry, lab., res. alley, bet. Ohio and New York, and East and New Jersey.

Cattman David F., door-keeper Metropolitan Theater, bds. 176 Virginia av.

Cottrell & Knight, (Thomas C. and John K.,) dealers in tinners' stock, tools and machines, 108 s. Delaware.

Cottrell Thomas, (C. & Knight,) 108 s. Delaware, res. 160 s. New Jersey.

Cottrell Tony, fireman, Peru & Indianapolis R. R., bds. 325 e. Ohio.

Couch Walter R., minister, (christian,) preacher at Oakland, Belleville, North Liberty, Arcadia, res. 393 Massachusetts av.

Coughlen Elizabeth J., res. 282 w. New York.

Coughlen William, (Merritt & C.,) res. 282 w. New York.

Coughlen William F., clerk, Merritt & Coughlen, bds. 282 w. New York.

Coullert John, lawyer, bds. 67 s. Misouri.

Coulon Charles, lawyer, res. Arsenal av.

Coulter Archibald, lab., res. 256 s. Delaware.

Coulter James, (C. & White,) 77 e. Market, res. 372 s. Alabama.

Coulter & White, (James C. & Charles H. W.,) plumbers, gas-fitters and fixtures, 77 e. Market.

Coulter William, lab., res. 256 s. Delaware.

Council John, res. 100 Jackson.

Counnach Layton, student, commercial college, bds. 180 Massachusetts av.

Counseler H., servant, 496 n. Meridian.

County Auditor's Office, Court House bldg., J. R. Wright, county auditor.

County Clerk's Office, in Court House bldg., W. C. Smock, county clerk.

County Jail, Court House square.

County Recorder's Office, Court House bldg., W. J. Elliott, recorder.

County Treasurer's Office, Court House square, F. Erdelmeyer, treas.

Court House, Marion co., e. Washington, bet. Delaware and Pennsylvania.

Cousins Mrs. Tathee, (col.,) wash-woman, res. Second, bet Howard and Lafayette R. R.

Courtney Catharine, dining-room girl, Indiana Female College, 146 n. Meridian.

Courtney Cornelius, lab., res. over 356 Winston.

Courtney Mary, waiter dining-room, Indiana Female College, 146 n. Meridian.

Coval Alexander, cooper, res. 84 Benton.

Covault Erastus J., salesman, 78 s. Meridian, bds. Bates House.

Covenanter Church, South, bet. Virginia av. and Noble.

Covert Isaac, silver-plater, res. 277 n. Noble.

Covert Wm. T., res. 443 s. Illinois.

Covington Delia, (col.,) res. 231 n. Minerva.

Covour Anna, res. 120 s. Noble.

Covour Catherine, (wid. Daniel,) res. 120 s. Noble.

Covour Isaac, carpenter, res. 120 s. Noble.

Cowen Alexander, res. 300 e. St. Clair.

Cowen Hariet, (wid. Wm.,) res. 240 s. Missouri.

Cox Ann, (wid. David,) res. 18 Chatham.

Cox Miss Ann, bds. 252 cor West and Market.

Cox A. J., salesman, 60 s. Meridian, res. 237 e. South.

Cox Albert W., patent right agt., res. 174 e. Walnut.

Cox Charles, dealer in stoves, tin and hollow-ware, 57 w. Washington, res. 71 s. Meridian.

Cox Charles H., salesman, 57 w. Washington, res. 71 s. Meridian.

Cox Criterd, brakesman, J. M. & I. R. R., res. 18 Chatham.

Cox David, tinner, 57 w. Washington, bds. 71 s. Meridian.

Cox Edward, works Geisendorff Woolen Factory, res. 149 n. Blake.

Cox Edwin, engineer, Merritt & Coughlen, res. n. Blake.

Cox John F., bds. 96 Fletcher av.

Cox Henry, carpenter, res. 224 w. Washington.

Cox Jacob, artist, over 26 and 28 w. Washington, res. 69 s. Meridian.

Cox Mrs. Jane, (wid.,) bds. 149 n. Blake.

Cox John A. M., sheet-iron worker, Sinker's, res. 275 s. Alabama.

Cox Lida A., (wid.,) res. 253 s. West.

Cox Lindly H., student, city academy, bds. 441 n. Mississippi.

Cox Milton, (Landers, Pee & Co.,) 58 s. Meridian, bds. Bates House.

Cox M. A., bds. Bates House.

Cox Miss Phœbe, lady boarder, 289 e. New York.

Cox Mrs. Sophia, (wid. Nathaniel,) res. 252, cor. Market and West.

Cox Thomas T., sheet iron-worker, Sinker's foundry, res. 114 s. Noble.

Cox T. J., picture dealer, e. Washington, bds. Pattison House.

Cox William, painter, res. over 270 e. Washington.

Cox William A., clerk, 49 and 53 w. Washington, res. 393 n. West.

Cox William C., (Tomlinson & C.,) 18 e. Washington, res. 30 w. St. Clair.

Coy Daniel, carriage-trimmer, 26 e. Georgia, res. 144 Virginia av.

Coylor H., helper, McLane, MacIntire & Hays.

Coyner James S., carpenter and builder, w. Pratt, bet. Illinois, res. 28 w. Pratt.

Coyner Luther, bds. 264 n. Tennessee.

Coynor M. L., asst. city engineer, Glenns' blk., bds. w. Ohio.

Coynor Martin L., railroad contractor, res. 449 e. St. Clair.

Cozad Justice L., supt. Bellefontaine R. R., res. 380 Massachusetts av.

Crabb Charles, engineer, 146 s. Pennnsylvania, bds. 24 s. Pennsylvania.

Crabb Wilson, lab., res. National rd., near White river bridge.

Crabben John, lab., res. s. side Bates.

Craft Mrs. A. G., (wid.,) res. 496 n. Tennesse.

Craft Frost, student, Greencastle College, bds. 496 n. Tennessee.

Craft Henry, lab., res. Madison R. R., near city limits.

Craft Hiram J., clerk, county treas. office, bds. 121 n. Delaware.

Craft John P., book-keeper, Sinker & Co., bds. 496 n. Tennessee.

Craft & Phipps, (W. H. C. & E. R. & C. R. Phipps,) watch-makers and jewelers, 14 n. Pennsylvania.

Craft Richard P., machinest, bds. 496 n. Tennessee.

Craft Smith, blacksmith, 231 w. Washington, res. 286 Indiana av.

Craft W. H., (C. & Phipps,) 14 n. Pennsylvania, res. 163 n. Alabama.

Craft Werner P., bds. 496 n. Tennessee.

Craig Alexander, clerk, 2 Morrison's blk., s. Meridian, res. 128 n. Illinois.

Craig S. A., (W. I. Haskit & Co.,) 14 w. Washington, bds. Pyle House.

Craig William, miller, res. 476 n. East.

Craig William R., book-keeper, Alford, Talbott & Co., res. 66 Fletcher av.

Craighead Robert D., student, Dr. Bobb's, over 15 e. Washington, bds. 440 n. Meridian.

Crail John B. T., farmer, res. bet. Michigan and National rds., beyond city limits.

Crail Sylvester B., expressman, 321 e. North.

Crain William M., grocer, n. e. cor. First and Tennessee, res. same.

Crain William N., (Taylor & C.,) 3 Bates House blk.

Cramer William, cabinet-maker, res. 333 s. East.

Crandle Stephen, turner, res. e. end Fletcher av., beyond city limits.

Crane Dennis, street-car driver, res. 6 Henry.

Crane George W., blacksmith, res. 94 w. Market.

Crane James D., photographer, 34 w. Louisiana, res. 256 s. Mississippi.

Crane James F., photographer, 34 w. Louisiana, bds. 46 Elm.

Crane Peter, engineer, Bellefontaine R. R., res. 379 Massachusetts av.

Crapo R. P., manf. and dealer in picture frames and mouldings, 196 e. Washington, res. same.

Crane William H., blacksmith, Indianapolis Agricultural Work, bds. 69 w. Market.

Craran Mat., lab., res. 155 High.

Crawford Eli, moulder, res. 19 School.

Crayton James, shoe-maker, 288 w. Washington.

Craven Corlens, lab., bds. 273 Green.

Craven John, res. 272 Green.

Cravens John R., (D. C Branham & Co.,) bds. Bates House.

Cravens Junius E., dental student, 76½ e. Market, bds. Pyle House.

Credlebaugh Miss Harriet E., artist, 327 e. Washington.

Creed Margaret, servant at 83 w. St. Clair.

Cress V. B., (V. B. Cress & Son,) bds. 9 Fletcher av.

Cress V. B. & Son, (Valentine B. & John B. C.,) groceries, cor. Noble and Fletcher av.

Cress John B., (V. B. C. & Son,) res. 9 Fletcher av.

Crestler Oliver, painter, res. 31 Vinton.

Cripps Stephen B., carpenter, bds. s. Illinois, Metter's saloon.

Criqui Michael, lab., res. Shelbyville pike, one-half miles s. corporation.

Christy William W., (col.,) driver, W. I. Woolen, res. 344 Blake.

Croan Henry, (col.,) lab., res. 181 Elm.

Croghan Henry, (col.,) porter, Fletcher's Bank, 30 e. Washington, res. 181 Elm.

Cromey Frederick, lab., res. 148 Huron.

Cronan John, watchman, res. 85 w. Mc-Carty.

Cronan Michael, lab., T. H. & I. B. R. Freight depot, bds. cor. s. Tennessee and Willow.

Cronan Patrick, lab., T. H. Freight depot, res. near cor. Tennessee and Willard.

Cronan Timothy, lab., T. H. & I. Freight depot, res. cor. Tennessee and McCarty.

Crough George W., horse-trader, res. 33 w. St. Clair.

Crane Jacob, wagon-driver, Mikel's Brewery, res. 25 s. West.

Crone Wm. H., blacksmith, 175 s. Tennessee, bds. 69 w. Market.

Crookston James, salesman, New York Store, bds Commercial Hotel.

Cropper James, watchman, Bellefontaine shop, bds. 149 Winston.

Cropper James H., farmer, res. 776 n. Tennessee.

Cropper Joseph, carpenter, bds. 135 n. Noble.

Cropper Roland, brick-mason, res. 40 Douglas.

Cropsey J. C., piano-fly finisher, 159 and 161 e. Washington, res. 359 n. Alabama.

Crosby Ann, servant, 113 n. Illinois.

Crosby Mary, servant, 270 n. Illinois.

Crosgood Michael, res. 20 Henry.

Crosley John, res. 69 w. Maryland.

Crosley Thomas, works Hereth & Bro., bds. Pattison House.

Cross Barnum C., inmate Deaf and Dumb Asylum.

Cross James R., carpenter, res. 339 w. Maryland.

Cross Jasper J., inmate Deaf and Dumb Asylum.

Cross Mrs. ——, res. with Martin M. Ray.

Cross Jesse C., inmate Deaf and Dumb Asylum.

Cross William, servant, 260 cor. West and Washington.

Crossland J. A., (C., Maguire & Co.,) 62 s. Meridian, res. n. e. cor. Illinois and Pratt.

Crossland Maguire & Co., (J. A. C., Douglass M., C. Hanna & J. M. Caldwell,) wholesale grocers, 52 s. Meridian.

Crossley F. B., saddler, 24 n. Delaware, bds. Pattison House.

Crosson D., barber, res. 385 n. New Jersey.

Crouch Mrs. Angeline, (wid.,) res. 242 w. Market.

Crouch George W., plasterer, res. 234 e. Louisiana.

Crouch John plasterer, res. 42 Helen.

Crouch John A., huckster, res. 442 Virginia av.

Crouch John D., cooper, res. second floor, 162 w. Washington.

Crouse Rinehold, stocking manfr., 86½ e. Washington, res. 456 e. Michigan.

Crow Mrs. Hannah, (wid. Mathew,) res. over 280 e. Washington.

Crowley Daniel, lab., res. 343 s. Delaware.

Crowley John, lab., bds. 372 s. Tennessee.

Crowling Julia, (wid.,) res. 372 s. Tennessee.

Crowley Thomas, lab., res. 54 Bicking.

Crowley William, drayman, res. 376 n. Missouri.

Crowthers Miss Susan, governess Orphan Asylum, res. 711 n. Tennessee.

Crozier Geo., watchman, New York Store, res. 350 n. Meridian.

Cruce Mrs. Murphy, (wid.,) res. 130 w. New York.

Crull David, carpenter, res. 22 Gregg.

Crusa Mrs. Susan, (wid. Christopher,) res. 165 Winston.

Cruse John P., contractor and builder, 322 e. Washington.

Cruse Solomon, farmer, res. 122 e. Pratt.

Crutchfield Stapleton, (col.,) lab., res. Camp Carrington.

Culbert Patrick, lab., res. 347 s. Missouri.
Culbertson Wilbur, student, bds. 476 n. East.
Culley Daniel B., book-keeper, res. 486 n. Pennsylvania.
Culley David V., book-keeper, bds. 19 e. Ohio.
Culley William, engineer, Dyrkit & Sons, cor. Tennessee and Georgia, res. 71 Norwood.
Culligan John, lab., res. 4 English blk., e. Washington.
Culligon John, lab., res. 14 Willard.
Cullings Owen, carpenter, res. n. w. cor. Third and Lafayette R. R.
Cullum Eberle, printer, W. & J. Braden, res. 168 w. Michigan.
Culvers ——, carpenter, res. 121 Forest av.
Cunnings Charles, res. 372 s. West.
Cunnings Miss Francis A., dress-maker, bds. 234 s. Pennsylvania.
Cummings James, carriage-painter, res. 18 w. Georgia.
Cummings James, pump-maker, res. 234 s. Pennsylvania.
Cummings Richard, bds. 234 s. Pennsylvania.
Cummings Waldo, student, Hollingsworth Business College, bds. 239 w. Market.
Cume Jacob B, car inspector, I. & C. R. R., res. 27 Lord.
Cunington Miss Emily, book-binder, bds. 12 California.
Cunington Mrs. Susan, (wid. William,) washing and ironing, res. 12 California.
Cunningham Frank, (J. A. Mann & Co.,) 61 and 69 w. Washington.
Cunningham James, drayman, T. F. Ryan, bds. 179 n. Tennessee.
Cunningham Miss Jennie, works 31 Kentucky av., bds. same.
Cunningham John, lab., res. 78 Maple.
Cunningham John, soldier, U. S. Arsenal, res. near Arsenal.
Cunningham John, wagon-maker, res. cor. Fifth and Railroad.
Cunningham Joseph, lab., res. 324 e. New York.
Cunningham J. B., civil engineer and surveyor, room 21 Talbott & New's blk., n. Pennsylvania, res. 65 w. Michigan.
Cunningham Margaret, laundress, Bates House.
Cunningham Margaret, servant, 479 n. Meridian.
Cunningham Maria, (wid. Frederick,) res. 40 Huron.
Cunningham Mary, inmate Home of the Friendless, w. s. n. Pennsylvania, beyond city limits.
Cunningham Lillie, servant, 166 e. Market.
Cunningham William F., bds. 57 Huron.

Curley Daniel, book-keeper, res. 436 n. Pennsylvania.
Curley Mrs. Mary P., teacher, fifth ward school, res. Mrs. Rebecca Maria Sweetser.
Curn Michael C., lab., res. 491 e. Georgia.
Curran Barbary, laundress, Bates House.
Curran Mrs. Bridget, (wid. John,) res. 354 Winston.
Curran Bridget, chambermaid, Sherman House, bds. same.
Curran David, printer, Journal office, bds. 56 Huron.
Curran Dennis, lab., bds. 354 Winston.
Curran E., wash-woman, Sherman House, bds. same.
Curran Elizabeth, servant, 139 n. Alabama.
Curran John, lab., res. on alley, n. St. Clair, bet. Charles and Bellefontaine R. R.
Curran John lab., res. Dougherty, bet. McKernan and Wright.
Curran Julia, servant, 139 n. Alabama.
Currans Mary, laundress, Bates House.
Currans Margaret, scrub girl, Bates House.
Curran Michael, lab., res. 356 Winston.
Curran Patrick, (Michael Lawless & Co.,) 138 s. Noble, bds. 56 Huron.
Curran Peter, tobacconist, bds. Ray House.
Curran Thomas, brick-maker, bds. 56 Huron.
Curry Hamilton, (col.,) cook. res. 588 n. Mississippi.
Curry James, (col.,) lab., bds. cor. Mississippi and Fifth.
Curry John A., (col.,) lab., res. n. e. cor. Third and Railroad.
Curry Michael, harness-maker, Hereth & Bro., res. 114 w. Georgia.
Curry Robert, brick-mason, bds. 370 e. Washington.
Curry Robert, brick-layer, res. 141 Meek.
Curry William, railroad-man, C. I. & C. R. R., res. 41 Hosbrook.
Curtain Mary, servant, 34 n. California.
Curtis Andrew, Justice of the Peace, 83½ e. Washington, res. 27 Fort Wayne av.
Curtis Casper, last-maker, res. 122 e. Merrill.
Curtis Charles, engineer, Geisendorff's, res. 122 e. Merrill.
Curtis Charles E., engineer, No. 2 Engine Fire Dept., res. 124 n. Delaware.
Curtis Joseph, (col.,) white-washer, res. 203 w. North.
Curtin Mrs. Mary, (wid.,) res. 80 Fayette.
Curtney Michael, lab., res. bet. Noble and Benton.
Curzon Joseph, architect, office s. e. cor. Meridian and Circle, res. 376 n. Illinois.
Cusley Ellis, farmer, res. 600 n. Illinois.
Cusen Garrett, dry goods and notions, 158 Indiana av., res. same.

Cusick Joseph, saloon and groceries, 75 s. West, res. same.

Cusick Julia, (wid. John,) res. 71 s. Maryland.

Cussick John, groceries, 75 s. West, res. same.

Custer Detrick, lab., res. 225 Bluff rd.

Custeter H. D., bds. Macy House.

Cutler David, res. 195 n. East.

Cutsinger Augustus, servant, Dr. Bobbs.

Cutsinger Charles, res. 23 Bates.

Cutsinger John, fireman, I., C. & L. R. R., res. bet. Noble and Benton.

Cutter A. F., railroad-man, bds. Ray House, e. South.

Cutter H. P., watchmaker and salesman, 24 e. Washington.

Cuykendall Warren A., engineer, res. 330 e. Louisiana.

D ADE TOWNSON, (col.,) lab., res. 228 n. Missouri.

Dade William (col.,) lab., res. 39 n. Harris.

Dadert William, lab., B. &. I. Depot, res. e. Michigan rd., beyond city limits.

Daerffel Herman, saloon, 199 s. Illinois, res. same.

Daffee Thomas, moulder, res. 199 e. Washington, up stairs.

Dagett & Co., (William D., Geo. C. Webster & J. W. Smither,) wholesale manfs. and dealers in confectionery, fruits and nuts, 26 s. Meridian.

Dagett William A., (D. & Co,) 26 s. Meridian, res. 280 n. New Jersey.

Daglish John, clerk, Bee Hive, res. 504 n. Mississippi.

Dahna William, clerk, 300 e. Washington, res. 215 Davidson.

Dailey Miss Jennie, ladies' boarding-house, 36 s. New Jersey.

Daily Bridget, servant, Palmer House.

Daily Catharine, servant 243 n. Pennsylvania.

Daily Eugene, lab., res. 246 s. West.

Daily Harrison, (H. D. & Co.,) 41 s. Meridian, Morrison's Opera Hall, res. cor. St. Mary and Fort Wayne av.

Daily H. & Co., (Harrison D. & William Hasson,) wholesale druggists, 41 s. Meridian.

Daily Josephine, servant, Sherman House.

Daily Julia, servant, Palmer House.

Daily Mary, (col.,) servant, 36 s. New Jersey.

Daisey Patrick, lab., res. 17 Maple.

Daily Philip M., salesman, H. Daily & Co., bds. Bates House.

Daily Telegraph Co., office 16 w. Maryland.

Daily Thomas, conductor, J. M. & I. R. R., bds. Sherman House.

Dain Robert C., paper-hanger, res. 423 n. New Jersey.

Dain Thomas, pump-maker, res. 114 e. St. Mary.

Dale Catherine, servant, 252 e. Washington.

Dale John, lab., res. 199 n. East.

Dales Elizabeth, (wid.,) res. 67 Eddy.

Dallas Miss Bell, clerk, 68 n. Illinois, res. 316 Indiana av.

Dattmer Frederick, chair-maker, res. 336 s. Delaware.

Dalton George, carriage-painter, res. 174 s. Tennessee.

Dalton Michael, lab., res. 391 s. Missouri.

Dalton Thomas, lab., Sinker's Foundry, res. 214 Buchanan.

Daly Mrs. Anlina, (wid. Peter,) res. rear 288 Kentucky.

Daly D. N., piano-varnisher, 159 and 161 e. Washington, bds. Pattison House.

Daly John, lab., res. 258 s. Delaware.

Daly Michael, lab., res. 258 s. Delaware.

Daly William, Insane Asylum, res. 343 Winston.

Dame Jason, Marble Yard, 71 e. Washington, res. 287 s. New Jersey.

Damond James, bar-tender, 284 w. Washington, res. same.

Danforth A. J., res. 432 n. Pennsylvania.

Daniels Charles, candy-maker, bds. 22 w. North.

Daniels D., salesman, New York Store, bds. 58 s. Pennsylvania.

Daniels Henry, (col.,) lab., res. 170 Douglas alley.

Daniel John, lab., res. 498 e. Georgia.

Daniels Samuel, res. 109 s. New Jersey.

Danningbur George, teamster, res. Madison rd., near toll-gate.

Darbecker John, barber, res. 77 n. New Jersey.

Darby John, (J. Hauck & Co.,) 11 w.Washington, res. w. New York.

Darby Mary, servant, Gen. Love, 81 n. Tennessee.

Darby S. F., saw-maker, res. 476 n. Alabama.

Danger Simon, plasterer, res. 313 e. Georgia.

Dark Charles, teller, Indianapolis Branch Banking Co., res. s. e. cor. Tennessee and Walnut.

Darnall William W., carpenter, res. 342 e. New York.

Darnell Calvin F., carpenter, res. 738 n. Illinois.

Darrigan John, lab., res. 37 Dougherty.

Darr William, brick-layer, res. 532 e. Georgia.

Darrow B. C., salesman, 38 s. Meridian, res. 24 w. Michigan.

Darter Jasper, lab., res. 1 Thomas.

Darrow James, trader, res. 19 Cherry.

Darrow Milton, compositor, Sentinel news room, res. 19 Cherry.

Daugherty Bernard, driver, City Ry., res. 126 New York.

Daugherity Frank L., Spinner, Merritt & Coughlen, bds. 272 w. Maryland.

Daubenspeck Nelson, stock dealer, res. 121 n. Delaware.

Daumont H., dealer in clocks, looking-glasses and pictures, 15 w. Washington, res. 439 n. Pennsylvania.

Daumont P. A., jewelry and watches, 47 s. Illinois, res. same.

Davenport Theodore, lab., res. 115 Huron.

Davenport Thomas, saw-maker, 217 s. New Jersey.

David George T., clerk, C. C. C. & I. R. R., res. 117 e. Washington.

David George, checkman Bellefontaine R. R., res. 273 e. Market.

David Thomas, butcher, res. 210 Union.

David N. C., bds. 110 Union.

David W. C., clerk, room 6 P. O. bldg., res. 273 e. Market.

David William, farmer, res. 723 n. Illinois.

Davidson George, carpenter, res. 188 Dougherty.

Davidson James, printer, res. 36 Massachusetts av.

Davidson John, collector, Indianapolis Journal, res. 170 Davidson.

Davidson N. N., propr. Highand Nurseries, Highland Home av., res. same.

Davidson Rufus, carpenter, res. 148 n. Blackford.

Davis Abel E., (Baxter & D.,) cor. West and Washington, res. 325 n. West.

Davis Amos, (col.,) lab., res. 747 n. Tennessee.

Davis Anna, (col.,) bds. 126 n. Missouri.

Davison Athen, carpenter, res. 360 e. St. Clair.

Davis Augustus G., traveling agt., 310 Indiana av.

Davis Bartholomew, bds. n. Mississippi, bet. Fourth and Fifth.

Davis Benjamin, road-master Terre Haute R. R., res. cor. East and Louisiana.

Davis C. B., (D. & Greene,) 27 s. Meridian, res. 139 Indiana av.

Davis Charles W., painter, bds. 35 Indiana av.

Davis Charles S., butcher, bds. 129 n. Pennsylvania.

Davis David, lab., res. Ninth, bet. Pittsfield and Lenox.

DAVIS EDWIN A.,
lawyer, U. S. commissioner and notary public, room 3, Talbott & New's blk., n. Pennsylvania, bds. Bates House.

Davis Edward W., butcher, bds. 129 n. Pennsylvania.

Davis Emma, servant, Palmer House.

Davis Ernest G., salesman, 13 n. Meridian, res. 139 Ind. av.

Davis Fleming, moulder, res. 118 Forrest av.

Davis George, watch-maker and jeweler, 37 w. Washington, res. 40 n. California.

Davis George, (col.,) porter, B. G. Stout & Bro., 7 and 8 Bates House blk.

Davis Gilbert W., clerk at office Florence Sewing Machine, 27 n. Pennsylvania, bds. 78 n. New Jersey.

Davis George W., painter, works 172 s. Tennessee.

DAVIS & GREENE,
(C. B. D. & James G.,) general insurance agts., 27 s. Meridian.

Davis Horace H., (H. H. D. & Co.,) 13 n. Meridian, res. 139 Indiana av.

DAVIS H. D.,
meat market, 71 e. Washington, res. 129 n. Pennsylvania.

Davis Horace H. & Co., (Horace H. & C. B. Davis,) general agts. American Button Hole Sewing Machine, 13 n. Meridian.

DAVIS ISAAC & CO.,
(Isaac D. & Berry Self,) hats, caps, furs and straw goods, 12 e. Washington.

Davis Ira, machinist, res. n. e. cor. Forest and Illinois.
Davis Irene, (col., wid.,) res. 32 Ann.
Davis Isaac, (Isaac D. & Co.,) 12 e. Washington, res. 426 n. Pennsylvania.
Davis J. M., (col.,) blacksmith, res. 242 Indiana av.
Davis Jacob, carpenter, res. 90 California.
Davis James E., shoe store, 239 e. Washington, res. 299 n. Liberty.
Davis Jane G., servant at 172 n. Meridian.
Davis James, res. 82 Greer.
Davis John R., shoe-maker, res. 299 n. Liberty.
Davis John M., engineer Bellefontaine R. R., res. 176 Davidson.
DAVIS JOSEPH W.,
steam gas fitter and brass founder, 110 s. Delaware, res. 221 n. Tennessee.
Davis Levi, butcher, 71 n. Pennsylvania, res. 120 n. Pennsylvania.
Davis M. J., (col.,) milliner, res. 242 Indiana av.
Davis Mrs. Mary, (wid. Owen,) res. 168 Winston.
Davis Miss Maria, bds. 199 e. Washington, up stairs.
Davis Mrs. Martha, (wid.,) res. 181 Virginia av.
Davis Milton, carpenter, res. 45 e. McCarty.
Davis Nathaniel, carriage smith, works S. W. Drew & Co., res. 128 w. First.
Davis Noble, res. 386 n. New Jersey.
Davis Oliver, bds. 273 n. Noble.
Davis P. L., mill-wright, res. 361 Massachusetts av.
Davis Q A., student, N. W. C. University, bds. 408 n. New Jersey.
Davis R P., carpenter, res. 215 Massachusetts av.
Davis Robert, brickmaker, res. 11 Cedar.
Davis Robert S., saw-grinder, res. 308 s. Illinois.
Davis Samuel, lab., res. 81 cor. Huron and Pine.

Davis Sarah A.,' (col.,) servant, 280 e. North.
Davis Smith, painter, bds. 147 w. Maryland.
DAVIES T. J.,
photograph-gallery, rooms, third floor Talbott & New's blk., n. Pennsylvania, res. 150 w. New York, cor. Mississippi.
Davis Thomas K., shoe-maker, res. 277 n. Liberty.
Davis Wesley, coach trimmer, 26 e. Georgia, res. n. Illinois, beyond city limits.
Davis William, heater, White River Iron Works, bds. California House.
Davis William A., engineer, Hand's Foundry, res. 68 s. Noble.
Davis William E., brick-layer, res. 123 Davidson.
Davis William H., student, N. W. C. University, res. 361 Massachusetts av.
Davis William M., (D. & Wright,) 88 e. Washington, res. 430 n. New Jersey.
Davis William W., engineer, C. C. & I. C. R. R., res. 37 Bates.
Davis William H., pump-maker, 133 n. Tennessee, res. 128 w. First.
DAVIS & WRIGHT,
auctioneers and com. mers., 88 e. Washington.
Davey Daniel, machinist, white River Iron Works, bds. s. West, bet. Meridian and McCarty.
Davy W. W., compositor, Sentinel news room.
Danald Matthew, drayman, Holland, Ostermeyer & Co., res. 236 Railroad.
Daney D., machinist, bds. 183 s. Illinois.
Dawson Henry, manfr. drain tile, res. 191 n. Liberty.
Dawson Luther C., machine-tender, res. 273 s. West.
Dawson Madison, lab., res. over 300 e. Washington.
Dawson Louisa, (wid. Daniel,) res. 113 Forest av.

Dawson T., saloon, 132 s. Illinois, res. 317 s. Delaware.

Dawson Thomas B., night watchman, res. 161 Maple.

Dawson William, driver, American Express Company, res. 140 n. Delaware.

Day Cynthia, servant, 163 n. New Jersey.

Day D. S., tinner, bds. 202 n. West.

Day D. T., shoe-maker, shop 302 s. Illinois, res. same.

Day John, (col.,) cook, Sherman House.

Day Richard L., agt., life insurance co., res. 547 n. Illinois.

Day William W., butcher, res. 438 e. St. Clair.

Daylish John, salesman, Tyler's Bee-Hive, res. 504 n. Meridian.

Dayton J. F., blacksmith, B. F. Haugh, bds. 307 n. Alabama.

Deaf and Dumb Asylum, e. Washington, beyond city limits.

Dean Charles, foundryman, bds. 154 s. Noble.

Dean Charles, brick-layer, res. 233 w. South.

Dean Charles C., (col.,) lab., res. e. s. n. Meridian, beyond city limits.

Dean David, (col.,) lab., bds. 160 Huron.

Dean Ellen, servant, 169 w. New York.

Dean Harrison, (col.,) lab., res. 89 Hosbrook.

Dean Henry, machinist, bds. 154 s. Noble.

Dean Fielden, (col.,) hod-carrier, res. 160 Huron.

Dean Margaret, servant, Frank Kennedy, 247 n. Meridian.

Dearinger David D., carpenter and builder, res. 437 n. Mississippi.

Deas Mend., servant 76 n. East.

Death James C., traveling agt., Scott, West w Co., 127 s. Meridian, res. Knightstown, Ind.

Deaver George W., clerk, res. 14 e. Michigan.

Debey Charles, lab., Central depot, res. 39 Meek.

Decatur House, and Basement Saloon, e. Washington, near railroad crossing.

Deegar Conrad, blacksmith, Bellefontaine shops, res. 248 Winston.

Decker Miss Belle, servant, Dr. Abbett, 85 Virginia av.

Decker L. H., tinner, 308 Virginia av., bds. end Virginia av.

Decker Mrs. Laura, (wid. John B.,) res. 181 n. Noble.

Dedrick George, student, bds. 194 n. Illinois.

Dedert Charles, hostler, John M. Lord, 297 n. Pennsylvania.

Deer Catharine, servant, 156 e. Washington.

Deer Phillip, hod-carrier, res. 250 Davidson.

Deer John, lab., res. 584 e. St. Clair.

Deery Alice, (wid. Henry,) res. 81 Jackson.

Deery John, expressman, res. 89 Jackson.

Deery Mrs. Bridget, (wid.,) res. 95 Jackson.

Deffauld Louis, piano-maker, res. 259 n. Liberty.

Degant John, clerk, bds. 309 e. Market.

DeGroat Chas. P., actor, bds. Macy House.

Dehave Edward C., porter, 187 w. Washington, res. 118 w. Georgia.

DeHaven Andrew J., charge of wall-paper department, Trade Palace, res. 118 w. Georgia.

DeHaven Jesse, plasterer, res. near Insane Aslum, s. s. National rd.

Deffart Austin, teamster, res. 27 Fayette.

Dehne & Bro., (Charles Dehne & William D.,) flour and feed, 300 e. Washington.

Dehne Charles, (D. & Bro.,) bds. East Street House.

Dehne William, (D. & Bro.,) res. 211 Davidson.

Deitch Clarance, clerk, 162 w. Washington, res. 173 e. Market.

Deitch Charles, clerk, 162 w. Washington, res. 173 e. Market.

Deitch Felix, dry goods, 162 w. Washington, res. 173 e. Market.

Deitch Joseph, horse-dealer, res. 85 n. Alabama.

Deitch Joseph L., wholesale liquor dealer, 14 s. Delaware, res 382 w. New York.

Deiter William, lab., res. beyond city limits.

Deilger Joseph, works Cabinet-Makers' Union, bds. 518 e. Washington.

Deitrich Miss Louise, Trade Palace, res. 123 w. Market.

Deitrich William, cigar dealer, res. 34 n. Delaware.

Deitz Adam, surgeon, res. 116 Ft. Wayne av.

Deitz Ferdinand, leather store, 17 s. Delaware, res. 390 e. Market.

Delafield Myer, (Rothschild & Co.,) 34 w. Louisiana, res. 227 s. Delaware.

Delaney Michael, lab., 133 n. Noble.

DELANO J. A., constable, res. 349 e. McCarty.

Delaney Michael, lab., res. 301 w. Merrill.

Delany John, lab., res. 258 s. Delaware.

Delany Margaret, (wid.,) 268 s. Tennessee.

Delany Peter, lab., res. 511 e. Tennessee.

Delany Tracy, servant, 128 n. Illinois.

Delany William, lab., rolling mill, res. 199 High.

Delany Thomas, lab., res. alley, bet. West and California and Georgia and Maryland.

Dellart Charles, upholster, 38 s. Illinois, bds s. East.

Dellart John C., saddler, bds. 65 s. East.

Dell Frank, bds. 135 e. Washington.

Dell Edward, clerk, 135 e. Washington, bds. same.

Dell James W., oil speculator, bds. Oriental House.

DELL WILLIAM, propr. Union Hall Hotel, Saloon and Restaurant, 135 e. Washington.

Dell William H., clerk, Union Hotel, bds. same.

Delong J. M., cooper, res. 314 e. Georgia.

DeLong Mrs. E. L., packer, Moore & Frink, res. 164 e. Washington.

Deller Frederick, painter, 184 n. Noble, res. same.

Delles Isabella, clerk, bds. 316 Indiana av.

Delles Jane, (wid.,) res. 316 Indiana av.

Delles Frank, bds. 151 Bluff rd.

Delles William, blacksmith, res. 316 Indiana av.

Dellington William H., (col.,) plasterer, res. w. s. Tennessee, bet. Fourth and Fifth.

Delzell Hugh, livery and sale stable, 42 e. Maryland, bds. Commercial Hotel.

Delzell Samuel, res. 276 n. Delaware.

Demint S. E., works Junction R. R., bds. Wiles House.

Demmy Martin, saddler, Sulgrove's, res. 219 w. North.

Demmy W. H., collar-maker, 20 w. Washington, res. 206 Huron.

Demmy William, saddler, res. 206 Huron.

DEMOCRATIC STATE CENTRAL COMMITTEE, headquarters at Washington Hall, w. Washington, near Metropolitan Theater, Lafe Develin, chairman, J. J. Bingham, secy.

Demos Leander, checkman, T. H. & I. Depot, res. 123 w. South.

Demond J., miller, bds. 366 w. Washington.

DeMotte Mrs. C. H., domestic supt. Indiana Female College, 146 n. Meridian, res. same.

DeMotte W. H., A. M., prest. and prof. of moral, mental and natural sciences, Indiana Female College, 146 n. Meridian, res. same.

Dennier Charles, cook, res. 310 e. Georgia.

Demunn George, railroader, res. 111 Meek.

Demmy Martin, harness-maker, 20 w. Washington, res. 219 w. North.

Denk Andrew, manfr. cider vinegar, 183 Indiana av., res. same.

Dennes Caroline, servant, J. N. New's, 425 n. Mississippi.

Deneen James M., tailor, 125 n. Liberty, res. same.

Deney Austin F., lawyer, room over 31 w. Washington, bds. s. e. city limits.

Deney Robert, U. S. claim agent, res. 18 Bates.

Dennis C. C., clerk, J. C. Green's, bds. 17½ Virginia av.

Dennis Charles C., book-keeper, Hume, Adams & Co., res. 230 s. Alabama.

Dennis John W., clerk, Gen'l Freight Office C. C. & I. C. Ry., res. 234 s. Alabama.

Dennis James M., artist, over 45 e. Washington, bds. 314 n. East.

Dennis Miss Mary F., bds. 111 Indiana av.

Dennis Peter, brick-layer, res. 26 Buchanan.

Denney Hosiab, works Insane Asylum, bds. National rd., n. White river bridge.

Denney Joseph W., mill-wright, res. 424 e. Vermont.

Denney Moses, teamster, res. 380 s. Missouri.

Denny James, mill-wright, bds. 189 n. Noble.

Denny Joseph W., mill-wright, res. n. w. cor. Walnut and Fayette.

Denny John E., (Ebert & D.,) 44 Kentucky av., res. 584 n. Mississippi.

Denzelmann Henry, piano-maker, works George Trayser, n. e. cor. New York and Davidson.

Deputy Clark, dental student with M. Wells, bds. 35 Kentucky av.

1eRuiter & Bro., (White & Derk,) wholesale oyster bay, 65 s. Illinois.

DeRuiter Derk, (W. DeRuiter & Bro.,) 65 s. Illinois, res. same.

DeRuiter Whitey, (D. R. & Bro.,) 65 s. Illinois.

Dersch John, lab., res. 157 Winston.

Derringer Allen, lab., res. n. Michigan rd., near Tenth.

Dervald Mathew, drayman, res. 236 Railroad.

Dervis N. J., (wid.,) res. 83½ e. Washington.

Desby Adrian, well-digger, res. 444 w. North.

Deschler J., (Western Furniture Co.,) 109 e. Washington.

Deschler Joseph, Astor Saloon, 15 n. Pennsylvania, res. 26 Cherry.

Desjardins Joseph, carpenter, res. 464 Virginia av.

Despa Ernest, painter, res. 50 Lockerbie.

Despo Isidore, carpenter, res. Harrison.

Despo Mrs. Wilhelmina, (wid. Ernest,) mid-wife, res. 60 Lockerbie, cor. Liberty.

Dessar Adolph, (D., Bro. & Co.,) 60 s. Meridian, res. New York City.

DESSAR, BRO. & CO., (Adolph, Joseph B., David & Lewis Dessar,) wholesale clothing and piece goods, 60 s. Meridian.

Dessar David, (D., Bro. & Co.,) 60 s. Meridian, res. New York City.

Dessar Joseph B., (D., Bro. & Co.,) 60 s. Meridian, res. 213 n. Illinois.

Deesar Lewis, (D., Bro. & Co.,) 60 s. Meridian, bds. 172 e. Ohio.

Detrick C. W., (Caldwell & D.,) 61 s. Illinois, bds. Wiles House.

Dettmer Frederick, chair-maker, res. 402 s. Delaware.

Deusch August, barber, bds. 280 e. Market.

Deusner William, carriage-maker, works S. W. Drew & Co., bds. 67 n. Alabama.

Develin Lafe, chairman Democratic State Central Committee, Washington Hall.

Dever Charles, driver M. U. Express Co., 42 and 44 e. Washington.

Dever James, res. 58 Massachusetts av.

Devenish Soloman, res. 219 e. South.

Devenport Mrs. Melinda, (wid.,) res. w. s. Minerva, bet. New York and Brewery.

Devenport Daniel, fireman, Sherman House, bds. same.

Devenport William, printer, res. w. s. Minerva, bet. New York and Wright's Brewery.

Devey John, salesman, 30 s. Meridian, bds. 213 s. Illinois.

Devine William, tailor, res. 160 s. Noble.

Dewald Frank, clerk, German Dry Goods Store, bds. Martin House, 33 w. Maryland.

Dewdney William, blacksmith, works Sinker & Co., res. 176 e. South.

Denight Mrs. C. L., (wid. Henry,) dress-maker, res. 20 Fatout's blk., w. Washington, up-stairs.

Dixon John, book-keeper, Smith, Howard & Co., Trade Palace, 26 and 28 w. Washington, bds. Bates House.

Dias Anthony, tailor, 8 w. Washington, bds. 73 n. Illinois.

Dial Frank. A., (Lindley & Co.,) over 8 e. Washington, res. 376 n. Tennessee.

Dibble Eddy M., book-keeper, res. 163 Spring.

Dickbout V. G., trunk-maker, 29 s. Illinois, res. 169 s. Eddy.

Dickens Mrs. Rachel, (wid,) res. 128 w. Ohio.

Dicker Sarah, asst. cook, Wiles House.

Dicker Miss Sophia, res. 70 n. California.

Dicker Mrs. Harriet, (wid.,) res. 70 n. California.

Dickert Jacob, cabinet-maker, res. 220 n. West.

Dickerson Frank., (col.,) lab., res. rear 75 s. Missouri.

Dickerson Sarah, (wid.,) res. 400 s. Missouri.

Dickey James B., carpenter, res. 47 Dougherty.

Dickey Thomas, news stand, p. o., bds. 47 Dougherty.

Dickison Irvin, teamster, res. cor. Ninth and Michigan rd.

Dickman Charles, saloon, 208 e. Washington, res. same.

Dickman Francis, farmer, 775 n. Illinois.

Dickmond Andy, carpenter, res. Kansas, s. city limits.

Dickson C. & Co., (Carlos, James C. & Wallace E. D.,) dye stuffs and woolen factory findings, 47 and 49 n. Tennessee.

Dickson Carlos, (C. D. & Co.,) 47 and 49 n. Tenessee, res. 74 w. Vermont.

Dickson James, (Butsch & D.,) 27 e. Georgia, res. 60 s. Pennsylvania.

DICKSON JAMES B., treasurer Metropolitan Theater and book-keeper V. Butsch & Dickson, res. n. Pennsylvania, bet. First and Second.

Dickson James C., (C. D. & Co.,) 47 and 49 n. Tennessee, res. 110 Indiana av.

Dickson Myron, salesman, 47 and 49 n. Tennessee, bds. 110 Indiana av.

Dickson Thomas M., book-keeper, W. B. Dickson, bds. 196 n. Tennessee.

Dickson Wallace E., (C. D. & Co.,) 47 and 49 n. Tennessee, bds. 110 Indiana av.

Dickson William B., lumber dealer, e. Market, res. 196 n. Tennessee.

Didion C., carpenter, res. 152 Madison.

Diekmann Charles W., engineer, Jeffersonville R. R., res. 91 n. East.

DIEKMANN FREDERICK W., carpenter, works Wabash, bet. Liberty and East, res. 91 n. East.

Diebert Charles, drives Merchants' Express Wagon, bds. 23 Kentucky av.

Diehl H. C., chief clerk, general freight office, C. C. & I. C. Ry., bds. 72 w. Maryland.

Dieter Ernest, shoe-maker, res. 25 Biddle.

Dieter John, tinner, bds. 25 Biddle.

Dietrichs Chas., jeweler, 76 n. Pennsylvania, res. 123 w. Market.

Dietrich Christian, cabinet-maker, res. 77 Davidson.

Dietrichs Miss Louisa, clerk, Trade Palace, bds. 123 w. Market.

Dietrichs Mrs. M., milliner, 68 e. Washington, res. 36 n. Pennsylvania.

Dietrichs William, German salesman, 33 e. Washington, res. 36 n. Pennsylvania.

Dietz C. L., utility at Theater, bds. 161 Ft. Wayne av.

Dietz Ferdinand, (D. & Reimer,) 17 s. Delaware, res. 390 e. Market.

Dietz Frederick, saloon-keeper, 255 e. Washington, res. National rd., beyond city limits.

Dietz Henry. bds. 251 w. Washington.

Dietz John, barber, 37 s. Illinois, bds. Ft. Wayne av.

Dietz Peter, saloon and boarding house, 60 s. Delaware, res same.

DIETZ & REISSNER, dealer in leather and oil findings, 17 s. Delaware.

Dietz Mrs. Sarah, (wid. H. W.,) res. 7 Massachusetts av.

Dietzel Charles, express-driver, res. 271 n. Liberty.

Ditzell Adam, expressman, res. 156 Davidson.

Dikeman William, carpenter, res. 91 n. East.

Diffinbaum Jacob, carpenter, res. 472 n. Alabama.

Dile Ann, (wid. Lawrance,) res. 229 s. West.

Dilg Charles A., sign and ornamental painter, 20 Virginia av., bds. Oriental House.

Dill E. B., (E. B. D. & Co.,) 87 e. Market, res. cor. Broadway and Cherry.

Dill Gertrude, (wid.,) res. 328 n. Illinois.

Dill E. B. & Co., (E. B. D. & W. C. Means,) Indianapolis Cider Vinegar manfrs., 87 e. Market.

Dill John P., compositor, Sentinel news room, res. 328 n. Illinois.

Dill Mary J., (wid. Charles,) res. 228 w. Maryland.

Dilley Mrs. (wid. Capt. Dilley,) res. 112 s. East.

Dilley John, engineer, bds. 213 s. Illinois.

Dillie Jasper, clerk, 7 Odd Fellows Hall, bds. 256 n. West.

Dillon Ann, res. 600 n. Illinois.

Dillon Daniel, lab., res. 61 Maple.

Dillon John, lab., res. 179 Madison av.

Dillon Mary A., occupant Deaf and Dumb Asylum.

Dillon Thomas, brick-layer, res. 463 n. East.

Dillon Thomas, brakeman, bds. Ray House.

Dillon Sarah, (wid. Patrick,) res. 30 Willard.

Dingeldey Theodore, principal German Deutsch School, bds. 124 n. Alabama.

DINNIN SAMUEL, Court Street Hall, bet. Pennsylvania and Delaware.

Dippel Conrad, piano case-maker, 159 and 161 e. Washington, res. 499 s. New Jersey.

Dippel Frederick, engineer, 159 and 161 e. Washington, res. 499 s. New Jersey.

Dipple Henry, clerk, res. 21 Wyoming.

Dipple Henry, bar-tender, 9 w. Washington, bds. 17 Kentucky av.

Deppel L., piano case-maker, 159 and 161 e. Washington, res. 499 s. New Jersey.

Dippey T, machinist, bds. Wiles House.

Dipple John, carpenter, works Bellefontaine shops, res. 425 e. Vermont.

Dipple Joseph, lab., res. 195 n. Noble.

Dishon J. M. & Bro., (James & William A.,) bill posters, office Journal bldg.

Dishon James M., city bill poster, res. 262 s. Missouri.

Dishon William, city bill poster, res. 326 s. Missouri.

Read Logan's History of Indianapolis, in after part of this book.

Dixon George. (col.,) lab., 225 w. Ohio.
Dixon John J., (col.,) lab., bds. Fourth, bet. Mississippi and Tennessee.
Dixon Homer W., res. 215 n. Mississippi.
Dixon James, tobacconist, bds. Ray House.
Dixon James, works Junction R. R., bds. Wiles House.
Dixon Miss Lou., res. 142 s. East.
Dixon Mrs. Minerva, (wid.,) dress-maker, bds. 60 w. Market.
Dobbins Miss. Thirza, student, female seminary, bds. 299 n. Liberty.
Dobson Jane, lab., Ricketts, near city limits.
Dochat Gotthart, stone-mason, res. 175 n. Minerva.
Dockweiller Jacob, works Bellefontaine R. R. Shop, res. 501 e. Market.
Dodd Harry, conductor, C. C. & I. R. R., bds. Sherman House.
Dodd J. W., res. 214 n. Illinois.
Dodd John, lab., res. 178 Meek.
Dodd William S., clerk, Judson & Dodd, bds. 214 n. Illinois.
Dodson James, engineer, T. H. R. R., res. 151 w. South.
DOEPFNER CHARLES F., justice of the peace, 139½ e. Washington, res. 52 s. Alabama.
Doerbaker John, barber, res. 77 n. New Jersey.
Doerr George, boarding-house, 267 e.Washington.
Doke James, agt. Wheeler & Wilson's Sewing Machine, bds. 34 Union.
Dohn Philip, furniture manfr. and dealer, 246 s. Meridian, res. same.
Dohn Peter, cabinet-maker, 246 s. Meridian.
Dolan James, lab., White River Iron Works, res. 313 w. Merrill.
Dolas John, carpenter, res. 54 Hosbrook.
Dolbey John, farmer, res. 44 Dougherty.
Dolph Mrs. Elizabeth A., (wid.,) res. n. Minerva, near City Hospital.
Dolson David L., clerk, Commercial Hotel, res. same.
Domanget Miss Rose, dress-maker, works 300 e. Market, bds. same.
Domon Jack, lab., res. 414 s. Illinois.
Domon Oliver, planer, res. 385 e. Georgia.
Domon Peter E., Delaware Saloon and Beer Hall, 18 s. Delaware, res. same.
Donahue Ellen, servant, Palmer House.
Donahue Honora, servant, Bates House.
Donahue James, fireman, C., I. & C. R. R., bds. 149 s. New Jersey.
Donahue Mary, chambermaid, Bates House.
Donahue Patrick, lab., res. 2 English's blk., e. Washington.
Donahue Peter, lab., res. 21 Maple.
Donahue Patrick, lab., res. 14 Willard.
Donahoe Patrick, lab., res. 209 e. Market.
Donahol Timothy, lab., res. 480 e. Georgia.

DONALDSON & ALVEY, (C. S. D. & J. H. A.,) jobbers of hats, caps, furs, gloves, straw goods, umbrellas and parasols, 54 s. Meridian. See card page 90.
Donaldson C. S., (D. & Alvey,) 54 s. Meridian, res. 180 n. Illinois.
Donaldson Edwin C., clerk, Donaldson & Alvey, bds. 180 n. Illinois.
Donaldson & Co., (Donaldson & Elms,) picture store, 57 s. Illinois.
Donavan Morris, switchman, Union R. R. Co., res. 114 Meek.
Donavan Obid, painter, works Webb & Glancey, res. 8 English's blk., e.Washington.
Donavan John, engineer, C. C. & I. C. R. R., res. 45 s. Benton.
Donovan William, moulder, res. 114 Meek.
Done Peter, lab., res. Kansas, beyond city limits.
Donley Francis, groceries, 347 s. Delaware, res. same.
Dopley John, tanner, bds. Wisconsin, s. city limits.
Donley Michael, boiler-maker, Sinker's Foundry, bds, 114 w. Georgia.
Donnan Mrs. Barbara, (wid. David,) res. 126 s. Tennessee.
Donnan Theodore, clerk, 56 s. Meridian, bds. 126 n. Tennessee.
Donnan Wallace, tinner, bds. 126 n. Tennessee.
Donough Daniel R., clerk, Union Depot Ticket Office, res. 335 s. Meridian.
Donovan Robert, carpenter and builder, res. cor. Christian av. and Broadway.
Dooley Bridget, servant, Martin M. Ray, n. Pennsylvania.
Doran Henry, lightning rod manfr., res. 21 cor. Pine and Forrest av.
Doran John, wholesale linen store, 69 s. Illinois, bds. Oriental House.
Doran M. W. E., life insurance agt., res. 21 cor. Pine and Forrest av.
Dorland Mrs. A., dress-maker, 67 n. Pennsylvania, bds. same.
Dorsey G. W., (col.,) servant, 340 n. Meridian.
Dorsey, Layman & Fletcher, hardware merchants, 64 e. Washington.
Dorsey Miss M. E., student, Indiana Female College, 146 n. Meridian, bds. same.
Dorsey Margaret, (col.,) servant, 340 n. Meridian.
Dorsey Thomas, contractor, res. 216 Bluff rd.
Dorsey Robert S., (D., Layman & Fletcher,) 64 e. Washington, res. Atlanta, Georgia.
Dorthy Morill, lab., res. 47 Benton.
Doty Harriet, (wid. Carey,) res. 281 e. Georgia.

Doty Lafayette, brick moulder, res. 117 s. Noble.

Doty Oliver, bar-tender, res. 281 e. Georgia.

Doty R. M., salesman, H. Daumont, res. 23 w. St. Joseph.

Dotson William, engineer, T. H. & I. R. R., bds. 272 w. Maryland.

Doty Miss Lucy A., bds. 176 n. Mississippi.

Dougherty Barney, tanner, res. s. city limits.

Dougherty Deborah, servant, Nichlas Davidson, Highland Home av.

Dougherty Miss Elizabeth, dress-maker, over Quaker Store, bds. 70 e. Ohio.

Dougherty James, lab., res. 5 Willard.

Dougherty John, res. 226 e. South.

Dougherty Mrs. Lucy, (wid.,) milliner, bds. 109 n. Illinois.

Dougherty Michael, tanner, res. Wisconsin, beyond city limits.

Dougherty Wm., lab., res. s. city limits.

Dougherty William, bds. 339 Winston.

Doughty John G., foreman, Journal Office, res. 27 Indiana av.

Doughty Otho, printer, res. 27 Indiana av.

Douglass Augustus, (col.,) barber, Dr. Franklin.

Douglass Andrew, lab., res. 323 s. East.

Douglass & Conner, publishers and proprietors Indianapolis Daily and Weekly Journal, cor. Market and Circle.

Douglass James G., (D. & Conner,) Journal Company, res. 129 w. New York.

Douglass S. M., (D. & Conner,) Journal bldg., res. 129 w. New York.

Douglas Benjamin W., machinist, res. 40 Hosbrook.

Douglas E. P., supt. sleeping car, B. R. R., bds. Sherman House.

Douglas Frank D., gen'l agent, Continental Life Insurance Co., of Hartford, Conn., bds. 143 n. Delaware.

Douglas Mrs. ——, (wid.,) res. 139 w. New York.

Douglas Miss Nellie, lady boarder, 289 e. New York.

Douglas Miss Sallie, bds. 139 w. New York.

Dove David M., carpenter, works Shover & Christian, res. 120 e. New York.

DOW & ALLEN, general agts. Lamb's Family Knitting Machine, dealers in knitting yarns, 18 n. Delaware.

Dow Eli S., (D. & Allen,) 18 n. Delaware, res. 107 n. Noble.

Downes Thomas, lab., res. 52 Maple.

Downs William, (col.,) barber, works 50 e. Washington, res. 70 Georgia.

Dowling James, lab., res. 313 w. Merrill.

Dowland ——, book-keeper, bds. Commercial Hotel.

Dowling W. W. & Co., editors and publishers, office second floor Journal bldg., res. 488 n. Mississippi.

Downey, Brouse, Butler & Co., (James E. D., Charles W. B., Ovid & Scott B., George W. Hoss & J. A. Brouse,) book and job printers and publishers, cor. Meridian and Circle.

Downey James E.; (D., Brouse, Butler & Co.,) cor. Meridian and Circle, res. 158 n. New Jersey.

Downey James, lab., res. Wisconsin, s. city limits.

Downey John, p. o., res. 183 e. Georgia.

Downey Mrs. M. E., (wid.,) res. 241 Virginia av.

Downey Robert, res. 92 e. Market.

Dox William A., salesman, 108 s. Meridian, bds. Spencer House.

Doxey Edward O., traveling agt., Mayhew & Branham, 129 s. Meridian, bds. Spencer House.

Doxon Miss L. V., teacher grade a, primary department, ninth ward school, res. 81 Christian av.

Doyle Andrew, brick-moulder, res. 307 w. South.

Doyle Ellen, laundress, Indiana Female College, 146 n. Meridian.

Doyle Miss Mary, manager cloak-room, Trade Palace, bds. n. w. cor. Meridian and Circle.

Dozenberger Oswell, tinner, 253 w. Washington, res. same.

Drake Chester B., brakeman, Indiana Central R. R., res. over 87 n. Noble.

Drake Edwin B., res. 28 s. Mississippi.

Drake Samuel, (col.,) lab., res. Railroad, bet. Fifth and Sixth.

Draper George, lab., res. 378 s. West.

Draper Joseph M., carriage-maker, res. 320 s. Delaware.

Draper Thomas, porter, Connely, Wiles & Co., res. 114 w. Georgia.

Dreher Matthias, (D., Miller & Co.,) res. 82 n. Liberty.

DREHER, MILLER & CO., (M. Dreher, H. W. Miller & Jas. Bolinger,) staple and fancy dry goods and notions, 250 e. Washington.

Dremus George, carriage-maker, res. 101 e. St. Joseph.

Drew John A., (Sulivan & Drew,) 10 e. Pearl, res. 88 Massachusetts av.

Drew Harry E., clerk, p. o., bds. 86 Massachusetts av.

Drew Samuel W., (S. W. D. & Co.,) res. e. Market Square.

DREW S. W. & CO., (S. W. D. & P. Sayer,) carriage manfrs., e. Market, bet. Delaware and Alabama.

Drew Vanvelt, (wid.,) res. 25 Maple.

Driftmeyer Henry, drayman, res. 176 s. Noble.

Driggs John, brick-mason. res. 248 cor. East and Louisiana.

Drinkout William, waiter, Union Depot Dining Hall, res. same.

Drinkout William, car-mender, C. C. & I. C. R. R., res. 113 s. Noble.

Driscol A. E., (wid. Wm. J.,) res. 426 s. Illinois.

Driscol Jerry, lab., res. 26 Willard.

Drotz E., (D. & Steinhaur,) 136 s. Pennsylvania, res. 258 s. Pennsylvania.

Drotz & Stienhaur, (Ernil D. & Michael S.,) files and rasps, 136 s. Pennsylvania.

Droege Charles A., salesman, 26 e. Washington, bds. 26 n. Mississippi.

Drought John, lab., res. 109 Elm.

Druff J. W., clerk, res. 333 s. Alabama.

Drum Robert, fence boss, Terre Haute R. R., res. 188 Virginia av.

Drummond Joseph M., teamster, res. 96 Greer.

Drusler William, wagon-maker, res. 276 w. Michigan.

Dryer J. W., druggist, cor. Noble and Washington, res. 26 n. Noble.

Dryer Peter, blacksmith, 377 Virginia av.

Dubach John, lab., U. S. Arsenal, bds. 65 s. East.

Duchene Charles, baker, res. 366 Virginia av.

Duck Andrew, lab., union factory, res. 96 s. East.

Dudley J. M., lumber merchant, bds. Macy House.

Dudley T., car service department, C. C. & I. C. R. R., bds. Bates House.

Duell Thomas W., engineer, Wishmeier's Mill, res. 433 e. Vermont.

Duffy John, tailor, 57 s. California, res. same.

Duffy Joseph, stone cutter, works Scott & Nichol, res. Clinton, bet. Ohio and New York.

Duffy Michael, tailor, Clinton, bet. Ohio and New York, res. same.

Dugan Catharine, servant, 473 n. Illinois.

Dugan Miss Mary, dress-maker, bds. 305 s. Pennsylvania.

Dugan Mary, servant, W. W. Lathrop, 310 n. Illinois.

Dugan Neal, lab., res. 60 Oak.

Dugan Thomas, 136 s. Illinois res. 305 s. Pennsylvania.

Duckert Eugene, (col.,) hair-dresser, bds. 235 n. Blake.

Duffy James, lab., res. cor. St. Clair and Missouri.

Dunavay Albert, (col.,) chair-bottomer, 187 Elm, res. same.

Dunavan James, drayman, res. 360 w. North.

Dunavan Lawrence, lab., res. 142 s. Noble.

Dumont Ebenezer, farmer, res. s. city limits.

Dunbar Charles F., book-keeper, 56 s. Meridian, res. 249 South.

Dunbar Henry, (col.,) lab., res. cor. Eighth and Michigan rd.

Dunbar Miss Hannah, tailoress, bds. 254 s. Pennsylvania.

Dunbar John M., s. s. National rd., w. White river bridge.

Dunbar Melgar, cash boy, Hume, Adams & Co., res. 254 s. Pennsylvania.

Dunbar Miss Nancy, tailoress, bds. 254 s. Pennsylvania.

Dunbar Miss Sarah, (wid. Melzar,) res. 254 s. Pennsylvania.

Dunbar Miss Sallie, tailoress, bds. 254 s. Pennsylvania

Dunbar William, lab., res. 719 n. Mississippi.

Duncan A. W., lab., res. 382 s. West.

Duncan David, carpenter, bds. cor. Michigan and California.

Duncan Mrs. Nancy, milliner and dress-maker, res. 426 e. North.

Duncan John S., lawyer, prosecuting attorney, room 3 Brown's blk., n. Pennsylvania, res. 240 n. Meridian.

Duncan John, brick-layer, res. 426 e. North.

Duncan R. B. & J. S., (Robert B. & John S. D.,) lawyers, Brown's blk., n. Pennsylvania.

Dungey ———, lab., George Stilz, Shelbyville pike, near corporation.

Dunkin F. M., student, commercial college, bds s. Tennessee.

Dunlop Elizabeth, (wid.,) res. 297 n. Meridian.

Dunlop Miss Julia, (col.,) bds. 190 n. Missouri.

Dunlap Joshua, (col.,) res. 190 n. Missouri.

Dunlap Mrs. Livingston, res. 25 Virginia av.

Dunlap Mary M., (wid. Robert,) res. 286 n. Pennsylvania.

Dunlea Charles, porter, Am. and U. S. Express Co.'s, 34 e. Washington, res. 35 n. Blake.

Dunleavy Patrick, lab., Frank Wright's Brewery, res. near Wright's Brewery.

Dulin Mrs. Elizabeth, (wid. Owen,) res. 332 s. Delaware.

DUNLOP J. S. & CO., insurance and real estate agts., 16 and 18 n. Meridian, up-stairs.

Dunlop J. S., (J. S. D. & Co.,) 16 and 18 n. Meridian. res. 283 n. Pennsylvania.

Dunlop Miss Lucy, (col.,) res. 190 n. Missouri.

Dunlop Miss Mat., bds. 51 n. Douglas alley.

Dunlop William, (col.,) waiter, Bates House.

Dunmire Anthony, groceries and provisions, e. Washington, beyond city limits, bds. same.

Dunmire Edward, shoe-maker, res. 171 Virginia av.

Dunmire Frederick, drayman, res. 266 e. Ohio.

Dunminge Robert, street-bolderer, bds. 104 n. California.

Dunn Edward, puddler, Indianapolis Rolling Mill, res. 275 s. Pennsylvania.

Dunn & Franco, (Mrs. M. D. & Mrs. Sarah F.,) millinery, 52 n. Illinois.

Dunn Geo. W., at insurance office of E. B. Martindale, over 2 w. Washington, res. 196 w. Ohio.

Dunn John C., (D. & Karney,) plumbers and gas-fitters, 70 n. Illinois, res. 544 n. Mississippi.

Dunn Jacob P., (William Love & Co.,) notary public, room 1 Talbott & New's blk., n. Pennsylvania, res. 410 n. Tennessee.

Dunn John E., salesman, Geisendorff & Co., res. 426 n. East.

Dunn & Karney, (John C. D. & John K.,) plumbers, and gas and steam-fitters, 70 n. Illinois.

Dunn Robert C., tinner, bds. 15 n. Illinois.

Dunn Tousey, bds. 410 n. Tennessee.

Dunn William A., employee, State House, res. 778 s. Mississippi.

Dunning Thomas, printer, bds. 144 n. Tennessee.

Durbin David T., clerk, res. 346 n. Meridian.

Durfee Miss Nancy, school-teacher, 3 miles n. of city, bds. 30 Biddle.

Durfeld John F., (J. W. Blake & Co.,) over 45 e. Washington, res. 2 miles n. w. of city, on Crawfordsville rd.

Durgin Lyman W., foreman Bellefontaine Shop, res. 425 e. Michigan, over 52.

Durham H. E., cigar-maker, res. 17 e. North.

Durhm Miss Lotta, res. 328 w. Washington.

Durkin Ellen, servant, 372 n. Meridian.

Durie Henry, switchman, res. 320 s. West.

Dury John, (E. H. Mayo & Co.,) 23 e. Washington, res. 184 Massachusetts av.

Dutton George works Gas Works, res. Madison rd., near toll-gate.

Dutton & Green, (H. C. D. & E. S. G.,) agts., Connecticut Mutual Life Insurance Co., 77½ e. Market, Eden's blk.

Dutton H. R., (D. & Green,) 77½ e. Market, Eden's blk., res. 708 n. Tennessee.

Duvall David C., salesman, 38 s. Illinois, res. 159 n. Illinois.

Duvall Z. P., policeman, sixth ward, res. 260 Railroad.

Duvall Mrs. Sarah, (wid. Joseph,) res. 337 s. Alabama.

Duzan James H., printer, res. 405 e. Washington.

Merchandise transferred from one depot to the other, or

Duzan William H., cabinet-maker, Charles Williams, rooms McOuat's blk.

Duzan William N., physician and surgeon, office n.Ill.,cor.Michigan, res. 163 n. Ill.

Dwyer John, teamster, res. 278 McCarty.

Dwyer Thomas, lab., res. 36 Bicking.

Dwyer William, shoe-maker, E. H. Mayo & Co., res. 50 Wyoming.

Dwyer William, lab., bds. 91 s. West.

Dye & Harris, (John T. D. & Addison C. H.,) lawyers, rooms 8 and 9, Talbott & New's blk., n. Pennsylvania.

Dye John T., (D. & Harris,) rooms 8 and 9, Talbott & New's blk., n. Pennsylvania, res. e. terminus Virginia av.

Dyer Charlotte, (wid. Volney,) res. Shelbyville pike, ½ mile s. corporation.

Dyer Frank P., salesman, 88 e. Washington, res. 27 w. Ohio.

Dynes Joel A., printer, Evening Commercial, res. 92 Broadway.

Dynes L. G., res. 192 Broadway.

EAGAN JOHANNA, chamber-maid at Bates House.

Eagen Daniel, lab., bds. 55 Fayette.

Eagen Patrick, lab., res. 52 Fayette.

Eagle J. D., (J. H. & Son,) bds. cor. Fort Wayne av. and Delaware.

Eagle J. H., (J. H. E. & Son,) res. cor. Delaware and Fort Wayne av.

EAGLE MACHINE WORKS, cor. Louisiana and Meridian, e. end Union Depot.

Eagle & Son, grocers and produce dealers, s. w. cor. Delaware and Fort Wayne av.

Ealy Mrs. Anna, res. n. e. cor. Mississippi and First.

Ealand John, works Junction R. R., bds. Wiles House.

Earl G. G., local agt., Merchants Despatch, 19 Virginia av., res. 412 n. East.

Earl Simeon, lab., res. s. West, beyond city limits.

Earley A., (col.,) lab., res. 223 e. Michigan.

Earley William A., clerk, Lesh & Tousey, bds. 89 Indiana av.

Early Miss Lizzie, bds. 51 Madison av.

Early Peter, lab., res. Stevens and Virginia av.

Early Samuel, (col.,) works at 24 n. Pennsylvania, bds. Robinson House.

Earnest Fred., expressman, 132 Union.

Earnshaw Frank, cabinet-maker, bds. Ray House.

Earnshaw Joseph, (Burke, E. & Co.,) res. 257 s. Pennsylvania.

Easter B. W., student, N. W. University, bds. 76 Plum.

Easter J. H., student, N. W. University, bds. 76 Plum.

EATON GEORGE A., (Smith, Howard & Co.,) 26 and 28 w. Washington, bds. Bates House.

Eaton John W., clerk, Smith, Harlan & Butler, res. 279 n. East.

Eberhart George, master of cabinet shop, Deaf and Dumb Asylum.

Eberley Joseph, servant, Dr. Bobbs, beyond city limits.

Eberline William, cabinet-maker, bds. 117 s. Illinois.

Ebert & Denny, (John E. & John D.,) carpenters and builders, 44 Kentucky av.

Ebert John, (E. & Denny,) 44 Kentucky av., res. 208 w. South.

Eberts John, collector for J. Butsch, res. 62 w. South.

Eccles William, (Geisendorff & Co.,) 22 w. Washington, res. 241 n. Alabama.

Eccleston Norris P., painter, 26 e. Georgia, bds. 18 w. Georgia.

Echols Harrison H., Clarkmann's Grocery, bds. 149 s. East.

Echols Henry H., clerk, cor. East and Virginia av., bds. 149 s. East.

Echlen Martha, servant, 125 e. Ohio.

Echols William, conductor, Bellefontaine R. R., res. 229 Winston.

Eck J. H., (McDonough & E.,) 144 s. Alabama, bds. 123 e. Vermont.

Eck Joseph, wagon-maker, res. near e. end New York.

Eckel Edward, gunsmith, res. 282 e. Washington.

Ecord Alvin, occupant Deaf and Dumb Asylum.

Eddy Morris R., book-keeper, Indiana National Bank, 2 e. Washington, bds. Bates House.

Eden Charlton, prest. and supt. Builders' and Manufacturers' Association, mill 225 n. Delaware, res. 340 n. Meridian.

Eden Lavina, (wid. James,) res. 28 Rose.

Eden Samuel C., carpenter, works planing mill, n. Delaware, res. 87 n. New Jersey.

Edmunds Edward, lab., res. 279 s. West.

Edmonds John, book-binder, Journal Office, bds. 350 n. Meridian.

Edmunds William, (Hendricks, E. & Co.,) 56 s. Meridian, res. 222 n. Illinois.

Edsall John, baggage-master, C., C. & I. C. R. R., bds. Commercial Hotel.

Edson Rev. A. H., minister, Second Presbyterian Church, cor. Pennsylvania and Vermont, res. 157 n. Tennessee.

Edward Beyerley, res. 194 Virginia av.

Edward J. A., lab., res. 430 s. Tennessee.

Edward William B., cattle-dealer, bds. 75 Kentucky av.

Edwards David, saloon, 300 n. Blake, bds. same.

Edwards E., saddles and harness, 33 s. Meridian, res. 75 Kentucky av.

Edwards John, (col.,) plasterer, res. 31 n. Harris.

Edwards Mrs. Martha, (wid. John,) boarding House, 75 Kentucky av.

Edwards R., painter, res. 398 s. West.

EDWARDS RICHARD, formerly of the directory publishing firm, Edwards & Boyd, long since played out, having gathered his traps and left for parts unknown.

Edwards Wesley, carriage-maker, res. 249 n. Mississippi.

Eerling Juda, bds. 216 w. New York.

Effinger John, shoe-maker, bds. 202 s. Illinois.

Egelus Frederick, carpenter, works Helwig's Factory, res. 130 and 132 n. Noble.

Egelus George, cash-boy, New York Store, res. 130 n. Noble.

Egger J., (E. & Muecke,) res. s. w. cor. Alabama and Maryland.

Egger & Muecke, (J. E. & William M.,) house and sign painters, 152 e. Washington.

Eggerton Charles, bar-keeper, Labelle Saloon, bds. 386 n. Tennessee.

EGGERT WILLIAM, homœopathic physician, surgeon and accoucher, office 75 e. Ohio, res. same.

Ehrensperger Frank, salesman, 66 s. Meridian, res. 126 n. East.

Ehrhart Joseph, baker, 80 e. Washington, bds. same.

Ebrick Frederick, soap and candle-maker, res. 233 Daugherty.

Eibell Frank, book-binder, bds. Wiles House.

Eibell Joseph, book-binder, bds. Wiles House.

Eighth Ward School House, cor Huron and Virginia av.

Eisselt Lewis, cook, 92 e. Washington, bds. same.

Eix Henry, (Pathos & E.,) 228 e. Washington, res. e. Washington, near corporation line.

Elbott Samuel, (col.,) school-teacher, bds. 229 n. Tennessee.

Elder Eli A., (E. & Ripley,) 49 n. Illinois, res. 133 w. New York.

Elder James, salesman, New York Store, bds. Oriental House.

Elder John R., agt. for Indiana and Illinois Central Railroad Co.'s Lands, office over 26 s. Meridian, res. 150 n. New Jersey.

Elder Miss Margaret, school-teacher, bds. 150 n. New Jersey.

Elder & Ripley (Eli A. & William G.,) groceries and provisions, 49 n. Illinois.

Elder William G., route agt., Daily Sentinel, 16½ e. Washington, res. 234 n. East.

Eldred Jas. E., occupant Deaf and Dumb Asylum.

Eldridge Jacob E., (E. & Van Buskirk,) res. 74 s. Mississippi.

ELDRIDGE & VAN BUSKIRK, (Jacob E. & Elias Van B.,) real estate agts., over 30 w. Washington. See card page 58.

Eleck Mrs. Lucy, (wid. Jacob,) bds. 293. Winston.

Elexander Joseph, carpenter, res. 173 Huron.

Elff Frank, barber-shop, 135 s. Illinois, res. 233 s. New Jersey.

Elkins Miss Nancy, (wid. Hiram,) res. 8 n. Liberty.

Ellenbogen E. N., (Strauss & E.,) 19 w. Washington, bds. Oriental House.

ELLIOTT & BLACK, (Byron K. E. & James B.,) attorneys at law, 24½ e. Washington.

Elliott Byron K., (E. & Black,) city attorney, 24½ e. Washington, res. 22 California.

Elliott Calvin A., bonded warehouse, No. 2, 143 s. Meridian, res. 180 n. West.

Elliott Charles, bds. Oriental House.

Elliott J. Perry, photographer, over 8 and 10 e. Washington, res. 293 n. Delaware.

Elliott John, painter, bds. Wiles House.

Elliott John M., salesman, 141 s. Meridian, bds. 54 s. Pennsylvania.

ELLIOTT JOHN T., (Hon.,) Judge Supreme Court of Indiana, office New State bldg., bds. Bates House, res. New Castle, Ind.

Elliott Jonathan, deputy sheriff, res. 77 n. Noble.

Elliott Joseph T., clerk, recorder's office, res. 22 Chatham.

Elliott Miss Sue, bds. 180 n. West.

Elliott N. K., conductor, C., C. & I. C. R. R., bds. Bates House.

Elliott P. H., attorney at law, res. 22 n. California.

ELLIOTT RUSSELL, paymaster, Bellefontaine R. R., res. 38 w. St. Clair.

Elliott & Smith, (T. S. E. & Francis S.,) commission buyers, 35 e. Market.

Elliott Taylor, city recorder, res. 22 Chatham.

Elliott T. B., (E. & Smith,) 35 e. Market, res. w. end Michigan.

Elliott W. D., clerk, recorder's office, bds. n. Tennessee, beyond city limits.

Elliott Wm. S., clerk, p. o., res. 98 n. East.

Elliott William J., county recorder, res. n. Tennessee, beyond city limits.

Ellis Mrs. Ellen, (wid.,) res. 32 Helen.

Ellis James, salesman, 24 s. Meridian, res. e. s. n. Meridian, beyond city limits.

Ellis James, (col.,) lab., res. w. Center.

Ellis John S., salesman, 22 s. Meridian, res. n. of city limits.

Ellis Thomas, cupalo-man, Sinker's Foundry, res. 35 Bradshaw.

Ellison Fred., clerk, C. C. C. & I. R. R., res. 367 s. Alabama.

Ellms Charles H., engineer, Bellefontaine R. R., 219 Davidson.

Ellsworth Samuel W., trader, res. 213 n. Liberty.

Elmer John W., shipping clerk, H. Dailey & Co., res. 192 e. McCarty.

Elmer Nettie, inmate Home for the Friendless, w. s. n. Pennsylvania, beyond city limits.

Elmer Wesley, clerk, res. 192 e. McCarty.

Elmore Thomas, (col.,) res. 78 Eddy.

Elstone J. W., physician, office 252 n. Illinois.

Elstrod Henry, cabinet-maker, works union factory, res. 184 Winston.

Elvin Gardner W., messenger, Peru Engine House, res 500 s. East.

Ely Henry, carpenter, bds. 148 Indiana av.

Ely Joseph, carpenter, res. cor. Plum and Cherry.

Embers Thomas, (col.,) barber, works 50 e. Washington, res. on Wabash alley.

Emenegger John, beer-brewer, res. 152 Madison av.

EMENEGGER MATHIAS, propr. Emenegger Hall, 111 and 113 e. Washington, res. same.

Emerson John B., book-keeper, bds. 239 w. Market.

Emerson B. B., (E., Beam & Thompson,) res. 239 w. Market.

Emmons J. B., saw-maker, bds. 51 s. Maple.

Emrich Andrew, tinner, shop 346 e. Washington, res. 109 Davidson.

Emerich Henry, cabinet-maker, foreman Helwich & Roberts, res. 109 Davidson.

Emerich Henry, (H. E. & Co.,) 86 w. Washington, res. 224 w. Maryland.

Emerich H. & Co., (Henry E., Frederick W. F. & John Osterman,) flour, feed, grain and seeds, 86 w. Washington.

Emerich Nicholas, groceries and provisions, 164 w. Michigan, res. same.

Emmons John, carpenter, res. 168 Winston.

Emmons Mrs. Sarah, (wid. John,) res. 168 Winston.

Emmons William, (E. & Williams,) marble cutter, n. Tennessee, bet. Washington and Market, res. 168 Winston.

EMMONS WILLIAM & CO., marble works, 27 n. Tennessee. See card in advertising department, page 6.

Empire Line Fast Freight, 96 Virginia av., W. S. Tarkington, agt.

Emslie J. A., prof. penmanship, bds. 23 Madison av.

Endecott John, (col.,) white-washer, res. 182 Douglas alley.

Ender Mrs. Mary, (wid.,) res. 327 s. Pennsylvania.

Endever Mrs. Mary, (wid.,) bds. 22 Circle.

Engelbach Herman, book stand, 2 s. Meridian, bds. Union Hall.

Engelhid W., shoe shop, 286 e. Washington, res. same.

Enggass H., merchant tailor, 113 s. Illinois, res. same.

England George, carpenter, bds. 226 w. New York.

Engle Mrs. Caroline, (wid.,) res. 262 s. Delaware.

Engle Rev. George B., clergyman Episcopal Church, res. 269 e. South.

Engle George B., Jr., local agt. Terre Haute R. R., bds. 269 e. South.

Engle Jackson, telegraph-operator, bds. 75 Kentucky av.

Engle Willis D., clerk, T. H. & I. R. R. Freight Depot, res. 269 e. South.

Engleman Mrs. Elizabeth, (wid. William,) res. National rd., beyond White river bridge.

English David W., printer, res. 253 n. West.

English E. G., vice-prest. Street Ry., Louisiana, res. 48 Circle.

English Orlando, printer, bds. 253 n. West.

English W. H., painter, res. 21 e. North.

English William H., prest. First National
Bank and treas. Citizens' Street Ry.,
s. e. cor. Washington and Meridian,
res. 48 Circle.
Enkinbrook Henry, drayman, res. 351 s.
Delaware.
Enners Henry, brick-layer, bds. 287 Mas-
sachusetts av.
Enners Louis, carriage-painter, works S.
W. Drew & Co., res. 237 n. Noble.
Enners Louis, butcher, res. 367 n. Noble.
Enners W., (Geisel & E.,) res. 369 n. Noble.
Enners Mrs. Wilmina, (wid. Phillip,) res.
287 Massachusetts av.
Enoch Mrs. Mary, res. 192 w. Ohio.
Enos B. V., (E. & Huebner,) 77½ e. Market,
res. 397 n. Alabama.
ENOS & HUEBNER,
(B. V. Enos & H. R. Huebner,) archi-
tects and supts., room 2 Eden's blk.,
77½ e. Market. See card, page 46.
Enos Robert, carpenter, bds. 397 n. Ala-
bama.
Enos F. H. K., clerk, Bellefontaine R. R.,
res. 350 n. Illinois.
Episcopal Church, cor. Illinois and New
York.
Episcopal Mission, 100 Fletcher av.
Equitable Fire Insurance Co., office room 4,
Odd Fellows Hall.
Erb Solomon, cooper, William Beard, res.
337 w. Maryland.
ERDELMEYER FRANK.,
drugs and medicines, 91 e. Washing-
ton, res. 263 e. Washington.
Erenest Buhler, book-binder, bds. 65 s.
East.
Erhart Krachenfels, carpenter, bds. 248
Winston.
Erie Transportation Co., 94 Virginia av.,
William T. Clark, agt.
Erick William, tinner, J. L. Frankem, bds.
25 e. Buchanan.
Ervin E. P., teamster, res. 405 s. East.
Ervin Thomas, lab., res. 337 s. Missouri.
Eschmeier Henry, pastor German Reformed
Church, res. 41 n. Alabama.

Eschmeir Otis, cash boy, New York Store,
bds. 41 n. Alabama.
Esken Mrs. Sarah, (wid. Drury,) res. end
Virginia av., beyond city limits.
Essmann Miss Caroline, bds. 340 Madison
av.
Essmann Joseph, .milk-carrier, res. 340
Madison av.
Essman William, propr. Illinois House, 283
s. Illinois, res. same.
Essigke August, meat market, 285 e. Wash-
ington, res. same.
Essigke Richard, dealer in fresh and salt
meats, 170 s. Illinois, opp. w. end Un-
ion depot, res. same.
Etchison A., (col.,) porter, Wiles House.
Etherton Samuel, carpenter, res. 23 Center.
Ettinger Gusta, flagman, res. 5 Graper.
Eudaly James, carpenter, res. 325 e. Ohio.
Eugene John, servant, 182 n. Meridian.
Euller Mrs. Margaret, (wid. Phillip,) res.
232 Railroad.
Eurich John L., saloon-keeper, res. 441 s.
Illinois.
Eurick Mrs. Rebecca, milliner and dress-
maker, res. 109 n. Illinois.
Eusey John, engineer, Bellefontaine R. R.,
res. 144 Winston.
Evans A., res. Jackson, near city limits.
Evans A. F., entry clerk, Evans & Brown,
bds. 54 s. Pennsylvania.
Evans Adolphus G., salesman, 75 s. Me-
ridian, bds. 257 Virginia av.
Evans Andrew, pump-maker, res. 237 Mas-
sachusetts av.
EVANS & BROWN,
(John D. E. & Daniel R. B.,) notions
and fancy goods, 75 s. Meridian.
Evans Charlotte, (col.,) bds. 73 Bright.
Evans George A., book-keeper, 75 s. Me-
ridian, res. 257 Virginia av.
Evans George T., (I. P. E. & Co.,) 124 s.
Delaware, res. 548 n. Meridian.
Evans Henry W., machinist, I. & C. Shops,
res. 25 Lord.
Evans Isaac P., (I. P. E. & Co.,) 124 s.
Delaware, res. Richmond, Ind.

A Fine Card of Exchange Stables on page 10. Advertising Department.

saac P., George T., h R. Evans,) manfrs.
Delaware.
r, res. 62 Grant.
Irown,) 75 s. Merid-
nsylvania.
?. E. & Co.,) 124 s.
n. Alabama.
eamstress, res. 75 s.

r, Hill & Wingate,

yer, res. 476 n. Me-

bds. Ray House.
(col., wid. James,)
isetts av.
er, presiding elder
hurch, Indianapolis
i. Liberty.
mason, res. 496 n.

E. & Co.,) 4 n. Dela-
Wayne av.
t-layer, res. 674 n.

ress-maker, bds. 237

. 181 w. Elizabeth.
Company, publishers
ommercial, cor. Me-

ttern-maker, Sinker
Alabama.
r, res. 142 s. West.
. New York.
k, 323 n. Alabama,
an.
I*,
ishington, res. same.
mith, res. 128 e. St.

arriage-painter, 123
es. n. Pennsylvania,
s.
ian and surgeon, 33
74 n. Pennsylvania.
music teacher, res.

bds. 78 Indiana av.
bds. 78 Indiana av.
eamstress, res. 183 n.

en'l agt., Enterprise
Co., Cin., office Jour-
w. Michigan.
inter, res. 78 Indiana

;, bds. 78 Indiana av.
i., res. 207 Kentucky

. res. 424 s. West.
e-maker, res. 221 w.

FABER CATHARINE, servant, David Benson, 206 s. Illinois.
FABER AUGUST, grocer, 405 s. West.
Faber L, shoe-maker, res. 278 Railroad.
Fagan John, yard-master, I. C. & L. R. R., res. 47 Bates.
Fagan John, brick-layer, res. 30 Helen.
Fahnestock Obed. bds. 92 s. Mississippi.
Fahnley Frederick, (Stiles, F. & McCrea,) 131 s. Meridian, res. 86 n. Illinois.
FAHRBACH PHILIP & CO., (Philip F. & ———,) proprs. Washington Hall Saloon, 78 and 80 w. Washington.
Fahrbach Philip, (P. F. & Co.,) 78 and 80 w. Washington, res. same.
Fahrion Christian, Western Furniture Co., res. 363 n. Noble.
Fahrion George, flour and feed dealer, 90 and 92 e. South, res. same.
Fair Christopher, carpenter, res. Seventh, bet. Illinois and Tennessee.
Fair Rachel, (col.,) servant, 176 e. Ohio.
Fairest Milton, carpenter, res. n. Pennsylvania, beyond city limits.
Fairbank Andrew, carpenter, res. 230 s. New Jersey.
Fairfield Miss Nellie, lady-boarder, 281 e. New York.
Faler Henry, engineer, Washington Foundry, res 127 e. Merrill.
Faljambe George B., messenger, American Express Co., res. 70 n. Liberty.
Falk Mrs. Ellen, (wid. William,) boarding, 199 w. Maryland, res. same.
Falkner J. H., master machinist, res. 29 n. Blake.
Fallon James J., Oriental Saloon, 67 s. Illinois, res. 128 s. Tennessee.
Falloon Wm. A., porter, Indiana Female College, 146 n. Meridian.
Fanan Thomas, lab., bds. 112 Meek.
Fanarn James, lab., res. 109 n. West.
Fanker Mary A., servant, 440 n. Meridian.
Farater James, lab., res. s. s., bet. Noble and Benton.
Faries T. C., dentist, 1 Odd Fellow's Hall, n. Pennsylvania, res. 144 e. New York.
Farles Joseph, jeweler, 231 e. South.
Farley Henry, teamster, Arsenal, res. 313 n. Noble.
Farley Richard, lab., res. Second, bet. Howard and Lafayette R. R.
FARLEY & SINKER, (Thomas F. & Albert S.,) proprs. American Saw Works, 98 s. Pennsylvania.
Farley Thomas, (F. & Sinker,) 98 s. Pennsylvania, res. 84 s. Pennsylvania.
Farlin Patrick, lab., res. 23, bet. Liberty and East.
Farlow Matilda C., occupant Deaf and Dumb Asylum.

Farman John H., stone-cutter, bds. 33 s. West.

Farman F. L., stone yard, res. 149 w. South.

Farmer Albert, works Indianapolis Rolling Mill, bds. 290 Madison av.

Farmer Miss Emma T., tailoress, bds. 290 Madison av.

Farmer Frank, stone yard, cor Mississippi and Louisiana, bds 23 Kentucky av.

Farmer J. B., patent right, res. 290 Madison av.

Farmer John H., stone-cutter, works yard cor. Mississippi and Kentucky av., res. 33 s. West.

Farmer Miss Mary E., tailoress, bds 290 Madison av.

Farmer Richard, (col.,) lab., res. West, bet. Ohio and Market.

Farnaer John A., contractor, res. 401 n. Pennsylvania.

Farnsworth C. O., reporter, res. 107 e. Walnut.

Farnsworth Theodore, physician and surgeon, 21½ w. Maryland, bds. Palmer House.

Farnsworth Thomas D., patent-wright dealer, res. 431 n. Tennessee.

Farrar John, (Farrar & Co.,) 208 w. Washington, res. 237 w. Ohio.

Farrell Catharine, servant, 65 w. Michigan.

Farrell Fergus, shipping clerk, res. 77 St. Clair.

Farrell Mrs. Mary, (wid. John,) res. 160 Davidson.

Farrer John, boot and shoe manfr., res. 237 w. Ohio.

Farriter John, res. 331 e. Louisiana.

Farrow James, (col.,) painter, res. over 212 e. Washington.

Fatout's Blk., s. w. cor. Washington and Missouri.

Fatout Charles, blacksmith, 231 w. Washington, cor. Maryland and Tennessee.

Fatout J. L., carpenter, bds. 238 n. West.

Fatout Percy H., carpenter, res. n. w. cor. Mississippi and North.

Fatout J. L. & M. K., carpenters and builders, Lafayette, bet. Michigan and North.

Fatout M. K., carpenter, res. 239 n. West.

Faucet David, livery and feed stable, 69 s. Mississippi, res. 147 w. Maryland.

Faut Frederick W., (H. Emmrich & Co.,) 86 w. Washington, res. n. East.

Fawkner Ida, occupant Deaf and Dumb Asylum.

Fawkner J. E., dealer in coal, lime, &c., 24 w. Maryland, res. 161 w. South.

Fay Amos F., (McCreery & F.,) 56 e. Washton, res. 255 n. East.

Fay Henry, with McCreery & Fay, bds. 255 n. East.

Fay John J., res. 101 n. Mississippi.

Fearnley John, carpenter, shop 23 Circle, res. 186 w. Vermont.

Feary Henry J., compositor, Sentinel news room, res. 129 Stevens.

Feary Jeremiah E., carpenter, 318 e. North, res. same.

Feary J. J., cigar-maker, bds. 318 e. North.

Feary Thomas, shoe-maker, 76 Jackson, res. same.

Featherhoff Warren, occupant Deaf and Dumb Asylum.

Featherston William E., auctioneer, 194 and 196 w. Washington, res. 165 Massachusetts av.

Feel Augustus, clerk, American Express, res. 43 Madison av.

Fehi Catharine, servant, Institute of the Blind, bds. same.

Fehi Susan, chamber maid, Institute of the Blind, bds same.

Feifer George, wood-sawyer, res. 150 e. St. Joseph.

Felbaum William, engineer, Lafayette R. R., res. s. w. cor. Mississippi and North.

Felbeck Mrs. Lena, (wid. John,) res. 11 Buchanan.

Felbush Conrad, teamster, res. 426 e. Vermont.

Feld George, painter, 249 w. Maryland, res. same.

For a Directory of Societies and Associations,

Feldpush John, lab., res. 168 Davidson.

Feles Charles, (col.,) servant, S. Fletcher, res. 225 e. Washington.

Felharber Daniel, shoe store, e. Washington, res. 21 n. New Jersey.

FELLER GEORGE, watch-maker and jeweler, 114 s. Illinois, res. same.

Fellows Miss Margaret, student, Indiana Female College, 146 n. Meridian, bds. same.

Fells Frederick, lab., res. 185 Harrison.

Feltman Herman, shoe-maker, 396 s. Delaware, res. same.

Fenniman William, brick yard, Madison rd., beyond city limits.

Fenton Catharine, servant, J. B. McChesney. 454 n. Tennessee.

Fenton Franklin, saw-maker, E. C. Atkins & Co., res. 131 e. St. Joseph.

Ferdinand Lewis, (col.,) lab., res. cor. Blackford and Michigan.

Fereth Adam, carpenter, res. 474 n. Alabama.

Ferguson Mrs. A. V., (wid.,) boarding house, 31 w. Ohio.

Ferguson Clem. A., watch-maker and jeweler, 7 w. Washington, res. n. e. cor. Meridian and Seventh.

Ferguson D. F., brick-layer, bds. 463 n. Meridian.

Ferguson Mrs. E. A., (wid.,) boarding house, 60 w. Market.

Ferguson E. A., brick-layer, res. 463 n. Meridian.

Ferguson George W., cabinet-maker, res. 19 Fayette.

Ferguson J. F., brick-layer, bds. 463 n. Meridian.

Ferguson James A., book-binder, Sentinel office, bds. 60 n. Market.

FERGUSON JAMES C., pork-packer, packing house e. s. Pennsylvania, bet. South and McCarty, res. 139 n. Meridian.

Ferguson Kilby, saw mill, Madison co., res. 251 e. McCarty.

Ferguson Ryan, Trade Palace, res. 155 n. Illinois.

Ferguson Robert, plasterer, res. 27 w. Pratt.

Ferguson William T., bds. 27 w. Pratt.

Ferling George, barber-shop, under First National Bank, s. e. cor. Washington and Meridian, res. 126 e. Maryland.

Feriter Morris, school teacher, res. 142 Bluff rd.

Ferity Bridget, servant, Palmer House.

Ferling William, cigar-maker, 108 s. Illinois.

Ferner Julius, salesman, J. G. Stiltz, res. 223 n. Noble.

Ferobe Joseph C., clerk, 25 n. Illinois, bds. same.

Ferrack John, lab., res. 18 Buchanan.

Ferres Mrs. Cornelia M., res. 254 e. Ohio.

Ferree & Co., (F. M. & J. Carpenter,) flour and feed, 23 Massachusetts av.

Ferree Jared D., printer, works Mirror office, res. 256 e. Ohio.

Ferree F. M., (F. & Co.,) res. 369 n. New Jersey.

Ferree Louis, teamster, res. 300 n. Blake.

Ferrel Bridget, servant, 150 n. New Jersey.

Ferrel Francis, tailor, 131 e. Washington, bds. same.

Ferrel Ezekiel J., agt. patent broom, res. 55 Massachusetts av.

Ferrell Andrew, bds. 241 Indiana av.

Ferrell Joseph K., res. 241 Indiana av.

Ferrell Patrick B., bds. 241 Indiana av.

Ferriter Patrick, lab., res. bet. East and Noble.

Ferriter Thomas, lab., res. 3 cor. Bates and Noble.

Ferry Henry, printer, res. 273 n. Liberty.

Ferry Jane, (wid. Hugh,) res. 85 e. Pratt.

Ferry John, brick-layer, res. 477 n. East.

Ferry Pamelia, (wid. John,) res. n. s. National rd., one mile from White river bridge.

Fertig Francis, house and sign painter, 6 e. Washington, res. 65 w. South.

Fesler James N., carpenter, works cor. South and Delaware, res. 138 s. Delaware.

Fesler William, carpenter, res. 212 Bluff rd.

Fetcher Mrs. Elizabeth, (wid.,) res. 227 Union.

Fetherling William, lab., res. 324 e. New York.

Fette Charles, machinist, Sinker's, res. 250 s. Alabama.

Fette George, cleaning and repairing clothes, 38 Virginia av., res. 123 Duncan.

Fette Conrad, tailor, res. 148 Virginia av.

Fetzer Jane, servant, 264 n. East.

Fibleman C. R. L., clerk, room 11, p. o. bldg., res. 11 Lockerbie.

Fil Cooney, lab., res. rear 277 n. Noble.

Fieber William, clerk, Schmidt's Brewery, res. 359 s. Alabama.

Fiel Augustus, clerk, Am. and U. S. Express Co.'s, res. 43 Madison av.

Field Edward S., (F., Braden & Co. and Chandler & F.,) res. e. s. n. Illinois, bet. Second and Third.

Field John, wagon-maker, res. 391 s. Illinois.

Fields John S., fireman, I. M. & I. R. R., bds. Ray House.

Fielhauer John, lab., res. 31 n. East.

Fifth Ward-School House, w. Maryland, Henry Colgan, principal.

Fike John W., farmer, res. Shelbyville pike, ¾ mile s. corporation.

Fike Peter, teamster, res. 318 Madison av.
Fike Thomas A., lab., bds. 318 Madison av.
File S. J., salesman, Bowen, Stewart & Co., bds. 122 n Illinois.
Fillbeck Miss Barbary, seamstress, W. A. Rockwood, 276 n. Illinois.
Finch C. & E. & Co., butcher shop, 276 w. Washington.
Finch Fabius M., (F. & F.,) rooms 6 and 7, Talbott & New's blk., n. Pennsylvania, res. 286 e. Ohio.
Finch & Finch, (Fabius M. & John A. F.,) lawyers, rooms 6 and 7, Talbott & New's blk., n. Pennsylvania.
Finch Miss F. A., teacher, D. grade primary department ninth ward school, bds. 286 e. Ohio.
Finch John A., (F. & F.,) rooms 6 and 7, Talbott & New's blk., n. Pennsylvania, bds. 286 e. Ohio.
Fines Julius, salesman, J. George Stiltz, res. 279 n. Liberty.
Fink Mrs. Mary, (wid. Fred.,) res. 51 McCarty.
Finley Frederick, millinery goods, res. 231 Virginia av.
Finley S. C., bds. 438 s. Illinois.
Finn Bridget, wash-women, res. 80 Maple.
Finn J., yardman, Bates House, bds. same.
Finn John, lab., res. 33 Dougherty.
Finn John, cooper, res. 126 Union.
Finn Miss Lizzie, bds. 126 Union.
Finney Mrs. Catharine, (wid. Michael,) washing and ironing, res. 161 Huron.
Finney E. W., lab., res. Shelbyville pike, ½ mile s. corporation.
Finney Jasper, salesman, 49 s. Meridian, res. 430 Virginia av.
Finler Frederick, bakery, bds. 114 Fort Wayne av.
First Baptist Church, n. e. cor. New York and Pennsylvania.
First English Lutheran Church, cor. New York and Alabama.
First National Bank, s. e. cor. Washington and Meridian, William H. English, prest., John C. New, cashr.

First Presbyterian Church, s. w. cor. New York and Pennsylvania.
First Universalist Church, cor. Maryland and Delaware, Wallace's blk.
First Ward School House cor. Vermont and New Jersey.
Fiscus Andrew, brick-layer, res. 140 Massachusetts av.
Fiscus Frank, brick-layer, res. 43 Chatham.
Fiscus John, brick-mason, bds. 392 n. Alabama.
Fiscus Thomas brick-mason, res. 280 e. St. Clair.
Fiscus William, brick-layer, res. 1 Vine.
Fish Charles, clerk, w. Washington, bds. 371 n. East.
Fish Frank, clerk, Roach, McDonald & Roach, bds. 367 n. East.
Fish George W., traveling agt., Grover & Baker Sewing Machine Co., 21 e. Washington.
Fish William S., job printer, Journal Office, res. 367 n. East.
FISHBACK JOHN, leather, hides, oil, shoe-findings and leather belting, 125 s. Meridian, res. cor. Walnut and Illinois.
Fishback William, clerk, 125 s. Meridian, bds. cor. Walnut and Illinois.
Fishback William P., (Porter, Harrison & F.,) Yohn's blk., cor. Washington and Meridian, res. n. s. e. Washington, fourth house e. city limits.
Fisher Andrew, music-teacher, res. 286 e. St. Clair.
Fisher Andrew, salesman, Helwig's furniture store, res. 406 n. East.
FISHER BENEDICT, propr. Union Depot Barber Shop, res. 189 s. Illinois.
Fisher Charles, cooper, res. 123 Spring.
FISHER CHARLES, justice of the peace and treas. Grand Lodge of Masons of Indiana, Yohn's blk., cor. Washington and Meridian, res. 26 w. North.

For a complete Church Directory, see Municipal Record.

Fisher David, clerk, fish-store, s. Illinois, bds. 239 Louisiana.

Fisher Ernstus, switchman, I. C. & L.Yard, bds. 269 s. New Jersey.

Fisher George, boot and shoe-maker, 119 Fort Wayne av., res. same.

Fisher James, bds. 26 w. North.

Fisher John, barber, bds. 335 Virginia av.

Fisher John E., bds. 269 s. New Jersey.

Fisher Mrs. Julia, actress, bds. Macy House.

Fisher P., lab., bds. cor. Washington and East.

Fisher Samuel, tailor, res. 269 s. New Jersey.

Fisher Mrs. Sarah, (wid.,) res. 105 Bluff rd.

Fisher William, lab., bds. cor. Washington and East.

Fisher Wright C., occupant Deaf and Dumb Asylum.

Fisher Wm. S., boot-maker, 10 s. Pennsylvania, res. same.

Fiske Celia, servant, 230 w. Ohio.

Fisk Mrs. E. I., notions, news room and circulating library, 62 n. Illinois, Miller's blk., res. same.

Fisk Henry C., salesman, 62 n. Illinois, res. same.

Fitch John E., book-keeper, Mayhew & Branham, res. 78 e. Pratt.

Fitch Lewis, cabinet-maker, bds. 174 w. New York.

Fitchey M. G., carpenter, res. 36 n. California.

Fitchey ——, carpenter, res. 210 w. Ohio.

Fitzgerald Catharine, laundress, Institute of the Blind, bds. same.

Fitzgerald David, lab., T. H. & I. R. R., bds. 387 n. Tennessee.

Fitzgerald Edmond, lab., res. 156 Meek.

Fitzgerald Isaac, stone-mason, res. 158 Blackford.

Fitzgerald John, tinner, 63 e. Washington, res. 399 s. Delaware.

Fitzgerald John, lab., T. H. & I. R. R., bds. 38 s. Tennessee.

Fitzerald Joseph, lab., res. 158 Blackford.

Fitzgerald Michael, soldier, U. S. Arsenal, res. same.

Fitzgerald P. H., student, commercial college, bds. cor. Washington and New Jersey.

Fitzgerald Patrick, carpenter, res. 298 s. Delaware.

Fitzgerald Wm. F., lab., rolling mill, res. 226 w. Merrill.

Fitzgerald William, lab., res. 188 Maple.

Fitzgibbon Michael, bds. Bates House.

Fitzhugh Lee M., salesman, 149 s. Meridian, res. 139 n. Alabama.

Fitzpatrick James, tailor, works 66 s. West, res. same.

Fitzpatrick ——, brick-mason, bds. Shelbyville pike, three-fourth mile s. corporation.

Fitzpatrick Joseph D., carpenter, res. 240 w. New York.

Fitzpatrick Peter, tailor, 66 s. West, res. same.

Flager Ryman, works arsenal, res. rear 228 Winston.

Flaherty John, lab., res. 688 n. Illinois, bet. Fourth and Fifth.

Flaharty Joseph, railroader, bds. 470 e. Georgia.

Flaherty Mary, nurse, 396 n. Meridian.

Flaherty Mrs. Sarah, (wid. Michael,) res. 323 w. Maryland.

Flaherty Thomas, clerk, 200 s. Delaware, bds. Ray House.

Flaig Matthew V., carpenter, works Warren Tate's Planing Mill, res. 186 n. New Jersey.

Flanner Charles W., salesman deliverer, Tyler's Bee-Hive, res. 801 n. Tennessee.

Flanner Jacob Tyler, clerk, Kahn & Bro., e. Washington, res. 801 n. Tennessee.

Flanner Mrs. O. A., (wid.,) res. 801 n. Tennessee.

Flapar John, colporteur, res. 287 n. Noble.

Flathers J. B., carpenter, res. 151 Maple.

Flatley P. B., lab., res. 39 s. Bright.

Flauh Leopold, expressman, res. n. Douglas.

Fleatz Charles, blacksmith, res. 187 Bluff rd.

Fleatz Charles H., tailor, 41 n. Illinois, res. 123 w. Market.

Fleit John, (col.,) works Bates House, res. rear 223 Massachusetts av.

Flemer Peter, drayman, res. 480 e. Georgia.

Fleming David, express-driver, res. 95 Bradshaw.

Fleming G. H., city gas inspector, bds. 24 w. Georgia.

Fleming John, press boy, Sentinel office, bds. West 40

Fleming John, hotel-tender, res. n. s. e. Georgia.

Fleming John T., agt. Macauley & Co., res. 133 Railroad.

Fleming Thomas, lab., bds. 91 s. West.

Fleming Thomas R. W., student, commercial college, bds. 289 s. East.

Fleming V. M., bds. 181 s. New Jersey.

Fleson Thomas, section boss, T. H. & I. R. R., res. 396 s. Missouri.

Fletcher Albert E., teller, (F. & Sharpe,) res. Vinton's blk., n. Pennsylvania.

FLETCHER'S BANK, 30 e. Washington, S. A. Fletcher & Co., proprs.

Fletcher Bertie, servant, 194 n. Illinois.

Fletcher Calvin, asst. secy. and treas. Indianapolis & Vincennes R. R., res. e. s. College, bet. Christian and Home avs.

Fletcher David, lab., res. rear 121 n Noble.

FLETCHER ELIJAH T., administrator and executor of the Calvin Fletcher estate, res. 410 n. Delaware.

Fletcher Henry F., clerk, American Express Office, res. 189 e. Market.

Fletcher Ingram, (F. & Sharpe,) 49 e. Washington, res. 462 n. Pennsylvania, cor. Pratt.

Fletcher John B., teamster, bds. 826 Virginia av.

Fletcher L. W., (W., Fletcher & Co.,) room 1 Vinton's blk., res. Franklin, Ind.

Fletcher Mrs. Lucinda, (wid.,) res. 72 w. Maryland.

Fletcher Mrs. Phœbe, (wid.,) seamstress, res. rear 121 n. Noble.

FLETCHER R. F., secy. Citizens' Street Ry., res. 477 n. Tennessee.

FLETCHER & SHARPE, (Ingram F. & Thomas H. S.,) bankers, 49 e. Washington.

FLETCHER S. A. & CO., Stoughton A. F., Sen. & Francis M. Churchman, props. Fletcher's Bank, 30 e. Washington.

Fletcher S. K., (Dorsey, Layman & F.,) 64 e. Washington, res. n. e. city limits.

Fletcher Stoughton A., Sen., Fletcher's Bank, 30 e. Washington, res. 180 e. Ohio.

Fletcher Stoughton A., Jr., Fletcher's Bank, 30 e. Washington, res. cor. Virginia av. and South.

Fletcher Thomas, stock-trader, res. 331 n. Alabama.

Fletcher William H., res. 326 Virginia av.

Fletcher William B., M. D., 135 n. Alabama, res 105 n. Alabama.

Fleury Louis, tailor, works 168 e. Washington, bds. 18 s. Delaware.

Flin Byron, porter, 62 e. Washington, res. 21 Dougherty.

Flinn George, shoe-maker, 29 s. West, res. same.

Flinn Thomas, city gas works, res. 336 s. Delaware.

Flick Wm. B., res. s. s. National rd., w. White river bridge.

Flock Samuel, carpenter, res. 40 Thomas.

Flowers Mrs. Jemima, (wid. Aaron,) res. 320 e. Washington.

Flowers Mrs. Naoma, (wid. Washington,) washing and ironing, res. 248 w. Market.

Flowers Samuel, carpenter, cor. Kentucky av. and Mississippi, res. 92 Kentucky av.

Floyd W. T., (col.,) bds. 63 s. Illinois.

Fly P. M., painter, bds. Wiles House.

Flynn Byron P., lab., res. 21 Dougherty.

Flynn D., gas house, res. 305 s. Delaware.

Flynn Dennis, brick-layer, res. 69 Maple.

Flynn Mrs. Johanna, (wid. John,) res. 336 s. Delaware.

Flynn Thomas, farmer, res. 81 Maple.

Flynn Thomas, lab, res. 336 s. Delaware.

Fodemyer Rudolph, chair-maker, res. 7 Buchanan.

Fogle Frederick, lab., res. 260 Winston.

Foland Valentine, cabinet-maker, res. 299 e. Merrill.

Foley John D., lab., works Vincennes R. R., res. near Arsenal.

Foley M., bds. 289 s. Delaware.

Foley Patrick, switchman, I. C. & L. yard, res. 269 e. Louisiana.

Foley Patrick, lab., res. 128 Winston.

Foley Patrick, lab., res. 91 Fayette.

Foley Timothy, striker, C. C. & I. C. shop, res. e. city limits.

Folkenig Charles, lab., McCord & Wheatly, res. 21 Coburn.

Follett J. B., (Martin, Hopkins & F.,) gen'l. ins. agt., res. 344 n. Alabama.

Folmer Godfried, butcher, bds. 207 w. Michigan.

FOLSOM EDWIN S., gen'l agt. Phœnix Mutual Life Ins. Co., of Hartford, Conn., room 3, Talbott & New's blk., n. Pennsylvania, bds. Pyle House.

Fondessar Wendal, blacksmith, res. 435 s. Illinois.

Foose Thomas. baker, 123 Meridian, bds. same.

Foote C. M., clerk, 24 e. Georgia, bds. 126 e. Ohio.

Foote Charles, machinist, bds. Wiles House.

Foote Miss Fanny, student, Indiana Female College, 146 n. Meridian, bds. same.

Foote Maria W., (wid. Jeremiah,) res. 18 e. Michigan.

Foote W. A., book-keeper, 56 and 58 e. Washington, bds. Pyle House.

Forbes J. R., watch-maker and jeweler, 34 Virginia av., res. 231 e. South.

Forbs James, collector, Indianapolis Journal, bds. 170 Davidson.

Forly C. H., trunk manfr., 109 s. Illinois, res. 175 e. Washington.

FORD E. A., gen'l passenger agt., C., C., C. & I. Ry. Line, office 53 s. Alabama, res. Cleveland, O.

Ford Miss Eliza T., teacher public schools, 188 w. Ohio.

Ford Fletcher W., carpenter, res. 307 e. Washington, 5 and 6 up stairs.

Ford T. S., carpenter, res. 114 Forrest av.

Ford John, wood-sawyer, res. 188 w. Ohio.

Ford Miss Laura, teacher, Fifth Ward School, res. 188 w. Ohio.

Ford Michael, shoe-maker, works 65 s. Meridian, res. 326 n. West.

Ford Nancy A., (wid. John E.,) res. 114 Forrest av.

Ford Tony, (col.,) lab., res. cor. Blackford and Michigan.

Ford William, lab., res. 134 Harrison.

Forge Mrs. Laura, (wid. Daniel,) res. rear 320 e. Washington.

Forginly John, lab., res. 498 e. Georgia.

Forsha Thomas, cigar-maker, 48 s. Pennsylvania, res. 76 Plum.

Forsyth Alexander, clerk, Oriental House, bds. same.

Fort John M., patent medicine dealer, bds. 89 s. Illinois.

Fortnight Ernest, cabinet-maker, res. 338 Virginia av.

Forwald John, lab., Cin. Engine Shop, res. rear 314 n. Noble.

Forwald William, carpenter, bds. 314 n. Noble.

Foster Mrs. Angeline, (wid. Roger,) res. old No. 17 n. New Jersey.

Foster A. S., foreman, boiler shop Eagle Machine Works, bds. Ray House.

FOSTER BENJAMIN F., (Rev.,) State Librarian and pastor First Universalist Church, office State House, res. 320 n. Illinois.

Foster Emely, res. 327 e. Washington.

Foster Chapin C., steward, Deaf and Dumb Asylum.

Foster Edgar J., (Hume, Adams & Co.,) 26 and 28 w. Washington, res. 339 n. Pennsylvania.

Foster George J., carpenter, res. 367 s.

Foster Isaac, carpenter, res. last house e. s. Short.

Foster John, brakesman, I. & C. R. R., res. 31 Buchanan.

Foster James H., painter, res. Pearl, bet. New Jersey and Alabama.

Foster James, lab., res. Pearl, bet. Alabama and New Jersey.

Foster Henry, engineer, I. C. & L. R. R., res. 534 e. Georgia.

Foster R., capitalist, res. 339 n. Pennsylvania.

Foster Robert, baker, 12 s. Missouri, bds. same.

FOSTER ROBERT S., (F. & Wiggins,) city treasurer, office Glenn's blk., res. 454 n. Delaware.

Foster Wallace, (Smith & F.,) 27 n. Pennsylvania, res. 88 e. Pratt.

Foster, Wiggins & Co., wholesale grocers, commission and storage merchants, 68 & 70 s. Delaware.

Foudray John E., (Wood & F.,) 16 n. Pennsylvania, res. 215 n. New Jersey.

Foudry J. S., harness-maker, 109 e. Washington, bds. 215 n. New Jersey.

Fourth Presbyterian Church, cor. Delaware and Market.

Fourth Ward School, cor. Blackford and Vermont.

Foust Charles J., salesman, Foster, Wiggins & Co., bds. 454 n. Delaware.

Foust Michael, teamster, res. 467 s. East.

Fout Frederick, feed store, cor. Washington and Tennessee, res. 222 n. East.

Fowler Benjamin, smithman, I. & C. R. R., res. 57 Harrison.

Fowler James P., carpenter, res. 312 e. Washington.

Fowler Miss Mary, dress-maker, bds. Second, bet. Tennessee and Mississippi.

Fowlers B. V., (W. & B. V. F.,) res. 300 n. Blake.

Fowlers W., (W. & B. V. F.,) res. 300 n. Blake.

Fowlers W. & Co., (W. & B. V. F.,) grocers, 300 n. Blake.

Fox Alois, shoe-maker, bds. Indiana av.

Fox Benjamin, lab., res. 70 cor. Hosbrook.

Fox Catharine, servant, May Gordon, 351 n. Alabama.

FOX JACOB, boot and shoe-fitter, over 8 Bates House blk., res. same.

Fox Jacob, shoe-maker, 33 w. Maryland.

Fox Jacob, shoe-maker, bds. 148 Indiana av.

Fox James, engineer, rolling mill, res. 278 Madison av.

Fox John, bar-tender, 202 e. Washington, res. 70 Hosbrook.

Fox Judson, carpenter, bds. 20 s. Pennsylvania.

Fox Mrs. Magdaline, (wid. Michael,) res. 177 n. Liberty.

Foy Owen, machinist, Sinker's Foundry, res. 88 Benton.

Francis George M., soldier, U. S. Arsenal, res. same.

Francis H. N., news agt., res. 22 Bates.

Francis James, (col.,) teamster, bds. 435 n. East.

Francis Jacob, porter, 34 s. Meridian, res. Clinton, bet. New Jersey and East.

Francis William, pilot on Ohio river, res. 22 Bates.

Francis Willman, (col.,) res. Howard, bet. Second and Third.

Franco Daniel, last-maker, res. Bluff rd.

Franco Mathew, last-maker, bds. Bluff rd.

Frank G. H., engineer, C. I. & C. R. R., bds. 149 s. New Jersey.

Frank Henry, (Spiegle, Thoms & Co.,) res. 118 w. Vermont.

Frank James, real estate agt., over 35 e. Washington, res. 461 n. Tennessee.

Frank F. L., conductor, C., C. & I. C. R. R., res. 379 e. Georgia.

Franks Francis L., (Miller & F.,) over 45 e. Washington, res. cor. Cherry and Plum.

Frankem I. L., stoves and tin-ware, 67 e. Washington.

Frankem Jonathan, res. 249 n. Illinois.

Frankenstein George, barber, works 326 s. Delaware, res. same.

Frankenstein Jacob, barber, 326 s. Delaware, res. same.

Frankie Andrew, works Union depot, res. 176 Union.

Franklin Ambrose, (col.,) lab., res. Minerva, near City Hospital.

Franklin Benjamin, (col.,) yardman, Oriental House.

Franklin Benjamin, (col.,) barber, res. Eighth, w. Lafayette R. R.

Franklin & Capp, (James E. F. & A. B. C.,) principals National Business College, 24½ e. Washington.

Franklin Cyntha, (col., wid.,) bds. 224 n. Missouri.

Franklin James E., (F. & Capp,) 24½ e. Washington, res. 195 n. Tennessee.

Franklin James E., student, commercial college, bds. 223 w. South.

Franklin John, pressman, Downey, Brouse, Butler & Co., bds. Mrs. Reed, n. Pennsylvania.

Franklin Life Insurance Co., of Indianapolis, cor. Illinois and Kentucky av., James M. Ray, prest., Edward P. Howe, secy., William S. Hubbard, vice-prest. and treas., B. F. Witt, general agt.

Franklin William, (col.,) white-washer, res. 161 Indiana av.

Franklin William H., (col.,) barber, n. e. cor. Washington and Meridian, under Indiana National Bank, res. 231 w. Ohio.

Franklin William T., carpenter, res. 223 w. South.

Frantz Jacob, works Maxwell, Fry & Turston, res. Clinton, bet. Vermont and New York.

Franz Peter, well-digger, res. 222 n. Noble.

Franzman Mrs. Amelia, (wid. Adam,) res. 292 c. Market.

Frary John C., compositor, Journal office, bds. 168 n. East.

Frauer Albert G., (Thayer & F.,) 248 e. Washington, res. city limits.

FRAUER, BIELER & CO., dealers in saddlery hardware and manfs. of harness, saddles and collars, etc., 109 e. Washington. See card, page 70.

Frauer Samuel C., druggist, 246 e. Washington, res. 257 e. New York.

Frauer E. C., druggist, 246 e. Washington, res. s. s. New York, bet. East and Liberty.

Frauer Herman, clerk, 246 e. Washington, res. 257 e. New York.

Frauer, Rudolph, (F., Bieler & Co.,) 109 e. Washington, res. 85 n. New Jersey.

Frazee Aaron, brick-layer, res. 317 Indiana av.

Frazee Frank, well-digger, res. 351, old number, e. McCarty.

Frazee George W., carpenter, res. 759 n. Mississippi.

FRAZER JAMES S., chief judge, Supreme Court of Indiana, office new State bldg., res. Warsaw, Ind.

Frazee John W., carpenter, res. 303 n. Delaware.

Frazee P., pay-master, C., C. C. & I. R. R., office 53 s. Alabama.

Frazee Samuel E., pay-master, I. & St. L. R. R., office Bellefontaine office, res. 176 n. Illinois.

Frazer John H., carpenter, works I. C. R. R. shops, res. 271 e. Market.

Frazer William, bridge builder, bds. 431 e. St. Clair.

Fredericks George W., brick-moulder, res. 126 Bluff rd.

Fredericks Godfrey, lab., res. 9 Willard.

Free Frederick R., res. Columbia, bet. East and New Jersey.

Free John W., cabinet-maker, Union factory, res. 25 bet. Liberty and East.

Freeman Miss Clara, bds. 341 s. Pennsylvania.

Freeman David, lab., res. 74 Wilkens.

Freeman George W., salesman, 40 s. Meridian, res. 412 n. Delaware.

Freeman Henry, machinist, bds. 341 s. Pennsylvania.

Freeman Joseph W., carpenter, res. 56 s. Noble.

Freeman Miss Mary, bds. 134 n. Meridian.

Freeman Michael, pattern-maker, Eagle Machine Works, res. 341 s. Pennsylvania.

Freelish William, stone-mason, res. 105 High.

Freese Anna, servant, 160 e. Market.

Freidenberg Alex., occupant Deaf and Dumb Asylum.

Freidenberg Amanda, occupant Deaf and Dumb Asylum.

Freitschk William, clerk, 29 w. Washington, bds. 17½ Virginia av.

Frelking John F., res. 469 n. New Jersey.

Frendley Mary, servant, 477 n. Delaware.

French Amos, occupant Deaf and Dumb Asylum.

French Mrs. Anna T., (wid.,) bds. 676 n. Mississsippi.

French Charles G., jeweler, res. e. Washington, near corporation line.

French William M., instructor, Deaf and Dumb Asylum.

Frenzel J. P., Sen., (F., Will & Co.,) 104 s. Illinois, res. 246 e. Market.

Frenzel J. P., Jr., messenger, Merchants' National Bank, 48 e. Washington, bds. 246 e. Market.

FRENZEL, WILL & CO., (John P. F., Francis W. & J. P. Simon,) tanners and dealers in hides, leather and shoe findings, 104 s. Illinois.

Frese C. & Co., (C. F. & C. F. Hahn,) dealer in hardware, cutlery, &c., 27 w. Washington.

Frese Charles, (C. F. & Co.,) 27 w. Washington, bds. 28 w. Georgia.

Frese Mathias, engraver, W. & J. Braden, bds. California House.

Freshour Casper, stone-mason, res. 228 s. New Jersey.

Frey A., Daily Telegraph Co., res. 340 s. Meridian.

Frick John, saloon, 151 Ft. Wayne av., res. cor. Massachusetts av. and Noble.

Frick J., grocery and produce dealer, 300 Massachusetts av., res. same.

Frick Philip, foreman, Jacob Voegtle, res. 15 s. Alabama.

Fricker Jacob, (Schmedel & F.,) res. Morris, bet. East and New Jersey.

Fridolin Buscher, boot and shoe manfr., 122 s. Illinois, res. 135 Bluff rd.

Friday John M., carpenter and builder, 254 railroad, res. same.

Friech Henry, saloon, res. National rd., near White river bridge.

Friedgen C. H., merchant tailor, 41 n. Illinois, res. 123 w. Market.

FRIEDGEN CORNELIUS, manfr. and dealer in fashionable boots and shoes, 36 w. Washington, res. 36 n. East. See card, page 14.

Friend G. gardner, Madison rd., near city.

Friend Christopher, gardner, Richards, res. 550 s. New Jersey.

Friend Mary, servant, W. O. Rockwood, 276 n. Illinois.

Fries Martin, lab., res. 253 Union.

Friersdorff Frederick, engineer, C. S. Cereys, res. California, bet. Maryland and Georgia.

Frink E. O., (F. & Moore,) 24 e. Georgia, res. 203 Massachusetts av.

Frink Hiram S., tailor, works 32 s. Meridian, res. 308 e. Ohio.

FRINK & MOORE, (S. C. F., E. O. F. & H. A. M.,) Union Novelty Works and Foundry, 24 e. Georgia.

Frink S. C., (F. & Moore,) 24 e. Georgia, res. 97 s. Meridian.

Frisman Leo. S., cook, Capital Saloon, 14 e. Washington, res. same.

Fristover Dorff, engineer, Cory & Co., res. California, bet. Maryland and Georgia.

Fritsche Carle, printer, bds. 467 n. Delaware.

Fritz Charles L., traveling agt., J. H. Vajen & Co., res. 137 Massachusetts av.

Fritz C. L., traveling agt., J. H. Vajen & Co., bds. 372 Massachusetts av.

Frizzell Allen, carpenter, res. 268 n. Blake.

Frizzell Bushrod, carpenter, res. 266 n. Blake.

Frizzell Jesse, well-digger, res. Eighth, bet. Lenox and Railroad.

Fromeyer Henry, salesman, 56 and 58 e. Washington, bds. 134 n. Mississippi.

Frommledt Peter, cabinet-maker, works Spiegle, Thoms & Co., bds. 252 e.Washington.

Froschauer Adam, lab., bds. 518 e. Washington.

Frost Homar, works Junction R. R., bds. Wiles House.

Frost Herman F., conductor, I. M. & I. R. R., bds. Bates House.

Fruchtenecht Herman, teacher, German Lutheran School, s. East, res. 265 e. New York.

Frumholt Peter, cooper, res. 167 Bluff rd.

Fry Albert, (col.,) hostler, res. 85 Eddy.

Fry J. M., painter, 68 n. Pennsylvania, bds. Wiles House.

Fry James C., porter, E. Over & Co., bds. Commercial Hotel.

Fry Miss R. N., boarding-house, 204 n. Illinois.

Fry Sarah, (wid. Robert,) res. 226 Massachusetts av.

Fry William H., (Maxwell, F. & Thurston,) 34 s. Meridian, res. cor. Meridian and King.

Fuchs Martin, bar-tender, Spencer House Saloon, bds. 280 e. Market.

Fugate J. L., (J. H. Vajen & Co.,) 21 w. Washington, res. 169 w. New York.

Fullekanick Henry, lab., bds. 79 s. Liberty.

Fullen S. W., salesman, 78 s. Meridian, bds. Sherman House.

Fuller Miss Catharine, res. over 230 c. Washington.

Fuller Miss Emeline, res. 27 s. Alabama.

Fuller Joseph A., operator Western Union Telegraph Office, bds. 75 Kentucky av.

Fuller Joseph H., lab., res. 27 s. Alabama.

Fulmer David P., silver-plater, res. 225 e. Market.

Fulmer Miss Fanny, milliner, works 122 n. East, res. 225 e. Market.

Fulmer Frederick, silver-plater, 39 Virginia av., res. 225 e. Market.

Fulmer Leander, silver-plater, 30 Virginia av., res. 225 e. Market.

Fulmer Leander, groceries and provisions, s. w. cor. Georgia and Benton, res. 399 Georgia.

Fulmer Rachel F., milliner, res. 225 e. Market.

Fullmore John, painter, bds. 248 s. Pennsylvania.

Fulton America, occupant Deaf and Dumb Asylum.

Fulton Frank P., printer, 79 w. Washington, bds. 214 Union.

Fulton Felix M., cabinet-maker, res. 214 Union.

Fulton Homer, cabinet-maker, bds. 214 Union.

Fulton Herman H., general clerk, T. H. & I. R. R. Freight Office, bds. Macy House.

Fulton Miss Jennie, bds. 214 Union.

Fulton Miss Sarah J., bds. 48 n. West.

Fulton Samuel S., clerk, Macy House, bds. same.

Fulton W. H., piano-maker, 159 and 161 e. Washington, res. 84 Massachusetts av.

Fulton William, fireman, I. C. & L. R. R., bds. 99 Benton.

Funkhouser D., (Jameson & F., 19 s. Meridian, res. 40 n. Mississippi.

Funnelle Miss Amanda, principal Normal Department Fourth Ward District School, bds. 60 n. California.

Furby Edith, servant, 74 e. North.

FURGASON ALBERT G., cooper, 321 e. Georgia, res. 123 s. Noble.

Furgeson J. A., (W. J. Holiday & Co.,) 59 s. Meridian, res. 270 n. Tennessee.

Furgason James, works Junction R. R., bds. Wiles House.

FURNAS JOHN & CO., (John F., Moses M. Collett & Horace McCay,) dealers in dry goods and notions, 68 e. Washington.

Furnas John, (J. F. & Co.,) 68 e. Washington, res. 518 n. Delaware.

Furn Franklin L., machinist, bds. 126 n. Mississippi.

Fuss John, carpenter, works H. Recker, bds. 60 s. Delaware.

Fyner C., lab., Hill's Nursery, Michigan rd.

GABERT E. M., student, commercial college, bds. 369 n. New Jersey.

Gabe Michael, lab., res. Kansas, s. city limits.

Gabel Charles D., carriage-smith, works S. W. Drew & Co., bds. s. e. cor. Winston and Michigan.

Gabel Conrad, carriage-maker, works S. W. Drew & Co., res. 196 n. Noble.

Gabel David, black-smith, bds. s. e. cor. Winston and Michigan.

Gabiœl & Talbott, cooper shop, near Frank Wright's Brewery.

Gaen Christian, works Cabinet-Makers' Union, res. 83 Davidson.

Gaen Mrs. Wilhelmina, (wid. Christian,) res. 83 Davidson.

Gage Mrs. Mary, res. 136 w. Michigan.

Gagg & Co., (Rudolph G. & Peter Leiber,) brewers, 215 s. Pennsylvania.

Gagg Rudolph, res. 174 Madison av.

Gahm John, groceries, provisions and saloon, 196 Indiana av., res. same.

Gains Miss M., (col.,) 247 cor. West and Ohio.

Gainey Mrs. Nancy, (wid. Meredith,) res. 32 n. East.

Gains P. O., carpenter, bds. 11 n. West.

Galaspie Miss Elizabeth, bds. 58. s. California.

Galbraith Arthur N., salesman, New York Store, res. 50 w. New York.

Galbaith Richard M., carriage-trimmer, works S. W. Drew & Co., res. 46 s. Illinois.

Galdon Marion, bds. 83 Indiana av.

Gall Albert, (G. & Rush,) 101 e. Washington, res. 65 n. New Jersey.

Gall Caroline A., (wid.) res. 65 n. New Jersey.

Gall Edmund, clerk, F. P. Rush, res. 65 n. Jersey.

GALL & RUSH, (Albert G. & Charles R.,) wholesale and retail dealers in carpets, oil cloths, wall paper, &c., 101 e. Washington.

Gallagher Francis, painter, res. 62 Massachusetts av.

Gallagher John, peddlar, res. 314 n. Noble.

Gallagher Julia, cook, Commercial Hotel.

Gallagher Mrs. Mary, (wid. Martin,) res. 59 n. Alabama.

Gallagher Mary, servant, 416 n. Illinois.

Gallagher Patrick, peddlar, res. 330 Railroad.

Gallagher Patrick, salesman, New York Store, bds. 36 w. Maryland.

Gallagher Patrick, lab., res. 5 Peru.

Gallahue Warren C., notion dealer, bds. 326 e. New York.

Gallahue Phœnix M., notion dealer, res. 328 e. New York.

Galliton Sarah, (col.,) res. 73 Bright.

Gallivan Margaret, servant, 413 n. Illinois.

Gallivan Michael, lab., res. 148 s. Noble.

Calloway Mrs. Catharine, res. 204 w. Vermont.

Galloway Frank. M., res. 204 w. Vermont. Indiana av.

Galloway Mrs. Jane, dress-maker, res. 83

Galloway John, painter, bds. 69 w. Market.

Galloway Miss Lizzie, res. 204 w. Vermont.

Gallup Edward P., (W. P. & E. P. Gallup,) 43 and 45 n. Tennessee, res. 78 n. Tennessee.

Gallup William P., (W. P. & E. P. Gallup,) 43 and 45 n. Tennessee, res. 78 n. Tennessee.

GALLUP W. P. & E. P., (William & Edward P. G.,) grain dealers, com. mers. and agts. Fairbanks' Scales, 43 n. Tennessee.

Galvin Albert, res. Little's Hotel.

Galvin Eliza, res. Little's Hotel, cor. New Jersey and Washington.

Galvin George W., lawyer, res. Little's Hotel, cor. New Jersey and Washington.

Galvin Mrs. Honnora, (wid. Math.,) res. 90 railroad.

Galzaulinchter John, lab., res. 340 Railroad.

Gamm John, groceries and saloon, 196 Indiana av., res. same.

Gammerdinger Jacob, blacksmith, res. 613 e. Washington.

Ganshaw Charles, bds. 144 Virginia av.

Ganter Cashum, confectionery and bakery, 233 e. Washington, res. same.

Ganter Daniel C., engineer, 188 e. Washington, res. 233 e. Washington.

Gapen Philip M., traveling agt., 48 s. Meridian, bds. 457 Bluff rd.

Garber Henry, works at Arsenal, res. 112 Benton.

Garden Miss Ella, student, Indiana Female College, 146 n. Meridian, bds. same.

Garden Mrs. Margaret, (wid. George,) res. e. Washington.

Gardner Brime, carpenter, res. 426 e. Georgia.

GARDNER & DECKER, tinners and dealers in stoves, 508 Virginia av.

Gardner Mrs. Sarah, (wid. Joseph,) res. 352 Virginia av.

Gardner William, (G. & Decker,) 308 Virginia av., res. end Virginia av.

Gardner Conrad, saloon, Stringtown, s. s. National rd.

Gardner James, cooper, res. 127 Duncan.

Gardner Joseph, tinner, res. 118 Indiana av.

Gardner Samuel B., cooper, res. w. New York.

Gardner Joseph, (col.,) lab., res. 129 n. California.

Gardner Thomas S., clerk, bds. 40 n. New Jersey.

Gardner Vinder, carpenter, Union Planing Mill, res. 31 California, cor. Indiana av.

Garham Mrs. Amanda, bds. n. e. cor. Mississippi and Michigan.

Garham William H., awning-maker, office 16 e. Washington, Bamberger's Hat Store, res. n. e. cor. Mississippi and Michigan.

Garity John, lab., White River Iron Works, bds. 111 w. South.

Garity Mary, servant, 469 n. Tennessee.

Garman James, res. 90 s. East.

Garmon Thomas, blacksmith, res. alley, rear 75 s. West.

Garner C. L., physician, office 58 e. Market, res. 270 w. Vermont.

Garner H. S., foreman Sentinel news room, bds. Palmer House.

Garner L. W., agt. H. Daumont, bds. 270 w. Vermont.

Garrall Willis A., res. cor. Fletcher av. and Cedar.

Garratt J., second-hand clothing store, 257 e. Washington, res. same.

Garrett David, box factory, 162 n. Noble, res. 166 n. Noble.

Garrett John, (col.,) lab., res. cor. Third and Howard.

Garretson George, works Junction R. R., bds. Wiles House.

Garrigus William, res. Shelbyville pike, one-fourth mile s. corporation.

Garrison Edward W., carpenter, res. 395 Massachusetts av.

Garrison George, agt. Hoosier Drug Store, bds. Wiles House.

Garrison William L., shoe-maker, 14 e. New York, bds. 208 Blake.

Garshwiler William, traveling agt., res. 32 w. South.

Gartler Elizabeth, servant, 65 s. East.

Garvey Ellen, servant, W. H. Talbott, 94 n. Meridian.

Garvey Kate, servant, W. H. Talbott, 94 n. Meridian.

Garvey Patrick, lab., res. 222 Eddy.

Gasper Frederick, grocer, 333 Virginia av., res. same.

Gass Charles, blacksmith, works Bremmerman & Renner, bds. 248 Winston.

Gass Mrs. Margaret, (wid. Henry,) res. 203 n. Delaware.

Gast Andrew, butcher, res. 116 e. St. Joseph.

Gaston Mrs. Delila, (wid. H. R.,) boarding house, 37 Kentucky av.

Gaston Edward, carriage-maker, 26 e. Georgia, res. 49 Kentucky av.

Gaston John M., physician, office 66 e. Market, res. 147 n. New Jersey.

Gaston Simpson, bar-tender, William Selkins, bds. 35 n. Alabama.

Gatch Conduce, book-keeper, 125 s. Meridian, bds. Avenue House.

Gate Fred., car-cleaner, res. 172 Union.

Gates Austin B., (G., Pray & Co.,) res. 91 n. Delaware.

Gates C., bar-tender, res. 377 e. Georgia.

Gates George N., brass-moulder, bds. 335 w. Maryland.

Gates John J., blacksmith, shop 82 s. New Jersey, res. 223 e. Market.

GATES, PRAY & CO., (B. G. Kelley, A. B. Gates & Wm. Pray,) livery, feed and sale stable, East Market Square.

Gath L., stone-wheeler, res. 27 California.
Gattenby John, carpenter, 229 s. Mississippi.
Gaul Albert, carpenter, res. 218 n. Alabama.
Gaulmeyer Conrad, carpenter, res. 164 Stevens.
Gauspohn Frederick, cabinet-maker, Spiegal & Thoms, res. 164 s. Noble.
Gavisty John, lab., bds. 111 w. South.
Gavin Miss Maggie, servant, 425 n. Pennsylvania, bds. same.
Gaw James, lab., 302 w. Market.
Gay Alford, (Aldrich & G.,) supt. Indiana Central Canal Co., res. 38 n. West.
Gay Leonard, foreman paper mill, 38 n. West.
Gaybert Mary, servant, 490 n. Meridian.
Gaylord Mary E., inmate Deaf and Dumb Asylum.
Gaylot William, lab., Insane Asylum, res. w. White river bridge.
Gayton Olmsted, (col.,) hod-carrier, res. First, bet. Howard and Lafayette R. R.
Gearin Jeremiah, lab., res. 356 s. West.
Geblar Gottlieb, painter, bds. 248 s. Pennsylvania.
Geerking Henry, lab., res. 81 s. Liberty.
Geeslin H. L., student, N. W. C. University, bds. 76 Plum.
Geffert Frederick, res. 265 Union.
Gehbauer Conrad, lab., res. 274 w. Market.
Gehrhart Mathew, saloon, 55 n. Alabama, res. 199 e. Market.
Gehring Conrad, German book store and news dealer, 147 e. Washington, res. same.
Gehring Frederick, printer, res. 119 e. St. Joseph.
Gehring Frank, blacksmith, res. 80 w. South.
Gehringer John, stage-carpenter, Metropolitan Theater, bds. n. Tennessee, cor. New York.
Geiger Geo. W., (Landers, P. & Co.,) 58 s. Meridian, res. 434 n. Tennessee.
Geiger J. W., salesman, New York Store, res. 119 e. Market.
GEIGER R. W., freight agt., C., C., C. & I. R. R., bds. 17½ Virginia av.
Geil John, lab., res. 81 n. Liberty.
Geis John, (G. & Knarzer,) 62 s. Delaware, res. same.
Geis Joseph, brewer, res. s. end Alabama.
Geis & Knarzer, saloon, 62 s. Delaware.
Geis Lawrence A., (G. & Weuner,) 99 e. Washington, res. same.
Geis & Weuner, saloon, 99 e. Washington.
Grise Frank A., groceries, 83 e. McCarty, res. same.
Geisel Christian, carpenter, Bellefontaine Shop, res. 222 Davidson.

GEISEL & ENNERS,
(—— G. & William E.,) groceries and saloon, s. e. cor. Noble and Massachusetts av.
Geisel George, blacksmith shop, Fort Wayne av., res. 146 Fort Wayne av.
Geisel Henry, (G. & Enners,) res. 291 Massachusetts av.
Geisel Henry, blacksmith, bds. 103 w. South.
Geisendorff Miss Alice, res. 170 w. New York.
Geisendorff Albert, bds. 170 w. New York.
Geisendorff C. E. & S. H., (Christian E. & Mrs. S. H. G.,) propr's Hoosier State Flouring Mills, w. Washington, n. White river bridge.
Geisendorff C. E. & Co., (C. E. & S. H. G. & Isaac Thalman,) wool dealers and manufrs. of woolen goods, 402 w. Washington.
Geisendorff Christian E., manufr., res. 170 w. New York.
Geisendorff Conrad, (C. E. G. & Co.,) res. 191 n. New Jersey.
GEISENDORFF & CO., (C. E. Geisendorff & Co., and William W. H. McCurdy, William Eccles,) dry goods, notions, cloths and hosiery, 22 w. Washington.
Geisendorff Geo. E., (G. & Co.,) 81 and 83 Masonic Hall, res. 257 n. Mississippi.
GEISENDORFF H. & CO., commission merchants, dealers in flour and feed, 81 and 83 Masonic Hall.
Geisendorff Harry, (G. & Co.,) 81 and 83 Masonic Hall, res. 122 n. Tennessee.
Geisendorff Lewis, salesman, Geisendorff Woolen Factory, res. 177 w. New York.
Geizendaner Mrs. Ann, (wid. Joseph,) res. 319 n. Noble.
Geizendanner John, baker, bds. 319 n. Noble.
Geizendanner William, (C. Hespelt & W. G.,) 150 w. Vermont, res. same.
Geldmer Louisa, servant, 272 Winston.
Gelsan George, bar-tender, 176 e. Washington, bds. same.
Gelzenbuchter Peter, clerk, 188 n. Noble, bds. same.
Gentile Arthur, bds. Joanturbyville, National rd.
George Miss Catharine, bds. 520 n. Mississippi.
George Frederick, engineer, P. & I. R. R., bds. 325 e. Ohio.
George Isaac, hub-turner, res. 187 w. South.
George James, sign-painter, bds. 163 w. Maryland.
George Mrs. Louisa, res. 623 n. Mississippi.

George Miss Julia, bds. 24 Mississippi.
George Robert, grocer, 184 w. Washington, res. 24 n. Mississippi.
George Mrs. Sarah, (wid. William G.,) res. 70 n. Liberty.
George Mrs. Sarah A., res. 520 n. Mississippi.
George Silas A., machinist, Central Shop, res. 289 Virginia av.
Gephart Augustus, upholsterer, 56 e.Washington, res. 209 n. Liberty.
Gerard C., gardener, res. 286 Winston.
Gerard Nicholas, tailor, res. 313 e. Washington.
Gerber Henry, lab., U. S. Arsenal, res. Benton, near Georgia.
Gerhardt F. R., druggist, 96 Russell, res. same.
German Catholic Church, s. s. Maryland, bet. Delaware and Pennsylvania.
German English Independent School, Maryland, bet. Delaware and Alabama.
German Evangelical Church, s. e. cor. Wabash and New Jersey.
German Methodist Episcopal Church, Ohio, bet. New Jersey and East.
German Lutheran School House, cor. East and Georgia.
German Mutual Fire Insurance Co., office 16 s. Delaware, F. Ritzinger, secy.
German Reformed Church, Alabama, bet. Market and Washington.
Gerro Felix, tailor, over 28 s. Meridian.
GEROLD C. A. & CO.,
    manufacturers and dealers in pianos, 32 s. Meridian, res. 195 n. East.
Gerstner A., merchant tailor, 173 e. Washington.
Gesine Mrs. Barbara, (wid. Martin,) res. 247 Davidson.
Gesking Mrs. Christiana, (wid. Fred.,) res. 381 Virginia av.
Gibbons John, lab., res. 65 n. Liberty.
Gibbs Duncan, (col.,) barber, res. 165 Indiana av.
Gibbs Jane, (col.,) hair-dresser, bds. 235 n. Blake.

Gibbs John, plasterer, res. 312 w. Washington.
Gibbs Martha, (col.,) servant, 474 n. Pennsylvania.
Gibbs William B, furniture repairer, works 84 e. Market, res. 102 n. Missouri.
Giblin David, lab., res. 60 Bates.
Gibson David, (Sobl, G. & Co.,) res. 27 California.
Gibson Daniel C., (Martin & G.,) 2 Blackford's blk., s. e. cor. Washington and Meridian, bds. Bates House.
Gibson Henry, blacksmith, res. 56 Bright.
Gibson James, marble-polisher, 36 Fayette.
Gibson Louis W., cooper, bds. Nagle House.
Gibson Mary, servant, 225 w. New York.
Gibson Samuel, works Junction R. R., bds. Wiles House.
Gibson Stuart, lab., res, end Fletcher av.
GIBSON WILLIAM T.,
    secy. Indiana Fire Insurance Co., room 5 Odd Fellows Hall, n. e. cor. Pennsylvania and Washington, res. 140 n. Alabama.
Gies Frank., book-binder, res. 163 Union.
Giger John W., clerk, New York Store, res. 219 e. Market.
Giger William, shoe-maker, res. California.
Gilbert Edward, general agt. Guardian Mutual Life Insurance Co., of New York, 4 Blackford's blk., s. e. cor. Washington and Meridian, res. 307 Indiana av.
Gilbert G., (col.,) servant, 130 n. Alabama.
Gilbreth Jacob, shoe-maker, 328 s. Delaware, res. same.
Gilchrist David, stone-mason, res. 298 e. Michigan.
Gildersleeve Miss. E. L., principal of collegiate dep't, Indiana Female College, 146 n. Meridian, bds. same.
GILKEY & JONES,
    (Oliver B. G. & Julius J.,) carpenters and builders, 36 Kentucky av.
Gilkey Oliver B., (Gilkey & Jones,) 36 Kentucky av., bds. 33 w. Maryland.

Gilkison William F., printer, res. 127 Meek.
Gillespie Anna, servant, 421 n. Illinois.
Gillespie Celia, servant, 171 Davidson.
Gillespie Mrs. Jane, (wid. James,) res. 116 n. Delaware.
Gillespie W. J., res. 76 e. Michigan.
Gillett Horace S., instructor Deaf and Dumb Asylum, res. 478 n. Pennsylvania.
Gillett Omer T., medicine student, 28 n. Delaware.
Gillett Samuel S., presiding elder, Wesley Chapel, bds. 60 n. California.
Gillis F. A., clerk, Union Depot Dining Hall, res. same.
Gilmore D. F., brick-mason, res. 329 Virginia av.
Gilmore Mrs. Francis, (col., wid. James,) bds. rear 223 Massachusetts av.
Gilvin Elliott L., grocer, cor. New Jersey and Virginia av., res. same.
Gimbel Martin, clerk, 37 s. Meridian, res. East.
Gimbel Michael, groceries and provisions, 329 s. East, res. same.
Ging Henry, saloon, res. 297 e. Ohio.
Ging Michael, saloon, under Little's Hotel, res. Virginia av.
Gingrich John, carriage-maker, 26 e. Georgia, res. 20 s. Delaware.
Ginnis Michael, saloon, res. 227 Virginia av.
Gints William, res. 46 Hosbrook.
Gipe William, brakeman, B. R. R. L., bds. 58 Benton.
Girton Frank B., teamster, bds. 291 e. Ohio.
Girtsendown John, bds. Oriental House.
Githens Charles O., engineer, B. R. L., bds. 132 e. Georgia.
Githins John C., lab., res. 90 Maple.
Githens Leonidas M., engineer, Greenleaf's Foundry, bds. 132 e. Louisiana.
Gitzwiler Frank., porter, R. L. & A. W. McOuat's, res. 251 Virginia av.
Given George W., machinist, works Arsenal, res. 321 n. Noble.
Givan Mrs. Margaret, (wid. James,) res. 246 e. Market.
Glass Henry, lab., res. w. Blake, bet. New York and Vermont.
Glass Odd, paper-maker, McClane, McIntire & Co.
Glasscock William, lab., res. 54 Bright.
Glavin Edward, moulder, res. 368 s. Tennessee.
Glazier Mrs. Catharine, (wid. Jacob,) res. 178 s. New Jersey.
Glazier Charles, flour and grain dealer, also general com. mer., 146 s. Pennsylvania, res. 129 Virginia av.
Glazier Daniel, engineer fire department, res. 185 s. New Jersey.
Glazier Frank., engineer fire department, res. 273 w. Washington.

Glazier John, driver, W. Chandler, bds. 217 w. Washington.
Glazier P. F., fireman, engine No. 1, bds. 273 w. Washington.
Glenn Mrs. Amanda, (wid. John,) res. 69 McCarty.
Glenn's Blk., s. s. Washington, bet. Meridian and Pennsylvania.
Glenn Bridget, servant, Solomon Kaufman.
Glenn Hugh, (W. & H. Glenn,) res. New York City.
Glenn William, (W. & H. Glenn,) 29 and 31 e. Washington, res. 292 n. Meridian.
GLENN W. & H.,
(William & Hugh G.,) proprs. New York Store, dealers in dry goods and notions, straw goods and trimmings, 29 and 31 e. Washington, Glenn's blk.
Gleson Anna, servant, 306 n. Delaware.
Gleson Martin, lab., C. C. & I. C. R. R., res. Michigan rd., beyond city limits.
Gleeson Thomas, bar-tender, Circle Restaurant, res. 15 n. Meridian.
Glessing Thomas B., artist, Metropolitan Theater, res. 237 w. New York.
Glick Herman, (G. & Schwartz,) 54 n. Illinois, res. 261 Massachusetts av.
GLICK & SCHWARTZ,
(Herman G. & Joseph S.,) hoop skirts and fancy goods, 54 n. Illinois.
Glickert John, shoe-maker, works 65 s. Meridian, bds. Martin House.
Globe House, 164 and 166 s. Illinois, opp. w. end Union Depot, Herman Gruenert, propr.
Glover Joseph M., Terra Cotta Works, s. w. cor. Mississippi and Tennessee, res. 282 n. Meridian.
Glutz Charles, carpenter, res. 413 s. Illinois.
Gochenour Samuel, conductor, B. R. R. L., bds. Sherman House.
Goddard Sarah, servant, Bingham's, 203 e. South.
Goddard Samuel, Sen., (G. & Sons,) res. 100 s. Mississippi.
Goddard Samuel, Jr., (G. & Sons,) res. 100 s. Mississippi.
Goddard & Sons, (Samuel, Sr., Samuel, Jr. & Thomas G.,) stone yard, cor. Kentucky av. and Georgia.
Godfrey Charles, inmate Deaf and Dumb Asylum.
Godfrey George B., railroader, res. e. city limits.
Godpeiter John W., clock-maker, res. 432 s. East.
Goe H. M., groceries, 352 w. New York, res. 354 w. New York.
Goe H. N., confectionery and ice cream saloon, 56 n. Illinois, res. 354 w. New York.
Goe H. S., spoke-turner, res. 56 Eddy.
Goe L. T., sign painter, 18 s. Meridian, res. 503 n. Mississippi.

Goebel John, cabinet-maker, res. 221 Bluff rd.

Gœbler William, notions and dry goods, res. 137 Ft. Wayne av.

Gœdker Rudolph, tailor, 128 n. Noble, res. same.

Gœpper Frederick, (F. G. & Co.,) 17 e. Washington, res. n. Meridian, e. s. beyond city limits.

GŒPPER F. & CO., (Frederick G. & George Mansfeld,) merchant tailors and clothiers, 17 e. Washington.

Goff Eliza, (col.,) res. 213 n. West.

Goff George, lab., bds. 276 w. Maryland.

Goff William W., (col.,) barber, bds. 213 n. West.

Gogen James, printer, Journal Office, res. 458 Virginia av.

Gogen William, sawyer, res. 43 s. New Jersey.

Gohn W. James, clerk, L. Q. Sherwood, bds. Palmer House.

Golaver Bridget, servant, 176 n. Illinois.

Golchan Elika, teamster, res. 356 s. Tennessee.

Goldman Maud, inmate Home of the Friendless, w. s. n. Pennsylvania, beyond city limits.

Golden Alfred, (col.,) servant, J. S. Newman, 243 n. Pennsylvania.

Golden Dennis, lab., res. 333 Virginia av.

Golden Patrick, railroader, res. 68 s. Noble.

Golder Howard, engineer, J., M. & I. R. R., bds. 75 Kentucky av.

Golding Andrew G., painter, bds. 82 California.

Golding William G., carriage-painter, res. 82 California.

Goldman Jacob, second-hand clothing, 277 s. Delaware, res. same.

Goldsberry Bayless S., hats, caps, furs and straw goods, 132 w. Washington, bds. 129 n. Illinois.

Goldsbury Livingston D., res. 296 Virginia av.

Goldsberry Samuel S., watch-maker, McLene & Herron, bds. Virginia av.

Goldsmith Charles, brakesman, T. II. & I. R. R., bds. 272 w. Maryland.

Goldsmith Miss Lou., Trade Palace, res. 24 w. New York.

Goliah Sampson, (col.,) lab., res. Missouri, bet. Indiana av. and North.

Good Eli, cigar-maker, bds. Neiman House.

Goode Mrs. Lucy B, (wid. Wolton,) bds. 152 n. Mississippi.

Goodfellow Peter, salesman, Spiegle, Thoms & Co., res. 204 n. Noble.

Goodhart Benjamin F., clerk, Redmond & Jordon, bds. 311 w. Washington.

Goodhart Benjamin F., (Smith & G.,) flour and feed, cor. Virginia av. and Delaware, res. 236 e. Vermont.

Goodier John R., student, City Academy, bds. over 280 e. Washington.

Goodman George, cabinet-maker, res. 40 Huron.

Goodman P. W., wheel-maker, bds. 13 s. Illinois.

Goodnoe Jonas D., lab., res. 124 e. Merrill.

Goodrich Mrs. Nancy, (col.,) res. Howard, bet. Second and Third.

Goodslip Robert, painter, res. 84 e. South.

Good Templars' Hall, s. w. cor. Washington and Meridian.

Goodwin A. Q., publisher Sparkling Gem, monthly temperance magazine, res. 171 n. Jackson.

Goodwin E., minister, res. 171 Jackson.

Goodwin G. K., salesman, Western Furniture Co., res. 40 Huron.

Goodwin Mrs. M. M. B., editress Sparkling Gem, and editress and publisher Christian Monitor, office New Journal bldg., res. 171 n. Jackson.

Goodwin R. M., (Morrow G. Hay,) room 3, Vinton's blk., res. 281 n. Pennsylvania.

Goodwin T. A., gen'l insurance agt., 35 e. Market, res. Washington, e. Asylum.

Goott John, tailor, 284 n. Liberty, res. same.

Gooth Edward, machinist, res. 364 s. Illinois.

GORDON GEORGE E., attorney at law, 6 Odd Fellows' Hall, res. 230 n. Pennsylvania.

Gordon Jonathan W., (G. & March,) room 4, Talbott & New's blk., n. Pennsylvania, res. 351 n. Alabama.

GORDON & MARCH, (Jonathan W. G. & Walter M.,) attorneys at law, room 4, Talbott & New's blk., n. Pennsylvania.

Gordon R., photograph gallery, 36½ e. Washington, res. 60 w. Market.

Gorham Wm. H., awning manufr., 16 e. Washington.

Gore James, res. 206 n. Delaware.

Gorman Mrs. Sarah J., (wid.,) res. Court, bet. East and New Jersey.

Gorman Thomas, blacksmith, Citizens' Street Ry. Co., res. Chesepeake.

Gorrell A. W., (H. F. West & Co.,) 37 s. Meridian, res. Fletcher av., near Cedar.

Goss William, clerk, Lukens & Hollowell, bds. 157 w. Maryland.

Goss Mrs. Caroline, (wid. William,) res. 121 Spring.

Goss Martin W., clerk, Union Star Line Office, res. 130 Virginia av.

Goss Louis, stone-mason, res. 329 Davidson.

Gossett T. F., salesman, 56 s. Meridian, bds. 169 n. Illinois.

Goth, Brown & Co., grocers and produce dealers, 489 n. New Jersey.

Goth Jacob, tinner, D. Root & Co., bds. 499 n. New Jersey.

Goth L., tinner, bds. 499 n. New Jersey.

Goth Peter, (G., Brown & Co.,) 489 n. New Jersey, res. 449 n. New Jersey.

Gott Charles H., farmer, res. 219 s. Tennessee.

Gott Thomas, farmer, res. 219 s. Tennessee.

Gottschalk Charles, cigar-maker, bds. 23 Kentucky av.

Gottschalk John, foreman, C. C. & I. C. shop, res. e. city limits.

Gottlieb Glock, lab., res. w. river bridge.

Gottpeter Henry, lab., res. 162 Buchanan.

Gough David, farmer, res. Kansas, s. city limits.

Gough Jacob M., blacksmith, bds. 80 s. Mississippi.

Gough John, apprentice, 277 w. Washington, bds. 68 s. California.

Goul Andrew, carpenter, res. 231 e. South.

Gould Adam, groceries, 405 w. Washington, res. same.

Gould G. B., student, commercial college, bds. 726 cor. New Jersey and Fifth.

Goulding John, lab., res. Sixth, bet. Tennessee and Mississippi.

Gould John J., lab., res. 46 Coburn.

Goulding John, lab., res. n. s. Sixth, bet. Illinois and Tennessee.

Gout Frederick, lab., T. H. & I. R. R. Engine House, res. 172 w. Union.

Grabe Jacob, carpenter, res. 356 s. Illinois.

Grabhorn Henry, varnisher, res. 415 e. Washington.

Graden William, res. end Virginia av., beyond city limits.

Grady Annie, cook, Bay House.

Grady Martin, lab., res. 28 Helen.

Grafenstein Frederick, butcher, 105 Massachusetts av., bds. 491 n. Alabama.

Grafenstein William, butcher, 105 Massachusetts av., res. 491 n. Alabama.

Grafford Susannah, (col.,) washing and ironing, res. 183 Douglas alley.

Grafton John I., clerk, supt's office M. U. Express Co., bds. Bates House.

Graham & Co., dealers in flour and feed, 62 n. Pennsylvania.

Graham George, gardener, U. S. Arsenal, res. Arsenal Grounds.

Graham J. J., (G. & Co.,) 62 n. Pennsylvania, res. 244 s. New Jersey.

Graham Miss Kate, head-laundress, Bates House.

Graham Samuel J., railroader, res. 374 n. Tennessee.

Graham William, brick-maker, res. 141 Huron.

Gramble Edwin G., farmer, res. 394 Virginia av.

Gramling Adam, salesman, 35 e. Washington, res. 39 Union.

Gramling Anton, retired school teacher, res. 210 n. Noble.

Gramling John, (J. & P. G.,) 35 e. Washington, res. 210 n. Noble.

GRAMLING J. & P., (John & Peter G.,) merchant tailors and dealers in ready-made clothing, 35 e. Washington.

Gramling Peter, (J. & P. G.,) 35 e. Washington, res. 212 n. Noble.

Grand Army of the Republic, office rooms 2 Ætna bldg.

Graney Dennis, lab., res. 175 Meek.

Graney Ellen, servant, 175 e. Ohio.

Graney Mary A., servant, e. s. n. Illinois, bet. Second and Third.

Graney Maggie, servant, 182 s. New Jersey.

Graney Thomas, lab., res. 96 Railroad.

Grandey J. C., painter, bds. Wiles House.

Grasbey Frederick, baggage-master, res. 77 s. Liberty.

Grass Adam, painter, res. Second, bet. Meridian and Illinois.

Gressfield Ezra, lab., res. Geisendorff, near Geisendorff's Woolen Factory.

Grasson William, packer, 68 s. Meridian, res. 124 Noble.

See Condensed R. R. Routes in last part of Book.

Graves Alfred, (col.,) lab., res. 164 Elm.
Graves Catharine, works City Laundry, res. 199 e. Washington.
Graves C. E., clerk, Merchants' Union Express Co., 42 and 44 e. Washington, res. 22 California.
Graves Highland, works Spiegle, Thoms & Co., res. 195 s. Alabama.
Graves Lewis W., farmer, res. 296 n. Meridian.
Graves Myra, brakeman, C., C. & I. C. C. R. R., bds. 58 Benton.
Graves Richard, fruit stand, cor. Kentucky av. and Tennessee, res. same.
Graves Virenda, (col.,) res. 164 Elm.
Gray George W., tailor, res. 172 Center.
Gray Henry, works J. Butsch, bds. 68 w. South.
Gray Jonathan, brick-layer, res. 293 n. Liberty.
Gray Robert, engineer, City Mills, res. 28 Lord.
Gray Robert, carpenter, res. 78 e. St. Clair.
Gray Robert P., (Lehr & G.,) 83½ e. Washington, res. 52 Greer.
Gray S. F., agt. Star Union Line and Allentown Line, 85 Virginia av., res. 70 e. St. Clair.
Gray Stephen, (McGinnis & G.,) 45 e. Washington, res. 84 Massachusetts av.
Gray Talbott, (col.,) waiter, Bates House.
Gray William, druggist, res. 235 n. Illinois.
Gray William, engineer, res. 57 Harrison.
Gray William, baggageman, C., C. & I. C. R. R., bds. 33 Meck.
Graydon Andrew, clerk, Central R. R. office, res. 287 e. Market.
Graydon Alexandria, retired merchant, res. 287 e. Market
Graydon William, clerk, 47 n. Illinois, bds. 492 n. Tennessee.
Greany John, lab., res. 274 s. Tennessee.
Greaney Patrick, grocer, 210 e. Washington, bds. 245 n. Liberty.
Great Western Horse Insurance Co., office 7 Vinton's blk., opp. p. o.
Greeley Michael, lab., res. 109 n. West.

Greeley Horace, (col.,) servant, Mrs. M. Achey, 17 Kentucky av.
Green A., chair-bottomer, res. 199 Huron.
Green Celia, (col.,) bds. West, bet. Ohio and Market.
Green D. M., salesman, 17 w. Washington, res. 364 n. Meridian.
Green E. S., (Dutton & G.,) 77½ e. Market, Eden's blk., res. 704 n. Tennessee.
Green Edmund, (col.,) servant, James Blake, 308 n. Tennessee.
Green George, tailor, 60 e. Market, res. n. Mississippi, beyond city limits.
Green Geo. W., clerk, car depot, C., C. & I. C. R. R., bds. Pyle House.
Green J. C., (J. C. G & Co.,) 98 e. Washington, res. 370 n. East.
Green J. C. & Co., druggists, 98 e. Washington.
Green Miss Jennie J., bds. 39 w. Market.
Green John, lab., res. 164 n. Delaware.
Green John, (col.,) lab., bds. 25 n. Illinois.
Green M. J., (wid. Bird,)res. 37 Maple.
Green Martha, res. 37 Maple.
Green Mary, servant, 182 Davidson.
Green N. Scott, individual book-keeper, First National Bank, bds. 364 n. Meridian.
Green P. M., (Cambell & G.,) 149 w. Washington, res. 130 n. Mississippi.
Green Mrs. Sarah, (wid.,) res. 145 n. Mississippi.
Green Thomas C., clerk, Davis & Green, bds. 364 n. Meridian.
Green Virginia, bds. West, bet. Ohio and Market.
Greenan Joseph, freight conductor, C., C. & I. C. R. R., bds. 90 s. Illinois.
Greenan Michael, fireman, C. C. & I. C. R., bds. 58 Benton.
Greenawalt John G., clerk, Indiana Military Agency, Gallup's bldg., res. 780 n. Illinois.
Greene James, (Davis & G.,) 27 s. Meridian, res. 364 n. Meridian.
Greenewald Henry, (G. & Schindler,) res. 174 e. Washington.

Greenewald & Schindler, (Henry G. & Robert S.,) Indiana Dry Goods Store, 174 e. Washington.

Greenfield Daniel C., deputy county clerk, county clerk's office, res. 323 w. Washington.

Greenfield Robert, produce buyer, Carlisle's Mills, res. 323 w. Washington.

Greenleaf Clement (A., G. & Co.,) 255 s. Tennessee, res. 303 s. Meridian.

Greenleaf & Co., founders and machinists, 325 s. Tennessee.

Greenleaf Edward, machinist, res. 416 s. Tennessee.

Greenleaf P. P., machinist, bds., 416 s. Tennessee.

Greenleaf William, machinist, bds. 416 s. Tennessee.

Greenlee James S., carpenter, res. 219 Virginia av.

Greenway John, shoe-maker, 41 e. Washington, res. 112 e. McCarty.

Greenwegen George, shoe-maker, 41 e. Washington, bds. Cincinnati House, s. Delaware.

Greenwood Joseph, teamster, res. end Virginia av., beyond city limits.

Greenrod Timothy, stone-cutter, res. 31 s. West.

Greensheet J. H., book-keeper, Wheat, Fletcher & Co., res. 110 Broadway.

Greer Elisha, huckster, res. 433 e. Vermont.

Greer James, poet, 242 s. Mississippi.

Greer Stephen H., clerk, n. e. cor. Noble and Market, bds. same.

Greesher William, clerk, res. 393 s. East.

Gregg James A., wagon-maker, res. 321 n. West.

Gregor Chackley F., carpenter, bds. 83 California.

Gregor Henry, belt-maker, Mooney & Co., res. 331 e. Georgia.

Gregor William, lab., res. 396 s. East.

Gregory Dennis, fur dealer, bds. 78 e. Market.

Gregory Miss May, lady boarder, 281 e. New York.

Gregory Miss Martha M., training school, bds. 115 Massachusetts av.

GREGORY ROBERT C., judge Supreme Court of Indiana, office New State bldg., bds. Bates House, res. Lafayette, Ind.

Grenwald John G., clerk, State Military Agency, res. 780 n. Illinois.

Gresbach August, brewer, bds. 94 e. South.

Greshaber John, boiler-maker, res. 349 s. Alabama.

Gresh B. J., professor string and brass music, res. 282 e. St. Clair.

Greuzard & Loucks, (Logan S. G. & C. L.,) house, sign and ornamental painters, 328 e. Washington.

Greuzard Logan S., (Loucks & G.,) 237 e. Washington, res. 455 Virginia av.

Greuzard Miss Rosa, utility at theater, bds. 454 Virginia av.

Grewlich William, cash-boy, New York Store, res. Fort Wayne av.

Grey Jessie, conductor, J. R. R., res. 293 s. New Jersey.

Grey Leonard, paper-finisher, McClene, McIntire & Hays.

Grey Robert, carpenter, res. 78 e. St. Clair.

Grieb John, lab., res. 126 Spring.

Grieb Gotlieb, stone-mason, res. 334 Railroad.

Griesheimer & Bro., (Moritz G. & Louis G.,) dealers in clothing and gents' furnishing goods, s. w. cor. Washington and Meridian.

Griesheimer Louis, (G. & Bros.,) 1 w. Washington, bds. Circle Restaurant.

Griesheimer M., (M. G. & Bros.,) 1 w. Washington, bds. Circle Restaurant.

Grieshamer John, bar-tender, 156 e. Washington, bds. same.

Grieves Clarance, printer, Evening Commercial, bds. 314 w. Merrill.

Grieves John S., printer, Evening Commercial, bds. 314 w. Merrill.

Griffenstien William, butcher, res. 491 n. Alabama.

Griffin Miss Bridget, servant, 184 w. Ohio.

Griffin James, lab., res. 2 Water.

Griffin John, lab., res. 75 Fayette.

Griffin Martin, lab., res. 115 Elm.

Griffin Martha, (col.,) res. w. North, near Bright.

Griffin Michael, drayman, res. 95 Fayette.

Griffin Mary A., servant, 154 s. New Jersey.

Griffin Mary M., servant, n. w. cor. Fourth and Illinois.

Griffin Mary, servant, 160 n. Meridian.

Griffin Patrick, lab., res. e. city limits.

Griffin Patrick, gardener, res. 376 s. Delaware.

Griffin Peter, compositor, Sentinel news room, bds. Palmer House.

Griffin Mrs. Sarah, (wid. James,) res. 362 s. Delaware.

Griffin Timothy, saloon, 48 s. Pennsylvania, res. 386 s. Delaware.

Griffin Thomas, lab., res. 142 s. Noble.

Griffith Mrs. Catharine, res. 231 n. East.

Griffith Charles, lab., res. 398 s. Tennessee.

Griffith Dennis, lab., res. 252 s. Missouri.

Griffith George, mail agt., L. & G. R. R., res. 645 n. Tennessee.

Griffith Humphrey, real estate owner, res. 78 n. Illinois.

Griffith J. L., brakesman, C., C. & I. C. R. R., bds. 61 s. Noble.

Griffith J. J. F., book-keeper, 41 s. Meridian, res. 126 e. Ohio.

Griffith James, engineer, I. C. & L. R. R., bds. 99 Benton.

Griffith James, works 5 Pearl, bds. Pearl, bet. Alabama and East.

Griffith Josiah R., res. 42 s. Mississippi.

Griffith Pleasant H., bds. 78 n. Illinois.

Griffith Sarah, servant, 330 e. Louisiana.

Grigsey James, carpenter, res. 114 Michigan rd.

Grigsly Samuel, works Hill's Nursery, res. near Arsenal av.

Grimes Williams H. H., carpenter, res. 325 n. West.

Grimm Casper, painter, bds. 174 e. St. Joseph.

Grimm Jacob, cistern-builder, res. 174 e. St. Joseph.

Grimm Jacob, Jr., blacksmith, bds. 174 e. St. Joseph.

Grimm Jacob, carriage-smith, works S. W. Drew & Co., res. 174 e. St. Joseph.

Grine John, bakery, 264 e. Washington, res. same.

Griner J., shoe-maker, res. 38 s. Alabama.

Grinsteiner George, undertaker, 276 e. Market, res. same.

Grinsteiner Joseph, hackman, bds. 276 e. Market.

Grior David, tailor, works 30 n. Pennsylvania, res. Bluff rd., beyond city limits.

Griswold Amanda, (wid. David,) res. 404 s. Illinois.

Griswoold Mathilda, (wid.,) res. 38 n. Douglas.

Griswold Thomas E., traveling agt., Kiefer & Vinton, 68 s. Meridian, bds. Oriental House.

Grobe Charles, eating-house, 12 w. Louisiana, res. same.

Graham A. C., messenger, American Express Co., res. 205 Union.

GROOMS A. C., book-keeper, Journal Office, res. 412 n. Jersey.

Grosch John, (G. & Strothman,) 37 s. Delaware, res. 203 n. Noble.

Grosch & Strothman, (John G. & William S.,) commission merchants, 37 s. Delaware.

Gross Andrew L., occupant Deaf and Dumb Asylum.

Grove Benjamin, dealer in lightning rods, res. 329 e. New York.

Grove Henry W., mill-wright, res. 80 cor. Huron and Pine.

Grove Samuel A., clerk, Rout & Bates, res. 329 e. New York.

GROVER & BAKER SEWING MACHINE CO., Thomas M. Cochrane, agt., 21 e. Washington.

Grubbs Daniel W., general insurance agt., 19 n. Meridian, res. 282 n. Illinois.

GRUENERT HERMAN, propr. Globe House, 164 s. Illinois.

GRUENERT JOHN H., propr. Jefferson House, s. s. South, bet. Pennsylvania and Delaware.

Grund G., striker, res. 137 Bluff rd.

Gruseman William, carpenter, res. 123 w. Fourth.

Guardian Baptist Mission Sunday School, over 194 and 196 w. Washington, meets 9 a. m., H. Knippenberg, supt.

Guenther C., shoe-maker, 168 s. Illinois, res. 142 e. Maryland.

Guenther, Ernesta F., res. s. e. cor. Tennessee and Third.

Guetig Henry, propr. Spencer House Saloon, res. 280 e. Market.

Guezett A., house and sign painter, res. 297 s. Delaware.

Guffin H. C., (G. & Parker,) n. Pennsylvania, res. Northwood, near N. W. C. University.

Guffin L. H., student, N. W. C. University, bds. 40 Christian av.

Guffin & Parker, (H. C. G. & R. P. P.,) attorneys at law, rooms 10 and 11, Talbott & New's blk., n. Pennsylvania.

Guisinger Frank, stage carpenter, bds. 144 n. Tennessee.

Gullett A., student, N. W. C. University, bds. cor. Plum and Vine.

See Cigar and Tobacco House, page 108.

Gulliver Aaron, barber, cor. Kentucky av. and Washington, res. same.

Gulliver Leo, (col.,) farmer, res. Tennessee, bet. Michigan and Vermont.

Gulliver William, (col.,) barber, cor. Kentucky av. and Washington, res. 75 Kentucky av.

Gum George R., plumber, 82 w. Washington, bds. Mrs. Reed, n. Pennsylvania.

Gumpf Cristopher, gardner, res. n s. National rd., w. White river bridge.

Gumphry Joseph, farmer, res. 112 n. Noble.

Gundelfinger Benjamin, res. 261 e. Market.

Gundelfinger Max, clerk, 1 w. Washington, bds. 157 e. Market.

Gurley J. P., hat-blocker, 44 s. Illinois, bds. 33 w. Maryland.

Gusietter Frederick, drives furniture wagon, res. 435 n. New Jersey.

Gustin George, Western Union Telegraph Office, bds. 275 n. New Jersey.

Gustin John, auctioneer, res. 27 e. North.

Gustin L., physician and surgeon, office cor. Illinois and Louisiana, res. 275 n. New Jersey.

Gustin Louis, fireman, I., C. & L. R.R., res. 82 s. Noble.

Gustin Robert, carpenter, bds. 275 n. New Jersey.

Gutchnecht Rudolph, shoe-maker, res. 562 n. Mississippi.

Guthmann John, printer, res. 157 Fort Wayne av.

Guthrie Edward A., compositor, Sentinel news room, res. 109 n. Illinois.

Guthrie Miss Emma, bds. 312 Indiana av.

Guthperle Peter, porter, Spiegle, Thoms & Co., res. 204 n. Noble.

Gutig Henry, barber, shop under Odd Fellows' Hall, res. 280 e. Market.

Guttschaup George, cigar-maker, bds. 19 Lord.

Guy James C., bds. 121 n. Delaware.

Gwin Eliza, (wid.,) res. 16 Henry.

HAAG CHARLES, peddler, res. 274 Massachusetts av.

Haas George, baker, res. 428 s. East.

Haciel Martin, section boss, I., P. & C. R. R., bds. 116 s. East.

Hack George, blacksmith, res. 463 n. Alabama.

Hack John, gardener, Deaf and Dumb Asylum.

Hacker Asbury T., res. 465 e. Georgia.

HACKER WILLIAM, grand secy. Masonic Order, State of Indiana, office Masonic Hall, bds. 89 Indiana av.

Hackersmith John, carpenter, res. 301 e. Georgia.

Hackstein Christian, lab., res. 166 Union.

Hackmann ——, cigar-maker, bds. 23 Kentucky av.

Hadley E., medical-student, bds. 302 n. Delaware.

HADLEY WILLIAM, city assessor, office Glenn's blk., e. Washington, res. 381 n. Delaware.

Hadley Wright J., student, City High School, bds. 381 n. Delaware.

HAEHL & MEANS, (John H. & Thomas A. M.,) gen'l agts. Great Western Life Insurance Co., of N. Y., 20 s. Delaware.

Hael Mrs. C., res. 704 n. Tennessee.

Haeman George, lab., Schmidt's Brewery, res. same.

HAERLE WILLIAM, ladies' furnishing goods, hosiery, fancy goods and notions, 4 w. Washington, res. 342 n. Illinois. See card in advertising department, page 2.

Haet Thomas, carpenter and builder, 26 Virginia av., res. 799 n. Tennessee.

Haffield Robert A., engineer, bds. 103 w. South.

Haffield Ulrich, teamster, res. 103 w..South.

Hagar Edward C., book-keeper, Fletcher's Bank, 30 e. Washington, bds. 17 w. Maryland.

Hagedon William H., Trade Palace, bds. 84 e. Michigan.

Hager Fanny, waitress, dining room, 33 w. Maryland.

Hagerdon H. F. E., brick-maker, res. 119 Buchanan.

Hagerhorst Christina, res. 197 s. Tennessee.

Hagerhorst William, machinist, Washington Foundry, res. 221 s. Alabama.

Hagerty Cornelius, lab., res. 32 Helen.

Haggerty James, currier, 125 s. Meridian, res. s. Meridian, near city limits.

Haggon John, lab., res. 279 Kentucky av.

Hahn Adolphus, commercial clothing store, n. e. cor. Illinois and Georgia, res. 184 Virginia av.

Hahn & Bals, (Charles F. H. & Charles H. G. B.,) wholesale dealers in wines, liquors and tobacco, 25 s. Meridian.

Hahn Charles F., (H. & Bals,) 25 s. Meridian, res. 97 n. Alabama.

Hahn Henry, boarding house, 65 s. East.

Hahn Jacob, bds. 227 s. Tennessee.

Hahn John, butcher, res. 10 Willard.

Hahn Lewis, butcher, res. 227 s. Tennessee.

Hahn Phillip, musician, Metropolitan Theater, res. 233 s. East.

Haid Frederick, butcher, 59 n. Noble, res. 1½ mile e. National rd.

Haines Elizabeth, cook, 107 Virginia av.

Haines Martha, (wid.,) res. 39 Elm.

Haines Thomas, road-master, Citizens' Street Ry., bds. Pyle House.

Hairman John, cabinet-maker, works Union Factory, res. 124 Winston.

Haisch John, printer, works 164 e. Washington, bds. Union Hall.

Hale A. C., dairyman, bds. end Virginia av.

Hale Dennis, tobacconist, bds. Ray House, e. South.

Hale H. J., Jr., machinist, 124 n. Missouri.

Hale Herman, stone-mason, bds. e. city limits.

Hale Henry J., machinist, res. 81 Massachusetts av.

HALE JUDSON, physician for diseases of the throat and lungs, n. Illinois, Miller's blk., second floor, res. 60 w. Market.

Hale Mrs. Margaret J., (wid. William,) res. 65 n. East.

Haley Oliver, engineer, Ben Franklin Office, res. 180 Dougherty.

Halceney H., lab., res. 184 w. New York.

Haley Pat., saloon-keeper, bds. 13 Willard.

Hall Adams, porter, Institute of the Blind, bds. same.

Hall Allen G., works Street R. R., res. 5 English's blk., e. Washington.

Hall B. R., upholsterer, bds. 423 e. St. Clair.

Hall Charles E., clerk, 31 n. Pennsylvania, bds. n. Illinois, beyond city limits.

Hall Mrs. C. S., res. 704 n. Tennessee.

HALL E. A., merchant tailor, 31 n. Pennsylvania, res. n. Illinois, beyond city limits.

Hall Earl G., patent-right business, res. 564 n. Tennessee.

Hall Edward R., (Lawyer & H.,) 49 s. New Jersey, res. Noblesville, Ind.

Hall Frank, farmer, res. Fifth, bet. Mississippi and Tennessee.

Hall Franklin, res. 283 Patterson.

Hall Georgia, (col.,) res. 129 n. Bright.

Hall George T., painter, bds. 240 e. Ohio.

Hall Mrs. Hanna, (wid. William Q.,) bds. 423 e. St. Clair.

Hall Harry L., asst. supt., L. & I. R. R., bds. Bates House.

Hall Henry, engineer, I., C. & L. R. R., res. 306 e. Georgia.

Hall Isaac B., book-keeper, bds. Ray House.

Hall James, (col.,) res. 107 Ash.

Hall Jerome, works Street R. R., bds. 5 English's blk., e. Washington.

Hall John, lab., res. 227 w. Market.

Hall John K., blacksmith, bds. 124 s. Meridian.

Hall Leonard A., heater, Rolling Mill, res. 12 Henry.

HALL NATHAN, (col.,) (Jones H. & Brown,) 16 s. Meridian, res. 258 n. Mississippi.

Hall Reginald H., (Rand & H.,) 24½ e. Washington, res. 210 n. Meridian.

Hall Robert, carpenter, Citizens' Street Ry., res. 120 s. New Jersey.

Hall Thomas Q., (Wilkens & H.,) 38 e. Washington, res. 125 e. Walnut.

Hall Wesley, lab., bds. Wiles House.

Hall William, machinist, C. & I. C. R. R. shops, res. 197 Bates.

Hall William, driver, Spiegle, Thoms & Co., res. Wabash, bet. New Jersey and East.

Hall William, (col.,) carpenter, res. 129 n. Bright.

Hall William, express-messenger, I. & C. R. R., res. 423 e. St. Clair.

Haley Jeremiah, hod-carrier, res. 68 Coburn.

Haley John, lab., res. 245 s. Missouri.

Haller Leon, salesman, Trade Palace, bds. Capital Restaurant.

Hallin Thomas, lab, res. Coburn, near New Jersey.

Hallihan Daniel, lab., res. 349 Winston.

Hallmich John, porter, Stewart & Morgan, 40 e. Washington.

Halper Martin H., printer, Journal Office, res. 229 e. Vermont.

Halstead Abraham, stone-cutter, res. 335 n. Pennsylvania.

Halsey Benjamin, farmer, res. s. s. Coburn, bet. Wright and East.

Halter Augustus, butcher, res. 207 w. Michigan.

Halter William, shoe-maker, res. n. s. National rd., near Insane Asylum.

Halterman Joseph, house-mover, bds. 26 s. West.

Hamilton Alfred, clerk, Willard & Stowell, bds. Pattison House.

Hamilton Benjamin, stove-moulder, Root's Foundry, res. 58 Greer.

HAMILTON CHARLOTTE, (wid. Kennard,) propr. Patterson House, 63 n. Alabama.

Hamilton David, engineer, C., C. & I. C. R. R., bds. 58 Benton.

Hamilton Eliza, (wid. John W.,) res. 138 e. Pratt.

Hamilton Elijah, lab., bds. Madison rd., near toll-gate.

Hamilton Miss Eliza, lady boarder, bds. 131 n. East.

Hamilton Miss Emma W., telegraph operator, bds. 63 n. Alabama.

Hamilton T. J., engineer, res. 50 Fletcher av.

Hamilton Frank W., dept. auditor Marion co., res. 291 s. New Jersey.

Hamilton Henry H., carpenter, res. 81 w. Elizabeth.

Hamilton J., works Junction R. R., bds. Wiles House.

Hamilton James, (King & Co.,) 50 s. Mississippi, res. 517 Maple.

Hamilton James B., brick-moulder, res. e. city limits.

Hamilton John A., foreman, Bellefontaine shops, res. e. city limits.

Hamilton Miss Julia F., student, High School, res. 63 n. Alabama.

Hamilton Mrs., house-keeper, Sherman House.

Hamilton Mary, (col.,) servant, 339 e. Market.

Hamilton Mrs. Nancy, res. Madison rd., near toll-gate.

Hamilton Patrick, lab., 301 w. Market.

Hamilton Robert A., machinist, King & Co., res. 517 Michigan.

Hamilton Samuel, machinist, res. 114 Michigan rd.

Hamilton Mrs. Sarah res. National rd., e. city limits.

Hamilton Thomas D., agt. Universal Life Insurance Co., res. 166 e. Market.

Hamilton William S., machinist, res. 74 s. Noble.

Hamilton W. H., foreman Sheet's bookbindery, res. 138 e. Pratt.

Hamlin Carlin, (H. & Johnson,) 62½ e. Washington, res. n. w. cor. Circle and Meridian.

Hamlin Richard, res. 26 Maple.

Hamlin & Johnson, (Carlin H. & Thomas C. J.,) attorneys at law and U. S. claim agts., rooms 62½ e. Washington.

Hamlin William H., Telegraph office, res. 129 Bates.

Hammil Andrew, blacksmith, res. 813 n. Mississippi.

Hammill Bernard, lab., 34 s. Meridian, res. 498 n. Mississippi.

Hammill Michael, lab., res. 271 McCarty.

Hammill Jacob, piano-varnisher, 159 and 161 e. Washington, res. 181 s. Meridian.

Hammill George, cigar-maker, bds. 193 s. New Jersey.

Hammond Abram A., ex-Governor, bds. Bates House.

Hammond & Howland, (Lupton J. H. & Livingston H.,) lawyers, room 4, Hereths' blk., n. Delaware.

Hammond John, (col.,) servant, Thomas Sharpe, 239 n. Pennsylvania.

Hammond Miss Julia, student, Indiana Female College, 146 n. Meridian, bds. same.

Hammond Margaret, servant, 229 n. New Jersey.

Hammond Sebea U., insurance agt., 19 n. Meridian, res. 174 w. Michigan.

Hammond Upton J., (H. & Howland,) 20½ n. Delaware, res. 273 n. Pennsylvania.

Hampton J. B., carriage-maker, res. 365 w. Vermont.

Hanah David, cooper, res. 466 e. Georgia.

Hanawa Thomas, brick-layer, res. 145 n. East.

Hancock Mary, (wid. Joseph,) res. 304 Massachusetts av.

Hand Adolphus C., brick-maker, res. Madison rd., near city limits.

Hand Jesse, student, commercial college, bds. 390 n. Delaware.

Hand Levi S., brick-maker, res. Shelbyville pike, 1 mile s. corporation.

Handy Jacob, engineer, C. I. & C. R. R., bds. 142 s. East.

HANEMAN J. & T., (John & Theodore H.,) grocers, 135 Massachusetts av.

Haneman John, (J. & T. H.,) res. 135 Massachusetts av.

Haneman Theodore, (J. & T. H.,) res. 135 Massachusetts av.

Hanes James, lab., bds. 149 s. New Jersey.

Haney Mrs. Mary (wid. John,) res. 334 s. Delaware.

Hangs Nicholas, works D. Root & Co., res. 328 s. Delaware.

Hahnorster Wilhelm cabinet-maker, bds. s. Meridian, bet. Louisiana and Georgia.

Hankins Mary, (wid., col.,) res. 116 Ash.

Hankinson Miss Martha, milliner, works 8 n. Pennsylvania.

Hanmen Ellen, servant, 466 n. Meridian.

Hanlin Mrs. Catharine, (wid. William,) res. 17 s. West.

Hanlon James, salesman, New York Store, res. North Tennessee.

Hanlon Mrs. Mary, (wid. Matthias,) res. 324 e. New York.

Hanly Mrs. E. M., millinery and dress-making, 64 n. Illinois, res. same.

Hanly Thomas, salesman, New York Store, bds. cor. Market and Illinois.

Hanna John, (H. & Knefler,) 20½ n. Delaware, res. Greencastle, Ind.

Hanna John L., deputy sheriff, res. 345 n. Noble.

HANNA & KNEFLER, (John H. & Fred. K.,) attorneys at law, 20½ n. Delaware, rooms 3 and 4 Hereths' blk.

Hannah Mrs. Louisa, (wid. George,) bds. 345 n. Noble.

Hanna Miss M. E., teacher, Institute of the Blind, res. same.

Hanna S. C., (Crossland, Maguire & Co.,) 52 s. Meridian, res. 388 n. Illinois.

Hanna V. C., (col.,) regular army, res. 172 n. Meridian.

Hannan Edward, lab., rolling mill, res. 188 High.

Hannaman William, Indiana Claim Agency, res. e. Washington, beyond city limits.

Hanneman Jacob, lab., res. Wabash, bet. Liberty and Noble.

HANNING JOHN G., plumber, gas and steam fitter and fixtures, 82 w. Washington, res. 135 e. St. Joseph. See card, page 10.

Hannon Miss Jennie, Trade Palace, bds. 359 s. Alabama.

Hanover Christian, wagon-maker, res. 2 Arch.

Hanrahan Catharine, (wid.,) res. 272 s. Tennessee.

Hanrahan Frank., lab., res. 278 s. Tennessee.

Hanrahan Miss Mary, tailor, over 28 s. Meridian, res. 272 s. Tennessee.

Hanrahan Miss Catharine, dress-maker, 36 n. Illinois, res. 272 s. Tennessee.

Hanrahan Patrick G., saloon, 267 s. Tennessee, res. same.

Hanrahan Michael, switchman, T. H. & I. R. R.

Hansen Arsmus, porter, 52 s. Meridian, res. 430 s. Tennessee.

Hansen John, painter, res. 42 Virginia av.

Hansen Miss Pamela, bds. 98 w. Vermont.

Hansen Peter, lab., bds. 172 Madison av.

Hanson Frank., lab., res. 51 McCarty.

Hanson Mat., shoe-maker, 331 s. Pennsylvania, res. same.

Hanson Peter, shoe-maker, 257 s. Delaware, bds. 259 s. Delaware.

Hanway Samuel S., contractor, res. 435 n. East.

Happenny Theodore S., res. 32 w. St. Clair.

Happy John, tinner, res. 58 Hosbrook.

Harbison A. D., engineer, Journal office, res. 186 w. Vermont.

Harbison R., master Transportation Union Depot, bds. 136 w. Vermont.

Harbison Mrs. Sarah, res. 136 w. Vermont.

Hard Frederick, butcher shop, 234 e. Washington, res. on Court, rear of shop.

Harden George, harness-maker, bds. 31 s. New Jersey.

Hardon Richard, (col.,) barber shop, 286 w. Washington, res. same.

Harden Thomas, coach-trimmer, works Geo. Dalton, res. 17 Kentucky av.

Hardesty E. J., train-master, J. M. & I. R. R., res. 335 s. Pennsylvania.

Hardesty Levi, retired, res. 310 n. Illinois.

Hardin A. G., turnkey at jail, bds. same.

Hardin Ezra C., carpenter, res. 231 e. Market.

Hardin Richard E., carpenter, res. 229 e. Market.

Hardin Samuel, confectioner, res. 231 e. Market.

Harding George C., local editor Sentinel, (H. & Morton,) cor. Meridian and Circle, res. 127 w. First.

Harding & Morton, (George C. H. & John R. M.,) publishers Saturday Evening Mirror, cor. Meridian and Circle.

Harding Jacob, printer, cor. Meridian and Circle, res. 511 n. Mississippi.

Harding Thomas W., lawyer, res. 17 Kentucky av.

Harding William, drayman, res. 230 Union.

Hardwick John, carpenter, res. 33 Fletcher av.

Hardy E. A., salesman, W. A. Bristor, bds. 68 s. Pennsylvania.

Hare Mark L., horse dealer, res. 171 Davidson.

Harfy Hannah, servant, 217 n. New Jersey.

Hargin John, compositor, Sentinel news room, res. 26 Blackford's blk.

Harich Frederick, servant, J. W. Vajen, 128 n. Meridian.

Harkness Mrs. A., boarding house, 346 n. Meridian.

Hark Frank, lab., res. 23 Bates.

Harkness John, printer, res. 179 n. Pennsylvania.

Harlon A. W., student, Kilgore & Helms, bds. 271 e. Market.

Harlan George W., (Smith, H. & Butler,) res. 199 Massachusetts av.

Harlan L. W., physician, res. 142 Virginia av.

Harlan Mrs. Susan, (wid. George,) res. 136 n. Tennessee.

Harley James, porter, Ray House.

Harman Mrs. Catharine, (wid. Conrad,) res. e. Washington, near Arsenal av.

Harmening Christian, drayman, res. 66 Railroad.

Harmening Christian, groceries, 283 s. Delaware, res. same.

Harmening Herman, lab., res. 76 Railroad.

Harmon Lorenz, lab., res. 44 Michigan rd., beyond city limits.

Harnes Miss Rosana, dress-maker, works 172 e. Washington, res. 39 w. McCarty.

Harney John, gas and steam-fitter, 70 n. Illinois, res. e. side Delaware, bet. Merrill and McCarty.

Harnung John, (J. T. & H.,) res. 351 s. Pennsylvania.

Harold I. W., salesman, 10 e. Washington, bds. 70 e. Market.

Harper J. P., chief engineer, I. & V. R. R., res. 434 n. Delaware.

Harper John L., (Ray, Mayhew & Co.,) 8 w. Louisiana, res. 269 e. Market.

Harper Henry, lab., res. 162 Bluff rd.

Harper Winfield S., printer, bds. 162 Bluff rd.

Harrah Miss Celeste, student, Ind. Female College, 146 n. Meridian, bds. same.

Harrold Isaac, clerk, Boston Store, bds. 70 e. Market.

Harrier Delana, dining-room girl, 30½ n. Pennsylvania.

Harrigan Michael, lab., White River Iron Works, bds. near city limits.

Harrimann Augustus, works Cabinet-Makers' Union, res. e. end New York.

Harriman M. V., baggage-master, J. M. & I. R. R., bds. Globe House.

Harrington John, lab., res. w. Seventh, near Michigan rd.

Harris Addison C., (Dye & H.,) notary public, rooms 8 and 9, Talbott & New's blk., n. Pennsylvania, res. n. Meridian, beyond city limits.

Harris Bug, (col.,) white-washer, res. 229 n. Minerva.

Harris C. E., carpenter, res. 140 e. North.

Harris Davis, lab., res. 30 Helen.

Harris Miss Frank, Trade Palace, bds. 126 Virginia av.

Harris Harvey J., feed and boarding-stable, 163 w. Washington, res. country.

Harris J. H., res. s. s. National rd., near Insane Asylum.

Harris Jacob M., soldier, U. S. Arsenal, res. same.

Harris Miss Jennie, bds. second floor, 152 w. Washington.

Harris John, varnisher, res. Wabash, bet. New Jersey and East.

Harris Jno. T., inmate Deaf and Dumb Asylum.

Harris Louis, hack-driver, res. Court, bet. East and New Jersey.

Harris Marion, works 163 w. Washington, res. Mount Jackson.

Harris Martha, servant, 385 n. Illinois.

Harris Mrs. Mary A., (wid. Pleasant,) servant, 141 n. Alabama.

Harris Obadiah, res. n. s. National rd., w. White river bridge.

Harris Sophia, (col.,) servant, 36 s. New Jersey.

Harris T. W., plasterer, res. 380 s. West.

Harris Theodore F., brakeman, I., C. & L. R. R.

HARRIS W. H., commander U. S. Arsenal, e. of city, bet. Michigan and North.

Harris William, (col.,) white-washer, res. 75 Bright.

Harrison ———, bds. 95 n. Pennsylvania.

Harrison Miss Aurelia, bds. 252 n. Meridian.

HARRISON A. & J. C. S., (Alfred & John C. S. H.,) proprs. Harrison's Bank, 15 e. Washington.

Harrison Alfred, (A. & J. C. S. H.,) 15 e. Washington, res. 252 n. Meridian.

Harrison B. X., salesman, New York Store, bds. Commercial Hotel.

Harrison's Bank, A. & J. C. S. Harrison, proprs., 15 e. Washington.

Harrison Benjamin F., (Porter, H. & Fishback,) Yohn's blk., cor. Washington and Meridian, res. 299 n. Alabama, cor. North.

Harrison Edward G., clerk, Harrison's Bank, bds. 252 n. Meridian.

Harrison Erbone C., brick-layer, res. 49 Ann.

Harrison F. P., engineer, I. C. & L. R. R., bds. Ray House.

Harrison George, occupant Deaf and Dumb Asylum.

Harrison John C. S., (A. & J. C. S. H.,) 15 e. Washington, res. 262 n. Meridian.

Harrison Jno. T., inmate Deaf and Dumb Asylum.

Harrison R. E., attorney at law, office 19 w. Washington, res. n. e. cor. Oak and Cherry.

Harrison T. C., lawyer and claim agt., 19 w. Washington, res. 23 Cherry.

Harrison Thomas, blacksmith, res. 6 Willard.

Harrison W. B., clerk, New York Store, bds. Commercial Hotel.

Harrison William H., (col.,) cook, Oriental House, bds. same.

Harrmann Francis J., undertaker, 26 s. Delaware, res. 272 e. Market.

Harry Edward, lab., res. end Virginia av., beyond city limits.

Harry Thomas, teamster, res. second floor, w. Washington.

Harshbarger Miss Sarah, bds. 119 Indiana av.

Harsin Charles B., carpenter, bds. w. s. s. West.

Harsman Henry, teamster, res. 186 Harrison.

Hart Abraham, dealer in rags and old iron, 320 Railroad, res. same.

Hart A. T., tinner, Tutewiler Bros., bds. Macy House.

Hart E. F., clerk, Am. & U. S. Express Co.'s, 34 e. Washington, res. 82 s. Illinois.

Hart James R., driver, Am. Express Co., bds. 82 s. Illinois.

Hart & Mathews, (T. J. H. & C. M.,) contractors and builders, shop 26 Virginia av.

Hart Michael, lab., res. 57 Dougherty.

Hart Robert M., res. 18 Chatham.

Hart T. J., (H. & Mathews,) 26 Virginia av., res. n. Tennessee, beyond city limits.

Hart Thomas, (col.,) lab., res. w. Center.

Hart Thomas, porter, 49 s. Meridian, bds. Webb House.

Hartavig Henry, drayman, res. 128 Davidson.

Hartcourt Theodore, cabinet-maker, res. 287 e. Georgia.

Harter John A., (Nickum, Parrot & H.,) res. 42 n. New Jersey.

Hartford Steam Boiler Inspection and Insurance Co., of Hartford, Conn., Davis & Greene, agts, 27 s. Meridian.

Harting & Bro., (Henry H. & Frederick H.,) brewers, cor Norwood and Bluff rd.

Harting Frederick, (H. & Bros.,) res. 62 Russell.

Harting Henry, (H. & Bros.,) res. 363 s. Illinois.

Hartman Charles, farmer, res. 119 n. New Jersey.

Hartman Christian, lab., res. 279 e. Ohio.

Hartman Christian, lab., res. 80 Railroad.

Hartman Mrs. Ellen, (wid. Charles,) res. 119 n. New Jersey.

Hartman Frederick, wagon-maker, 377 Virginia av., res. 377 e. Georgia.

Hartman Herman, porter, H. F. West & Co., 37 s. Meridian.

Hartman Henry, porter, 68 s. Meridian, res. 330 s. Alabama.

Hartman Henry, works Central depot, res. 122 Union.

Hartman Mathew, plasterer, res. 262 n. Alabama.

Hartman Valentine, cigar-maker, bds. 90 Union.

Hartman William, plasterer, res. over 351 e. Market.

Hartman William, bar-keeper, 13 e. Washington, res. same.

Hartney Patrick, salesman, 89 e. Market, bds. 61 Ft. Wayne av.

Hair Work, all kinds, at 50 South Illinois Street. Card on page 82.

Hartpence James, Everet blk., 20 s. Meridian, bds. cor. Illinois and Market.

Hartpence J. Walter, dealer in cigars and tobacco, 20 s. Meridian, res. cor. Illinois and Market.

Hartpence William R., confectioner, cigars and tobacco, s. e. cor. Georgia and Illinois.

HARTWELL E., chief clerk, Bates House, n. w. cor. Washington and Illinois, res. same.

Hartwig John, porter, 52 s. Meridian, res. 290 s. Alabama.

Harty Michael, lab., res. 447 s. Tennessee.

Hartzler Eliza Ann, res. n. s. National rd., w. White river bridge.

Harvey Alonzo D., traveling agt., Indiana Insurance Co., bds. 89 n. Delaware.

Harvey Alvin C., real estate, bds. 89 n. Delaware.

Harvey Gideon, (col.,) works Buell's Family Medical Depot, res. s. s. Wabash, bet. New Jersey and East.

Harvey James R., brick-layer, res. 250 n. Minerva.

Harvey Miss Marian, teacher, C Primary, Ninth Ward School, bds. 146 n. Meridian.

Harvey J. S., (H. & Vanhorn,) 101 e. Washington, res. 236 e. New York.

Harvey Silas L., dept. county clerk, bds. 230 e. New York.

Harvey Thomas B., physician and surgeon, office 53 e. Market, res. 302 n. Delaware.

HARVEY & VANHORN, (J. S. H. & Menolus H.,) attorneys at law, 101 e. Washington.

Harwood Irwin M., cabinet-maker, res. 67 Madison av.

Haselton Charles, C., C. & I. C. R. R., bds. 58 Benton.

Haselton Charles, shoe-maker, bds. 345 n. Alabama.

Haselton W. H., clerk, U. S. Pension Office, bds. 300 n. Alabama.

Haskit William I., (W. I. H. & Co.,) 14 w. Washington, res. n. Meridian.

HASKIT W. I. & CO., (William I. H., S. A. Craig & E. B. Martindale,) wholesale and retail druggists, 14 w. Washington.

Hasling Leonard, works Sinker & Co., res. 378 e. Washington.

Hasseld Ernest, painter, works Spiegle, Thoms & Co., bds. 98 n. East.

Hasselberry Chris., lab., res. 86 Eddy.

Hasselman Louis W., res. s. w. cor. Meridian and Vermont.

Hasselman Otto U., bds. s. w. cor Meridian and Vermont.

Hastings Edwin L., foreman, Journal Office, res. n. Illinois, bet. First and Second.

Hasson C. E., salesman, 12 e. Washington, res. 504 n. Delaware.

Hasson James, res. n. e. cor. St. Clair and Delaware.

Hasson William, (H., Daily & Co.,) 41 s. Meridian, res. 444 n. Meridian.

Haston C. B., res. 77 e. St. Joseph.

Hasty John, telegraph repairer, bds. 192 Virginia av.

Hatfield Calvin, res. McKernan row.

Hatfield Frederick, lab., res. n. Mississippi, bet. Fourth and Fifth.

Hatfield John B., foreman, U. S. Arsenal.

Hathaway Alfred, (col.,) hostler, Gates & Pray, res. 130 n. East.

Hathaway Frank, lab., National rd., near White river bridge.

Hathaway J. W., student, commercial college, bds. 44 s. Tennessee.

Hathaway John, (col.,) lab., res. near City Hospital.

Hatten Elliott, bds. 144 n. Tennessee.

Hatten John S., meat market, 399 n. Illinois, res. n. e. cor. Mississippi and First.

Hatten Miss Mary J., seamstress, res. e. s. Blake, bet. Washington and New York.

Hatten William, tinner, bds. 144 n. Tennessee.

Hattenbach Joseph, dealer in tobacco and cigars, 51 s. Illinois, bds. 33 w. Maryland.

Hattendorp Henry, merchant tailor, res. 317 e. Washington.

Hattman John George, cook, Capital Restaurant, 14 e. Washington, res. 101 n. Noble, cor. Ohio.

Hauck John, (J. H. & Co.,) 11 w. Washington, res. 373 n. East.

Hauck John & Co.,(John H. & John Darby,) groceries and produce dealers, 11 w. Washington.

Haueisen Frederick G., agt. Mutual Life Insurance Co., res. 78 n. Tennessee.

Haueisen Robert, clerk, 29 w. Washington, bds. 32 n. Mississippi.

Haueisen W., (C. Mayer & Co.,) 29 w. Washington, res. 32 n. Mississippi.

Haufler John, lab., res. Indiana av., near Fall creek.

Haug Michael, saloon, 138 s. Pennsylvania, res. same.

Haugh Adam, capitalist, res. 208 n. Alabama.

Haugh Alex, finisher, B. F. Hays, bds. 244 e. Vermont.

HAUGH B. F. & CO., (Benjamin F. H. & Joseph R. H.,) manfrs. iron railings and jails, 74 s. Pennsylvania.

Haugh Benjamin F., (B. F. H. & Co.,) 74 s. Pennsylvania, res. 504 n. Pennsylvania.

Haugh Charles E., book-binder, bds. 224 e. Vermont.

Haugh Emanuel, machinist, 74 s. Pennsylvania, res. 244 e. Vermont.

Haugh Joseph R., cashr. Citizens' National Bank, res. 175 n. New Jersey.

Haugh William A., machinist, B. F. Haugh, bds. 244 e. Verment.

HAUGHEY THEODORE P., prest. Indianapolis National Bank, n. e. cor. Pennsylvania and Washington, res. 242 n. Pennsylvania.

Haupt Robert, notion store, 151 e. Washington, res. 17 Chatham.

Hausshelt Charles, printer, res. 60 Hosbrook.

Hauk John, confectioner, res. 373 n. East.

Hauk W. V., physician, res. w. s. College av., bet. Forest Home and Christian av.

Hawkey John W., brick-mason, res. 136 Winston.

Hawkey Nathan B., brick-mason, res. 136 Winston.

Hawkins Albert, clerk, Sherman House, bds. same.

Hawkins Benjamin, (col.,) lab., res. 174 Douglas alley.

Hawkins Edward, (col.,) cook, Sherman House.

Hawkins Frank, (col.,) lab., res. Missouri, bet. Indiana av. and North.

Hawkins Mrs., nurse, 422 n. New Jersey.

Hawkins Mary, (col.,) servant, 164 Virginia av.

Hawkins James, Spiegle, Thoms & Co., res. 128 s. East.

Hawkins Jesse F., trader, res. 208 w. Washington.

Hawkins John S., carpenter, C., C. & I. C. R. R. Shop, res. 186 Meek.

HAWKINS WILLIAM M., propr. Sherman House, Louisiana, opp. Union Depot.

Hawkins William M., Jr., clerk, Sherman House, bds. same.

Hawley Miss L. D., matron, Institute of the Blind, res. same.

Hawley Miss P. W., teacher, Institute of the Blind. res. same.

Hawthorn Charles E., retired merchant, res. 132 n. Alabama.

HAY & CO., (Campbell H. & Edward A. Cobb,) drugs and medicines, chemicals and toilet articles, 48 w. Washington.

Hay Campbell, (H. & Co.,) 48 w. Washington, bds. Macy House.

Hay John C., book-keeper, Wm. Sumner & Co., 10 w. Washington, bds. Macy House.

Hay Lawrence G., receiver Sinking Fund of Ind., office New State bldg., cor. Tennessee and Washington, res. 21 s. Pennsylvania.

Hay W. H., (Morrow, Goodwin & H.,) lawyers, room 3, Vinton's blk., res. 222 n. Tennessee.

HAY W. H., state agt. Charter Oak Life Insurance Co., of Hartford, Conn., 6 Blackford's blk., s. e. cor. Washington and Meridian.

Hayden Harry, salesman, 41 s. Meridian, bds. 378 n. Meridian.

Hayden J. J., attorney at law, New State bldg., res. 378 n. Meridian.

Hayden William, (col.,) lab., res. 47 Peru.

Haynes Lewis, traveling agt. Fairbank's scales, 43 and 45 n. Tennessee, bds. Spencer House.

Haynes Miss Lizzie, bds. 39 Elm.

Haynes Mrs. Martha, (wid. James,) res. 39 Elm.

Haynes Philip, (Carter & H.,) 40 w. Washington, res. 169 n. Illinois.

Haynes & Suddith, fish dealers, 107 s. Illinois.

Haynes Thomas, (H. & Suddith,) 107 s. Illinois, bds. Pyle House.

Haynes Wm. H., foreman, Ben Franklin Office, bds. Oriental House.

Hayman S. B., bill-clerk, U. S. and Am. Express Co.'s, 34 e. Washington, bds. 54 s. Pennsylvania.

Haywood Alfred, manufr. artificial limbs, etc., 237 e. Washington, res. same.

Hays Barton S., artist, studio n. Pennsylvania, up-stairs, res. country.

Hays Betty, (col.,) servant, 262 n. Meridian.

Hays E. M., (H., Rosenthal & Co.,) 64 s. Meridian, res. 223 e. Ohio.

Hays Francis M., occupant Deaf and Dumb Asylum.

Hays Isaac C., (Snyder & H.,) 17 n. Meridian, res. 340 n. Alabama.

Hays Margaret, laundress, Bates House.

HAYS, ROSENTHAL & CO., (E. M. H., H. R. & Moses R.,) wholesale clothing, 64 s. Meridian.

Hays S. D., engineer, res. 81 w. McCarty.

Hays Miss Sarah, seamstress, res. Geisendorff, near Geisendorff's Woolen Factory.

Hays Thos., (McLene, MacIntire & H.,) end w. Maryland, res. 83 w. St. Clair.

Hays W. M., agt. Erie Trans. Line, res. 16 e. Michigan.

Haze James, (col.,) lab., res. w. Center.

Hazelrigg H. G., G. M. Masonic Order, res. Lebanon, Ind.

Hazelton Miss Alice, student, N. W. C. University, bds. 383 Massachusetts av.

Hazelton Margaret, over 270 e. Washington.

Hazzard Miss Belle, bds. 79 w. Ohio.

Hazzard John W., bds. 79 w. Ohio.

Hazzard Miles, agt. Security Life Insurance and Annuity Co., bds. Pattison House.

Hazzard Samuel P., western agt. B. & O. R. R., res. 166 n. West.

Headen Samuel, carpenter, bds. 144 n. Tennessee.

Heaf August, propr. New York Dye House, 14 s. Pennsylvania, res. same.

Heaf John, dyer, 14 s. Pennsylvania, res. 55 s. California.

Healy Mrs. Anna, (wid. Jesse,) dressmaker, 35 n. Alabama, res. same.

Healy Oliver, engineer, Ben Franklin Office, res. 180 Dougherty.

Healey Patrick, bar-keeper, Oriental Saloon, bds. 13 Willard.

Hebble John W., propr. Bicking House, 89 s. Illinois.

Hearth John H., carpenter, res. 243 w. New York.

Hearth George L., clerk, bds. 243 w. New York.

Heartline George, teamster, Spiegle, Thoms & Co., bds. 116 s. East.

Heaten Eli, bds. 378 Indiana av.

Heath Carydon. A., traveling agt., J. C. Green & Co., res. 66 n. East.

Heath John, res. 37 Chatham.

Heath Sylvester, student, bds. 37 Chatham.

Hebble Oran Z., bds. 89 s. Illinois.

Heber T. L., clerk, 68 e. Washington, res. cor. Jackson and Christian av.

Hecht Betty, servant, 160 n. Noble.

Hecht Jordan, porter, Hays, Rosental & Co., 64 s. Meridian.

Heck Peter, lab., George Stiltz.

Heck Peter, file-maker, res. 80 s. Delaware.

Heckel Frank, bar-tender, Spencer House Saloon, bds. 280 o. Market.

Heckle Joseph, coach-trimmer, 26 e. Georgia, res. 306 e. Washington.

HECKMAN CHRISTOPHER, propr. City Flouring Mills, e. Washington, near Railroad, res. 413 e. Washington.

Heckman George, cigar-maker, 39 w. Washington, res. 19 Lord.

Heckman William, (col.,) servant, 302 n. Delaware.

Henchon William, carpenter, res. 252 e. South.

Hedge Jesse, works Coburn & Jones, res. Wabash, bet. New Jersey and East.

Hedge Samuel V., occupant Deaf and Dumb Asylum.

Hedges Elijah, foreman, W. W. Weaver, res. 39 n. Illinois.

Hedges Isaac L., revenue inspector liquors, res. country.

Hedges James, res. 140 n. Tennessee.

Hedges Vinton, tinner, 193 w. Washington, res. 140 s. Tennessee.

Hedrich Miss Augustus, servant.

Hedrich George E., cabinet-maker, res. 231 n. Noble.

Hedrich John C., carver, res. 229 n. Noble.

Hedrich Peter, cabinet-maker, res. 231 n. Noble.

Hedrick John, works Spiegle, Thoms & Co., res. 120 n. Noble.

Hedrick Wm. A., salesman, New York Store, bds. Macy House.

Heeb Charles, saloon, 20 n. Delaware.

Heevey Barney, lab., res. n. s. Coburn, bet. Wright and McKernan.

Hefferman N., (wid. John,) res. 490 s. West.

Heide Lewis, butcher, 71 s. Noble, res. 171 n. Noble.

Heider Herman, clerk, res. over 198 e. Washington.

Heider Mrs. Pauline, (wid. Julius,) dressmaker, res. over 198 e. Washington.

Heidenreich Christ., tailor, res. 128 Huron.

HEIDLINGER JOHN A., manfr. and dealer in cigars and tobacco, 39 w. Washington, res. 14 n. Mississippi. See card, page 104.

Heine Henry, shoe-maker, works 32 e. Washington, res. 304 Virginia av.

Hein Charles, works Spiegle, Thoms & Co., res. 160 n. Liberty.

Heim Henry C., res. 552 e. Washington.
Heim Jacob F., res. 552 e. Washington.
Heim John R., res. 552 e. Washington.
Heinbaugh George, sawyer, Union Factory, res. rear 287 n. Noble.
Heinebach Samuel, printer, res. 121 Spring.
Heiner Anthony, railroader, res. 60 s. Noble.
Heiner Barbary, (wid.,) res. 31 Bradshaw.
Heiner John M., clerk, 156 s. Pennsylvania, res. 31 Bradshaw.
Heirler Jacob, I. C. & L. R. R. Shop, res. 97 Bates.
HEISER CHARLES, saloon, 76 s. Delaware, bds. 176 s. Illinois.
Heiser Henry, plasterer, res. 356 n. Noble.
Heiskell W. L., dentist, 67 n. Pennsylvania, bds. Pyle House.
Heitkam Charles, saloon, 80 s. Delaware, res. same.
HEITKAM G. H., merchant tailor and dealer in clothing and furnishing goods, 8 w. Washington, res. n. Winston, near corporation line.
Heitkam Henry, barber, res. 184 s. Delaware.
Heitkam John, Cabinet-Makers' Union, res. 112 Winston.
Heits Louis, blacksmith, res. 62 Hosbrook.
Heizer Cyrus C., township trustee, res. e. city limits.
Heizman Mathias, saw filer, 63 s. Pennsylvania, bds. California House.
Heizer Conrad, carpenter, res. 377 e. Michigan.
Heizer John, lab., res. 350 Railroad.
Heizer Thomas G., butcher, res. 64 California.
Helcher Charles, cabinet-maker, res. 72 Coburn.
Helle Jacob, tinner, works McCreery & Fay, bds. Patterson House.
Helle Louis, house painter, res. 248 s. Pennsylvania.

Helm James H., brick-mason, bds. Ray House.
HELM ADAM, carpenter and builder, res. 206 n. Liberty, cor. North, shop on cor. of alley, in rear of same.
Helm James, brick-layer, bds. 366 w. Washington.
HELM JOHN, drovers and railroad exchange grocery and saloon, 272 Winston.
Helm H. A., stone-mason, res. e. citylimits.
Helms L. A., (Kilgore & H.,) Miller's blk., bds. 60 w. Market.
Helms Thomas M., chair-maker, Spiegle, Thoms & Co., res. 105 n. Noble.
Helmstetter John, tailor, res. 68 s. Illinois.
Helton James, lab., Arsenal, bds. 232 n. Noble.
HELWIG CHARLES, wholesale and retail dealer and manfr. of furniture, 115 and 117 e. Washington, factory cor. New York and Canal, res. 122 w. New York.
Helwig Jacob, shoe-maker, bds. 479 s. Illinois.
Helwig John, porter, Stewart & Morgan, res. 347 n. New Jersey.
Hemily George E., lab., res. 461 s. New Jersey.
Henderson Catharine, student, Female College.
Henderson Charles A., traveling agt., Kiefer & Vinton, 68 s. Meridian, bds. Oriental House.
Henderson George, machinist, bds. 404 s. Illinois.
Henderson Miss Helen, student, Ind. Female College, 146 n. Meridian, bds. same.
Henderson Lawrence, lab., Bellefontaine Shop, res. 23 John.
Henderson William R., student, Hendrick & Hord's Office, bds. 134 n. Meridian.
HENDERSON WILLIAM, prest. Indianapolis Insurance Co., res. 134 n. Meridian.

Smokers' Emporium Complete.   See page 108.

Hendricks A. W. L., res. 125 e. Ohio.

Hendricks Abram W., (H., Hord & Hendricks,) 24½ e. Washington, res. 296 n. Meridian.

HENDRICKS, EDMUNDS & CO., (V. K. H., William E. & T. S. Stone,) jobbers in boots and shoes, 56 s. Meridian.

Hendricks Miss Eliza S., bds. 419 n. Illinois.

Hendricks Emma, servant, 81 w. Vermont.

Hendricks Henry, brakesman, C. I. & C. R. R., bds. 142 s. East.

HENDRICKS, HORD & HENDRICKS, (Thomas A. H., Oscar B. H. & Abram W. Hendricks,) attorneys at law, 24½ e. Washington.

Hendricks Isaac, well-digger, res. 72 Railroad.

Hendricks James C., carpenter, res. 202 n. Blake.

Hendricks M. D., solicitor and teacher of mathematics, National Business College, 24½ e. Washington, bds. 32½ n. Pennsylvania.

Hendricks Miss Sarah, student, Ind. Female College, bds. same.

Hendricks Miss Sarah D., bds. 419 n. Illinois.

Hendricks Thomas A., (H., Hord & Hendricks,) U. S. senator, 24½ e. Washington.

Hendricks V. K., (H., Edmunds & Co.,) 56 s. Meridian, res. 419 n. Illinois.

Hennessy Daniel, lab., Gas Works, res. 276 s. Alabama.

Hennessy John, lab., res. 97 s. New Jersey.

Hennessy John, machinist, bds. Ray House.

Hennessy John, switchman, T. H. R. R., bds. 76 Huron.

Henning Frederick A., barber, s. Illinois, res. 357 e. Market.

Henning Gotlieb F., clerk, p. o., res. Wabash, bet. Liberty and Noble.

Henning Henry R., carpenter, works H. Recker, res. 357 e. Market.

Henninger E., (E. & G. H.,) 110 s. Illinois, res. 398 n. West.

Henninger G., (H. & Bro.,) 115 s. Illinois, res. 398 n. West.

Henninger G. & E., groceries and fancy goods, 115 s. Illinois.

HENRIE JOHN W., supt. Union Depot Dining Hall, w. end depot, res. same.

Henrie Peter, watchman, bds. 286 s. East.

Henry Charles D., cigar-maker, bds. Oriental House.

Henry Elizabeth, servant, 296 n. Meridian.

Henry Marshel G., printer, res. 75 s. Noble.

Henry Lawrence, lab., res. 286 s. East.

Henry J. K., carpenter, res. 253 s. Mississippi.

Henry John, bds. 286 s. East.

Henry Patrick, carpenter, bds. 272 w. Maryland.

Henry Miss Sarah, seamstress, works 146 Davidson, bds. 161 Davidson.

Henshaw Jerry, (col.,) lab., res. 81 s. Missouri.

Hensil John, fireman, B. R. R., bds. 272 Winston.

Henson Charles, clerk, res. 39 e. McCarty.

Henson Hiram, carriage-painter, res. 157 Davidson.

Henson Mrs. Sarah, (wid. Hiram,) res. 8 n. Liberty.

Hensler Henry, grocery and saloon, 301 Massachusetts av., res. same.

Hensler Isaac N., blacksmith, res. s. s. National rd., near Insane Asylum.

Hensley John T., carpenter, res. 381 e. Georgia.

Hensley Miss Susan, seamstress, bds. 174 Virginia av.

Hensf Henry, lab., res. e. Pearl.

Hepp John, clerk, Taylor & Sherwood, res. s. s. Michigan, bet. Liberty and Noble.

Herd Mrs. Gertrude, (wid. Alanson,) bds. Patterson House.

Herder John M., cabinet-maker, res. 3 e. Pearl.

Hereter H., res. 41 Kentucky av.

Hereth Adam, (A. H. & Co.,) 24 n. Delaware, bds. Pyle House.

Hereth Ann, servant, 223 e. Vermont.

Hereth David, bell-boy, Bates House, res. same.

Hereth Henry, treas. Carpenters' Union, res. 241 w. New York.

Hereth J. C. & Bro., (John C. & Adam Hereth,) saddle and harness manfrs., 24 n. Delaware.

Hereth John C., (Hereth & Bro.,) res. 277 n. East.

Hereth John L., carpenter, res. 155 Spring.

Hereth Peter P., carpenter, res. 64 Bates.

Hereth Philip, saddler, works Hereth & Co., res. 161 Davidson.

Hering Philip, piano-tuner, res. 235 e. Vermont.

Herfard Miss B., bds. 220 n. Tennessee.

Hernf Valentine, expressman, res. 140 Davidson.

Herly John, expressman, bds. 22 California.

Herrens Mrs. Mary, (wid.,) res. 38 Dunlop.

Herrman Charles, toll-keeper, w. Washington, res. same.

Herrmann Gabriel, salesman, 26 e. Delaware, bds. 272 e. Market.

Herrington Dennis, lab., res. 166 s. East.

Herrman Ignatius, works Oil Mill, res. 266 Union.

Herrmann Jacob, carpenter, res. 277 Winston.

Herrmann Jacob F., undertaker, 26 s. Delaware, res. 272 e. Market.

Herrington Ellen, dining-room girl, Sherman House, bds. same.

Herrington Mary, dining-room girl, Sherman House, bds. same.

Herron Fred. M., (McLene & H.,) Bates House blk., res. 416 n. Illinois.

Herron Michael, lab., res. 24 w. McCarty.

Hersh Nathan, merchant, res. 139 n. Delaware.

Hershey Wilson S., engineer, Wilkins & Hall's Shop, bds. Nagele House.

Hershman F. M., inmate Deaf and Dumb Asylum.

Hert William, fireman, B. R. R., res. over 248 n. Noble.

Hertsh Ferdinand, works Charles Werbe & Co., bds. 300 e. Market.

Heshbarger Elizabeth, chamber-maid, Wiles House.

Hespelt Charles, (C. H. & Co.,) 150 w. Vermont, res. same.

HESPELT CHARLES & CO.,
National Bakery, 150 w. Vermont, cor. Mississippi.

Hess August, confectionery, res. 288 Madison av.

Hess Augustus, book-binder, Meikel's, res. 126 w. Ohio.

HESS CHARLES,
principal Ind. Normal Academy of Music, 253 s. Meridian, office 35 e. Washington, res. 263 s. Meridian.

Hess Coleman, lab., Sinker's Foundry, res. Madison rd., near city limits.

Hess Henry E., book-keeper, Martin & Hopkins, res. 263 s. Meridian.

Hess Gotfried, baker, res. 126 w. Ohio.

Hess James W., merchant, res. 385 n. Illinois.

Hesse George, varnisher, res. 153 Huron.

Heston Charles, lab., res. 141 n. Noble.

Hesse Henry, varnisher, Burk & Woolens', bds. 298 s. Illinois.

Hessling Barnhard, tailor, 225 Winston, res. same.

Hester Mrs. Permelia, (wid.,) boarding house, 35 Indiana av.

Hester W. W., asst. physician Insane Asylum, two miles w. city, res. same.

Heston Thomas, (col.,) lab., res. 179 Eddy.

Hetherington B. F., (H. & Co.,) 244 s. Pennsylvania, res. 239 s. Delaware.

HETHERINGTON & CO.,
(Benjamin F. H., F. Berner & J. Kindel,) machine works, 244 s. Pennsylvania.

Hetherington Christopher, lab., res. 111 Forrest av.

Hetselgesser Lucian W., cor. Illinois and South, bds. 595 e. Washington.

HETSELGESSER SAMUEL,
south side livery and sale stable, cor. South and Illinois, res. 395 e. Washington.

Hever Theodore, clerk, Quaker Store, bds. 98 Broadway.

Hewes Charles W., Jr., salesman, Bowen, Stewart & Co., res. cor. Michigan and Pennsylvania.

Hewes Charles W., (Rev.,) prest. Indianapolis Female Institute, n. e. cor. Pennsylvania and Meridian.

Hewes W. C., machinist, res. 25 Biddle.

Hewser Catharine, servant, 275 e. New York.

Hewett William, harness-maker, 17 Virginia av., res. 205 Huron.

HEWLING MISS CLARA,
ladies' boarding house, 79 w. South.

Heyer Frank, switchman, B. R. R., res. s. Liberty.

Heyman Henry, (H. & Schwabacher,) 41 s. Delaware, res. 18 s. Mississippi.

Heyman Herman, clerk, 41 s. Delaware, bds. 18 s. Mississippi.

HEYMAN & SCHWABACHER,
(Henry H. & Joseph S.,) wholesale dealers in wines and liquors, 41 s. Delaware.

A New Firm of Coal and Salt Dealers, on page 26.

Hiatte Calvin, inmate Deaf and Dumb Asylum.

Hiatte John, bar-tender, Bates House Saloon, bds. Bates House.

Hiatte Naomi S., inmate Deaf and Dumb Asylum.

Hibbard H. W., freight agt. T. H. & I. R. R., bds. Bates House.

Hibben, Ethelbert C., attorney at law, res. 322 w. New York.--

HIBBEN, TARKINGTON & CO., (James S. H., William C. T., Coleman B. Patterson & Willis S. Webb,) jobbers in dry goods and notions, 112 s. Meridian.

Hibben, James S., (H., Tarkington & Co.,) 112 s. Meridian, res. n. Tennessee.

Hickey John, switchman, res. 23 Willard.

Hickman John W., (R. G. Thomas & Co.,) 155 w. Washington, res. 116 w. Maryland.

Hicks Miss Elizabeth, res. 338 w. North.

Hicks J. M., patent right agt., res. 175 Eddy.

Hicks John C., carpenter, res. Broadway, near city limits.

Hicks Joseph, stone-cutter, res. 30 Grant.

Hicks Mrs. Sarah A., (wid.,) res. 338 w. North.

Hicks William, lab., res. 338 w. North.

Hickson Mrs. Lizzie J., dress-making, room 3, Fatout's blk., w. Washington.

Hier Charles, switchman, J. M. & I. R. R., res. 317 s. Pennsylvania.

Hierd Jacob, gardener, res. Madison rd.

Hiet George, cooper, res. 398 e. Georgia.

Higden William, carpenter, res. 105 Bradshaw.

Higel Christian, carder, Merritt & Coughlen's woolen factory, res. 59 s. California.

Higgins C. B., agt. American Express Co., Union depot.

Higgins Charles J., (Asher, Adams & H.,) 76 e. Market, bds. 427 n. Pennsylvania.

Higgins Monroe, (col.,) waiter, Bates House.

Higgins Thomas, lab., res. 327 s. Delaware.

Higgins William B., silver-plater, 8 w. Washington, res. Morrison, bet. Delaware and Alabama.

Highland Conley, cabinet-maker, W. J. Woolen.

Highstreet John, lab., res. Madison rd., near toll-gate.

Hight William, (col.,) teamster, bds. 179 Douglas alley.

Hild August, lab., Spiegle, Thoms & Co., res. 287 Davidson.

Hild William, iron moulder, Sinker & Co., res. 287 Davidson.

Hildebrand Clayton S., watch-maker, Mc-Lene & Herron, res. 51 Madison.

Hildebrand J. A., bar-keeper, 40 w. Louisiana, bds. Sheridan House.

Hilderbrand Henry, carpenter and builder, res. 308 n. Delaware.

Hilderbrand J. M., stone-cutter, res. 951 n. West.

Hilderbrand J. F., traveling agt., R. P. Crapo.

Hilderbrand John J., stone-cutter, res. s. Noble.

Hilderbrand J. S., (J. H. Vagen & Co.,) 25 w. Washington, res. 51 Madison av.

Hilderbrand William, stone-mason, res. 46 Massachusetts av.

Hilgemeir C., (H. & Co.,) 367 s. Delaware, res. 43 Wyoming.

Hilgemeir & Co., (C. H. & R. Meggs,) groceries and produce, 367 s. Delaware.

Hilkene H. W., harness-maker, bds. Court, bet. East and New Jersey.

Hilkenbach William, shipping clerk, 149 s. Meridian, res. 494 n. Mississippi.

Hilker Henry, gardener, res. 122 e. St. Joseph.

Hill Charles M., store-keeper, Bates House, bds. same.

Hill & Carter, (col.,) (John F. H. & Edward C.,) barbers and hair-dressers, 14 Bates House, n. Illinois.

Hill Miss Ellen, res. 225 n. New Jersey.

Hill Ellison C., (H. & Vinnedge,) 3 w. Washington, res. 477 n. Meridian.

Hill George W., (H. & Wingate,) res. 110 s. East.

Hill James, paper-hanger, bds. 148 Indiana av,

Hill James, groceries and produce, 346 w. Washington, res. same.

Hill James B., (J. F. & Co.,) res. Michigan rd., e. city.

Hill John F., (J. F. H. & Co.,) res. 84 n. Alabama.

Hill John F., (col.,) (H. & Carter,) 14 Bates House, res. 756 n. Tennessee.

Hill John F. & Co., beech-wood nursery, Michigan rd.

Hills Lucian, gen'l freight agt. B. R. R., res. 208 n. Illinois.

Hill Lucy, nurse, n. Illinois.

Hill Matson, book-keeper, Reynolds & Holliday, 13 s. Meridian, bds. Pyle House.

Hill Nathan, hostler, 16 n. Pennsylvania.

Hill S. H., foreman, Journal Office, res. 183 w. New York.

Hill Samuel, stock dealer, res. 50 Cherry.

Hill & Vinnedge, (Ellison C. H. & George W. V.,) dealers in boots and shoes, 3 w. Washington.

Hill & Wingate, (George W. H. & William D. W.,) planing mill and lumber yard, cor. East and Georgia.

Hill William O., insurance agt., res. 40 n. Pennsylvania.

Hilldreth Joseph C., conductor, B. R. R., bds. Palmer House.

Hillman Charles, carpenter, res. 32 Water.

Hillman Frederick, freight receiver, Peru depot, res. 36 Water.

Hillman John, lab., res. 238 Union.

Hillman Michael, nurseryman, res. 793 n. Illinois.

Hillman Sophia, servant, F. Smith, Tennessee, bet. Third and Fourth.

Hillman William, porter, 74 and 76 s. Meridian, res. 226 Bluff rd.

Hillman William, (W. H. & C. K.,) groceries and provisions, 401 Virginia av., res. 36 Water.

Hilt Franklin, coach-blacksmith, res. 159 Spring.

Hilton W. W., boarding-house, 86 s. Illinois.

Hinchman Jesse G., real estate agt., 24½ e. Washington, res. 210 e. Ohio.

Hindman Sarah, (wid,) res. 73 w. Georgia.

Hindman William, bell-boy, Palmer House, bds. same.

Hine Henry, painter, works 152 e. Washington, res. 160 n. Liberty.

Hines Andrew, lab., res. rear 321 Davidson.

Hines Cyrus C., judge Marion co. civil circuit court, office Langsdale's blk., res. 428 n. Tennessee.

Hines Jesse, mason, res. 83 e. St. Clair.

Hinesley A. J., (Budd & H.,) 18 w. Pearl, res. 485 n. Tennessee.

Hinckley David J., auditor, C., C., C. & I. R. R., bds. Oriental House.

HINESLEY WILLIAM,
propr. exchange livery and sale stables, 35 n. Illinois, res. 469 n. Tennessee. See card in advertising department, page 10.

HINESLEY & WOOD,
(William H. & Herman W.,) livery, sale and board stables, 21 w. Pearl.

Hinkley Christopher, spinner, Merritt & Coughlen, w. Washington.

Hinkley Oliver W., book-keeper, Indianapolis Branch Banking Co., res. room 8, Vinton's blk., n. Pennsylvania.

Hinkley Wood, clerk, Fletcher & Sharp's Bank, bds. 109 Virginia av.

Hinniger Michael, machinist, Sinker's.

Hinsdale Miss Emma, (Quimby & H.,) 59 n. Illinois, res. same.

Hinton James S., (col.,) barber, res. 229 n. West.

Hinton Rebecca, servant, 187 n. Alabama.

Hippard George F., salesman, Bowen, Stewart & Co., res. 104 w. Vermont.

Hippard Mrs. Mary A., (wid.,) res. 104 w. Vermont.

Hipler William, varnisher, Spiegle, Thoms & Co., res. 347 n. Noble.

Hipple Edward, carpenter, works Warren Tates' planing mill, res. 136 n. New Jersey.

Hire Frederick, switchman, Bellefontaine Yard, res. cor. Meek and Liberty.

Hirsh L., salesman, 3 Palmer House, bds. 18 Circle.

Hirt Albert, saw gummer, res. 383 s. Illinois.

Hiser William, painter, res. 82 Indiana av.

Hisler John, res. 43 Harrison.

Hiss Sebastian, lab., res. 505 n. Illinois.

Hitchcock Alexander, collector, res. 186 e. St. Joseph.

Hitchen John, shoeing shop, 44 e. Maryland, res. 277 Massachusetts av.

Hitchen Miss Marintha, bds. 439 n. Illinois.

Hitchen Theodore, book-keeper, 146 s. Pennsylvania, res. 267 s. New Jersey.

Hizer Elizabeth, (wid. Edward,) res. cor. Plum and Vine.

Hoag C. J., gen'l agt. Provident Life Ins. and Trust Co., of Philadelphia, over 8 e. Washington.

Hoag Russell, bar-tender, 72 w. Washington, res. 36 Massachusetts av.

A New China Store and Queensware Jobbing House, on page 88.

Hoagland John D., messenger, res. 176 n. Mississippi.

Hoak John, bar-tender, 255 e. Washington, res. same.

Hoalts John, bds. end Virginia av., beyond city limits.

Hobacker Anna, servant, 212 n. Noble.

Hobbs Solomon, clerk, res. 384 n. West.

Hobbs Walter, clerk, 98 e. Washington, bds. 230 s. Alabama.

Hobbs William, engineer, I. C. & L. R. R., bds. Ray House.

Hobmeister Nicholas, grocer, 150 n. Noble, cor. New York, res. same.

Hoche Joseph W., carpenter, res. 112 Madison av.

Hochstetter Christian, German Lutheran minister.

Hockersmith Joseph, agt. Buffalo Scales, res. 301 e. Georgia.

Hockersmith Thomas, conductor, I. & C. R. R., res. 58 Greer.

Hodapp William, piano-maker, works Geo. Trayser, n. e. cor. New York and Davidson, res. 18 s. Delaware.

Hodges Ambrose, carpenter, res. 267 Davidson.

Hodges Andrew, carpenter, res. 354 Railroad.

HODGES JAMES A., actor, Metropolitan Theater, res. 127 Huron.

Hodgson I., architect and supt., room 1, Brown's blk., n. Pennsylvania, res. 433 n. Illinois.

Hodler Gotlieb, porter, 68 s. Meridian, res. 123 e. McCarty.

HOEFGEN EMANUEL, janitor, Gymnasium Billiard Hall, res. 12 Indiana av.

Hoefgeu Samuel B., lawyer, over 20 e. Washington, res. 17½ Virginia av.

Hoefler G. A. R., varnisher, piano factory, 32 s. Meridian, res. 178 s. Illinois. ●

Hoefner August, shoe-maker, 127 w. Washington, res. same.

Hoegus William, carpenter, res. 299 Indiana av.

Hoemeyer Frederick, saw-filer, bds. Concordia House.

Hoeckmann Henry, lab., res. on alley n. Michigan, bet. East and Liberty.

Hoereth John A., carpenter, works John G. Hoereth, res. 474 n. Alabama.

Hoereth John G., carpenter, res. 263 n. East.

Hofacker Charles, lab., Bellefontaine Shop, res. 271 n. Noble.

Hofacker Gotlob, shoe shop, 262 e. Washington, res. same.

Hoff Fred., lab., res. 159 Union.

Hoffeld R. C., cigars and tobacco, 11 n. Pennsylvania, res. 126 Virginia av.

Hoffman Casper, blacksmith, res. 534 n. Alabama.

Hoffman G. W., harness-maker, 24 n. Delaware, bds. 263 e. Washington.

Hoffman Henry, boot-maker, res. 137 Bluff rd.

Hoffmann Michael, (Otto & H.,) res. 131 Bluff rd.

Hoffman M., machinist, Sinker & Co.

Hoffman Samuel B., carpenter, res. McCarty.

Hoffmann Philip, groceries and provisions, cor. Sixth and Tennessee, res. same.

Hofmeister Mrs. Margaret, (wid.,) res. 150 n. Noble.

Hoffmeyer Frederick, driver, M. U. Express Co., 42 and 44 e. Washington, res. 224 n. Davidson.

Hoffmeyer William, breweryman, res. 376 e. New York.

Hoffmire Henry, tailor, res. 195 n. Liberty.

Hoffne Frederick, butcher, res. near White river bridge.

Hogan Bridget, servant, 260 n. Illinois.

Hogan Edward, (Millender & H.,) 27 s. Illinois, bds. 82 s. Illinois.

Hogan Johana, servant, 311 s. Delaware.

Hogan John, lab., res. National rd., e. city limits.

Hogan Mrs. Mary A., dress-maker, 80 s. Illinois, bds. 82 s. Illinois.

Hogan Miss Mary, student, Ind. Female College, 146 n. Meridian, bds. same.

Hogan Philip, tobacconist, bds. Wiles House.

Hogan Mrs. Sarah G., works Capital Tobacco Works, bds. Georgia, bet. Meridian and Illinois.

Hogeland, Durfeel & Conklin, (Israel H., J. F. D. & H. N. C.,) manfrs. of the Hogeland Washing Machine and dealers in patents, 75 s. Illinois.

Hogerty Pat., teamster, res. 261 s. Tennessee.

Hogshire W. R., res. 283 n. Meridian.

Hohl Christopher G., book-keeper, 25 s. Meridian, res. Massachusetts av.

Hohug Charles, insurance agt., res. 120 n. Mississippi.

Hoke Lewis A., salesman, 21 w. Washington, bds. 372 Massachusetts av.

Holahan Patrick, lab., Gas Works, res. 128 s. Tennessee.

Holbrook H. C., (Ryan & H.,) 48 s. Meridian, res. 314 w. New York.

Holbrook Preston, (D. Cady & Co.,) 9 n. Pennsylvania, res. 96 New York, bet. Meridian and Illinois.

Holden George, brakeman, C., C. & I. C. R. R.

Holderman Henry, farmer, res. Shelbyville pike, one-half mile s. corporation.

Holderman John, salesman, H. Daumont, bds. 126 e. Market.

Holderman Montgomery, clerk, H. Daumont, bds. 67 n. Alabama.

Holbrook Thomas E., res. 242 n. Illinois.
Holdman Henry, lab., res. rear 335 n. Noble.
Holdman John, stone-mason, bds. rear 335 n. Noble.
Holl W. H., driver, Spiegle, Thoms & Co., res. Wabash, bet. New Jersey and East.
Holladay Elias G., (H. & Lingenfelter,) 16½ s. Meridian, res. 296 Virginia av.
Holladay & Lingenfelter, real estate agts., 16½ s. Meridian.
Hollahan John, bell boy, Sherman House, bds. same.
Holland Arsa, box-maker, works 162 n. Noble, bds. 166 n. Noble.
Holland Ellen, (col.,) cook, Sherman House,
Holland Calvin R., harness-maker, bds. 126 w. Sixth.
Holland Catharine, (wid.,) bds. 20 California.
Holland Charles W., lab., res. 20 California.
Holland Cris, (col.,) cook, Sherman House.
Holland George B., minister, M. E. Church, res. 126 w. Sixth.
Holland George G., blacksmith, bds. 126 w. Sixth.
Holland George L., painter, res. 44 Coburn.
Holland John, lab., T. H. R. R., res. 303 s. Delaware.
Holland John, clerk, 75 s. West, res. 333 s. Delaware.
Holland John, lab., res. 291 s. East.
Holland John W., (H., Ostermeyer & Co.,) res. 112 n. Pennsylvania.
HOLLAND, OSTERMEYER & Co (John W. H. & Fred. O.,) wholesale grocers and tea dealers, 27 and 29 e. Maryland.
Holland Thomas, lab., C., C. & I. C. R. R. freight house, res. Meek, cor. Ketey.
Holland T. F., book-keeper, 27 and 29 e. Maryland, res. 383 n. Illinois.
Holler Phillip, machinist, works Indiana Central R. R. shops, res. 205 n. Noble.
Holler William, second-hand store, 274 e. Washington, res. same.

HOLLENBECK C. EDWIN, propr. of the Bryant & Stratton Business College and Telegraph Institute, s. e. cor. Washington and Meridian, res. 169 n. Illinois.
Holliday Cort F., (Reynolds & H.,) 13 s. Meridian, res. 131 n. Meridian.
Holliday E. G., gardener, res. end Virginia av, beyond city limits.
Holliday Mrs. Eliza, boarding house, res. 56 w. New York.
Holliday F. T., res. 242 n. Alabama.
Holliday Rev. Fernandes C., res. 131 n. Meridian.
Holliday J. D., salesman, 59 s. Meridian, res. cor. Delaware and St. Clair.
Holliday John H., city editor.
Holliday Wilbur F., (Reynolds & H.,) 13 s. Meridian, res. 131 n. Meridian.
Holliday William, (W. J. H. & Co., Murphy, Johnston & Co.,) 59 s. Meridian, res. 241 n. Meridian.
Holliday Mrs. William A., (wid.,) res. 242 n. Alabama.
Holliday William J. & Co., (William J. H., John W. Murphy, John A. Furgason & Henry W. Voigt,) heavy hardware, iron and steel, 59 s. Meridian.
Hollingsworth Jonathan, farmer, res. 526 n. Mississippi.
Hollingsworth Zeth, wagon-yard, 276 w. Washington, bds. Nagel House.
Hollingsworth & Co.'s National Business College, 24½ e. Washington, Franklin & Capp, principals.
Hollman Herman, butcher, Canal, bet. Maryland and Georgia, res. same.
Hollman Jeremiah, lab., res. 44 Elizabeth.
Hollman Merritt S., agt. Merritt & Co., books and stationery, bds. 322 n. Illinois.
Hollman Mrs., (wid. Jacob,) res. 31 Bradshaw.
Hollow Philip H., stone-mason res. 349 n. Noble.
Holloway William R., (Douglass & Conner,) Journal Co., bds. 287 n. Alabama.

Holloway Allen T., salesman, 127 s. Meridian, bds. cor. Maryland and Tennessee.

Holloway Henry C., (A. Jones & Co.,) 74 and 76 s. Meridian, res. 426 n. Delaware.

Hollowell Amos K., clerk, 34 s. Meridian, bds. 441 n. Mississippi.

Hollowell James, groceries and produce, w. Washington, res. same.

Hollowell James S., (Lukens & H.,) 26 and 28 s. Tennessee, res. 172 Virginia av.

Hollowell N., clerk, bds. Martin House, 33. w. Maryland.

Hollweg Louis, dealer in glass and queensware, 48 s. Meridian, basement.

Holly Henry, works Sinker's Foundry, res. 264 Madison av.

Holly & Schrader, boot and shoe manfrs. and dealers, 85 w. Washington, cor. Tennessee.

Holly Theodore, (H. & Schrader,) 85 w. Washington, res. n. blake.

Holly William, stone-mason, bds. 264 Madison av.

HOLMAN G. G.,
gen'l com. mer., 6 Bates House blk., w. Washington, res. w. s. Weston, third house n. carporation.

Holman J. A., attorney at law, room 12, Talbott & New's blk., n. Pennsylvania, res. Western av., with G. G. Holman.

Holman Merritt S., salesman, 5 e. Washington, res. 322 n. Illinois.

HOLMES ANDREW J.,
secy. Indiana State Board of Agriculture, office State House, res. Rochester, Ind.

Holmes Erastus, painter, res. 37 Rose.

Holmes Henry A., mason, res. 64 s. Calfornia.

Holmes James, carpenter, Bellefontaine shop, bds. 248 Winston.

Holmes Joseph, carpenter, Bellefontaine shop, bds. 248 Winston.

Holmes Jonathan, res. 526 n. Meridian.

Holmes Miss Mollie, lady boarder, 207 s. Tennessee.

Holmes Robert, inmate Deaf and Dumb Asylum.

Holsker Ben., watchman, res. 505 s. Tennessee.

Holsker Henry, lab., bds. 505 s. Tennessee.

Holstein Charles L., attorney at law, 24½ e. Washington, bds. Macy House.

Holt Charles, machinist, bds. 169. s. Tennessee.

Holt Francis, clerk, Indianapolis Gas-Light and Coke Co., cor. Maryland and Pennsylvania.

Holt John R., carpenter, res. 37 Blake.

HOLT MRS. LOUISA M.,
(wid. Joshua F.,) res. n. e. cor. East and Vermont.

Holtsman Israel, lab., res. 205 Kentucky av.

Holtorf J. C., clerk, U. S. and American Express Co.'s, 34 e. Washington, bds. Pyle House.

Holzbacher Augustus, cigar-maker, G. F. Meyer, res. 86 Indiana av.

Holzbacher John, cigar-maker, bds. Concordia House.

Holzerman Louis, clerk, 29 w. Washington, bds. 283 s. Pennsylvania.

Hoskins Robert S., gravel-roofer, res. 271 e. Ohio.

Homan Jeremiah, cistern-builder and cementer, res. 130 s. East.

Homan William J., cistern and cement-builder, 82 w. Washington, res. 130 s. East.

Homburg Henry, baker, res. cor. Union and Pipps.

Homburg K., physician, office 194½ e. Washington, res. same.

Homburg William F., stone-cutter, bds. Macy House.

Home Fire Insurance Co., of Columbus, Ohio, Davis & Green, agts., 27 s. Meridian.

Home of the Friendless, n. Pennsylvania, beyond city limits.

Homudh Frederick, drayman, res. 3 Charles.

Homyer William, slater and tinner, bds. Pearl.

Honberger Christian, carpenter, res. 70 Jackson.

Hondihon Timothy, lab., White River Iron Works, bds. 262 s. Tennessee.

Hook and Ladder Co., n. New Jersey, bet. Washington and New Jersey.

Hooker E. M. B., printer, H. C. Chandler.

Hoover Alexander F., clerk, p. o., res. 135 n. East.

Hoover Asa, (col.,) sexton, Second Presbyterian Church, res. Walnut, bet. Meridian and Illinois.

Hoover Miss Catharine, student, Ind. Female College, 146 n. Meridian, bds. same.

Hoover Daniel, groceries and produce, cor. New York and Douglas, res. same.

Hoover Jacob B., teamster, res. 524 n. Mississippi.

Hoover W., boiler-maker, B. R. R. Shop, bds. 241 n. Liberty.

Hopkins H. C., (Martin & H.,) gen'l ins. agt., res. 224 n. Alabama.

Hopkins James H., foreman N. & J. Braden's book bindery, res. 340 w. Washington.

Hopkins John B., tinner, res. 35 Center.

Hoppe E. B., policeman, fifth ward, res. 251 w. Washington.

Hopp Aaron, lab., res. 298 Kentucky av.

Hoppe George, propr. Lafayette House, 179 s. Meridian.

Hoppe John, tinner, DeRoot & Co., bds. 58 Hosbrook.

Hoppe Jesse, (col.,) porter, Tutewiler Bros.

Hoppe Lewis M., carpenter, res. Jackson, second house n. Street R. R.

Hopson Samuel, lab., 600 n. Illinois.

Hord J. M., real estate agt., 24½ e. Washington, res. 577 n. Tennessee.

Hord Oscar B., (Hendricks, H. & Hendricks,) 24½ e. Washington, res. n. w. cor. New York and California.

HORN, ANDERSON & CO., (M. A. H. & C. J. S. A.,) wholesale and retail grocers and tea dealers, 31 w. Washington.

Horn H. J., with Horn, Anderson & Co., res. 72 n. Mississippi.

Horn M. A., (H. Anderson & Co.,) 31 w. Washington, res. 72 n. Mississippi.

Horian James, wagon-maker, s. s. National rd., near Insane Asylum.

Horney Susan L., matron, Home of the Friendless, bds. same.

Horniday John E., carpenter, res. 365 n. Alabama.

Horniday Thomas B., policeman, first ward, res. 365 n. Alabama.

Hosbrook D. Bates, civil engineer, res. 439 n. Illinois.

Hoshour Samuel K., professor languages, N. W. C. University, res. 172 n. East.

Hoskins Robert S., (Sims, Miller & H.,) Canal, near Kentucky av., res. 271 e. Ohio.

Hosman John W., (D. A. Branson & Co.,) rooms over 23 n. East.

Hoss David, lab., Peru Depot, res. 453 Virginia av.

Hoss J. C., (J. W. Bower & Co.,) 67 and 78 Massachusetts av., bds. 180 e. Vermont.

Hoss Nelson, deputy assessor, res. 35 Cherry.

Hoss George W., supt. public instruction, (Downey, Brouse, Butler & Co.,) res. Jackson, bet. Forrest Home av. and Butler.

Host Frederick, watchman, Planing Mills, res. 475 w. Michigan.

Hottmann John G., cook, Capital Restaurant, res. 101 n. Noble.

Hotz George & Co., (G. H. & W. Pope,) merchant tailors, 124 s. Illinois.

Houck Franklin, blacksmith, cor. Indiana av. and Mississippi.

Houck N. J., blacksmith, bds. 124 s. Meridian.

Hound Mrs. Amelia, (wid. William,) res. 21 n. New Jersey.

Hough Charles, piano action and tune regulator, 159 and 161 e. Washington, res. Pattison House.

Hould Mrs. Mary, (wid.,) res. over 182 e. Washington.

Houpt Reuben, clothier, res. 17 Chatham.

House Ben D., notary public, 16½ e. Washington, res. 193 s. New Jersey.

Houston J. T., (J. C. Green & Co.,) res. 370 n. East.

Houston Robert, res. 370 n. East.

Houts Christeniza, servant, w. s. n. Illinois, bet. Sixth and Seventh.

Hovey J. W., general merchant at Oakland, res. same.

Howard A. B., clerk and telegraph operator, Jeffersonville Depot, bds. 164 Virginia av.

Howard Alice, (col.,) servant, 76 n. New Jersey.

Howard Bridget, wash-woman, Sherman House, bds same.

Howard D. W., res. 56 Thomas.

Howard E., physician and surgeon, 80 s. Illinois, res. 326 n. Illinois.

Howard Miss Elizabeth, boarding house, 298 s. Illinois, res. same.

Howard Frank. A., blacksmith, bds. 343 s. East.

Howard George W., finisher, Osgood, Smith & Co., bds. Ray House.

Howard Edward B., (Smith, H. & Co.,) 26 and 28 w. Washington, bds. Bates House.

Howard James, (col.,) lab. bds. 276 e. North.

Howard Liberty, telegraph operator, res. 164 Virginia av.

Howard Mary, (col.,) servant, res. 8 cor. Noble and Fletcher av.

Howard Robert, (col.,) lab., res. North, bet. Blake and Douglas.

Howard William H., soldier at Arsenal, res. near Arsenal.

Howder Jacob, currier, 78 e. Washington.

Howes Charles A., (H. & Bro.,) 50 cor. Virginia av. and New Jersey, res. 78 Huron.

Howe Edward P., corresponding secy. of Franklin Life Insurance Co., res. 420 n. Pennsylvania.

Howes Henry, (Howes & Bro.,) res. 78 Huron.

Howe Joseph, res. 33 Harrison av.

Howe Robert, 175 w. Ohio.

Howe Miss Louisa, 175 w. Ohio.

Howe William H., real estate agt., res. 33 Harrison av.

Howell Elizabeth saloon and grocery, res. n. s. National rd., one-half mile from bridge.

Howell John, book-keeper, Foster, Wiggins, & Co., res. First, beyond city limits.

Howell Thomas F., res. 376 s. West.

Howes & Bro., (Charles & Henry H.,) meat market, cor. Virginia av. and New Jersey.

Howes Charles H. & Bro., res. 78 Huron.

Howes Henry, (H. & Bro.,) cor. Virginia av. and New Jersey, res. 78 Huron.

Howie James, lab., res. 453 e. Market.

Howie James, pattern-maker, Root's Foundry, res. 127 Stevens.

Howie William, machinist, works B. R. R. Shop, res. 453 e. Market.

Howk Fred., blacksmith, cor. Indiana av. and Mississippi, res. 196 w. Vermont.

Howk Newton J., carriage-maker, bds. 196 w. Vermont.

Howland Miss Alice, student, Ind. Female College, 146 n. Meridian, bds. same.

Howland James C., dental student, 39½ s. Meridian, res. n. Pennsylvania, bet. First and Tinker.

Howland J. A., pressman, Downey, Brouse, Butler & Co, bds. 377 n. East.

HOWLAND JOHN D., clerk, U. S. Circuit and District Courts, room 11, p. o. bldg., n. Pennsylvania, res. 98 w. Vermont.

Howland Livingston, (Hammond & H.,) 20½ n. Delaware, res. 109 Virginia av.

Howland Miss Mary, student, Ind. Female College, bds. 230 n. Tennessee.

Howsley David, (col.,) lab., res. Tennessee, bet. Michigan and Vermont.

Hoyt Miss Clara, teacher, B. & C. Int. first ward school, res. 84 Massachusetts av.

Hoyt Harriet, (wid. Benjamin,) res. 84 Massachusetts av.

Hoyt James, base ballist, bds. Bates House.

HOYLE CLINTON D., pump manufacturer, well and cistern-cleaner, 14 Virginia av., res. 321 e. Ohio.

Hubbard Wm., lab., res. 273 s. Tennessee.

Hubbard William S., (Whitsitt & H.,) res. w. s. Meridian, bet. Second and Third.

Huber Jacob, (Becker & H.,) 77 e. Washington, res. same.

HUBER JACOB, propr. Crystal Palace Saloon and Restaurant, 44 w. Washington, res. same.

Hudson Mrs. E. G. & Tobitha Potter, dress making, 3 Indiana av.

Hudson Miss Mary, bds. 121 w. Vermont.

Hudson James W., res. n. s. Jones, near Dacotah.

Hudson Simon, blacksmith, res. 242 e. Washington.

Hudson Thomas, lab., res. 140 cor. Elm and Grove.

Huebner H. R., (Enos & H.,) architects, 77½ e. Market, res. 346 n. Noble.

HUEGELE JOHN, saloon and billiard hall, 13 e. Washington, res. same. See card, advertising depmt., page 2.

Huett William, harness-maker, res. 100 Huron.

Huey David, bds. 14 s. Delaware.

Huey David E., cabinet-maker, works Spiegle, Thoms & Co., bds. 293 Winston.

Huey Milton S., varnisher, Spiegle, Thoms & Co., res. 293 Winston.

Huey Temperance, (wid. William,) res. 310 e. Louisiana.

Huff Andrew, lab., bds. n. s. National rd., w. White river bridge.

Huff Andrew L., brakesman, B. R. R., res. 331 n. Noble.

Huff David, lab., res. 24 Rose.

HUFF J. T., grocer and provision dealer, 298 n. Pennsylvania, res. same.

Huffer Frank, saddler, 23 s. Meridian, bds. 69 Fletcher av.

Huffer James M., (H. & Son,) 23 s. Meridian, res. 69 Fletcher av.

Huffer John J., (H. & Son,) 23 s. Meridian, bds. 69 Fletcher av.

Huffer & Son, (James M. & John J. H.,) saddlers, 23 s. Meridian.

Huffington M. A., teamster, res. 31 Dougherty.

Huffman John, gardner, res. Shelbyville pike, 1¼ mile s. corporation.

Huffman John T., moulder, Union Novelty Works, res. 332 w. Maryland.

Huffman John H., leather tanner, res. 263 e. Washington.

Huffman Mary C., occupant Deaf and Dumb Asylum.

Huffman Valentine, lab., res. 110 s. Noble.

Huffman William, saddler, res. 263 e. Washington.

Huffmyer William, driver, City Brewery, res. 376 e. New York.

Hufftailing Hiram, freight conductor C., C. & I. C. R. R., bds. 58 Benton.

Hug Mrs. Christine, (wid. Martin,) res. 81 n. New Jersey.

Hug Mrs. Sarah K., (wid. Joseph,) res. 66 n. Noble.

Hughbanks Phebe, (col.,) servant, J. Sloan, 230 n. Tennessee.

Hughes Mrs. Eliza, (wid. Nixon,) res. 161 Davidson.

Hughes Miss Elizabeth, ladies' boarding house, res. 169 n. Noble.

Hughes Isom, engineer, J. M. & I. R. R!, res. 237 s. Delaware.

Hughes Joseph, hostler, 27 s. Pennsylvania, bds. 24 s. Pennsylvania.

Hughes Miss Lizzie, bds. 251 n. Liberty, cor. Michigan.

Hughes Mrs. Missouri, (wid. Leander,) res. 27 n. Noble.

Hughes Samuel A., conductor, C., C. & I. C. R. R., bds. Bates House.

Hugler Samuel, lab., res. rear 313 Massachusetts av.

Hugo Mrs. Charlotte, (wid. Charles,) res. 79 n. Noble.

Hugo Henry August, plasterer, res. 359 s. East.

Hull Absalom D., cigar-maker, res. 179 n. Noble.

Hull Armstrong, carpenter, res. 748 n. Tennessee.

Hully Charles, drayman, res. 146 Union.

Hull Mrs. Jane, (wid.,) res. 725 n. Tennessee.

Hultz August, lab., res. end Virginia av., beyond city limits.

HUME, ADAMS & CO., (James M. H., William L. A. & Edgar J. Foster,) carpets and wall papers, Trade Palace, 26 and 28 w. Washington.

Hume Mrs. Bulah A., (wid.,) res. 6 California.

Hume James M., (H., Adams & Co.,) 26 and 28 w. Washington, res. e. Ohio.

Hume James E., occupant Deaf and Dumb Asylum.

Hume Mrs. Maddison, (wid.,) bds. 673 n. Tennessee.

Hume Newton, paper-hanger, res. 673 n. Tennessee.

Humel George, cigar-maker, bds. 193 s. New Jersey.

Humphrey John, bds. 168 w. Michigan.

Humphrey John W., cooper, res. 294 Indiana av.

Humphrey Miss Rachel, bds. 383 e. Michigan.

Humphreys Charles A., traveling agt., Stewart & Morgan, bds. Palmer House.

Humphreys John, 89 w. Walnut.

Humphreys William W., deputy clerk U. S. Circuit and District Courts, room 11, p. o. bldg., n. Pennsylvania, bds. 126 n. Tennessee.

Hunsinger James, bds. 105 s. New Jersey.

Hunt Albert, machinist, res. 119 w. South.

Hunt Andrew, turner, bds. 390 n. Delaware.

Hunt August, farmer, res. 370 n. Delaware.

HUNT AARON L., auctioneer, 85 e. Washington, res. 294 n. Pennsylvania.

Hunt Bertha, servant, 544 n. Tennessee.

Hunt Charles, engineer, Capitol Tobacco Works, res. 79 w. So.th.

Hunt E. W., printer, res. 165 n. Mississippi.

HUNT CHARLES C., cigars and tobacco, 61 e. Washington, res. 366 s. Alabama.

Hunt Harry C., clerk, 85 e. Washington, bds. 294 n. Pennsylvania.

Hunt Miss Jennie, cloak and dress-maker, Tyler's Bee-Hive, bds. Pyle House, n. Meridian.

Hunt John P., book-keeper, res. 82 w. Market.

Hunt Lemuel C., printer, res. 270 n. Patterson.

Hunt Mary, (wid. John,) res. 520 s. Illinois.

Hunt Walter W., book-keeper, 85 e. Washington, bds. 294 n. Pennsylvania.

Hunt P. G. C., dentist, 76½ e. Market, res. 172 n. Delaware.

Hunter James, (col.,) lab., res. 134 Douglas.

Hunter James H., clerk, Indiana Military Agency, bds. 254 n. Tennessee.

Hunter John L., inmate Deaf and Dumb Asylum.

Hunter Marselis, bds. 340 n. West.

Hunter Ralph, piano planer, 159 and 161 e. Washington, res. 340 n. West.

Hunter Thomas, cooper, res. California, near Helen.

Hunting Edward B., salesman, 108 s. Meridian, bds. Spencer House.

Huntington James M., carpenter, res. 476 n. Mississippi.

Huntley Norton, lab., res. 19 e. North.

Huntzinger James W., student, commercial college.

Hurd Mrs. Clarisa L., (wid. Daniel,) boarding, 144 n. Tennessee.

Hurd John, lab., res. Michigan rd., beyond city limits.

Hurd Mrs. Lizzie, (wid. Eugene,) bds. 269 n. West.

Hurley Frank., teamster, res. 132 Maple.

Hurley J. W., physician and surgeon, res. Shelbyville pike, 1 mile s. corporation.

Hurley Michael, driver, Indiana Transfer Co., res. 23 Elm.

Hurley Patrick, hack-driver, res. 1 cor. North and California.

Hurley Richard, hack-driver, bds. 89 s. Illinois.

Hurley Thomas, teamster, res. cor. Elizabeth and Dunlop.

Hurrle Ignatz, tailor, 168 e. Washington, res. 63 n. Noble.

Hurst Herman, tailor, res. 317 s. Pennsylvania.

Hurt Albert, saw-maker, res. 383 s. Illinois.

Hurt James R., brakeman, L. & C. R. R., res. over 212 e. Washington.

Husbands Lindsay, (col.,) white-washer, res. 167 Indiana av.

Huschild C., (Daily Telegraph Co.,) 16 w. Maryland.

Hust Jacob, butcher, res. 94 Eddy.

Huskinson Thomas, carpenter, res. 145 n. New Jersey.

Hust George C., butcher shop, 576 e. Washington. res. same.

Husted Hiram C., tanner, res. 255 e. McCarty.

Hustis John, engineer, T. H. & I. R. R., bds. Macy House.

Huston C. B., salesman, 66 e. Washington, res. 77 e. St. Joseph.

Huston George W., gen'l stock agt., C. & I. J. and C. H. & D. R. R., cor. McGill and Louisiana.

Huston Fielding, (col.,) lab., res. 230 w. Vermont.

Huston James M., carpenter, res. e. Washington, beyond city limits.

Huston Joel, stationary engineer, res. 552 n. Mississippi.

Huston Mrs. ———, works Journal bindery, res. over 10 Bates House blk.

Hustow Eunice, (wid. Elijah,) res. 283 e. Georgia.

Hutchins H. H., book-keeper, J. K. Sharpe, res. e. Market, beyond city limits.

Hutchins H. S., (Lemon & H. H. S.,) groceries and provisions, 187 w. Washington, res. 386 n. Mississippi.

Hutchinson Charles P., supt. Sentinel establishment, 16½ o. Washington, res. 289 n. New Jersey.

Hutchinson David, engineer, J. M. & I. R. R., res. 192 e. McCarty.

Hutchinson E. B., clerk, office gen'l supt. C. C. & I. C. R. R., bds Macy House.

Hutchinson Miss Ann E., dress-maker, 299 n. East. res. same.

Hutchison B., conductor, C., C. & I. C. R. R., bds. Sherman House.

Hutchison Margaret J., servant, 157 n. Illinois.

HUTCHISON WILLIAM, machinist, Bellefontaine shop, res. 383 Massachusetts av.

Hutson James, res. 66 Jones.

Hutt John, grocer, 323 cor. Noble and Virginia av., res. same.

Hutton Eliza J., seamstress, res. 655 n. Tennessee.

Hutton E. L. & Co., groceries and provisions, 94 n. Illinois.

Hutton Edwin L., (H. E. H. & Co.,) 94 n. Illinois, res. same.

Hutton Geo., carpenter, res. 187 Dougherty.

Hyatt Miss Jennie, seamstress, res. 85 n. Missouri.

Hyatt John, bar-keeper, Bates House, bds. same.

Hyde Rev. N. A., agt. Home Missionary Society, res. 116 n. Alabama.

Hyland James, contractor, res. 730 n. Illinois.

Hyland Michael, contractor, res. 673 n. Illinois.

Hyman Mrs. Helena, dress-maker, 141 n. Delaware, res. same.

Hyman Robinson, traveling agt. for patent gate fastenings, res. 141 n. Delaware.

Hyner Amelia, (wid.,) res. 344 Indiana av.

Hyne William H., moulder, Root's Foundry, res. 257 Coburn.

ICHNER WILLIAM, lab., 240 w. Market.

Iden William, bar-keeper, St. Nicholas Saloon, bds. same.

Idler William, master mechanic, T. H. & I. R. R. shops, res. 171 w. South.

Igo John W., boarding house, 44 s. Tennessee, res. same.

Igoe Martin, lawyer, office 83½ e. Washington, res. 34 Lockerbie.

ILG GEORGE, propr. Union House, cor. Illinois and South.

Iliff Charles E., salesman, 16 e. Washington, bds. 73 n. Alabama.

Iliff Mrs. R. W., (wid. Richard W.,) res. 73 n. Alabama.

Iliff L. S., (R. W. I. & Son,) 24 w. Louisiana, bds. 73 n. Alabama.

Iliff R. W. & Son, confectioners and fruit dealers, 24 w. Louisiana.

Imille Max, house and sign painter, res. 143 s. New Jersey.

ILLINOIS HOUSE, Wm. Essman, propr., 183 s. Illinois.

Ince Annie, (wid.,) res. 228 Massachusetts av.

Ince Thomas, soldier, U. S. Arsenal, res. same.

INDIANA BANKING CO., (F. A. W. Davis, Willis S. Webb, John L. Ketcham, W. W. Woollen, Samuel C. Vance, John P. Banta & William Needham,) bankers, 28 e. Washington.

Indiana Female College, n. Meridian, cor. New York, W. H. Demotte, principal.

INDIANA FIRE INSURANCE CO., room 5 Odd Fellows Hall.

Indiana & Illinois Central Railroad Co., office 36½ s. Meridian.

INDIANA NATIONAL BANK, n. e. cor. Washington and Meridian, George Tousey, prest., D. M. Taylor, cashier.

Indiana Military Agency, William Hanneman, agt., room 8, Gallup's bldg., s. e. cor. Tennessee and Market.

Indiana State Offices, New State bldg., s. w. cor. Washington and Tennessee.

INDIANA TRANSFER CO., 40 e. Maryland, C. W. Bucking, supt. See card in advertising department, page 4.

INDIANAPOLIS BRANCH BANKING CO., Fletcher & Sharp, proprs., organized 1856. Capital $200,000, deposits received and discounts made daily, from 8 A. M. to 4 P. M., office 49 e. Washington, cor. Pennsylvania.

Indianapolis Builders' and Manufacturers' Association, 225 n. Delaware.

Indianapolis Chamber of Commerce, Vinton's blk., opp. p. o.

Indianapolis, Cincinnati and Lafayette Freight Depot and Offices, s. Delaware, cor. Louisiana.

Indianapolis Coal & Mining Co., 19 Circle N. Carpenter, supt.

INDIANA DIRECTORY PUBLISHING OFFICE, 16½ e. Washington, Logan & Co., publishers. See card.

Indianapolis Female Bible Society, office at Todd, Carmichael & Williams', Glenn's blk.

Indianapolis Female Institute, n. e. cor. Pennsylvania and Michigan.

INDIANAPOLIS GAS LIGHT & COKE CO., s. Pennsylvania, cor. Louisiana, office cor. Maryland and Pennsylvania.

INDIANAPOLIS GYMNASIUM, Billiard Hall, cor. Meridian and Maryland.

Read Logan's History of Indianapolis, in after part of this book.

INDIANAPOLIS INSURANCE CO., office in Company's bldg., cor. Virginia av. and Pennsylvania.

Indianapolis Journal, daily and weekly, Douglass & Conner, proprs. and publishers, Journal bldg., e. Market, cor. Circle.

Indianapolis Mission Sunday School Chapel, cor. Union and Madison av.

INDIANAPOLIS NATIONAL BANK, n. e. cor. Washington and Pennsylvania, Odd Fellows Hall, Theodore P. Haughey, prest., F. Williams, cashr.

INDIANAPOLIS ROLLING MILL COMPANY, office Blake's row, John M. Lord, prest. and supt.

INDIANAPOLIS SENTINEL, daily and weekly, office 16½ e. Washington, R. J. Bright, publisher and propr.

Indianapolis Tobacco Works, 87 e. South, R. May & Co., proprs.

Indianapolis and Vincennes Railroad Co., office cor. Illinois and Kentucky av., A. E. Burnside, prest., D. R. Larned, secy. and treas., C. Fletcher, ass't secy. and treas., J. P. Harper, chief engineer.

INDIANAPOLIS WAGON AND AGRICULTURAL WORKS, office and manufactory 172 s. Tennessee, W. H. Jones, prest.

Indicut Miss Lizzie, (col.,) bds. 66 Missouri.

Indles John, carpenter, res. 14 Jackson.

Ingerson Charles, brakeman, C., C. & I. C. R. R., bds. 58 Benton.

Ingersoll B. F., scroll sawyer, Builders' & Manufactrers' Society, res. 129 e. South.

Ingersoll Charles, engineer, 159 and 161 e. Washington, res. 224 e. Market.

Ingersoll E. P., minister, res. 383 n. Pennsylvania.

Ingersoll Miss Mary, third ass't, City High School, bds. 271 Virginia av.

Ingersoll Miss Selma, teacher, bds. 271 Virginia av.

Inglas John, employee C., C. & I. C. R. R. Shops, bds. n. e. cor. Georgia and Liberty.

Ingle J. O., telegraph-operator, 11 s. Meridian, res. 75 Kentucky av.

Ingle Mark W., (Masten & I.,) 28 s. Meridian, res. 126 n. Tennessee.

Inglehart Frank, clerk, 92 e. Washington, bds. same.

Ingleking Fred., driver, res. 143 Bluff rd.

Ingleking William, driver, res. 208 Union.

Ingraham C. B., photograph gallery, 32½ e. Washington, res. same.

Ingraham J. P. T., (Rev.,) pastor, Christ Church, res. 65 Circle.

Inglicker John, lab., res. 453 s. Missouri.

Insprucker John A., shoe-maker, bds. 237 w. Ohio.

Inwalle Benjamin J., saloon, 367 Virginia av., res. same.

Inwall Henry, bar-tender, res. 3 Rabb's blk., e. Washington.

Ireland William H., stair-builder, bds. 195 s. Alabama.

Irick Adam, gas-fitter, bds. 18 w. Georgia.

Irick Henry, soldier, U. S. Arsenal.

Irick Joseph, stone-cutter, res. 167 Union.

Irick M. C., carriage-painter, 123 e. Washington, bds. 210 n. Winston.

Irick Morris, blacksmith, res. 210 Winston.

Irick William, printer, bds. 18 w. Georgia.

Irick William H., res. 326 n. New Jersey.

Irons Mrs. Catharine, (wid. Steven,) res. 193 w. Maryland.

Irons Henry T., book-binder, W. J. Braden, res. 193 w. Maryland.

Irving A. B., (I. Bros.,) 12 n. Pennsylvania, res. 195 cor. New York and Massachusetts av.

Irving Brothers, (C. L. & A. B. I.,) dealers in pianos, 12 n. Pennsylvania.

Irving Benjamin, teamster, res. National rd., w. White river bridge.

Irving C. L., (I. Bros.,) 12 n. Pennsylvania, res. 283 n. Alabama.

Irving D. K., salesman, New York Store, bds. 58 s. Pennsylvania.

Irwin Joseph W., carpenter, res. Eighth, bet. Railroad and Lenox.

Irwin Roll C., compositor, Downey, Brouse, Butler & Co., bds. Mrs. Reed, n. Pennsylvania.

Irwin W. B., carriage-blacksmith, 123 e. Washington, bds. 35 Circle.

Isensee Albert, locksmith and bell-hanger, res. 72 n. California.

Isensee Miss Sarah, bds. 321 n. Liberty.

Isgrigg & Bracken, (James A. I. & Thomas E. B.,) lumber yard, 180 w. Market.

Isgrigg James A., (I. & Bracken,) 180 w. Market, res. 413 w. New York.

Ishmell Frederick, lab., res. 43 Dacotah.

Iska Gustavus, lab., Washington Foundry, res. 427 Virginia av.

Iske William, packer, 16 w. Washington.

Ittenbach Frank, (Smith, I. & Co.,) bds. 140 Madison av.

Ittenbach Gerard, (Smith, I. & Co..) res. 140 Madison av.

Ivory Peter, teamster, res. 427 e. St. Clair.

JACK CHARLES, engineer, McLene, MacIntire & Hays, bds. 302 w. Maryland.

Jack Charles T., engineer, bds. 114 s. Noble.

Jack M. W., boarding house, 74 n. Pennsylvania.

Jackes Daniel, fireman, C. I. & C. R. R., bds. 142 s. East.

Jackman Herman, tailor, res. 110 Virginia av.

Jackson Alexis M., trader, bds. 89 n. Delaware.

Jackson Andrew, (col.,) servant, 262 n. Meridian.

Jackson Andrew, egg-packer, res. 449 n. Mississippi.

Jackson Charles P., res. 17½ Virginia av.

Jackson James, section-master, J. M. & I. R. R., res. 241 Union.

Jackson John, clerk, bds. 223 w. Ohio.

Jackson Mrs. Rachel, (col.,) wash-women, res. 207 w. North.

Jackson Sarah, (wid. Jesse,) res. n. s. National rd., half mile from river bridge.

Jackson Thomas, (Van Camp, J. & Co.,) res. 223 w. Ohio.

Jackson Thomas, currier, Mooney & Co., res. cor. alley and Tennessee, bet. Georgia and Maryland.

Jackson William, slate-roofer, res. 186 Davidson.

Jackson Willis, (col.,) servant, Col. D. G. Rose, res. 126 w. Michigan.

JACKSON WILLIAM N., ticket agt., Union Depot, bds. 82 w. North.

Jacob Israel, (wid. Joseph,) res. 156 n. East.

Jacobs Charles P., (Barbour & J.,) 14 n. Delaware, res. 77 w. second.

Jacobs Mrs. Elizabeth, (wid. William,) res. Court, bet. East and New Jersey.

Jacobs Frederick, res. 369 s. Delaware.

Jacobs Joseph, wholesale notions, over 6 w. Louisiana, res. 156 n. East.

Jacobs Milton, engineer, Journal office, bds. 98 n. East.

Jacobs Richard, trunk-maker, res. 440 Virginia av.

Jacobs Stephen, trunk-maker, bds. 440 Virginia av.

Jacoli Frederick, meat shop, 367 s. Delaware, res. same.

Jacobs Milton, bds. 145 s. New Jersey.

Jacobs Valentine, saloon-keeper res. 145 s. New Jersey.

Jacoby David R., patent-right agt., res. 35 w. Georgia.

Jacoby Jerome, confectioner, 26 s. Meridian, res. 35 w. Georgia.

Jacques Sarah, (wid.,) res. 76 Massachusetts av.

Jaire Alexander, telegraph operator, bds. e. Georgia.

James Miss Amanda A., res. cor. Illinois and Seventh.

James Miss Betty, servant, Ray House.

James Elizabeth, waiter, Dining Room Ray House.

James E. M., (col.,) driver, McCreery & Fay, res. cor. Vermont and West.

James Frank., (col.,) lab., res. 133 s. Tennessee.

James J. W., shoe-maker, res. 620 n. Illinois.

James Miss Lou, res. 180 Virginia av.

James M. C., salesman, New York Store, res. 69 w. New York.

James Oliver, plasterer, res. 225 w. Vermont.

James Robert, (col.,) lab., res. 86 n. Missouri.

James Seth C., marble-worker, works 136 s. Meridian, res. s. Alabama.

JAMES & SPEER, (Thomas S. J. & H. P. S.,) marble dealers, 136 s. Meridian.

James S. C., marble-cutter, res. 80 Virginia av.

James Thomas S., (J. & Speer,) 136 s. Meridian, bds. Ray House.

James William, (col.,) lab.; res. Camp Carrington.

James William B., switchman Union R. R. Co., bds 127 s. New Jersey.

James W. T., res. 35 Fletcher av.

JAMESON ALEX. C., secy. Indianapolis Insurance Co., res. 287 n. Delaware.

Jameson Frank, porter, Palmer House.

Jameson & Funkhouser, (P. H. J. & D. F.,) physicians and surgeons, 19 s. Meridian.

Jameson L. H., wood-measurer, res. 139 w. South.

Jameson Patrick H., (J. & Funkhouser,) 19 s. Meridian, res. 249 n. Alabama.

Jameson Richard, res. n. s. National rd., w. White river bridge.

Janeway Arthur, miller, res. 312 w. Washington.

Janeway John, pattern-maker, Moore & Frink, res. in rear of same.

Jaritz Thomas, painter, bds. 28 Kentucky av.

Jarrell Miss Frances E., dress and cloak-maker, 36 n. Ills., bds. 148 Indiana av.

Jasper Aldridge, (col.,) lab., res. Second, bet. Howard and Lafayette R. R.

Jaybert Fred., lab. res. 228 Union.

Jeffers James T., soldier U. S. Arsenal, res. same.

Jeffers William, lab., r. rear 74 s. West.

JEFFERS WILLIAM A., propr. City Bath House and Barber Shop, 16 w. Pearl, res. same.

Jefferson Benjamin, (col.,) carpenter, res. w. Center.

Jeffersonville, Madison & Indianapolis Freight Depot and Office, South, bet. Pennsylvania and Delaware.

Jefferson Edmund, broom-maker, bds. 82 e. St. Clair.

Jefferson House, s. w. cor. South and Pennsylvania, John H. Gruenert, propr.

Jefferson Robert, carpenter, res. 247 n. Minerva.

Jeffreys Miss Cordelia, seamstress, bds 299 e. Merrill.

Jeffries Mrs. Mary, (wid. John,) res. Madison rd., near toll-gate.

Jehrling John P., cleaner and repairer of clothes, 3 Virginia av., res. 125 e. McCarty.

Jemison James, lab., res. 8 Hosbrook.

Jemison John, harness and saddlery, 180 w. Washington, res. same.

Jenken Samuel W., book-keeper, Lukens & Hollowell, res. 165 Huron.

Jenkins A. W., res. 72 Massachusetts av.

Jenkins Charles W., conductor on switch track Ind. Central R. R., res. 294 e. Market.

Jenkins Dennis H., messenger American Express, res. 331 s. Meridian.

Jenkins Ebenezer, painter, 9 Massachusetts av., res. 129 e. North.

Jenkins H. E., painter, bds. 11 n. West.

Jenkins James, blacksmith, bds. 169 s. Tennessee.

Jenkins John, moulder, res. 294 e. Market.

Jenkins John R., painter, works 9 Massachusetts av., res. 129 e. North.

Jenkins J. W., painter, bds. 127 e. North.

Jenkins Mrs. Julia A., res. alley bet. Fourth and Fifth, near Lafayette R. R.

Jenkins Nellie, servant, 233 E. Michigan.

Jenkins Rebecca, servant, 254 s. Alabama.

Jenkins Mrs. Sarah, (wid. Nathaniel,) res. 166 e. Market.

Jenkins Thomas, (col.,) res. 157 Maple.

Jenkins William F., farmer, res. 512 n. Illinois.

Jenkins William J., tobacconist, J. Cahill & Co., bds. Ray House.

Jenison Alexander F., (J. A. F. & J. H.,) 19 n. Illinois, res. 19 w. Ohio.

JENISON A. F. & J. H., (Alexander F. & John H.,) groceries and provisions, 19 n. Illinois.

Jenison George M., (George M. J. & Co.,) 24 e. Washington, res. 356 n. Illinois.

JENISON GEORGE M. & CO., watches, jewelry, silver-ware and watch-makers' tools, 24 e. Washington. See card, back of title-page.

Jenison John H., (Jenison A. F. & J. H.,) 19 n. Illinois, res. 19 w. Ohio.

Jenks C. J., brakesman, J., M. & I. R. R., bds. Ray House.

Jenks George N., engineer, I. & C. R. R., res. n. s. e. Georgia.

Jenks Susan E., occupant Deaf and Dumb Asylum.

Jennings Benjamin, works at J. Cahall & Co.'s. Ray House.

Jennings Benjamin F., works at J. Cahall & Co.'s, bds. 23 s. Mississippi.

Jennings Patrick, school-teacher, res. 248 Davidson.

Jennings Presly, butcher, res. cor. Morrison and Delaware.

Jennings William T., foreman, Munson & Johnson, res. 277 w. Michigan.

Jessie Samuel, fireman, J., M. & I. R. R., bds. 146 e. McCarty.

Jewish Synagogue, Market, near East.

Jillson J. M., clerk, C., C., C. & I. R. R., bds. Pyle House.

Jimber Henry, teamster, res. 132 Bluff rd.

Jines Henry, (col.,) 247 n. Meridian.

Jines William, lab., res. 83 n. Missouri.

Joachimi August, res. 26 Biddle.

Joachimi Julius A., cigar-maker, res. 26 Biddle.

Job Alzier, wagon-maker, res. 99 Huron.

Joeke Adolph, teamster, res. cor. Cedar and Elm.

Johns Charles, agt. Soldiers' Relief Fund, res. 273 n. Mississippi.

Johns Samuel, bds. 392 n. Alabama.

Johns Samuel E., book-binder, Wm. Sheets, res. 181 n. Delaware.

Johns N., inmate Deaf and Dumb Asylum.

Johnson Aaron R., huckster in provisions, res. 127 Indiana av.

Johnson Adelaide, occupant Deaf and Dumb Asylum.

Johnson Albert, clerk, bds. 167 w. Maryland.

Johnson Albert, tobacconist, bds. Ray House, e. South.

Johnson Alexander T., carpenter, res. 394 n. West.

Johnson Andy, fireman, Sherman House, bds. same.

Johnson Angeline, occupant Deaf and Dumb Asylum.

Johnson Mrs. Ann, milliner and dressmaker, res. 251 s. Alabama.

Johnson Miss Ann M., res. 57 cor. Noble and Huron.

Johnson A. W., carpenter, res. 57 cor. Noble and Huron.

Johnson Benjamin, lab., res. 279 s. Tennessee.

Johnson Benjamin, (col.,) lab., res. cor. Heward and Second.

Johnson Benjamin F., carpenter, res. 800 n. Tennessee.

Johnson B. F., hack-driver, res. 331 n. Blake.

Johnson Berry N., salesman, 112 s. Meridian, bds. Sherman House.

Johnson Miss Carrie, bds. 139 w. Market.

Johnson Charles, (col.,) porter, H. C. Chandler, bds. 144 n. Douglas.

Johnson Charles R., fish-dealer, 341 s. Meridian, res. 476 s. Illinois.

Johnson Christ., lab., bds. 172 Madison av.

Johnson Mrs. Cynthiana, res. 434 w. North.

Johnson C. F., inmate Deaf and Dumb Asylum.

Johnson Edmund C., res. 341 s. Meridian.

Johnson Edward, lawyer, res. 474 n. Pennsylvania.

Johnson Edward, (col.,) lab., res. 100 Indiana av.

Johnson Miss Emily, ass't teacher City High School, bds. 138 Massachusetts av.

Johnson Edward, (col.,) servant, 222 e. South.

Johnson Edward, book-peddler, bds. Wiles House.

Johnson Mrs. Elizabeth, (wid. John B.,) res. 167 w. Maryland.

Johnson Elizabeth M., occupant Deaf and Dumb Asylum.

Johnson Mrs. Ellen, (wid. T. B.,) res. 27 Massachusetts av.

Johnson Emily Jane,, (col.,) bds. 141 n. Bright.

Johnson Gabriel, (col.,) lab., res. cor. Sixth and Lafayette R. R.

Johnson George H., clerk, 64 e. Washington, res. 370 s. Alabama.

Johnson G. W., fireman, J., M. & I. R. R., bds. Ray House.

Johnson Henrietta, (col.,) res. 224 Huron.

Johnson Isaac I., notary public and lawyer, 17½ w. Washingtrn, bds. Palmer House.

Johnson James, (col.,) porter, C. M. Lunt's office, bds. Wiles House.

Johnson James, carpenter, res. 394 n.West.

JOHNSON JAMES, carpenter, bds. 69 w. Market.

Johnson James A., carpenter, res. 476 s. Illinois.

Johnson James W., teamster, bds. 154 s. New Jersey.

Johnson Jennie Miss, dress-maker, 68 s. Illinois, res. same.

Johnson Jesse, with H. S. Prier, bds. 14 e. Washington.

Johnson John, tailor, res. 311 Massachusetts av.

Johnson John, (col.,) barber, 303 e. Washington, res. same.

Johnson John, (col.,) porter, 14 Bates House, bds. Douglas alley.

Johnson John E., gardener, Hill's nurseries, Michigan rd., res. same.

Johnson John S., carpenter, res. 309 s. Meridian.

Johnson John W., writing teacher, Purdy's College, res. 491 n. Mississippi.

Johnson J. B., bridge carpenter, Vincennes R. R., bds. 103 s. New Jersey.
Johnson J. F., tobacconist, bds. Ray House, e. South.
Johnson Joseph, carpenter, bds. 183 s. Illinois.
Johnson Julia, (col.,) servant, 564 n. Illinois.
Johnson Julius W., plasterer and bricklayer, res. 95 Benton.
Johnson Lewis, (col.,) lab., res. 224 n. Missouri.
Johnson Lizzie, (col.,) servant, 222 e. South.
Johnson Miss Lou. J., bds. 341 s. Meridian.
Johnson Lucy, (col.,) cook, Wiles House.
Johnson Marquis L.,(J. & Turner,) 7 Blackford's blk., s. e. cor. Washington and Meridian, res. 546 n. Illinois.
Johnson Miss Martha G., bds. 127 Indiana av.
Johnson Mrs. Mary, (wid. John,) res. 313 Massachusetts av.
Johnson Mrs. Mary A., (wid. Thomas,) res. 175 e. Louisiana.
Johnson Mary A.,(col.,) (wid.,)'res. Eighth, bet. Lenox and Knox.
Johnson Mary F., (wid. T. H.,) res. 23 e. North.
Johnson Milo, carpenter, res. 98 Broadway.
Johnson M. L., inmate Deaf and Dumb Asylum.
Johnson Noah, (col.,) lab., res. camp Carrington.
Johnson Miss Oregon, dress-maker, works 172 e. Washington, res. 39 w. McCarty.
Johnson Peter W. H., (col.,) lab., res. 7 Athon.
Johnson Philip A., carpenter, works Eden's Shop, n. Delaware, res. 256 n. East.
Johnson Quillis, tinner, cor. Maria and Smith.
Johnson Isaac, (col.,) waiter, Bates House.
Johnson Rachel, (wid., col.,) res. 270 Massachusetts av.
Johnson Riley, occupant Deaf and Dumb Asylum.
Johnson Robert, clerk, M. U. Express Co., bds. 27 Massachusetts av.
Johnson Robt. B., tabaconist, J. Cahall & Co., bds. 341 s. Meridian.
Johnson Miss R., res. 57 cor. Noble and Huron.
Johnson Samuel, (Munson & Johnson,) res. 220 n. New Jersey.
Johnson Samuel L., compositor, Sentinel news room, res. 142 n. Mississippi.
Johnson Mrs. Sarah, (col.,) wash-women, res. 149 n. Bright.
Johnson Mrs. Sarah M., (wid. James B.,) seamstress, 135 n. Noble, res. same.

Johnson Richard, res. 471 s. Illinois.
Johnson Sidney H., contractor, res. n. w. cor. St. Joseph and New Jersey.
Johnson Sophia, (col.,) servant, 287 e. Market.
Johnson Miss Susan, school-teacher, bds. e. s. Liberty, bet. Meek and Georgia.
Johnson Thomas C., (Hamlin & J.,) 62½ e. Washington, res. 81 e. Michigan.
Johnson T. E., attorney at law and notary public, Blackford's blk., s. e. cor. Washington and Meridian, res. 474 n. Pennsylvania.
JOHNSON & TURNER, (Marquis L. J. & A. H. T.,) gen'l agts., Continental Life Insurance Co., of New York, 7 Blackford's blk., over First National Bank, s. e. cor. Washington and Meridian.
Johnson Warren, (col.,) lab., res. rear 420 e. St. Clair.
Johnson Wesley, moulder, works D. Root & Co., res. 318 s. Delaware.
Johnson William, (col.,) waiter, Wiles House.
Johnson William, (col.,) lab., res. 160 Douglas alley.
Johnson William, farmer, res. 332 Blake.
Johnson William, hack-driver, res. 236 n. Blake.
Johnson William, farmer, res. 328 n. Blake.
Johnson William F., carpenter, res. 374 n. Delaware.
Johnson William G., clerk, 68 e. Washington, res. Orphan Asylum.
Johnson William H., (col.,) lab., res. 249 n. West.
Johnson William H. H., real estate agt., res. 38 w. North.
Johnson William S., tailor, over 30 w. Washington, res. 315 e. Ohio.
Johnson William S., farmer, s. s. National rd., near Insane Asylum.
Johnson W. Scott, bds. 328 n. Illinois.
Johnson ———, mail carrier, bds. 774 n. Tennessee.
Johnston Charles, bds. 21 Fletcher av.
Johnston George H., res. 21 Fletcher av.
Johnston George W., clerk, People's Dispatch Fast Freight Line, 42 and 44 e. Washington, bds. Pyle House.
Johnston House, n. s. National rd., two miles w. river bridge.
Johnston John C., bds. 320 n. Alabama.
Johnston John F., surgeon dentist, 39½ s. Meridian, res. n. Pennsylvania, bet. First and Tinker.
Johnston John H., lawyer, res. 320 n. Alabama.
Johnston Lewis, (col.,) hostler, 10 e. Pearl, res. 224 n. Mississippi.
Johnston Robert, clerk, supts. office M. U. Express Co., res. Massachusetts av.

Johnston R. G., clerk, pension office, bds. 38 w. St. Clair.

Johnston Samuel A., (Munson & J.,) 62 e. Washington, res. 220 n. New Jersey.

Johnston William J., (Munson & J.,) 62 e. Washington, res. 86 e. Vermont.

Johnston William W., (Murphy, J. & Co.,) 49 s. Meridian, res. 546 n. Meridian.

Jolley James, night-watchman, I. C. & L. R. R. Shop, res. 86 Bates.

Jolly John, lab., res. 14 Lord.

Jolly William, brakesman, I. & C. R. R., res. 24 Lord.

Jones Alexander, (col.,) farmer, res. 824 n. Illinois.

Jones Aquilla, Sr., (A. J. & Co.,) treas. Indianapolis Rolling Mill Co., res. 187 n. Pennsylvania.

Jones Aquilla, Jr., (Vinnedge, J. & Co.,) 66 s. Meridian, res. 187 n. Pennsylvania.

JONES A. & CO., (Aquilla J., H. Clay, E. P. J., John W. J. & H. Holloway,) wholesale grocers, 74 and 76 s. Meridian. See card, page 30.

Jones Barton D., (Anderson & J.,) 19 n. Meridian, res. 188 n. Delaware.

Jones Benjamin, (col.,) servant, 498 n. Illinois.

Jones Benjamin F., clerk, 74 and 76 s. Meridian, res. 187 n. Pennsylvania.

Jones Casper M., Jr., clerk, 188 e. Washington, bds. 2 s. Alabama.

Jones Charles, (col.,) lab., res. n. Minerva.

Jones C. H., (col.,) cook, Rockwell's Dining Rooms.

JONES & CHILD, (L. M. B. J. & M. C., Jr.,) agts. Winnesheik Fire Insurance Co.

Jones Curtis, salesman, res. 130 e. St. Joseph.

Jones Edward B., engineer, B. R. R. res. cor. Massachusetts av. and Second.

Jones Edward M., (col.,) teamster, res. 205 n. West.

Jones Evan, expressman, res. 131 Union.

Jones Elizabeth M., occupant Deaf and Dumb Asylum.

Jones Elisha P., (A. J. & Co.,) 74 and 76 s. Meridian, res. 187 n. Pennsylvania.

Jones Flemming J., broom-maker, res. cor. Illinois and Seventh.

Jones Geo. W., farmer, res. 787 n. Illinois.

Jones Griffin B., carpenter, res. 19 Short.

JONES, HALL & BROWN, (John W. J., Nathan H. & C. W. B.,) barbers and hair dressers, 16 s. Meridian.

Jones Henry H., (col.,) barber, res. w. s. Douglas, bet. Washington and New York.

JONES HENRY G., photographer with B. L. Rider, 16½ e. Washington, bds. 60 w. Market. See card.

Jones Hester A., (wid. Wm.,) res. 395 s. West.

Jones Horace, telegraph-operator, T. H. & I. R. R. Freight Depot, res. 157 n. Alabama.

Jones Jesse, gen'l agency business, 17½ w. Washington, res. 488 n. Illinois.

Jones John, (col.,) lab., bds. end Fletcher av., beyond city limits.

Jones John, hostler, 16 n. Pennsylvania.

Jones John G., machine agt., res. 119 Indiana av.

Jones John L., bds. 430 n. New Jersey.

Jones John P., traveling agt., res. 157 n. Alabama.

Jones John P., lab., res. end Virginia av., beyond city limits.

Jones J. P., clerk, 13 w. Maryland, res. 235 e. South.

Jones John S., carpenter, res. end Virginia av.

Jones John W., (A. J. & Co.,) 74 and 76 s. Meridian, bds. 187 n. Pennsylvania.

Jones John W., teamster, res. 412 s. West.

Jones John W., ((col.,) (J., Hall & Brown,) 16 s., Meridian, res. n. Mississippi.

Jones John W., yard-master T. H. & I. R. R. 132 w. First.

George M. Jenison & Co.   Card on back of title page.

Jones J. W., resides 51 Maple.

Jones Joseph, barber, works 143 w. Washington, res. same, up-stairs.

Jones Julius, (Gilky & J.,) 36 Kentucky av., bds. 69 w. Market.

Jones Lemuel, carpenter, res. 70 n. Delaware.

Jones L. M. B., (J. & Childs,) 25 w. Washington, bds. Bates House.

Jones Miss Lizzie A., bds. 131 Union.

Jones L. W., salesman, 123 s. Meridian, bds. Sherman House.

Jones Miss Maria H., teacher, branch of Eighth Ward school, res. 201 n. Liberty.

Jones Marshall, (col.,) teamster. res. 462 s. Tennessee.

Jones Martha, (col.,) servant 434 n. Delaware.

Jones Mary, laundress, Bates House.

Jones Mrs. Mary A., (wid. Cadwallader,) res. 188 s. Mississippi.

Jones Robert, (col.,) barber, res. 228 w. Vermont.

Jones Robert, (col.,) servant, 133 w. New York.

Jones Robert A., stair-builder, 232 Winston, res. 299 Winston.

Jones R. L., (col.,) barber, 14 Bates House, bds. Missouri, bet. Vermont and Michigan.

Jones Miss Sallie, Trade Palace, bds. 160 e. Market.

Jones Samuel, carpenter, res. 655 n. Tennessee.

Jones Miss Sarah, clerk Trade Palace, bds. 67 n. Alabama.

Jones Miss Sarah M., student, Ind. Female College, 146 n. Meridian, bds same.

Jones Spicer, farmer, res. 136 n. Tennessee.

Jones Stephen, tobacconist, bds. Ray House.

Jones Stephen G., works at 175 w. Cumberland, bds. Ray House.

Jones Steward, express messenger, Merchants' Union, bds. 144 E. New York.

Jones Sullivan, well-digger, res. 170 w. Georgia

Jones T. C., planer, bds. 35 Fletcher av.

Jones Walter D., student, commercial college, bds. 44 s. Tennessee.

Jones William A., soldier, U. S. Arsenal, bds. same.

Jones William B., switch-tender, Union R. R. Co., bds. 123 s. New Jersey.

Jones William H., (Coburn & J.,) agt. Indianapolis Agricultural Works, Tennessee, bet. Louisiana and South, res. 273 n. Ills.

Jones William M., freight agt. I. & C. R. R., res. 144 e. New York.

Jones W. T., works at Osgood & Smith's, res. 35 Fletcher av.

Jones William W., 3 Odd Fellows' Hall, res. 332 n. Alabama.

Jordan Miss Anna M., clerk, Willard & Stowell, res. over 40 s. Illinois.

Jordan Miss Ella, res. 2d floor 186 w. Washington.

Jordan Lewis, (Perkins, J. & Perkins,) room 4 Ætna bldg., n. Pennsylvania, res. n. Meridian.

Jordan Michael, tobacconist, bds. Ray House.

Jordan P. G., delivery clerk, American and United States Express Cos.' 34 e Washington, res. 492 n. Mississippi.

Jordan Thomas, grain dealer, bds. 31 w. Market.

Jordan Thomas, bds. 213 s. Ill.

Jordan William (Stelzel), Jordan & Co.,) 33½ w. Washington, res. 206 Ind. av.

Jordan Mrs. Elizabeth, bds. 175 n. Tennessee.

Jordan Gilmore, clerk, Second Auditor's Office, res. 186 n. Tennessee.

Jordan John, groceries, w. Washington, res. 172 n. Mississippi.

Jordan John, (col.,) bds 224 w. New York

Jordan P. works on Junction R. R., bds· Wiles House.

Jordan & Redmond, (John J. & Samuel R.,) grocers, 158 w. Washington.

Jordan ———, res. 649 n. Tennessee.

Jorion N., carpenter, res. 317 Davidson.

Jose N., furniture dealer, 8 s. Pennsylvania, res. s. city limits.

Joseph Richard C., land claim agt., office s. w. cor. Meridian and Washington, res. 29 n. California.

Josey N., frame-maker, H. Daumont, res. s. city limits.

Jottangen George, blacksmith, res. 290 e. Louisiana.

Jongeon Mrs. Mary, (wid. Leon,) seamstress, res. 214 Huron.

Journal bldg., e. Market, cor. Circle.

Jout Wm., machinist, bds. Martin House, 33 w. Maryland.

Jowett Samuel, moulder, bds. 42 Henry.

Jowett William, saw-grinder, bds. Martin House.

Joyce Benjamin, lab., res. Howard, bet. First and Second.

Joyce Elizabeth, servant, 189 e. Ohio.

Judah Jno. M., dep'y clerk supreme court, bds. 88 w. Ohio.

Judd Frederick, carder, res. 233 n. Blake.

Judge James, lab., res. 47 Wyoming.

Judson Andrew, brick-mason, bds. 201 Davidson.

Judson Chas., book-keeper, Judson & Dodd, res. 135 n. Illinois.

Judson Henry, clerk, res. 146 w. New York.

Judson Mrs. Rebecca, (wid.,) bds. 135 n. Illinois.

Judson William, bds. cor. Meridian and New York.

Julow Mrs. Amelia, (wid. Henry,) res. 176 Union.

Julow Henry, shoe-maker, res. 373 s. Illinois.

Julow Mrs. Wilhelmina, (wid. William,) res. 50 Lockerbie.

Junken Samuel W., book-keeper, 26 and 28 s. Tennessee, res. 165 Huron.

Justice J. F., blacksmith, bds. 2 Arch.

Justice James M., soldier, U. S. Arsenal, res. same.

Justice L. L., carpenter, res. 123 s. New Jersey.

Justice Sylvester, bds. 123 s. New Jersey.

KAAGAN HUBERT, plasterer, res. 49 Bradshaw.

Kab Miss Catharine, servant, 519 n. Meridian.

Kaegle Mrs. Hannah, (wid. Frederick,) res. 341 e. Ohio.

Kafader Joseph, stone-cutter, res. 461 s. Illinois.

Kafinan Louis, butcher, bds. 252 s. Delaware.

Kahler Frank, clerk, Smith & Goodhart, res. Noble, bet. Ohio and New York.

Kahler James, shoemaker, res. bet. E and Wright, s. Coburn.

Kahn Abraham, clothing, 33 w. Washington, res. 226 e. New York.

Kahn Adolphus, clothier, 6 w. Washington, res. 184 Virginia av.

Kahn Charles, meat market, 207 west Michigan, res. same.

Kahn Edward, machinist, Eagle Machine Works, bds. 80 s. Mississippi.

Kahn Isaac, merchant, res. 139 n. Delaware.

Kahn Jacob, gentlemens' furnishing goods, res. 193 n. East.

Kahn Jacob, clerk, bds, 69 w. Market.

Kahn Leon, (S. K. & Bro.,) 45 and 47 e. Washington, res. 164 n. East.

Kahn Lyon, salesman, 133 s. Illinois, bds. 184 Virginia av.

Kahn Samuel, (S. K. & Bro.,) 45 and 47 e. Washington, res. 283 e. Market.

Kahn S. & Bro., (Samuel & Leon K.,) German Dry Goods Store, 45 and 47 e. Washington.

Kaiser Christ, butcher, bds. 285 e. Washington.

Kaissar John, machinist, bds. 23 Kentucky av.

Kalb Frederick, grocery and saloon, 310 Winston, res. same.

Kalb Henry, lab., res. 164 e. St. Joseph.

Kalb John, tinner, res. 164 e. St. Joseph.

Kale John, lab., bds. 376 e. Market.

Kaleter Martin, butcher, res, 338 Madison av.

Kaling Henrietta, (wid.,) res. 167 e. St. Joseph.

Kalleen Jane, servant, J. S. Newman, 243 n. Pennsylvania.

Kambell John, cooper, bds. 213 s. Illinois.

Kamel James, (col.,) lab., res. 48 Henry.

Kamm Gotleib, saloon, 560 Virginia av. res. same.

Kane Dennis, blacksmith, res. 900 e. Georgia.

Kane Patrick, clerk, bds. 325 s. Delaware.

Kannan Augustus, marble carver, res. 104 Hosbrook.

Kautlin Mrs. Mary, bds. 23 Madison av.

KAPPES J. HENRY.
(E. C. Atkins & Co., and Indianapolis Piano-Forte Manufacturing Co.,) 161 e. Washington, res. 132 e. North.

Kares Joseph, carpenter, works Cincinnati car-shop, res. 113 Davidson.

Karitzer Frederick, lab., bds. 197 Harrison.

Karitzer Henry, lab., bds. 197 Harrison.

Karkfoff Charles, street sprinkler, res. 25 Coburn.

Karle Christian, (K. & Co., & Schneider & Co.,) 83 e. Washington, res. 82 s. Delaware.

Karle Christian & Co., boots and shoes, 83 e. Washington.

See Condensed R. R. Routes in last part of Book.

Kasana Theresa, servant, F. Goepper.
Kasberg Joseph, book-binder, W. Sheets, res. 71 Hosbrook.
Kasberg Peter, (Russel & K.,) res. 71 Hosbrook.
Kasimer Seiter, cooper, res 188 Madison av.
Kassabaum Frederick, lab., res. 592 e. St. Clair.
Kastle Jacob, baker, res. 267 n. Noble.
Kaufman Aaron, salesman, 213 e. Washington, res. 389 n. Pennsylvania.
Kaufman Abby, inmate of Deaf and Dumb Asylum.
Kaufman Adam, collar-maker, 76½ s. Delaware, res. same.
Kaufman B., clothier, 111 s. Illinois, res. same.
Kaufman Louis, (Barthol & K.,) res. 267 n. East.
Kaufman Morris, butcher, n. e. cor. West and Indiana av. res. same.
KAUFMAN S., wholesale hats and caps, 116 s. Meridian, res. n. Pennsylvania, outside city limits.
Kaufman William, butcher, 194 s. Illinois, bds. same.
Kay Joseph, wagon-maker, res. 211 Missouri.
Kay Robert, wagon-maker, Ft. Wayne av. res. 295 Indiana av.
Kayman B., res. 182 Virginia av.
Keaf John, carpenter, I. & C. shops, res. 43 Harrison.
Kenfer Jacob machinist, res. 230 s. Pennsylvania.
Kearn John, res. on Georgia, bet. Delaware and Pennsylvania.
Kearns Catharine, servant, Palmer House.
Kearney John, gas fitting, Miller's Block, res. 307 s. Delaware.
Keaser J. M., inmate of Deaf and Dumb Asylum.
Keating Jeffrey, lab., res. 207 High.
Keating Miss L. A., school-teacher, 250 Daugherty, res. same.
Keay William, stone cutter, res. 378 n. East.
Keay William F., clerk, U. S. Arsenal, bds. 378 n. East, near St. Clair.
Keedey J. A., inmate Deaf and Dumb Asylum.
Keedey Susan, inmate Deaf and Dumb Asylum.
Keefe Daniel, porter, Sentinel establishment, 16½ e. Washington.
Keeffe Daniel O., sergeant U. S. Arsenal, res. Arsenal grounds.
Keeffe Patrick, soldier, U. S. Arsenal, res. same.
Keehn Miss Mary E., attending school, bds. 204 n. Illinois.
Keel Henry, carpenter, bds. 330 Railroad.
Keely Daniel, brick-mason, bds. 370 e. New York.

Keely Miss Ellen, music teacher, 124 n. East, res. same.
Keely F. M., carpenter, bds. 74 Lockerbie.
Keely Henry S., brick-layer, res. 146 Winston.
Keely Isaac, brick-mason, res. 370 c. New York.
Keely Jefferson, carpenter, bds. 74 Lockerbie.
Keely John, brick-mason, res. 124 n. East.
Keely Joseph, carpenter, shop Michigan, bet. Alabama and New Jersey, res. 74 Lockerbie.
Keely Mrs. Lou., (wid. Alfred,) res. 2d floor 152 w. Washington.
Keely Marion, carpenter, res. 74 Lockerbie.
Keely Oliver, brick-mason, res. 301 e. Ohio.
Keely Samuel, brick-mason, res. bet. Michigan and National rd., beyond city limits.
Keely Miss Sarah E., teacher of music, bds. 146 n. Meridian.
Keely William, brick-mason, res. 309 e. Ohio.
Keemer James, (col.,) servant, 175 e. Ohio.
Keen George, bar-keeper, Empire Saloon, 23 n. Illinois.
Keenan Benjamin, jewelry dealer, bds. Wiles House.
Keenan John, teamster, res. 105 s. Noble.
Keenan Margaret, (wid. Thomas,) res. 105 s. Noble.
Keenan Philip, jewelry-dealer, bds. Wiles House.
Keenan William, teamster, res. 105 s. Noble.
Keepers S. W., fireman, J., M. & I. R. R., bds. Ray House.
Keers Samuel, flour-packer, Geisendorff Mills, res. 25 n. Blake.
Kees Hiram, engineer, I., C. & L. R. R., res. 165 Bates.
Keesee Mrs. Mary E., (wid.,) res. 300 n. Blake.
Keesey Andrew H., painter, 19 s. East, res. 22 s. East.
Keeting J. J., res. 90 s. Illinois.
Kegel Mary, clerk, 24 n. Pennsylvania, res. w. Ohio, bet. Noble and Liberty.
Kehler Louisa, (wid. Gotlieb,) res. 156 e. St. Joseph.
Kehling William, butcher, 137 s. Illinois, bds. same.
Keiser Charles, cigar-maker, res. 182 s. Delaware.
Keiser George L., grocer, 225 w. Washington, res. same.
Keistner Henry, shoe-maker, works 127 w. Washington, res. Tennessee, bet. South and Maryland.
Kellerher William carpenter, res. Minerva, bet. New York and Vermont.
Keith James, res. w. White river bridge.
Keith Julia, servant, 95 n. New Jersey.

Karle John, shoe-maker, res. 160 bluff rd.
Karle Joseph J., shoe-maker, res. 59.e.South.
Keith Samuel, (col.,) lab., res. end Laird.
Keightley John A., clerk, Dailey & Co., res. 176 n. East.
Keleman Jeremiah E., lab., res. 267 w. Washington.
Kell George, painter, bds. 52 s. Pennsylvania.
Keller Daniel, stone-cutter, res. 466 s. East.
Keller Frederick, (Daily Telegraph Co.,) res. 129 w. Maryland.
Keller Susan, servant, 32 n. East.
Keller William, lab., Rolling Mill, res. 230 s. New Jersey.
Keller Z. P., engineer, res. 159 Meek.
Kellersher David, res. Minerva, bet. New York and Vermont.
Kellerher Miss Ellen, seamstress, res. Minerva, bet. New York and Vermont.
Kellerher John, carpenter, res. Minerva, bet. New York and Vermont.
Kellerher William, carpenter, res. Minerva, bet. New York and Vermont.
Kellermeier Louisa, servant, 186 n. New Jersey.
Kelley Albert, brakesman, C., C. & I. C. R. R., bds. 33 Meek.
Kelley Andrew, compositor, book and job room, Sentinel Office, bds. 24 Buchanan.
Kelly Benjamin G., (Gates, Pray & Co.,) gen'l agt., Buffalo Scale Works Co., bds. 91 n. Delaware.
Kelley Cornelius, carriage-painter, works S. W. Drew & Co., res. 206 e. Ohio.
Kelley Cornelius, lab., res. 240 s. Missouri.
Kelley Elisha, (col.,) lab., res. 598 n. Mississippi.
Kelley Mrs. Eliza, (wid. Ambrose,) res. 181 s. New Jersey.
Kelley Hugh J., carriage-painter, works S. W. Drew & Co., res. 216 e. Washington.
Kelley John B., (Moran & K.,) 12 s. Pennsylvania, res. 315 Virginia av.

Kelley John, lab., res. 430 s. Illinois.
Kelley Mary, (wid. Henry,) w. Maryland, bet. California and Helen.
Kelley Mrs., (wid. Patrick,) res. 24 Buchanan.
Kelley Patrick, lab., res. 280 s. Tennessee.
Kelley Robert, lab., res. 153 w. South.
Kelley Thomas, porter, Commercial Hotel.
Kelley Thomas, fireman, B. R. R., bds. 270 Railroad.
Kelley Timothy, clerk, res. w. Maryland, bet. California and Helen.
Kelley William, lab., res. 430 s. Illinois.
Kellogg Newton, edge tool manfr., 411 w. Washington, res. 47 n. West.
Kelly Bernando, soldier, U. S. Arsenal, res. same.
Kelly Daniel, fireman, B. R. R., bds. 272 Winston.
Kelly James, peddler, res. 128 Bluff rd.
Kelly Kate, dining-room girl, Sherman House, bds. same.
Kelly Laura, (col.,) servant, 36 New Jersey.
Kelly R. H., coal-dealer, office 33 s. Meridian, res. 483 n. Meridian.
Kelly William, res. 225 Eddy.
Kelly Wm. J., inmate Deaf and Dumb Asylum.
Kelser Peter, bds. cor. Sixth and Michigan rd.
Kelsey S. R., student, commercial college, bds. 1152 s. New Jersey.
Kemker Charles, (J. C. Brinkmeyer & Co.,) 80 s Meridian, res. 190 n. East.
Kemp Alice M., (col.,) servant, 32 s. Illinois.
Kemp Armsterd, (col.,) lab., res. 237 Michigan.
Kemp Grace, (col.,) servant, 232 n. Illinois.
Kemp Jasper, lab., res. 245 Bluff rd.
Kempf Robert, harness-maker, 109 e. Washington, bds. 60 s. Delaware.
Kemper Lorenz D., carpenter, res. 192 s. New Jersey.

For a complete Church Directory, see Municipal Record.

Kemper John M., carpenter, shop, South, bet. Alabama and New Jersey, res. 192 s. New Jersey.

Kemper Wm. H., (Yandes & K.,) res. 45 Madison av.

Komton Eliza, (wid. Thomas,) res. National rd., near Insane Asylum.

Kenady John M., teamster, res. 340 Indiana av.

Kend John, cigar-maker, bds. 252 e. Washington.

Kendall John, printer, res. 281 w. Merrill.

Kendrick Robert, artist, res. 73 n. East.

Kendrick William H., physician and surgeon, 73 n. East, res. same.

KENEASTER, N. D., propr. Bates House, n. w. cor. Washington and Illinois, res. same. See card, advertising dept., page 5.

Kennedy Byram & Co., (R. Frank K., Norman S. B. & Edward G. Cornelius,) jobbers in dry goods and notions, 108 s. Meridian.

Kennedy James, nurseryman, cor. Delaware and Market, res. beyond city limits.

Kennedy James, lab., res. 43 Benton.

Kennedy John, lab., res. 373 e. New York.

Kennedy Patrick, works Rolling Mill, res. 157 s. Alabama.

Kennedy R. Frank, (K., Byram & Co.,) 108 s. Meridian, res. 247 n. Meridian.

Kennedy Thomas, res. 179 e. South.

Kenney Mrs. Catharine, (wid. Nicholas,) res. 144 Steven.

Kenney Thomas, tailor, 25½ w. Washington, res. 58 s. West.

Kennington John, lab., Gas Works, res. 286 s. Alabama.

Kenington Moses, blacksmith, res. cor. Georgia and West.

Kennington Robert, saloon and bowling alley, 178 s. Delaware, res. 325 s. Pennsylvania.

Kenroy James, carriage-painter, bds 269 n. West.

Kensel George, porter, 43 s. Delaware.

Kenseler Patrick, railroad section-boss, res. Howard, bet. First and Second.

Kentman M., res. 236 Massachusetts av.

Kenton John, blacksmith, res. 26 Center.

Kenton James, blacksmith, res. 41 Ellen.

Kenyon John H., dairyman, res. Shelbyville pike, ¼ mile s. corporation.

Kepner M. J., inmate Deaf and Dumb Asylum.

Kepple Henry, lab., res. 272 s. Illinois.

Kepple Joshua, lab., res. 270 s. Tennessee.

Kepple Martin, eating house, 36 w. Louisiana, opp. Union Depot, res. same.

Ker John, (col.,) gardener, res. bet. Cedar and Elm.

Kercheval W. J., book-keeper, 64 e. Washington, res. 75 n. Pratt.

Kerfoot Mrs. L. B., res. 378 n. New Jersey.

Kerfoot Richard, salesman, 32 w. Washington, res. 78 n. New Jersey.

Kerkhoff Fred., checkman, Madison Depot, res. 271 Union.

Kerlin Frederick, chair-maker, res. 145 Bluff rd.

Kerlin James M., dry goods, 186 w. Washington, res. 526 n. Illinois.

Kern Casper, cabinet-maker, works at Spiegel, Thoms & Co.'s, res. 392 e. Michigan.

Kern Charles, soda-water-maker, works n. e. cor. Railroad and Michigan, bds. 392 e. Michigan.

Kern Jacob, (L. & J. K.,) 26 Fort Wayne av., res. 288 e. Michigan,

Kern Louis, (L. & J. K.,) 26 Fort Wayne av., bds. Winston, bet. Michigan and North.

Kern L. & J., (Louis & Jacob K.,) soda-water manfs, 26 Fort Wayne av.

Kern Mary, dining-room girl, 30½ n. Pennsylvania.

Kerper Charles, boarding-house, 73 w. Maryland.

Kersey John, (col.,) barber, 50 e. Washington, res. West, bet. Michigan and Vermont.

Kersey Mrs. Martha T., matron Orphan Asylum, res. Orphan Asylum, 711 n. Tennessee, cor. Fifth.

Kersey Oliver, carpenter, res. 240 Union.

Kersey Miss Priscilla, milliner, works 44 s. Illinois, bds. 157 Davidson.

Kersey Shubal C., carpenter, res. 711 n. Tennessee.

Kessner Fred., clerk, res. 311 s. Pennsylvania.

Ketcham John L., (K. & Mitchell and Indiana Banking Co.,) over 21 e. Washington, res. 164 Merrill.

KETCHAM & MITCHELL, (John L. K. & James L. M.,) attorneys at law, over 21 e. Washington.

Ketcham William A., law student, Ketcham & Mitchell, bds. 165 e. Merrill.

Kettenbach Edward, (K. & Newmeyer,) bds. 279 Massachusetts av.

Kettenbach Henry, retired grocer, res. 279 Massachusetts av.

Kettenbach & Newmeyer, groceries, flour and feed, 273 and 277 Massachusetts av.

Kettenbach William F., clerk, Kettenbach & Newmeyer, 277 Massachusetts av., bds. 279 Massachusetts av.

Ketzel Charles, works at J. Cahall & Co.'s, bds. Ray House.

Ketzel Christian, works at J. Cahall & Co.'s, bds. Ray House.

Keyser George, plumber, 82 w. Washington, res. w. Vermont, bet. Blackford and Bright.

Keveney John, soldier U. S. Arsenal, res. same.

Kevers John H., groceries and provisions, 525 n. Mississippi, res. same.

Key Thomas H., soldier U. S. Arsenal, res. same.

Keyser Jno. N., carpenter, res. 369 w. Vermont.

Kiefer Augustus, (K. & Vinton,) 68 s. Meridian, residence 483 n. Illinois.

Kiefer Jacob, bds. 483 n. Illinois.

Kiefer L. A., (K. & Son,) 2 Odd Fellows' Hall, bds. 463 n. Delaware.

Kiefer Miss Phœbe, bds. 483 n. Illinois.

Kiefer & Son, watch-makers and jewelers, 2 Odd Fellows's Hall.

KIEFER & VINTON, (Augustus K. & A. E. V.,) wholesale druggists, 68 s. Meridian.

Kiesel John, baker, works cor. New York & Delaware, bds same.

Kightly John A., salesman, 39 s. Meridian, bds. 176 n. East.

Kiker John C., carpenter, res. rear 285 n. Noble.

Kiley Daniel, engineer, res. 115 Davidson.

Kiley John, engineer, res. 115 Davidson.

KILGORE & HELMS, (J. D. K. & Lewis A. H.,) dentists, Miller's blk., over 70 n. Illinois.

Kilgore J. D., (K. & Helms,) Miller's blk., n. Illinois, res. 204 n. Illinois.

Kilgore J. W., carpenter, res. 34 Thomas.

Kilkeney Jacob, salesman, res. 124 e. St. Joseph.

Killinger John G., cabinet-maker, 326 e. Market, res. 328 e. Market.

Killorme Thomas, drayman, J. H. Ross, res. 359 w. Washington.

KIMBALL EBEN W., attorney at law, notary public, and U. S. commissioner, 46 e. Washington, res. 382 n. Meridian.

KIMBALL NATHAN, Treasurer of State, office new State bldg., cor. Tennessee and Washington, res. 475 n. Illinois.

Kimball James N., deputy Treasurer of State, office cor. Tennessee and Washington, res. 475 n. Illinois.

Kimble Thomas V., (Roll, K. & Aikman,) 123 s. Meridian, res. 275 Indiana av.

Kindal Joseph, foreman, 24 e. Georgia, res. 19 Madison av.

Kinder Mrs. Maria W., (wid. Isaac,) res. 27 Lockerbie.

Kindler Chas., locksmith and bell-hanger, 60 n. Illinois, res. 225 s. West.

Kinester Henry, cigar-maker, res. 167 Maple.

Kiney Isaiah, blacksmith, bds. 424 Virginia av.

Kiney Robert, freight conductor I., C. & L. R. R., bds. 58 Benton.

Kincy Thomas, tailor, res. 58 s. West.

Kincy Walter, lab., res. 486 e. Georgia.

Kiney William, tinner, bds. 20 s. Pennsylvania.

King & Co., (Jacob K. & James Hamilton,) founders and machinists, 97 s. Mississippi.

King Cornelius, lumber dealer, cor. St. Clair and Peru R. R., res. n. city limits.

King David, ice dealer, res. 261 n. Mississippi.

KING EDWARD, vice-prest. and asst. treas. C , C. C. & Indianapolis R. R. Co., office 53 s. Alabama, res. on national rd., 2 miles e. city.

King George, operator, B. R. R., bds. 109 Virginia av.

King George, butcher, res. 392 s. Tennessee.

King Geo., carpenter, res. 272 e. St. Clair.

King G. E., clerk Bellefontaine R. R. office, bds. 109 Virginia av.

King Honora, servant, Palmer Pouse.

King I. S., physician, office and res. 25 s. West.

King Jacob, (K. & Co.,) res. 217 w. South.

King James H., salesman, 38 e. Washington, res. 113 Indiana av.

King James M., (J. W. Blake & Co.,) over 45 e. Washington, res. 248 s. Meridian.

King James W., bailiff, res. 248 s. Meridian.

King Jerome H., brakesman, Indiana Central, bds. Commercial Hotel.

King John, lab., res. 374 s. West.

King John G., carpenter, res. 374 s. West.

King John W., wool dealer, res. 69 n. Alabama.

King Mrs. Kate, (wife John H,) seamstress, shop and res. 51 Peru.

King Mrs. Lizzie, (wid. George,) res. 424 Virginia av.

King Margaret, kitchen girl, Bates House.

King Miss Martha J., bds. 294 n. Tennessee.

King Matthias, stone-cutter, res. 156 Stevens.

King Miss Mary, clerk, 4 w. Washington, res. 113 Indiana av.

King Peter, moulder, Root's, res. 385 s. Delaware.

King Robert, soldier, U. S. Arsenal, res. same.

King Mrs. Sarah, bds. 261 n. Mississippi.

King William, turner, bds. 20 s. Pennsylvania.

Kingan Thomas D., (Nofsinger, K. & Co.,) bds. Bates House.

Kingham Joseph, broom-maker, 253 Massachusetts av.

Kingleman William, 35 w. Washington, res. 134 w. Washington.

Kingman Frank N., insurance agt., bds. 510 n. Delaware.

Kingman Nelson book-keeper, 66 e. Washington, res. 510 n. Delaware.

Kingsbury F. H., gen. traveling agt., Star Union Line, 85 Virginia av., bds. 97 w. Maryland.

Kingsbury John E., clock-maker, 237 Massachusetts av., res. same.

KINGSLEY R. S., groceries and produce, 200 s. Illinois, cor. South, bds. 198 s. Illinois.

Kingston Samuel, painter, res. 231 s. Mississippi.

Kinitzer Henry, cigar-maker, res. 191 Maple.

Kinley Samuel J., carpenter, res. 392 s. Missouri.

Kinney Cornelius, work Cincinnati Freight Depot, res. 270 w. St. Clair.

Kinney Joanna, servant, 78 e. Ohio.

Kinsell George, lab., res. 233 w. McCarty.

Kintz Adam, hostler, 23 s. Delaware, res. 483 s. New Jersey.

Kipp Albert, clk., 29 w. Washington, bds. 29 Massachusetts av.

Kirby James H., plasterer, res. 297 n. Mississippi.

Kirby Mrs. Sarah, (wid. John H.,) res. 308 e. Ohio.

Kirk N., res. 75 n. Pennsylvania.

Kirby & Stevens, house and sign painters, 38 Kentucky av.

Kirby Mrs. Susan, (wid. Zachariah,) seamstress, res. 153 Huron.

Kirby William L., salesman, 131 s. Meridian, bds. Sherman House.

Kirk Daniel A., turner, Spiegle, Thoms & Co., res. 131 Meek.

Kirk Mrs. E., milliner, 75 n. Pennsylvania, res. same.

Kirkwood Adam, fireman, C., C. & I. C. R. R., bds. 149 s. New Jersey.

Kirkwood John, bds. 28 Lord.

Kirlin Miss Anna, res. 526 n. Illinois.

Kirlin James, dry goods, 186 w. Washington res. 526 n. Illinois.

Kirlin John, lab., res. Stevens bet. Green and Virginia av.

Kirly James, painter, 36 Kentucky av., res. 404 s. Missouri.

Kisch John, sawyer, res. 104 Bluff Road.

Kise John W., teamster, res. 94 Dunlap.

Kise L. S., teamster, res. n. Smith.

Kiser Catharine, (wid.) res. 68 Massachusetts av.

Kiser Charles, meat-market, Fourth bet. Tennessee and Mississippi, res. same.

Kishner Frederick, salesman, 125 s. Meridian, res. 311 s. Pennsylvania.

KISSELL FREDERICK, saloon, 98 Russel, res. same.

Kissell Jacob W., res. 22 s. West.

Kistner Adam, propr. California House, 184 s. Illinois, res. same.

Kistner John G., dealer in boots and shoes, 83 s. Illinois, res. 336 s. Meridian.

Kitchel Moses, boarding house, 18 w. Georgia, res. same.

Kitchen John M., physician and surgeon, Vinton's blk. opp. P. O., res. 147 n. Pennsylvania.

Kitler John H., varnisher, res. 22 Bates.

Kitley Miss Lucy A., student, N. W. Christian University, bds. 297 Winston.

Kittle Josiah H., carpenter, res. 172 Buchanan.

Kitsmiller William, engineer, 29 s. Illinois, res. 244 w. Washington.

Kizer Adam, shoe-maker, res. 127 e. St. Mary's.

Kizer Herman, upholsterer, 38 e. Washington, bds. Union Hall.

Klair Fred, saloon-keeper, res. 177 Union.

Klauke Mrs. Margaret, (wid. John A.,) bds. 260 n. Noble.

Klein John George, (K. & Vandergotten,) 37 s. Illinois, res. 281 n. Liberty.

Klein Mrs. Veronica, (wid. Michael,) res. 63 n. Noble.

Klemm Louis, teacher, German English School, bds. 67 n. Tennessee.

Kline Frederick, bar-tender, 397 cor. Meridian and McCarty, res. same.

Kline Henry, lab., res. e. Georgia.

Kline Jane, occupant Deaf and Dumb Asylum.

Kline Joseph, inmate Deaf and Dumb Asylum.

Kline Joseph, clerk, 67 e. Washington, res. 297 s. New Jersey.

Kline J. George, barber, 37 s. Illinois, res. 321 n. Liberty.

Kline Madison, clerk, C. A. Furgason, bds. Pyle House.

Kline Nicholas, shoe shop, 283 Massachusetts av., res. 351 Spring.

Kline Solomon, carpenter, res. 389 n. West.

Kline W. H., clerk, 3 Odd Fellow's Hall, res. 361 n. Spring.

Klineshmit Christian, street-sprinkler, res. 284 e. Market.

Klingensmith Frederick, lab., bds. 275 Davidson.

Klingensmith Israel, (Burns & K.,) 115 e. Washington, bds. 478 n. Tennessee.

Klingensmith Jacob, commercial broker, res. 478 n. Tennessee.

Klumpp David F., brewer, 297 w. Washington, res. 202 w. Maryland.

Klusmann Louis, salesman, 8 w. Washington, res. 123 St. Mary.

Knapp Miss Ann, music-teacher, bds. 483 n. Mississippi.

Knapp Gardner, book-keeper, Evening Commercial, cor. Circle and Meridian, res. 483 n. Mississippi.

Knauf Adam D., baker, 257 Massachusetts av., res. same.

Knaur George, gardener, res. and garden, s. s. National rd., near Insane Asylum.

Knarzer George, (Geis & K.,) 62 s. Delaware, bds. same.

Knaur John, lab., bds. National rd., near Insane Asylum.

Knaur William, lab., bds. s. s. National rd., near Insane Asylum.

Knefler Charles, book-keeper, 64 s. Meridian, bds. 18 Circle.

Knefler Fred., (Hanna & K.,) 20½ n. Delaware, res. 466 n. Pennsylvania.

Kneip John, carpenter, res. 294 n. Liberty.

Knertzer Frank, blacksmith, res. 338 e. Ohio.

Knierim Henry, painter, bds. 272 Winston.

Knight E., boarding-house, 124 s. Meridian.

Knight Jasper N., painter, res. s. w. cor. Fourth and Tennessee.

Knight John, (Cottrell & K.,) 108 s. Delaware, res. 304 n. Delaware.

Knight William, moulder, bds. 111 w. South.

Knighton Charles J., planing mill, cor. Market and Winston, res. 781 n. Illinois.

Knipe William, porter, New York Store, bds. n. Tennessee.

KNIPPENBERG HENRY,
(E. C. Atkins & Co.,) Sheffield Saw Works, 210, 212, 214 and 216 s. Illinois, res. 165 Massachusetts av. See card on outside.

Knippenberg J., book-keeper, 159 and 161 e. Washington, res. 132 e. North.

Knodle A., boots and shoes, 32 e. Washington, res. 8 Indiana av.

Knodle Dora, (wid.,) res. 154 e. St. Joseph.

Knodle George, salesman, 32 e. Washington, res. 80 w. Ohio.

Knoss William, Miller, res. 297 c. New York.

Knotts N. K., painter, 27 s. Illinois, res. 289 w. Michigan.

Knox Clinton, train-boy, J., M. & I. R. R., bds. Sherman House.

Knox Francis A., (col.,) barber-shop, under Bee-Hive Store, res. Howard, bet. Second and Third.

Knox John W., soldier, U. S. Arsenal, res. same.

Knox R. E., works 10 w. Washington, bds. Mrs. Morrison's, n. Pennsylvania.

Koahler William, coffee-house, e. Market, res. 106 Davidson.

Koch George, shoe-maker, works 267 Massachusetts av., bds. 350 n. Noble.

Koch H. H., grocer, 196 cor. Noble and South, res. same.

Kochler August, piano sounding board-maker, 159 and 161 e. Washington, bds. Jæger-Halle.

Koehler John, (K. & Ladz,) res. 244 n. Noble.

Koehler & Ladz, grocery and saloon, 247 n. Noble.

Koehne Benjamin, bar-tender, Palmer House, bds. same.

Koehne Charles, (H. Lieber & Co.,) 21 n. Pennsylvania, res. 467 n. Delaware, bet. Pratt and St. Joseph.

Koehnen Mary, servant, 342 n. Illinois.

Koehring Bernhard, cooper, 287 n. Liberty, res. same.

Koehring Charles, lab., res. 93 Elm.

Koerner Michael, lab., res. over 178 e. Washington.

Koester J. M., works Hill's nursery, bds. 518 e. Washington.

Koestner D., lab., res. 225 Bluff rd.

Koestner T., lab., res. 265 Union.

Kofman Mrs. Caroline, (wid. Samuel,) res. 261 e. Market.

Kogemeier John, lab., res. 116 Winston.

Kohl Peter, porter, Hume, Adams & Co., bds. California House.

Kohn Joseph, clothier, 80 w. Washington, res. same.

Kolasheck George, lab., res. 22 Wyoming.

Kolb Henry, tinner, bds. 164 e. St. Joseph.

Kolb John, tinner, bds. 164 e. St. Joseph.

Kolb Louis, job turner, e. South, bet. Pennsylvania and Meridian, res. 17 e. South.

Kolb Philip, lab., res. 127 e. St. Mary.

Kolb William, boarding-house, 23 and 25 Kentucky av.

Kolb William, clerk, 10 w. Louisiana, bds. 138 s. Meridian.

Koller E. H., grocer, 206 e. Washington, res. Arsenal, near Insane Asylum.

Kolthoff Margaret, servant, 82 w. Vermont.

Kolthoff Mary, servant, 82 w. Vermont.

Kolthoff Sophia, servant, 324 n. Meridian.

Konkle Bernard, clerk, cigar-store, res. 253 Union.

Konontz Herman, asst. cook, Bates House, res. same.

Konsela Mrs. Maria, groceries and saloon, cor. Seventh and Michigan rd., res. same.

Koontz George W., clerk, Post Office, res. 30 n. East.

Koontz J. A., student, commercial college, bds. 726 n. Tennessee.

Korn Martin, tanner, works 47 and 49 s. Delaware, res. 247 Davidson.

Korner Christ., tailor, res. 228 s. Delaware.

Kraft Miss Mary, res. 207 w. Michigan.

Kortepeter William, tailor, works over 182 e. Washington, res. 430 s. East.

Kortpeter Henry, car-inspector, T. H. & I. R. R., res. 162 Buchanan.

Koss Charles, porter, Kennedy, Byram & Co., res. 121 n. Spring.

Koster Charles, (K. & Maas,) 141 e. Washington, res. 181 Blake.

Koster & Maas, cigar-manfrs. and dealers, 141 e. Washington.

Kothe William, grocer, 130 Davidson, res. same.

Kotteman William, finisher, 38 e. Washington, res. 327 e. Michigan.

Kough Michael, works Street R. R. Co., res. 385 e. Ohio.

Kowan William, street-contractor, res. 169 n. East.

Krag August, traveling agent, bds. 22 w. North.

Kramer Andrew, shoe-maker, works 175 e. Washington, res. 199 n. Liberty.

KRAMER HENRY, butcher, 80 Fort Wayne av., res. same.

Kramer William, bds. n. e. cor. West and Indiana av.

Krasky Theodore, works glue factory, res. cor. Eighth and Lafayette R. R.

Krause Henry, cooper, res. Bluff rd., near McCarty.

Krauss Christian, works Cabinet Makers' Union, res. e. end New York.

Krauss George, clerk, Gall & Rush, res. 140 n. East.

Krauss Jacob, res. 140 n. East.

Krauss John, clerk, Gall & Rush, res. 140 n. East.

Krauth Elmer, salesman, 14 w. Washington, res. 27 w. First.

Krauth Ernest, salesman, 14 w. Washington, res. 27 w. First.

Kreamer Gotleib, soldier, U. S. Arsenal, res. same.

Kregar William, carpenter, res. 92 s. Russel.

Kregelo Charles E., groceries, bds. 228 n. West.

Kregelo David, res. 228 n. West.

Kregelo Jacob, carpenter, res., 82 e. St. Clair.

Kreger Christ, groceries, res. 343 e. McCarty.

Kreger Henry, currier, Mooney & Co., res. 331 e. Georgia.

Kreger William, currier, Mooney & Co., res. e. Ohio bet. New Jersey and East.

Kregers Frederick, lab., res. 175 Union.

Kreider R. G., clerk, shoe-store Glenns' Block, res. 218 e. South.

Kretsch Peter, manfr. and dealer in tobacco and cigars, 141 s. Illinois, res. 325 s. Meridian.

Kreutzer John, tailor, res, n. w. cor. Fourth and Tennessee.

Kreis J. R., beer-garden, s. city limits.
Krieger Henry, belt-maker, res. 331 e. Georgia.
Kriger Frederick, tailor, 335 Virginia av., res. 483 s. New Jersey.
Kring Caleb, carpenter, res. 376 s. West.
Kring John L., carpenter and stair builder, Byrkit & Son, cor. Tennessee and Georgia, res. 374 s. West.
Krist Delmain, lab., res. 296 n. Noble.
Kristner Henry, glove-maker, 127 w. Washington, res. Tennessee, bet. South and Maryland.
Kroff George, clerk, 104 s. Illinois, res. 176 s. Illinois.
Krome Augustus, teacher, German Lutheran school, res. 280 e. Georgia.
Krome Christ, res. 280 e. Georgia.
Krouse Jacob, lab., 325 e. Merrill.
Kruder R. G., salesman, D. D. Chore, Glenns' blk., res. 218 e. South.
Krug Gotlieb C., grocer, 24 e. Georgia, res. 67 s. Noble.
Kruger Christian, (W. H. & C. K.,) 401 Virginia av., res. 343 e. McCarty.
Kruger Henry, tailor, 191 n. Noble, res. same.
Kruger Joseph, cistern builder, res. 267 e. Market.
Kruger Joseph, jr., gas fitter, works Coulter & White's, bds. 267 e. Market.
Krugg Eliza, servant, 199 n. Pennsylvania.
Krumm Jacob, tailor, Philadelphia Dye-House, bds. 50 n. Illinois.
Kruse Christian, carpenter, res. 15 e. McCarty.
Kruse Henry, stone-mason, res. 84 s. Liberty.
Kruse John, lab., res. 199 e. Washington, 2d floor.
Krussy Henry, cooper, res. 116 bluff rd.
Kudfeter William, tailor, res. 430 s. East.
Kuder Herman, salesman, 2 Bates House blk., bds. Mr. Morse, circle.
Kuehn Ernst, tailor, res. 503 n. Illinois.
Kuerst Henry, carpenter, res. 182 Madison av.

Kuerst August, lab.,
Kuhlenberg Bernard Illinois.
Kuhlman Charles, Robinson & Co.,
Kuhlman Mrs. Christ
Kuhlman E. H. L., f pike, ½ mile s. c
Kuhn August, sales bds. Mozart Hal
Kuhn Philip, grocery av., res. same.
Kuhn William, propr n. East, cor. Nev
Kugelman Henry, co dorff's Woolen F
Kugelman William, 35 w. Washing land.
Kull Frederick, carp
Kung M. A., miller same.
Kunkel Charles, lab
Kunkel George, cur res. on Bluff rd.
Kunkel Henry, car ginia av.
Kunkel Jacob, cur res. 451 s. Illin
Kunkel John, lab., r
Kunkel John, lab., b
Kunkel J., cigar-ma res. Concordia F
Kunrey Helen, milli same.
Kuntz Jacob, carpen
Kuntz Herman, st bds. 9 s. Alaban
Kunz Nicholas H., s bds. 9 s. Alaban
Kuplman Charles, p maker, 159 an res. 118 n. Nob
Kurts H. P., blacks sissippi.
Kutemeir Charles, Market.

Kuss Dora, servant, 156 n. East.
Kuster Theodore, railroader, res. 265 Union.
Kutzleb Robert, painter, res. 247 s. Delaware.
Kyle John, pedlar, res. 117 Oak.
Kyser George W., plumber and gas fitter, res. 369 w. Vermont.

LAAZ JACOB, (KOEHLER & LAAZ,) 247 n. Noble, res. 266 n. Noble.
Labarre Lewis, moulder, at Root's foundry, res. 79 Elm.
Lace Edward, works Junction R. R., bds. Wiles House.
Lack Henry, mattrass manfr., 21 s. Meridian, bds. California House.
Lack Rudolph L., teller at Harrison's Bank, res. 623, n. Illinois.
Lackey Joseph, farmer, res. 496 Virginia av.
Lacy George J., paper-maker, McLene, McIntire & Hays, res. 375 w. Washington.
Lacy Lucy, (col.,) washer, res. 156 Douglas alley.
Ladz Mrs. Ann C., (wid. John,) res. 266 n. Noble.
Laddy John, lab., res. 51 Wyoming.
Ladies Christian Monitor, Mrs. M. M. B. Goodwin editress and proprietress, office Journal bldg.
LaDow D., (LaD. & Lewis,) 120 s. Illinois, bds. 426 s. Illinois.
LADOW & LEWIS, proprs. Indianapolis marble-works, 120 s. Illinois.
Latz Charles, bar-tender, Circle Restaurant, res. 15 n. Meridian.
Lafayette & Indianapolis Freight Depot, cor. North and Canal.
Lafayette House, 197 s. Meridian, George Happe, propr.
Lafferty Charles C., patent-right agt., res. over 223 w. Washington.
Lagmann John F., works U. S. Arsenal, bds. 518 e. Washington.
Lahman Frederick, shoe-maker, bds. 31 Madison av.
Luhman John, lab., Schmidt's brewery, res. same.
Laible Andrew, butcher, bds. e. Washington.
Laing David, carpenter, res. 80 s. Mississippi.
Lair Jacob, works at Arsenal, res. 151 Winston.
Laird C. P., insurance solicitor, res. 36 Cherry.
Laird John P., carpenter, res. 68 s. Noble.
Laird Robert, tailor, bds. 554 n. Illinois.
Laird Harrison, tinner, bds. 554 n. Illinois.
Lake Ellis R., huckster, res. 265 Bluff rd.

Laird William H., book-keeper, 68 s. Meridian, res. 554 n. Illinois.
Lake John S., sealer, res. Bluff rd., s. city limits.
Lake Joseph, machinist, bds. 183 s. Illinois.
Lake Miss Maggie, bds. 299 Indiana av.
Lally Thomas, tailor, over 28 s. Meridian, res. 525 w. South.
Lamb Amos, salesman, 75 s. Meridian, bds.
Lamb Peter, lab., res. 253 s. Tennessee.
LAMB SAMUEL, sheriff Supreme Court, office new state bldg., cor. Tennessee and Washington, res. n. e. cor. Pratt and Delaware.
Lamb William C., law student, Supreme Court rooms, cor. Tennessee and Washington, bds. 162 n. New Jersey.
Lambert David, lab., res. 36 Rose.
Lambert Eli F., lab., res. end Virginia av., beyond city limits.
LAMBERT JAMES M., proprietor Ray House, cor. South and Delaware. See card, page 13, advertising department.
Lambert Joseph, lab., res. 373 w. Washington.
Lambert Peter, (col.,) lab., Minerva, bet North and Elizabeth.
Lamotte Charles, (L. & Son,) 192 Massachusetts av., res. same.
Lamotte Joseph, (L. &. Son,) 192 Massachusetts av., res. same.
Lamotte & Son, (Joseph & Charles L.,) dealers in stoves and tin-ware, 192 Massachusetts av.
Lampheiner August, saloon, 191 e. Washington, res. same.
Landcraft Jacob, tailor, res. 44 Dunlap.
Landers Miss Anna, milliner, works 152 e. Washington, bds. n. Delaware, bet. Market and Ohio.
Landers Elizabeth, servant, 422 n. Illinois.
Landers Frank, (L., Pee & Co.,) 58 s. Meridian, res. 402 n. Pennsylvania.
Landers Jacob, livery and sale stable, 32 s. Pennsylvania, res. 128 w. Maryland.
Landers James, res. 687 e. St. Clair.
Landers John, clerk American Express Co., bds. 213 s. Illinois.
LANDERS, PEE & CO., (Frank L., George W. P., Alexander B. Conduitt, Milton Cox, John C. McCutchen, George W. Geiger and Joseph P. Shipp,) wholesale dry goods, 58 s. Meridian.
Landis Jacob, livery stable, bet. Washington and Maryland, res. 128 w. Maryland.
Landis Milton M., asst. supt. and agt. White Line Central Transit Co., res. 506 n. Meridian.

Wholesale and Retail Tobacconist.   See page 108.

Landis J. M., inmate Deaf and Dumb Asylum.

Landon William, lab., rear Lukens & Hallowell, s. Tennessee.

Landreth Miss Anna, milliner, works at Miss Wink's, cor. Washington and Alabama, bds. 89 n. Delaware.

Lane Edith, (wid., col.,) res. 25 Vine.

Lane John, conductor Bellefontaine R. R., res. 313 s. East.

Lane John, (col.,) servant, 462 n. Pennsylvania, cor. Pratt.

Lane John A., salesman, 146 s. Pennsylvania, bds 369 n. Alabama.

Lane Uriah, lab., res. 369 n. Alabama.

Lane William, street sprinkler, res. 80 s. Liberty.

Lang Charles, works at Meikel's brewery, res. 64 s. West.

Laug Daniel, (L. & Smith,) 146 e. Maryland, res. 168 Davidson.

Lang Daniel A., carpenter, (McCreery & Fay,) 56 e. Washington, res. 166 Davidson.

Lang Frederick, lab., res. 71 Harrison.

Lang Fred., porter, Browning & Sloan's drug house, res. 77 w. Third.

Lang Fred. J., porter, Auditor of State's office, cor. Tennessee and Washington, res. cor. s. California and Georgia.

LANG LOUIS,
wine house and bottled liquors, 29 s. Meridian, res. 221 e. Ohio.

Lang Samuel, tinner, bds. 80 s. Mississippi.

Lang & Smith, (D. A. L. & H. H. S.,) house carpenters and joiners, 146 e. Maryland.

Lang William W., book-binder, Journal Office, res. 80 s. Mississippi.

Langan William C, special agt. American Express Co., bds. Bates House.

Langbein Joseph, groceries, toys and fancy goods, 200 e. Washington, res same.

Langenberg, Henry H., (L., Vogt & Rozier,) 244 and 246 w. Washington, res. Bluff rd, beyond city limits.

Langdon Caroline, (wid.,) seamstress, res. w. Maria.

Langdon Mrs. Mary A., (wid.,) bds. 175 Bluff rd.

Langenberg Mrs. Caroline, (wid. William,) res. rear 141 n. Noble.

Langenberg Mrs. Margaret, (wid. Christian,) res. 175 w. South.

Langenberg, Vogt & Rozier, (Henry H. L., Frederick V. and Aaron R.,) groceries and provisions, 244 and 246 w. Washington.

Langhorn A. T., telegraph operator, C., C. & I. C. R. R., bds. 229 s. Alabama.

Langley William, works for Sullivan & Drew, res. Boyd's blk., Massachusetts av.

Langsdale J. M. W., res. 225 e. Ohio.

Langsdale Mrs. Mary M., (wid. John,) servant, 127 n. Alabama.

Langsdale Thomas, rubber, Indianapolis piano factory.

Langston Abby, chambermaid, Bicking House, 89 s. Illinois.

Lanhan John, lab, res. 376 s. Illlinois.

Lanigan John, clerk, 32 w. Louisiana, bds. same.

Lanlertson Geo., physician, res. 121 Duncan.

Lannay Miss Virginia, student, Indiana Female College, 146 n. Meridian, bds. same.

Lannes David G., clerk, A. Clem & Bro., bds. 126 e. Ohio.

Lanpheter Jno., barber shop, 323 w. Washington, res. same.

Lansberger Andrew, gardener, bds. 518 e. Washington.

Lansingkamp William, coppersmith, res. 176 s. Delaware.

Lanthan C. W., copper-smith, res. 184 s. Delaware.

Lapp Alice, servant, 298 e. Ohio.

Lapp John, engineer, res. 497 s. New Jersey.

Laport M. J., sawyer, bds. 266 s. Illinois.

Large Michael, lab., res. 332 Indiana av.

Large Theodore S., fireman, I. C. R. R., bds. 230 n. East.

Larger Jerome, brakesman, C., C. & I. C. R. R., bds. 58 Benton.

Larimore James, lab., bds. end Huron, beyond city limits.

Larimore Thomas F., lab., end Huron, beyond city limits.

Larkin John, lab., res. Ellen.

Larkin M. L., brick-layer, res. 147 Ash.

Larnes John W., (col.,) barber, 286 w. Washington.

Larr Mrs. Elizabeth, (wid. John,) res. 136 n. Noble.

Larr Henry, carpenter, res. 347 e. New York.

Larr Samuel, watchman, I. & C. Depot, res. 263 s. East.

Latham Charlbs, clerk, Fletcher's Bank, bds. e. Washington, beyond city limits.

Latham Charles C., soldier, U. S. Arsenal, res. Arsenal.

Latham George W., machinist, res. 8 Lord.

Latham Henry, clerk, Indianapolis National Bank, res. e. Washington, near corporation.

Latham W. H., A. M., M. D., instructor, Deaf and Dumb Asylum, res. e. Washington, e. city limits.

Latshaw J. L., (Minnick & L.,) 17½ w. Washington, res. 92 s. Mississppi.

Lauck Mrs. Mary, (wid. Michael,) res. 391 s. Delaware.

Lauer Charles, saloon, 202 e. Washington, res. 15 Bluff rd.

Laughlin Eli, student, commercial college, bds. 133 Virginia av.

Laughlin Miss Jane, student, N. W. C. University, res. 113 Massachusetts av.

Laughlin John, lab., res. 55 Fayette.

Laughlin Margaret, servant, 284 n. Meridian.

Lauler William, porter, Union Depot, res. 288 s. East.

Laughlin Miss Mary, student, Training School, fourth Ward, res. 113 Massachusetts av.

Laurie Miss Susan, student, res. 113 Massachusetts av.

Laurie William, salesman, New York Store, bds. n. Liberty.

Lavery John, salesman, 10 w. Pearl, bds. 315 s. Delaware.

Law Mrs. Caroline L., (wid.,) res. Fifth, bet. Mississippi and Railroad.

Laubon H. W., clerk, C., C., C. & I. R. R., bds. Winston.

Lawler Ellen A., nurse, Institute of the Blind, bds. same.

Lawler James, expressman, res. 288 s. East.

Lawler Mary, (wid. Richard,) res. s. s. bet. Noble and Benton.

Lawler William, engineer, res. 289 s. East.

Lawless Michael, (Michael L. & Co.,) 138 s. Noble, res. same.

Lawless Michael & Co., (Michael L. & Patrick Curren,) groceries, 138 s. Noble.

Lawrence Arthur V., commission merchant, groceries and egg packer, 173 w. Washington, res. 211 w. Ohio.

Lawrence James, (col.,) barber, 14 Bates House, res. 55 Maple.

Lawson Aaron, farmer, res. 35 Jones.

Lawson Mrs. Elizabeth, (wid.,) res. cor. Patterson and North.

Lawson Joseph, res. w. Market, rear State House.

Lawson Milton T., farmer, res. cor. Patterson and North.

Lawson Peter, res. Broadway, near city limits.

Lawton Watson H., checkman, Bellefontaine outer Depot, bds. 149 Winston.

Lawyer & Hall, (Peter C. L. & Edward K. H.,) grain-dealers, 49 s. New Jersey.

Lawyer John A., engineer, 49 s. New Jersey.

Lawyer Peter C., (L. & Hall,) 49 s. New Jersey, bds. Little's Hotel.

Lax Mrs. Elizabeth, (wid. Endrulix,) res. 191 n. East.

Lax Jacob, printer, works Journal Office, res. 191 n. East.

Laycock Chas. F., carpenter, res. 300 s. Missouri.

Layman John, works Schmidt's Brewery, bds. same.

LAYMAN J. F., (Dorsey, L. & Fletcher,) 64 e. Washington, res. 379 n. Pennsylvania. See card, page 130.

Layoery James, lab., res. 82 Bates.

Laythem George, clerk, bds. Wiles House.

Layton Timothy M., shoe-maker, bds. 364 n. Mississippi.

Leabarr Lewis, moulder, res. 150 Huron.

Leach Alfred P., student, bds. 164 Virginia av.

Leach George, bds. 230 n. West.

Leach James, porter, Cottrell & Knight, bds. 268 s. East.

Leach Jeremiah, lab., bds. 276 s. West.

Leach Joseph, cloth manufacturer, res. 276 s. West.

Leach Sarah J., occupant Deaf and Dumb Asylum.

Leanaker Sada, servant, 78 w. Michigan.

LEARNED CHARLES, dealer in lath machines and agt. for Marvin's patent safes, 57 s. Illinois, res. 630 n. Illinois.

Leary Edward, lab., res. Bicking.

Leary James B., student, commercial college, bds. Macy House.

Leary Patrick C., lawyer, bds. Pyle House.

Leary John O., messenger-boy, West. Un. Tel. Co., 11 s. Meridian, bds. 114 Meek.

Leas Barbary, (wid. Jacob,) res. 454 s. Illinois.

Leathers & Carter, (William W. L. & George C.,) lawyers and notaries public, room 3 Odd Fellows' Hall, n. e. cor. Washington and Pennsylvania.

Leathers William W., (L. & Carter,) room 3 Odd Fellows' Hall, res. 273 n. New Jersey.

Leavaf Peter, boss brewer, res. 246 s. Pennsylvania.

Leavitt William, carpenter, res. 302½ e. North.

Lechene Charles, shoe-maker, works 32 e. Washington, res. 160 Madison av.

Leck Robert M., clerk, 37 e. Washington, res. 480 n. Mississippi.

Leckner Max, salesman, Stewart & Morgan, res. 36 n. Delaware.

Leclair Henry, engineer, B. R. R., bds. 272 Winston.

Lee Benjamin E., salesman, 37 e. Washington, bds. s. Meridian, bet. Maryland and Georgia.

Lee Edward S., physician, res. cor. New York and Blake.

LEE HENRY H., China Tea store and prescription drug store, 18 and 20 Bates House, new China tea store, 7 Odd Fellows' Hall, res. 189 n. Illinois.

Lee James W., (L. & Replogle,) n. w. cor. Washington and Noble, res. 161 Spring.

LEE MANDAVILLE G., editor, Evening Commercial, cor. Meridian and Circle, res. 483 n. Mississippi.

Lee Michael, plasterer, res. 319 e. Merrill.

Lee Robert D., occupant Deaf and Dumb Asylum.

Lee William E., saloon, 48 Virginia av., res. 173 s. Tennessee.

Lee Mrs. R. J., matron, City Hospital.

Leeds F. M., works Osgood & Smith, res. 131 Merrill.

Leeds George E., produce dealer, res. 256 n. Mississippi.

Leeds L. B., bds. 131 e. Merrill.

Leenon John D. S., carriage-painter, works A. W. Drew & Co., bds. 89 n. Delaware.

Lefever Samuel, contractor, 145 w. South.

Leibhardt Joseph, dyer, Merrit & Coughlen.

Leitz Theodore H., artist, res. n. East.

Lelewer David, (David L. & Bro.,) 114 s. Meridian, res. s. Delaware, near South.

LELEWER D. & BROTHER, (David & Isaac L.,) fur manfs., 114 s. Meridian. See card, page 94.

Lelewer Isaac, (David L. & Bro.,) 114 s. Meridian, res. 227 s. Delaware.

Lelsh Mrs. Elizabeth A., res. 94 n. California.

Lehr F. A., (L. & Gray,) 83½ e. Washington, res. 419 n. New Jersey.

Lehr & Gray, (Ferdinand L. & Robert P. G.,) real estate agts., 83½ e. Washington.

Lehr Philip, carpenter, res. 163 Davidson.

Lehritter C. & Co., (C. & John A. L.,) capital saloon and restaurant, 14 e. Washington.

Lehritter Conrad, (C. L. & Co.,) 14 e. Washington, res. 213 e. Ohio.

Lehritter George, saloon and restaurant, 143 e. Washington, res. same.

Lehritter John A., (C. L. & Co.,) 14 e. Washington, bds. 81 n. New Jersey.

Leibe George, shoe-maker, res. 128 Spring.

Leitham George W., machinist, res. 8 Lord.

Lemman Mrs. John, res. 72 e. Ohio.

Lemoine Louis, painter, res. 274 n. Noble.

Lemoine Victor, sign-painter, res. s. w. cor. Mississippi and Third.

Lemmen Mrs. Jane, (wid. John,) dressmaker, 72 e. Ohio, res. same.

Lemon A. E., clerk, Ind. Fire Ins. Co., 5 Odd Fellows Hall, res. 305 e. New York.

Lemon Charles P., fireman, Ind. Central R. R., res. 305 e. New York.

Lemmon Londa A., carpenter, res. 72 e. Ohio.

Lemon Daniel A., (D. A. L. & Co.,) 187 w. Washington, res. 46 n. Mississippi.

Lemon D. A. & Co., (D. A. L. & H. S. Hutchens,) groceries, 187 w. Washington.

Lemon O. V., messenger, American Express Co., res. Richmond.

Lemon Peter H., lawyer, res. 305 e. New York.

Lemons William, brick-layer, res. 158 Winston.

Lemping John, varnisher, Spiegle, Thoms & Co., bds. 182 Davidson.

Lenark Joseph, fur-dealer, 31 w. Washington, bds. 78 e. Market.

Lendhan John, lab., res. 135 Huron.

Lendormi Mrs. Disirel, (wid. Basil,) res. 434 e. North.

Lendormi Pauline, policeman, 9th ward, res. 434 e. North.

Lenk Mathias, foreman, Schmidt's brewery, res. same.

Lennert Mrs. Sarah E., embroidery, stamping and fancy goods, 20 n. Pennsylvania, res. 38 s. Illinois, up-stairs.

LENOX EDWARD, merchant tailor, 33 s. Illinois, res. same, see card page 86.

Lerisman Henry, grocer, res. 492 Virginia av.

Lenton James, teamster, res. e. s. Blake, bet. New York and Vermont.

Lentz Christian, servant, 263 n. East.

Lentz John, packer, 37 s. Meridian, res. s. e. cor. East and Stevens.

Lentz William, packer, H. F. West & Co., res. s. e. cor. East and Stevens.

Leon Adolph, boots and shoes, 27 n. Illinois, res. 301 s. Delaware.

Leonard Mrs. Abigal, (wid. James,) res. 183 n. Liberty.

Leonard Homer, student, Purdy's Commercial College, bds. 297 Winston.

Leonard James, (Mattler & L.,) 65 w. Washington, res. 213 s. Illinois.

Leonard John, stone-mason, res. 26 Orient.

Leonard Michael, works Gates, Pray & Co., bds. Mrs. Woller's, n. Pennsylvania.

Leonard Morris, lab., res. 16 Willard.

Leonard William F., horse-broker, res. 297 Winston.

Leonhart Herman, cooper, bds. 90 Union.

Leofer Miss M. E., teacher of German, Ind. Female College, cor. Meridian and New York.

Leparn D., fireman, C., C. & I. C. R. R., res. 421 e. Georgia.

Lepp Henry, tailor, shop Massachusetts av., res. 320 e. Ohio.

Leppert E. J., occupant Deaf and Dumb Asylum.

Leppert Leebold, tailor, 17 e. Washington, res. on Bluff rd.

Leppert Nicholas, blacksmith, I. & C. shops, res. 23 Lord.

Lerkamp John, clerk, (John Helm,) bds. 272 Winston.

Leser John, (Rose & L.,) 90 e. Washington, res. 156 n. Davidson.

Lesh Aaron B., (L., Tousey & Co.,) 43 s. Delaware. res. 94 n. California.

Lesh Lewis, (L., Tousey & Co.,) 43 s. Delaware, res. 48 n. California, old number.

LESH, TOUSEY & CO., Aaron B. & Lewis L. & Wood T.,) pork-packers and com. mers., 43 s. Delaware.

Leslie Samuel, works Union Starch Factory, bds. 292 Winston.

Lesman August, lab., res. 413 Virginia av.

Lesman C., lab., res. bet. Pine and Cedar.

Lesman Lizzie, res. 9 Forest av.

Lester George S., boots and shoes, 15 s. Meridian, bds. Commercial Hotel.

Letard M'lle. F., teacher of French and German, Ind. Female College, 146 n. Meridian, bds. same.

Lethan Victor, painter, cor. Second and Missouri, res. same.

Letral Toney, fireman, P. & I. R. R., bds. 108 s. New Jersey.

Letz Theobold, artist, Miller & Frank's over 45 e. Washington, res. 81 n. East.

Levien Sigment, travelling agt., res. 212 e. Vermont.

Levy Henry, second-hand clothing, 199 e. Washington, res. same.

Lewellyn Arthur, (col.,) servant, 410 n. Delaware.

Lewellyn Richard, carpenter, works Vincent & Thompson, bds. 178 Davidson.

Lewis Anderson, (col.,) blacksmith, res. 21 Minerva.

Lewis Anna, (col.,) servant, W. C. Tarkington.

Lewis Archibald M., carpenter, res. Geisendorff, near Geisendorff Woolen Factory.

Lewis Cyrus, (col.,) lab., res. Canal, bet. Maryland and Georgia.

Lewis Edgar, railroader, bds. 166 Buchanan.

LEWIS GEORGE W., salesman, 98 e. Washington, res. 312 e. Louisiana.

Lewis Hiram L., teamster, res. 407 s. East.

Lewis John, teamster, res. 151 bluff rd.

Lewis John, (col.,) waiter, Bates House.

Lewis John, inmate Deaf and Dumb Asylum.

Lewis Jonathan W., carpenter, res. 318 e. New York.

Lewis Louisa, (col.,) cook, 27 n. New Jersey.

Lewis Tompkins A., supt. Gt. W. Ex. Co., 80 Virginia av., res. n. w. cor. Meridian and First.

Lewis Walter W., bds. 14 e. Mississippi.

Lewis William, (col.,) lab., res. 157 Maple.

Lewis W. H., (LaDow & L.,) 120 s. Illinois, bds. Oriental House.

Lewis W. H. H., printer, res. 32 e. Ohio.

Lewitt William H., machinist, Grover & Baker Sewing Machine Co.'s Rooms, 21 e. Washington.

Lex Jacob, printer, Journal bldg., bds. 191 n. East.

Lex Lewis, printer, Journal bldg., bds. 191 n. East.

Lexauer Edward, groceries, 125 e. Washington, res. same.

Liautey John, shoe-maker, 139 e. Washington, bds. 137 e. Washington.

Liceman William, lab., res. rear 9 Peru.

Lich Henry G., pastor, German M. E. Church, res. 224 e. Ohio.

Lickhart George, baggage-master, T. H. & St. Louis R. R., res. 395 s. Delaware.

Liddy Frederick U., salesman, Trade Palace, bds. Pyle House.

Liden Thomas, railroader, res. 388 s. Missouri.

Lieber H. & Co., (Herman L. & Charles Koehne,) picture-frames, looking-glasses, &c., 21 n. Pennsylvania.

Lieber Herman L., (H. L. & Co.,) 21 n. Pennsylvania, res. 404 n. Delaware.

Lieber Peter, city brewery, 213 s. Pennsylvania.

Lieble George, shoe-maker, works 204 e. Washington, res. 126 Spring.

Liebrich Lewis, porter, Browning's drug store, res. 330 w. North.

Liechenfelt Henry, turner, bds. 272 e. Washington.

Liegel Martin, breweryman, res. cor. South and Meridian.

Lietz Theobold, portrait-painter, office A. R. Miller's Gallery, res. 83 n. East.

Lightfoot Thomas, (col.,) lab., res. Camp Carrington.

Lightford J. G., machinist, res. 73 s. Pennsylvania.

Lilly Eiy, chemist, 38 s. Meridian.

Likens Mahala H., occupant Deaf and Dumb Asylum.

Likert Simon, express-driver, res. 271 n. Liberty.

Lilienkamp Ernest, tailor, works over 182 e. Washington, bds. Union Hall.

Lilly Herman, printer, res. 108 s. Meridian.

Lilly John O. D., agt. Car Spring Co., res. n. Tennesee, bet. Second and Third.

Lilly Joseph D., pump-maker, res. 459 s. Missouri.

Lilly Miss Mary E., bds. 73 w. Maryland.

Linas Daniel, stone-cutter, res. 23 Rose.

Linch Martin, turner, Spiegle, Thoms & Co., bds. 27, bet. s. Liberty and East.

Linch Michael, lab., bds. 27, bet. s. Liberty and East.

Linchan John, lab., res. 347 s. Illinois.

Lincoln Charles, clerk, 38 w. Washington, bds. 73 n. Illinois.

Lindeman Frank, clerk, 125 e. Washington, res. 293 e. Ohio.

Lindenbower William H., real estate agt., office Temperance Hall, res. 682 n. Mississippi.

Linder J. L., grocer, 395 s. East, res. same.

Lindeman Bernard, lab., res. 475 e. Market.

Lindis M. M., asst. supt. White Lime C. T. Co., res. 506 n. Meridian.

LINDLEY & CO., (Hiram L. & Frank A. Dial,) real estate and insurance agts., over 8 e. Washington.

Lindley Miss Delia, milliner, over 8 w. Washington, bds. 202 n. Davidson.

Lindley Henry J., book-keeper, McKernan & Pierce, res. 71 Indiana av.

Lindley Hiram, (L. & Co.,) over 8 e. Washington, res. 74 e. North.

Lindley Miss Jane L., school-teacher, Fourth Ward School, res. 203 Davidson.

Lindley Lemuel G., conductor, B. R. R., res. 203 Davidson.

Lindman William, moulder, Root's Foundry, res. 109 Benton.

Lindsay Lavina, inmate Deaf and Dumb Asylum.

Line Isaac M., brick-layer, res. 291 n. Liberty.

Linens Daniel, brakesman, C., C. & I. C. R. R., bds. 58 Benton.

Liner Charles, brakeman, C., C. & I. C. R. R., bds. 424 on C. R. R.

Lines & Smelser, (J. W. L. & F. S.,) wholesale dealers in tobacco and cigars, 6 w. Louisiana.

Lines J. W., (L. & Smelser,) 6 w. Louisiana, bds. Bates House.

Lingenfelter Archibald, Jr., carpenter, res. Shelbyville pike, one mile s. corporation.

Lingenfelter Ashford, Sr., carpenter, res. 271 Davidson.

Lingenfelter Ashford, Jr., carpenter, bds. 271 Davidson.

Lingenfelter Jefferson, carpenter, res. 271 Davidson.

Lingenfelter John W., carpenter, res. 32 Bradshaw.

Lingenfelter W. H., boarding-house, 35 Circle.

Lingenfelter ———, (Holladay & L.,) 16½ s. Meridian.

Link Andrew S., cabinet-maker, res. 280 n. Noble.

Link George, lab., bds. 75 s. West.

Link Mary, servant,.225 s. Delaware.

Link Nathan, (col.,) cook, Bates House.

Link Olander, lab., res. 77 w. McCarty.

Linnell Charles, works Junction R. R., bds. Wiles House.

Linsemann Charles, clerk, Emenegger's Saloon, 113 e. Washington, res. same.

Linser John H., bar-tender, Emenegger's Hotel, bds. same.

Linsey Aaron, cooper, bds. 269 n. West.

Lintner Abraham, clerk, 184 Indiana av., bds. 269 n. West.

Lintner Amos H., groceries, 182 Indiana av., res. same.

Lindner Miss Ann, res. 269 n. West.

Lintner C. H., dry goods, 184 Indiana av., bds. 285 n. West.

Lintner Daniel S., groceries and produce, cor. North and Dunlop, res. same.

Lintner John, res. 269 n. West.

Lintner John, groceries and provisions, 395 s. East, res. same.

Linton James W., soda business, res. 179 Indiana av.

Lintz Benjamin, lab., bds. Court, bet. East and New Jersey.

Lintz Benjamin, porter, Stewart & Morgan, bds. 62 s. Delaware.

Lintz Mrs. Delia, (wid.,) dealer in Boots and Shoes, 25 w. Washington, res. 70 w. New York.

Lintz G., gardener, res. n. s. National rd., w. White river bridge.

Lintz John, lab., res. 112 Stevens.

Lintz John, servant, Robert Butler.

Lintz John K., clerk, 25 w. Washington, bds. 70 w. New York.

Lintz William F, porter, West's queensware store.

Lintzman Louisa, servant, George Stiltz, near corporation.

Lions Adolph, shoe-maker, res. 301 s. Delaware.

Lipp Emanuel, carpenter, bds. 31 w. Ohio.

Lipp Henry, carpenter, res. 315 Virginia av.

Lipp Henry A., merchant tailor, 13 Massachusetts av., res. 320 e. Ohio.

Lippert Mrs. Elizabeth, (wid. Henry,) res. 222 Railroad.

Lish Arnold, bds. 94 n. California.

Lister Roll, brakesman, I., C. & L. R. R., bds. Sherman House.

Little George, moulder, res. s. Missouri near Rolling Mill.

Little Joseph C., roller, Rolling Mill, res. 230 s. Mississippi.

Little H. C., inmate Deaf and Dumb Asylum.

Litte's Hotel, s. e. cor. Washington and New Jersey, Richard Pryor, propr.

Little Washington, painter, res. 74 n. Liberty.

Litton Preston, grocer, 504 n. Illlinois, res. same.

Livengood Edward, conductor Bellefontaine R. R., res. 383 e. Michigan.

Livingston H. B., salesman, 2 Bates House blk., res. 78 n Pennsylvania.

Livingston Miss Josephine, bds. 275 Bluff rd.

Lloyd Gideon, real estate agt., over 49 Washington, cor. Pennsylvania and Washington, res. 241 n. Tennessee.

Lloyd S. C., teamster, Roberts' lumber yard, bds. 241 n. Tennessee.

Lobee Christopher, driver, Simpson, bds. 325 s. Delaware.

Locie Samuel, stationary engineer, bds. 58 Benton.

Locke Eric, banker and broker, over 19 n. Meridian, res. 76 California, bet. Vermont and Michigan.

Locke James, lab., res. 444 s. Illinois.

Locke Josiah, capitalist, res. 463 n. Pennsylvania.

Locke Otho, clerk, 65 s. Illinois, bds. same.

Locke L. S., painter, works 175 s. Tennessee, res. 444 s. Illinois.

Locke William M., boarding-house, 266 s. Illinois.

Lockland Mrs. Elizabeth, (wid.,) boarding-house, 111 w. south.

Lockley Arthur, (col.,) teamster, res. 39 n. Harris.

LOCKHART WILSON, M. D., supt. Insane Asylum, National rd., two miles west of city.

Locklaer Mrs. Lavina, (col.,) washerwoman, res. Lafayette R. R., bet First and Second.

Lockley Mrs. Elizabeth, (wid.,) Elizabeth, near City Hospital.

Lockwood Henry, cooper, res. 324 e. Louisiana.

Lockwood Nelson, cooper, res. Minerva, bet. Vermont and New York.

Loeble Wm., lab., res. Bluff rd., s. city limits.

Loehman Charles, grocer, res. 376 Virginia av.

Loeper James W., machine draftsman, room 4 Vinton's blk., res. 173 n. Tennessee.

Loeper Max, Jr., physician and surgeon, 188 e. Washington, res. same.

Loeper William, Sr., physician and surgeon, 88 e. Washington, res. same.

LOGAN ABRAM L., (L. & Co.,) 16½ e. Washington, res. same.

Logan Bernard, grocer and produce dealer, 191 w. South, res. same.

LOGAN & BROWN, (Reuben D. L. & Benjamin B.,) attorneys and counselors at law, notaries public and collecting agts., over 4 w. Washington. See card, page 62.

LOGAN & CO., publishers Indianapolis, Terre Haute, Fort Wayne and other City Directories; also, State Gazetteers and R. R. Directories, U. S. P. O. Directory; and publishers Western Commercial Review and R. R. Journal; office, 16½ e. Washington. See card.

Logan John A., works Singer's sewing machines, bds. 321 s. Missouri.

Logan Judge, lawyer, bds. 268 e. St. Clair.

Logan Mathew, shipping clerk, Singer Manufacturing Co., res. 23 Fayette.

Logan Patrick, lab., 321 s. Missouri.

Logan Mrs. Mary, (col., wid.,) res. rear 276 e. North.

Logan Reuben D., (L. & Brown,) over 4 w. Washington, res. 422 n. East.

Logan Samuel L., traveling agt. Grover & Baker Sewing Machine Co., 21 e. Washington.

Logan Thomas J., carpenter, res. 171 Meek.

Logan Mrs. W., (wid. Martin,) res. 12 Sinker.

Logsdew Nancy J., (wid. David,) res. 7 Kentucky av.

Logsdon Thomas, painter, bds. 506 e. Washington.

Logue J. H., harness-maker, 24 n. Delaware, bds. 152 n. Meridian.

Lohman William, drayman, Anderson, Bullock & Schofield, res. 105 s. Mississippi.

Lohrman Paul, (Frauer, Bieler & Co.,) 109 e. Washington, res. 25 w. St. Clair.

Loines Timothy, lab., res. 46 Wyoming.

Lollendine Leonard F., runner, Oriental House, bds. same.

Lolly Ann, servant, 163 n. Tennessee.

Lolly Thomas, tailor, res. 225 w. South.

Loman Charles, carpenter, res. 577 e. St. Clair.

Loman James, egg-packer, 18 w. Pearl, res. 152 e. St. Clair.

Loman Nelson, pump-maker, works 87 Massachusetts av., bds. cor. Delaware and St. Clair.

Louden Andrew, book-binder, bds. 572 n. Tennessee.

Louden James S., clerk, Journal Office, bds. 572 n. Tennessee.

Lonergan John, groceries, 154 n. e. cor. Pine and Noble, res. same.

Lonergan Morris, boiler-maker, bds. 154 n. e. cor. Pine and Noble.

Long & Birch, (Mathew L. & Richard B.,) undertakers, 15 Circle, bet. Meridian and Market.

Long Miss Caroline, bds. 81 w. Michigan.

Long D. D., (S. Smith & Co.,) res. 249 s. New Jersey.

Long Eli C., grainer, works 9 Massachu-setts av., res. 81 w. Michigan.

Long E. F., salesman, New York Store, bds. 58 s. Pennsylvania.

Long George, pastor, Presbyterian Church, Clermont, res. 202 e. Market.

Long G. T., boot and shoe-maker, res. 475 n. East.

Long Isaac S., lumber dealer, res. 264 n. Blake.

Long James, plasterer, res. 74 Bicking.

LONG JAMES H.,
(col.,) barber shop, shampooing and hair dressing saloon, cor. Meridian and Circle, res. cor. Tennessee and Sixth. See card.

Long Joseph D., local editor Journal, bds. Oriental House.

Long Joseph, shoe-maker, res. Western av., near city limits.

Long Mathew, (L. & Birch,) 15 Circle, res. n. New Jersey.

Long Oliver L., grainer, works 9 Massa-chusetts av., bds. 81 w. Michigan.

Long Robert, (L. & Birch,) 15 Circle, res. 353 n. New Jersey.

Long, Snyder & Co., (David D. L., Adam S. & Madison Munday,) malt dealers, 214 and 216 s. Delaware.

Long Thomas, grocer, 127 Indiana av., res. 119 Indiana av.

LONG THOMAS F.,
feather renovator, 55 Indiana av., res. 462 e. Georgia.

Long William C., works Osgood & Smith, bds. 154 s. Illinois.

Longdorff Henry, res. 302 n. Blake.

Longdorff Mrs. Martha, res. over 320 e. Washington.

Longdorff William, carpenter, res. 111 Mas-sachusetts av.

Longrich Edward, tailor, works Goepper & Co., res. 284 e. North.

Longrich Mrs. Margaret, (wid. Edward,) bds. 284 e. North.

Loomis George B., music-teacher, public schools, res. 125 e. Vermont.

Loomis J. K., conductor, J., M. & I. R. R., bds. Ray House.

Loomis W. H., city councilman, res. 29 School.

Loomis Margaret, servant, 165 n. Alabama.

Loose Miss Annie, res. 117 n. Missouri.

Loose Samuel, local engineer, C. & I. C. R. R.

Lord Alice, lady boarder, over 270 e. Wash-ington.

LORD JOHN M.,
prest. and supt. Indianapolis Rolling Mill Co., res. 297 n. Pennsylvania.

Losee Thomas V., master-machinist, C. I. & L. R. R. shop, res. 326 e. Georgia.

Losey John, cooper, 102 s. East, res. 112 s. East.

Lord John P., book-keeper, Ind. Banking Co., 28 e. Washington, bds. 297 n. Pennsylvania.

Lord Ralph K., blacksmith, White River Iron Works, res. s. w. cor. South and Tennessee.

Losey M. D., book-keeper, 38 e. Washing-ton, res. 112 s. East.

LOSIE J. M. & CO.,
(J. M. L. & ———,) maufr. of patent spring bed-bottoms, 83 e. Washington. See card.

Louch Alfred A., painter, works George W. Dalton, cor. Kentucky av. and Ten-nessee.

Louck Mrs. Mary, (wid. Michael,) res. 391 s. Delaware.

Loucks & Bruner, grocers and produce-dealers, cor. Cherry and Broadway.

Loucks Calvin R., painter, 327 e. Wash-ington, res. Michigan rd., beyond city limits.

Loucks Charles, carpenter, res. 78 Benton.

Loucks Christopher B., carpenter, res. 186 Bates.

Loucks George, (L. & Greuzard,) 327 e. Washington, bds. 182 Bates.

Loucks & Greuzard. (George W. L., & L. S. G.,) painters, 327 e. Washington.

Loucks James, (Bruner & L.,) res. 400 n. New Jersey.

Loucks Joseph, moulder, bds. 187 Bates.

Loucks W. W., carpenter, res. 341 n. Ala-bama.

Louden Andrew A., res. 572 n. Tennessee.

Louden Henry A., clerk, Journal office, bds. 572 n. Tennessee.

Louder S. T., salesman, 19 s. Meridian, res. 15 e. Ohio.

Loughnen Dennis, lab., res. 40 Ellen.

Louid Edward, turner, res. over 232 e. Washington.

Louis Anderson, (col.,) blacksmith, res. cor. North and Minerva.

Louis Anna, (wid. Bradley L.,) washer-woman, res. 224 n. Missouri.

Loucks Mrs. Elizabeth, (wid. David,) tailoress, res. 147 Union.

Louney William, boiler-maker, bds. 111 Huron.

Louney Edward, lab., res. 111 Huron.

Louney Miss Margaret, res. 111 Huron.

Louney, Michael, carpenter, bds. 111 Hu-ron.

Louney William, lab., res. 111 Huron.

Loury Harry, blacksmith, bds. California House.

Louthan David K., baker, works 188 e. Washington, res. 26 n. Pennsylvania.

Louts John, painter, bds. 314 e. Georgia.

Love John, res. 81 n. Tennessee.

Love William, (William Love & Co.,) room 1, Talbott & New's blk., n. Pennsyl-vania, res. 506 e. Washington.

LOVE WILLIAM & CO., (William L. & Jacob P. Dunn,) real estate brokers, room 1, Talbott & New's blk., n. Pennsylvania.

Lovejoy A. A., supt. Vincennes R. R., bds. Spencer House.

Lovejoy J. H., printer, H. C. Chandler & Co., res. 35 s. West.

Lovell Bass, (col.,) huckster, res. 126 Benton.

Lowe Albert, (col.,) lab., res. w. Center.

Lowe Charles G., (Lowe & Son,) 30 s. New Jersey, res. 318 n. Liberty.

LOWE GEORGE, carriage repository, 46 n. Pensylvania, res. 321 n. Pennsylvania.

Lowe George, lab., res. s. New Jersey.

Lowe James, bds. 399 s. East.

Lowe Nahum H., sr., (Lowe & Son,) 30 s. New Jersey, res. 308 e. North.

Lowe Nahum H., Jr., carpenter, bds. 308 e. North.

Lowe N. H. & Son, (N. H. & Charles G· L.,) carpenters and builders, 30 s. New Jersey.

LOWE WILLIAM A., attorney at law, over 20 e. Washington, Sentinel bldg., res. 44 Christian av., cor. Jackson. See card page 68.

Lowe William W., res. 560 n. Illinois.

Lowery John, miller, res. 359 w. Washington.

Lowder Samuel, salesman, 49 s. Meridian, res. 15 e. Ohio.

Lowen John, wood-chopper, res. 59 Hosbrook.

Lower John, lab., res. 27 w. McCarty.

Lower John, foreman, Coburn & Jones, res. 386 n. Delaware.

Lower John W., foreman, Coburn & Jones' lumber yard, bds. 386 n. Delaware.

Lowman Georgiana, occupant Deaf and Dumb Asylum.

Lowman Nelson D., blacksmith, res. 112 e. St. Clair.

Lowman William, blacksmith, res. 112 e. St. Clair.

Lowrie William, clerk, New York Store, bds. 181 n. Liberty.

Lowry Wiley W., druggist, 65 Massachusetts av., res. 73 Massachuseets av.

Loy D. M., foreman tin-shop, D. Root & Co., bds. 126 e. Maryland.

Lozier John H., (Rev.,) pastor, Asbury Chapel, res. e. Washington, beyond city limits.

Luallen James, (col.,) lab., res. n. Douglas Alley.

Luallen John, (col.,) servant, 282 w. New York.

Lucas Benjamin F., I. M. P., res. 82 s. Benton.

Lucas James, (col.,) white-washer, res. 233 n. West.

Lucas J. G., mill-wright, 132 s. Pennsylvania, res. 84 s. Illinois.

Lucas Walter A., book-keeper, Geisendorff & Co., bds. Oriental House.

Lucesi John, terre cotta maker, bds. 23 Kentucky av.

Lucia John, lab., res. 358 s. West.

Lucia Morris, railroader, res. 228 s. West.

Lucia Morris, lab., res. 339 s. Missouri.

Lucitt Bridget, pantry girl, Sherman House, bds. same.

Lucky Willis, porter, Globe House, bds. same.

Luddington W. H. H., traveling agt., Wheeler & Wilson's Sewing Machines, 10 w. Washington, res. 316 s. Delaware.

Ludlow George, carpenter, res. 495 Virginia av.

Ludlow Jason C., foreman, Warren Tates' Planing Mill, res. 136 n. New Jersey.

Ludlow John, meat market, 34 n. Pennsylvania, res. 268 s. New Jersey.

Ludlow Silas, traveling agt., A. Jones & Co., res. 97 Jackson.

Ludlow Stephen W., clerk, Post Office, bds. 60 Market.

Ludlum J. E., res. 49 Chatham.

Ludorff Lewis, (L. L. & Co.,) 42 s. Meridian, res. 320 s. Meridian.

Ludwig Lewis, res. 178 s. Illinois.

Ludorff L. & Co., (Lewis L. & B. E. Thonssen,) wholesale dealers in notions and general furnishing goods, 42 s. Meridian.

Ludwig James, dyer, res. Geisendorff, near Geisendorff's Woolen Factory.

Ludwig Otto, wines and liquors, 181 e. Washington, res. 111 e. Washington.

Ludwig Lewis, res. 178 s. Illinois.

Ludwig Samuel, groceries, 142 Fort Wayne av., res. same.

Lueders Miss Catharine, (Lueders Sisters,) 74½ e. Market, res. 484 n. Mississippi.

Lueders Miss Cornelia, (Lueders Sisters,) 74½ e. Market, res. 484 n. Mississippi.

Lueders Miss Eliza, (Lueders Sisters,) 74½ e. Market, res. 484 n. Mississippi.

Lueders Miss Louisa, (Lueders Sisters,) 74½ e. Market, res. 484 n. Mississippi.

Lueders Sisters, (Catharine, Cornelia, Eliza & Louisa L.,) stamping and embroidering, 74½ e. Market.

Lueders Thomas C., res. 484 n. Mississippi.

Luging James, dyer, res. 21 Douglas.

Lukey Christopher, lab., Coburn & Jones' Lumber Yard, res. 474 e. Washington.

Lukens Benjamin, res. 612 n. Illinois.

Lukens & Hollowell, (R. L. L. & I. S. H.,) agricultural Implements, 26 and 28 s. Tennessee.

Lukens Robert L, (L. & H. Hollowell,) 26 and 28 s. Tennessee, res. 281 Virginia av.

Lukens Richard, agl. implements, 25 s. Tennessee, res. 281 Virginia av.

Luley Calvin, clerk, 152 w. Washington, res. 74 e. Pratt.

Lumpkins Henry, (col.,) lab., bds. Railroad, bet. Fifth and Sixth.

LUNT JAMES M., gen'l supt. C., C. & I. C. R. R., office s. e. cor. Virginia av. and Delaware, res. 360 n. Alabama.

Luony Amanda, (wid. Dennis,) res. cor. West and Georgia.

Lupton Elizabeth, res. cor. West and Georgia, beyond city limits.

Lupton George, dentist, res. 21 Indiana av.

Luphart Joseph, dyer, Merritt & Coughlen.

Lupton Miss Rebecca, res. n. Pennsylvania, beyond city limits.

Lupton William C., painter, res. 290 e. Ohio.

Lureingler George, (col.,) hod-carrier, res. 75 s. Missouri.

Luther Alford, painter, res. 267 n. Mississippi.

Luther Robert, wagon-maker, res. 22 California.

Lutimer Herman, lab., Henry Weghorst, s. East, near city limits.

Lutman Samuel, conductor, C., C. & I. C. R. R., bds. Sherman House.

Lutz George, shoe-maker, res. 400 Virginia av.

Lutz John J., soldier, U. S. Arsenal, res. same.

Lyden Thomas, works railroad repair shop, bds. 199 w. Maryland.

Lyer Peter, blacksmith, res. 390 Virginia av.

Lynn Josephine, servant, 144 n. East.

Lybrand Christopher, machinist, res. 223 s. Tennessee.

Lydon Thomas, lab., T. H. & I. R. R. Engine House, 388 s. Missouri.

Lymann John H., manfr. boots and shoes, 9 n. Illinois, res. 223 w. Washington.

Lynch Ann, servant, 23 w. Ohio.

Lynch Bridget, wash-women, Sherman House, bds. same.

Lynch Catharine, wash-women, Commercial Hotel.

Lynch Jacob, (L. & L.,) 83 Kentucky av. res. 28 Chadwick.

Lynch John, lab., White River Iron Works, res. 349 s. Missouri.

Lynch J. S., grain-buyer, bds. Wiles House.

Lynch & Lilly, (Jacob H. L. & Joseph D. L.,) pump manfrs., 83 Kentucky av.

Lynch Martin, turner, bds. 281 e. Georgia.

Lynch Michael, brick-layer, res. e. s. n. Illinois, bet. Third and Fourth.

Lynch Michael P., clerk, 68 s. Meridian, bds. Oriental House.

Lynch Owen, lab., res. 20 California.

Lynch Patrick, lab., bds. 115 n. Noble.

Lynch Patrick, engineer, Sinker's Foundry, res. 109 Harrison.

Lynch Patrick, porter, Spencer House, bds. same.

Lynch Wesley, carpenter, res. 556 n. Alabama.

Lynn Daniel, lab., res. 41 Dacotah.

Lynn James, machinist, Sinker's, res. 346 s. Alabama.

Lynn Miss Mary E., dress-maker, over 199 e. Washington, res. same.

Lynn P. A., clerk, Union Line, office 85 Virginia av., bds. Pyle House.

Lynn Robert, lab., res. 123 Maple.

Lynn William A., cooper, res. 426 Virginia av.

Lynn Winfield S., salesman, Browning & Sloan, bds. Oriental House.

Lyon Miss Catharine, wash-woman, res. 269 s. Pennsylvania.

Lyons Annie, servant, Palmer House.

Lyons Charles, engineer, B. R. R., res. 265 Davidson.

Lyon Daniel, works Junction R. R., bds. Wiles House.

Lyons George, works Pork House, res. 298 Madison av.

Lyons James, lab., res. 145 n. Mississippi.

Lyons John, boiler-maker, Sinker & Co.
Lyons John, lab., res. 243 s. Missouri.
Lyons John, second-hand furniture, 243 e. Washington, res. same.
Lyons Julia, chamber-maid, Bates House.
Lyons Mrs. Mary A., (wid.,) res. 500 n. Tennessee.
Lyons Patrick, works City Gas Works, res. 147 s. Alabama.
Lyons William, lab., 341 s. Delaware.
Lyons William G. W., foreman, Furgason's pork house, res. 298 Madison av.
Lyter Elvira A., occupant Deaf and Dumb Asylum.
Lytle Alexander, groceries and provisions, 52 Indiana av., res. same.
Lytle Miss Phebe A., works Capital Tobacco Works, res. 325 s. Meridian.
Lytle Robert J., carpenter, res. 392 s. Missouri.

McADAMS MISS BELL, bds. 51 Douglas Alley.
McAndrews Walter, bar-keeper, 132 s. Illinois, bds. Neiman House.
McAllie Jacob, wagon-maker, res. 234 w. Michigan.
McAllister James W., soldier, U. S. Arsenal, res. same.
McAllister William, medical student, 3 Virginia av., bds. 936 s. Alabama.
McAlpine, machinist, bds. 452 e. Michigan.
McAlvano John, painter, res. 144 w. New York.
McArthur James, salesman, New York Store, bds. 82 e. Washington.
McArthur John B., councilman, fourth ward, res. 270 n. West.
McAvir James, gas-fitter, works 82 e. Market.
McBaker Thomas, tailor, res. 170 e. Michigan.
McBeth Alexander, stone-cutter, res. rear 172 w. Washington.
McBride John, saloon, 159 w. Washington, bds. same.

McBride Michael, pedler, res. 274 n. Liberty.
McBride Riley, carpenter, res. 237 w. Merrill.
McCabe John, bar-tender, 62 w. Maryland, bds. same.
McCabe Matthew, (Simpson & McC.,) saloon, 52 s. s. Illinois, res. 9 Forest av.
McCaferry Thomas, lab., res. 320 s. West.
McCain G. W., book-agt., res. 676 n. Mississippi.
McCain James, carpenter, bds. 73 n. Illinois.
McCain John, engineer, res. 224 s. Noble.
McCall C. C., telegraph operator, bds. 348 n. Alabama.
McCall Hugh, servant, at 112 n. Meridian.
McCall Neenith, inmate Home for the Friendless, w. s. n. Pennsylvania, beyond city limits.
McCallay Jacob, res. 234 w. Michigan.
McCann Miss Catharine, res. 27 Lockerbie.
McCann Dennis, lab., res. 3 Bates
McCann James A., student, City Academy, res. 69 n. East.
McCann Patrick, lab., res. 100 s. East.
McCann Samuel D., physician and surgeon, office 69 n. East, res. same.
McCarey Robert, (col.,) barber, bds. 756 n. Tennessee.
McCarr Patrick, lab., res. 100 s. East.
McCarthy Bridget, servant, 420 n. Alabama.
McCarthy H. B., actor, res. 80 n. Mississippi.
McCarthy John, works Spiegel, Thoms & Co.
McCarthy Thomas, teamster, bds. 57 Wyoming.
McCarthy Timothy, teamster, res. 57 Wyoming.
McCarthy William, lab., res. 320 s. Delaware.
McCarthy William, iron-moulder, Sinker & Co., res. 137 Davidson.
McCarty Mrs. Catharine, (wid. Michael,) res. 199 n. East.

McCarty Charles, lab., res. 190 Harrison.
McCarty Hannah, servant, 523 n. Tennessee.
McCarty James, works rolling mill, bds. Burns House.
McCarty James, lab., res. 243 s. Tennessee.
McCarty James, lab., Bellefontaine shops, bds. 248 Winston.
McCarty John, turner, res. 281 Georgia.
McCarty Joseph, metre and service register, gas works, res. cor. Delaware and South.
McCarty Mrs. Margaret, (wid.) res. 122 n. Pennsylvania.
McCarty Mrs. Mary, (wid.,) res. 2 n. Douglas Alley.
McCarty Mrs. Mary, (wid. Daniel,) res. 376 e. Market.
McCarty Michael, lab., res. near Jeffersonville Round-House.
McCarty Nicholas, office s. w. cor. Washington and Meridian, res. 122 n. Pennsylvania.
McCarty O. P., clerk, general ticket office, C. C., & I. C. R. W., bds. 73 w. Maryland.
McCarty Stephen, lab., res. 393 e. Michigan.
McCARTY THOMAS B., Auditor of State, office new State bldg. cor. Tennessee and Washington, res 194 n. Illinois.
McCarty Timothy, lab., res. 57 Wyoming.
McCarty Timothy, driver on street cars, bds. 88 s. Mississippi.
McCarty William, moulder, Sinker & Co.
McCary Robert, (col.,) barber, 14 Bates House, res. 196 n. Missouri.
McCay Elizabeth, (wid. Theodore,) res. 314 e. Georgia.
McCay M. H., (John Furnas & Co.,) 68 e. Washington, res. near Georgia.
McCay Robert, propr. Favorite Saloon, 560 Virginia av., res. same.
McChesney Edward, baggage-master, C., C. & I. C. R. R., bds. 454 n. Tennessee.
McChesney J. B., treasurer, C. C. & I. C. R. W., res. 455 n. Tennessee.
McChesney Sarah, (wid.,) res. 133 n. Pennsylvania.
McChesney William L., asst. book-keeper, A. Jones & Co., 74 and 76 s. Meridian, bds. 454 n. Tennessee.
McClain Albert, painter, res. 12 w. North.
McClain John S., clerk, 225 w. Washington, res. same.
McClain Miss Martha Ann, seamstress, res. Michigan rd., beyond city limits.
McClain Miss Mary, res. 275 s. Noble.
McClain Moses, drives express wagon, bds. 457 e. Georgia.
McClain Mrs. Susan, (wid. Jacob,) res. 234 Huron.
McClain William C., carpenter, res. 317 e. Ohio.

McClain Miss Sarah, bds. 144 n. Tennessee.
McClaren John, printer, res. 399 n. Alabama.
McClay C. S., clerk, 7 and 9 e. Washington, bds. Spencer House.
McClellan John, clerk, res. 331 w. Maryland.
McClelland Joel C., res. 196 e. St. Joseph.
McClelland Robert, carpenter, works Belfontaine R. R. shops, res. 68 Davidson.
McClendock William, lab., res. 322 s. East.
McClintock Edward, res. 307 n. Alabama.
McClintock William, lab., res. 303 s. Delaware.
McCloskey George, boarding house, 315 e. Ohio.
McCloskey John, carpenter, res. 88 s. Mississippi.
McCloskey John, carpenter, res. 140 w. Vermont.
McCloskey J. H., clerk, 2 Odd Fellows' Hall, res. 80 Indiana av.
McCloud Mahala, (col ,) washing and ironing, res. n. Missouri.
McCloud Thomas, shoemaker, bds. 61 s. Noble.
McClure Alexander, boiler-maker, res. 227 w. Merrill.
McClure George H., carpenter, res. James, in Meikel's division.
McClure J. E., salesman, 89 e. Market, bds. 61 Ft. Wayne av.
McClure Joseph F., carpenter, res. e. s. Mississippi, bet. Third and Fourth.
McClure M. D., yard boss, Rolling Mill, bds. 347 s. Alabama.
McClure Theophilus, printer, Journal Office, res. 66 w. New York.
McClusty John, lab., res. 80 Indiana av.
McCole Mary, servant, J. Tarlton, 492 n. Tennessee.
McComb Samuel, telegraph operator, bds. Oriental House.
McConnell William, works Junction R. R., bds. Wiles House.
McCool William, box-maker, works cor. Delaware and South, res. 62 Greer.
McCool William, carpenter, res. 349, old number, e. McCarty.
McCord Benjamin R., res. 92 e. New York.
McCord R. B., (McCord & Wheatley,) 186 s. Alabama res. e. New York.
McCORD & WHEATLEY, (R. B. McC. & William M. W.,,) dealers in pine and poplar lumber, 186 s. Alabama.
McCorkle William, saloon and restaurant, 141 w. Washington.
McCormick Allen, res. 257 s. Mississippi.
McCORMICK EDWARD, Bourbon Saloon, 62 w. Maryland, res. s. Illinois.
McCormick Ephraim, teamster, res. over 308 e. Washington.

McCORMICK GEORGE, propr. Commercial Hotel, n. e. cor. Illinois and Georgia.

McCormick J. A., res. 257 s. Mississippi.

McCormick James, tobacconist, bds. Ray House.

McCormick Jediah R., carpenter and builder, cor. St. Clair and Railroad, res. 400 n. Mississippi.

McCormick John, nurseryman, n. s. National rd., one mile w. White river bridge.

McCormick John L., carpenter and builder, res. 726 n. Tennessee.

McCormick William, clerk, Commercial Hotel, bds. same.

McCormick W. H., conductor, C., I. & L. R. R., res. 240 s. Alabama.

McCormick W. L., works Junction R. R., bds. Wiles House.

McCowen Mary, (col.,) servant, 456 n. Meridian.

McCoy Benjamin R., lumber merchant, yard cor. South and Delaware, res. 77 Kentucky av.

McCoy Boykin, (col.,) blacksmith, bds. n. Michigan rd., near Tenth.

McCoy Charles, traveling agt. Wheeler & Wilson's sewing machines.

McCoy John, physician and surgeon, 151 e. Washington, bds. Pattison House.

McCoy Robert, photographer, res. 299 e. New York.

McCrea Rollin H., (Stiles, Fahnly & McC.,) 131 s. Meridian, bds. Sherman House.

McCready Frank, tinner, works Tutewiler & Bros., bds. 240 e. Vermont.

McCready James B., book-keeper, Indiana National Bank, 2 e. Washington, res. 240 e. Vermont.

McCreery A. A., salesman, 39 s. Meridian, bds. Pyle House,

McCREERY & FAY. (John McC. & Amos F. F.,) housekeepers' emporium, 56 and 58 e. Washington. See cards, pages 96, 120 and 200.

McCreery John, (McC. & Fay,) 56 and 58 e. Washington, res. Springfield, Ills.

McCrossan Samuel, lab., res. 234 n. Mississippi.

McCubbins Miss Mary W., res. cor. Patterson and North.

McCue Anthony, lab., 114 n. Tennessee.

McCue Farrell, carpenter, bds. w. s. Mississippi, bet. First and Second.

McCue James, bar-keeper, 52 s. Illinois, bds. 259 s. west.

McCue Thomas, lab., res. 104 Cherry.

McCuit Mrs. Ellen, (wid.,) res. cor. Patterson and Elizabeth.

McCullough Jacob S., book-keeper, 112 s. Meridian, res. 308 e. New York.

McCune Henry W., book-keeper, bds. 228 n. West.

McCurron Thomas, lab., res. 107 Forest av.

McCurdy Mrs. Catharine, (wid. Alexander,) res. 230 e. Vermont.

McCurdy George W., auction and commission merchant, cor. Washington and Virginia av., res. 230 e. Vermont.

McCurdy William H. H., (Geisendorff & Co.,) 22 w. Washington, bds. 355 n. East.

McCutchan Allen, night-watchman, C., C. & I. C. freight depot, res. e. s. Liberty, bet. Meek and Georgia.

McCutchan Miss Elizabeth, res. e. s. Liberty, bet. Meek and Georgia.

McCutcheon Carmill, carpenter, res. 214 railroad.

McCutcheon George R., yard-master Peru R. R., res. 432 e. North.

McCutcheon J. C., (Landers, Pee & Co.,) 58 s. Meridian, res. 226 n. Meridian.

McDola Osa, conductor construction train, T. H. & I. R. R., res. 79 w. Lousiana.

McDaniel James R., driver engine No. 1, bds. Nagle House.

McDaniel Reason, teamster, res. 280 w. St. Clair.

McDermott Ellen, servant, 180 e. Ohio.

McDermott James, works Sinker & Co., res. 133 w. Maryland.

McDermott Joseph, stove-mounter, res. 159 s. Alabama.
McDermott Mrs. Mary, (wid.,) servant, S. C. Vance's, e. end Market.
McDermott Thomas, lab., res. 321 s. Missouri.
McDevitt Edward, machinist, Sinker & Co., bds. Ray House.
McDole Oscar H., conductor, T. H. & I. R. R., res. 79 Louisiana.
McDonald Miss Alice, ladies' boarding, 139 w. Market.
McDonald Curran E., (C. Werbe & Co.,) deputy U. S. marshal, res. 300 e. Market.
McDonald Hon. David, judge U. S. District Court for District of Ind., court rooms, p. o. bldg., res. 203 n. Pennsylvania.
McDonald E. M., (McD., Roache & McD.,) room 3 Ætna bldg., n. Pennsylvania, res. n. e. cor. St. Clair and Meridian.
McDonald George, clerk, Lee's drug store, bds. 204 n. Illinois.
McDonald James, pressman, Journal Office, res. 329 w. Maryland.
McDonald Joseph E., (McD., Roache & McD..) room 8 Ætna bldg., n. Pennsylvania, res. 229 n. Pennsylvania.
McDonald Mac, salesman, 43 s. Delaware, bds. 229 n. Pennsylvania.
McDonald Martin, carder, Geisendorff & Co., res. 329 w. Maryland.
McDonald M. A., inmate Deaf and Dumb Asylum.
McDonald Patrick, teamster, res. 133 s. New Jersey.
McDonald Patrick, lab., res. 20 Willard.
McDonald, Roache & McDonald, (Joseph E. McD., A. L. R, & E. M. McD.,) attorneys at law, room 3 Ætna bldg, n. Pennsylvania.
McDonough D. B., (McD. & Eck,) 144 s. Alabama, res. 123 e. Vermont.
McDonough & Eck, (D. B. McD. & John H. E.,) lime, plaster and hair, 144 s. Alabama.
McDougal Mrs. Louisa, res. 156 n. Illinois.
McDougal William, brakesman, B. R. R., res. over 180 e. Washington.
McDowell John, commission merchant, bds. 17 Kentucky av.
McDowell Joseph, book-keeper, Bowen, Stewart & Co., res. 75 n. Illinois.
McElroy William, weaver, Merritt & Coughlen.
McElvano John, (Cornelius & McE.,) res. 144 w. New York.
McElwee John, carpenter, Sinker's machine shop, res. 217 n. Mississippi.
McFadden Lewis L., deputy sheriff, bds. 195 Davidson.
McFadden William, lab., T. H. & I. R. R. Freight Depot, res. 16 Root.
McFall David, res. 55 e. Maryland.

McFarland A. H., carriage-maker, bds. Union Hall.
McFarland Miss C., res. 26 e. St. Clair.
McFarland Christina, servant, 132 n. Alabama.
McFarland John L., pump-maker, bds. 271 Virginia av.
McFarland Miss Laura, res. 26 e. St. Clair.
McFarland Robert, carpenter, res. 164 Dougherty.
McFarland W. H., compositor, Sentinel news room, bds. Oriental House.
McFarren James, res. 22 Fletcher av.
McGaiha Marianna, chamber-maid, Indiana Female College, 146 n. Meridian.
McGarahan James, lab., bds. Ray House, e. South.
McGarahan Thomas, tobacconist, bds. Ray House.
McGaroh Rebecca, servant, 38 w. Market.
McGaw John A., cigars and tobacco, 16 Bates House, res. 182 n. Mississippi.
McGee Bruce, clerk, 36 w. Washington, bds. Mrs. Morrison's, n. Pennsylvania.
McGee David, carpenter, res. 387 s. Missouri.
McGee Edward, boiler-maker, Sinker's, res. 215 s. Alabama.
McGee Mrs. Rachel, (wid. Samuel, bds. 344 n. Noble.
McGee Thomas, book agt., res. 308 s. West.
McGee William, engineer, res. rear 260 s. Alabama.
McGerrie G., works dining-room, Ray House.
McGibbon Mrs. Mary, house-keeper, Hess' Academy of Music.
McGiffen Samuel, broom-maker, res. 74 e. St. Clair.
McGill & Obenchain, (William C. McG. & Timothy L. O.,) groceries, s. e. cor. St. Clair and Illinois.
McGill William C., (McG. & Obenchain.) s. e. cor. St. Clair and Illinois, res. 413 n. Tennessee.
McGinnis Miss Alice, tailoress, over 28 s. Meridian, res. 83 s. West.
McGinnis Charles E., (McG. & Gray,) 45 Virginia av., res. 41 Virginia av.
McGinnis Edward, salesman, 43 Virginia av., res. 41 Virginia av.
McGinnis Mrs. Eliza, (wid.,) seamstress, res. e. s. Douglas, bet. Washington and New York.
McGINNIS GEORGE F., county auditor, res. Perry Township.
McGINNIS & GRAY, (Charles E. McG. & Stephen G.,) merchant tailors and clothiers, 45 Virginia av. See card, page 124.
McGinnis John, groceries, flour, feed and liquor, 280 e. Washington, res. same.
McGinnis John, coal-cart driver, 23 Virginia av., res. 49 s. West.

McGinnis John F., lumber merchant, res. 109 s. New Jersey.

McGinnis Nicholas, tailor, over 83 s. Meridian, res. 83 s. West.

McGinnis Oliver, works Junction R. R., bds. Wiles House.

McGinnis Owen, 45 Virginia av., res. 41 Virginia av.

McGinnis Peter, tailor, over 28 s. Meridian, res. 83 s. West.

McGinnis Miss Sarah, tailoress, over 28 s. Meridian, res. 83 s. West.

McGinnis William, freight-conductor, C., C. & I. C. R. R., res. 99 e. Georgia.

McGinnis Wilson, brakesman, bds. 99 e. Georgia.

McGinty Martin, railroad-flagman, res. 243 Kentucky av.

McGinty Mary, servant, 419 n. Illinois.

McGlen Michael, lab., res. 150 Douglas.

McGlew T., book agt., res. 316 s. West.

McGlochlan Christopher, stove-moulder, Root's, res. 296 s. East.

McGowan Daniel, works Junction R. R., bds. Wiles House.

McGowan Thomas, works Junction R. R., bds. Wiles House.

McGrath Daniel, lab., res. 290 e. Georgia.

McGrath Dennis, lab., res. 474 e. Georgia.

McGrew J. T., salesman, Hume, Adams & Co., res. 293 Virginia av.

McGruder Moses, (col.,) lab., res. 174 Douglas alley.

McGrynn Martin, works Junction R. R., bds. Wiles House.

McGuire Mrs. Hannah, (wid.,) res. 408 Indiana av.

McGuire John, lab., res. 268 Merrill.

McGuire Miss Maria, bds. 408 Indiana av.

McGuire Richard, gas-fitter, bds. Washington, bet. Tennessee and Mississippi.

McHugh John T., hat-blocker, 44 s. Illinois, bds. 104 Cherry.

McHutcheon Peter, Trade Palace, res. 323 n. Liberty.

MacIntire H. N., instructor, Deaf and Dumb Asylum.

MacIntire John, (McLene, MacI. & Hays,) w. end Maryland, res. 25 s. West.

McIntire John, soldier, U. S. Arsenal, res. same.

McIntire Lucius, heater, rolling mill, res. 18 Henry.

McIntire Robert, tobacconist, bds. Ray House, e. South.

McIntire Thomas, (McLene, MacI. & Hays,) supt. Deaf and Dumb Asylum, e. end Washington, res. same.

McIntosh Donald, boots and shoes, 63 Indiana av., res. same.

McIntosh Enos, (col.,) minister, bds. 229 n. West.

McIver Mrs. Elizabeth, (wid. John,) res. 148 n. East.

McIver John C., hats, caps, furs and straw goods, 22 e. Washington, res. 148 n. East.

McJantine Alexander, carriage-maker, res. 59 e. McCarty.

McKabe John, saloon, res. 35 Wyoming.

McKabe Joseph, lab., bds. n. s. National rd., w. White river bridge.

McKalvey Mrs. Ann, (wid. Joseph,) boarding house, 89 s. Pennsylvania.

McKay James, gas-fitter, 77 e. Market, res. cor. Washington and Liberty.

McKay M. H., (John Furnas & Co.,) 68 e. Market, res. cor. Broadway and Forrest Home av.

McKean John, engineer, rolling mill, res. 228 s. Noble.

McKee James, gas-fitter, res. 307 e. Washington.

McKee John W., agt. Grover & Baker Sewing Machine Co., res. 76 Plum.

McKee Robert, gardener, res. s. e. cor. Elm and Pine.

McKeehan Benjamin, boss track layer, I., M. & J. R. R., res. 333 s. Pennsylvania.

McKeehan Benjamin M., messenger, adjutant-general's office, res. s. Pennsylvania.

McKeehan James, railroading, bds. 333 s. Pennsylvania.

McKeehan John, stock-yard master, C., C. & I. C. R. R., res. 61 s. Noble.

McKeehan Michael, wood-engraver, res. 55 Bates.

McKeely D. S., conductor, B. R. R., bds. Sherman House.

McKeely Frank, brakesman, Bellefontaine R. R., bds. 270 Railroad.

McKena Dennis, lab., res. 3 Bates, cor. Noble.

McKeeny Oscar, engineer, T. H. & I. R. R., res. 27 Henry.

McKenzie, Mrs. Rachel, res. Blake, bet. Vermont and Michigan.

McKenzie S. L., belt-maker, Mooney & Co., bds. 18 w. Georgia.

McKenzie William, carpenter, res. Blake, bet. Vermont and Michigan.

McKeon M. M., engraver on wood, res. 55 Bates.

McKernan David S., clerk, P. O., res. 117 w. New York.

McKernan Michael, lab., res. 96 Railroad.

McKernan James H., (McK. & Pierce,) 2 Blake row, bds. Oriental House.

McKERNAN & PIERCE, (James H. McK. & Winslow S. P.,) dealers in real estate, room 1, 2d floor Blake row.

McKibben J. R., carpenter and house-builder, res. 402 n. East.

McKinney George, lab., builders and manufacturers planing mill, res. n. e. cor. Third and Illinois.

McKinley A. D., lab., res. 150 Ft. Wayne av.
McKinney H., clerk, Little's Hotel.
McKinney John A., lab., res. 25 s. Mississippi.
McKnight Mrs. Mattie, (wid. William,) washing and ironing, 27 California.
McLofflin Miron, blacksmith, bds. 404 s. Illinois.
McLane William, carpenter, res. 82 Benton.
McLane William C., carpenter, res. 244 s. East.
McLaren Duncan, groceries, 252 s. Tennessee.
McLaren Emily, (wid. Duncan,) res. 254 s. Tennessee.
McLaren John, printer, bds. 280 n. Alabama.
McLaughlin Christopher, moulder, res. 296 s. East.
McLaughlin John A., gunsmith, res. 360 s. Alabama.
McLaughlin Philip, cooper, 102 s. East, bds. 8 n. Liberty.
McLaughlin, Thomas H., lab, res. 163 Stevens.
McLean James W., mechanic, res. 11 e. South.
McLean Miss M. A., bds. 228 n. Tennessee.
McLENE & HERRON, (Jeremiah McL. & Fred M. H.,) watches, jewelry, silver-ware, and watchmaker's material, 1 Bates House blk., cor. Washington and Illinois.
McLENE, McINTIRE & HAYS, (Jeremiah McL., John and Thomas McI., & Thomas H.,) paper mill, w. end Maryland.
McLene Jeremiah, (McL. & Herron, and McL., MacIntyre & Hayes,) 1 Bates House blk., res 139 n. Pennsylvania.
McLue Dennis, lab., res. 23 Maple.
McMahan Anna, waiter, dining room, Wiles House.
McMahan Catharine, (wid. Martin,) res. 48 Henry.
McMahan Dennis, lab., res. 71 s. Liberty.
McMahan John, fireman, I., C. & L. R. R., res. 197 Bates.
McMahan Thomas, lab., res. over 356 Winston.
McMahan Sarah, (wid.,) res. 85 Maple.
McMahan T. C., cabinet-maker, bds. 65 s. East.
McMannmon Bryan, lab., res. 122 Stevens.
McManhan Catherine, (wid.,) res. 41 Henry.
McMasters Robert, bds. 82 e. St. Clair.
McMillin Charles, clerk, rolling mill coal office, bds. 74 e. Vermont.
McMillin James, chair-maker, bds. 199 Huron.
McMillin Samuel H., pawn-broker, 17½ w. Washington, res. 74 e. Vermont.
McMillin Thomas, clerk, D. R. R. Co., bds. 74 e. Vermont.

McMillin & Co., (James McM. & William F. Combs,) real estate brokers, 17 w. Washington.
McMullen Henry, bds. 75 n. Illinois.
McMullen J. W., clerk, 42 n. Pennsylvania, res. 30½ n. Pennsylvania.
McMullen Otho H., occupant Deaf and Dumb Asylum.
McMurray Robert, cigar-maker, res. e. side n. Illinois, bet. Third and Fourth.
McMurray Samuel B., carpenter, bds. e. s. n. Illinois, bet. Third and Fourth.
McNab Philip, physician, office and res. 149 s. New Jersey.
McNamarra Frank, lab., res. near rolling mill.
McNamarra James, lab., bds. 38 s. Tennessee.
McNamarra John, salesman, New York Store, bds. Oriental House.
McNamara John E, servant, 209 w. South.
McNamarra Mary, chambermaid, Institute of the Blind, bds. same.
McNamarra Michael, conductor, Cincinnati ; R. R., res. 165 e. South.
McNmarra William, pressman, Sentinel office, bds. 60 n. Pennsylvania.
McNamarra William C., stone-cutter, bds. 38 s. Tennessee.
McNeal Barnet F., lab., res. bet. Michigan and National rd., beyond city limits.
McNeely Charles, salesman, Spiegel, Thoms & Co., bds. Wiles House.
McNeely Delia, servant, 332 w. Washington.
McNeely Henry, lab., res 50 Elm.
McNeely John, carpenter, shop 18 e. Pearl, res. 74 w. First.
McNeely Miss Martha, teacher, eighth ward school, bds. 201 n. Liberty.
McNeely John R., clerk, C., C. & I. C. R. R. freight depot, res. First, bet. Illinois and Tennessee.
McNeely Elisha, barrel factory, St. Clair, bet. Railroad and Canal, res. 232 Illinois.
McNoughton Miss Mollie, bds. 296 w. New York.
McNutt Alonzo, brakesman, Bellfontaine R. R. bds. 229 Winston.
McNatty Peter, speculator, bds. 204 n. Illinois.
McOunt Andrew W., (R. L. & A. W. McO.,) 61 and 63 w. Washington, res. n. e. cor. New York and East.
McOunt George, bds. n. e. cor. New York and East.
McOunt Mrs. Janet S., (wid. Thomas,) res. n. e. cor. New York and East.
McOunt R. L. & A. W., dealers in stoves and house furnishing goods, 61 and 63 w. Washington.

McOuat R. L., 61 and 63 w. Washington, res. 76 w. Market.

McOuat Sarah, (wid. James,) res. 300 Pattison.

McPeck David I, salesman, res. 276 n. West.

McPherson Caroline, servant, W. H. Jones, 273 n. Illinois.

McPHERSON R. C., division supt Merchants' Union Express Co., 42 and 44 e. Washington, bds. Bates House.

McPherson William M., painter, bds. 184 n. Tennessee.

McQuade Patrick, expressman, bds. 79 Fayette.

McQuality William, works Hinesley's livery stable, bds. 69 w. Market.

McRoy Wm., weaver, bds. 336 w. Washington.

McShepard James B., clerk, res. 215 w. Maryland.

McSweeny Annie dress-maker, bds. 70 e. Market.

McSweeny Miss M., dress-maker, bds 70 e. Market.

McVeigh Hugh, clerk, 159 and 161 e. Washington, res. 437 n. Mississippi.

McVey David, blacksmith, 277 w. Washington, res. 58 s. California.

McVey Joseph, carpenter, res. 24 Coburn.

McVey Mary, servant, 21 n. East.

McVey William, clerk, Featherston's auction rooms, res. 437 n. Mississippi.

McVicker Achor W., cutter, Taylor & Crain, 3 Bates House blk., res. 176 w. Ohio.

McWorkman Henry, clerk, p. o., rooms Eden's blk., e. Market.

Maas Jacob, boarding-house, 18 Circle.

Maas Louis, (Koster & M.,) 141 e. Washington, res. 12 n. New Jersey.

Mabb Miss Maria, rooms 2d floor 186 w. Washington.

Mabrey Randall C., farmer, res. 285 Massachusetts av.

Macauley John T., book-bindery, 13 w. Maryland, up stairs, bds. 18 w. North.

Macauley Daniel, (M. & Co.,) Mayor of Indianapolis, office Glenns' blk., res. 18 w. North.

Macbeth Robert, blacksmith, bds. 103 w. South.

Machel Gustave, lab., res. 85 n. Noble.

Machett Robert, carpenter, res. 169 e. St. Joseph.

Machin Edward, lab., res. 280 Railroad.

Mack John, lab., res. 193 High.

Mack Michael H., brakesman, Bellefontaine R. R., bds. 270 Railroad.

Mack Miss Nellie, boarding, 83 n. Missousouri.

Mack Philip, lab., res. 300 w. Maryland.

Mack William, pressman, Sentinel Office, bds. 165 e. South.

Maconica James, carpenter, res. 120 Christian av.

Macy David, prest. Peru & I. R. R., 101 e. Washington, res. 216 n. Delaware.

MACY HOUSE, s. e. cor. Illinois and Market, A. W. Melsheimer, propr. See card, advertising dept., page 11.

Macy W. W., student, city academy, bds. 76 Fort Wayne av.

Madden Catharine, servant, 245 n. Illinois.

Madden Mrs. E., (wid.,) res. 37 Ellen.

Madden Joseph, plasterer, res. 37 Ellen.

Madden Miss Mary E., res. 37 Ellen.

Madden Michael, lab., res. 239 s. Tennessee.

Madden Thomas, deputy col. internal revenue, sixth district, room 15, P. O. bldg., res. 131 w. First.

Madden Thomas J., brick-layer, res. 112 Meek.

Madison Charles, (col.,) lab., bds. 257 n. West.

Magee Henry, lab., res. 263 Davidson.

Magee John, lab., res. 263 Davidson.

Magee Philip, carpenter, res. 263 Davidson.

Magraugh Daniel, cellar-digger, res. 291 e. Georgia.

Magraugh Dennis, lab., res. 474 e. Georgia.

Maguire Charles, salesman, New York Store, res. 50 w. New York.

Maguire Douglass, (Crossland, M. & Co.,) 52 s. Meridian, res. 78 e. Ohio.

Maguire George, plasterer, res. 460 Virginia av.

Mahan W. H., traveling agt., Rikhoff & Bro., res. 28 w. Pratt.

Maher William, tobacconist, J. Cahall & Co., bds. Ray House.

Mahoney Daniel, street-grader, res. 51 Ellen.

Mahoney Fanny, servant, 191 n. New Jersey.

Mahoney John, flagman, B. R. R., res. 10 Buchanan.

Mahorney John T., (col.,) manfr. of ornamental hair work, 55 s. Illinois, res. 235 n. Blake.

Mai August, carpenter, works Many & Sons, res. 349 s. Pennsylvania.

Mai Frederick, lab., Schmidt's Brewery, res. same.

Maier Jacob, barber, 143 e. Washington, res. 147½ e. Washington.

Mair Francis, carpenter, res. 335 s. Delaware.

Major Stephen F., clerk p. o., res. 221 e. North.

Makepeace Horace B., salesman, 26 s. Meridian, res. 54 Massachusetts av.

Maker Thomas J., painter, res. 319 Massachusetts av.

Malay James, marble-cutter, res. 31 Henry.

Malkt Martin, engineer, res. 576 s. Illinois.

Mallory Mrs. Jane, (col.,) res. 267 n. Mississippi.

Malone Abner J., carpenter, res. 128 Virginia av.

Malone Abner J., Jr., machinist, bds. 128 Virginia av.

Malone L. D., (col.,) carpenter, res. 141 n. Bright.

Malone Patrick, lab., res. 27 Wyoming.

Malone William, clerk, 25 w. Washington, bds. 128 Virginia av.

Maloney Edward, res. 52 Huron.

Maloney James, (J. M. & Roth,) res. 43 Ellsworth.

Maloney John, shoe-maker, res. 259 s. Mississippi.

Maloney John, blacksmith, res. Columbia, bet. East and New Jersey.

Maloney Mary, servant, 75 w. Ohio.

Malott V. T., cash. Merchants' National Bank, 48 e. Washington, res. 298 n. Delaware.

Malound Thomas, lab., res. 331 e. Louisiana.

Maloy James, stone-cutter, res. 29 Henry.

Malpas Henry, bleachery, rooms 17 and 18 Miller's blk., n. Illinois.

Mande Charles, res. n. s. National rd., w. White river bridge.

Mandering Michael, brakesman, I., C. & L. R. R., res. w. s. Noble, bet. Georgia and I., C. & L. R. R.

Mangle Joseph, moulder, bds. Globe House.

Mangold Frederick, saw-grinder, res. 130 e. St. Mary.

Mangold Jane, (wid. Henry,) res. 130 e. St. Mary.

Manhattan Fire Insurance Co., of New York, Davis & Greene, agts., 27 s. Meridian.

Manhattan Life Insurance Co., of New York, Davis & Greene, agts., 27 s. Meridian.

Manheimer David, auctioneer, 13 w. Washington, res. 172 e. Ohio.

Manheimer J. C., student, commercial college, res. 172 e. Ohio.

Manheimer Louis, clerk, 13 w. Washington, res. 172 e. Ohio.

Manker Lewis, physician, res. National rd., near Insane Asylum.

Manker William, painter, bds. 23 Kentucky av.

Manlove John T., res. Bethel pike, half-mile from end Virginia av.

Manlove W. R., (Stanton & M.,) 14 n. Delaware, res. 346 n. Meridian.

Mann Alford J., carpenter, res. 53 cor. Pine and Fletcher av.

Mann Henry C., (col.,) barber shop, 10 s. Delaware, res. 361 e. New York.

MANN J. A. & CO., (Joseph A. M. & F. Cunningham,) tobacconists, 67 and 69 w. Washington.

Mann James B., grocery and provision store, cor. East and Virginia av., res. 149 s. East.

Mann Joseph A., tobacconist, bds. Ray House e. South.

Mann Lauren, carriage-maker, bds. 206 e. Ohio.

Mann William, (col.,) barber, bds. 242 w. Ohio.

Manner Michael, works Junction R. R., bds. Wiles House.

Manning Michael J., broker, n. e. cor. Washington and Illinois, bds. Palmer House.

Manning Thomas S., carriage-painter, works S. W. Drew & Co., res. 76 w. Ohio.

Mansfield George, (Goepper & Co.,) 17 e. Washington, res. 336 n. East.

Mansfield John L., res. 295 n. East.

Mansfield Julius, tailor, res. 26 Chatham.

Mansfield Oscar, clerk, 64 e. Washington, res. 295 n. East.

Mansfield Thomas, blacksmith, res. 165 w. Maryland.

Manson M., shoe-maker, 350 s. Delaware, res. same.
Mansur C. W., salesman, 21 w. Washington, bds. 19 e. Ohio.
Mansur Isaiah, prest. Citizens' National Bank, 4 e. Washington, res. cor. Vermont and Meridian.
Mansur John, farmer, res. 18 e. Vermont.
Mansur William L., res. 19 e. Ohio.
Many A. J., carpenter, res. 125 n. Noble.
Many Charles, carpenter, res. rear 356 Winston.
Many Charles J., (J. B. Many & Son,) res. 125 n. Noble.
Many Camilla, carpenter, res. 214 Railroad.
Many Gerard, teacher of French, bds. 125 n. Noble.
Many John, switchman, res. 31 Maple.
Many John, groceries, cor. Virginia av. and Noble, res. same.
Many John B., (J. B. M. & Son,) res. 125 n. Noble.
MANY JOHN B. & SON, (J. B. & Charles J. M.,) carpenters and builders, 120 Spring.
Mapes Caleb F., horse-trainer, res. 124 n. Blackford.
Mapes Henry, bleacher, Miller's blk., res. 159 n. Mississippi.
Mapes S. H., physician, res. 232 Michigan.
March Walter, (Gordon & M.,) room 4, Talbott & New's blk., n. Pennsylvania, res. 168 e. St. Clair.
Marchel Mary A., servant, 493 n. Meridian.
Marchant Isaac, clock-maker, 368 w. Washington.
Marchant Isaac, Sr., bds. w. Washington, bet. White River and Canal.
Marchant Isaac, Jr., book-keeper, Merritt & Coughlen, res. w. Washington, near toll-gate.
Marcus Elias, carpenter, res. 191 w. Maryland.
Mardick James Y., groceries, cor. Georgia and Benton, res. same.
Mardock J. F., lottery agt., 22 w. Maryland, res. 347 s. Pennsylvania.

Marer John P., lab., res. 69 Elizabeth.
Marian Catherine, servant, W. H. Latham's e. Washington.
Marion County Jail, s. w. cor. Alabama and Market.
Marion Engine House, No. 2, cor. New York and Massachusetts av.
Market Fire Insurance Co., of New York, J. S. Dunlop & Co., agts., 16 and 18 n. Meridian.
Market Nicholas, peddler, res. 460 s. Missouri.
Marks J. H., steward, Palmer House, res. same.
Marks Peter, (col.,) lab., bds. 53 Hosbrook.
Markwood T. M., (Baar & M.,) 20 w. Maryland, res. same.
Marlan Miss Elizabeth, dress-maker, cor. Illinois and Maryland, res. same.
Marmont Hall, cor. Illinois and Georgia.
Marmont Hugo, (Schoettle & M.,) saloon, 102 s. Illinois, res. same.
Marnarn Kate, (wid. Timothy,) res. alley rear 75 s. West.
Marone & Behringer, (Toney M. & Joseph B.,) saloon, 145 w. Washington.
Marone John, res. 145 w. Washington.
Marone Toney M., (M. & Behringer,) 145 w. Washington, res. same, up stairs.
Marot J. R., second-hand store, 87 e. Washington, res. 36 n. Delaware.
Marot Lewis, with J. R. Marot, 87 e. Washington, res. 36 n. Delaware.
Maroney Margaret, servant, Palmer House.
Marguert Jacob, butcher, res. 255 n. Noble.
Marquis George, res. 372 s. West.
Marra Annie, servant, Rev. E. P. Ingersoll, 383 n. Pennsylvania.
Marrow Wilson, lawyer, res. 282 n. Pennsylvania.
Marsee John M, (M. & Son,) bds. 203 s. New Jersey.
Marsee Joseph, (M. & Son,) res. 203 s. New Jersey.
Marsee & Son, (Joseph & John M.,) steam planing mill, s. New Jersey, near Maryland.

Marsee Louis, cigar store, near Union Hall, res. 12 n. New Jersey.

Marsh Alfred S., occupant Deaf and Dumb Asylum.

Marsh David M., traveling agt., Asher & Adams, res. 370 n. West.

Marsh E. J., compositor, book and job room Sentinel office, bds. s. e. cor. Market and Circle.

MARSH H. & H· B., (Herman & Henry B. Marsh,) occulists and aurists, room 2, Miller's blk., n. Illinois.

Marsh Henry B., (H. & H. B. M.,) Miller's blk., n. Illinois, res. 519 n. Meridian.

Marsh Herman, (H. & H. B. M.,) Miller's blk, n. Illinois, res. 519 n. Meridian.

Marsh Miss Minnie, milliner, over 6 w. Washington, res. 89 Indiana av.

Marsh P. James, claim-broker, n. e. cor. Washington and Illinois, bds. Palmer House.

Marsh William S., harness-maker, Carr & Bro., res. 89 Indiana av.

Marshal Benjamin, porter, Grover & Baker S. M. Co., res. 337 n. New Jersey.

Marshall Benjamin, teamster, res. 319 n. East.

Marshall Mrs. C., dress-making, 58 n. Illinois, bds. Macy House.

Marshall Charles H., minister, Fourth Presbyterian Church, res. 80 Chistian av.

Marshall Chas. L., clerk, Martin & Hopkins, insurance agts., bds. 222 n. Alabama.

Marshall Charles M., bath-house, 16 w. Pearl, res. 16 s. Mississippi.

Marshall E., teamster, res. 32 Massachusetts av.

Marshall Edward, soldier, U. S. Arsenal, res. same.

Marshall Elizabeth, occupant Deaf and Dumb Asylum.

Marshall Emma, (wid., col.,) res. 130 Massachusetts av.

Marshall H. J., carriage-painter, 26 e. Georgia, bds. 24 w. Georgia.

Marshall James M., with Martin, Hopkins, & Follett, res. 124 Broadway.

Marshall John, engine-driver No. 2, res. 46 Massachusetts av.

Marshall Joseph, carpenter, works Mahoney & Ross, bds. 38 s. Tennessee.

Marshall Levi, carpenter, Bellefontaine Shop, res. 344 Winston.

Marshall Mary Jane, occupant Deaf and Dumb Asylum.

Marshall N. Frank, paper-hanger, res. 15 Indiana av.

Marshall P. J., occupant Deaf and Dumb Asylum.

Marshall Susan A., occupant Deaf and Dumb Asylum.

Marshall Isaac, res. 29 w. Georgia.

Marshall William, teacher, Deaf and Dumb Asylum. bds. J. N. Phipp, near Arsenal av.

Marshall Worthington, clerk, 78 Massachusetts av., bds. rear 269 e. North.

Marshall W. S. A. M., instructor, Deaf and Dumb Asylum.

Marshall W. J., (J. W. Bowers & Co.,) 67 and 78 Massachusetts av., bds. 180 e. Vermont.

MARTIN MRS. B., confectioner, 80 e. Washington, res. same.

Martin Charles, foundryman, bds. 174 Virginia av.

Martin Edward B., carpenter, res. 323 Davidson.

Martin George W., painter, bds. 392 n. Alabama.

Martin & Gibson, (John T. M. & Daniel C. G.,) gen'l agts. Western Life Insurance Co., of Cincinnati, Ohio, 2 Blackford's blk., s. e. cor. Washington and Meridian.

Martin Gilbert, blacksmith, res. n. Michigan rd., near Tenth.

Martin Gustav, clerk, C. Freese & Co., bds. California House.

Martin H. C., (M., Hopkins & Follett,) office first floor Journal bldg., res. 224 n. Alabama.

Martin, Hopkins & Follett, (Henry C. M., Henry C. H. & J. B. F.,) gen'l fire insurance agts., office first floor Journal bldg.

Martin James Otis, clerk, Martin, Hopkins & Follett, bds. 224 n. Alabama.

Martin Jesse, boarding-house, 34 w. Maryland.

Martin John, brick-mason, res. 54 Orient, bet. Michigan and National rd.

Martin John G., bds. Bates House.

Martin John H., (col.,) lab., res. 570 n. Mississippi.

Martin J. R., teamster, res. end Virginia av., beyond city limits.

Martin John T., (Martin & Gibson,) 2 Blackford's blk., s. e. cor. Washington and Meridian, bds. Macy House.

Martin Joseph T., (M. & Myers,) 117 w. Washington, res. 14 Kentucky av.

Martin Kallesh, butcher, with Fred. Borst, res. 338 Madison av.

Martin Lewis, clerk, 113 and 115 w.Washington, res. same.

Martin Luther R., real estate and stock broker, conveyancer and commissioner of Deeds, 10½ e. Washington, res. 97 e. Michigan.

Martin Mrs. Mary, (wid. John,) bds. 36 w. Michigan.

Martin & Myers, (J. T. M. & J. M. M.,) tinners, 117 w. Washington.

Martin Robert, cooper, res. 127 Duncan.

Martin Wesley, (col.,) lab., res. cor. North and Bright.

Martin William, carpenter, bds. cor. Cumberland and Pearl.

Martin William, res. 220 s. Noble.

Martin William, bell-boy, Bates House, bds. same.

Martindale Andy, res. 83 Bradshaw.

Martindale C. F., salesman, S. Kaufman, 116 s. Meridian, bds. s. e. part city, near Virginia av.

MARTINDALE ELIJAH B., (Morton, M. & Tarkington and W. J. Haskit & Co.,) attorney at law and agt. Home Life Insurance Co., of N. Y., office over 2 w. Washington, res. w. s. n. Meridian, beyond city limits.

Martindale Julia A., (wid. Austin,) res. 194 w. Georgia.

Martindale Moses A., occupant Deaf and Dumb Asylum.

Martindale William, book-keeper, Lines & Smelser, res. 83 Bradshaw.

Martland Andrew M., res. 227 n. Illinois.

Martz Charles W., student, N. W. C. University, bds. 361 Massachusetts av.

Martz Miss Carrie C., dress-maker, 90 s. East, res. same.

Martz Henry K., mill-wright, res. 189 n. Noble.

Martz James M., student, N. W. C. University, bds. 361 Massachusetts av.

Martz Mrs. Sarah, (wid. Peter,) res. 90 s. East.

Martz Sarah, servant, 384 n. Tennessee.

Martz Sophia, servant, 98 w. Vermont.

Marvin D. G., job printer, Journal Office, bds. 98 n. East.

Marvin Sarah, (wid. Thomas,) res. 249 s. Tennessee.

Maskill Catharine, servant, 25 w. First.

Maskill Dennis, lab., res. n. Tennessee, bet. First and Second.

MASON MRS. A. L., boarding-house, 17½ Virginia av.

Mason Francis, (wid. Robert,) dress-maker, res. 201 Meek.

Mason George, butcher, res. 297 s. Missouri.

Mason Hampton, barber, 143 w. Washington, res. 209 w. North.

Mason James, carpenter, res. 161 Davidson.

Mason James P., traveling agt., res. 407 n. East.

Mason Johnston, (col.,) lab., res. rear 343 Massachusetts av.

Mason Madison, (M. M. & Son,) s. e. cor. Illinois and Washington, res. 309 w. North.

Mason M. & Son, (col.,) barbers and hair-dressers, s. e. cor. Illinois and Washington.

Mason Louisa, (col.,) servant, 335 n. Liberty.

Mason Mrs. Maria, house-keeper, 222 n. Illinois.

Mason Samuel, res. n. s. Ohio, bet. Illinois and Meridian.

Mason Susan, (wid. Alexander,) res. 52 s. Pennsylvania.

Mason William C., clerk, p. o., bds. 17½ Virginia av.

Mason W. L., rev. inspector tobacco and cigars, room 14 P. O. bldg., res. Kentucky av.

Masoner Simon, well-digger, res. 108 Hosbrook.

Masonic Hall, s. e. cor. Washington and Tennessee.

Massey Jackson, (col.,) porter, 24 s. Meridian, bds. 70½ n. Illinois.

Massey Melinda, (col.,) servant, 704 n. Illinois.

Massey Miss M. S., res. 500 n. Tennessee.

Massey Timothy, boot and shoe-maker, 66 Massachusetts av.

Masten Benjamin F., (M. & Ingle,) 28 s. Meridian, res. Lafayette, Ind.

MASTEN & INGLE, (Benjamin F. M. & Mark W. I.,) agts., Saginaw Salt Works, and proprs. Otter Creek Coal Yard, 28 s. Meridian. See card, page 25.

Mat Edward, tinner, bds. 23 Kentucky av.

Matcke Edward, baker, bds. 117 s. Illinois.

Mather Ann M., (wid. John,) res. 227 s. Pennsylvania.

Matheus Cyrus, (Hart & M.,) 26 Virginia av., res. 338 s. East.

Matheus Elias C., carriage-trimmer, 123 c. Washington, bds. Union Hall.

Mathews Iris, carpenter, res. 337 s. East.

Mathews John W., salesman, New York Store, bds. 126 e. Ohio.

Mathews Mrs. Martha, (wid. Granville M.,) seamstress 237 n. Noble, res. same.

Mathews William, carpenter, res. 96 Indiana av.

Matler Mrs. Anna M., (wid. John,) res. 314 e. Ohio.

Matler & Leonard, saloon, 65 w. Washington.

Matler Stephen, (M. & Leonard,) 65 w. Washington, res. 314 c. Ohio.

Matlock James M., book-keeper, 49 s. Meridian, res. 328 n. Alabama.

Matlock Dan. C., Trade Palace, bds. Pyle House, room 24.

Matlock Miss Susan, res. 361 w. Vermont.

Matlock William, clerk, 22 w. Maryland, res. 244 n. Mississippi.

Matlock William, res. 361 w. Vermont.

Matlock William A., driver, street railway, bds. 244 n. Mississippi.

Matlock William W., clerk, res. 244 n. Mississippi.

Matthe Charles, blacksmith, bds. 292 e. Market.
Matthe Mrs. F., (wid.,) res. 335 n. West.
Matthe Mrs. Margaret, (wid. Charles,) res. 292 e. Market.
Mather Anna, dress-maker, bds. 189 Bates.
Mather John, engineer, I., C. & L. R. R. shop, res. 189 Bates.
MATTHES CLEMENS, propr. capital saloon, 92 e. Washington, res. same.
Matthias Jacob, plasterer, res. 246 n. East.
Matthias Mary, servant, 235 e. Vermont.
Mattocks Mrs. Ada, dress-maker, bds. Louisiana, bet. Tennessee and Illinois.
Matton Rudolph, blacksmith, res. 13 Waters.
Matson Edward T., moulder, Root's foundry, res. 129 Stevens.
Matson John, shoe-maker, res. 42 Massachusetts av.
Matson S. S., shoe-maker, 5 w. Washington.
Matson William, lab., res. 374 s. Tennessee.
Matz John, boots and shoes, 182 w. Washington.
Mauk Martin, tailor, res. 99 n. Noble.
Maurer John, moulder, res. 50 Green.
Maurice J. N., boot and shoe-maker, 71 n. Pennsylvania, res. 5 Dougherty.
Mauzy James S., salesman, 127 s. Meridian, bds. cor. Maryland and Tennessee.
Max Mr., res. 329 s. Pennsylvania.
Maxwell Charles D., cash boy, Tyler's Bee Hive, res. w. First.
Maxwell, Fry & Thurston, (John M. M. & W. H. F., Jr., & W. B. F.,) iron merchants, 34 s. Meridian.
Maxwell John C., freight agt., B. & O. R. R., res. 29 w. First.
Maxwell John M., (M., Fry & Thurston,) 34 s. Meridian. res. 330 n. Meridian.
Maxwell Samusl A., cash boy, Tyler's Bee Hive, res. w. First.
Maxwell W. D., farmer, res. First, bet. Meridian and Illinois.
May Alvin D., mailing clerk, Daily and Weekly Sentinel, 16½ e. Washington.
May Andrew, lumber dealer, res. 125 s. East.
May Augustus, carpenter, res. 133 e. McCarty,
May Edwin A., architect, res. 173 n. Pennsylvania.
May Henry, drayman, bds. 365 s. Delaware.
May Herman, soldier, U. S. Arsenal, res. same.
May J. A., (J. A. M. & Co.,) bds. 26 s. Mississippi.
MAY J. A. & CO., (J. A. & R. A. M.,) manfrs. plug tobacco, 85 and 87 e. South.
May John, (Stoble & May,) grocers, 365 s. Delaware, res. 360 s. Alabama.

May Lawrence, salesman, 103 e. Washington, bds. Emenegger's Hotel.
May Margaret, servant, F. M. Brown, 322 n. Illinois.
May P. M., tobacconist, bds. Ray House.
May R. A., (J. A. M. & Co.,) res. 429 n. Meridian.
Mayer Charles, (C. M. & Co.,) 29 w. Washington, res. 285 n. Illinois.
Mayer Charles & Co., (C. M. & W. Hauieson,) dealers in toys, fancy goods and notions, 29 w. Washington.
Mayer Francis, carpenter, res. 335 s. Delaware.
Mayer Jacob, works Root's foundry, bds. 23 Kentucky av.
Mayer John F., dealer in umbrellas and parasols, 69 e. Washington, res. 123 e. St. Joseph.
Mayer Joseph, (Rheinheimer & Co.,) 3 Palmer House, bds. 18 Circle.
Mayer J. Henry, driver, Ind. Transfer Co., res. 71 s. Pennsylvania.
Mayer Leopold, salesman, 3 Palmer House, bds. 18 Circle.
Mayer M., cigars and tobacco, 96 s. Illinois, res. same.
Mayer X. F., saloon and restaurant, 156 e. Washington, res. same.
Mayerhoff Mrs. Mary, (wid. Henry,) res. 242 s. Alabama.
Mayers Charles, brakesman, I., C. & L. R. R., bds. Ray House.
Mayers Charles, blacksmith, bds. California House.
Mayers George, clerk, res. 170 Buchanan.
Mayher William, tobacconist, (J. Cahall & Co.,) bds. Ray House.
Mayhew & Branham, (Enoch C. M. & Edward B.,) wholesale boots and shoes, 129 s. Meridian.
Mayhew Elisha C., farmer, Michigan rd., north of corporation line.
Mayhew Enoch C., (M. & Branham,) 129 s. Meridian.
Mayhew Frank, messenger boy, Western Union Telegraph Co., 11 s. Meridian.
Mayhew James N., salesman, 50 e. Washington, res. 512 e. Washington.
Mayhew O. F., solicitor of patents, office with sec'y State Board Agriculture, State House, res. 25 Circle.
Mayhew Parish L., (Ray, M. & Co.,) 8 w. Louisiana, bds. 59 w. Maryland.
Mayhew Royal H., entry clerk, 108 s. Meridian, bds. 17½ Virginia av.
Mayhew James, driver, Ind. Transfer Co., bds. 185 w. Maryland.
Maynard C. E., telegraph operator, bds. Ray House.
MAYO E. H. & CO., (Edwin H. M. & ——,) boots, shoes and rubber goods, 23 e. Washington. See card, page 72.

Mayo Edward H., (E. H. M. & Co.,) 23 e. Washington, res. 562 n. Pennsylvania.

Mayo H. S., (E. H. M. & Co.,) 23 e. Washington.

Mayport Miller, sawyer, res. 34 Vinton.

Mays Alfred, (col.,) barber, shop 162 Indiana av., res. Camp Carrington.

Mays Calvin, (col.,) barber, res. Howard, bet. Second and Third.

Mays Philip, barber, 162 Indiana av., bds. Camp Carrington.

Mays Thomas A., student, commercial college, bds. 26 n. Pennsylvania.

Mead Frank, machinist, res. 39 McCarty.

Mead James, mill-wright, McCord & Wheatley's, res. 50 Forrest av.

Mead Laura E., occupant Deaf and Dumb Asylum.

Mead Peter, (col.,) lab., bds. 94 Elm.

Mead William, runner, Neiman House, bds. same.

Mead William H., traveling agt., Mayhew & Branham, 129 s. Meridian, bds. Sherman House.

Meadows William H., carpenter, res. 19 Fatout's blk., w. Washington.

Meager Miss Annosia, servant, 413 w. New York.

Meagher Thomas, blacksmith, bds. Globe House.

Means John, res. 94 w. Market.

Means Thomas A., (Haehl & M.,) 20 s. Delaware, res. 293 Virginia av.

Means W. C., (E. B. Dill & Co.,) 87 e. Market, res. 238 Madison av.

Mears George W., physician, office s. w. cor. Meridian and Washington, res. 210 n. Meridian.

Mears Henry B., Varnish Works, s. e. cor. Kentucky av. and Mississippi, bds. 210 n. Meridian.

Mears Miss Rilla, lady-boarder, over 274 e. Washington.

Meason William, works Junction R. R., bds. Wiles House.

Meek Alonzo, engineer, I., C. & L. R. R., bds. 99 Benton.

Meek Cornwell, retired merchant.

Meek Robert L., railroader, res. 117 s. Noble.

Mechan Dennis, lab., bds. cor. Norwood and Tennessee.

Meehan Peter M., paper-hanger, bds. Wiles House.

Meeky Emma, servant, 79 Massachusetts -av.

Meconi Dennis, lab., res. 80 Elm.

MEDINA FRANK J., manufacturer and dealer in human hair work, 50 s. Illinois, res. same. See card, page 52.

Medor Mrs. Margaret, (wid. John,) res. 208 w. Vermont.

Medsker William F., attorney at law, room 4, Talbott & New's blk., bds. 162 n. New Jersey.

Megge Richard, res. 37 Wyoming.

Meier & Brother, (Valentine & Joseph M. M.,) ale bottlers, 76 s. West.

Meier & Co., (Lewis M. & William Buschmann,) dry goods, &c., 151 Fort Wayne av.

Meier Charles M., saloon, 156 e. Washington, res. third floor Rabb's blk.

Meier Joseph M., (Meier & Bro.,) res. 76 s. West.

Meier Lewis, (M. & Co.,) 151 Fort Wayne av., bds. 469 n. New Jersey.

Meier Valentine, (M. & Brother,) res. 76 s. West.

Meigs Charles D., book-keeper, 5 e. Washington, bds. s. e. cor. Circle and Market.

Meikel Miss Carrie, res. 113 n. Mississippi.

Meikel Charles P., printer, Journal bldg., res. 500 n. West.

Meikel Frederick J., (J. M. & F. J. M. & Co,) 13 w. Maryland, res. 113 n. Mississippi.

Meikel J. M., (J. M. & F. J. M. & Co.,) 13 w. Maryland, res. 113 n. Mississippi.

Meikel J. M. & F. J. & Co., job printers, stationers, blank book manufacturers, paper dealers, 13 w. Maryland.

Meikel John P., brewery, 297 w. Washington, res. 213 w. Maryland.

Meikel Mrs. Mary C., (wid.,) res. 113 n. Mississippi.

Meiners Cornelius, lumber dealer, res. 240 n. Illinois.

Meinke August, currier, 17 s. Delaware, bds. 60 s. Delaware.

Meirhoff Mary, (wid. Henry,) res. 242 s. Alabama.

Meisser Frank, butcher, bds. 277 Virginia av.

Meler John, brewer, res. 185 Madison av.

Melker Martin, engineer, Carpenters' Union, res. 575 s. Illinois.

Melling Charles, lab., res. 47 Douglas.

Melville Robert B, tailor, 2 Bates House blk., res. 79 n. California.

MELSHEIMER AUGUSTUS W., propr. Macy House, 45 n. Illinois, cor. Market. See card, page 11, adv. department.

Melton Thomas, works 175 w. Cumberland, bds. 26 s. Mississippi.

Mendel Moses, salesman, Commercial Clothing Store, bds. 184 Virginia av.

Mengas Frank, cigar store, 153 e. Washington, res. 182 s. Delaware.

MENNINGER DANIEL, Labelle Saloon, 20 Kentucky av., res. 386 n. Tennessee.

Merchant C., carpenter, res. 461 n. Alabama

Merchants Despatch Fast Freight Line, office 19 Virginia av.

Merchants Fire Insurance Co., of Hartford, Conn., Davis & Green, agts., 27 s. Meridian.

MERCHANTS' & MANUFACTURERS' EXCHANGE, 27 s. Meridian, James Green, secretary.

MERCHANTS' NATIONAL BANK, 48 e. Washington, John S. Newman, prest., V. T. Malott, cashr.

MERCHANTS' POLICE, office 85 e. Washington, up-stairs, A. D. Rose, captain.

MERCHANTS' UNION EXPRESS Co., office 42 and 44 e. Washington, Charles A. Parsons, agt., R. B. McPherson, div. supt.

Merche H. B., artist, 19 Miller's blk., res. 519 n. Meridian.

Meredith Edward, foreman, E. C. Atkins & Co.'s saw factory, res. 235 s. Mississippi.

Meredith R. O., carpenter, res. cor. Oak and Cherry.

Meredith Samuel C., mail clerk, Journal Office, res. 212 Blackford.

Meredith William, printer, res. 124 n. Missouri.

Merousky Henry, lab., res. Fourth, bet. Railroad and Canal.

Merick William, stableman, Citizens' Street Ry., bds. Neiman House.

Mermann Mary, cook, Ray House.

Merrifield Charles E., groceries, cor. Tennessee and New York, res. 135 w. New York.

MERRILL & CO., (Samuel M. & Mrs. J. M. Moores,) publishers, booksellers and stationers, 5 e. Washington.

Merrill Miss Catharine, res. s. w. cor. Alabama and Merrill.

Merrill Miss Ella, bds. 244 w. New York.

Merrill Mrs. Lucinda, (wid. J. F.,) res. 244 w. New York.

Merrill Miss Mina, res. n. e. cor. Alabama and Merrill.

Merrill Miss Minerva A., bds. 244 w. New York.

Merrill Nicholas, shoe-maker, res. 288 w. Washington.

Merrill Samuel, (Merrill & Co.,) 5 e. Washington, res. n. e. cor. Alabama and Merrill.

Merrill William H. D., plumber, res. 244 w. New York.

MERRITT & COUGHLEN, (George M. & William C.,) woolen manfrs. and dealers in woolen and cotton factory findings, w. end Washington, near White River.

Merritt George, (M. & Coughlen,) res. 172 n. West.

Merritt, Joseph J., (M. & Rosengarten,) 32 n. Pennsylvania, bds. 31 Cherry.

Merritt & Rosengarten, (Joseph J. M. & Albert R.,) news stand and periodical nepot, 32 n. Pennsylvania.

Merriweather Cameron, (col.,) lab., res. rear 378 n. Meridian.

Merryhew Arter, shoe-maker, res. 505 n. Meridian.

Merryman Daniel H., salesman, res. 146 Ft. Wayne av.

Merryman W. G., clerk, 298 n. Pennsylvania, bds. 213 n. Pennsylvania.

Merther William, butcher, n. e. cor. Noble and New York, res. 358 e. New York.

Merz Fredarica, commercial editor, Daily Telegraph, res. over 170 e. Washington.

Mescal Joseph, lab., Bellefontaine shop, res. 30 John.

Meskamp William. lab., res. 42 Elm.

Messenger Adna C., carpenter, res. 397 w. New York.

Messenger Lyman, carpenter, res. 318 Massachusetts av.

Messersmith Mike, occupant Deaf and Dumb Asylum.

Messick John, book-heeper, 24 s. Meridian, res. James Ellis, n. Meridian.

Messick Thomas B., money order clerk, P. O. Rooms, Eden's blk.

Messler Christina, (wid. Frederick,) res. 426 s. East.

Metcalf George W., traveling agt., Fairbanks' scales, 43 and 45 n. Tennessee.

METROPOLITAN THEATRE, n. e. cor. Washington and Tennessee, V. Butsch, propr.

Metzger Alexander, real estate, claim, ins., foreign exchange and general collecting agt., 6 Odd Fellows Hall, res. 385 n. Pennsylvania.

Metzger Mrs. Catharine, (wid. George,) res. 382 e. Michigan.

Metzger Charles, tailor, 225 n. Noble, res. same.

Metzger Conrad, shoe-maker, works 170 e. Washington, res. 225 n. Noble.

Metzger Englebert J., propr. Daily Telegraph, res. 79 n. East.

Metzger Jacob, brewer, bds. 404 n. Delaware.

Metzger Henry, brewer, 297 w. Washington.

Metzger J., (Daily Telegraph Co.) res. cor. Delaware and St. Clair.

Metzger John, bar-tender, Selking's saloon, res. 31 n. East.

METZNER A, drugs and medicines, 127 e. Washington, res. same.

Meyer Mrs. Caroline, res. 110 w. Vermont.

Meyer Miss Caroline, seamstress, works 146 Davidson, res. 180 n. Noble.

Meyer Charles F., propr. brick-yard, res. end Virginia av., beyond city limits.

Meyer, C. L., carpenter, res. 275 e. Ohio.

Meyer Emir, book-keeper, Merchants National Bank, 48 e. Washington, bds. 126 e. Ohio.

Meyer Frank, drayman, (Connelly, Wiles & Co.,) res. 278 n. Liberty.

Meyer Frederick, works starch factory, bds. on Michigan rd., East.

Meyer F. W., clerk, 397 s. Meridian, bds. 224 Union.

Meyer George F., (G. F. M. & Co.,) 35 w. Washington, res. 180 n. Delaware.

MEYER GEORGE F. & CO., (G. F. M. & Wm. Kugleman,) manfrs. and dealers in cigars and tobacco, 35 w. Washington.

Meyer Henry, salesman, 45 and 47 e. Washington, res. 641 n. Tennessee.

Meyer Jacob, barber, res. 12 s. Alabama.

Meyer Louisa C., bds. 78 w. North.

Meyer Ludwig, drayman for Eagle Machine Works, res. 98 Davidson.

Meyer Martin, umbrella making, fancy trimming, 19 s. Alabama, res. same.

Meyer William, finisher, Eagle Machine Works, res. 98 Davidson.

Meyers Mrs. Alethea C., (wid. William,) seamstress, res. 114 Railroad.

Meyers Christopher, brass moulder, res. 89 s. Liberty.

Meyers George, bar-keeper, 189 s. Meridian, bds. same.

Meyers Helena, servant, 451 n. Tennessee.

Meyers J. G., real estate, res. 485 n. Alabama.

Meyers J. W., teacher, public schools, res. Fifth, bet. Mississippi and Tennessee.

Meyers Oscar, printer, res. 399 n. Alabama.

Meyers Philip, machinist, res. 383 s. Missouri.

Michael Mrs. Elizabeth, (wid.,) res. 246 Madison av.

Michael John P., brewer, at 297 w. Washington, res. 215 w. Maryland.

Michael Philip, brewery, w. Washington, res. s. Mississippi, bet. Rockwood and McCarty.

Michelfelder John, express driver, Union Factory, res. 377 e. Michigan.

Michelby John B., carpenter, bds. 656 n. Tennessee.

Mick James F., dealer in feathers, ginseng, beeswax and rags, 21 w. Maryland, res. 170 Jackson.

Mick William E, groceries and provisions, 251 n. Illinois, res. 26 Gregg.

Middaugh Charles L., painter, bds. 33 Ellsworth.

Middaugh James W., fireman, C., C. & I. R. R., res. 483 e. Georgia.

Middleton James (col.,) lab., res. 239 Massachusetts av.

Mier Christian H., chair-maker, res. 31 s. New Jersey.

Miers Charles, printer, res. 130 n. Blackford.

Migga Richard, (Hilgemeir & Migga,) grocers, 367 s. Delaware, res. 38 Wyoming.

Mihlenbeck Albert, clerk, Gall & Rush, res. 336 e. Market.

Milan John, servant, Mrs. Ferguson, 60 w. Market.

Milan Miss Mary, bds. 226 w. New York.

Mileham Joseph N., master car repairs, Bellefontaine shops, res. 261 Davidson.

Miles, Anthony, (col.,) lab., res. 32 Bradshaw.

Miles Christopher, carpenter, bds. 183 s. Illinois.

Miles James H., carpenter, res. w. side Mississippi, bet. First and Second.

Miles Oscar, printer, Capital Job Office, res. 280 n. Alabama.

Miley John S., traveling agt., Foster, Wiggins & Co., res. 77 Jackson.

Millender & Hogan, (William B. M. & Edward H.,) painters, glaziers and calcy-miners, 27 s. Illinois.

Millender William B., (M. & Hogan,) 27 s. Illinois, res. 72 w. Maryland.

Miller Adam R., (M. & Franks,) over 55 e. Washington, bds. 143 n. Delaware.

Miller Albert A., Trade Palace, bds. 239 n. Pennsylvania.

Miller Amanda, (wid. Jacob,) res. 423 w. Washington.

Miller Andrew J., lab., res. 395 n. West.

Miller Anthony, carpenter, 227 e. Vermont, res. same.

Miller B., tailor, res. 412 s. Illinois.

Miller B. W., asst. assessor int. rev., room 14, P. O. bldg., bds. 373 n. Delaware.

Miller Benjamin, lab., bds. 75 s. West.

Miller Mrs. Catharine, (wid. John,) res. 573 e. St. Clair.

Miller Charles, porter, 101 e. Washington.

Miller Charles, lab., res. 330 Madison av.

Miller Charles E., res. 133 n. Mississippi.

Miller Charles, carpenter, res. 47 Orient, bet. Michigan and National rd., beyond city limits.

Miller Christ., carpenter, 123 e. McCarty.

Miller Christian, lab., res. 219 Union.

Miller Christian, watch-maker, works 226 e. Washington, res. same.

Miller Christian, carpenter, res. 489 s. East.

Miller Christian, (M. & Paule,) res. 230 Davidson.

Miller C., (col., lab.,) res. 340 w. North.

Miller C. W., messenger, res. 317 n. Delaware.

Miller Daniel, sawyer, res. 385 e. Michigan.

Miller David H., physician, bds. 298 e. Ohio.

Miller E. W., drayman, res. 170 Madison av.

MILLER E. T.,
druggist, cor. Illinois and Maryland,
res. 30 Indiana av.

Miller E. M., (wid.,) res. 373 n. Delaware.

MILLER & FRANKS,
(Adam R. M. & Francis L. F.,) photographers and artists, over 45 e. Washington.

Miller Frank X., cooper, res. 249 s. Delaware.

Miller Frederick, cooper, bds. w. Washington.

Miller Frederick, carpenter, res. 21 Biddle.

Miller Frederick A., blacksmith, res. 172 s. Noble.

Miller George, (M., Mitchell & Stough,) cor. Kentucky av. and Georgia, res. 88 Kentucky av.

Miller George W., apprentice Greenleaf Machinery Works, bds. 211 Union.

Miller George B., blacksmith, res. 211 Union.

Miller George L., mill-wright, res. 290 Winston.

Miller Geo. W., prest. and supt. Carpenters' Union, cor. Meridian and South, res. 256 s. Meridian.

Miller George W., carriage-maker, res. 666 n. Mississippi.

Miller Harrison S., gas-fitter, res. 157 Davidson.

Miller Henry, stair-builder, res. 360 n. East.

Miller Henry, currier, Mooney & Co., res. 304 s. Illinois.

Miller Henry, lab., res. 206 w. Vermont.

Miller Henry, saloon, 248 n. Noble, cor. Michigan, res. 324 e. Michigan.

Miller Henry, brick-maker, res. 18 John.

Miller H. F., teacher, res. 18 Gregg.

Miller Henry L., res. South, bet. Meridian and Pennsylvania.

Miller Henry W., (Dreher, M. & Co.,) res. 304 e. Ohio.

MILLER JACOB,
cigar manfr. and dealer, 138 s. Illinois, res. 61 s. Russell.

Miller Jacob, shoe-maker, works 65 s. Meridian, bds. Martin House.

Miller Jacob V., carpenter, res. cor. Illinois and Indiana av.

Miller Jeremiah, groceries, res. n. s. National rd., w. White river bridge.

Miller Jesse, corder, bds. 206 w. Vermont.

Miller John, machinist, res. 50 Fayette.

Miller John, breweryman, res. s. Tennessee.

Miller John, gardener, res. n. s. National rd., w. White river bridge.

Miller John, saloon and boarding, 123 s. Illinois, res. same.

Miller John, clerk, bds. 346 n. Meridian.

Miller Joseph, bds. 293 Indiana av.

Miller John A., book-keeper, Vinnedge, Jones & Co., 66 s. Meridian, bds. 188 s. Mississippi.

Miller John A. D., carpenter, res. 468 n. East.

Miller John S., machine-hand, bds. 265 s. Meridian.

Miller J. Frank, Merchants' Police, res. 260 n. Noble.

Miller J. F., teacher, M. E. Church School, 212 e. Ohio, res. same.

Miller Mrs. J. R., seamstress, res. 231 w. Vermont.

Miller J. S., bds. Macy House.

Miller Laurence, cabinet-maker, works 83 e. Market, res. 128 e. Maryland.

Miller Leonard, tailor and renovator, res. 412 s. Illinois.

Miller Levi, student, N. W. C. University, bds. 22 Gregg.

Miller Louis, blacksmith, res. National rd., beyond city limits.

Miller Louisa, (wid. William,) res. 116 n. Noble.

Miller Margaret M. (wid. Mathew,) res. 149 cor. New Jersey and Louisiana.

MILLER MARK D.,
Farmers and Mechanics Saloon, 320 e. Washington, res. 157 Davidson.

Miller Mary, bds. 206 w. Vermont.

Miller Mary, servant, 284 e. Michigan.

Miller Mary E., milliner and dress-maker, 32 Virginia av., res. same.

Miller Miss Mary F., seamstress, res. 157 Davidson.

Miller Miss Melinda, milliner, works 152 e. Washington, res. 307 e. Washington.

Miller Milton R., machinist, res. foot of Michigan, beyond city limits.

Miller, Mitchell & Stough, (George M., William M. & Charles A. S.,) carriage manfrs., cor. Kentucky av. and Georgia.

Miller Noah, salesman, Farmers' Store, bds. 89 n. Delaware.

Miller Osiat, printer, bds. 84 Massachusetts av.

Miller O. S., printer, Journal bldg., bds. 12 Indiana av.

Miller Oliver T., occupant Deaf and Dumb Asylum.

Miller & Paule, (Christian M. & Henry P.,) contractors and builders, 231 Railroad.

Miller Peter, works Cabinet Makers' Union, res. 525 e. Market.

Miller P. W., res. 133 Mississippi.

Miller Reinhold A., watch-maker, 226 e. Washington, res. same.

Miller Miss S., seamstress, res. 157 Davidson.

Miller Sebastian, clerk, 138 s. Illinois, bds. 61 Russell.

Miller S. K., salesman, 85 e. Market, bds. 512 n. Mississippi.

Miller S. S., plasterer, bds. Court, bet. Alabama and New Jersey.

Miller Theodore, lab., res. 330 Madison av.

Miller Thomas, railroader, P. & I. R. R., res. bet. Liberty and East.

Miller Thomas J., painter, bds. 307 e. Washington, No. 2, up stairs.

Miller Thomas P., invalid, res. 157 Davidson.

Miller Valentine, currier, 125 s. Meridian, res. 140 Davidson.

Miller William, shoe-maker, bds. 79 s. Liberty.

Miller William, saw-maker, works E. C. Atkins & Co., bds. Concordia House.

Miller William W., student, Purdy's College, bds. 31 Kentucky av.

Miller William B., (Sims, M. & Hoskins,) Canal, near Kentucky av., res 246 n. Blake.

Miller Mrs., (wid.,) res. 293 Indiana av.

Milligan Francis, wagon-maker, res. 79 Elm.

Milligan Frank, (col.,) waiter, Bates House.

Milner D., mailing clerk, Journal office, bds. 173 Daugherty.

Milner J., lawyer, office 94 e. Washington, bds. 89 n. Delaware.

Milner John E., teamster, res. w. Seventh near Lenox.

Mills D. S., physician, res. 82 s. Illinois.

Mills David, (D. M. & Co.,) livery and feed stables, res. 142 n. East.

Mills John, master mechanic, bds. 333 s. Pennsylvania.

Mills Layton, (L. M. & Co.,) res 180 Massachusetts av.

Mills Mahala, servant, A. S. Walker, 81 w. Vermont.

Mills William G., printer, bds. 152 n. Meridian.

Milton Hiram T., carpenter, res. 338 Indiana av.

Minch Mrs. Mary, (wid. Henry,) res. 266 Winston.

Miner Margaret, (wid. Milton T.,) bds. 33 w. Maryland.

Miner William, carpenter, res. 16 w. Maryland.

Miner Willis R., book-keeper, Connelly, Wiles & Co., bds. Palmer House.

Minger Christopher, telegraph repairer, bds. 18 s. Delaware.

Mingevan Patrick, brakesman, T. H. & I. R. R., res. cor. West and Georgia.

Minick D. C., (M. & Latshaw,) 17½ w. Washington, res. same.

Minick Hiram, policeman, sixth ward, res. 147 Union.

Minick & Latshaw, (David M. & L. T. L.,) real estate agts., 17½ w. Washington.

Minihin Thomas, lab., res. 197 Meek.

Mint James, (col.,) servant, 139 n. Alabama.

Minthorn John J., (Adams & M.,) res. 268 e. St. Clair.

MIRROR, (WEEKLY,) Harding & Morton, publishers, cor. Meridian and Circle.

Miselton Philip, lab., res. Court, bet. Alabama and New Jersey.

Mission Illinois Street Church, cor. Illinois and Russell.

Mission Sabbath School, cor. Madison av. and Merrill.

Mitchell Adolphus O., clerk, Japan Tea Store, res. 244 n. Illinois.

Mitchell Bryant, (col.,) lab., res. 158 n. Douglas Alley.

Mitchell Burn, (col.,) porter, Daggett & Co., res. 230 n. Missouri.

MITCHELL JACOB, merchant tailor and draper, 2 Bates House blk., w. Washington, res. 174 e. Ohio.

Mitchell James L., lawyer, (Ketchum & M.,) over 21 e. Washington, res. e. end Market.

Mitchell Mrs. Jane, (wid.,) bds. 169 n. Illinois.

Mitchell Joseph G., occupant Deaf and Dumb Asylum.

Mitchell Mary A., servant, J. N. Phipps, near Arsenal av.

Mitchell Mrs. Percilla, (col.,) res. Eighth, bet. Lenese and Knox.

MITCHELL & RAMELSBURG FURNITURE CO., 39 s. Illinois. See card on front fly-leaf, page 2.

Mitchell Robert, brick-moulder, res. 114 Michigan rd., beyond city limits.

Mitchell Robert, carriage painter, bds. Ray House, e South.

Mitchell Simeon J., conveyer of the mail, Indianapolis and Brooklyn, res. 297 n. Mississippi.

Mitchell William, (col.,) lab., res. Fourth, bet. Mississippi and Tennessee.

Mitchell Wm., (M. & Rammelsburg,) manager Mitchell & Rammelsburg furniture Co., 39 s. Illinois, res. 32 s. Mississippi.

Mitchell William M., (Miller, M. & Stough,) cor. Kentucky av. and Georgia, res. 244 n. Illinois.

Mitchell W. H., school teacher, bds. 297 n. Mississippi.

Mittay Charles, lab., res. 835 e. New York.

Mittay Christian, lab., res. 335 e.New York.

Mittay Christian G., drives ale wagon, res. 347 e. New York.

Mittay Henry, drives for George Fahrion, 90 e. South, bds. same.

Mittay John C., ale peddler, Frank Wright's brewery, res. 847 e. New York.

Mittee Samuel E., railroader, P. & I. R. R., res. 233 cor. Grove and Huron.

Mitten George, engineer, I., C. & L. R. R., res. 75 Davidson.

Mix Lyman, produce dealer, res. 76 n. Noble.

Mix Lemuel, produce shipper, bds. 236 e. Market.

Mock Leonidas G., brakesman, Bellefontaine R. R., res. 222 Winston.

Mock Martin, clerk, Joseph Staub, res. 127 Davidson.

Mock Morris, clerk, M. U. Ex. Co., res. 275 s. Tennessee.

Mock Mrs. Sarah, (wid. George,) res. 222 Winston.

Mode Michael, (C. Karle & Co.,) 83 e. Washington, res. 118 n. Liberty.

Moffit Miss Emma G., bds. 177 n. Tennessee.

Moffit Charles, piano pattern maker, 159 and 161 e. Washington, res. 70 Fletcher av.

Moffitt John, (Willis & Moffitt,) 166 Indiana av., res. near City Hospital.

Moffitt John, printer, Braden's, res. 297 s. New Jersey.

MOFFITT O. I.,
restaurant and ice cream saloon, 24 n. Pennsylvania, res. 237 s. New Jersey.

Moffitt Robert, printer, M. & J. Braden, bds. Oriental House.

Moffitt Sarah, (wid. John,) res. 237 n. New Jersey.

Moffitt William, salesman, Browning & Sloan, res. 177 n. Tennessee.

Mahoney Patrick, lab., res. 298 s. Delaware.

Mohr George, works cabinet-maker's union, bds. 518 e. Washington.

Moisseemo Von, image-maker, res. 295 e. New York.

Mokler Charles, pictures and frames, 79 s. Illinois, res. same.

Molin Thomas, railroader, bds. 470 e. Georgia.

Monahan Charles, lab., res. 368 s. Tennessee.

Monahan John, boarding house, 300 s. Tennessee.

Monahan Patrick, boots and shoes, res. 271 e. Merrill.

Monahan Patrick, lab., res. 368 s. Tennessee.

Monahan Timothy, salesman, 41 e. Washington, res. 474 e. Georgia.

Monan Michael, lab., res. bet. Liberty and East.

Monfort Cornelius, carriage-maker, res. 780 n. Tennessee.

MONNINGER DANIEL,
saloon, 20 Kentucky av., res. 388 n. Tennessee.

Monroe Edwin, basket-maker, 362 e. New York, res. same.

Monroe F. T., printer, bds. Martin House, 33 w. Maryland.

Monroe John, carpenter, res. 330 e. Vermont.

Monroe John L., carpenter, res. 431 e. St. Clair.

Monroe Samuel, teamster on Junction R. R., res. 319 e. North.

Monroe Simon, teamster, res. 252 Massachusetts av.

Montague Miss Jane, dress-maker, works 172 e. Washington, res. 105 s. New Jersey.

Montague Martha, (wid. William,) res. 105 s. New Jersey.

Montague Miss Mary, tailoress, res. 105 s. New Jersey.

Monteith John, carpenter, res. 127 e. South.

Monteith Taylor, carpenter, bds. 127 e. South.

Monteith William, carpenter, bds. 127 e. South.

Montgomery Andrew, shoe-maker, res. 505 n. Meridian.

Montgomery Joseph, works at 175 w. Cumberland, bds. Ray House.

Montgomery Thomas, lab., res. 39 e. McCarty.

Montgomery Wm., drives express wagon, res. 312 Madison av.

Montgomery William, cooper, res. 1 mile w. White river bridge, n. s. National rd.

Montgovern John S., cigar-maker, J. A. Heidlinger, res. 17 s. Mississippi.

MOODY BROS.,
(Edward R. & Charles W. M.,) drugs and medicines, 51 and 180 Indiana.

Moody Charles W., (Moody Bros.,) 51 and 180 Indiana av., bds. Pyle House.

Moody Edward, (Moody Bros.,) 51 and 180 Indiana av., res. 126 w. Vermont.

Moody George A., clerk, 180 Indiana av.

Moody Lucinda, servant, 238 n. West.

Moody Michael, shoe store, 83 e. Washington, res. 118 n. Liberty.

MOONEY & CO.,
(James E. M. & A. S. Mount,) leather, hides, oil, rubber and leather belting, 147 s. Meridian.

Mooney James E., (M. & Co.,) 147 s. Meridian, bds. 152 s. Mississippi.

Mooney John, salesman, New York Store, res. 213 n. Mississippi.

Mooney Thomas, fireman, T. H. & I. R. R., bds. Nagele House.

Moore Aaron, (col.,) lab., res. w. Ohio.

Moore Alfred C., road-master, C., C. & I. C. R. R., res. e. s. Liberty, bet. Meek and Georgia.

Moore Miss Catharine M., student, Indiana Female College, 146 n. Meridian, bds. same.

Moore Charles, merchant, res. 175 s. New Jersey.

Moore Edmund, lab., res. 142 Elm.

Moore Channey G., asst. assessor internal revenue, room 14, p. o. bldg., res. 242 n. Pennsylvania.

Moore Duncan, soldier, U. S. Arsenal, res. same.

Moore Eliza J., occupant Deaf and Dumb Asylum.

Moore Emma, (wid.,) res. 80 n. Pennsylvania.

Moore Miss Fannie, works Ben. Franklin office, bds. 24 s. Illinois.

Moore Frank., compositor, Downey, Brouse, Butler & Co., bds. 171 n. West.

Moore Frank., tinner, I. L. Frankem, bds. Pyle House.

Moore George, railroader, res. 195 w. South.

Moore George D., Indianapolis Agricultural works.

Moore George T., clerk, bds. Macy House.

Moore Geo. W., at gen'l ticket office, C., C. & I. C. R. R., res. 222 e. Louisiana.

Moore Granville C., clerk, office Supt. Public Instruction, res. 366 w. Vermont.

Moore Hardin F., works J. Cahall & Co., bds. Ray House.

Moore Henry, carriage painter, 123 e. Washington, res. 124 e. New York.

Moore Henry H., physician and surgeon, 298 e. Ohio, res. same.

Moore H. A., (Frink & M.,) 24 e. Georgia, res. 97 s. Meridian.

Moore James, lab., res. 59 Jones.

Moore James, engineer, C., C. & I. J. R. R., bds. 142 s. East.

Moore James, lab., White River Iron Works, res. 37 Jones.

Moore James L., pump-maker, works 14 Virginia av., bds. 321 e. Ohio.

Moore Jane, (col.,) bds. 126 w. Michigan.

Moore John, boiler-maker, res. 229 s. Alabama.

Moore John, carpenter, bds. 144 n. Tennessee.

Moore John G., ale-bottler, res. 378 e. Michigan.

Moore John W., plasterer, res. 267 w. Merrill.

Moore Joseph, huckster, res. 31 s. Bright.

Moore Joseph A., (Alford, Talbott & Co.,) 2 Morrison's Opera blk., s. Meridian, res. 433 n. Pennsylvania.

Moore Joshua, cloth-finisher, res. 528 s. Illinois.

Moore J., teamster, res. 246 s. Missouri.

Moore J. L., pump-maker, bds. 321 e. Ohio.

Moore Mrs. J. M., (wid. Joseph,) res. 23 e. Michigan.

Moore Miss Maggie, res. 31 s. Bright.

Moore Mary, servant, Blind Asylum, bds. same.

Moore Mary J., (wid.,) res. 267 w. Merrill.

Moore M. H., carriage-trimmer, works S. W. Drew & Co., res. 119 n. New Jersey.

Moore Nicholas, lab., res. 384 s. Delaware.

Moore Patrick, lab., res. 294 Madison av.

Moore & Co., bakery and confectioners, 131 s. Illinois.

Moore Phillip, (M. & Co.,) 131 s. Illinois, res. same.

Moore P. H., piano-forte-maker and tuner, res. 27 Ellsworth.

Moore Richard, tailor, res. 67 s. West.

Moore Robert C., painter, res. 104 s. Pennsylvania.

Moore Miss Sarah, res. 31 s. Bright.

Moore Sophia, (col.,) res. w. Ohio.

Moore S. H., physician, 37 Virginia av., res. 323 Virginia av.

Moore Thomas, soap manfr., res. n. s. National rd., half mile from bridge.

Moore Thomas C., blacksmith, res. 553 Virginia av.

Moore Thomas C., book-keeper, 49 s. Meridian, res. 23 e. Michigan.

Moore Thomas D., cooper, res. Carey's blk.

Moore William, cooper, 102 s. East, res. 275 w. Washington.

Moore William, horse dealer, res. 185 n. Noble.

Moore William H., plasterer, res. 387 Massachusetts av.

Moores John A., carpenter, res. n. s. National rd., w. White river bridge.

Moores Mrs. J. M., (Merrill & Co.,) 5 e. Washington, res. s. w. cor. Alabama and Merrill.

Moorman O. W., student, City Academy, bds. 76 Fort Wayne av.

Moore John, carpenter, res. 74 n. Pennsylvania.

Moran Mrs. Ellen, (wid. Thomas,) boarding, 38 s. Tennessee.

Moran Catharine, servant, Institute of the Blind, bds. same.

Moran John, lab., res. 92 s. Liberty.

Moran John, engineer, C., C. & I. C. R. R., res. 165 Meek.

Moran & Kelley, (Samuel M. & John B. K.,) house, sign and ornamental painters, 12 s. Pennsylvania.

Moran Michael, lab., bds. n. s. National rd., w. White river bridge.

Moran Samuel B., (M. & Kelley,) 12 s. Pennsylvania, res. 140 w. Vermont.

Morback Charles, boot-maker, bds. 78 s. Delaware.

Morback Peter, boot and shoe-maker, 78 s. Delaware, res. same.

Morell William, clerk, New York Store, bds. 70 e. Market.

Morell William, lab., res. 395 s. West.

Morford Emeline, (wid. Thomas,) res. 276 s. Tennessee.

Morgan Daniel, switchman, res. 308 Madison av.

Morgan Daniel B., mill-wright, res. 322 w. Washington.

Morgan David E., heater, Rolling Mill, res. 248 s. Missouri.

Morgan Dennis, egg-packer, bds. Court, bet. East and New Jersey.

Morgan Ellen, servant, 113 s. Meridian.

Morgan L. L., carpenter, bds. 420 s. Illinois.

Morgan Miss Mary, dress-maker, 316 e. New York, res. same.

Morgan Patrick, lab., I. & C. R. R., bds. end Lord.

Morgan Paulina, (wid. John,) res. 33 e. McCarty.

Morgan Sarah M., (wid. George W.,) dress-maker, res. over 167 w. Washington.

Morgan S. C., with Grover & Baker Sewing Machine Co., res. 322 n. Alabama.

Morgan Stephen W., (Stewart & M.,) 40 e. Washington, res. in country.

Morgan William, lab., bds. 759 n. Mississippi.

Morganveck V., grocer, 21 Chatham, res. same.

Moriarty Betsy, servant, n. e. cor. New York and East.

Moriarty Daniel, lab., res. 248 s. Delaware.

Moriarty James, brick-layer, res. 493 s. East.

Moriarty John, lab., res. n. s. e. Georgia.

Moriarty John, lab., res. near National rd., beyond city limits.

Moriarty Patrick, lab., res. 33 Bates.

Moriarty William, lab., res. 229 w. Merrill.

Moriarty William C., cashr. and book-keeper, Sentinel Establishment, 16½ e. Washington, bds. Palmer House.

Moritz Amelia C., inmate Deaf and Dumb Asylum.

Morley David, lab., res. w. Seventh, near Lenox.

Morley Edward B., constable, res. 303 Indiana av.

Morley Thomas, lab., res. 226 s. Missouri.

Morrer John, moulder, res. 839 s. Pennsylvania.

Morris Alfred, coach-trimmer, 26 e. Georgia, bds. Pattison House.

Morris Artemus, carpenter, res. 142 e. McCarty.

Morris Mrs. A. W., (wid.,) res. 115 s. Meridian.

Morris Betsey, (wid., col.,) res. 129 n. California.

MORRIS CHARLES G., drugs and medicines, 521 n. Illinois, bds. 112 n. Jackson.

Morris Elizabeth, res. 625 n. Meridian.

Morris Grigsby, (col.,) cook, Spencer House, res. 81 w. Georgia.

Morris Harmony, huckster, res. 330 Indiana av.

Morris John, shoe-maker, res. 5 Dougherty.

Morris Henry W., clerk, 59 w. Washington, res. 186 n. Mississippi.

Morris James W., teller, Citizens' National Bank, 4 e. Washington, res. 112 Jackson.

Morris John C., clerk, res. 9 Cherry.

Morris John D., freight agt., I., C. & L. R. R., res. 112 Jackson.

Morris John I., (H. F. West & Co.,) 37 s. Meridian, res. Ft. Wayne rd., beyond city limits.

Morris Joseph, lab., res. 239 Bluff rd.

Morris Miss Mary, student, Indiana Female College, 146 n. Meridian, bds. same.

Morris Mary E., (wid. Frank,) res. 226 Massachussetts av.

Morris Sanford, salesman, 10 e. Washington, res. 275 w. Vermont.

Morris S. B., lab., res. 79 Norwood.

MORRIS THOMAS A., prest. I. & St. L. R. R., office 33 s. Alabama, res. Western av., n. city limits.

Morris William B., express-messenger, res. 210 Huron.

Morris William H., heater, Rolling Mill, res. 266 s. Illinois.

Morris William J., plasterer, res. 169 Ft. Wayne av.

Morrison Alexander, stone-cutter, res. 177 Meek.

Morrison Alexander F., res. cor. Ft. Wayne av. and St. Mary.

Morrison Ann, (wid. A. F.,) res. 52 n. Pennsylvania.

Morrison Charles, clerk, 49 s. Meridian, res. Ft. Wayne av., cor. St. Mary.

Morrison E. S., salesman, 117 e. Washington, bds. 17½ Virginia av.

Morrison Mrs. Hettie, (wid.,) bds. 175 e. Ohio.

Morrison Hetty A., clerk, p. o., bds. Pattison House.

Morrison Jacob, traveling agent, res. n. Pennsylvania, beyond city limits.

Morrison James, attorney at law, 24½ e. Washington, res. cor. Maryland and Fort Wayne av.

Morrison James, teamster, bds. 135 Union.

Morrison J. A., agent Pennsylvania R. R., 85 Virginia av., res. 219 n. New Jersey.

Morrison John, bds. 148 Indiana av.

Morrison John I., lawyer, room 6 Talbott & New's blk., n. Pennsylvania, res. 298 n. Tennessee.

Morrison Michael, teamster, res. 135 Union.

Morrison Michael, Jr., laborer, bds. 135 Union.

Morrison Miss M. F., student, Indiana Female College, 146 n. Meridian, bds. same.

MORRISON'S OPERA HALL, W. H. Morrison, propr., n. e. cor. Meridian and Maryland.

Morrison Robert I., deputy treasurer of state, bds. 298 n. Tennessee.

Morrison S., lab., res. 428 s. Missouri.

Morrison William, teamster, res. 429 e. St. Clair.

Morrison William, lab., bds. 135 Union.

Morrison William A., secy. Ind. & Ill. C. R. R., office 26 s. Meridian, bds. 52 n. Pennsylvania.

Morrison William II., book-binder, bds. 144 n. Tennessee.

Morrison William H., propr. Morrison's Opera Hall, (Alford, Talbott & Co.,) res. 63 Circle.

Morrison William Henry, civil engineer, over 46 e. Washington.

Morrison W. Lewis, book-keeper, Stewart & Morgan, res. cor. Fort Wayne av. and St. Mary.

Morrow Miss Emma L., seamstress, James Blake, 308 n. Tennessee.

MORROW, GOODWIN & HAY, (Wilson M., Robert M. G. & William H. H.,) attorneys at law, room 3 Vinton's blk., opp. P. O.

Morrow Thomas, lab., 327 w. Market.

Morrow Thomas E., carpenter, res. 217 Coburn.

Morrow Willson, (M., Goodwin & Hay,) 3 Vinton's blk., res. 282 n. Pennsylvania.

Morse Charles A., machinist, res. 204 Winston.

Morse Joseph, (Rev.,) res. 203 s. New Jersey.

Morse L. C., (col.,) barber, bds. 63 s. Illinois.

Morse Robert S., carpenter, res. 68 Indiana av.

Morse Thomas J., carpenter, res. cor. Vermont and West.

Morton Alfred, (col.,) lab., res. Minerva, near City Hospital.

Morton Miss Catharine E., res. 215 w Ohio.

Morton George T., attorney at law, room 1, Talbott & New's blk., n. Pennsylvania, bds. Pyle House.

Morton John, bricklayer, res. 67 Norwood.

Morton John R., (Harding & M.,) cor. Meridian and Circle.

Morton Joseph, (col.,) lab., res. West, bet. Ohio and Market.

Morton J. M., clerk, 149 s. Meridian, bds. Oriental House.

MORTON, MARTINDALE & TARKINGTON, (Oliver P. M., Elijah B. M., & John S. T.,) attorneys at law, Bee Hive blk., over 2 w. Washington. See card, p. 64.

Morton Miss Minta, bds. cor. Seventh and Tennessee.

Morton Oliver P., (M., Martindale & Tarkington,) U. S. Senator, bds. Bates House.

Morton Robert, lab., res. 32 Bicking.

Morton Peter H., traveling agent, res. 23 w. St. Joseph.

Morton Thomas R., clerk, adjutant-general's office, res. 295 w. Ohio.

Morton Wm., 32 Bicking, s. of Delaware.

Moses Lucius W., optician, 50 e. Washington, res. 87 e. Michigan.

Mosier George, meat market, 295 s. Missouri, res. same.

Mosier Theodore, foreman I. &. C. Car Works, res. 111 Forrest av.

Moss Albert, brewer, bds. 30 s. Alabama.

Moss Alexander, (col.,) res. cor. Elizabeth and Blake.

Moss Andrew, machinist, res. 227 e. Market.

Moss Casper, brewer, res. 30 s. Alabama.

Moss Edmund, occupant Deaf and Dumb Asylum.

Moss Mrs. M., (wid. Lewis,) dress-maker, res. 188 n. Tennessee.

Moss Nathan, (col.,) barber, res. w. north.

Moss Solomon, (col.,) servant, J. Martin, 33 w. Maryland.

Mossler A. I., 114 s. Meridian, res. 82 n. East.

Mossler L. I., (L. I. M. & Bro.,) 114 s. Meridian, res. 79 Massachusetts av.

Mossler L. I. & Bro., (L. I. & Solomon M.,) wholesale clothing, 114 s. Meridian.

Mossler Morris L., book-keeper, 114 s. Meridian, res. same.

Mossler Solomon, (L. I. & Bro.,) 114 s. Meridian, res. 82 n. East.

Moth Peter, engineer, res. 165 e. St. Joseph.

Motherhead A. M., (Greenleaf & Co.,) res. 126 e. Ohio.

Motherhead John L., (Greenleaf & Co.,) res. 128 s. Meridian.

Mote D., student, commercial college, bds. 44 s. Tennessee.

Mottery Catharine, student, bds. 200 s. Meridian.

MOTTERY FERDINAND, Concordia House, 200 s. Meridian.

Mottery Minnie, student, bds. 200 s. Meridian.

Mottler Miss Louisa, bds. 327 s. Pennsylvania.

Motz John, barber, res. 84 e. South.

Moulton Charles W., engineer, I. & C. R. R., res. 26 Fletcher av.

Moulton Daniel S., clerk, American Express Co., res. 219 e. South.

Moulton Emily, (col ,) servant, 512 n. Illinois.

Moulton Miss Mary, servant, Mrs. A. Buchet, 42 Kentucky av.

Mount A. S., (Mooney & Co.,) 147 s. Meridian, res. 455 n. Tennessee.

Mount C. Frank, telegraph operator, bds. 455 n. Tennessee.

Mount Mrs. G. A., boarding house, 148 Indiana av.

Mount Jacob, clerk, Spiegle, Thoms & Co., bds. 116 s. East.
Mount William P., works Mooney & Co., bds. 455 n. Tennessse.
Mountain Michael, lab., res. 80 s. West.
Mounts Henry, clerk J. M. & I. R. R., bds. Ray House, c. South.
Mowerer Andrew, hod-carrier, res. 475 e. Washington.
Maper J., carpenter, bds. 392 n. Alabama.
Moyst William H., saddler, 23 s. Meridian, bds. 3 e. Maryland.
Mozart Hall, 35 and 37 s. Delaware.
Muar Henry, bell boy, Sherman House, bds. same.
Muchell John, lab., res. n. e. cor. East and Buchanan.
Mucho William, cigar-maker, William Wallace, res. 249 s. Pennsylvania.
Mucherberger John, box-maker, in rear 174 e. Washington, res. over the same.
Muxke William, (Egger & M.,) res. over 152 e. Washington.
MUELLER CHARLES G., saloon, 25 and 27 s. Delaware, res. same.
Mueller Christian, carpenter, res. 439 s. East.
MUELLER EDWARD, (Union Starch Factory,) traveling agt., Holland, Ostermeyer & Co., res. 305 e. Market.
Mueller L. H., apothecary and chemist, 187 e. Washington, res. same.
Mueller William, shoe-maker, works 286 e. Washington, bds. Liberty, one-half square s. Washington.
Mueller William, teacher, German English school, bds. 138 s. New Jersey.
Muhlenback August, (M. & Obermeyer,) 2 Palmer House, res. 198 e. Washington.
Muhlenback Frederick, photographer, over Bee Hive, 2 w. Washington, res. same.
Muhlenback & Obermeyer, (August M. & W. M. O.,) dealers in hats, caps, &c., 2 Palmer House and 198 e. Washington.
Muhlman Christian, cabinet-maker, res. 488 s. New Jersey.
Muir James W., clerk, at 20 e. Washington, bds. Pyle House.
Mulbarger W. H., carriage-maker, res. 384 s. West.
Mulchay Margaret, (wid. Daniel,) res. 488 e. Georgia.
Mulchay Michael, lab., res. 87 s. Noble.
Mulchay Patrick, lab., res. 488 e. Georgia.
Mull Jacob, mail agt., Bellefontaine R. R., res. 273 n. Tennessee.
Mullaney Dennis, clerk, 48 s. Meridian, bds. 355 n. Illinois.
Mullaney Edward, foundryman, res. 52 cor. Noble and Huron.
Mullaney Mrs. Mary, (wid.,) res. 355 n. Illinois.

Mullaney P. J., salesman, 141 s. Meridian, res. 355 n. Illinois.
Mullen John, res 270 Madison av.
Mullen Michael, porter, Commercial Hotel.
Mullen William, lab., res. 521 n. Tennessee.
Mullen William F., cash boy, Bee Hive store, res. 521 n. Tennessee.
Mullen Mrs., (wid. Dradger,) res. 20 Dougherty.
Mullencoff Soprohnia, servant, 172 n. West.
Muller Augustus, school teacher, res. 29 Fletcher's av.
Muller Frederick C., res. 398 e. Washington.
Muller George F., meat shop, 237 s. Alabama, res. same.
Mullen John A., butcher, res. 235 s. Alabama.
Mulligan Thomas D., stereotyper, Journal office, bds. Oriental House.
Mulligan Timothy, shoe-maker, res. 474 e. Georgia.
Mulliken John, wood agt., Ind. Central R. R., res. 71 Davidson.
Mulliken Miss Sarah A., dress-maker, 68 c. Washington, over Quaker store, res. n. 71 Davidson.
Munce James, plasterer, res. 404 Virginia av.
Munce M., plasterer, res. 440 Virginia av.
Munce William, plasterer, res. 442 Virginia av.
Munhall L. W., dentist. 35½ e. Market, bds. Macy House.
MUNINGER & CO., (Conrad M. & Jacob Schwaub,) saloon, 167 w. Washington.
Muninger Conrad, (M. & Co.,) 567 w. Washington, res. 292 w. Maryland.
Munroe Alex., salesman, New York Store, bds. 58 s. Pennsylvania.
Munroe James, (col.,) lab., res. 124 n. Delaware.
Munroe Miss Jane, bds. Johana Turbyville, National rd., near White River Bridge.
Munsell Ezra, painter, res. 63 Peru.
Munsell Henry, carriage-maker, n. w. cor. Massachusetts av. and St. Clair, res. 71 Peru.
Munsell Henry T., engineer, Bellefontaine R. R., bds. 71 Peru.
Munsell Newton, brakesman, Bellefontaine R. R., res. 71 Peru.
Munson Charles H., (M. & Johnson,) 62 e. Washington, res. 286 n. Alabama.
Munson David, propr., Munson's patent lighning rod, 62 e. Washington, res. 228 e. Market.
MUNSON & JOHNSON, (Charles H. M. & W. G. J.,) dealers in stoves and tin-ware, 62 e. Washington.
Munson Lewis, capitalist, res. 286 n. Alabama.

Munson William L., grocer, 51 n. Alabama, bds. 286 n. Alabama.

Munson W. G., salesman, 62 e. Washington, res. 228 e. Market.

Murdock George T., book-keeper, 70 n. Illinois, bds. 385 s. Illinois.

Murdock James F., agt. State lottery, res. 347 s. Pennsylvania.

Murdock Joseph, moulder, 385 s. Illinois.

Muremill Miss, servant, at 68 Bates.

Murphy Ann, servant, at 123 n. Illinois.

Murphy Bridget, dining room girl, Sherman House, bds. same.

Murphy Bridget, servant, 128 n. Meridian.

Murphy Charlotte, servant, at 376 n. Illinois.

Murphy Miss Chloe A., teacher, first ward school, bds. cor. New York and East.

Murphy Daniel E., groceries and produce, 396 w. North, res. same.

Murphy Edward, employee, Merchants Union Express Co., res. 176 s. Illinois.

Murphy Frank, lab., res. 365 s. Missouri.

Murphy James, lab., res. 278 e. Louisiana.

Murphy James, brakesman, Bellefontaine R. R., bds. 270 Railroad.

Murphy James, res. 17 Elizabeth.

Murphy Jesse T., policeman, ninth ward, res. 179 n. Noble.

Murphy John, lab., I., C. & L. R. R.. res. Michigan rd., beyond city limits.

Murphy John, express driver, res. 27 California.

Murphy John, lab., bds. 91 Fayette.

Murphy John W.. bds. 396 W. North.

MURPHY JOHN W.,
(M. Johnston & Co., and W. J. Holliday & Co.,) 49 s. Meridian, res. 166 n. Meridian.

MURPHY, JOHNSTON & CO.,
(John W. M., William W. J. & William J. Holliday,) wholesale dry goods and notions, 49 s. Meridian.

Murphy Lizzie, waiter, dining room, Commercial Hotel.

Murphy Margaret, servant, 333 n. Illinois.

Murphy Margaret, servant, at 38 w. St. Clair.

Murphy Mary, kitchen girl, Bates House.

Murphy Mary, pantry girl, Sherman House, bds. same.

Murphy Maurice, lab., T. H. & R. R. shop, res. n. s. Meek.

Murphy Michael, lab., res. near Jeffersonville Road House.

Murphy Michael, lab., 232 s. Missouri.

Murphy Michael, policeman, Seventh Ward, res. 190 n. Blackford.

Murphy Milton, engineer, Starch Factory, res. 316 e. New York.

Murphy Patrick, expressman, res. 66 Indiana av.

Murphy Patrick, lab., res. s. s. e. Georgia, n. corporation line.

Murphy Patrick, lab., T. H. & I. R. R. Freight Depot, res. s. Missouri, near McCarty.

Murphy Patrick J., shoe-maker, 9 n. Illinois, bds. 69 w. Market.

Murphy Rebecca, (wid. Jonathan,) dressmaker, works 17 n. East.

Murphy Samuel, res. 42 Fletcher av.

Murphy T., (col.,) lab., bds. 276 e. North.

Murphy Tobias M., life insurance agt., res. 321 e. Georgia.

Murphy William, lab., res. near Jeffersonville Round House.

Murphy William H., clerk, 42 n. Pennsylvania, bds. 43 Fletcher av.

Murray C. W., cooper, res. 440 n. East.

Murray James, clerk, bds. 335 n. East.

Murray & White, lumber dealers, 321 s. Tennessee.

Murray William, agt. picture store, 79 s. Illinois, bds. same.

Murrell William R., salesman, New York Store, bds. 69 w. New York.

Murtaugh George F., foreman, Capitol Tobacco Works, bds. 144 n. Tennessee.

Murtough Sarah, laundress, Institute of the Blind, bds. same.

Musbom Nicholas, tobacconist, bds. Ray House, e. South.

Musgrave C. inmate Deaf and Dumb Asylum

Musgrave Moses, woolen manfr., res. 63 s. California.

Musgrave O. L., carder and spinner, bds. 725 n. Tennessee.

Musgrave P. D., physician, res. n. e. cor. Tennessee and Fifth.

Musgrave W. agt. Munson's Lightning Rods, bds. 725 n. Tennessee.

Music Hall, 80 s. Delaware, Charles Heitkam, propr.

Musser William, printer, Journal Office, res. 43 Dougherty.

Mussman & Bro., (William & Dietrich M.,) groceries, 244 s. Meridian.

Mussmann Dietrich, (A. & D. M.,) 254 s. Meridian, res. same.

Mussman Frederick, clerk, W. & D. M., bds. 244 s. Meridian.

Mussman William, (W. & D. M.,) 244 s. Meridian, res. same.

Mutzler John, brewer, Smith's brewery, res. 4 Buchanan.

Muzzy Bennett, express driver, res. 12 California.

Muzzy ———, book-keeper, J. Cahall & Co., res. 26 s. Mississippi.

Myer Christ., tailor, res. 73 s. Liberty.

Myer C. F., lab., bds. 293 e. Washington.

Myer Frank, drayman, 149 s. Meridian, res. 284 Liberty.

Myer Frederick, lab., res 144 Union.

Myer Frederick, lab., Starch Factory, bds. Michigan rd., beyond city limits.

Myer G., (M. & Co.,) bds. Palmer House.

Myer Henry, clerk, German Dry Goods Store, res. 641 n. Tennessee.

Myer Henry, cab-finisher, 105 e. Washington.

Myer Martha J., (wid. Charles,) res. 172 w. Washington, second floor.

Myer, Reinheimer & Co., clothiers, 133 s Illinois.

Myer William, blacksmith, res. 426 e. Georgia.

Myer Amos H., occupant Deaf and Dumb Asylum.

Myers August, carpenter, res. 349 s. Pennsylvania.

Myers C., brass-founder, J. W. Davis, res. 71 s. Liberty.

Myers Charles S., printer, Journal bldg., res. 43 Blackford.

Myers Charles, toll gate-keeper, Madison rd.

Myers C. F., picture frame-maker, res. 227 n. Liberty.

Myers Frank, moulder, res. at 138 Winston.

Myers Frederick, carpenter, res. 326 e. Vermont.

Myers George, lab., bds. e. city.

Myers George, (col.,) barber, bds. 63 s. Illinois.

Myers Irwin M., delivery clerk, feed store, res. 271 Indiana av.

Myers Jacob C., carpenter, res. 280 e. North.

Myers James M., real estate agt., 24½ w. Washington, res. 245 n. Illinois.

Myers Jane, occupant Deaf and Dumb Asylum.

Myers John, teamster, res. 171 Eddy.

Myers John A., (Martin & M.,) 117 w. Washington, res. 219 w. Washington.

Myers John G., real estate agency, 12 s. Pennsylvania, res. 485 n. Alabama.

Myers John H., carpenter, res. 327 Winston.

Myers Joseph, carpenter, res. 426 s. Illinois.

Myers Julia, (wid. Charles,) res. rear 230 s. New Jersey.

Myers Miss Lizzie, bds. 266 s. Pennsylvania.

Myers L. F., confectioner, res. 322 n. New Jersey.

Myers M., presiding elder German Evangelical Church, res. 180 n. Noble.

Myers Oscar, printer, Journal Office, res. 399 n. Alabama.

Myers Smith H., clerk, 3 w. Washington, bds. 422 n. Illinois.

Myers William, clerk, cor. McCarty and Meridian, res. 224 Union.

Myers William H., rout agt. Daily Sentinel, 16½ e. Washington, res. 322 n. New Jersey.

NAEGLE JOSEH F., salesman, 68 s. Meridian, bds. Commercial Hotel.

Naer George, brewer, res. s. Alabama, bet. Merrill and McCarty.

Nagle August, propr. Nagle House, 272 w. Maryland.

Nagle Miss Margaret, seamstress, bds. 296 n. Liberty.

Nahn Wm., shoe-maker, works 17 w. Washington, res. 380 e. Michigan.

Nally William, tailor, over 25 w. Washington, res. same.

Naltner A., (A. Seidensticker & Co.,) 14 s. Delaware, res. 186 e. McCarty.

Nan Valentine, lab., res. 159 High.

Napton James, stone-cutter, bds. 458 e. Georgia.

Nardin Frederick P., cabinet-maker, res. 50 Fletcher av.

Nathan Joseph, porter, Macy House, bds. same.

Nathan Sharff, clerk, Rauh & Bros., res. 31 Kentucky av.

National Livery and Sale Stables, Court, bet. Pennsylvania and Delaware.

NATIONAL VARIETIES, Court, bet. Pennsylvania and Delaware, S. Dinnin, propr.

Naughton Patrick, grocer, 210 e. Washington, res. 245 n. Liberty.

Naughton Peter, clerk, 210 e. Washington, bds. 245 n. Liberty.

Navin John N., veterinary surgeon, 164 w. Washington, res. State, bet. Mississippi and Tennessee.

Nawl Samuel, (col.,) lab., res. n. Douglas alley.

Naylor M. D. Miss, teacher, Institute of the Blind, res. same.

NEAB CONRAD, plumber, gas and steam fitter, 70 n. Illinois, bds. Palmer House.

Neal A. C., printer, Journal office, res. 286 Virginia av.

Neal Edward, contractor, res. 140 E. St. Joseph.

Neal Jennie, inmate, Home of the Friendless, w. s. n. Pennsylvania, beyond city limits.

Neal Leonard, tailor, 19 w. Washington, res. s. West.

Neal William, (col.,) express driver, res. 165 w. Elizabeth.

Neall George H., produce dealer, bds. 76 n. Noble.

Neall Jonathan R., egg dealer, 230 e. Washington, res. 76 n. Noble.

Nearney Alfred, silver-plater, bds. 225 e. Market.

Nebergall John, carpenter, works John B. Many, res. 266 Winston.

Nechsler David, butcher, 306 s. Meridian.

Neelberg Louis, foundryman, res. cor. Noble and Virginia av.

Nedrick William A., clerk, New York Store, bds. Wiles House.

Needham William, (Indiana Banking Co.,) res. Franklin, Ind.

Neeld, Nathan M., (Hibben, Tarkington & Co.,) 112 s. Meridian, bds. 139 n. Meridian.

Neeman Christian, carpenter, (Stelhorn & Co.,) res. 231 Davidson.

Neeman Christian, shoe-maker, 267 Massachusetts av., res. 350 n. Noble.

Neeman Christian, lab., res. 70 Lockerbie.

Neeman Bridget, chambermaid, Sherman House, bds. same.

Neeman Henry, (Boedker & N.,) bds. 272 Winston.

Neff Albert H., cooper, res. w. Maria.

Neffla Frederick N., (N. & Macer,) meat market, 300 n. Blake, bds. 275 s. West.

Negley P. L., law student with Elliott & Black, 24½ e. Washington, bds. n. Delaware.

Neibling Maria, occupant Deaf and Dumb Asylum.

Neiger, Frederick, wagon-maker, res. 344 n. Noble.

Neighbors Charles, expressman, res. 19 Henry.

Neighbors Robert, drayman, res. 151 Union.

Neiman Christian, res. 231 Davidson.

Neiman Daniel S., bar-tender, bds. Nieman House.

Neiman Jacob S., driver Citizen's Street Railway, res. 33 w. McCarty.

Neiman John S., clerk, Trade Palace, bds. Neiman House.

Neiman Joseph, tailor, res. 42 Dunlap.

NEIMAN LAHA MRS., Propts. Neiman House, 130 s. Illinois.

Neiman T. J., trunk-maker, 16½ s. Meridian, res. 42 n. Douglas.

Neifing Nicholas, lab., res. 690 n. Illinois.

Neis Louis, carpenter, res. 460 n. East.

Nelias Charles, tailor, res. 65 w. South.

Nell Enelia, (wid. John,) res. 199 e. Washington, up stairs.

Nelson Edward, machinist, res. 167 Meek.

Nelson Miss Ellen, (col.,) res. 126 n. Missouri.

Nelson Henry H., agt. Morrison's Opera Hall, res. 125 n. Mississippi.

Nelson H. L., watch-maker, 24 e. Washington, res. 318 n. Alabama.

Nelson James, carpenter, res. w. s. n. Pennsylvania, beyond city limits.

Nelson Johanna, servant at 275 n. Meridian.

Nelson John, servant, W. H. Talbott, 94 n. Meridian.

Nelson Louisa, (col.,) res. 134 Bright.

Nelson Sanday, (col.,) lab., res. 126 n. Missouri.

Nelson Thomas, builder, res. 27 Massachusetts av.

Nelson Thomas A., salesman, New York Store, bds. 27 Massachusetts av.

Neltner Joseph, teamster, bds. 167 Union.

Nemeyer C. W., railroader, res. 108 s. Noble.

Nenaber Betsy, (wid.,) res. 297 e. Georgia.

Nenan Hannah, servant, W. P. Noble, e. Market, near corporation line.

Nentz John, cigar-maker, bds. Neiman House.

Nestner Christina, (wid. Frederick,) res. 426 s. East.

Nething Louis, works Root's foundry, res. 375 n. Alabama.

Nettler Lewis, Empire Restaurant, 23 n. Illinois, res. same.

Neubacher Lewis, brass finisher, res. 290 s. Alabama.

Nevegold Frederick, White River Iron Works, res. 88 s. Mississippi.

Neveux Jules, carriage painter, works S. W. Drew & Co., bds. 272 n. Noble.

New Barney, chair finisher, bds. 146 e. McCarty.

New Daniel, blacksmith, res. 121 s. New Jersey.

New Frank R., bds. 426 n. Illinois.

NEW GEORGE W., physician and surgeon, 15 Miller's blk., up stairs, res. 426 n. Illinois.

New John B., minister, res. 82 n. Illinois.

New John C., cashier First National Bank, res. 248 n. Pennsylvania.

New Leopold, soldier U. S. Arsenal, res. Arsenal.

New Martha, (wid.,) res. 119 s. New Jersey.

New Valentine, packer, John Woodbridge, res. High.

New York Life Ins. Co., W. W. Byington, general agt., n. w. cor. Meridian and Washington.

Newan Ann, servant, e. Market.

Newbacher Lewis, brass foundry, res. 264 S. Alabama.

Newby Milton, brakesman, bds. Ray House.

Newby ———, (col.,) engineer, res. 558 n. Mississippi.

Newcomb Horatio C., associate editor Indianapolis Journal, res. 564 n. Illinois.

Newcomb Jesse J., upholsterer, Bates House, bds. same.

Newcomb Richard H., salesman 302 n. Illinois, res. n. e. cor. North and Illinois.

Newcomb William C., salesman, 49 s. Meridian, res. 446 n. New Jersey.

NEWCOMER, F. S., Physician, office room 6, Blake's row, res. 82 w. North.

Newell John W., res. 234 w. Washington.

Newell L. S., agt. for Appleton's American Cyclopædia, office Vinton blk., bds. Pyle House.

Newell Robert A., carpenter and builder, North, bet. Illinois and Tennesse, bds. 255 n. Mississippi.

Newhart Henrietta, servant, 75 n. Alabama.

Newland R. A., music teacher, Institute of the Blind, res. same.

Newman David, salesman, Raub Bros., bds. 182 e. Washington.

Newman Henry, salesman, 173 w. Washington, res. same.

Newman Miss H., res. 56 Massachusetts av.

Newman Isaac L., broom-maker, res. 372 n. East.

NEWMAN JOHN S., prest. Merchants' National Bank, 48 e. Washington, res. 243 n. Pennsylvania, cor. Michigan.

Newman Omer, res. 325 n. Pennsylvania.

Newman Pauline, hoop-skirt manfr., 95 e. Washington, res. 79 Massachusetts av.

Newman Peter, lab., res. 305 s. Missouri.

Newman William T., lab., res. 20 Douglas.

Newmeyer Julius A., (Kettenback & N.,) bds. 279 Massachusetts av.

Newn William, shoe-maker, res. Minerva, bet. New York and Michigan.

Newson Joseph, (R. Z. Thomas & Co.,) 155 w. Washington, res. 441 n. Mississippi.

Newton Miss Caroline, lady boarder, 281 e. New York.

Newton George A., clerk, I. C. & L. R. R., 385 w. Michigan.

NEWTON MRS. MARIA L., (wid. Norman,) dress-maker and milliner, 36 e. Market, res. 17 n. East.

Newton Philo A., hat and bonnet bleacher, res. Center, bet. Dunlop and Ellen.

Nice Lewis, groceries, 460 n. East, res. same.

Nicely Wilson, physician, 73 n. Illinois, bds. same.

Niccum J. G., blacksmith, res. 53 Maple.

Nichol James M., teller, Ind. National Bank, 2 e. Washington, res. 415 n. Meridian.

NICHOL JOSEPH W., attorney at law and notary public, rooms 1 and 2 Talbott & New's blk., n. Pennsylvania, bds. 17 Virginia av.

Nicolai Charles, saddler, 326 e. Washington, res. same.

Nicolai Henry, butcher, res. 116 e. St. Joseph.

Nicolai L., butcher, 306 Virginia av.

Nicolai M., dress-maker, bds. 226 e. Washington.

Nicholas Addison, grocer, 99 Massachusetts av., res. same.

Nicholas Robert, (col.,) brick-layer, res. Howard, bet. Third and Fourth.

Nicholas Mrs. America, servant, last house w. Michigan.

Nichols Bernard, image-maker, res. 295 e. New York.

Nichols John, res. end Virginia av., beyond city limits.

Nichols Robert, (col.,) res. 330 w. North.

Nichols Thomas M., dentist. 29½ w. Washington, res. Virginia av., beyond city limits.

Nichols Willard, printer, Journal office, res. 73 e. St. Clair.

Nichols Willard C., employee, State Librarian's office, bds. 73 e. St. Clair.

Nichols William, lab., res. 318 w. North.

Nichols W. L., (col.,) porter, J. H. Vajen.

Nicholson David, (Scott & N.,) Kentucky av., res. 160 w. Georgia.

Nicholson Edwin, clerk, res. 261 w. Washington.

Nicholson Jane, (wid.,) res. Broadway, outside city limits.

Nicholson Miss J., servant, 170 w. Market.

Nicholson Miss Mary, principal first ward school, res. cor. Broadway and Forest Home av.

Nicholson J. C., painter, res. 380 s. West.

Nicholson William T., car inspector for I. & C. R. R., res. 22 Lord.

Nickum John R., (Parrott, N. & Co.,) 188 e. Washington, res. 155 n. Tennessee.

Niddy Mrs. Catharine, (wid. John,) res. National rd., one mile from White River bridge.

Nife William, clerk, New York Store, bds. 144 n. Tennessee.

Nifong Jerome, teamster, res. 37 Vinton.

Nichans Joseph, res. 349 s. Delaware.

Niermeyer Henry, shoe-maker, works 156 w. Washington, bds. Court, bet. East and New Jersey.

Niemeyer Henry F., clerk, 102 s. Noble, res. same.

Niemeyer William, Sr., groceries, 102 s. Noble, res. same.

Neimeyer William, Jr., railroader, bds. 102 s. Noble.

Nilius Charles, tailor, 142 s. Illinois, res. 14 Eddy.

Nine Catharine, servant, 473 n. Delaware.

Ninth Ward School, n. s. Vermont, bet. Davidson and Railroad, Mrs. M. Richardson, principal.

Nitch Theresa, (wid. Albert,) res. 220 s. East.

Nixon J. Howard, (Rev.,) res. 77 e. Michigan.

Noble A. F., military claim agt., room 5 Yohn's blk., bds. with W. P. Noble, near terminus e. Market.

Noble James, copartner, Miller & Franks, res. 139 n. Delaware.

Noble James, retired merchant, res. 143 n. Delaware.

NOBLE LAZARUS, Clerk Supreme Court, office s. w. cor. w. Washington and Tennessee, res. 88 w. Ohio.

Noble William H. L., general freight agt., I., C. & L. R. R., res. Madison rd., near city limits.

Noble Winston P., real estate dealer, res. e. Market, near corporation line.

Noe Andrew'J., car painter, works Ind. Central R. R. shop, res. 21 n. East.

Noe Marshal, planner, carpenter association, res. 284 n. New Jersey.

Noe Mrs. Mary, (wid. Andrew J.,) dressmaker, 21 n. East, res. same.

Noel E. B., (E. L. & C. B. N.,) 86 Virginia av., res. 252 s. New Jersey.

Noel E. L., (E. L. & E. B. N.,) 86 Virginia av., res. 252 s. New Jersey.

Noel E. B. & E. L., grain dealers and commission merchants,86 Virginia av.

Noel S. V. B., bds. 252 s. New Jersey.

Noers George, lab., Meikel's Brewery, res. 72 s. West.

Nofsinger Francis B., physician and surgeon, res. 49 Indiana av.

Nofsinger J. B., (N., Kingan & Co.,) porkpackers, res. Indiana av., near angle.

NOFSINGER, KINGAN & CO., (W. R. & J. B. Nofsinger, and Thomas D. Kingan,) beef and ;pork-packers and provision dealers, on White River, foot Georgia.

Nofsinger William R., (N., Kingan & Co.,) res. National rd., one mile e. city limits.

Noftsker David, lab., res. 271 w. Merrill.

Nogle Augustus, propr. Nagle House, 272 w. Maryland.

Nolan Mrs. Anna, (wid. Thomas,) seamstress, res. 65 n. California.

Nolan Joshua D., res. 756 n. Tennessee.

Nolan J., shoe-maker, res. 120 e. Merrill.

Nolan Michael, boot and shoe-maker, 63 Indiana av., bds. 223 s. West.

Nolan Nancy, (wid..) Stringtown, near river bridge.

Nolan Solomon C., cabinet-maker, res. 114 s. Noble.

Nolder Charles, lab., res. 127 e. St. Joseph.

Nomas John, grocer, cor. Virginia av. and Noble, bds. same.

Nooe Daniel M., carriage-smith, res. 121 s. New Jergey.

Nooe Martha, (wid. Aquilla,) res. 119 s. New Jersey.

Nordman Henry, cooper, 263 s. West, res. same.

Normal Academy of Music, 263 s. Meridian, office 35 e. Washington, Charles W. Hess, principal.

Norman J., brush-maker, works Schmedel & Fricker, res. Second, bet Tennessee and Mississippi.

Norris Alfred, (col.,) teamster, res. Michigan rd., beyond city limits.

Norris James C., salesman, 131 s. Meridian, bds. 91 Broadway.

Norris Mrs. ———, (wid.,) res. 94 Broadway.

Norte George, cooper, res. 3 Willard.

North Pinkney A., carpenter, res. cor. Blake and Elizabeth.

North Street M. E. Church, n. Alabama, cor. North.

North-Western Christian University, on Forest Home av., end of Plum, beyond city limits, Elijah H. Goodwin, prest.

North-Western Market, s. w. cor. Ohio and Tennessee.

Northan Asa, propr. Brittan's Scientific Lightning Rod, bds. Neiman House.

Northcraft ———, traveling agt., W. H. Haskit & Co., bds. Martin House, 33 w. Maryland.

NORTHROP W. W., gen'l agt. Security Life Ins. and Annuity Co., office, room 2, Blake Row, res. 310 n. Illinois.

Northway George M., plasterer, res. 186 n. New Jersey.

Northway John W., plasterer, res. 306 e. North.

NORTH-WESTERN FARMER, edited and published by T. A. Bland, cor. Meridian and Circle, issued mothly.

Northnan Frederick, cooper, res. 263 s. West.

Norton James, hostler, W. Hincsley, 38 s. Tennessee.

Norton J. B., actor, bds. Macy House.

Norton Luther, carpenter, res. 417 e. St. Clair.

Norton William, res. 461 n. Alabama.

Norton William, brakeman, Bellefontaine R. R., res. 174 Davidson.

Norvell Hannegan C., salesman, Taylor & Crain, bds. 10 e. Market.

Norwood George, res. 129 n. Illinois.

Norwood Margaret res. 120 w. Maryland.

Notmire C., carpenter, res. 293 e. Ohio.

Notter Mary, (col.,) servant, 252 n. Meridian.

Notter Stephen, lab., Rickerts, Madison rd., near city limits.

Nottyer Christian, carpenter, works Warren Tate's factory, res, 293 e. Ohio.

Now Mary, servant, 272 e. Washington.

Nowland E. R., clerk., 30 w. Louisiana, bds. 283 e. South.

Nowland P. B. L., fruit store, 30 w. Louisiana, bds. 283 e. South.

Nowland J. H. B., res. 288 e. South.

Null Miss Laura, bds. 194 w. Vermont.

Null Samuel L., painter, res. 194 w. Vermont.

Null Thomas E., book-binder, bds. Wiles House.

Nupp Michael, boiler-maker, C., C. & I. C. R. R. shop, res. 19 Meck.

Nutman Henry, cooper, res. 273 s. West.

Nutter Kate, brush-maker, works Schmedel & Fricker, res. Morris, bet. East and New Jersey.

Nutter Lena, brush-maker, works Schmidel & Fricker, res. Morris, bet. New Jersey and East.

Nutting Rufus, (N. & Wood,) 17½ w. Washington, res. 368 n. East.

Nutting & Wood, (Rufus N. & D. L. W.,) gen'l agts. Mutual Benefit Life Insurance Co., 17½ w. Washington.

Nutts Albert, baker, works 188 e. Washington, res. 121 Massachusetts av.

Nutts Jacob, baker, 128 e. Washington, res. 121 Massachusetts av.

Nurce Thomas, lab., bds. 105 w. New York.

Nutzel John, meat market, 175 Madison av., res. same.

Nydegger Frederick, carpenter, 110 e. St. Marys.

Nydegger Frederick, jr., cabinet-maker, bds. 110 e. St. Mary.

Nye Benjamin, carriage-painter, S. W. Drew & Co., res. 244 n. Mississippi.

Nye Michael W., tailor, res. 244 n. Mississippi.

OAKEY JOSEPH, patent-right agt., res. 326 n. East.

Oakwood August, cigar-maker, bds. 108 s. Illinois.

OATMAN MERRITT J., State agt. Singer Sewing Machines, 16 n. Delaware, res. 712 n. Tennessee.

Obedurf Emma, servant, res. 9 cor. New York and California.

Obenchain Timothy L., (McGill & O.,) s. e. cor. St. Clair and Illinois, res. 417 n. Tennessee.

Obermeyer Levi, res. 444 n. East.

Obermeyer Mrs. M. A., dress and mantuamaking, 50 s. Illinois, res. same.

Obermyer W. A., (Muhlenbech & O.,) 2 Palmer House and 98 e. Washington, res. 50 s. Illinois.

O'Brien Catharine, occupant Deaf and Dumb Asylum.

O'Brien Chris. H., clerk, p. o., res. 140 Massachusetts av.

O'Brien Mrs. Eleanor, (wid.,) res. 574 n. Mississippi.

O'Brien John, lab., res. 80 Bates.

O'Brien John, lab., res. 372 s. Delaware.

O'Brien John, lab., res. 258 s. Delaware.

O'Brien John, lab., res. rear 74 s. West on alley.

O'Brien John H., real estate agt., res. 574 n. Mississippi.

O'Brien Jerry, tinner, 62 e. Washington, res. 28 Wyoming.

O'Brien Joseph, lab., res. 73 w. McCarty.

O'Brien Michael, carpenter, res. Bellefontaine R. R., n. St. Clair.

O'Brien Margaret, servant 410 n. Meridian.

O'Brien Richard, varnisher, res. 77 s. East.

O'Brien Miss Sarah E., bds. 574 n. Mississippi.

O'Brien Thomas, lab., res. Clinton, bet. New York and Ohio.

O'Brien Thomas, telegraph operator, Bellefontaine R. R. office, res. Second, near St. Clair.

O'Brien Thomas, engineer, w. Marshal, near West.

O'Brien Timothy, traveling agt. Columbus & Indianapolis Central, R. R. res. 282 s. Delaware.

O'Brien Thomas, steam engineer, res. 274 w. Market.

O'Bringer Mary, servant, 226 c. New York.

O'Callaghan Daniel, lab., res. 275 s. West.

O'Callaghan Michael, lab., res. 36 Lord.

Oekerman Andy, foreman, 105 E. Washington, res. 20 n. Noble.

O'Connard Michael, lab., res. 198 Minerva.

O'Connell Bridget, chambermaid, Commercial Hotel.

O'Connell Dennis, lab., res. 232 Madison av.

O'Connell G., lab., bds. 232 Madison.

O'Connell James, dairyman, res. 40 Lord.

O'Connell John, works, Junction R. R., bds. Wiles House.

O'Connell John, lab., bds. 232 Madison av.

O'Connell Morris, lab., res. 224 s. West.

O'Connell Thomas, lab., res. 450 Benton.

O'Connell William, stone-cutter, res. 48 Wyoming.

O'Connor Daniel, lab., res. 36 Douglas.

O'Connor Edward, lab., res. 294 s. Delaware.

O'Connor John, lab., res. 191 Meek.

O'Connor John, lab., res. 288 s. Delaware.

O'Connor John, lab., res. 167 Meek.

O'Connor John, Jr., lab., bds. 167 Meek.

O'Connor Macks, lab., res. 1 Elizabeth.

O'Connor Maurice, lab., res. alley bet. East and Noble.

O'Connor Michael, lab., res. Minerva, bet. New York and Vermont.

O'Connor Michael, book-keeper, T. F. Ryan, res. 487 n. Illinois.

O'Connor Michael, porter, Spencer House, bds. same.

O'Connor Michael, agt., Sand's Chicago Ales, 54 s. Illinois, bds. 90 s. Illinois.

O'Connor M., Sr., lab., res. 237 Coburn.

O'Connor Michael, Jr., contractor, res. 73 s. Noble.

O'Connor Marty, lab., res. 290 s. Delaware.

O'Connor Peter, lab., bds. 130 s. Noble.

O'Connor P. I., salesman, New York Store, bds. Commercial Hotel.

O'Connor Stephen, blacksmith, works, D. Root & Co., res. 330 s. Delaware.

O'Connor Thomas, shoe-maker, s. Delaware, res. same.

O'Day Nara, cook, Bicking House, 89 s. Illinois.

ODD FELLOWS' HALL, n. e. cor. Washington and Pennsylvania.

ODD FELLOWS' TALISMAN, cor. Circle and Meridian, R. J. Strickland, editor and propr.

Odell James T., gilder, res. 145 Huron.

Odell Thomas B., bds. Oriental House.

Odell William S., clerk, 10 w. Washington, bds. 34 Union.

O'Donald Ellen, servant, at 476 n. Meridian.

O'Donald Mary, servant, at 475 n. Illinois.

O'Donald William, brakesman, I., C. &. L. R. R., bds. Ray House.

O'Donnell Margaret, servant, 222 n. New Jersey.

O'Donnell Patrick, clerk, 69 s. Illinois, bds. Oriental House.

O'Dowd Annie, baker, Blind Asylum, bds. same.

O'Driscoll John, printer, res. 30½ n. Pennsylvania.

Oehler Andrew, watch-maker and jeweler, 20 s. Delaware, res. same.

Oehler David, saloon, 84 Russell, res. same.

Oehler Roman, watches, clocks and jewelry, 183 w. Washington, res. same.

Oeschle Miss Kate, assistant teacher, German, ninth ward school, res. 146 n. Meridian.

O'Farrell Edward, boiler-maker, res. 340 s. Alabama.

Off Christian, (C. O., & Bro.,) res. 297 n. Noble.

OFF CHRISTIAN & BROTHER, (Christian & Jacob O.,) lumber merchants, n. e. cor. Noble and North.

Off Gottleib, lumber dealer, n. e. cor. North and Michigan, res. 324 n. Noble.

Off Jacob, (C. Off & Bro.,) res. 291 n. Noble.

Ofterhyde William, turner, res. 234 Davidson.

Ogden William S., chief clerk, general freight office, T. H. & I. R. R., res. 422 n. Meridian.

Oglesby J. H., res. 16 e. Michigan.

Oglesby Joseph E, clerk, White Line freight office, bds. 16 e. Michigan.

Oglesby Stephen, (col.,) bds. 235 w. Ohio.

Ogri Louis, engineer at Cabinet-Maker's Union, res. 525 e. Market.

O'Hanlon Francis, contractor, res. 179 n. Tennessee.

O'Hanlon James J., clerk, New York Store, bds. 179 n. Tennessee.

O'Hanlon Miss Mary C., bds. 179 n. Tennessee.

O'Hara Mrs. Eva, (wid.,) res. 121 W. Vermont.

O'Hara Frank, fireman, C., C. & I. C. R. R., bds. 58 Benton.

O'Hara John, shoe-maker, res. 386 s. West.

O'Hara Mathew, tailor, res. 233 s. West.

O'Haver Patterson, lab., res. 65 n. Bright.

Ohleyer George, basket-maker, res. 156 Bluff rd.

Ohoron Mike, lab., res. 331 s. Missouri.

Ohorvald A., lab., res. 243 s. West.

Ohr A. D., ticket clerk, Union Depot, res. 431 n. Meridian.

Ohr Henry, clerk, res. 126 n. Delaware.

Ohr John H., agt., Adams Express Co., 42 and 44 e. Washington, res. 448 n. Meridian.

Ohrw Rebecca, clerk, Carter & Haynes, res. 337 s. Delaware.

Oiler Philip, works, Osgood, Smith & Co., bds. Ballard House.

Oiler William, shoe-maker, 257 s. Delaware, res. 259 s. Delaware.

O'Keane Dennis, blacksmith, res. 400 e. Georgia.

O'Keane P. J., salesman, 10 w. Pearl, bds. 225 s. Delaware.

O'Keif Timothy, lab., res. 264 s. Tennessee.

Okey Edward H., carpenter, res. 359 n. New Jersey.

Okey Joseph B., patent-right agt., res. 326 n. East.

Okey Philip, fence-builder, res. 77 Oak.

O'Lair Peter, brick-mason, res. 27 Vine.

O'Laughlin Patrick, lab., res. 258 s. Delaware.

O'Lavy Bridget, servant, 324 n. Delaware.

O'Leary Daniel, employe Merchants' Union Express Co., res. 261 s. Illinois.

O'LEARY JEREMIAH, saloon, 103 s. Illinois, res. same.

O'Leary John, saloon 103 s. Illinois, bds. same.

O'Leary Mary, laundress, Bates House.

O'Leary Michael, lab., res. 372 s. Delaware.

Olin C. C., general insurance agt., office Eden's blk., res. n. Tennessee, out city limits.

Olin Edward, book-keeper, Singer Sewing Machine, bds. Pattison House.

Olin F. W., clerk, 22 e. Washington, res. n. Tennessee, north of city limits.

Oliver Charles, tobacconist, res. 39 Center.

Oliver D. H., [physician, 31 Virginia av., res. 28 Gregg.

Oliver Mrs. Hannah, (wid. Abram,) res. Madison av., near toll-gate.

Oliver Theodore, lab., res. 315 s. Missouri.

Olmstead Minerva, (wid.,) res. 15 Willard.

Olro Henry, Taylor & Chandler's foundry, res. 233 w. Michigan.

Olrry William, saloon, res. 166 s. East.

Olscr Peter, brick-layer, res. Union, bet. McCarty and Fipps.

Olverson Albert, printer, works Journal office, bds. 177 w. Maryland.

O'Mara James, porter, M. U. Ex. Co., res. 40 Douglas.

O'Mara P., boiler-maker, res. 157 High.

O'Mara Richard, express driver, res. 239 n. Douglas.

O'Minehan Andy, lab., res. 167 Madison av.

O'Mor Richard, res. Menerva, bet. New York and Vermont.

O'Neal James H., flagman, bds. 83 w. Louisiana.

O'Neal John, pork-packer, bds. Ray House, e. South.

ONeal Joseph, miller. bds. 366 w. Washington.

O'Neal Michael, lab., res. 164 Meek.

O'Neal Miss Nellie, milliner, works 152 e. Washington, res. 143 w. McCarty.

O'Neal Patrick, lab., res. 190 Harrison.

O'Neal Robert, lab., res. 155 Meek.

O'Neal Thomas, lab., res. 169 Meek.

O'Neal Timothy, lab., res. 168 Meek.

O'Neal William, carpenter, res. 279 w. Merrill.

O'Neal Miss Catharine, lady boarder, over 320 e. Washington.

O'Neil Charlotte, (wid. Richard,) res. 306 n. Delaware.

O'Neil Miss Ettie, milliner, Mrs. M. J. Catlin, res. over 49 s. Illinois.

O'Neil John, lab., res. 211 e. Market.

O'Neil Michael, cutter, J. & P. Gramling, res. 149 e. McCarty.

O'Neil Thomas, lab., res. 199 Meek.

Orbison William H., (E. H. Mayo & Co.,) bds. 121 n. Delaware.

O'Reily Michael, shoe-maker, res. 414 s. Tennessee.

O'Reily Timothy, lab., res. 287 s. Tennessee.

Orma Mrs. Catharine, (wid. Chas.,) boarding, res. 126 n. Mississippi.

Ormsby Miss Emma, works Capital Tobacco Works, bds. Wiles House.

Orphan Asylum, s. e. cor. Tennessee and Fifth.

Orr Andrew, printer, res. 278 n. Alabama.

Orr John E., salesman, John N. Conklin, bds. 36 n. Delaware.

Orrell Jasper, operator, W. U. telegraph office, Union Depot, res. Fatout blk., w. Washington.

Osborn A. M., assistant civil engineer, room 21 Talbott & New's blk., n. Pennsylvania, res. 204 n. Illinois, cor. Vermont.

Osborn Mrs. Flizabeth, bds. 219 n. Mississippi.

Osborn George W., salesman, 3 Odd Fellows' Hall, bds. 225 n. Liberty.

Osborn John, porter, John N. Conklin.

Osborn John H., canvassing for Asher & Adams, res. 225 n. Liberty.

Osborn Jordan, occupant Deaf and Dumb Asylum.

Osborn Miss Lizzie, clerk, 64 n. Illinois, bds. 78 n. Pennsylvania.

Osgood Judson R., (O., Smith & Co.,) res. 84 e. Michigan.

OSGOOD, SMITH & CO., (Judson R. O., Samuel F. S. & Jacob Woodburn,) manfrs. of wheels, spokes, hubs, &c., 230 s. Illinois.

O'Shea Thomas, lab., res, 116 Plum.

Ossenfort Frederick, porter, 74 and 76 s. Meridian, res. 316 Winston.

Osterman John, (H. Emmerich & Co.,) 86 w. Washington, res. w. Market, bet. Tennessee and Mississippi.

Ostermeyer Mrs. Christian, (wid. Louis,) res. 263 n. Liberty.

Ostermeyer Anthony, lab., bds. 87 e. South.

Ostermeyer Christian F., groceries and dry goods, 350 e. Ohio, cor. Noble, res. same.

Ostermeyer Frederick, (Holland, O. & Co.,) 27 and 29 e. Maryland, res. e. city limits.

Ostermeyer Henry, carpenter, res. 153 Huron.

Ostermeyer Lewis, drayman, res. 9. Charles.

Ostermiller Otto, switchman, res. 17 Henry.

O'Sullivan Andrew, lab., res. 260 s. Delaware.

O'Sullivan Daniel, lab., res. 106 Meek.

O'Sullivan Daniel, lab., res. 290 s. Delaware.

O'Sullivan Florence, lab., res. 277 s. Delaware.

O'Sullivan Jeremiah, lab., res. 175 Meek.

O'Sullivan Michael N., contractor, res. 190 Harrison.

O'Sullivan Timothy, lab., res. 180 Maple.

O'Sullivan William, lab., res. 456 s. East.

Oswald Godfried, painter, res. 336 Railroad.

Otis William H., bds. Bates House.

Ott Charles, collar-maker, 24 n. Delaware.

Ott John, carpenter, res. south end Dacotah.

Ott Michael, collar-maker, 20 w. Washington, res. s. East.

Otte William, carpenter, works Ind. Central R. R. shop, res. 190 n. Noble.

Otten David, saloon, 131 w. Washington, res. 127 Spring.

Otto August, lithographer, res .81 Plum.

Otto Charles, brick-mason, res. Orient, bet. Michigan and National rd.

Otto Fred, lab., res. 210 Madison av.

Otto Fritz, porter, Bowen, Stewart & Co.

Otto & Hoffman, groceries, 170 Bluff rd.

Otto Matilda, servant, 13 e. South.

Otto Philip, (O. & Hofmann,) res. 170 Bluff rd.

Otto William, carpenter, res. 190 n. Noble.

Otwell Francis, policeman, seventh ward, res. 102 s. Benton.

Otwell Frank A., salesman, Lukens & Hollowell, 26 and 28 s. Tennessee, res. 60 Fletcher av.

Otwell James L., conductor street car, bds. Virginia av.

Otwell William, marble-cutter, bds. 236 Virginia av.

Ould John, butcher, bds. 252 s. Delaware.

Oulen Peter, cigar-maker, res. 139 Ft. Wayne av.

Ounspan Benjamin, soldier, U. S. Arsenal, res. same.

Over Ewald, (E. O. & Co.) 68 s. Meridian, res. 79 n. Alabama.

OVER E. & CO.,
(Ewald O. and Henry Schnull,) iron and steel merchants, and agts. Union Safe Factory of Cincinnati, O., 68 s. Meridian.

Overfelt Joseph, works Bellefountaine R. R. Depot, res. 392 s. Delaware.

Overfelt Philip, works Bellefountaine R. R. Depot, res. 392 s. Delaware.

Overley William, conductor, B. Line R. R., res. 248 cor. East and Lousiana.

Overman Robert, carpenter, res. 374 w. Vermont.

Overstreet John A., spoke-turner, bds. 10 w. Georgia.

Overstreet James M., works Osgood, Smith & Co., res. 10 W. Georgia.

Owen H. C., sawyer, res. 357 s. Delaware.

Owen William J., sawyer, res. 357 s Delaware.

Owens E., farmer, res. 360 n. New Jersey.

Owens Ephraim, lab., res. Boyd's blk. Massachusetts av.

Owens B. F., clerk, A. D. Streight, Yohn's blk., cor Meridian and Washington, res. 480 n. Mississippi.

Owens James, moulder, Sinker & Co.

Owens James M., plasterer, res. 175 Bluff road.

Owings Miss Emma, dress-maker, 361 e. Market, res. same.

Owings James H., canvasser, bds. 139 e. South.

Owings Joseph, messenger boy, Bellefontaine R. R. office, bds. 139 e. South.

Owings Mrs. Lydia, (wid. William,) nurse, res. 371 e. Market.

Owings Nathaniel, res. 139 e. South.

P AFF MARY, (wid. William,) res. 405 s. East.

Paff William, res. 153 n. West.

Paena Henry, currier, 125 s. Meridian, res. 584 n. Alabama.

Padgett Albert, train-boy, T. H. & I. R. R. bds. Sherman House.

Page Mrs. Louisa, house-keeper, Bates House, bds. same.

Paine D. L., printer, res. 71 c. St. Clair.

Paine Henry, tanner, res. 548 Alabama.

Paine George, clerk, plaining mills, bds. 351 s. Meridian.

Paine Peter, (col.,) farmer, res. Blackford alley.

Painter John, trader, res. s. e. cor Second and Illinois.

Painter Edward R., compositor, Downey, Brouse, Butler & Co., bds. Pattison House.

Painter Miss, Mary, bds. 297 n. Meridian.

Palmer Abraham, (col.,) servant, end Virginia av., beyond city limits.

Palmer Benjamin G., jeweler, res. 178 e. South.

Palmer Charles C., capitalist, res. 57 w. Maryland.

Palmer Cyrus O., res. 129 n. mississippi.

Palmer E. L., book-binder and blank-book manfs. Co., s. Illinois, res. same.

PALMER HOUSE,
s. w. cor. Washington and Illinois, Alonzo Blair, propr. See card, page 7, adv'ng dep.

Palmer James, waiter, Bates House, bds. same.

Palmer John, bds. 183 s. Illinois.

Palmer L. F., painter, bds. 140 s. East.

Palmer Mrs. Margaret, (wid. Daniel C.,) res. 289 Virginia av.

Palmer Marshal E., res. 57 w. Maryland.

Palmer Mrs. M. V., bds. 31 w. Ohio.

Palmer N. B. retired capitalist, res. 57 w. Maryland.

Palmer Trumble, G. deputy auditor of State, department public accounts, office, new State bldg., res. 173 n. Illinois.

Pallet William, conductor P. & I. R. R., res. on Cady st. bet. Georgia and Bates.

Panman Gaudaloup, blacksmith, bds. 282 e. Washington.

Pape William, lab., bds. 174 w. Ohio.

Papenhouse Henry, porter, Union Depot, res. 17 Meek.

Pardick Elizabeth, servant 96 n. East.

Pardick Herman, carpenter, 166 Stevens.

PARISETTE JOSEPH,
confectionery and ice-cream saloon, 25 n. Illinois.

Parish Joseph, bds. Bates House.

Park Hiram, J., cook, res. 122 Benton.

Park William, carpenter, res. 46 Thomas.

Parker A. G., piano-tuner, Benham Bros. & Co.

Parker & Bloomer, (Eben A. P. & Isaac L. B.,) lawyers, over 23 e. Washington.

Parker C. C., traveling agt., res. 163 s. Tennessee.

Parker Eben A., (P. & Bloomer,) over 23 e. Washington, res. 75 California.

Parker Edward F., lawyer, 8½ e. Washington, res. 248 n. East.

Parker Ellis L., student, N. W. Christian University, bds. 320 e. Vermont.

Parker George, (col.,) lab., res s. side Elizabeth, bet Blake and Minerva.

PARKER GEORGE W.,
sheriff, marion county, res. County Jail.

Parker George W., roller, White River Iron Works, bds., California House.

Parker Jackson, (col.,) teamster, res. 130 n. California.
Parker John, lab., res. 19 Hosbrook.
Parker John, farmer, res. 309 e. New York.
Parker Jacob, (col.,) teamster, res. 130 n. California.
Parker James, harness-maker, 17 Virginia av., res. 19 Hosbrook.
Parker Lucy, (col.,) servant, res Ann.
Parker Margaret, (wid.,) res. 641 n. Tennessee.
Parker Martha, (col.,) res. near City Hospital.
Parker Mary, (col.,) servant at N. A. Randall, 21 w. Market.
Parker R. P., (Guffin & P.,) rooms 10 and 11 Talbott & New's blk., res. Shelbyville rd., outside city limits.
Parker R. R., shirts and men's furnishing goods, 30 w. Washington, res. 90 n. Mississippi.
Parker Sarah, hoop-skirt maker, 34 w. Washington, res. 179 e. south.
Parker Wilson, brick-mason, res. 163 s. Tennessee.
Parkinson E. M., traveling agt. Fairbanks' Scales, 43 and 45 n. Tennessee, bds. Spencer House.
Parkman Charles B., sec'y Indianapolis Rolling Mill, res. 230 n. West.
Parmelee William H., railroad-man, res. 364 n. Mississippi.
Parr Wm., physician, res. 378 n. Delaware.
Parrott Horace P., (P., Nickum & Co.,) res. 349 n. Delaware.
PARROTT, NICKUM & CO., (Horace P., John R. N. & John A. Harter,) steam cracker bakery, 188 c. Washington.
Parrott Richard, butcher, e. s. Mississippi, bet. First and Second.
Parrott Samuel, res. 36 s. West.
Parry M. A., (wid.,) res. 103 n. Meridian.
Parry Roger, blacksmith, res. 12 Henry.
Parsley Asberry, teamster, res. 545 n. Mississippi.
PARSONS CHARLES H., agt. M. U. Ex. Co., 42 and 44 e. Washington, res. 115 n. New Jersey.
Parsons John, student, bds. 40 Christian av.
Parsons John J., life insurance agt., res. 234 w. New York.
Parsons William J., traveling agt., Scott, West & Co., 127 s. Meridian, bds. 33 w. Maryland.
Partello W. H., prompter Metropolitan Theater, bds. 17 Virginia av.
Parvin Celestine, inmate Deaf and Dumb Asylum.
PARVIN THEOPHILUS, physician, office 135 n. Alabama, res. 143 n. Alabama.
Parvis P. A, inmate Deaf and Dumb Asylum.

Pascoe James E., boiler-maker, res. 450 e. Georgia.
Pasquier John B., carpenter, res. 414 e. Michigan.
Passmore Alonzo, (col.,) blacksmith, res. Douglas alley.
Patchin Clement, patent medicine dealer, res. 82 n. Pennsylvania.
Pathos & Eix, (A. P. & H. E.,) saloon, 228 e. Washington.
Paton Elisha B., carpenter, res. 524 e. Georgia.
Patten George, res. 467 s. Illinois.
Patterson Catherine, (wid.,) res. 142 Massachusetts av.
Patterson Charles W., farmer, res. w. end North.
Patterson Mrs. Clemence, dress-maker, 25 Massachussetts av., res. same.
Patterson Frank, salesman, 5 w. Washington, bds. Pyle House.
Patterson George, bds. 142 Massachusetts av.
Patterson House, 63 n. Alabama, Mrs. Charlotte Hamilton, proprietress.
Patterson Isaac, farmer, res. e. s. n. Meridian, beyond city limits.
Patterson John, carpenter, res. 362 s. Illinois.
Patterson John L., carpenter, res. 25 Massachusetts av.
Patterson John P., (Alford, Talbott & Co.,) 2 Morrison's blk., res. 163 n. New Jersey.
Patterson Joseph D., pork-packer, res. 404 n. Illinois.
Patterson Robert, carpenter, res. 78 Lockerbie.
Patterson Robert M., city civil engineer, office, Glenns' blk., res. 123 n. Illinois.
Patterson R. H., ice merchant, res. w. end North.
Patterson Samuel J., farmer, res. w. end North.
Patterson Mrs. ——, (wid.,) cor. Massachussetts av. and Alabama.
Patterson William, lawyer, office 18½ e. Washington, res. 280 e. Ohio.
Patterson William, wagon and agricultural works, bds. Pattison House.
Patterson William, stable-man Citizen's Street Railway, bds. Neiman House.
Patterson William, clerk, P. O., bds. 142 Massachusetts av.
Patterson William A., moulder, res. 28 n. East.
Patterson William H., salesman, 45 and 47 c. Washington, res. 520 n. Mississippi.
Patterson William O., hopper clerk, P. O., bds. 140 Massachusetts av.
Pattison Augustus E., (Hibben, Tarkington & Co.,) 112 s. Meridian, res. 413 n. Pennsylvania.

Pattison Coleman B., (Hibben, Tarkington & Co.,) 112 s. Meridian, res. 405 n. Illinois.

Pattison House, 63 n. Alabama.

Pattison R. D., brakesman, C., C. & I. C. R. R., bds. 149 s. New Jersey.

Pattison T. N., capitalist, res. 416 n. Pennsylvania.

Pattison William A., supt. Indianapolis Wagon and Agricultural Works, bds. Alabama, bet. Market and Ohio.

Patty Sarah, servant, 74 Lockerbie.

PAUL HENRY, lieutenant police, res. 17 e. McCarty.

Paule Henry, (Miller & P.,) res. 181 Davidson.

Pauling George, driver, Geisendorff & Co., bds. 441 n. Illinois.

Paver J. M., route agt., Merchant's Union Express, res. 230 w. Ohio.

Paxton Mrs. Elizabeth, res. 22 Circle.

Payne Daniel, machinist, res. 71 e. St. Clair.

Payne John, (col.,) lab., res. Sixth, bet. Mississippi and Railroad.

Payne John R., carpenter, res. 307 e. Washing, No. 7 up-stairs.

Payne Mrs. Laura, (wid.,) servant, 140 n. Alabama.

Payne William, boarding house, 20 s. Pennsylvania.

Paynter Joseph R, carpenter, res. 82 w. Market.

Payton Elisha B., carpenter, res. 7 English blk., e. Washington.

Payton Monroe, works Street R. R. Co., bds. 7 English blk., e. Washington.

Peabody John, stock-dealer, res. 424 n. Delaware.

Peacock James, book-keeper L. Q. Sherwood, res. 25 w. First.

Peacock Mary A. H., dress-maker, res. 354 w. North.

Peacock William, shoe-maker, res. cor. w. Sixth and Canal.

Peak Andrew A., cooper, res. Helen, near river.

Peak David, carpenter, res. 302 w. Maryland.

Peak Mrs. Sarah, (wid. Lafayette,) res. 59 Indiana av.

Peak William J., fireman, Corey & Co., res. Helen.

Peal Charles, cooper, res. 51 Orient, bet. Michigan and National rd., beyond city limits.

Peal Christina, servant L. Hetselgesser, c. Washington, beyond city limits.

Peal Henry, blacksmith, res. Orient, bet. Michigan and National rd., beyond city limits.

Peal William F., Union Starch Factory, res. s. s. c. National rd.

Pearce Albert, engineer I., C. & L. R. R., bds. 99 Benton.

Pearce Alfred E., baker, works 188 e. Washington, bds. 26 n. Pennsylvania.

Pearce Mrs. F. A., (wid. William A.,) res. 93 n. New Jersey.

Pearce Margaret, kitchen girl, Bates House.

Pearce S. J., printer, Sentinel book and job room, bds. 144 n. Tennessee.

Pearce William H., paper-hanger, res. rear 308 e. Ohio.

Pearsall P. R., prof. of music, res. 24 w. Georgia.

PEARSON & CO., (John P. ———) House of Lords Saloon, 78 w. Washington.

PEARSON CHARLES D., physician, office 39½ w. Washington, res. 296 w. New York.

Pearson Charles D., salesman, 22 e. Washington, bds. 296 w. New York.

Pearson James, carpenter, bds. Martin House, 33 w. Maryland.

Pearson James W., student, with Dr· Charles D. Pearson, bds. 296 w. New York.

Pearson John, (P. & Co,) 78 w. Washington res. 135 e. St. Joseph.

Pearson John, civil engineer, J. B. Cunningham's office, res. 65 w. Michigan.

Pearson John H., (Hanning, Ramsey & Co.,) res. 135 e. St. Joseph.

Pearson Jonas O., machinist, res. 223 n. Mississippi.

Pearson Joseph, stone-cutter, res. cor. Blackford and Vermont.

Pearson Levi W., brick-mason, res. 268 n. Alabama.

Pease Mrs. N. K., saleswoman, Grover & Baker S. M. Co.'s rooms, bds. 204 n. Illinois.

Pease Theodore W., book agt., res. 275 s. Noble.

Pearse William, paper-hanger, Hume, Adams & Co., res. n. Noble, near Vermont.

Peck E. A., res. 465 Virginia av.

Peck Edwin J., capitalist, res. 59 w. Maryland.

Peck Mrs. Eliza, (wid. George W.,) servant, 144 e. New York.

Peck George, res. 301 w. Market.

Peck Thomas H. S., foreman, Root's foundry, res. 488 n. Tennessee.

Peck William, boarding house, 67 n. Alabama.

Peckham Charles S., traveling agt., Fairbanks scales, 43 and 45 n. Tennessee, bds. Spencer House.

Peckham Calib, architect, room 6 Blake's row, res. 378 s. West.

Peckham C. H., carpenter, res. 380 n. Delaware.

Peden Mrs. Catharine, (wid. Abner W.,) res. 314 e. Ohio.

Peden Joseph S. bar-keeper, 26 w. Louisiana, res. 314 e. Ohio.

Pedelo Robert J., moulder, Root's foundry, res. 20 Coburn.

Pee Emmet, bds. 81 w. Ohio.

Pee George W., (Landers. Pee & Co.,) 116 s. Meridian, res. 81 w. Ohio.

Peebles M., (wid. John,) res. 295 n. Alabama.

Peek Moses, (col.,) servant, at 612 n. Illinois.

Pegan Miss Martha A., milliner, works 129 Massachusetts av., bds. same.

Peine William, cash boy, New York Store, 548 n. Alabama.

Peil Isaac, painter, res. Stringtown, one mile west National rd., n. s.

Peltier Leon, stone-cutter, res. 55 Hosbrook.

Pena Ahiza, carpenter, res 540 s. Illinois.

Pence Mrs. Caroline, (wid. John,) tailoress, res. 151 Union.

Pance William M., salesman, 14 w. Washington, bds. 128 w. Maryland.

Pender Louis, stone-cutter, res. 80 Elm.

Pendergist William, lab., res. 273 e. North.

Pendergrast J. O., carpenter, res. s. s. National rd., half-mile w. bridge.

Pendleton Ralph C. J., clerk, supt. office, C., C. & I. C. R. R., res. 441 e. St. Clair.

Pendery N. S., physician, office room 10 and 11 Eden's blk., 85 e. Market, res. same.

Penn George W., secretary, Carpenter's Union, bds. 257 s. Meridian.

Penniche Maurice, dealer in government goods, 154 e. Washington, res. 211 Union.

Pentecost H. O., compositor, Sentinel news room, bds. Palmer House.

Pentecost Mahlon B., res. 274 n. Alabama.

Peoples Nancy, (wid. William,) res. 295 n. Alabama.

Pepper Edward, machinist, res. 451 s. Missouri.

Percell Peter, tinner, 62 e. Washington, res. 146 w. Vermont.

Perdue George W., fireman, Bellefontaine R. R., bds. 7 Peru.

Perdue Mrs. Rebecca, (wid. Milton,) res. 7 Peru.

Perhamus John T., salesman. 54 s. Meridian, res. 35 w. St. Clair.

Perigo Mrs. Eliza, (wid.,) bds 73 n. Illinois.

Perkins Amos G., lawyer, res. 244 n. East.

Perkins Charles, currier, 49 s. Delaware, res. Michigan rd., beyond city limits.

Perkins E. H., printer, Sentinel office, res. 67 Daugherty.

Perkins Garret, res. 244 n. East.

Perkins James A., boiler-maker, res. 15, cor. Pine and Elm.

Perkins John H., clerk, 125 w. Washington, bds. 97 s. Illinois.

PERKINS, JORDAN & PER-KINS, (Samuel E. P., Lewis J. & Samuel E. Perkins, Jr.,) attorneys at law, room 4 Aetna bldg., n. Pennsylvania.

Perkins Samuel E., (P., Jordan & Perkins,) room 4, Aetna bldg., n. Pennsylvania, res. 274 w. New York.

Perkins Samuel E., Jr., (P., Jordan & P.,) room 4, Aetna bldg., n. Pennsylvania, bds. cor. New York and California.

Perkison Patrick, lab., res. 21 Maple.

Permont Cass, lab., 69 McCarty.

Persoll Mrs. Martha, (wid,) res. w. Mariah.

PERRIN GEORGE K., attorney at law and collecting agt., rooms 5 and 6, College Hall bldg., cor. Pennsylvania and Washington, res. 293 n. New Jersey. See card, page 66.

Perrine P. R., agt. Star Shuttle Sewing Machine, 79 e. Market, res. 293 n. Alabama.

Perrine Theodore F., coal and lime, res. 291 n. Alabama.

Perrine T. B., engraver, 84 Virginia av., res. 60 Massachusetts av.

Perry James H., carpenter and builder, res. 427 n. Mississippi.

Perry John C., salesman, A. Jones & Co., res. 22 w. Georgia.

Perry Jackson, res. 22 w. Georgia.
Perry Julia, (col.,) res. w. Ohio.
Perry Lida, servant, Elizabeth Hollowell, res. n. s. National rd., half-mile from bridge.
Perry Matthew, moulder, Sinker's, res. 405 s. Delaware.
Perry Rodger, blacksmith, T. H. & I. R. R. shops, res. 12 Henry.
Perry William B., carder, res. 44 Dunlap.
Perryman William E, student, commercial college, bds. 726 n. Tennessee.
Peters A. R., traveling agt., Miller & Franks, bds. 150 w. Washington.
Peters C. W., clerk, Furgeson's Pork House, bet. South and McCarty.
Peters Elizabeth (col.,) seamstress, res. Douglas alley.
Peters Joseph, lab., res. 315 Massachusetts av.
Peters William, clerk, Furgeson's Pork House, bds. 166 n. West.
Peterson Ausmirs, shoe-maker, 257 s. Delaware, bds. 259 s. Delaware.
Peterson Charles, bds. 68 w. South.
Peterson Christopher, bds. end Virginia av., beyond city limits.
Peterson H., carpenter, bds. 172 Madison av.
Peterson John, clerk, (McCreery & Fay,) res. 168 Spring.
Peterson Lars, shoe-maker, works 350 s. Delaware, res. Union, near sixth ward school.
Peterson L., lab., 172 Madison av.
Peterson Margaret, inmate Home of the Friendless, w. s. n. Pennsylvania, beyond city limits.
Petre John, lab., res 142 Elm.
Petre John, saloon and boarding house, 272 e. Washington
Petri's Hall, 264 e. Washington, John Petri, propr.
Pettey Betsey, res. over 255 e. Washington.
Pettey James, teamster, for S. S. Bates, bet. Cady and Hodge.

Petty Charles, machinist, res. 250 s. Alabama.
Petty Julius, farmer, res. 350 Indiana av.
Pettier Eugene, stone-cutter, res. 55 Hosbrook.
Pettit Rev. Joseph, pastor St. Peter's Catholic church, res. s. w. cor. Virginia av. and Dougherty.
Pettit Willis H. book-keeper, Citizen's National Bank, 4 e. Washington, bds.
Pyle House.
Pfuendler N., sexton Fourth Presbyterian Church.
Pfaff J. L., clerk, bds. 153 n. West.
Pfaff Lucian, salesman, D. H. Chase's shoe store.
Pfaff Nancy J., bds. 153 n. West.
Pfaff W. A., (Burton & Pfaff,) 38 s. Meridian, res. 153 West.
Pfafflin Theodore, groceries, cor. Vermont and Mississippi, res. 25 w. Michigan.
Pfafflin William, 39 Washington, bds. Oriental House.
Pfarback Andrew, carpenter, bds. 228 s. New Jersey.
Pfarback Phillip, plasterer, res. 230 s. New Jersey.
Pfarer John, res. 428 s. East.
Pfeiffer H. A., salesman, New York Store, bds. Oriental House.
Pfeiffer William printer, 16 w. Maryland. res. 334 s. Alabama.
Pfetzer John, tailor, res. 52 Coburn.
Pfleger George, lab., res. 18 Vinston.
Pfleger Jacob, tailor, 121 Davidson, res. same.
Pfleger Jacob, Jr., carpenter, Miller & Paule, res. 121 Davidson.
Pfleger Jacob K., carpenter, works Miller & Paule, res. 121 Davidson.
Pfleger Lewis, expressman, bds. 18 Vinton.
Pfeiffer H. A., clerk New York Store, bds. Oriental House.
Pfiening William, gilder, works Leiber & Co., n. Pennsylvania, res. 191 n. East.
Pfingst George F., salesman, 4 w. Washington, bds. 342 n. Illinois.

Pfingst Mrs. Eliza, bds. 342 n. Illinois.

Phalen Timothy, flagman, C., C. & I. C. R. R., res. 72 Benton.

Phelen Patrick, boiler-maker, Sinker's shop, res. 301 Virginia av.

Phelix Charles, painter, bds. 562 Indiana av.

Phelps A. B., student commercial college, bds. 188 s. Mississippi.

Phelps Allen E., harness-maker, bds. 278 n. Mississippi.

Phelps Sewel, lab., res. 280 w. Merrill.

Phelps Simon B., engineer, C,. C. C. & I. C. R. R., res. 332 e. Louisiana.

Phillabaum Miss Lucinda, seamstress, bds. 171 n. West.

Phillips Deborah. A., occupant Deaf and Dumb Asylum.

Phillips Miss E. J., actress, Metropolitan Theater, bds. Macy House.

Phillips George II., messenger, American Express Co., bds 56 w. New York.

Phillips James, conductor, J. M. & I. R. R., bds. Bates House.

Phillips Jesse, (col.,) lab., res. Lafayette R. R., bet. First and Second.

Phillips Thomas, tailor, res. 174 w. Ohio.

Phipps C. R., (Craft & P.,) 14 n. Pennsylvania, bds. e. Washington, outside city limits.

Phipps E. R., (Craft & P.,) 14 n. Pennsylvania, res. 286 n. Pennsylvania.

Phipps Fanny, (wid. Michael,) res 247 s. Missouri.

Phipps Henry, teamster, res. 324 e. New York.

Phipps Isaac N., retired real estate dealer, res. bet. e. Washington and Arsenal av.

Phipps John M., pysician and surgeon, res. 233 n. Noble.

Phipps Joseph, clerk, bds. 182 s. New Jersey.

Phipps Leonidas M., deputy assessor Internal Revenue, p. o. bldg., res. 187 n. Alabama.

Phipps Matilda, (wid. Samuel,) 501 s. East.

Phipps Rebecca, (wid.,) res 154 n. West.

Phipps William C., assessor Center township, res. Pendleton pike, 3 miles n. e. city, bds. 233 n. Noble.

Piana Phillip, (col.,) servant, 180 e. Ohio.

Pickerill Frank, pump-maker, res. 86 e. Market.

Pickerill G. W., physician and surgeon, 30½ n. Pennsylvania, res. cor. Plum and Cherry.

Pickerill Samuel J., pump-dealer, res. 104 Plum.

Piel Henry, blacksmith, 787 n. Illinois.

Pierce Alfred F., student, commercial college, bds. 452 s. New Jersey.

Pierce Charles, printer, bds. 144 n. Tennessee.

Pierce Charles, carpenter, bds. 69 w. Market.

Pierce D., lab., bds. 179 Douglas alley.

Pierce Henry D., clerk, McKernan & Pierce, bds. cor. Meridian and Second.

Pierce James, teamster, res. 177 n. Liberty.

Pierce John, lab,, res. 235 w. Merrill.

Pierce William, engineer, res. 436 s. West.

Pierce Winslow S., (McKernan & P.,) 2 Blake's row, res. 544 n. Meridian.

Piermont Miss Anna, bds. 69 McCarty.

Pierson Irving J., cutter, 8 w. Washington, bds. Macy House.

Pierson James, carpenter, res. 432 e. St. Clair.

Pierson John C., brick-mason, res. s. side Second, bet. Mississippi and Tennessee.

Pierson L. W., brick-layer, res. 268 n. Alabama.

Pierson Stephen D., tailor, 118 n. Noble, res. same.

Pigg Francis W., painter, res. 35 n. Harris.

Pigg James M., carpenter, res. 101 cor. Cedar and Forest av.

Pigg John, pump-maker and well-digger, res. 232 e. Louisiana.

Pigg Sarah, (wid. David,) res. 232 e. Louisiana.

Pigton Wm. B., (col.,) lab., res. 249 n. West.

Pike Mary M., occupant Deaf and Dumb Asylum.

Pilbeam George W., carpenter, res. 390 s. Tennessee.

Pile H. F. II., saloon, 359 s. Delaware, res. 130 e. McCarty.

Pilkel Louis, stone-cutter, res. 55 Hosbrook.

Pinkerton I. A., attorney at law, rooms 8 and 9, Talbott & New's blk., bds. 162 n. New Jersey.

Pinkerton James P., clerk, at supreme clerk's office, bds. John Smith, n. New Jersey.

Pinkerton James A., (col.,) lab,) res. 75 Bright.

Pinney W. H. H., farmer, res. 176 s. New Jersey.

Piper Edwin S., saw-maker, works E. C. Atkins & Co., res. 234 e. Vermont.

Piper William, music teacher, bds. 164 Virginia av.

Piscator Augustus, cutlery manfr., 12 s. Delaware, res. same.

Pitman George W., tobacconist, res. State, bet. Mississippi and Tennessee.

Pitman Mrs. Hannah, (wid. Eli,) res. State, bet. Mississippi and Tennessee.

Pitman Miss Mary E., res. State, bet. Mississippi and Tennessee.

Pittman Robert C., boarding-house, 14 s. Mississippi.

Pittman G. S., carpenter, res. 287 s. East, cor. Georgia.

Pittman Miss Martha, tailoress, res. 14 n. Mississippi.

Pitts George W., ice dealer, res. 370 n. Tennessee.

Pitts Mrs. Fredonia, (wid. Francis,) res. over 10 s. Mississippi.

Pitts Z. A., brakesman, I. & J. R. R., res. 75 McCarty.

Pitts W. S., tobacconist, bds. Ray House.

Pitzer W. H., salesman, 48 s. Meridian, res. 314 w. New York.

Place Jeremiah E., occupant, Deaf and Dumb Asylum.

Plank James, freight conductor, C., C. & I. C. R. R., bds. 58 Benton.

Plank Isaac, switchman, Bellefontaine R. R., res. 384 c. Market.

Plansbarn Noah, brakesman, B. Line R. R., bds. 103 s. New Jersey.

Plant C. H., cabinet-maker, res. Kentucky av., bet. Washington and Tennessee.

Plant George, engineer, T. H. & I. R. R., res. 274 s. Mississippi.

Plant John W., sawyer, Spiegel & Thoms, res. 261 e. Washington.

Plant Susanna, (wid. George,) res. 261 e. Washington.

Platz Valentine, works U. S. Arsenal, res. 455 e. Market.

Plesslin C. F., piano key maker, 159 and 161 e. Washington, bds. Pattison House.

Plessner Otto, blacksmith, 26 e. Georgia, bds. 144 Virginia av.

Plimpton Charles H., checkman, C., C. & I. C. R. R., res. 393 e. Georgia.

Ploch John, lab., bds. 518 e. Washington.

Plogsterth Victor, grocer, 207 Davidson, res. same.

Plumb H H., salesman, 6 e. Washington, bds. 224 e. Market.

Plumb William, baker, res. 254 Massachusetts av.

Plummer Edward, painter, bds. 216 e. Market.

Plummer Edwin, carriage-maker, B. C. Shaw, res. 216 e. Market.

Plummer Mrs Eleanor, (wid. Hiram,) res. 216 e. Market.

Plummer Hiram, brakesman, Jeffersonville R. R., res. 216 e. Market.

Plummer Mahala, servant, 217 Massachusetts av.

Plummer William, blacksmith, res. 216 e. Market.

Plummer William, brakesman, Peru R. R., res. 276 Railroad.

Poe John M., res. 503 n. Mississippi.

Poehler & Co., (Henry & Lewis P.,) groceries, cor. Ray and Bluff rd.

Poehler Henry, (L. & H. P.,) res. 375 s. Illinois.

Poehler Lewis, (P. & Co.,) res. cor. Bluff rd. and Ray.

Pohler Christ., lab., res. 385 Virginia av.

Pohler William, lab., Peru coal yard, res.

389 Virginia av.

Pohlman Mary, (wid. Theodore,) res. 46 e. South.

Pohne Mrs. P., (wid.,) res. 72 e. Maryland.

Poland Miss Hattie, bds. 139 w. Market.

Poland John, (Coffman & P.,) res. 306 w. Washington.

Poleman Dora, servant, Henry Veghorst, s. East, near corporation line.

Police Office, room 1, Glenns' blk., e. Washington.

Polson James, lab., res. 117 n. Missouri.

POLSTER FREDERICK, saloon, 192 n. Mississippi, res. same.

Pool Adoniram J., engineer, Ind. Central R. R., res. 73 Davidson.

Poole John E., secretary, Eagle Machine Works, res. 237 s Meridian.

Pool Miss Lettie, dress-maker, Boyd's blk., Massachusetts av., res. same.

Pool Mrs. Sarah C., (wid. Matthias,) res. Boyd's blk., Massachusetts av.

Pool William, works street railroad, res Boyd's blk.

Poorman Daniel S., teamster, res. 158 Huron.

Porerum Joseph S., carpenter, res. 414 n. Delaware.

Pope A. G., salesman, 59 s. Meridian, res. 282 n. Alabama.

Pope Abner, farmer, res. 74 w. North.

Pope Abner J., bds. 74 w. North.

POPE CHARLES R., bds. Bates House.

Pope Christian, brick-moulder, res. Harrison.

Pope Ester, servant, Palmer House, bds. same.

Pope George William, brick-maker, res. 67 Harrison.

Pope Henry, chair-maker, bds. 383 Virginia av.

Pope Henry, paper-maker, res. 199 n. West.

Pope Henry T., carpenter, bds. 199 n. West.

Pope James P., bds. 139 Huron.

Pope Mrs. Mary, (wid. William,) bds. 139 Huron.

Pope Richard, (col.,) laborer, res. end Virginia av., beyond city limits.

Pope William, (George Hotz & Co.,) 124 s. Illinois, bds. California House.

Popensticker Goolp, lab., res. 100 Huron.

Popp Paul, cabinet-maker, 276 e. Washington, bds. 118 n. Noble.

Pork George, shoe-maker, bds. 31 Court.

Porter Albert G., (P., Harrison & Fishback,) res. 257 n. Delaware.

Porter Amanda, (wid. John,) res. over 199 c. Washington.

Porter Miss Eliza, ironer in City Laundry, bds. 199 c. Washington.

Porter Miss Emeline, (col.,) servant, William Wick.

PORTER, HARRISON & FISH-
* BACK, (A. G. P., Benjamin H. & William P. F.,) lawyers, Yohn's blk., n. e. cor. Meridian and Washington.
Porter John, tobacco presser, 199 e. Washington.
Porter John H., occupant Deaf and Dumb Asylum.
Porter Margaret, bds. 373 e. Georgia.
Porter Omer T., (P., Vance & Beck,) 85 e. Market, bds. 24 w. New York.
PORTER THEODORE R.,
custom tailor, over 24 w. Washington, bds. Macy House. See card, page 60.
Porter Thomas, cash-boy New York Store, 161 s. Delaware.
PORTER, VANCE & BECK,
(Omar T. P., S. M. V. & S. T. Beck,) flour and produce merchants, 85 e. Market.
Porter W. L., cooper, bds. w. Washington.
Porter William H., railroader, J., M. & I. R. R., res. 361 s. Delaware.
Porter William M., (col.,) barber-shop, 63 s. Illinois, and under Spencer House, res. 63 s. Illinois.
Posner Moretz, clerk, 114 s. Meridian, res. s. Delaware, near South.
Post C. C., agt., Pitts., Ft. W. & C. R. R., bds. Bates House.
Porton Charles W., porter Brackbush & Co., res. e. Washington, beyond city limits.
Pothas A., (P. & Eix,) res. cor. Liberty and Washington.
Potman Benjamin, varnisher, res. 106 n. Spring.
Pottage Benjamin, hardware, cutlery, tools and carriage trimming, 77½ w. Washington, res. 127 w. Market.
Pottage Charles, salesman, 77½ w. Washington, res. 9 Ellsworth.
Pottage Thomas W., clerk, 77½ w. Washington, res. 127 w. Market.
Pottage William, moulder, bds. 302 w. Maryland.
Potter ——, book-keeper, 24½ w. Washington, bds. 32 n. Pennsylvania.
Potter George H., driver Citizen's Street Railway, bds. Neiman House.
Potter George W., (col.,) white-washer, res. Second, bet. Howard and Lafayette R. R.
Potter John, (col.,) servant, 190 e. Market.
Potter John L., carpenter, res. 77 Jones.
Potter Miss Mary, bds. 448 n. Meridian.
Potter N. C., book-keeper, Great Western Horse Insurance Co., res. 290 e. St. Clair.
Potts Charles, Sr., miller, bds. 82 n. Liberty.
Potts Charles, Jr., miller, bds. 82 n. Liberty.
Potts Mrs. Mary A., (wid. Albert,) res. 115 w. New York.

POUND WILLIAM,
local editor Evening Commercial, and correspondent Cincinnati Gazette, cor. Meridian and Circle, res. 43 Fletcher av.
Pouder Milton, stock agt., Baltimore & Ohio R. R., res. 144 n. East.
Powell Charles, lab., Bellefontaine R. R. Shop, res. e. of e. end Michigan.
Powell David, railroader, res. 434 n. New Jersey.
Powell James, (col.,) lab., 154 n. West.
Power Jacob B., ex-policeman, res. 71 n. East.
Power John, lab., res. 76 Maple.
Power J. K., actor, bds. Macy House.
Powers Mrs. B. F., teacher of vocal culture, Indiana Female College, 146 n. Meridian, bds. same.
Powers Mrs., servant, Palmer House.
Powers Patrick, works Sinker's foundry, res. 271 s. Pennsylvania.
Powers Mrs. Peggy, (wid.,) res. 55 Fayette.
Powers Stephen, lab., res. 65 Maple.
Powers Thomas, works Sinker's foundry, res. 273 s. Pennsylvania.
Powers Thomas, lab., res. bet. Liberty and East.
Powley Henry, carpenter, (Miller & Powley,) res. 181 Davidson.
Prager Henry, stone-mason, res. 330 Railroad.
Prail Frederick J., brick-mason, res. 214 Winston.
Prange Anthony F., (C. P. & Co.,) res. over 318 e. Washington.
Prange Charles, (C. P. & Co.,) res. e. city, on Michigan rd.
Prange Charles & Co., (Charles & Anthony F. P. & Henry Buddenbaum,) groceries and dry goods, 318 e. Washington.
Prasse Henry, grocer, 446 Virginia av. res. same.
Prather Austin B., book-keeper, Horn, Anderson & Co., res. 76 n. Mississippi.
Prather Miss C., bds. second floor, 152 w. Washington.
Pratt Oliver, machinist, bds. 239 s. Delaware.
Pratt William B., book-keeper, Osgood, Smith & Co, res. 3 miles s. of city.
Pray Enos G., cancer doctor, res. 102 Broadway.
Pray J. J., Trade Palace, res. cor. Christian av. and Broadway.
Pray William, (Gates, P. & Co.,) res. 79 n. Alabama.
Preer J. H., student commercial college, bds. cor. Washington and New Jersey.
Presbyterian Reformed Church, 250 e. South.
Presley Otis, carriage-blacksmith, bds. 89 s. Pennsylvania.

Presley John T., propr. saw-mill, near Claremont, I., C. & L. R. R., res. 119 s. East.

Presse Henry, res. 108 s. Noble.

Pressel Albert, drayman, E. Over & Co., res. 110 Plum.

Pressel Anna, (wid. Augustus,) res. 102 Oak.

Pressel Charlotte, (wid. Philip,) res. 110 Plum.

Pressel Mrs. Mary, (wid.,) res. 248 n. Blake.

Pressel Nancy, (wid. Augustus,) res. 102 Oak.

Pressell William, carpenter, res. 97 Broadway.

Preston Elliott, switchman, res. 474 s. Tennessee.

Preston Miss Julia, res. 118 Huron.

Preston Margaret, (wid. Alfred,) seamstress, res. 218 Huron.

Preston Miss Mary, actress, Metropolitan Theater, bds. Macy House.

Preston S. N., book-keeper, 11 s. Meridian, bds. 78 w. North.

Prettyman James, (col.,) white-washer, bds. Missouri, bet. Indiana av. and North.

Preynitz William, carpenter, res. 327 e. Georgia.

Price Mrs. E. J., (wid. Isaac,) bds. 30 w. Pratt.

Price Frank M., clerk, A. Clem & Bros., bds. 278 e. Michigan.

Price Mrs. Lutitia, res. 348 Indiana av.

Price William, teamster, res. 379 n. West.

Prickley William, carpenter, bds. 109 Davidson.

PRIER H. J., State agt., McCormick's Reaper and Mower, 244 e. Washington, bds. Little Hotel.

Prince George, (col.,) lab., bds. 94 Elm.

Prince Hannibal, (col.,) gardener, res. 94 Elm.

Princel Henry, lab., res. 181 Madison av.

Prindall Lewis, lab., res. 518 s. Illinois.

Prindle Mrs. Margaret, seamstress, res. 294 n. Liberty.

Prinker August, groceries, 174 w. New York, res. same.

Prinsler Augustus, lab., res 226 w. Maryland.

Printler Harmon, lab., res. 362 Virginia av.

Prinz John D., salesman, Alford, Talbott & Co., res. 83 n. Noble.

Privett Mary, servant, 138 e. New York.

Pronger Frederic, city express driver, res. 193 Davidson.

Pross George, brick-layer, res. 269 e. North.

Proper Joseph driver, Citizens Street Ry., res. 67 w. Georgia.

Prosser Ann, (wid. Henry,) res. 84 e. South.

Protzman John, bds. 42 s. Illinois.

Prosser John, Philadelphia Dye House, 50 n. Illinois, res. same.

Protzman Miss Belle, principal dress-maker, 52 s. Illinois, bds. same.

Prunk D. H., physician, office 30 n. Mississippi, res. 372 w. New York.

Pruitt Paulina J., occupant Deaf and Dumb Asylum.

PRYOR RICHARD, propr., Little's Hotel, s. e. cor. Washington and New Jersey.

Pugh Miss Catharine, lady boarder, 27 n. New Jersey.

Pugh William, painter, works 241 w. Washington, res. Pearl, bet. Canal and California.

Pullman George, tailor, res. 249 Davidson.

Purcell Bizarro, engineer, res. 114 Railroad.

Purcell Charles, carpenter, res. 247 w. New York.

Purcell Mrs. Sarah, (wid. Charles,) res. 7 Massachusetts av.

Purcell Sarah E.. (col.,) servant, at 162 n. Illinois.

Purdy David, occupant Deaf and Dumb Asylum.

Purdy Judson. teacher, Purdy's Business College, Eden's Hall, Market, bet. Pennsylvania and Delaware, bds. 248 n. Illinois.

Purdy William, propr. Purdy's Business College, Eden's Hall, Market, bet. Pennsylvania and Delaware, res. 248 n. Illinois.

Pursell A. Evans, dentist, room 5, Wiley's blk., n. Pennsylvania, res. 278 n. Mississippi.

Pursell Mrs. Elizabeth, (wid.,) dress-maker, res. 34 w. Ohio.

Pursell Miss Emily K., bds. 47 w. New York.

Pursell Jonathan, shoe-maker, works at 32 e. Washington, res. 247 w. New York.

Pursell R. P., lab., res. e. Georgia, bet. Delaware and Pennsylvania.

Pursey Francis J., painter, res. 21 Peru.

Putnam Benjamin, varnisher, res. bet. Noble and Benton.

Putnam Ellen, (wid.,) printer, res. 16 Centre.

Putnam Miss Lydia R., assistant editor, Christian Monitor, res. 16 Centre.

Putnam Mrs. Sarah, (wid. Silas,) res. 16 Centre.

PYBURN MRS. AGNES, physician and surgeon, res. e. side s. West, bet. Louisiana and Georgia.

Pyle House 95 n. Meridian, John Pyle, prop.

PYLE JOHN, propr. Pyle House, res. 95 n. Meridian.

Pyle John E., book-keeper, res. 119 Massachusetts av.

Pyle William L., res. 620 n. Illinois.

QUAKER, OR FRIENDS CHURCH, s. e. cor. Delaware and St. Clair.
Quarmby Joseph, res. 321 n. Noble.
Quigley B., (wid. Patrick,) res. 52 Eddy.
Quigley Mrs. Sophia, (wid.,) bds. 231 n. Mississippi.
Quillans William, tobacconist, bds. Ray House.
Quimby Miss Harriet N., (Quimby & Hinsdale,) 59 n. Illinois, res. same.
Quimby & Hinsdale, (Harriet N. Q. & Emma H.,) milliners, 59 n. Illinois.
Quinius Rev. H., minister, German Lutheran, res. n. s. Ohio, bet. Illinois and Meridian.
Quinius John, clerk, 33 c. Washington, res. w. Ohio, bet. Meridian and Illinois.
Quinlin James, driver, J. H. Ross, bds. 359 w. Washington.
Quinlin John, tailor, over 28 s. Meridian, bds. 199 w. Maryland.
Quinlin Michael, soldier, U. S. Arsenal, res. same.
Quinn Edwin, boot and shoe-maker, 75 w. South, res. same.
Quinn James, lab., res. 300 s. East.
Quinn Miss Jane, servant, J. O. D. Lilly, n. Tennessee, bet. Second and Third.
Quinn John, foreman, Allen's Livery Stables, res. 303 s. Pennsylvania.
Quinn John, saloon and boarding house, 245 and 247 w. Maryland.
Quirk Charles, lab., res. end Virginia av.
Quirk Christian, lab., res. end Virginia av.
Quisser Frank, butcher, works 131 Massachusetts av., res. 336 Virginia av.
Quisser Julius, butcher shop, 131 Massachusetts av., res. 336 Virginia av.

RAAB JOHN, teamster, res. 346 n. Noble.
Raab Sebastian, shoe-shop, 93 e. South, res. 242 s. Delaware.
Radasill Allison, inmate Deaf and Dumb Asylum.
Radford James, (col.,) waiter, Bates House.
Rady Patrick, lab., West, near cor. South.
Raeffal Peter, lab., res. 36 Union.
Rafert Andrew F., carpenter and builder, cor. Walnut and Ft. Wayne av.
Rafert Charles, checkman, I., P. & C. R. R., res. 139 Merrill.
Rafert Christian, carpenter and job shop, 81 e. Pratt, res. 83 e. Pratt.
Rafert Ernest, drayman, res. 93 Union.
Rafert Henry, res. 117 e. St. Mary.
Rafert William, drayman, res. 242 Madison av.
Rafert William, lab., res. 268 s. Alabama.
Ragen Charles, railroader, bds. 470 e. Georgia.
Ragemeyer Henry, lab., res. 115 e. St. Joseph.

Ragsdale Mrs. Martha A., (wid. Anderson,) res. 397 Massachusetts av.
Rhaling Charles, shoe-maker, works 218 e. Washington, res. Court, bet. East and New Jersey.
Raible Charles, cabinet-maker, and boarding house, res. 518 E. Washington.
Raible John, tailor, 113 Spring, res. same.
Raible L., cabinet-maker, res. 132 Spring.
Raidy Michael, American Express employe, res. 434 s. Meridian.
Raidy Patrick, lab., bds. 240 s. West.
Railsback Adelaide, res. w. s. Blake, bet. New York and Vermont.
Railsback Miss Sarah, teacher branch eighth ward school, in Asbury Chapel, bds. 227 Virginia av.
Railway Passenger's Assurance Co., Hartford, Conn., J. S. Dunlop & Co., agts., 16 and 18 n. Meridian.
RAKESTRAW T. M., boot and shoe-maker, 64 n. Pennsylvania, res. same.
Rale John, lab., res. 392 s. Missouri.
Ralph A. J., vice prest. American Horse Insurance Co., bds. 24 w. New York.
Rammel Eli, minister, res. end Virginia av.
Ramsarer Christian, lab., res. n. s. National rd., near Insane Asylum.
Ramsay Alexander, assistant book-keeper, 82 w. Washington, res. 135 e. St. Joseph.
Ramsay Charles, bds. Bates House.
Ramsey J. F., furniture, 39 s. Illinois, res. 260 n. Illinois.
Ramsey James A., teller, First National Bank, bds. 260 n. Illinois.
Ramsey John F., real estate dealer, res. 260 n. Illinois.
Ramsey John W., clerk, bds. 260 n. Illinois.
Ramsey Thomas, shoe-maker, res. 487 Virginia av.
Ramsey A. H. B., salesman, Horn, Anderson & Co., bds. 186 n. Tennessee.
Ramsey Walter L., plumber, 82 w. Washington, res. 135 e. St. Joseph.
Ramsey William, gas-fitter, 82 w. Washington, res. 135 e. St. Joseph.
Ran Mrs. Kate, (col., wid.,) washer-woman, res. 163 Indiana av.
Ranefel H. P., res. 13 e. St. Joseph.
Rand Edward L., soldier, U. S. Arsenal, res. same.
Rand Frederick, (R. & Hall,) 24½ e. Washington, res. 270 n. Illinois.
Rand & Hall, (Frederick R. & Reginald H. H.,) lawyers, 24½ e. Washington.
Randall Berry G. G., clerk, 31 s. Illinois, bds. 31 w. Market.
Randall George, carpenter, res. 784 n. Illinois.
Randall H. P., assessor, res. 19 e. St. Joseph.

RANDALL NELSON A.,
oyster and fruit dealer, 31 s. Illinois,
res. 31 w. Market.

Randolph Lat, teamster, res. w. city limits.

Randolph Reuben, res. w. of city limits.

Rank Peter, baker, 98 e. South, res. same.

Rank P. D., (R. Moon & Co.,) 131 s. Illinois, res. same.

Rankin Albert, plasterer, res. 422 n. New Jersey.

Rankin Austin D., engineer, T. H. & I. R. R., res. 183 w. south.

Rankin John R., printer, bds. 126 n. Pennsylvania.

Rankins Elisha, tinner, Munson & Johnson's, bds. 118 s. New Jersey.

RANSDELL DANIEL M.,
city clerk, office Glenns' blk., e. Washington, res. 346 n. Meridian.

Raper George, student commercial college, bds. 44 s. Tennessee.

Rapp Frederick J., plow-maker, res. 240 e. Market.

Rare Robert, shoe-maker, bds. end Virginia av.

Rarich Henry, miller, bds. National rd., w. White river.

Rariden Miss M. C., teacher of history and mathematics, Indiana Female College, 146 n. Meridian, bds. same.

Rarme John A., salesman, 30 w. Washington, res. 2 Magill.

RASCHIG CHARLES M.,
cigars and tobacco, 11 e. Washington, res. 200 n. Tennessee, cor. Vermont. See card, page 108.

Raschig Edward, auditor American Express Co., res. 126 e. North.

Rasener C. H., cabinet-maker, res. 511 s. New Jersey.

Rassman Charles, saloon, e. Washington, near Arsenal av., res. same.

Rasener Christina, dress-maker, bds. 480 s. Tennessee.

Rasener Frederick W., dry goods and groceries, 288 e. Washington, res. e. on Michigan rd.

Rasener Herman, res. 231 n. Liberty.

Rasener A. F., clerk, C., C. C. & I. R. R., res. 155 Union.

Rasener William, lab., res. 155 Union.

Ratcliff John, teamster, bds. 291 e. Ohio.

Ratti Francis A., Sr., res. 318 n. East.

Ratti Francis A., Jr., foreman press room, Sentinel office, res. 318 n. East.

Ratti Joseph, foreman book and job room, Sentinel office, res. 318 n. East.

Rauh Benhard, (B. Brothers,) 1 Palmer House, res. 165 n. Tennessee.

Rauh Brothers, clothiers and gents' furnishing goods, 1 Palmer House.

Rauschen Henry, lab., res. 366 s. Illinois.

Raver Charles, checkman Peru depot, res. 139 e. Merrill.

Rawlings C. C., telegraph operator, B. & I. R. R., bds. 17½ Virginia av.

Rawlings James M., teamster, bds. 139 Huron.

Rawzell Jacob F., cooper, bds. 68 w. St. Joseph.

Ray Allison D., traveling agt. Munson's lightning rods, res. 187 Buchanan.

Ray Austin, traveling agt., res. 86 Indiana av.

RAY CHARLES A.,
judge Supreme Court of Indiana, Supreme Court bldg., res. 140 and 144 n. Illinois.

Ray George, section foreman, I., C. & L. R. R., bds. 99 Benton.

Ray H. C., notary public, room 12, Talbott & New's blk., n. Pennsylvania, res. with Martin M. Ray.

Ray H. J., cigars and tobacco, 290 e. Washington, res. same.

Ray Mrs. Harriet, (wid. James N.,) res. 10 Water.

RAY HOUSE,
James M. Lambert, propr., s. e. cor. Delaware and South. See card, page 13, adv. dept.

Ray Isaac, carpenter, res. 44 Forest av.

Ray James M., (R., Mayhew & Co.) prest. Bank of the State of Indiana, res. 112 n. Meridian.

Ray John W., (R. & Ritter,) 24½ e. Washington, res. National rd., beyond city limits.

Ray, Mayhew & Co., wholesale dealers in boots and shoes, 8 w. Louisiana.

Ray Mrs. Mary, (wid.,) res. 32 w. Ohio.

RAY M. M.,
attorney at law, room 12 Talbott & New's blk., n. Pennsylvania, res. cor. Pennsylvania and Seventh.

Ray Mrs. Nancy, (wid. David,) res. 44 Forest av.

RAY & RITTER,
(John W. R. & E. F. R.,) attorneys at law, 24½ e. Washington.

Ray Mrs. Sarah, (wid. George W.,) res. 163 n. Noble.

Ray W. S., student, N. W. C. University, bds n. Pennsylvania, outside city limits.

Rayder George, fireman, Bellefontaine R. R., bds. 456 e. Michigan.

Raymond Henry, book-keeper, res. 47 Coburn.

Raymond J. N., book-keeper, res. 21 e. St. Joseph.

Raymond Samuel, blacksmith, shop 60 e. Maryland, bds. Beard House.

Raymond W. C., actor, bds. 27 w. Ohio.

Raynor C. H., with McCreery & Fay, res. 523 n. Tennessee.

Raynor Jacob, (col.,) driver, Hume, Adams & Co.

Razier George, printer, bds. 146 Blackford.

Razier Percy, printer, bds. 146 n. Blackford.

Read Julia Ann, (wid. Alexander,) servant, National rd., half-mile from bridge, n. s.

Reading F. C., foreman, B. C. Shaw, 26 c. Georgia.

Reading W. V., coach-trimmer, 26 e. Georgia, bds. 126 c. Maryland.

Reagan Edward, boiler-maker, Sinker & Co, res. 138 s. Tennessee.

Reagan J. D., book-keeper, 18 w. Pearl, res. 21 e. St. Joseph.

Reagan Lot, physician, office and res. 12 s. Mississippi.

Reagan Maggie, servant, Palmer House.

Reagan Michael, lab., res. 13 Willard.

Realey Frederick, watchman, res. 290 s. Illinois.

Ream Albert, brakesman, P. & I. R. R., bds. 142 s. East.

Reame Joseph, clerk, 60 s. Meridian.

Reariden Elizabeth, cook, 128 n. Meridian.

Reariden John, painter, bds. 201 Davidson.

Reasener C. F., shoe-maker, res. 46 Michigan rd.

Reasener, Henry, car inspector, C., C. & I. C. R. R., bds 293 e. Washington.

Reasener F. W., grocery, 288 e. Washington, res. e. city limits.

Reasoner, Shepmyer & Co., (William F. R. & Andrew S.,) dry goods, groceries and provisions, 546 e. Washington.

Reasoner William F., (R., Shepmeyer & Co., 546 e. Washington, res. in rear same.

Reaume William H., salesman, Anderson, Bullock & Schofield, bds. Oriental House.

Rebentish Charles, shoe-maker, res 187 c. South.

Reber Godfried, stone-cutter, res. 268 s. Delaware.

Rech George, clerk, 44 w. Louisiana, bds. 118 s. Illinois.

Reck Mrs. Martha, res. 77 w. First.

Reckel Gertrude, (wid. Godfried,) res. 269 e. Ohio.

Reckel Miss Mary, seamstress, 279 e. Ohio, res. same.

Recker Hubert, carpenter, shop n. Liberty, near Market, res. 507 e. Market.

Recker John, bleacher, bds. 175 Virginia av.

Records Isaac, janitor County offices, bds. 228 e. Louisiana.

Records John C., hat-blocker, 44 s. Illinois, bds. 17 Virginia av.

Records R. P., railroader, bds. 58 Benton.

Red Edward, (col.,) 73 Ann.

Redfield D. A., publisher, res. 71 w. Michigan.

Redford John E., trader, res. 21 Massachusetts av.

Redford Mrs. Catharine, (wife John E.,) milliner and dress-making, 21 Massachusetts av., res. same.

Redmond Dennis deputy marshal, Union Depot, res. 179 w. South.

Redmond Margaret, (wid. John,) res. 243 w. Maryland.

Redmond O. A., printer, Journal bldg., bds. Commercial Hotel.

Redmond Samuel, res. 311 w. Washington.

Reid Mrs Ann, (wid. John,) res. near Jeffersonville Round House.

Reed Anson T., (A. R. & Co.,) bds. 63 w. Maryland.

REED A. & CO., (Anson T. R. & James Boyle,) soda-water manfs. 212 w. Washington.

Reed Benjamin F., mail-agt., Central R. R., res. 31 w. Michigan.

Reed Earl, clerk, 27 w. Washington, bds. 37 Kentucky av.

Reed E. R., engraver, 50 e. Washington, res. 17 w. Maryland.

Reed Mrs. Elizabeth, (wid.,) bds. 293 Indiana av.

Reed Enoch, marble-cutter, works H. W. Roberts, bds. 270 n. Liberty.

Reed Frank, soda-water-maker, res. 63 w. Maryland.

Reed George, lab., res. 365 e. Market.

Reed George, plasterer, bds. Patterson House.

Reed George D., machinist, res. 185 Bates.

Reed Henry, painter, bds 69 w. Market.

Reed Howard H., railroader, bds. 31 w. Michigan.

Reed Jeremiah, (col.,) barber, bds. Oriental House.

Reed John, traveling agt., G. W. McCurdy, bds. 134 n. East.

Reed Johnson, res. 48 Wyoming.

Reed Miss Lou., dress-maker, res. over 320 e. Washington.

Reed Mrs. Martha J., (wid. John W.,) res. 134 n. East

Reed Michael, lab., res. 36 n. Douglas.

Reed Mrs. S. A., boarding house, 30½ n. Pennsylvania.

Reed Samuel B., bds. 185 Bates.

Reed Thaddeus C., civil engineer, bds. 31. w. Michigan.

Rees Valentine, carpenter, Spiegel & Thoms, res. 420 s. East.

Reed William, bds. 267 e. Washington.

Reeder Ephraim C., grocer, 298 e. Washington, res. same.

Rees Henry, physician and surgeon, office cor. Alabama and Washington, res. 236 n. East.

Rees Addison, lawyer, bds. 289 Winston.

Reese Charles, (H. R. & Co.,) 113 w. Washington, res. same.

Reese Charles, Sr., cabinet-maker, works Spiegle, Thoms & Co., res. 188 n. Noble.

Reese George, lab., res. 235 Madison av.
Reese Henry, (H. R. & Co.,(113 w. Washington, res. same.
Reese Henry & Co., (H. B. & Chas. R.,) grocers, 113 and 115 w. Washington.
Reese John, cabinet-maker, res. 145 Fort Wayne av.
Reese John, lab., res. n. s. National rd., w. river bridge.
Reese Mrs. Sarah T. Bolton, bds. 289 Winston.
Reese Edward, barber, bds. 77 s. Illinois.
Reeves Carey C., works Carpenter's Union, res. 510 e. Washington.
REEVES FRANK J., traveling agt., bds. 510 e. Washington.
Reeves Sarah, (wid. William,) res. 469 n. Meridian.
Reeves Thomas, lab., res. 53 Dacotah.
Reger Charles W., works Cabinet-Makers' Union, res. 79 Davidson.
Reggar Joseph, carpenter, Bellefontaine shops, res. 7 Charles.
Regula Conrad A., clerk, F. M. Brown, 322 n. Illinois.
Rehling Charles, (Rentschler & R.,) 188 s. Illinois, res. same.
Rehling William, boots and shoes, 257 s. Delaware, res. same.
Reich Gideon, overseer city prisoners, res. 83 Elm.
Richwein John, lab., res. 199 Davidson.
Richwein Philip, bar-tender, Astor Saloon, 15 n. Pennsylvania, res. Wabash, bet. Liberty and Noble.
Reick Augustus, policeman, eighth ward, res. 490 Virginia av.
Reihl Charles II., brick-mason, res. 31 Indiana av.
Reid Earl, bds. end Virginia av., beyond city limits.
Reid Erasmus, gardener, res. end Virginia av., beyond city limits.
Reid G., teamster, bds. 355 w. Washington.
Reid Julia A., (wid. Irvin,) res. 188 Virginia av.
Reid Wesley, res. end Virginia av., beyond city limits.
Reidy Michael, lab., res. 345 s. Meridian.
Reilly John, employee, Am. Ex. Co., res. 414 s. Tennessee.
Reily H. H., res. 43 Bluff rd.
Rein Mary, res. 315 s. Delaware.
Reinacher Jacob, janitor, Metropolitan Theater, res. 331 n. New Jersey.
Reinard Frederic, tanner and currier, res. 131 w. Fourth.
Reiners John, book-keeper, J. H. Vajen & Co., bds. 128 n. Meridian.
Reinert Gotleib, butcher, 153 w. Washington, res. same.
Reinfels Henry, lab., res. 272 Union.
Reingen Alfred, plasterer, res. w. side Tennessee, bet. Fifth and Sixth.

Reinhardt L., boot and shoe-maker, res. 172 e. Market.
Reinhardt S. W., carpenter, res. 309 e. Merrill.
Reinhart Valentine, cabinet-maker, res. 277 Bluff rd.
Reinka Frederick, machinist, bds. 183 s. Illinois.
Reinken Eliza, servant, at 158 n. New Jersey.
Reinken Henry, cigars and tobacco, 266 e. Washington, res. same.
Reinken John, cigar-maker, works 266 e. Washington, bds. same.
REINMAN REINHART, wine and beer hall, 35 and 37 s. Delaware, res. same.
Reisner Albert, (Deitz & R.,) 17 s. Delaware, res. Blake, bet. Vermont and New York.
Reisner Charles, blacksmith, res. Arch.
Reisner Christian H., chair-maker, res. 511 s. New Jersey.
Reisner G. A., (Comingore & R.,) 17 w. Washington, res. 170 Winston.
Reisner Herman, works last factory, s. Illinois, res. 231 n. Liberty.
Reisner Mrs. Mary C., (wid. John J.,) res. 170 Winston.
Reising Lewis, gas-fitter, works J. W. Davis, res. 338 s. Delaware.
Reister Catharine, (wid. John,) res. 308 Massachusetts av.
Reiter Henry, teamster, res. 95 Elm.
Reitz Charles, res. 287 s. Pennsylvania.
Reitz Frank A., bds. 552 e. Washington.
Reitz Henry, res. 287 s. Pennsylvania.
Reitzel Carrie, dress-maker, works 39 n. Alabama, res. 417 s. Illinois.
Reley James, (col.,) lab., res. 217 n. Minerva.
Remas Victor, gardener, res. 270 s. Noble.
Remeley Joseph, book-store, e. Washington, bds. 120 w. Market.
Renard Eugene, stone-mason, res. 323 e. New York.
Renard Eugene, saloon, 299 e. Washington, res. same.
Renard John, stone-mason, res. 323 e. New York.
Rend Robert, carpenter, res. 30 n. New Jersey.
Render Mary, servant, 467 n. Delaware.
Renehan James, undertaker, res. near cor. North and Indiana av.
Renehan Joseph, lab., res. 74 Fayette.
Renner Christian, blacksmith, res. 127 Bluff rd.
Renner Jacob, porter, Hume & Adams, res. Fourth, bet. Mississippi and Tennessee.
Renner John B., (Brennerman & R.,) 123 e. Washington, res. 34 s. Alabama.
Rennett George F., sleeping car conductor, C., C. & I. C. R. W., res. 70 e. Maryland.

Reno Robert S., carpenter, works on Court, bet. New Jersey and Alabama, res. 30 n. New Jersey.

Rentsch Edward, groceries and produce dealer, 172 s. Illinois, res. same.

Rentsch Herman, grocery and produce dealer, 145 e. Washington, res. same.

Rentschler Adam, moulder, Frink & Moore, res. same.

Rentschler Catharine, servant, 133 n. Liberty.

Rentschler Frederick, blacksmith, works Helwig factory, res. 106 Spring.

Rentschler John G., (R. & Rehling,) 188 s. Illinois, res. same.

Rentschler Martin, carriage-maker, works S. W. Drew & Co., res. 134 n. Liberty.

RENTSCHLER & REHLING, (John R. & Charles R.,) groceries and produce dealers, 188 s. Illinois.

Renzinbrink William, machinist, res. 363 s. Tennessee.

Replogle John, (Lee & R.,) saloon, n. w. cor. Washington and Noble, bds. 161 Spring.

REPUBLICAN STATE CEN- TRAL COMMITTEE ROOMS, old State Bank bldg., cor. Kentucky av. and Illinois, A. H. Connor, chairman, John F. Wood, sec'y.

Resener Christian F., carpenter, res. 161 n. New Jersey.

Resener Henry F., carpenter, res. 235 Winston.

Resner F. & W., (William F. & Frederick R.,) groceries and dry goods, 179 n. East.

Resner Henry, shoe-maker, res. 370 Virginia av.

Resner T., (T. &. W. R.,) res. 179 n. East.

Resner William F., (F. & W. R.,) res. 331 e. Ohio.

REUTTI THEODORE, saloon and beer garden, 252 e. Washington, res. same.

Revel William, engineer, C., C. & I. C. R. R., res. 303 e. Georgia.

Revels Willis, (col.,) physician, res. 205 n. West.

Rexfald Eugene M., express messenger, Merchants' Union, res. 25 w. St. Clair.

Reynolds C. E., clerk, 19 Virginia av., bds. 325 n. Delaware.

Reynolds Chesley, expressman, res. 79 Ash.

Reynolds Edward, (Wiles & R.,) res. 160 Virginia av.

Reynolds Frank, yard-master Bellefontaine R. R., res. 156 n. Liberty.

REYNOLDS & HOLLIDAY, (John B. R., Cort. F. & Wilbur F. H.,) kerosene lamps, oil and lamp trimmings, 13 s. Meridian. See card, page 106.

Reynolds Isaac, tobacconist, bds. Ray House.

Reynolds John, book-keeper, James Sulgrove & Son, 20 w. Washington, res. 287 n. Alabama.

Reynolds John B., (R. & Holliday,) 13 s. Meridian, res. 160 Virginia av.

Reynolds J. W., carpenter, res. 115 w. South.

Reynolds Miss Lucy, bds. 115 n. Missouri.

Reynolds Mathew, cigar-maker, 6 Hunt, res. 439 s. Illinois.

Reynolds Samuel, carpenter, bds. 323 n. Delaware.

Reynolds T. C., carpenter, res. 17 Vine.

Reynolds Thomas, stone-cutter, res. 215 n. Michigan.

Reynolds Thomas B., (Wiles & R.,) 48 n. Pennsylvania, res. 160 Virginia av.

Reynolds N. W., wholesale cigar-manfr., Seidensticker's blk., res. 440 n. Illinois.

Reynolds A. L., carpenter, res. 119 Ash.

Reynolds William, checkman, T. H. & I. freight house, res. n. Delaware, bet. North and Walnut.

Rheinhart Louis, shoe-maker, res. 172 e. Market.

Rheinheimer N., (R. & W.,) 3 Palmer House, res. 275 s. Delaware.

Rheinheimer & Co., clothiers, 3 Palmer House.

Rheinhold Jacob, carpenter, res. 373 w. Vermont.

Rhoads Charles W., watchman, city fire-alarm tower, res. 231 w. New York.

Rhoads Hiram H., teamster, res. 364 w. North.

Rhoads Mrs. Maranda, seamstress, res. 285 Blake.

Rhoads Susan, (col.,) washer, res. 350 w. North.

Rhoads William, lab., res. 311 w. Market.

Rhodes Elizabeth, (col.,) servant, 350 w. North.

Rhodes Hiram, teamster, res. 379 Vinton.

Rhodes Jane, house-cleaner, res. Tennessee, bet. Michigan and Vermont.

Rhodes James, (col.,) dining-room boy, Oriental House.

Rhodes John W., 82 e. St. Clair.

RHODIUS MRS. GEORGE, propr. Circle Restaurant, 15 n. Meridian, res. same.

Rice A., clerk, 100 e. Washington, bds. Mozart Hall.

Rice Miss Bertha, bds. 277 s. Delaware.

Rice Elizabeth, (wid.,) res. 3 Rockwood.

Rice Gustave, dealer in dry goods and notions, 100 e. Washington, bds. 19 Circle.

Rice George H., pump-maker, res. Wabash, bet. Liberty and Noble.

Rice Isaac, lab., res. 415 e. Washington.

Rice James, lab., res. 113 n. West.
Rice James A., book-keeper, bds. 123 n. New Jersey.
Rice John, lab., bds. 376 e. Market.
Rice Lucy, (wid. William,) res. 7 Dacotah.
Rice Mary, servant, D. W. Grubbs, 282 n. Illinois.
Rich Harriet, res. cor. New York and Blake.
Rich Miss Jane, res. cor. New York and Blake.
Richard Frank, stone-cutter, res. 485 e. Georgia.
Richards E. N., (R. & Thomas,) 399 n. New Jersey, bds. 30 e. Pratt.
Richards E., (E. & O. T.,) res. 30 w. Pratt.
Richards Frederick W., printer, at Journal Offie, res. 31 Hosbrook.
Richards John, carpenter, res. 425 n. East.
Richards Miss Sarah, seamstress, bds. 175 e. Ohio.
Richards & Thomas, (E. N. R. & O. T.,) grocery and produce dealers, 399 n. New Jersey.
Richardson Benjamin A., clerk, Indianapolis Gas Light and Coke Co., s. e. cor. Maryland and Pennsylvania, bds. 17½ Virginia av.
Richardson Edward, horse-trader, bds. 171 n. Davidson.
Richardson Frank, salesman Singer Manufacturing Co., bds. 118 n. Delaware.
Richardson Miss H., teacher, bds. 248 n. Illinois.
Richardson I. J. horse-dealer, bds. 171 Davidson.
Richardson John, lab., res. 122 Maple.
Richardson Miss Mary M., principal ninth ward school, bds. 171 Davidson.
Richmeyer William, blacksmith, bds. cor. Washington and Liberty.
Richey Miss Alice, assistant teacher fifth ward school, res. 124 n. Missouri.
Richey Mrs. Charlotte, (wid. John,) res. 124 n. Missouri.
Richey James, hostler, bds. 198 s. Illinois.
Richison Tempy, (wid. James,) res. 55 Jones.
Richison Daniel A., teamster, res. 378 n. West.
Richer Julius, tinsmith, res. 324 s. Delaware.

RICHMAN CHARLES,
chief engineer, fire department, res. 16 Fletcher av.
Richmond Mrs. E. L., milliner, 8 n. Pennsylvania, res. cor. Delaware and Massachusetts av.
Richmond John, lab., res. 51 Maple.
Richter Anton, lab., res. Lord.
Richter Adolph J., boot and shoe-maker, 217 e. Washington, res. same.
Richter August, street commissioner, res. 310 Virginia av.

Richter C., brick-layer, res. 146 Huron.
Richter F., (R. & Schradluke,) res. 317 s. Illinois.
Richter Forence, saloon-keeper, res. 303 s. Meridian.
Richter Frederick, stone-mason, res. Shelbyville pike, one-half mile s. corporation.
Richter Harry, blacksmith, res. 261 s. Mississippi.
Richter Herman, (Western Furniture Co.,) res. 256 Winston.
Richter & Schradluke, grocers, s. w. cor. Illinois and Russell.
Richter Simeon, bds. 146 Huron.
Richter William, grocery and saloon, 416 Virginia av., res. same.
Rickard Henry, bds. Bates House.
Rickards Miss Amelia, seamstress, 314 e. Market, res. same.
Rickards Mrs. Kezia, (wid. R.,) res. 176 n. Missouri.
Rickards Miss Sarah, seamstress, 314 e. Market, res. same.
Rickards Thomas, carpenter, 127 e. Market, res. 314 e. Market.
Rickard Henry, (R. & Talbott,) 78 s. Meridian, bds. Bates House.
Rickard Mrs. Rebecca, milliner, res. 314 e. Market.
Rickard & Talbott, (Henry R. & Charles H. T.,) wholesale hats, caps and furs, 78 s. Meridian.
Rickards B. A., inmate Deaf and Dumb Asylum.
Ricker Wilhelmina, servant, J. Frank, 461 n. Tennessee.
Rickers Andrew J., inmate Deaf and Dumb Asylum.
Rickers John, inmate Deaf and Dumb Asylum.

RICKETTS DILLARD,
prest. J., M. & I. R. R., res. Madison rd., near city limits.
Ricketts W. H., foreman, Journal bindery, res. 73 w. Maryland.
Ricketts William C., carpenter, works 127 e. Washington, res. 314 e. Market.
Riddle Mrs. Sarah, (wid.,) res. w. side Minerva, bet. New York and Brewery.

RIDER B. L.,
photograph and fine art gallery, 16½ e. Washington, res. 708 n. Tennessee. See card.
Rider Israel, Baptist minister, bds. 144 n. Tennessee.
Rider William, gardener, res. 23 Ellsworth.

RIDENOUR JONATHAN M.,
vice-prest. C., C. & I. J. R. R., office 110 and 112 Virginia av., res. n. s. Michigan rd., one-half mile beyond city limits.
Ridenour Henry, teacher, high school, res. 31 w. St. Clair.

Ridgeway J. F., physician, office 88 e. Market, res. 151 n. New Jersey.

Ridgeway Otis N., works 37 w. Washington, bds. 44 s. Tennessee.

Riegger Mrs. Caroline, (wid. George,) seamstress, res. 275 e. New York.

Rielly Hugh, lab., res. 340 Winston.

Rielly Michael, shoe-maker, res. 414 s. Tennessee.

Riemenschnider H., stocking factory, 86½ e. Washington, res. 83 n. New Jersey.

Rien Martin, brakesman, Bellefontaine R. R., bds. 270 Railroad.

Riepple Charles, butcher, res. 158 Huron.

Rifle Abraham, carpenter, res. 127 St. Mary.

Rifle Martin, file-maker, bds. 36 Union.

Riggs C. M., attorney at law, over 45 e. Washington, res. 197 n. Illinois.

Riggs John, butcher, res. Wabash, bet. Liberty and Noble.

Riggs John, cash boy, New York Store, bds. 7 Charles.

Right C. M., pump-maker, res. 230 s. Noble.

Rigley John, stone-cutter, res. e. of east end Michigan.

RIKHOFF & BRO.,
(John G. & Herman R.,) rectifiers and wholesale liquor dealers, and agts. for Finley & Wilder's Toledo Ale, 77 s. Meridian. See card, page 92.

Rikhoff H., (R. & Bro.,) 77 s. Meri dian.

Rikhoff John G., (R. & Bro.,) 77 s. Meridian, res. Cincinnati, Ohio.

Riley A. T., student, commercial college, bds. 444 n. New Jersey.

Riley B. F., clerk, county treasurer's office, res. 289 w. Vermont.

Riley Calvin, student, Bryant's Commercial College, bds. 444 n. New Jersey.

Riley Edward, lab., res. 167 Madison av.

Riley Ellen, chambermaid, Sherman House, bds. same.

Riley Eline J., (col.,) servant, C. Hamlin, n. w. cor. Meridian and Circle.

Riley John, lab., res. 575 Maple.

Riley John H., res. 66 s. Eddy.

Riley Mrs. Melinda, guitar teacher, 42 Kentucky av., res. same.

Riley Patrick, depot marshal, Union Depot, bds. California House.

Riley R. H., coal dealer, 33 s. Meridian, res. 443 n. Meridian.

Riley T., lab., res. alley rear 75 s. West.

Riley William, teamster, res. 59 Eddy.

Rinefelt Henry, lab., res. 264 Union.

Ring Catharine, cook, 30½ n. Pennsylvania.

Ring Mary, servant, at 233 n. Illinois.

Ring John, lab., res. 181 Dougherty.

Ringer Jacob, lab., res. 330 n. New Jersey.

Ringer John Q., car inspector, res. 160 e. St. Joseph.

Rink Sarah, inmate Home of the Friendless, w. s. n. Pennsylvania, beyond city limits.

Rinkle David, saloon, 94 e. South, res. same.

Rinkle Harris, res. 406 s. Tennessee.

Ripley William J., (Elder & R.,) 40 n. Illinois, res. 227 w. New York.

Risnar Albert, tanner, res. w. side Blake, bet. New York and Vermont.

Ritchey James, lab., 275 s. Tennessee, bds. cor. South and Illinois.

Ritchey Mrs. Sarah, dress-maker, res. 22 Douglas.

Rittenhouse George L., egg and apple packer, res. 479 n. Meridian.

Ritter E. F., (Ray & R.,) attorney at law, 24½ e. Washington, res. 415 n. East.

Ritter Frederick, teamster, bds. toll-gate, Madison rd.

Ritzinger Augustus W., clerk, Savings Bank, 38 e. Washington, res. 226 e. Ohio.

Ritzinger F., secretary, German Mutual Fire Ins. Co., agt. Hamburg & Bremer steamer, office 16 s. Delaware, res. 226 e. Ohio.

Ritzinger Frank L., teller, Fletcher's Bank, 30 e. Washington, bds. 226 e. Ohio.

RITZINGER J. B.,
propr. Savings' Bank, 38 e. Washington, res. 226 e. Ohio.

Roach A. C., (R. & Thistlethwaite,) Journal bldg., res. 68 Bates.

Roache A. L., (R., McDonald & Roache,) room 3, Aetna bldg., n. Pennsylvania, res. 613 n. Pennsylvania.

Roach Catharine, servant, 154 n. West.

Roach Charles, engineer, Tate's Sash Factory, res. 297 s. East.

Roach John, teamster, bds. National rd., half mile from bridge.

Roach James, teamster, res. s. s. National rd., beyond river bridge.

Roach Mary, servant, Jacob King's, 217 w. South.

Roach Michael, lab., res. 25 s. Bright.

Roach Milton, clerk, (Roach & T.,) bds. 68 Bates.

Roach Niclas, engineer, Frank Wright's Brewery, res. 25 n. Bright.

Roach & Thistlethwaite, (C. R. & J. P. T.,) book-publishers, second floor Journal bldg.

Roan John, lab., res. 332 s. Delaware.

Roback A. C., conductor, T. H. R. R., res. 26 s. West.

Roback Eli, book-binder, Sentinel office, res. 231 n. Mississippi.

Roback Henry H., brick-moulder, res. 78 Forest av.

Roback Mrs. Sarah, (wid.,) res. 231 n. Mississippi.

Robb Isaac, (col.,) res. Tenth, n. city limits.

Rober Godfrey, stone-cutter, res. 268 s. Delaware

Roberts Benjamin, (col.,) carpenter, res. 243 n. West.

Roberts Chapel, Rev. Mendenhall pastor, n. e. cor. Pennsylvania and Market.

Roberts Franklin, teamster, res. 309 w. Market.

Roberts Henry, marble-cutter, res. 198 n. Mississippi.

Roberts Hezekiah W., marble-shop, Indiana av., res. 270 n. Liberty.

Roberts James L., (col.,) waiter, Bates House.

Roberts Jackson, lab., res. 25 s. Bright.

Roberts J. A., student, N. W. C. University, res. Western av., new city limits.

Roberts Jefferson, lab., res. 265 e. St. Clair.

Roberts John, (col.,) barber, under Palmer House, bds. Pyle House.

Roberts John, lumber-dealer, cor. Indiana av. and Canal, res. 274 n. Mississippi.

ROBERTS JOSEPH T., lawyer, 75 e. Washington, bds. 408 Indiana av.

Roberts Julia, servant, at 520 n. Illinois.

Roberts Leonidas, railroader, bds. 103 s. New Jersey.

Roberts Lydia, inmate Deaf and Dumb Asylum.

Roberts Mrs. Mary, (wid.,) res. 286 w. Market.

Roberts Michael, lab., res. 207 Kentucky av.

Roberts Silas W., lab., res. 286 w. Market.

Roberts Turner W., (col.,) propr. Roberts' House, 66 Missouri.

Roberts William, lumber yard, s. Meridian, bds. 309 s. Meridian.

Roberts William, lab., res. 301 w. Market

Robertson A. M. & Bros., dealers in dry goods, 96 e. Washington.

Robertson A. M., (R. & Bros.,) 96 e. Washington.

Robertson & Close, (J. E. R. & W. A. C.,) Boston Dry Goods Store, 10 e. Washington.

Robertson Fountain, (R. & Bros.,) 96 e. Washington, res. same.

Robertson James H, salesman, 10 e. Washington, bds. 177 n. Alabama.

Robertson J. E., (R. & Close,) 10 e. Washington, res. 177 n. Alabama.

Robertson Mary, servant at 564 n. Pennsylvania.

Robertson William, machinist, res. 223 Union.

Robins Catharine, (wid. Daniel,) res. 213 w. Market.

Robins Charles J., livery, 314 n. New Jersey, res. 316 n. New Jersey.

Robins Frank, boot and shoe-maker, res. 222 w. Maryland.

Robins James, traveling agent, Moody & Bros, res. 174 w. Ohio.

Robins F., Jr., bds. 222 w. Maryland.

Robins J. C., horse dealer, res. 316 n. New Jersey.

Robinson A. M., inmate Deaf and Dumb Asylum.

Robinson A J., traveling agent, Fairbanks' scales, bds. Spencer House.

Robinson Miss Alice, milliner, res. 153 e. Washington.

Robinson C. B., supt. Union Depot, res. 381 s. Alabama.

Robinson C. F., (wid. William,) res. 209 n. Pennsylvania.

Robinson Charles, gas-fitter, 77 e. Market, res. cor. Alabama and McCarty.

Robinson Frederick, telegraph operator, bds. 381 s. Alabama.

Robinson G., painter and glazier, res. 400 s. Illinois.

Robinson Horace, watchman, Bellefontaine depot, bds. 290 Railroad.

Robinson J. B., trunk-maker 29 s. Illinois, res. 107 Massachusetts av.

Robinson J. W., plasterer, res. 339 s. Alabama.

Robinson J. C. inmate Deaf and Dumb Asylum.

Rabinson Jerome, clerk, B. & L. R. R. office, res. 339 s. Alabama.

Robinson John, machinist, Bellefontaine shops, res. 454 c. Michigan.

Robinson John R., carpenter, res. 23 California.

Robinson John L., tobacconist, bds. Ray House, e. South.

Robinson Joseph H., street contractor, res. n. w. city limits.

Robinson Lafayette W., armorer, at U. S. Arsenal, res. 107 Massachusetts av.

Robinson Miss Martha A., teacher, high school, bds. 24 w. New York.

Robinson Martin S., clerk, bds. Pyle House.

Robinson Miss Mattie S., assistant intermediate, high school bldg., bds. 24 w. New York.

Robinson Matthew B., farmer, res. 107 Massachusetts av.

Robinson Melissa, (wid.,) res. near rolling mill.

Robinson Miss Minnie A., dress-maker, res. 107 Massachusetts av.

Robinson R. D., minister, Trinity Church, res. 104 e. St. Mary.

Robinson S. H., night watchman, C., C. C. & I. R. R., res. e. Michigan.

Robinson Samuel M., carpenter, res. 110 n. Missouri.

Robinson Mrs. Sarah, (wid.,) bds. 322 w. New York.

Robinson Miss Susan A., seamstress, bds. 619 n. Illinois.

Robinson T. S., tobacconist, bds. Ray House.

Robinson W. H., engineer, res. 250 s. Missouri.

ROBINSON WILLIAM J. H., supt. Indianapolis Piano Manfr. Co., res. 163 e. Washington.

Robison Anthony, (col.,) lab., res. 420 e. St. Clair.

Robison Elisha, (col.,) teamster, bds. cor. Mariah and Minerva.

Robison Mrs. Francis A., res. 37 Ellen.

Robison G., (col.,) lab., res. 434 n. East.

Robinson James, (col.,) porter, Schooley's grocery, res. Camp Carrington.

Robison Joseph, teamster, res. cor. Peterson and North.

Robison Mittey, (wid., col.,) res. 86 n. Missouri.

Robison Robert W., carpenter, res. 110 n. Missouri.

Robinson W. G., (col.,) saloon, 154 Indiana av., res. same.

Rocap Francis, carpenter, Bellefontaine shop, res. 201 Davidson.

Roche Morris J., shoe-maker, bds. 144 n. Tennessee.

Rockey Henry S., res. 202 e. Ohio.

Rockwell Miss Annie, Rockwell's Dining Rooms, 46 s. Meridian.

Rockwell Jones, (Rockwell & Co.,) 46 s. Meridian, bds. same.

Rockwell Prindle S., (Rockwell & Co.,) 46 s. Meridian.

Rockwell Silas, (Rockwell & Co.,) 46 S. Meridian.

Rockwood William O., treasurer Cincinnati R. R., res. 276 n. Illinois.

Rodam James, lab., res. 409 s. Delaware.

Rodenberger Samuel, carpenter, res. 342 Winston.

Rodenwald Henry, groceries and provisions, 441 Virginia av., res. same.

Rodenwald H. H., clerk, bds. 441 Virginia av.

Roder John, lab., T. H. & I. R. R. engine house, res. Union.

Rodgers W. C., fuel agt., B. & I. R. R., bds. Oriental House.

Rodgers William, works Junction R. R. bds. Wiles House.

Rodibaugh Adam, farmer, res. n. e. cor. Fourth and Tennessee.

Rodius Andrew, barber, works under First National Bank, res. 370 s. Delaware.

Roe Martin, lab., res. 241 s. Tennessee.

Rohr F., printer, H. C. Chandler & Co., bds. 128 s. Illinois.

Roesner Augustus, porter, 14 w. Washington, bds. California House.

Roesener Anthony, Indiana Transfer Co., res. 23 e. McCarty.

Roesner Charles, blacksmith, s. w. cor. Massachusetts av. and Noble, res. n. w. cor. Broadway and Arch.

ROESENER E. H., Indiana Transfer Co., res. 71 s. Pennsylvania.

Roeth Adam, tailor, 207 e. Washington, bds. same.

Roetis Christian, lab., res. 265 Union.

Rogers Benjamin F., switchman, Peru R. R. yard, res. 372 e. New York.

Rogers Benjamin F., tobacconist, bds. Ray House.

Rodgers Mrs. Catharine, (wid. James W.,) res. 30 Water.

Rogers G. M., agt. Connecticut Mutual Life Insurance Co., res. 409 n. East.

Rogers Harry, physician, res. 253 s. West.

Rogers James, lab., bds. 253 s. West.

Rogers John, carriage blacksmith, 123 e. Washington, bds. Hosbrook.

Rogers Jones, lab., res. Helen, bet. Georgia and Maryland.

Rogers J. Newel, cashier Tyler's Bee-Hive, 2 w. Washington, res. 154 s. New Jersey.

Rogers Levi, brick-maker, res. Arsenal av.

Rogers Sarah, (wid. Alexander,) res. 2 Ann.

ROGERS WILLIAM C, assistant engineer Bellefontaine R. R., bds. Oriental House.

Rogers William S., soldier, U. S. Arsenal, res. same.

Rogge Ernest, tailor, res. 335 Virginia av.

Rogge Rudolph, tailor, 335 Virginia av., res. same.

Roll Isaac H., (R., Kimble & Aikman,) 123 s. Meridian, res. 203 n. Illinois.

Roll, Kimble & Aikman, (Isaac H. R , Thomas V. K. & John B. A.,) jobbers in hardware, cutlery, &c., 123 s. Meridian.

Roll Rebecca, (wid.,) res. 351 n. New Jersey.

ROLL WILLIAM H., dealer in carpets, wall-paper and shades, 38 s. Illinois, res. 117 w. Maryland.

Rolland Samuel, (col ,) waiter, Bates House.

Rolling Mill Coal Co., cor. Tennessee and South, David Titcomb, agt.

Romaine Charles, teacher in Bryant & Stratten's Telegraph Institute, bds. 188 s. Mississippi.

Roman Elizabeth, servant, at 49 Indiana av.

Romerill Charles, plasterer, res. 342 n. East.

Ronand John, night watchman, Giesendorff's Factory, res. 30 Dunlop.

Ronand Michael, lab., res. 30 Dunlop.

Ronand Timothy, warperer, bds. 30 Dunlop.

Roney Charles S., brick-mason and cistern-builder, res. 183 n. East.

Roney Emily, nurse, res. 140 n. Alabama.

Roney Michael, lab., res. 131 s. Tennessee.

Rooker A. J., painter, res. 37 Douglas.

Rooker Albert, treasurer, Robert Patterson, bds. 373 w. Washington.

Rooker Calvin F., deputy clerk, clerk's office, res. 778 n. Illinois.

Rooker George, painter, basement, 191 w. Washington.

Rooker John S., painter, res. 144 Indiana av.

Rooker Rudolph, tailor, bds. 349 s. Alabama.

Rooker Peter, saloon, res. 250 w. Maryland.

Rooker S. D., painter, res. 104 s. California.

Roop John A., wagon-maker, works agricultural works, res. 46 n. New Jersey.

Roos Jacob, meat-shop, 137 s. Illinois, res. same.

Root Charles, lab., res. s. s. Lockerbie, bet. Liberty and Noble.

ROOT D. & CO.,
(Deloss & Jerome B. R.,) manufacturers of stoves, hollow-ware, steam engine, mill-gearing, dealers in tinner's stock, 66 e. Washington, foundry 183 s. Pennsylvania. See card, p. 14, adv. dept.

Root Deloss (D. R. & Co.,) 66 e. Washington, res. 441 n. Meridian.

Root Miss Emily, teacher, fourth ward school.

Root Jerome B., (D. R. & Co.,) 66 e. Washington, res. 511 n. Illinois.

Ropkey Ernest, lab., end Virginia av., beyond city limits.

Ropkey Mrs. Aelena, (wid. E. F.,) res. 64 e. McCarty.

Ropkey Louis, lab., bds. Noble, bet. New York and Ohio.

Ropkey Therman, peddler, res. 483 e. Georgia.

Ropp Fred., brewer, bds. Jefferson House.

Rorebrock G. W., lab., res. 433 Virginia av.

Rorgart Anthon, lab., res. 342 s. Delaware.

Rorick Edward, bell-boy, Spencer House, bds. same.

Rorick Thomas, steward, Spencer House, res. 72 w. Louisiana.

Rose Charles, (R. & Leser,) 323 e. Washington, res. same.

ROSE DAVID G.,
post-master, rooms Macy House, office n. end P. O. bldg.

Rose Frank B., printer, bds. 67 Madison av.

Rose Frank, engineer, res. 48 Fletcher av.

Rose John N., shoe-maker, 242 Coburn.

Rose Jennie, bds. 27 s. Alabama.

Rose John M., maufr. Plummer's patent boots and shoes, 22 n. Pennsylvania, res. 242 Coburn.

Rose & Leser, dyers and scourers, 90 e. Washington.

Rose Mary R., (wid.,) res. 49 Rose.

Rosebrock George, lab., res. 445 Virginia av.

Rosebrock Frederick, groceries and provisions, 492 Virginia av., res. same.

Rose Thomas, shoe-maker, bds. 241 Coburn.

Rosenbaum Christopher, teamster, res. 21 Elm.

Rosenbaum Wm., porter, Institute of the Blind, bds. same.

Rosenberry John, tailor, res. Court, bet. Alabama and New Jersey.

Rosengarten Albert, (Merritt & R.,) 32 n. Pennsylvania, res. 31 Cherry.

Rosengarten Louis, dealer in rags and old iron, 33 n. Noble, res. same.

Rosengarten Mary, (wid.,) res. 31 Cherry.

Rosenthal H., (Hays, R. & Co.,) 64 s. Meridian, res. 160 n. East.

Rosenthal Moses, (Hays, R. & Co.,) 64 s. Meridian, res. 229 e. Ohio.

Roshier Adam, termster, bds. 435 n. East.

Rosmire Charles, teamster, res. 70 cor. Cedar and Elm.

Ross A. M., inmate Deaf and Dumb Asylum.

Ross Alfred, carpenter, bds. 172 e. Washington.

Ross Amos P., solicitor, Phoenix Mutual Life Ins. Co., room 3, Talbott & New's blk., n. Pennsylvania, res. 284 n. New Jersey.

Ross Charles, (col.,) lab., bds. 94 Elm.

Ross D. M., (Anderson & R.,) 77 w. Washington, res. 80 s. Tennessee.

Ross Miss Dessah, dress-maker, works 172 e. Washington, bds. over the same.

Ross Henry J., res. 65 and 67 Indiana av.

Ross J. B., salesman, New York Store, bds. Commercial Hotel.

Ross James, painter, res. 58 Huron.

Ross James J., cooper, Solomon Beard, res. 335 w. Maryland.

Ross Jackson, lab., res. 143 n. Bright.

Ross John J., works Junction R. R., bds. Wiles House.

Ross John H., dealer in all kinds of coal, office 24 e. Prarl, res. 294 n. Tennessee.

Ross Miss Lova, lady boarder, over 230 e. Washington.

Ross Mary E., (wid. William,) res. 11 Willard.

Ross Mrs. Mariah, (wid. Isaac,) res. over 172 e. Washington.

Ross Norman M., res. 128 s. Meridian, old No. 56.

Ross Thomas, lab., Tay's stove manufactory.

Ross William, carriage trimmer, 123 e. Washington, bds. Union Hall.

Ross William, works Junction R. R., bds. Wiles House.

Rossman Miss Bell, seamstress, works and bds. 35 n. East.

Rosswinkle George, cigars and tobacco, 281 n. East, res. same.

Roth Bence, salesman, 54 n. Illinois, bds. 261 Massachusetts av.

Roth John R., (R. & Meir,) bds. Emmeneger's Hotel.

Roth Matthew, carpenter, res. 15 Henry.

Roth & Meir, (John R. & Henry M.,) merchant tailors, 207 e. Washington.

Rothschild & Co., clothiers, 34 w. Louisiana.

Rothschild Henry, dealer in ready-made clothing, 125 w. Washington, bds. bet. Meridian and Illinois.

Rothschild Joseph, (R. & Co.,) 34 w. Louisiana, res. Brazil, Ind.

Rothert John, clerk, 333 Virginia av., bds. same.

Rothrock Valentine, supt. Osgood, Smith & Co., res. 181 s. New Jersey.

Rottler F. M., harness-maker, 109 e. Washington, bds. 115 e. Washington.

Rough Austin, machinist, C, C. & I. C. shop, res. 42, on Central R. R.

Rouhette Arthur, lab., res. over 300 e. Washington.

Roundtra Thomas, (col.,) barber, bds. 361 e. New York.

Rouse Hiram J., butcher, with J. Ludlow, 34 n. Pennsylvania.

Routon Galloway F., carpenter, res. 366 n. West.

Rout Thomas C., (R. & Bates,) res. 22 Lockerbie.

Routh Banca, clerk, Joseph Swartz, 261 Massachusetts av., bds. same.

Routh E., salesman, bds. Commercial Hotel.

Routier Mrs. Gusta (wid. John,) bds. cor. Elm and Cedar.

Routier Peter, carpenter and builder, s. e. cor. Cedar and Virginia av., res. 394 Virginia av.

Rouge J. K., student, commercial college, bds. 444 n. New Jersey.

Row John, teamster, res. 239 Bluff rd.

Rowe Benjamin, blacksmith, bds. 287 Indiana av.

Rowe J. J., machinist, res. 38 Grant.

Rowe Samuel P., clerk, at Dorsey, Layman & Fletcher's, res. 284 e. Michigan.

Rowe William, cutter, rolling mill, res. 232 s. Alabama.

Rowe William E., yard master, Indiana Central R. R., res. 230 n. East.

Rowell Mrs. Love T., (wid. Charles T.,) res. 147 n. New Jersey.

Rowland John D., student, commercial college, bds. 726 n. Tennessee.

Rowland John, machinist, Phœnix Foundry, res. 30 Dunlop.

ROWLAND JOHN, watchman and night engineer, Geisendorff's Woolen Mill, res. 30 Dunlap.

Rowland John, student, Bryant & Stratton's Commercial College, bds. 726 n. Tennessee.

Rowland Michael, res. 30 Dunlap. res. 30 Dunlap.

Rowland Thomas, cooper, res. 423 w. New York.

Rowland Peter, miller, Geisendorff's mill,

Rowland Timothy, warehouse-man, Geisendorff factory, res. 30 Dunlap.

Rowland William, works Sinker's foundry, res. 30 Dunlap.

Rouser George, baker, 70 s. West, res. same.

Royer George, fireman, Bellefontaine R. R., res. 214 Railroad.

Royer Jacob, miller, res. 137 Virginia av.

Rozier Aaron, (Langenberg, Vogt & R.,) 244 w. Washington, res. 146 n. Blackford.

Rubush Alexander, brick-layer, res. n. s. e. Georgia, bet. Cady and Benton.

Rubush Meyher S., brick-layer, bds. 424 Virginia av.

Rubush William R., brick-layer, res. 424 Virginia av.

Ruckle N. R., printer, bds. 17 w. Maryland.

Ruckles Jacob, clerk, res. 346 e. Market.

Ruckersfeldt Charles, clerk, res. 183 w. New York.

Rudisil Miss Margaret, artist, bds. 146 n. Meridian.

Ruedy J. J., German physician, res. 15 n. New Jersey.

Ruhl William, groceries, provisions and saloon, cor. Illinois and Seventh, res. same.

Rumann Augustus, saloon-keeper, res. 334 Virginia av.

Rummel J. A., lab., res. 213 s. Tennessee.

Rummel Jabob, lab., res. 162 Bluff rd.

Rummel John A., roller, rolling mill, res. 11 Willard.

Rupp John, groceries and produce, cor. West and Kentucky av., res. same.

Rupp W. F., merchant tailor, 131 e. Washington, res. same.

Ruschaupt August, (Wands & R.,) 81 e. Washington, res. 56 Massachusetts av.

Ruschaupt Frederick, (Wittenberg & Co.,) 37 e. Washington, res. 273 n. Delaware.

Rush Charles, (Gall & R.,) 101 e. Washington.

Rush Frederick P, forwarding and commission merchant, 99 s. Delaware, res. 105 n. Meridian.

Rush Thomas, clerk, 2 Palmer House blk., bds. 85 w. Maryland.

Rush William P., physician, office 32 s. Meridian, res. 85 w. Maryland.

Ruske Henry A., lab., res. 68 s. East.

Russell Alexander W., clerk, p. o., bds. 296 s. Meridian.

Russell Annie E., clerk, p. o., bds. 204 n. Illinois.

Russell Miss Belle, bds. 97 w. South.

Russell Conrad, stone-mason, res. 417 e. Washington.

Russell David, soldier, U. S. Arsenal, res same.

Russell David, (R. & Kasberg,) res. 359 e. Market.

Russell Miss Emma, bds. n. w. cor. Meridian and Circle.

Russell H. C., res. 23 w. Georgia.

Russell James, railroad contractor, res. 121 w. New York.

Russell James M, hopper clerk, p. o., res. 296 s. Meridian.

Russell Miss Jennie, bds. 316 w. Washington.

Russell John S., carpenter, res. 354 s. Delaware.

RUSSELL & KASBERG, (Davis R. & Peter K.,) founders, cor. Benton and Market. See card, page 114.

Russell Laven M., policeman, eighth ward, res. 82 s. Noble.

Russell Lott, (col.,) lab., res. Tennessee, bet. Michigan and Vermont.

Russell Noel V., conductor, Indiana Central Ry., res. 175 s. New Jersey.

Russell Samuel, lab., res. 128 n. Blackford.

Russell William H., foreman, barber shop, 50 e. Washington, res. 212 Vermont.

Rute Miss Trese, bds. 179 n. Alabama.

Ruth Adolph, bar-keeper, 29 s. Meridian, bds. 221 e. Ohio.

Ruth Joseph, engineer, I. C. & L. R. R., bds. 99 Benton.

Rutledge Miss L. E., teacher, ninth ward school, bds. 115 Massachusetts av.

Ruth Louis, bar-tender, Washington Hall Saloon, res. 57 Madison av.

Ryan Mrs. Ellen B., (wid. John,) seamstress, res. 75 s. Mississippi.

Ryan Ellen, dress-maker, bds. 217 e. Georgia.

Ryan Francis, paper-hanger, Hume, Adams & Co., res. 126 Indiana av.

Ryan Francis M., carpenter, bds. 172 w. Michigan.

Ryan George W., lab., bds. Blake, near Washington.

Ryan George W., (John B. Ryan & Bro.,) under 14 n. Pennsylvania, res. 481 s. New Jersey.

Ryan Hannah, dining-room girl, Sherman House, bds. same.

RYAN & HOLBROOK, (James R. R. & H. C. H.,) wholesale dealers in wines, liquors and cigars, 48 s. Meridian.

Ryan James, porter, Sherman House, bds. same.

Ryan James, lab., res. 119 w. Washington.

Ryan James B., (R. & Holbrook,) 48 s. Meridian, res. 158 n. Mississippi.

Ryan John, lab., res. 28 Willard.

Ryan John, lab., res. 278 s. Delaware.

Ryan John, machinist, res. 277 e. Georgia.

Ryan John B., (John B. R. & Bro.,) under 14 n. Pennsylvania, res. 336 n. West.

RYAN JOHN B. & BRO., (John B & George W. R.,) house and sign-painters, under 14 n. Pennsylvania.

Ryan Mrs. Julia, (wid. Anthony,) res. 57 Peru.

Ryan Mrs. M. B., (wid. J. A.,) res. 209 Virginia av.

Ryan Mary, chambermaid, Bates House.

Ryan Mary, servant, 11 e. South.

Ryan Margaret, (wid.,) res. 227 e. Georgia.

Ryan Michael, lab., res. 34 Helen.

Ryan Michael, lab., rolling mill, res. 64 Bicking.

Ryan Michael, lab., Minerva, near Vermont.

Ryan Michael, lab., Bellefontain R. R. shop, res. 358 Winston.

Ryan Patrick, lab., res. 14 Water.

Ryan Richard J., lawyer, bds. 355 n. Illinois.

Ryan T. F., propr. U. S. Bonded Warehouse and wholesale liquor dealer, 141 s. Meridian, res. 355 n. Meridian.

Ryan Thomas, lab., res. over 280 e. Washington.

Ryan Walter, cooper, res. 317 w. Washington.

Ryan William J., porter, p. o., bds. 75 s. Mississippi.

Ryan William, carriage blacksmith, 26 e. Georgia, bds. Pyle House.

Ryland James R., works at 175 w. Cumberland, bds. Ray House.

Rynders J. C. F., book-keeper, J. H. Vagen, bds. 128 n. Meridian.

SABBE HENRY, (C. Schroeder & Sabbe,) groceries, 299 s. Delaware.

Saaf Albert, , lab., res. 103 n. Noble.

Sackett C. O., printer, H. C. Chandler & Co., bds. 44 n. Pennyslvania.

Sackett F. E., salesman, D. Root & Co., bds. 510 n. Delaware.

Sackett William, carpenter, bds. 89 Indiana av.

Saddith George A., fish store, s. Illinois, res. 239 Louisiana.

Sage Charles, attorney at law, 327 w. Washington, res. same.

Sage John, lab., res. 24 w. McCarty.

Saghorn James, res. 125 e. Washington.

Sager William, lab., res. 131 Ft. Wayne av.

Sahn Ludwig, grocery dealer, 142 Ft. Wayne av., res. same.

Sahn Miss Pauline, tailoress, works over 168 e. Washington, res. 142 Ft. Wayne av.

Sahr Franklin L., book-keeper, Stiles, Fahnley & Co., bds. 190 Virginia av.

Sailors, Brother & Co., (James L., Mason P. & H. M. S.,) dry goods and merchant tailors, 197 w. Washington.

Sailors Henry C., book-keeper, Coburn & Jones, bds. Oriental House.

Sailors H. M., (Sailors, Bro. & Co.,) 197 w. Washington, res. 50 Ellsworth.

Sailors James L., (S., Bro. & Co,) 197 w. Washington, res. 50 Ellsworth.

Sailors Mason P., (S., Bro. & Co.,) 197 w. Washington, res. s. w. cor. Ellsworth and Vermont.

Sailors William A., tobacconist, res. 202 w. Washington.

St. Clair Miss Ollie, bds. 139 w. Market.

St. Clair William, lab., T. H. & I. engine house, res. near same.

St. John Hiram, prest. American Horse Insurance Co.

St. John's Academy, kept under direction of Sisters of Providence, cor. Tennessee and Georgia.

St. John's Church, (Catholic,) n. s. Georgia, bet. Illinois and Tennessee.

St. John's Home for Invalids, Sisters of Providence, 125 and 127 s. Tennessee.

St. Johns James, teamster, res. 185 Bluff rd.

St. John's School, n. s. Georgia, bet. Illinois and Tennessee.

St. Mary's Church, (German,) e. Maryland, bet. Pennsylvania and Delaware.

St. Peter's Roman Catholic Church, s. w. cor. Virginia av. and Dougherty.

Sally Thomas, tailor, res. 225 w. South.

Salter William H., res. 222 n. Delaware.

Saltmarsh William L., carpenter, s. Delaware, bet. Georgia and Railroad, res. 155 n. Illinois.

Salskaun Theodore, cooper, bds. 567 e. St. Clair.

Sample James C., traveling agt. Wheeler & Wilson Sewing Machine, res. 52 Cherry.

Sampson William, carpenter, res. 268 s. Illinois.

Sanburn Abram G., painter, res. 176 Blackford.

Sanburn Abram G., Jr., painter, bds. 176 Blackford.

Sanders Carrie, seamstress, bds. 105 s. New Jersey.

Sanders Enoch G., painter, bds. 129 n. Liberty.

Sanders Frederick, propr. brick-yard, end Virginia av., beyond city limits.

Sanders Herman, piano-maker, res. 134 Spring.

Sanders Jane, (wid. John,) res. 468 s. Illinois.

Sanders John, (col.,) white-washer, res. 233 n. West.

SANDERS JOHN E., Cabinet Saloon, Palmer House, res. 185 w. South.

Sanders Theodore, book-keeper, 178 e. Washington, bds., John Mueller, s. Delaware.

Sanders John P., carpenter, res. 282 n. Liberty.

Sanders Richard, (col.,) lab., res. 276 e. North.

Sanders William, (col.,) blacksmith, res. cor. Ellen and Indiana av.

Sandrock Adam, saloon, 134 s. Meridian, res. same.

Sandrock Adam H., saloon, 276 e. Washington, res. same.

Sands Isaac, stove-mounter, res. 231 w. South.

Sands Miss Melvina, tailoress, over 28 s. Meridian. res. 231 w. South.

Sanford Francis A., occupant Deaf and Dumb Asylum.

Sanger Joseph, lab., res. 14 Lord.

Sangerties Foster A., boiler-maker, res. 28 Fletcher's av.

Sansom James J., occupant Deaf and Dumb Asylum.

Santo Edward, groceries and saloon, cor. North and Indiana av., res. same.

Santo Henry, porter, Union Depot, res. 266 n. West.

Sapp W. D., clerk, Spencer House, bds. same.

Sargent F. L., res. e. s. Blake, bet. Washington and New York.

Sater C. C., student commercial college, bds. 44 s. Tennessee.

Sauer John, lab., res. 27 w. McCarty.

Saulay C., harness-maker, 24 n. Delaware, bds. cor. New York and Tennessee.

Saules John, lab, res. 394 s. Delaware.

Saulsbury Percival, carpenter, res. 351 n. Pennsylvania.

Saunders Isreal, freight conductor, C., C. & I. C. R. R., bds. 605 e. Washington.

Saw-Mill Mission Church, (Methodist,) s. w. cor. North and Railroad.

Sawyer J. S., salesman, 52 s. Meridian, res. 170 w. Market.

Sawyers Miss Anna, bds. 201 e. Market.

Sawyers Edward, teamster, bds. National rd., near White river bridge.

Sawyers Samuel, driver, Citizens' Street R. R., res. 16 Willard.

Saxe Charles, currier, res. Michigan rd., beyond city limits.

Sayer Philip, (S. W. Drew & Co.,) res. 431 e. Vermont.

Sayers John, harness-maker, bds. 94 s. Liberty.

Sayers Thomas, switchman, C., C. & I. C. yard, res. 94 s. Liberty.

Sayler Henry B., res. 230 n. West.

Saylor Jackson, heater, rolling-mill, res. 270 s. Illinois.

Sayles Charles F., book-keeper, 6 e. Washington, bds. Pyle House, n. Meridian.

Scalf Peter, farmer, res. National 'rd., one mile w. White river bridge.

Scanlon James, paper-maker, Field, Braden & S.,) res. 261 w. Washington.

Scantlin John M., merchant police, res. 79 w. Elizabeth.

SCARLETT CHARLES E., editor and publisher Ind. State Commercial and Home Advocate, office in Vinton's blk., e. Market, opposite Journal office, res. Lafayette, Ind.

Schackelford John, bds. 297 n. Delaware.

Schad Christian, tailor, over 24 w. Washington, res. 331 e. Vermont.

Schad George, works Cabinet-Maker's Union, res. 106 Spring.

Schad Gotleib, carriage-maker, res. 101 n. Davidson.

Schadel Adolph, brass-finisher, res. 272 s. Illinois.

Schader John A., locksmith, res. 126 n. Mississippi.

Schafer Adam, piano-top-maker, 159 and 161 e. Washington, bds. California House.

Schafer Henry, cigar-maker, G. F. Meyer & Co., res. 289 e. Washington.

Schafer William, porter, Andrew Wallace.

Schafer John B., carriage-painter, works B. C. Shaw, res. over 230 e. Washington.

Schaffer Peter, drayman, res. 567 e. St. Clair.

Schaffner Albert, hostler, 27 e. Pearl, bds. 52 s. Pennsylvania.

Schaffner Charles J., lab., res. 361 n. Noble.

Schaler Frederick, blacksmith, res. 87 w. South.

Schaler Henry, blacksmith, res. 225 s. Alabama.

Schaler John, boiler-maker, res. 129 e. Merrill.

Schaler Joseph, boiler-maker, Washington Foundry, res. 225 s. Alabama.

Schalsebuk M. P., tinner, res. 76 Garden.

Schaneman William, lab., res. 148 Bluff rd.

Schansee Patrick, lab., res. 139 s. Graper.

Schapp Elizabeth, (wid. John,) res. 140 Union.

Scharff Nathan, salesman, Rauh Bros., res. 31 Kentucky av.

Schaub E., saloon, 168 w. Washington, res. same.

Schaub George, shoe shop, 170 e. Washington, res. 221 n. Noble.

Schaub Henry, jr., saloon, 176 e. Washington, res. same.

Schaub Jacob, shoe-maker, works 170 e. Washington, res. 191 n. Noble.

Schaub John, lab., res. 225 n. Noble.

Schaub John, Jr., blacksmith, bds. 225 Noble.

Schaub Peter, expressman, res. 217 n. Noble.

Schauf Faltine, carpenter, res. 313 e. Market.

Schauf Kate, servant, 215 e. Ohio.

Scheele Edward, physician, res. 90 s. Meridian.

Schied Charles, cooper, res. 333 w. Maryland.

Scheigert Frederick, policeman, fifth ward, res. 265 s. Illinois.

Schelbach Wilhelmina, (wid. Godfried,) res. 265 e. New York.

Scheldmire Christian, engineer, C., C. & I. C. R. R., res. 195 Meek.

Schellschmidt Adolph, musician, Metropolitan band, res. 246 e. Ohio.

Schellschmidt Ferdinand, musician, city band, res. 511 e. Market.

Scheltmaer Anton, shoe-maker, res. 375 e. Michigan.

Scheltmaer Mrs. Caroline, (wid. Frederick,) res. 375 e. Michigan.

Schendel Frederick, carpenter, res. 33 n. East.

Schermerhorn F. D., general agt., Merchants' Despatch, 19 Virginia av., res. 548 n. Tennessee.

Schetter Christopher, (S. & Simpson,) res. 283 s. Pennsylvania.

SCHETTER & SIMPSON, (Christopher S. & John S.,) wholesale and retail groceries and provisions, s. w. cor. South and Delaware.

Schener Cooney, lab., bds. 282 e. New York.

Schener Mrs. Elizabeth, (wid. John,) res. 382 e New York.

Schener John, lab., res. 382 e. New York.

Schiau John, lab., res. 116 Stevens.

Schibner Sophia, servant, 252 e. Washington.

Schickendance Jacob, gardener, res. Shelbyville pike, one mile s. corporation.

Schiefselle Christian, lab., res. 15 Bluff rd.

Schierling Nicholas, lab., res. 292 n. Liberty.

Schildmeyer Anthony A., boot and shoe store, 313 e. Washington, res. 375 e. Michigan.

Schildmeyer Fred, merchant tailor, 182 e. Washington, res. 310 e. Market.

Schildmeyer Christian, railrouder, res. 195 Meek.

Schildmeyer George, clerk, 198 e. Washington, res. 310 e. Market.

Schildmeyer Henry, carriage-painter, res. cor. John and Winston.

Schillenberg Frederick, stove-maker, res. 506 s. East.

Schillinger George, lab., res. 161 Spring.

Schillinger George, Jr., porter, 108 s. Meridian, bds. 167 Spring.

Schilmeyer Jacob, blacksmith, res. 343 n. New Jersey.

Schiltmeyer Charles, drayman, res. 39 Peru.

Schindler Mrs. Caroline, (wid. Robert,) res. Court, bet. New Jersey and Alabama.

Schindler Oscar, salesman, 178 e. Washington, res. Court, bet. New Jersey and Alabama.

Schindler Robert, (Greenewald & S.,) res. Court, in rear of 174 e. Washington.

Schissler David, clerk, S. Binkley, bds. 316 s. Illinois.

Schley George J., printer, H. C. Chandler & Co., res. 153 n. Tennessee.

Schley George, commercial editor, Indianapols Sentinel, res. 159 n. Illinois.

Schliebitz Frederick W., watches, clocks and jewelry, 227 e. Washington.

Schloss Joseph, porter, 64 s. Meridian, bds. 223 e. Ohio.

Schloss Sophia, servant, 223 e. Ohio.

Schlosser Michael, brewer, res. 184 Madison av.

Schlotzhaur Adam, grocery and saloon, s. w. cor. Michigan and Liberty, res. same.

Schlotzhauer Valentine, cabinet-maker, works Union Factory, res. n. w. cor. New York and Davidson.

Schmahl Henry, moulder, D. Root & Co., res. 270 s. Delaware.

Schmalholz Casper, bar-tender, Capital Saloon, bds. same.

Schmalholz Rudolph, saddler, works 224 e. Washington, res. 64 n. Noble.

SCHMEDEL & FRICKER,
(H. S. & Jacob F.,) brush manufs. and dealers, 194 e. Washington. See card, page 36.

Schmedel H., (S. & Fricker,) res. 77 Lockerbie.

Schmidt Charley, wiper, T. H. & I. R. R., res. 126 Milburn.

Schmidt Christian, dead animal wagon, res. s. West, near city limits.

Schmidt Cornelius, plasterer, bds. 252 e. Washington.

Schmidt Harold, clerk, 306 e. Washington, res. 133 e. Washington.

Schmidt Jacob, barber, 37 s. Illinois.

Schmidt John, butcher, bds. 272 e. Washington.

Schmidt Joseph, carpenter, res. 294 n. Noble.

Schmidt Leopold, turner, works Cabinet-Maker's Union, res. Wabash, bet. Liberty and Noble.

Schmidt Lorenzo, clerk, 14 s. Delaware, bds. 111 and 113 e. Washington.

Schmidt Ludwig, shoe-maker, res. 128 e. Merrill.

Schmidt Matthew, cabinet-maker, res. 265 s. West.

Schmidt Peter, carpenter, works H. Recker, res. 394 e. Market.

Schmidt Robert, tanner, res. 95 s. New Jersey.

Schmidt Rudolph, wine and liquors, 133 e. Washington, res same.

Schmidt William, carpenter, res. 49 Jones.

Schmidt William, butcher, res. 23 Charles.

SCHMIDT'S BREWERY,
n. w. cor. Wyoming and High, Christian F. Schmidt, propr.

Schmitt Christian, stone-cutter, res. 131 Stevens.

Schmitt Geerge, lab., res. 220 Railroad.

Schmitt George, painter, 78 s. Delaware, res. same.

Schmitt John, blacksmith, res. 50 Hosbrook.

Schmitt Leonard, brewer, res. 29 McCarty.

Schmitts August, cabinet-maker, bds. 65 s. East.

Schmitts William H., carpenter, works H. Recker, res. 153 Winston.

Schmuck Peter, quarter-master general, cor. Market and Tennessee, res. same.

Schmucker Lewis, cabinet-maker, bds. 253 n. Noble.

SCHNEIDER & CO.,
(John S. & Christian Karle,) proprs. Phoenix Brass and Bell Foundry, 26 Union R. R. track. See card, page 38.

Schneider Conrad, driver, beer wagon, res. 67 Wyoming.

Schneider Frederick, belt-maker, 125 s. Meridian, res. 161 s. Pennsylvania.

Schneider John, (J. S. & Co.,) 26 e. Louisiana, res. 195 s. East.

Schnell Mrs. Mary, (wid. Louis,) res. 33 n. Noble.

Schnull Henry, (E. Over & Co.,) 68 s. Meridian, res. 124 n. Alabama.

Schoettle Christian, (S. & Marmont,) 102 s. Illinois, res. same.

Schoettle & Marmont, saloon, cor. Illinois and Georgia.

Schoff Abram, file-maker, bds. cor. Noble and Ohio.

Schoff Margaret, res. n. Meridian, out city limits.

Schofield James B., salesman, 62 s. Meridian, bds. Bates House.

Schofield Nat. M., (Anderson, Bullock & S.,) 62 s. Meridian, res. Franklin, Indiana.

Schofield S. A., teacher, Institute for the Blind, bds. same.

Schofield Thomas, spinner, Geisendorff's Mills, res. 408 w. Washington.

Scholtz Melissa, (wid.,) bds. 392 n. Alabama.

Schomberg George, varnisher, bds. Wabash, bet. New Jersey and East.

Schomberg William, shoe-shop, 23 n. New Jersey, res. 134 Davidson.

Schonacker Miss Clara, (Mary & C. S.,) bds. 134 n. Illinois.

Schonacker Mrs. H., res. 134 n. Illinois.

Schonacker M. & C. S., (Mary & Clara S.,) ornamental hair brading, 134 n. Illinois.

Schonacker Louis, clerk, T. H. &*I. R.
freight depot, res. 134 n. Illinois.
Schonacker Miss Mary, (M. & Clara S.,)
bds. 134 n. Illinois.
SCHOOLEY THOMAS,
groceries and provisions, 523 n. Illinois, res. 520 n. Illinois.
Schoonmaker P. H., (A. Hereth & Co.,) 24 n. Delaware, bds. Pyle House.
Schopp George, shoe-maker, res. 140 Union.
Schopp Mary, res. with F. G. Goepper.
Schoppenhorst Mrs. Mena, (wid. William,) res. 38 Lockerbie.
Schott Charles, lab., res. 525 s. Illinois.
Schove William, lab., res. 270 n. Noble.
Schovedore Joseph, cabinet-maker,· res. 256 Winston.
Schowe E. F., blacksmith, B. F. Haugh, res. 1 Water.
Schowe Frederick, blacksmith, res. 1 Water.
Schowe F. W, carpenter, res. 338 s. Alabama.
Schowe Frederick, lab., res. 350 Virginia av.
Schowe Henry J., lab., res. 9 Water.
Schrader Anthony, works Evans' Linseed Mill, res. 276 n. Liberty.
Schrader August, tailor, res. 219 Coburn.
Schrader C., salesman, 36 s. Meridian, res. n. Mississippi.
Schrader Chris·ian, (S. & Loehman,) res. cor. McCarty and Virginia ave.
Schrader Frederick, (Holley & S.,) 85 w. Washington, res. n. Mississippi.
Schrader Frekerick, cooper, res. 322 n. Noble.
Schrader & Loehman, (Christian S & L.,) grocers, 380 cor. Cedar and Virginia av.
Schrader Rudolph, machinist, works Sinker & Co., res. 332 e. Market.
Schrader William, bar-tender, res. 172 s. Meridian.
Schradeuke John, (Rickter & S.,) res. 165 Stevens.
Schrag Leonhart, cooper, res. s. Illinois, near Bluff rd.
Schrake Mrs. Mary, (wid. Christopher,) res. 253 n. Noble.
Schramm Charles, book-keeper, Spiegel, Thoms & Co., res. 223 e. Vermont.
Schramm J. C. A., book-keeper, res. 223 e. Vermont.
Schreiner M., works Spiegel, Thoms & Co., res. 126 n. Noble.
Schrever ——, porter, Stewart & Morgan, res. e. Washington.
Schrexner William, porter, Stewart & Morgan, res. e. Washington.
Schreyer John, heater Indianapolis Rolling Mills, res. 159 Bluff rd.
Schribner John, teamster, bds. 292 w. Maryland

Schroder William, bar-tender, cor. McCarty and Meridian, res. 173 Bluff rd.
Schroeder Charles, (S. & Sabbe,) groceries, 299 s. Delaware, res. same.
Schroeder F. E., merchant tailor, 121 s. Illinois, res. 219 Coburn.
Schroer William, works 32 s. Meridian, bds. 250 s. Alabama.
Schroyer Charles F., carpenter, 53 s. California.
Schrutz Joseph, lab., res. 30 Coburn
Schnaler Henry, blacksmith, res. 225 s. Alabama
Schucko Charles, machinist, res. 50 Bradshaw
Schuh G., moulder, works 29 c. Georgia, bds. Court, bet. East and New Jersey.
Schugun Patrick, res. 579 Maple.
Schuler Eidel, carpenter, res. 301 Winston.
Schuler George, butcher, res. 124 Bluff rd.
Schulmeyer Fred. W.., lab., res. 109 e. St. Mary.
Schulmeyer Louis E., salesman, Stewart & Morgan, res. St. Soseph.
Schulmier Henry, butcher, bds. 252 s. Delaware.
Schulter Herman, flagman Delaware st, res. 436 s. East
Schultheis John, carpenter, res. 406 s. Illinois
Schultz Henry, cigar-dealer, 112 Virginia av. bds. 176 s. Delaware.
Schultz John, works Cabinet-Makers'Union res. 475 e. Market.
Schultz Mary, servant, 67 n. New Jersey.
Schumm Christopher, works beer-garden, 252 e. Washington, res same.
Schurich Frederick, saloon, res. National rd., w. White river bridge.
Schurr Charles, tinner, 103 e. Washington, bds. on Russell.
Schurr Leonard, watch and clock-maker, 74 Indiana av., res. same.
Schussler Abel, brick-mason, res. 93 n. New Jersey.
Schussler Conrad, watchman, Eagle Machine Works, res. 93 n. New Jrrsey.
Schussler John, carver, res. 93 n. New Jersey.
Schustar John, tailor, res. 521 e. Market.
Schwab Barbara, bds. 235 s Delaware.
Schwab Leinhart, groceries, 235 s. Delaware, res. same.
Schuabacher Joseph, (Heyman & S.,) 41 s. Delaware, bds. Bates House.
Schwader Christ., machinist, res. 124 e. McCarty.
Schwalb Henry, printer, res. McOuat's blk.
Schwam George, lab., Michael's brewery, res. 72 s. West.
Schwartz Charles, salesman, 37 e. Washington, Georgia, bds. bet. Illinois and Meridian.

Schwartz Joseph, (Glick & S.,) 54 n. Illinois, res. 261 Massachusetts av.

Schwartz Henry, tailor, 289 e. Ohio, res. same.

Schwartz Joseph, teamster, res. s. s. Coburn, bet. Wright and East.

Schwaub Jacob, (Munninger & Co.,) 167 w. Washington, res. same.

Schwear Christian, clerk, 576 e. Washington, res. same.

Schwear C. H., (S. & Spear,) res. 376 e. Washington.

SCHWEAR & SPEAR,
(C. H. S. & Fred Spear,) dry goods and groceries, 576 e. Washington.

Schwegel Daniel, collar-maker, res. 201 s. Pennsylvania.

Schweigert Michael, wagon-maker, res. 22 Ray.

Schweinhart Andrew, carriage-painter, bds. rear 299 n. East.

Schweinhart Daniel, brick-layer, res. rear 299 n. East.

Schweinhart Edmund, shoe-maker, 299 n. East, res. 68 e. St. Mary.

Schweinhart Mrs. Susan, (wid. Peter,) res. rear 299 n. East.

Schweinberger William, meat-shop, 329 s. Delaware, res. same.

Schwerluck Bennet, tailor, 356 s. Alabama, res. same.

Schuiche, Charles, grocery and producedealer, 224 Bluff rd., res. same.

Schwomeyer Charles H., groceries and produce, cor. Meridian and McCarty, res. same.

Schwomeyer Christian, drayman, res. 380 e. Michigan.

Schwomeyer Henry, cooper, 308 and 318 n. Noble, res. same.

Schwomeyer William, cooper, works William Schwomeyer, res. 311 n. Noble.

Scellard Mary, chamber-maid, Oriental House, res. same.

Scott Aaron, fireman I. P. & C. R. R., res. 142 s. East.

Scott Adam, (S. & Nicholson,) 118 n. East.

Scott Albert A., salesman, Bates House, res. 472 n. East.

Scott Alice, (col.,) servant at John Ridenour's, cor. Asylum av. and Michigan rd..

Scott Amos, teamster, res. 225 n. New Jersey.

Scott Andrew J., lab., w. s. Tennessee, bet. Fourth and Fifth

Scott Charles A., patent-right dealer, over 32 w. Washington, bds. Commercial Hotel.

Scott C. S., blacksmith, 472 n. East.

Scott Mrs. Drucilla, (col., wid.,) res. Second, bet. Howard and Lafayette R. R.

Scott Miss Fanny, student, Indiana Female College, 146 n. Meridian, bds. the same.

Scott Harvey B., teamster, res. 222 s. East.

Scott James, cigar-maker, res. w. McGill.

Scott James P., (Williams, S. & Co.,) 4 w. Louisiana.

Scott John, (col.,) lab., res. cor. Third and Howard.

Scott John, book-keeper Sohl, Gibson & Co., res. 279 w. Michigan.

Scott John, (col.,) lab., res. 592 n. Mississippi.

SCOTT JOHN N.,
lawyer and city judge, office Glenns' blk., res. 179 n. Alabama.

Scott J. W., (S., West & Co.,) 127 s. Meridian, res. Richmond, Ind.

Scott Joseph, (col.,) lab., res. 229 w. Elizabeth.

Scott & Nicholson, (Adam S. & David N.,) stone-cutters, yard Kentucky av., bet. Missouri and West.

Scott N. H., clerk, C., C. C. & L. R. R., res. 216 e. Ohio.

Scott Kinsley C., occupant Deaf and Dumb Asylum.

Scott Mrs. Mary, (wid. George,) works Journal office, bds. 240 e. Ohio.

Scott Robert H., with engineer corps, on Vincennes R. R., res. 107 Meek.

Scott Robert R., clerk, 109 w. Washington, res. 210 w. Ohio.

Scott Samuel T., agt. Peoples' Dispatch Fast Freight Line, 42 and 44 e. Washington, res. 260 e. Ohio.

Scott Thomas J, carpenter, bds. 222 s. East.

SCOTT, WEST & CO.,
(J. W. S., J. C. W. & J. A. Burbank,) wholesale dealers in china, glass, queensware, fruit jars, lamps, &c., 127 s. Meridian. See card, page 88.

Scott William, fireman, C., C. & I. C. R. R., res. 315 e. Ohio.

Scott William, carpenter, res. 415 s. Tennessee.

Scott Winfield H., clerk, Bellefontaine R. R. depot, res. 260 e. Ohio.

Scotton Mrs. Julia, (wid. John B.,) dressmaker, works 172 e. Washington, res. Tinker, bet. Tennessee and Illinois.

Scovill Mrs. Clarissa, (wid. Andrew,) bds. 353 n. Noble.

Scovill George W., collector, McCreery & Fay, res. 353 n. Noble.

Scribner George B., beer and soda-water manfr., res. 216 Blackford.

Scribner Samuel, sport, bds. Empire Saloon.

Scribner William, res. 307 s. Pennsylvania.

Scudder Mrs. Helen M., (wid. John,) dressmaking, 83 n. New Jersey, res. same.

Scudder Henry, teamster, Hoosier Mills, bds. 391 w. Washington.

Scudder Mrs. John, dress and cloak-maker, 29 e. Ohio.

Scudder John, works Black's livery stable, on Pearl, bds. 70 n. East.

Scudder John, trader in horses, res. 29 e. Ohio.

SCUDDER M. R., deputy city marshal, res. over 77 e. Washington.

Scudder Miss Stephanna, dress-maker, works 83 n. New Jersey, res. same.

Sculley Michael, lab., res. alley rear 75 s. West.

Savick William, tailor, res. 111 n. Noble.

Seamer Conrad C., upholsterer, res. 181 Meek.

Seaman Edwin, clerk, William Sheets, bds. w. Maryland.

SEATON E. A., hats, caps, furs and straw goods, 25 n. Pennsylvania, res. 25 Gregg. See card, page 162.

Seaton J. A., clerk, at 25 n. Pennsylvania, bds. 25 Gregg.

Seaton Lafayette, blacksmith, bds. California House.

Seaton W. D., clerk, at 25 n. Pennsylvania, bds. Pyle House.

Seay Jeremiah, carpenter, bds. 498 e. Washington.

Secker Ferdinand, lab., Henry Weghorst, s. East. near corporation.

Second Presbyterian Church, s. w. cor. Pennsylvania and New York.

Second Universalist Church, n. side Michigan, bet. Illinois and Tennessee.

Second Ward School House, n. Delaware, bet. Vermont and Michigan.

Secor Sidney B., printer, Journal office, res. 27 Fatout's blk., up-stairs, w. Washington.

SECREST CHARLES, justice of the peace, over 45 e. Washington, res. 317 s. Alabama.

Secrest Henry, confectioner, Daggett & Co., res. cor. Hosbrook and Cedar.

Secrest John, lab., res. n. s. National rd.

SECRETARY OF STATE, office new State bldg., w. Washington, Nelson Trussler, secretary, Thomas J. Trussler, deputy.

Security Life Ins. and Annuity Co., of New York, office Blake bldg., w. Washington, W. W. Northrop, general agt.

Sedam Charles, (col.,) lab., res. n. Meridian, beyond city limits.

Seddelmeyer Martin C., salesman, 6 e. Washington, bds. 500 n. Alabama.

SEDGWICK RODERICK, fancy dry goods, 68 n. Illinois, res. 129 n. Mississippi.

Seeber S. S., clerk, Trade Palace, bds. Macy House.

Seeberger Miss Louise, teacher, primary German, ninth ward school, bds. 126 Virginia av.

Sechofer Frank, cabinet-maker, res. 236 Massachusetts av.

Seele Christina, cook, n. e. cor. New York and East.

Seele Henry, works Union Starch Factory, res. 308 n. Liberty.

Seeman Christian, res. 615 e. National rd.

Sees George M., tailor, works J. & P. Gramling, res. 388 e. Market.

Sees Godfried, shoe-maker, res. 320 e. Ohio.

Sees Mrs. Mary, (wid. William,) bds. 136 n. Tennessee.

Segar Louis, peddler, res. 133 n. Liberty.

Segemeir William, grocery and produce dealer, 185 s. Meridian, res. same.

Seger John, wagon-maker, bds. 269 n. West.

Seger J. M., wagon-maker, 178 Indiana av., bds. 269 n. West.

Seibel Philip P., cooper, res. 385 n. noble.

Seibert David, blacksmith, res. 205 e. Market.

Seibert Frederick, painter, res. 297 Winston.

Seibert Hiram, street contractor, res. 143 s. East.

Seibert Royal F., blacksmith, works 302 e. Washington, res. 11 n. Liberty.

Seibert R. S., fireman, No. 2 engine, fire dept., bds. 70 e. Market.

Seibert Samuel M., blacksmith, shop 302 e. Washington, res. 11 n. Liberty.

Seibert Thomas B., lab., res. 11 n. Liberty.

Seidensticker Adolph, (A. S. & Co.,) 14 s. Delaware, res. 332 e. Ohio.

Seidensticker A. & Co., (Adolph S. & A. Noltner,) real estate, collecting and law office, 14 s. Delaware.

Seidensticker Frederick, saloon, 176 s. Illinois, res. same.

Seiders W. H., State agt. for Southern Ind., Aetna Fire Ins. Co., Aetna bldg., n. Pennsylvania, bds. Sherman House.

Seidl Miss Josephine, teacher, primary German, ninth ward school, bds. cor. New York and East.

Seifert August, clerk, fruit stand, cor. Meridian and Washington.

Seifert Mrs. Susanna, (wid.William Cross,) res. 384 e. Michigan.

SEIG GEORGE B., groceries, liquors and provisions, 28 n. Illinois, res. 91 e. Michigan.

Seigrest S., pastor, St. Mary's Church, res. 75 e. Maryland.

Seitz Charles, confectioner, 112 s. Illinois, res. same.

Seitz Frederick, saloon, 117 s. Illinois, res. same.

Seiss C. A. tailor, bds. Court, bet. East and New Jersey.

Self Berry, (Isaac Davis & Co.,) 12 e. Washington, res. 85 e. Pratt.

Sellers Charles H. billiard-keeper, Exchange Saloon, bds. Bates House.

SELKING WILLIAM,
saloon, restaurant, cigars and tobacco, 33 n. Pennsylvania, res. 35 s. Alabama. See card, page 112.
Sellers Daniel E., saddlery and harness, 17 Virginia av., res. 17½ Virginia av.
Sellers John H., propr. billiard room, 33½ n. Illinois, bds. Bates House.
Selman A. G., physician and surgeon, 21 Virginia av., res. 222 e. South.
Selman Christian, groceries, 615 e. National rd., res. same.
Selman John, student, 21 Virginia av., bds. 222 e. South.
Selman Thomas H., bds. 222 e. South.
Sells Michael, stock-broker, res. 176 s. New Jersey.
Semen Charles, carpenter, res. 140 Broadway.
Semen Edward, clerk, bds. 15 w. Maryland.
Sene Mrs. Hannah, (wid. Morris,) res. 398 s. Delaware.
Senior Zachariah, boot-fitter, 71 w. Maryland, res. same.
Senour J., (J. S. & Co.,) 5 w. Washington, res. 115 n. Illinois.
SENOUR J. & CO.,
City Shoe Store, 5 w. Washington.
Senour W., (J. S. & W.,) 5 w. Washington, bds. Pyle House.
Seph Bastian, varnisher, 74 w. Washington, res. 19 Meek.
Seph Mathias, car-oiler, C., C. & I. C. R R., res. 19 Meek.
Seringer L., cabinet-maker, res. 164 n. Davidson.
Sers Martin, lab., T. H. & I. R. R. freight house, res. 124 Meek.
Sers Thomas, lab., res. 118 Meek.
Server Alexander, butcher, res 324 West.
Server Caroline, (wid. John,) res. 29 Grant.
Server Elliott, lab., res. 374 s. West.
Server Frank, lab., res. 376 s. West.
Server Granville, salesman, 64 e. Washington, res. 15 Arch.
Server William W., lab., res. 124 n. Blackford.
Sento Henry, lab., res. 266 n. West.
Setter John, res. 78 Lockerbie.
Seventh Presbyterian Church, cor. Elm and Cedar.
Seventh Ward School House, near cor. Georgia and East.
Sevens John F., boiler-maker, res. 118 Benton.
Severinghouse Carrie, servant, 104 St. Mary.
Sewall Elmer C., salesman, 129 s. Meridian, bds. Avenue House.
Server Albert, night-watch, T. H. & I. R. R. engine house, res. Bluff rd.
Sewer Louis, lab., piano factory, res. 23 w. Wyoming.

Sex H. J., base-ballist, bds. Bates House.
Sexton Miss Rubie H., student, Indiana Female College, bds. same.
SEXAUER EDWARD,
grocery and produce dealer, 125 e. Washington, res. same.
Seybold Mrs. Alice, (wid. Mahlon,) res. 233 e. Ohio.
Seybeld James H., marble shop, Market, opp. p. o., res. 233 e. Ohio.
Seymour Elisha, bds. Bates House.
Shaaf Able, file-cutter, res. cor. Ohio and Noble.
Shackelford J. S., passenger agt., C., C. & I. C R. R., bds. cor. North and Delaware.
Shackelton Joseph, pattern-maker, res. 283 s. East.
Shackley William, brakesman, C., C. & I. C. R., bds. 58 Benton.
Shand Catharine, servant, 158 n. New Jersey.
Shad Gotlieb, wagon-maker, res. 101 Davidson.
Shade Miss Fanny, res. 97 w. Georgia.
Shae James, lab., res. 343 s. Missouri.
Shae Julia, laundress, Indiana Female College, 146 n. Meridian.
Shafer Ann, servant, W. W. Byington, 78 w. North.
Shafer & Barrett, butchers, 92 n. Illinois.
Shafer Christian, lab., bds. 183 w. Washington.
Shafer George W., painter, bds. 83 California.
Shafer Henry, cigar-maker, res. over 203 e. Washington.
Shafer Isaiah, book-keeper, Hill & Wingate, res. Louisiana, bet. East and Noble.
Shafer John, (S. & Perrott,) 92 n. Illinois, res. beyond city limits, bet. Bluff rd. and Canal.
Shafer John, shoe-maker, res. n. s. New York, bet. Blake and Minerva.
Shafer & Perrott, (John S. & Richard P.,) meat-market, 92 n. Illinois.
Shafer William, porter, Andrew Wallace, res. n. Tennessee, beyond city limits.
Shaffer Adolphus, shoe-maker, bds. s. Mississippi.
Shaffer Frederick W., tanner, res. 11 Fourth.
Shaffer Henry, harness-maker, res. Huron.
Shaffer Mrs. Nancy A., (wid. Jacob,) res. over 429 e. Washington.
Shaler Henry, boiler-maker, Washington foundry, res. 286 e. Louisiana.
Shallenberger A., carpenter, res. 468 n. Delaware.
Shallenberger J. R., student, commercial college, bds. 726 New Jersey, cor. Fifth.
Shaltz John, machinist, res. 435 s. Illinois.

Shampay Alfred, porter, Anderson, Bullock & Schofield, res. 104 Indiana av.

Shank Benjamin, auctioneer, res. 62 Bicking.

Shannon Mrs. Sarah T., (wid. Patrick C.,) boarding house, res. 126 e. Ohio.

Share George K., (G. K. S. & Co.,) 408 Meridian, res. 214 n. Alabman.

SHARE GEORGE K. & CO., (George K. S. & George Stetworth,) jobbers in saddlery and coach hardware, and harness trimmings, 40 s. Meridian.

Share Louis, brush-maker, res. 518 e. Washington.

Share Michael, gardener, res. Kansas, beyond city limits.

Sharey Conobs, lab., res. 105 w. New York.

Sharrer David, carpenter, res. 250 Indiana av.

Sharpe James, Bee Line R. R., bds. cor. Noble and New Jersey.

Sharpe John S., clerk J. K. Sharpe, res. 193 s. New Jersey.

Sharp Stephen, engineer I. P. Evans & Co., res. 255 s. Alabama.

SHARPE A. W., tobacconist and smokers' emporium, 28 n. Pennsylvania, res. 193 s. New Jersey.

Sharpe Ebenezer, (Benham Bros. & Co.,) with Fletcher & Sharpe, s. w. cor. Washington and Pennsylvania, res. 564 n. Pennsylvania.

Sharpe C. L., clerk, 28 n. Pennsylvania, bds. 193 s. New Jersey.

Sharpe George, cigar-maker, bds. 122 s. Noble.

SHARPE J. K., boot, shoe and leather manfr., and dealer in hides, leather, oil and shoefindings, 47 and 49 s Delaware, res. on Michigan rd., near Deaf and Dumb Asylum, e. of city.

Sharpe John S., salesman, J. K. Sharpe, res. 193 s. New Jersey.

Sharpe Thomas H., (Fletcher & S.,) s. w. cor. Washington and Pennsylvania, res. 239 n. Pennsylvania.

Sharpless Pennell, (E. E. Case & Co.,) 84 w. Washington, res. 71 n. California.

Sharpner Gotleib, carpenter, res. Seventh, near Lafayette R. R. track.

Shatwell Mahaley, (wid.,) res. 1 Rockwood.

Shaub John, painter, res. 497 n. Alabama.

Shaughnessey John, clerk, 23 w. Washington.

Shaughnessey Patrick, lab., res. 243 Kentucky av.

Shaw Augustus D., switchman, Bellefontaine R. R. yard, res. 222 Winston.

Shaw Miss Belle, bds. cor. Huron and Pine.

Shaw Miss Elizabeth, res. 80 Huron.

SHAW BENJAMIN C., carriage manfr, 26, 28 and 30 e. Georgia, res. 41 Madison av. See card, page 128.

Shaw George W., merchant policeman, bds. cor. Huron and Pine.

Shaw Henry C., coach-trimmer, 26 e. Georgia, bds. 41 Madison av.

Shaw Henry G., carriage-maker, 26 e. Georgia, res. 219 Buchanan.

Shaw John P., clerk, res. 438 s. West.

Shaw Mrs. L., (wid.,) seamstress, res. 753 n. Mississippi.

Shaw Lemuel, lab., res. 400 s. Missouri.

Shaw Lucien, law student with Ray. & Ritter, 24½ e. Washington, bds cor. Market and Circle.

Shawver Alexander, Sr., carpenter, res. Broadway, near city limits.

Shawver Alexander, Jr., carpenter, bds. Broadway, near city limits.

Shawver Amos P., saddler, 20 w. Washington, res. 197 Indiana av.

Shawver Christian, saddler, 9 Bates House blk., res. 297 Indiana av.

Shawver Christopher J., saddler, res. 297 Indiana av.

Shay Florence, lab., bds. 497 e. Georgia.

Shay John, lab., res. cor. Union and Phipps.

Shay Mary, washer-woman, Sherman House, bds. same.

Shay Mary, (wid. John,) res. 162 Meek.

Shay Michael, lab., res. 197 Meek.

Shay Thomas, lab., bds. 497 e. Georgia.

Shea Bridget, servant, 261 Davidson.

Shea Ellen, servant, T. A. Louis, n. w. cor. Meridian and First.

Shea Honora, servant, F. D. Schermerhorn, 548 n. Tennessee.

Shea Johanna, servant, 280 e. Washington.

Shea Josephine, servant, B. Tousey, n. e. cor. Tennessee and Third.

Shea John, lab., res. 228 Winston.

Shea John, lab., T. H. & I. R. R. freight depot, bds. Union, bet. Illinois and Meridian.

Shea Julia, laundress, Bates House.

Shea Mary, laundress, Bates House.

Shea Michael, street contractor, res. 520 n. Delaware.

Shea Patrick, lab., res. 373 e. New York.

Shea Thomas, lab., 358 Winston.

Shea Thomas, (Tchen & S.,) res 358 Winston.

Shead Gotlieb, carriage-maker, work S. W. Drew & Co., res. 101 Davidson.

Sheale Frederick, helper, T. H. & I R. R. shop, res. 37 Henry.

Shean Dennis, lab., res. 72 Railroad.

Shenn Mrs. Ellen, res. s. s. bet. Noble and Benton.

Shear Adam, shoe-maker, res. 23 Grant.

Shear Frederick, teamster, res. 495 s. Illinois.

Shearer John, lab., bds. 191 n. Liberty.

Shearer Mrs. Mary, nurse, Orphan Asylum, res. 711 n. Tennessee.

Shealy Fred., lah., res. 452 s. Illinois.

Sheay James, lab., works U. S. Arsenal, res. near Arsenal.

Sheehan Daniel, lab., res. 237 s. West.

Sheeks David, lawyer, res. 439 n. New Jersey.

Sheets David, grocery, 241 w. McCarty, res. same.

Sheets Harrison H., res. 95 n. Pennsylvania.

Sheets James M., res. 225 w. Washington.

Sheets William, blank-book manfr., stationer and paper-manfr., 79 w. Washington, res. 95 n. Pennsylvania.

Sheeley Eli, res. 453 e Market.

SHEFFIELD SAW WORKS, E. C. Atkins & Co., proprs., 210, 212, 214 and 216 s. Illinois. See card on first page, inside front cover.

Shehan Jeremiah, lab., res. 288 Railroad.

Shehan Thomas, lab., res. 288 Railroad.

Shehan Timothy, lab., res. 72 Benton.

Shelburg Miss Mary, lady boarder, rooms 17 Fatout's blk.

Shelburn Miss Mary, (col.,) bds. w. s. Douglas, bet. Washington and New York.

Shelburn Richard, (col.,) lab., Douglas, and New York.

Sheldon Frank, assistant foreman, Sentinel news room, bds. Palmer House.

Sheldmair Frederick, drayman, res. 58 Peru.

Shall Christian, teamster, res. 575 s. Illinois.

Shellenbarger John R., student, commercial college, bds. 726 n. Tennessee.

Shelley Christian H., express messenger, res. 162 w. Louisiana.

Shelt John, wood carver, Wilkin's & Hall, res. w. Cumberland.

Shelt William W., salesman, 60 s. Meridian, bds. Bates House.

Shelter Lawrence, baker, res. 314 n. New Jersey.

Shepard Abner H., carpenter, res. cor. Merrill and Kentucky av.

Shepard Mrs. Ann, dress-maker, 381 n. New Jersey, res. same.

Shepard Charles, res. 102 e. Pratt.

Shepard James E., clerk, C., C. C. & I. C. R. R., res. 270 s. Alabama.

Shepard James McB., book-keeper, res. 213 w. Maryland.

Shepard John, carpenter, bds., cor. Merrill and Kentucky av.

Shepard John, (col.,) lab. res. w. Center.

Shepard John W., inmate Deaf and Dumb Asylum.

Shepard Thomas, carpenter, res. cor. Merrill and Kentucky av.

Shepmyer Andrew, (Reasoner S. & Co.,) 546 e. Washington, res. in rear.

Sherer Adam, shoe-maker, 34 n. Illinois, res. 23 Grant.

Sheridan Bernard, moulder, res. 243 s. Mississippi.

Sheridan Bridget, pastry cook, Bates House.

Sheridan House, Mrs Charlotte Smith, propr., one square n. Union depot.

Sheridan John, bell-boy, Bates House, bds. same.

Sheridan Kate, kitchen girl, Bates House.

Sheridan P. H., salesman, New York Store, bds. 58 s. Pennsylvania.

Sherling Nicholas, messenger Republican State Central Committe rooms, res. 292 n. Liberty.

Sherlock Jennie, servant, at 156 n. Illinois.

Sherman Elizabeth, (wid.,) res. 95 Oak.

Sherman Gustavus, res. 258 n. Pennsylvania.

Sherman House, opp. Union depot, William Hawkins, propr.

Sherman Leroy, clerk, 21 w. Maryland, res. 321 e. Ohio.

Sherman Paul, harness-maker, res. 62 Indiana av.

Shermer Miss Lena, bds. cor. Market and Tennessee.

Sherrer John, lab., Schmidt's brewery, res. 52 Wyoming.

Sherrer Louisa, dress-maker, over 167 w. Washington, res. same.

Sherrill James, occupant Deaf and Dumb Asylum.

SHERWOOD L. Q., agency Russell's Reaper and Mower, warerooms, 79 and 81 n. Illinois, res. 556 n. Illinois.

Sherwood Solomon T., carpenter, res. 131 Union.

Sherwood William O., (Taylor & S.,) cor. Virginia av. and Pennsylvania, res. 21 n. West.

Shields Aaron, (col.,) lab., res. Mississippi, bet. Third and Fourth.

Shields Elizabeth, servant, 282 w. New York.

Shieds James, cutter, at 81 n. Pennsylvania, bds. Commercial Hotel.

Shields James D., cattle-broker, res. 26 Biddle.

Shields Mrs. Marcella, (wid.,) seamstress, res. n. s. New York, bet. Blake and Minerva.

Shields Patrick, carriage-driver, res. Wabash, bet. New Jersey and East.

Shields Robert, cattle-broker, bds. 109 Virginia av.

Shields Robert, blacksmith, White River Iron Works, bds. 110 w. New York.

Shikk Georgiana, waiter, dining-room, Macy House, bds. same.

Shields William, lab., res. 27 s. Alabama.

Shiler Henry, cabinet-maker, bds. 174 w. New York.

SHILLING & BROTHER, (Ederich & Henry,) chair-manfrs., rear 134 e. McCarty.

Shilling Charles, lab., res. end Virginia av., beyond city limits.

Shilling C. D, trunk-maker, 55 w. Washington, bds. 299 n. New Jersey.

Shilling Ederich, (S. & Bro.,) res. rear 134 e. McCarty.

Shilling Frederick, teamster, res. 487 s. New Jersey.

Shilling Henry, (S. & Bro.,) res. rear 134 e. McCarty.

Shilling Henry, brick-maker, res. 367 Virginia av.

SHILLING R. L., manfr. and dealer in trunks, valises and traveling bags, 55 w. Washinton, and 12 Kentucky av., res. 299 n. New Jersey.

Shilling R. O., trunk-maker, 55 w. Washington, res. 120 n. New Tennessee.

Shilling William, engineer, res. 276 w. Michigan.

Shilt Elizabeth, res. cor. Cumberland and Pearl.

Shimer Caleb D., res. 215 Union.

Shindler Robert A., res. 167 e. Washington.

Shine Charles, cooper, res. 333 w. Maryland.

Shine Margaret, (wid. Patrick,) washerwoman, res. 307 w. Market.

Shipley George G., heater, rolling mill, res. 281 s. Tennessee.

Shipley James, nurseryman, cor. Delaware and Market, res. in Illinois.

Shipley J. J., lab., res. 297 s. Tennessee.

Shipp Joseph P., (Landers, Pee & Co.,) 58 s. Meridian, res. n. Pennsylvania, bet. Walnut and St. Clair, with D. Braden.

Shipp Joseph, piano-tuner, bds. 749 n. Illinois.

Shipp S. M., book-keeper, 78 s. Meridian, bds. Bates House.

Shire Darby, carpenter, res. 82 w. Market.

Shire Philip, cigar-maker, 61 e. Washington, bds. 87 n. Pennsylvania.

Shirley Thornton, (col.,) porter, Oriental House.

Shmalholz John, lab., res. 64 n. Noble.

Shmidt John, cigar-maker, res. 27 w. McCarty.

Shmidt L., brewer, res. 29 w. McCarty.

Shmidt William, peddler, bds. 325 s. Tennessee.

Shockency John, bar-tender, res. 46 Bicking.

Shoecraft Silas, lab., res. 67 Eddy.

Shoef Abel, lab., res. 103 n. Noble.

Shoemaker Miss Amanda, teacher, first ward school.

Shoemaker F., real estate agent, over 49 e. Washington, res. 45 Fletcher av.

Shoemaker George, clerk, 145 e. Washington, bds. same.

Shoemaker John, cabinet-maker, res. 45 Fletcher av.

Shoemaker Michael, works Spiegel, Thoms & Co., bds. 475 e. Market.

Shoemaker Obediah, lab., res. 2 Rockwood.

Shoemire Lewis, res. Ft. Wayne av.

Shomberg William F., shoe-maker, res. 131 Davidson.

Shomphy Alfred, works hardware store, res. 142 Indiana av.

Shanley Jacob, res. 142 s. East.

Shonsy Mrs. Catharine, res. 179 Madison av.

Shopp Mrs. Elizabeth, (wid.,) res. 140 Union.

Shopp George, shoe-maker, bds. 140 Union.

Shoppe William, bds. George Reyeres.

Shoef George, shoe-maker, res. 114 s. Noble.

Short H. N., lawyer, office cor. Virginia av. and Washington, res. 69 n. Alabama.

Short Joshua, lab., res. 412 s. Illinois.

Shortridge A. C., supt. public schools, office Vinton blk., n. Pennsylvania, res. Jackson, near city limits.

Shortridge Ambrose F., collector, res. 198 n. Illinois.

Shortridge George, student, N. W. University, bds. 92 Broadway.

Shoughnessey James, works J. Cahall & Co., bds. 46 s. Grove.

Shoup Calvin E., fireman, C., C. & I. C. R. R., bds. s. Noble.

Shouse Louisa, milliner, res. e. Washington.

Shover Charles E., carpenter, bds. 255 n. Mississippi.

Shover & Christian, (James E. S. & Wilmer F. C.,) carpenters and builders, 278 n. Delaware.

Shover James E., (S. & Christian,) carpenters and builders, 278 n. Delaware, res. 255 n. Mississippi.

SHOWALTER CHRISTIAN, groceries and provisions, 252 Indiana av., res. 258 Indiana av.

Showley Jacob, res. 142 s. East.

Shrader Frank, railroader, res. 193 Bates.

Shrewsbury Samuel, clerk, 34 s. Meridian, bds. Pyle House.

Shroar H. H., (C. A. Gerold & Co.,) piano manuf., 32 s. Meridian, res. 260 s. Alabama.

Shoart William, piano-maker, bds. 260 s. Alabama.

Shubert George, teamster, res. 328 n. West.

Shuckra Michael, railroader, res. 138 Meck.

Shue Wolf, moulder, works 24 e. Georgia.

Shuey Mrs. Malinda, (wid. Jeremiah,) res. 269 e. North.

Shunk Miss Susan, bds. 494 n. Mississippi.

Shultah Michael, carpenter, res. 491 s. Illinois.

Shuls Philip, works Central depot, res. 144 Union.

Shulte Frank, tanner, res. 7 Ellsworth.

Shultz Alfred, groceries and provisions, 332 w. Washington, res. same.

Shultz August, brass-finisher, res. 361 s. Alabama.

Shultz George, blacksmith, res. 32 Henry.

Shultz Elizabeth, servant, 175 e. Market.

Shultz John, lab., res. 471 e. Georgia.

Shuster George, tailor, works 168 e. Washington, bds. 521 e. Market.

Shuvein Anna, servant, 160 s. New Jersey.

Shy Mrs. Eliza, (wid. H.,) res. back 373 w. Washington.

Shy Timothy, lab., res. e. Georgia, near corporation line.

Silley Carrie, occupant Deaf and Dumb Asylum.

Sickels W. W., res. 351 n. East.

Siddall J. P., physician and surgeon, 166 Virginia av., res. 227 e. Louisiana.

SIDES D. T., gen'l agt. Washington Life Ins. Co., office 16½ s. Meridian, res. 37 Fletcher av.

Siedel Miss Amelia, school-mistress, res. 318 New York.

Siedel Mrs. Louisa, (wid. E.,) seamstress, res. 318 e. New York.

Siersdorfer Louis, boots and shoes, 41 e. Washington, res. 187 Virginia av.

Sigel Lucinda, servant, at 523 n. Tennessee.

Sights William, baker, works cor. East and New York, bds. same.

Sikes Joseph, (col.,) lab., bds. 225 w. Ohio.

Sikner Miss Mary, servant, res. 176 w. Ohio.

Silley Joseph D., pump-maker, res. end s. Missouri, near corporation line.

Sillman Thomas, bds. 222 e. South.

Silvers Austin H., blacksmith, 202 w. Washington.

Silvers Mrs. R. A., milliner and dress-maker, 25½ Massachusetts av., res. Market, bet. Canal and West.

Silvers William, carriage-maker, res. over 223 w. Washington.

Simco William, (col.,) carriage-driver, res. 235 n. Minerva.

Simmelink Mrs. Mary, (wid. William,) res. 299 e. Ohio.

Simmonds Lewis D., carpenter, res. 325 n. Liberty.

Simmons Anderson, (col.,) lab., res. 201 n. Minerva.

Simmons H., optician, 43 s. Illinois, res. same.

Simms Charles, (col.,) hostler, Maria, near City Hospital.

Simon A., porter, Holland, Ostemeyer & Co., res. e. city limits.

Simon Fidel, saloon, 211 w. Washington, res. same.

Simon Frederick, grocer, 188 n. Noble, res. same.

Simon John D., tanner, e. Market, near Benton, res. 344 e. Market.

Simon J. P., (Frenzel, Will & Co.,) 104 s. Illinois, res. 344 e. Market.

Simonds Christian, lab., res. 263 n. Noble.

Simonds G. B., gen'l supt. White River Iron Co., res. 552 n. Meridian.

Simpson Elizabeth, servant, 143 n. Alabama.

Simpson Miss Elizabeth, dining-room girl, at 58 Benton.

Simpson Frederick, (col.,) brick-setter, end Fletchee av., beyond city limits.

Simpson James P., carpenter, res. 454 e. Georgia.

Simpson Jeptha E., book-keeper, 14 w. Washington, bds. Pyle House, n. Meridian.

Simpson John, (Schetter & S.,) bds. Ray House.

Simpson John E., assistant supt. T. H. & I. R. R., bds. cor. Virginia av. and Alabama.

Simpson Nicholas, flour and feed, 100 s. Illinois, res. 263 s. Delaware.

Simpson Oliver, lab., res. 78 Lockerbie.

Simpson Oliver, salesman, T. Schooley, bds. 520 n. Illinois.

Simpson Richard, flour and feed, 10 Pearl, res. 325 s. Delaware.

Simpson Samuel, bds. end Virginia av., beyond city limits.

Simpson & McCabe, saloon, 52 s. Illnois.

Sims Charles N., pastor, Wesley Chapel, res. 239 n. New Jersey.

Sims Jacob, salesman, Dessar, Bro. & Co., res. 79 w. Ohio.

Sims J. M., (S., Miller & Hoskins,) Canal, near Kentucky av., res. 423 n. Mississippi.

Sims John M., tar and gravel roofer, bds. 378 n. West.

Sims John, carpenter, res. 394 n. Mississippi.

SIMS, MILLER & HOSKINS, (J. M. S., W. B. M. & R. S. H.,) gravel roofers, Canal, near Kentucky av. See card, page 18.

Sindlinger, Gotlieb, meat-market, 104 s Illinois, res. same.

Single Apton, bottler, 29 s. Meridian, bds. 221 e. Ohio.

Sink Francis C., works Coburn & Jones, res. Wabash, bet. New Jersey and East, n. side.

Singleton William, white-washer, res. 131 n. Bright.

Sinker Alfred P., (Farley & S.,) 136 s. Pennsylvania, res. Western av., near city limits.

Sinker E. P., (Sinker & Co.,) res. 84 w. Vermont.

SINKER & CO., (E. P. S., Daniel Yandes & William Allen,) Western Machine Works, s. Pennsylvania, one square e. Union Depot.

SINKER JAMES M., carpenter and builder, res. 240 n. Mississippi, shop in rear. See card, page 80.

Sinks George, res. 75 w. First.

Simons Miss Tillie, milliner, over 8 w. Washington, bds. 203 n. Davidson.

Sipe J., conductor, Bellefontaine R. R., bds. Spencer House.

Sipe William A., (Bills & S.,) lawyer, 20½ n. Delaware, Hereth blk., bds. Pyle House,

Sipf Murmie, laundress, Institute of the Blind, bds. same.

Sipp Charles A., machinist, Taylor & Chandler, res. 512 n. Mississippi.

Sipp Miss Emma, servant, 430 Virginia av.

Sipple Jahu A., lab., bds. Carey's blk.

Sire Henrietta, lab., I. & C. shops, res. 200 Bates.

Sirp Elizabeth, servant, 175 n. New Jersey.

Sisco Harry C., foreman, Osgood, Smith & Co., res. 445 s. Illinois.

Sitar Fred, collar-maker, res. 278 s. Pennsylvania.

Skeen Samuel F., clerk, 192 e. Washington, bds. 35 n. East.

Skillen James, (S. & Rush,) Aetna Mills, 354 w. Washington, res. 48 n. West.

Skillen Miss Jennie, bds. 48 n. West.

Skillen & Rush, (J. S. & F. P. R.,) Aetna Flouring Mills, 354 w. Washington.

Skinner E., bar-keeper, 101 s. Illinois, bds. same.

SKINNER ELLISON C., propr. Excelsior Dye House, 62 s. Illinois, res. 124 w. Sixth.

Skinner John J., brick-layer, res. 82 Benton.

Skrovluk John, groceries, cor. Illinois and Bluff rd., res. 165 Stevens.

Slack Alfred H., fancy notions, 66 n. Illinois, res. same.

Slack E. F., clerk, over 27 s. Meridian, bds. Macy House.

Slair Christian, boot and shoe-maker, res. 128 Ft. Wayne av.

Slanabell John, lab., res. 512 n. Tennessee.

Slaniger John, carpenter, res. cor. Pearl and Cumberland.

Slate B. F., teamster, Wheatley & McCord, res. 215 Coburn.

Slater Jasper R., mail agt., Jeffersonville R. R., res. 41 Bradshaw.

Slaughter John W., carpenter, res. 41 Grant.

Slaughter Milton, carpenter, res. 203 Meek.

Slaven James, railroader, res. 89 s. Pennsylvania.

Sloan Edward W., supt. American Ex. Co., res. 451 n. Tennessee.

Sloan George W., (Browning & S.,) 7 and 9 e. Washington, res. 486 n. Meridian.

Sloan Frank, lab., bds. 163 n. Noble.

Sloan James K., carpenter, res. 638 n. Mississippi.

Sloan John, res. 280 n. Tennessee.

Sloan Miss Margaret, milliner, Dunn & Feanco, bds. 89 Indiana av.

Sloan Robert, bundle wrapper, Tyler's Bee Hive, res. 230 n. Tennessee.

Sloan Mrs. S. H., (wid. Alfred,) res. 29 School.

Slouch George, (col..) lab., res. n. California.

Slusher Henry, watch-maker, res. s. e. cor. Blake and New York.

Slusher Henry, huckster, res. 239 s. East.

Smalcyergaug John, currier, res. 67 s. Illinois.

Small Charles A., res. 88 Michigan rd.

Small David, res. 89 Jackson.

Small Elisha, grocery clerk, bds. 70 e. Market.

Small Elizabeth, (wid.,) res. 88 Michigan road.

Small F., printer, Journal office, bds. Palmer House.

Small Francis, engineer, McClain, McIntire & Hays.

Small Henry, tailor, 8 e. Washington, up stairs, res. 252 n. Mississippi.

Small Jerome, engineer, I. & C. R. R., bds. 111 Meek.

Small William, salesman, N. Y. Store, bds. n. Delaware.

Smallwood Mrs. Elizabeth, (wid. James,) res. rear 121 n. Noble.

Smallwood William, lab., res. rear 121 n. Noble.

Smelser Frank, (Lines & S.,) bds. 243 n. East.

Smelser James W. (J. W. S. & Bro.,) res. 243 n. East.

Smelser Marshall E., clerk, 212 e. Washington. res. 243 n. East.

Smelser Max, painter, res. 143 n. New Jersey.

Smelser O. P., (wid. Jacob,) res. 112 Plum.

Smerts Jacob, varnisher, bds. 415 e. Washington.

Smidt Ludwig, shoe-maker, res. 138 e. Merrill.

Smidt Nicholas, cigar-maker, 61 e. Washington, res. 29 w. McCarty.

Smith Miss Addie, school teacher, No. 1 Centre township, bds. 173 Massachusetts av.

Smith Adaline, ladies' boarding-house, res. 273 n. Noble.

Smith Albert, lab., bds. 132 Huron.

Smith Alexandria, carriage-painter, works S. W. Drew & Co., bds. one door n. Pattison House.

Smith Mrs. Alice P., (wid. William B,) res. s. s. New York, bet. Delaware and Alabama.

Smith Miss Anna T., dress-maker, 34 n. Delaware, res. 171 s. Alabama.

Smith Miss Anna M., school-teacher, res. 47 n. Alabama.

Smith Andrew, conductor, I., P. & C. R. R., bds. Spencer House.

Smith Athlick, dancing-master, res. 146 Buchanan.

Smith August, butcher, works 221 Massachusetts av., res. 23 Charles.

Smith Augustus, fireman, C., C. & I. C. R. R., bds. 61 s. Noble.

Smith Bella, lady boarder, 36 s. New Jersey.

Smith Benjamin, engineer, Jeffersonville R. R., res. 301 s. East.

Smith Butler K., (S., Harlan & Butler,) res. 279 n. East.

Smith C. B., trunk-maker, 16½ s. Meridian, bds. 385 w. New York.

Smith C. W., gen. freight agt., C., C. & I. C. R. R., res. 325 n. Alabama.

Smith Catharine, servant, 166 n. Meridian.

Smith Caroline, servant, 81 n. New Jersey.

Smith Charles, lab., rolling mill, res. 267 s. Tennessee.

Smith Charles, butcher, works 221 Massachusetts av., bds. 23 Charles.

Smith Charles, agt. soap factory, res. 215 Union.

Smith Charles, lab., res. 126 Maple.

Smith Charles, teamster, res. end Virginia av., beyond city limits.

Smith Charles, overseer rolling mill, res. 326 w. Maryland.

Smith Charles W., oil dealer, res. 35 Kentucky av.

SMITH CHARLES W., Jr., room 5 Yohn's blk., cor. Washington and Meridian, res. 148 n. Mississippi.

Smith Mrs. Charlotte, propr. Sheridan House..

Smith Christina, (wid. Henry,) Michigan rd., beyond city limits.

Smith Christian, (S., Ittenbach & Co.,) stone-cutter, res. 131 Stevens.

Smith Columbus, (col.,) lab., res. Athon, near City Hospital.

Smith Conrad, cabinet-maker, res. 424 s. East.

Smith David, butcher, res. 317 w. Washington.

Smith David, shoe-maker, res. 446 Indiana av.

Smith E. W., lab., res. 64 Grant.

Smith Eben, (Strong & S.,) res. 409 n. Pennsylvania.

Smith Edward, works Junction R. R., bds. Wiles House.

Smith Mrs. Ellen, (wid. Washington,) res. 171 s. Alabama.

Smith Mrs. Eliza J., (wid. Isaac,) res. 153 n. Tennessee.

Smith Enoch H., baker, works 188 e. Washington, res. 11 s. Alabama.

Smith Emma, servant, 144 n. East.

Smith Miss Emma, bds. 316 w. Washington.

Smith F. E., grocery clerk, bds. 372 w. New York.

Smith Francis, (Elliott & S.,) 35 e. Market, res. n. Tennessee.

Smith Frank, real estate agt., res. n. Tennessee, bet. Third and Fourth.

Smith Frank, compositor, book and job rooms, Sentinel office, res. n. Illinois.

Smith Frank, lab., res. 400 s. Tennessee.

SMITH & FOSTER, (J. W. S. & Wallace F.,) gents' furnishing goods, 27 n. Pennsylvania.

Smith Fount P., traveling agt., res. 320 e. Vermont.

Smith Frederick, (Smith & Pfifflin,) 200 n. Mississippi, res. 468 n. Tennessee.

Smith Frederick G., engineer, I., C. & L. R. R., bds. 99 Benton.

Smith Frederick, painter, works Spiegel, Thoms & Co., res 60 Railroad.

Smith Fuller, res. 105 Virginia av.

Smith G. W. B., printer. res. 39 Virginia av.

Smith & Goodhart, (W. Q. S. & B. F. G.,) storage and commission merchants, s. e. cor. Delaware and Virginia av.

Smith George C., harness-maker, bds. 35 Circle.

Smith George, works Frink & Moore, bds. rear 203 Massachusetts av.

Smith George T., traveling agt., Chicago wholesale house, res. 229 n. New Jersey.

Smith George M., drayman, res. 56 Maxwell.

Smith H. C., railroader, res. s. Missouri.

Smith H. H., (Lang & S.,) 146 e. Maryland, res. 42 Forest av.

Smith Rev. Harry, Ind. editor of The Standard, (Chicago,) res. cor. Massachusetts av. and Alabama.

Smith, Harlan & Butler, groceries and dry goods, 199 Massachusetts av.

Smith Henry, bar-tender, 13 e. Washington, bds. same.

Smith Henry W., (col.,) servant, n. e. cor. Illinois and Pratt.

Smith Henry B., freight agt., Peru & Indianapolis R. R., res. s. side New York, bet. Delaware and Alabama.

Smith Herman, salesman, 22 s. Meridian, res. 31 n. Liberty.

Smith Herman, varnisher, 38 e. Washington, res. n. Pennsylvania, outside city limits.

Smith Hezekiah, minister, res. 39 w. St. Joseph.

Smith Hugh H., shoe-maker, res. 47 n. Alabama.

Smith Ira, salesman, 71 and 73 w. Washington, bds. Wiles House.

Smith Isaac, lab., res. n. s. National rd., w. White river bridge.

Smith John, (col.,) lab., res. 43 Peru.

SMITH, ITTENBACH & CO., (Christian S., Gerard I. & Frank I.,) dealers in cut, dressed and building stones. See card, page 6.

Smith Herman, porter, Wood & Boyd, res. 31 n. Liberty.

Smith J. L., salesman, Spiegel & Thoms, bds. Wiles House.

Smith J. H., shipping clerk, 52 s. Meridian, bds. Pyle House.

Smith Joseph W., (S. & Foster,) general agt. Florence Sewing Machines, for Ind., 27 n. Pennsylvania, res. 78 n. New Jersey.

Smith J. W., clerk, 68 e. Washington, bds. Pattisan House.

Smith Jacob, book-binder, bds. 86 California.

Smith Jacob, lab., res. 32 Jones.

Smith Jacob, (col.,) lab., res. cor. Third and Howard.

Smith Jacob, (col.,) lab., res. 751 n. Mississippi.

Smith Jacob W., book-binder, W. & J. Braden, res. 86 n. James.

Smith James, supt. Home of the Friendless, w. s. Pennsylvania, beyond city limits.

Smith James, carpenter, res. end Harrison.

Smith James, works at 175 w. Cumberland, bds. Ray House.

Smith James, salesman, New York Store, bds. Commercial Hotel.

Smith James, lab., res. end Virginia av., beyond city limits.

Smith James, engineer, P. & I. R. R., res. 96 Bates.

Smith James C., carpenter, res. 196 n. Mississippi.

Smith James G., res. 62 Bates.

Smith James H., tobacconist, bds. 183 s. Illinois.

Smith James H., traveling agt., res. 463 e. Georgia.

Smith James H. V., salesman, 5 c. Washington, res. 225 s. New Jersey.

Smith James S., painter, res. 307 e. McCarty.

Smith Mrs. James R., (wid.,) res. 178 s. New Jersey.

Smith James W., school-teacher, res. 368 c. New York.

Smith James M., (col.,) waiter, Bates House.

Smith John, lab., bds. 232 s. Tennessee.

Smith John, carpenter, res. 11 Dacotah.

Smith John, minister, Baptist Church, res. 104 Massachusetts av.

Smith John, farmer, res. National rd., one mile from White river bridge.

Smith John, works street car stables, res. 72 Fayette.

Smith John, (col.,) lab., res. Second, bet. Howard and Lafayette R. R.

Smith John, (col.,) bds. 66 Douglas alley.

Smith John, brick-moulder, bds. end Virginia av., beyond city limits.

Smith John, blacksmith, bds. cor. Cumberland and Pearl.

Smith John C., conductor, Indianapolis & Cincinnati R. R., res. 171 s. New Jersey.

Smith John C., carpenter, res. 86 California.

Smith John C., agt. life ins., res. 229 n. New Jersey.

Smith John G., blacksmith, Pennsylvania, bet. Washington and Maryland, res. 162 n. New Jersey.

Smith John W., porter, 56 and 58 e. Washington, res. 62 e. Bates.

Smith John W., clerk, Quaker Store, bds. Pattison House.

Smith Jonathan, printer, Journal office, bds. Circle Restaurant.

Smith Jordan, (col.,) lab., res. Tennessee, bet. Michigan and Vermont.

Smith Joseph, machinist, res. 34 Elm.

Smith Joseph, fruit stand, s. w. cor. Meridian and Washington, res. same.

Smith Joseph, res. 409 n. Pennsylvania.

Smith Josiah, real estate agt., 16½ s. Meridian, res. 385 w. New York.

Smith Julius H. C., book-binder, res. 329 n. Illinois.

Smith Kate, ladies' boarding house, 251 n. Liberty.

Smith L., porter, Bellefontaine R. R. office, res. 72 Davidson.

Smith Peter, cabinet-maker, res. 394 e. Market.

Smith Mrs. Lizzie, millinery and dressmaking, 40 s. Illinois, bds. Pyle House.

Smith Miss Lizzie J., ladies' boarding house, 51 n. Douglas alley.

Smith Martin, works at 175 w. Cumberland, bds. Harrison, near Virginia av.

Smith Mrs. Margaret, (wid. George,) res. rear 203 Massachusetts av.

Smith Mrs. Martha, (wid.,) res. 162 n. Mississippi.

Smith Mrs. Mary, (wid. John,) bds. 378 w. Washington.

Smith Mary E., (wid. Samuel,) res. 394 s. West.

Smith Mary G., cook, at 204 n. Illinois.

Smith Mrs. Mary, (wid. O. H.,) res. 75 w. Ohio.

Smith Marion, lab., res. 572 w. North.

Smith Miss Mattie, salesman, Quaker Store, res. 34 n. Delaware.

Smith Maranda, (col.,) servant, 415 n. East.

Smith Millie, (col., wid,) bds. w. s. Douglas, bet. Washington and New York.

Smith Miss Mollie, servant, 145 s. New Jersey.

Smith Nathaniel, tanner, res. 368 e. New York.

SMITH N. R. & CO., (Morton R. S. & George A. Eaton,) dry goods, Trade Palace, 26 and 28 w. Washinton. See card, page i and front stencil.

Smith Norton R., (N. R. Smith & Co.,) 26 and 28 w. Washington, bds. Bates House, res. Brooklyn, N. Y.

Smith Patrick, boss, rolling mill, res. 232 s. Tennessee.

Smith Robert, (col.,) lab., bds. cor. Seventh and Lafayette R. R. track.

Smith Robert A., printer, Journal office, bds. 69 w. Market.

Smith Robert C., bds. 145 Mississippi.

Smith R. L., wholesale trunk factory, 16½ s. Meridian, res. 385 w. New York.

Smith Mrs. S. P., (wid. James.)

Smith Mrs. Sarah E., bds. 73 n. Illinois.

Smith Sarah A., res. Center.

Smith Mrs. Sarah, (wid.,) res. 191 n. New Jersey.

Smith Sarah A., tailoress, res. 14 n. Mississippi.

Smith Mrs. Sarah, matron, Home of the Friendless, w. s. n. Pennsylvania, beyond city limits.

Smith Samuel, paper carrier, res. 22 s. East.

Smith Samuel, shoe-maker, 28 s. West, bds. same.

Smith Samuel F., (Osgood, S. & Co.,) res. 30 w. Maryland.

Smith Samuel S., tobacconist, res. 2 Union.

Smith Samuel, (col.,) lab., res. 86 n. Missouri.

Smith Sophia, (wid.,) res. Bates, near corporation line.

Smith Sophia, (wid.,) res. 148 e. Pratt.

Smith Squire, cooper, res. 14 s. Mississippi.

Smith Thomas, employe I., C. & L. R. R., bds. 162 n. Mississippi.

Smith Thomas, bds. 232 s. Tennessee.

Smith Timothy, res. 266 s. Tennessee.

Smith Walter S., student, N. W. Christian University, bds. 279 n. East.

Smith William, book-binder, res. 162 n. Mississippi.

Smith William, conductor, I., C. & L. R. R., bds. Sherman House.

Smith William, 43 s. Delaware.

Smith William, wagon-maker, res. s. s. Bates, bet. Cady and Hedge.

Smith William, butcher, 221 Massachusetts av., res. 23 Charles.

Smith William, blacksmith, B. F. Haugh, res. 320 n. Alabama.

Smith William, night watch, I., C. & L. R. R. shops, res. Bates.

Smith William, retired merchant tailor, res. 97 n. Delaware.

SMITH W. A., saloon, 40 w. Louisiana, bds. Sheridan House.

Smith W. C., bds. Oriental House.

Smith William C., harness-maker, 24 n. Delaware, bds. 341 n. Alabama.

Smith William H., book-keeper, Mooney & Co., res. 162 n. New Jersey.

Smith William J., tobacconist, bds. 2 Union.

Smith Mrs. W. J., (wid.,) bds. 372 w. New York.

Smith W. L., clerk, 68 e. Washington, bds. 39 Virginia av.

Smith W. P., carpenter, bds. 111 w. South.

Smith William P., deputy county surveyor, bds. Michigan rd., n. of corporation line.

Smith William S., clerk, McDonald's coal and lime yard, res. 619 n. Illinois.

Smith William W., railroader, res. 203 s. Missouri.

Smith William Q., Jr., bds. 131 e. Merrill.

Smith William Q., (S. & Goodhart,) res. 180 n. East.

Smither Henry C., salesman, 76 w. Washington, res. 368 n. Mississidpi.

Smither J. W., (Daggett & Co.,) 26 s. Meridian, res. 34 w. North.

Smither John, res. 184 n. Tennessee.

Smithers Theodore F., messenger, Merchants' Union Express, bds. 184 n. Tennessee.

SMITHMYER JOHN L., architect and U. S. patent agt., Vinton's blk., opp. p. o., res. Bates House. See card, page 44.

Smithson Mrs. Rosanna, (wid.,) res. e. s. Blake, bet. Washington and New York.

Smitz Jacob, clothes dyer, 39 w. Georgia, res. same.

Smock E. O., photographer, res. Bradshaw, beyond city limits.

Smock George, auctioneer, res. 40 n. East.

Smock H. A., painter, bds. Oriental House.

Smock Marcellus L. J., driver, Merchants' Union Express Co., res. 206 Meek.

Smock Mrs. Martha, (wid. Abraham,) dress-maker, res. 12 Fatout's blk.

Smock Newton, express messenger, Merchants' Union Express Co., res. 79 n. New Jersey.

Smock Richard T., works State Factory, res. 320 w. Washington.

Smock William, lab., res. 117 s. Noble.

Smock Richard M., deputy clerk, county clerk's office, res. on Fall creek pike.

Smock Samuel, auctioneer, res. 36 n. New Jersey.

Smock Miss Sarah C., student, Baptist Institute, bds. 233 e. Michigan.

SMOCK WILLIAM C., clerk, Marion county, office court house square, res. 233 e. Michigan.

Smock William H., brakesman, Bellefontaine R. R., res. 344 n. Noble.

Snell Lewis, tail sawyer, at Weishmeyer's mill, bds. rear 287 n. Noble.

Snider A. J., bds. end Virginia av., beyond city limits.

Snider Charles R., clerk, W. H. Snider's, cor. South and East.

Snider Charles D., clerk, W. H. Snider, cor. South and East.

Snider D. W., res. end Virginia av., beyond corporation line.

Snider George W., book-keeper, Anderson, Bullock & Schofield, bds. Pyle House.

Snider Power, lab., res. cor. McCarty and Madison av.

Snider William H., druggist, cor. South and East, res. same.

Snow Mrs. Elizabeth, (wid. William,) res. e. end e. Michigan.

Snow William S., machinist, res. 327 n. New Jersey.

Snowden Ellen, bds. Rev. B. F. Foster, 320 n. Illinois.

Snyder Adam, porter, D. Root & Co., res. 106 e. St. Mary.

Snyder Charles, grocer, res. 85 Bradshaw.

Snyder C., porter, 91 e. Washington.

Snyder Conrad, carpenter, res. 247 n. Liberty.

Snyder David E., (S. & Hays,) general agt., New England Mutual Life Ins. Co., of Boston, Mass., 17 n. Meridian.

Snyder Fred. M , machinist, Greenleaf, res. 244 s. Alabama.

SNYDER & HAYS, (David E. S. & Isaac C. H.,) Fire and Life Insurance agts., 17 n. Meridian.

Snyder John, clerk, 31 s. Illinois, bds. 24 w. Georgia.

Snyder John F., carpenter, res. 508 n. Mississippi.

Snyder Mrs. L. C., milliner and dressmaker, res. 508 n. Mississippi.

Snyder Maria, (wid. John,) res. National rd., half mile from bridge.

Snyder Michael, lab., res. Kansas, s. city limits.

Snyder Nicholas, lab., res. 31 Buchanan.

Snyder Peter, lab., res. 132 e. St. Joseph.

Snyder Samuel, foreman, 25 w. Washington, bds. 35 w. Georgia.

Snyder Stephen, bds. 437 s. Illinois.

Sobbe Charles, carpenter, Stelhorn & Neeman, res. s. e. Winston and Michigan.

Sobbe Henry, carpenter, works Stelhorn & Neeman, bds. 231 Davidson.

Socks Philip, carter, res. 70 s. California.

Socwell H. M., grocer, 232 e. Washington, res. 266 e. Market.

Soehner Charles, Sr., res. 90 n. Illinois.

Soehner Charles, Jr., clerk, 131 s. Meridian, res. 90 n. Illinois.

Sogemeier August, grocery, cor. Ray and Meridian, bds. same.

Sohl, Gibson & Co., (Levi S., David G. & Alfred J. Sohl,) manfs. White Rose and Bank Mills flour, 352 w. Washington.

Sohl Levi, (S., Gibson & Co.,) res. cor. West and Michigan.

Solomon Abraham, bds. 172 n. New Jersey.

Solomon Charles, cigar dealer, 25 s. Illinois, res. same.

Solomon Henry, cigar dealer, 25 s. Illinois, res. same.

Solomon Joseph, (J. & M. S.) 25 s. Illinois, res. 73 Kentucky av.

Solomon J. & M.) loan office, 25 s. Illinois.

Solomon Morris, (J. & M. S.,) 25 s. Illinois, res. 172 n. New Jersey.

Solomon Sarah, servant, Dr. Bobbs, beyond city limits.

Sommer Ludwig, works Cabinet-Maker's Union, bds. 518 e. Washington.

Sommerlad Christopher, varnisher, Speigle, Thoms & Co., res. 315 s. Delaware.

Sonderegger Frank, painter, res. 215 n. Noble.

Sonnefield W., teamster, res. 66 s. Noble.

Soper S. R., trading merchant, res. 90 s. Meridian.

Soule Charles E., compositor, Sentinel news room, res. Blake, bet. Ohio and New York.

Soup Edward, cabinet-maker, res. 242 Bluff rd.

Sourbeer Columbus, moulder, bds. 169 s. Tennessee.

SOUTH SIDE LIVERY AND SALE STABLES, cor. South and Illinois, S. & L. W. Hetselgesser, props.

Southard Albert B., conductor, I., P. & C. R. R., res. Peru.

Southard J. P., book-keeper, res. 148 e. Vermont.

Southard Macy, gen'l ticket agt , I., P. & C. R. R., office, 101 e. Washington.

Southard Matthew R., retired merchant, res. 80 w. St. Clair.

Southart James W., carpenter, res. 123 Meek.

Southern Christian, res. 243 w. McCarty.

Southworth P. T., patent-right dealer, bds. Wiles House.

Spades M. H., notions, white goods, hosiery, and trimmings.

Spahr Frank L., book-keeper, 131 s. Meridian, bds. 190 Virginia av.

Spann John M., (John S. Spann & Co.,) 2 Brown's blk., res. 163 n. Pennsylvania.

SPANN JOHN S. & CO., (John S. S., John Carter & John M. Spann,) real estate brokers, room 2 Brown's blk., n. Pennsylvania.

Spann Mrs. Sarah J., (wid.,) boarding house, 240 e. Ohio.

Spar William, teamster, res. 326 w. Washington.

Sparks William, res. 8 cor. Noble and Fletcher av.

Spaulding George, (col.,) lab., res. Douglas alley.

SPAULDING JOHN L., propr. City Laundry and Shirt Manufactory, 22 and 24 s. New Jersey. See card, adv. dept., page 18.

Spaulding Ralph, (col.,) lab., res. 300 w. Market.

Speake Mrs. Jane, (wid.,) res. 67 w. New York.

Spears Sarah, (col.,) res. 142 Douglas.

Speckman Henry, tobacconist and cigar dealer, 108 s. Illinois, res. same.

Speer H. P., (James & S.,) 136 s. Meridian, res. 333 s. Alabama.

Speer Miss Mary, student, Indiana Female College, 146 n. Meridian, bds. same.

Spehn Andrew, lab., res. 203 Union.

Spellman Frederick, works starch factory, bds. n. Noble, near New York.

Spellman John, merchant's police, res. 350 Spring.

Spencer B. F., clerk 192 e. Washington, res. over 188 e. Washington.

Spencer C. F., salesman, Tyler's Bee Hive, bds. 40 s. Illinois.

Spencer Charles, (col.,) works s. e. cor. Washington and Meridian, bds. 225 n. Tennessee.

Spencer Cassius C., turner W. C. Burk's factory, bds. 254 n. Tennessee.

Spencer Miss Emma F., attending Indiana Female College, bds. 78 w. North.

SPENCER HOUSE, cor. Illinois and Louisiana, w end Union depot, J. W. Canan, propr.

Spencer James. (col.,) eating saloon, s. e. cor. Washington and Meridian, res. 225 n. Tennessee.

Spencer Milton, grocer, 192 e Washington, bds. 224 e. Market.

Spencer Philip, bar-tender, 252 e. Washington, bds same.

Spencer Samuel, clerk, H. M. Socwell, bds. 266 e. Market.

Spencer Samuel, (col.,) works s. e. cor. Washington and Meridian, bds. 225 n. Tennessee.

Spencer Stephen, hatter, res. 359 s. Alabama.

Spencer William, soldier, U. S. Arsenal, res. same.

Spencer William, (col.,) lab., res. alley, bet. Fourth and Fifth, near Lafayette R. R.

Spencer Belle, (wid.,) bds. 201 Meek.

Speth Morris, carpenter, works 127 e. Maryland, bds. 314 e. Market.

Spicer August, breweryman, res. 152 Madison av.

Spicer Albert, bar-keeper, bds. Commercial Hotel.

Spicer Alfred S., clerk, bds. 57 and 59 n. Davidson.

Spicer B. M. & Co., (Broomfield M. S. & ——,) real estate agents, over 32 w. Washington.

Spicer Broomfield M., (B. M. S. & Co.,) over 32 w. Washington, res. 57 and 59 n. Davidson.

Spicer Edward M., carpenter and builder, bds. 57 and 59 n. Davidson.

Spier Frederick, (S. & Schwear,) res 580 e. Washington.

Spiegel Augustus, (S., Thoms & Co.,) res. 219 n. Liberty.

Spiegel Christian, (S. & Thoms,) s. East· res. 310 n. East.

Spiegel Edward, cabinet-maker, Spiegel & Thoms, bds. 310 n. East.

Spiegel Frank, bds. 310 n. East.

SPIEGEL, THOMS & CO., (Christian S., Augustus S., Frederick T. and Henry Frank,) wholesale and retail furniture manfrs. and dealers, 71 and 73 w Washington, factory s. East. See card, adv. dept., page 12.

Spinden Fred., occupant Deaf and Dumb Asylum.

Spiries Dolfare, (col.,) carriage-driver, res. 27 Dunlop.

Spittle Joseph, machinist, Bellefontaine shop, res. 139 Davidson.

Spitzfadden Peter, meat market, 97 e. Washington, res. 252 s. Delaware.

Spitznager L., barber, res. 154 Blu'l rd.

Splan Jonas, teamster, res. 89 s. West.

Splan Michael, lab., res. 95 s. West.

Splann Timothy, lab., res. 365 e Market.

Splann Timothy, cartman, 24 e. Maryland, res. 77 s. West.

Splan Thomas, lab., res. 342 Winston.

Sponable Mrs. Mary J., res. 175 n. Tennessee.

Sponsel Courald, brewer, Madison rd., near city limits, res. same.

Sponsel Henry, groceries, 353 s. Delaware, res. same.

Spooner Gen. Benjamin J., U. S. Marshal for Indiana, room 6 p. o. bldg, res. Lawrenceburg, Ind.

Spooner John C., deputy U. S. Marshal, room 6 p. o. bldg, res. Lawrenceburg, Ind.

Sprague Melvin, carpenter, res. 325 n. Pennsylvania.

Sprang Adam, stone-cutter, res. 128 n. Liberty.

Spratt J. E., clerk, cor. Tennessee and New York, res. 22 Lockerbie.

Spratt Simon, watch-maker, 14 n. Pennsylvania, bds. 84 Massachusetts av.

Spray Miss Jennie, saleswoman, 34 w. Washington, res. 91 s. Pennsylvania.

Spray Joseph, driver, Indiana Transfer Co., res. 91 s. Pennsylvania.

Spray Miss Lizzie, saleswoman, 34 w. Washington, res. 91 s. Pennsylvania.

Sprincel J., peddler, bds. 375 s. Tennessee.

Springs Edward, (col.,) lab., res. 350 w. North.

Springer David, carpenter, shop 260 Massachusetts av, res. 13 Chatham.

Springer E., carpenter, bds. 13 Chatham.

Springer Howard, porter, 29 w. Washington, res. 47 Ft. Wayne av.

Springer James E., agt. life insurance, res. 115 Meek.

Springer John, pattern-maker, Root's foundry, res. 140 s. East.

Springer M. B., moulder and foundryman, 159 and 161 e. Washington, res. 131 Meek.

Springer W. H., candy-maker, res. 22 w. North.

Springsteen Abram, brick-mason, res. 268 e. Market.

Springsteen J. & Son., painters, 216 e. Washington, res. 117 Spring.

Springsteen Jefferson, deputy marshal, Union depot, res. 117 Spring.

Springsteen John, painter, res. 117 Spring.

Springsteen Jacob, Jr., painter, bds. 117 Spring.

Sproudel George, tobacconist, res. 11 Ellsworth.

Sproule James E., res. 32 s. Mississippi.

Sproule Robert S., associate editor Daily and Weekly Sentinel, over 16 e. Washington.

Sproule William K., book-keeper, Rikhoff & Bro., res. 92 s. Mississippi.

Spurgeon Joseph, painter, res. 185 n. Liberty.

Spurgeon Robert S., clerk, E. B. Martindale, res. 185 n. Liberty.

Srochn George C., clerk, res. 26 Fayette.

Sroube John A., carpenter, res. 23 Fletcher av.

Staats George, supt. Odd Fellows' Hall, res. 10 c. Michigan.

Stabler Michael, teamster, res. 133 Spring.

Stacy Henry, supt. gas-works, res. 155 s. Delaware.

STACY M. D.,
watch-maker and jeweler, 36 e. Washington, res. 77 Massachusetts av.

STACY MILTON H.,
finisher, Merritt & Coughlin's Woolen Factory, res. w. end Washington.

Stafer John, railroader, res. 42 s. Liberty.

Stafford Daniel, (col.,) engineer, res. 41 n. Geisendorff

Stager Jacob, lab., res. Court, bet. Alabama and New Jersey.

Stagg Charles W., attorney at law and notary, Yohn's blk., res. 267 w. Vermont.

Stagg Mrs. E. P., (wid.) res. 146 w. New York.

Stagg John R., agt. Osgood & Smith, res. 238 s. Alabama.

Stahl Louis, painter, res. 263 s. Delaware, up-stairs.

Stahlhut Frederick, saloon, 8 s. Delaware, res. 664 n. Tennessee.

Stahlhut Frederick, carpenter, res. 228 Railroad.

Stake Charles, engineer, C. C. & I. C. R. R. res. 33 Meek.

Stake John, grinder, last factory, bds. 65 s. East.

Stake Joseph, painter, res. 21 Meek.

Stakeley Benjamin, box factory, 195 e. Washington, res. 164 Winston.

Stallard Clara, (wid. Dr. W. H.,) res. 339 Virginia av.

Stallberg August, hats and caps, 218 Virginia av., res. same.

Stanbaugh M. C., inmate Deaf and Dumb Asylum.

Stanbridge William, cigar-maker, bds. 44 w. Maryland.

Standon Thomas, lab., res. Eighth, bet. Knox and Lenox.

Stanly Mrs. H. M., (wid.,) midwife, res. e. s. Blake, bet. Washington and New York.

Stanridge George L. K., carpenter, bds. 89 n. Delaware.

Stanridge Henry J., boarding-house, 89 n. Delaware.

Stanton Ambrose P., (S. & Manlove,) 14 n. Delaware, Langdale's bldg., res. 111 Indiana av.

Stanton Charles F., carpenter, res. 177 Indiana av.

STANTON & MANLOVE,
(A. P. S. & W. R. M.,) attorneys at law, 14 n. Delaware.

Stanton P., railroader, res. 14 Buchanan.

Staples Harrison, (col.,) lab., res. 181 w. Elizabeth.

Staples Joshua, civil engineer, Vincennes R. R., res. 70 n. Mississippi.

Stapp Henry, (col.,) teamster, res. Wabash, bet. New Jersey and East.

Stapp J. H., real estate and collecting agency, 12 s. Pennsylvania, res. cor. Tennessee and Sixth.

Stapp Thomas B., res. s. e. cor. Mississippi and Fifth.

Star Union Line, 85 Virginia av., S. F. Gray, agt.

Starbuck I., brick-layer, bds. 317 Indiana av

Starch William, groceries, cor. Blake and Elizabeth, res. same.

Stark Christopher, wagon-maker, res. 96 s. East.

Stark Miss Fanny, music-teacher, bds. cor. Massachusetts av. and Alabama.

Stark Herman, shoe-maker, res. rear 230 s. New Jersey.

Stark John, last-maker, bds. 65 s. East.

Stark Mrs., (wid.,) res. cor. Massachusetts av. and Alabama.

Starlin Agnes, (col.,) servant, 141 s. New Jersey.

Starling Mrs. S. S., teacher of painting and drawing, Indiana Female College, 146 n. Meridian, bds. same.

Starr Miss E. A., teacher, Institute for the Blind, res. same.

Starr John, book-keeper, Cottrell & Knight, res. 4 Arch.

Starr John C., carpenter, res. 25 Henry.

Starr Jonathan, book-keeper, Cottrell & Knight, 108 s. Delaware, bds. 163 Spring.

Starts James H., works Crown Hill Cemetery, bds. n. Mississippi, bet. Fourth and Fifth.

STARTS WILLIAM, groceries and provisions, n. Mississippi, bet. Fourth and Fifth, res. same.

Staton John W., lab., bds. 312 Madison av.

Staton Mrs. Mary A. (wid.,) bds. 312 Madison av.

Stall J., heater, rolling mill, res. 241 s. Mississippi.

Staub Alexander, tinner, bds. 200 n. Noble.

Staub Mrs. Catharine, (wid. Anton,) res. 200 n. Noble.

Staub George W., tinner, Tutewiler Bros., bds. 200 n. Noble.

Staub Joseph, merchant tailor, No. 2 Odd Fellows Hall, res. 200 n. Noble.

Stayton Thomas, (col.) lab., res. 53 Hosbrook.

Steacker Frederick, painter, res. 228 Spring.

Steacy Miss Sarah, book-binder, Journal office, bds. 177 s. New Jersey.

Stealey Herbert, carpenter, res. 237 Madison av.

Stealey Israel, physician, office 78 s. Illinois, res. same.

Stealey Alonza, bds. 78 s. Illinois.

Stebbins Sarah, (wid. John,) res. 33 Henry.

Stechham Lewis, upholsterer, Speigle & Thoms, res. 128 e. Washington.

Stechhan Otto, upholsterer, Speigle & Thoms, res. 178 e. Washington.

Stedman Elmah P., clerk, I., C. & L. R. R., res. cor. Bates and Benton.

Stedman Henry S., clerk, Benham Bros. & Co., res. Jackson, cor. Bond.

Stedman Percival, clerk, I., C. & L. R. R., res. 174 Jackson.

Steeg Philip W., res. 226 Dougherty.

Steel Edwin, apprentice stone-cutter, res. 31 s. West.

Steel Marshal, (col.,) lab., res. 235 n. Minerva

Steele F. R., book-keeper, North Western Farmer, cor. Meridian and Circle, bds. Mrs. Reed's, n. Pennsylvania.

Steele Francis M., student, Bryant & Stratton's Commercial College, bds. 36 n. Pennsylvania.

Steele T. J., printer, Journal office, res. 321 n. New Jersey.

Steele William H., carpenter, res. 321 n. Jersey.

Steelsmith Simon, farmer, bds. 512 n. Mississippi.

Steffens Charles, brass-finisher, res. 269 s. Alabama.

Stegmaier Adam, baker, res. 264 s. Pennsylvania.

Stein Ferdinand, barber, 28 Virginia av., res. same.

Stein Miss Julia, clerk, Carter & Haynes, s. Illinois.

Steinbech Rev. Charles, res. 109 Stevens.

Steiernagle George, cigar-maker, bds. 23 Kentucky av.

Steinhauser Bruno, paper box manf., 168 e. Washington, res. over 182 e. Washington.

Steinhauer Christopher, file-maker, bds. 264 w. Pennsylvania.

Steinhauer L., lab., Smith's brewery.

Steinhauer M. (Drots & S.,) 136 s. Pennsylvania, res. 260 s. Pennsylvania.

Steinhiller August, piano-varnisher, 159 and 161 e. Washington, res. 316 Railroad.

Steinhilper Mrs. Ann, (wid. Martin,) res. 316 Railroad.

Steinkent Henry, upholsterer, 38 e. Washington, res. cor. Ohio and Mississippi.

Steinman George C., tailor, bds. 60 s. Delaware.

Steinman John, cutter, Jos. Staub, res. 139 Virginia av.

Steinmeyer Mary, servant, H. Taylor, near e. end Market.

Steiert John, machinist, res. 31 Madison av.

Steirt Leopold, lab., res. 252 Railroad.

Stellagona J,, butcher, res. 442 s. Illinois.

Stellenkamp Theodore, barber, 182 s. Illinois, res. same.

Stelborn Christian, carpenter, res. n. w. cor. Noble and North.

Stelhorn Frederick, carpenter, S. & Noeman, res. 185 Davidson.

Stelzel John, barber, 33½ w. Washington, res. 376 e. Ohio.

Stelzel, Jordan & Co., barbers and hair dressers, 33½ w. Washington, up-stairs.

Hair work, all kinds, at Medina's, 50 South Illinois Street.

Steoble Catharine, servant, N. S. Byram, 466 n. Meridian.

Stephens A. J., shoe-maker, works at 65 s. Meridian, bds. Martin House.

Stephens Alexander D., compositor, Sentinel news room, res. 213 n. Pennsylvania.

Stephens Captain, carpenter, bds. 144 n. Tennessee.

Stephens Miss H. N., jewelry and notions, 32 s. Illinois, res. same.

Stephens Joseph, shoemaker, shop over 8 Bates House blk., bds. Martin House, Maryland.

Stephens Thomas D., weaver, res. 149 n. California.

Stephens Thaddeus, physician, bds. 526 n. Illinois.

Stephenson John, cooper, res. 213 n. Missouri.

Stephenson John W., (B. & S.,) res. 248 Bluff rd.

Sterges Miss Adalide, (wid.,) res. e. side Blake, bet. Washington and New York.

Sterges Levick, shoe-maker, res. e. side Blake, bet. Washington and New York.

Stern Israel, saloon, cor. Indiana av. and Illinois, res same.

Stern M. G. T., school-teacher, res. 30 Chatham.

Sterrett Almina, (wid.,) res. 405 n. Pennsylvania.

Stevens Albert, conductor, Ind. Central R. R., bds. 58 Benton.

Stevens George, conductor, C., C. & I. C. R. R., bds. 58 Benton.

Stevens Henry C., paper-hanger, res. 516 n. Mississippi.

Stevens James N., policeman, second ward, res. 460 n. Delaware.

Stevens L. B., brick-maker, res. 87 Union.

Stevens Mary, waiter, dining-room, Macy House, bds. same.

Stevens Marinda, (wid. William,) res. 213 n. Pennsylvania.

Stevens T. M., physician, office over Harrison's bank, bds. 526 n. Illinois.

Stevens William B., paper-maker, res. 327 w. Maryland.

Stevenson David, res. 442 n. Illinois.

Stevenson John, res. 213 n. Missouri.

Steward Axiom, (col.,) cook, Soldiers' Home, res. 229 n. Tennessee.

Steward Benjamin F., retired farmer, res. 21 Lockerbie.

Steward John, fireman, Bellefontaine R. R., bds. 71 Peru.

Stewart Robert M., carpenter, shop n. side Vermont, bet. Alabama and New Jersey, res. 115 Massachusetts av.

Stewart Mrs. S. W., (wid. William,) res. 117 n. Illinois.

Stewart Mrs. Sophia W., (Bowen, S. & Co.,) res. n. Illinois.

Stewart Miss Alice M., student, Ind. Female College, 146 n. Meridian, bds. the same.

Stewart Mrs. Anne, res. 226 n. Meridian.

Stewart Miss Anna, res. 452 e. Georgia.

Stewart Charles G., (Bowen, S. & Co.,) 18 w. Washington, res. 141 n. Alabama.

Stewart Daniel, (S. & Morgan,) 40 e. Washington, res. 265 n. Illinois.

Stewart David B., teamster, bds. 311 Indiana av.

Stewart David, machinist, res. 452 e. Georgia.

Stewart Miss Elizabeth, student, Ind. Female College, 146 n. Meridian, bds. the same.

Stewart Mrs. Elizabeth, res. 311 Indiana av.

Stewart Frederick S., salesman, Bowen, Stewart & Co., res. 198 n. East.

Stewart George, (col.,) barber, 14 Bates House, bds. Missouri, bet. Vermont and Michigan.

Stewart H., (col.,) servant, at 220 n. Tennessee.

Stewart Henry, stone-cutter, bds. Lord, near city limits.

Stewart James, (col.,) porter, 40 s. Meridian.

Stewart Miss Nellie, bds. 311 Indiana av.

For a complete Church Directory, see Municipal Record.

Stewart James, (col.,) hod-carrier, res. 4 Rhode Island.

Stewart John, hackman, res. 329 e. Michigan.

STEWART & MORGAN, (Daniel S., Stephen W. M. & Thomas G. Barry,) wholesale and retail druggists, 40 e. Washington.

Stebbens Thomas E., brick-layer, res. 763 n. Mississippi.

Stibert Charles, carpenter, res. 279 s. Delaware.

Stibing Philip, works Ind. Central R. R. shops, res. 211 n. Noble.

Sibings William, engineer, C. & I. C. R. R., res. 127 Meek.

Stich Floriber, carpenter, res. 281 s. New Jersey.

Stidell John, book-binder, Sentinel office, res. cor. Massachusetts av. and Liberty.

Stiedel George, file-cutter, res. 216 Noble.

Stiegman Charles, (S. & Weis,) res. 144 Madison av.

Steigman & Weis, (Charles S. & Peter W.,) dry goods and groceries, 150 Madison av.

STIERLE CHARLES & CO., Eagle Brass Works, 244 s. Pennsylvania, bds. cor. South and Meridian. See card, page 210.

Stiles Daniel J., (S., Fahnley & McCrea,) 131 s. Meridian, res. 190 Virginia av.

Stiles, Fahnley & McCrea, (Daniel J. S., Frederick F. & Rollin H. McC.,) wholesale millinery, straw and fancy goods, 131 s. Meridian.

Stiles James, shoe-maker, 41 e. Washington, res. s. w. cor. Tennessee and South.

Stiles William, pork-butcher, res. 27 s. Alabama.

Stilwell Chas. B., patent-right-dealer, bds. Bates House.

STILWELL GEORGE W., attorney at law, room over 62½ e. Washington, res. Little's Hotel.

Stilwell James R., minister, M. E. Church, agt. Freedmen's Aid Society, res. 76 n. New Jersey.

Stilwell John D., collecting agt., bds. Little's Hotel.

Stillwell W. M., steward, Institute of the Blind, res. same.

Stilt John, barber, res. Columbia.

Stiltz John, salesman, 91 e. Washington, bds. same.

Stiltz J. George, seed and agricultural implements, 78 e. Washington, res. e. of city limits.

Stiltz Mrs. Nancy, (wid. Christian,) res. 36 n. East.

Stilz Frederick, clerk, H. Hensler & Co., bds. 301 Massachusetts av.

Stimpson Maria E., bds. 284 n. Noble.

Stilz John G., (H. Hensler & Co.,) bds. Michigan, bet. Liberty and Noble.

Stine A., second hand clothing, 177 Virginia av., res. same.

Stine Joseph, boot and shoe dealer, 106 Bluff rd., res. same.

Stineman John, tailor, works, 2 Odd Fellows' Hall, res. 139 Virginia av.

Stiner John, brakesman, I., C. & L. R. R., bds. 99 Bent n.

Stinerout Drehart, lab., res. 40 Jones.

Stirk Daniel P., blacksmith, East, near Virginia av., res. Clinton, bet. Ohio and New York.

Stirk Mrs. Margaret, (wid.,) res. Clinton, bet. Ohio and New York.

Stirk Thomas, blacksmith, res. Market, near Blackford.

Stoecker William, dyer, 190 w. Washington, res. same.

Stoper Joseph, engineer, bds. 42 s. Liberty.

Stokely Benjamin, machinist, res. 164 Winston.

Stokes R. M., works Byrkit & Sons', planing mills, bds. 126 n. Tennessee.

Stokes Jacob C., carpenter, res. 124 Bluff rd.

Stolhood Charles, carpenter, res. First, bet. Illinois and Meridian.

Stolte Henry, student, commercial college, bds. 365 s. Delaware.

Stolte William, (S. & May,) grocers, 365 s. Delaware, res. same.

Stolworthy G. W., cutter, 19 w. Washington, res. 320 n. Delaware.

Stolz Charles, shoe-maker, 138 Bluff rd., res. same.

Stolz John, belt-maker, Mooney & Co., res. Bluff rd.

Stom Jacob, farmer, res. one mile from river bridge, w. on National rd.

Stone T. S., (Hendricks, Edmunds & Co.,) 56 s. Meridian, res. Worcester, Mass.

Stone Thomas J., book-binder, Journal office, bds. 147 Virginia av.

Stone W. O., salesman, 56 s. Meridian, res. 113 n. Illinois.

Stoneman & Tuttle, (William H. S. & Benjamin F. T.,) wholesale grocers, cor. Meridian and Louisiana, opp. Union depot.

Stoneman William H., (S. & Tuttle,) cor. Meridian and Louisiana, bds. 76 n. New Jersey.

Stoner Abraham L., carpenter and joiner, res. 237 n. Noble.

Stoops Miss Catharine, dress-maker, works 87 n. Delaware, bds. same.

Store Arnott S., carpenter, Meikel's Brewery, 297 w. Washington, res. same.

Storer Emil, salesman, 36 w. Washington, res. 36 n. East.

Stormer Henry C., farmer, bds. e. s. Blake, bet. Washington and New York.

Storz William, piano-maker, works George Trayser, n.e. cor. New York and Davidson, bds. 18 s. Delaware.

Stott John H., machinist, bds. 293 w. Vermont.

Stough Charles A., (Miller, Mitchell & S.,) cor. Kentucky av. and Georgia, res. 202 w. Maryland.

Stough Jacob L., painter, cor. Kentucky av. and Georgia, res. 211 w. Maryland.

STOUT B. G. & BRO., (Benjamin G. & Richard C. Stout,) wholesale and retail grocers, 7 and 8 Bates House blk., w. Washington.

Stout Benjamin G., (B. G. S. & Bro.,) 7. and 8 Bates House blk., res. 144 n. Mississippi.

Stout Carheart, coal agt., 133 w. South.

Stout D. E., salesman, 60 s. Meridian, bds. Palmer House.

Stout David L., (O. B. S. & Bro.,) 7 and 8 Bates House blk., bds. Palmer House.

Stout Mrs. Elizabeth, (wid. John,) res. 336 e. New York.

Stout Furman, (F. S. & Sons,) res. 331 w. Washington.

Stout F. & Son, (Furman & George W. S.,) groceries, 331 w. Washington.

Stout George W., (F. Stout & Son,) res. 331 w. Washington.

Stout Harvey, clerk, bds. 115 Meek.

Stout Ira H., lab., res. 95 Hosbrook.

Stout John B., printer, works Sheets, res. 133 w. South.

Stout John R., salesman, B. G. Stout & Bro., res. 246 n. Illinois.

Stout Oliver B., (O. B. S. & Bro.,) 7 and 8 Bates House blk., res. 218 e. Market.

Stout Remsen, engineer White River Iron Works, res. 382 S. Illinois.

Stout Richard C., (B. G. S. & Bro.,) 7 and 8 Bates House blk., res. 173 w. New York.

Stowell Myron A., (Willard & S.,) 4 and 5 Bates House blk., res. 78. w. Michigan.

Stoword James, (col.,) lab., res. 243 n. West.

Strable Michael, engineer, I., P. & C. R. R., bds. 103 s. New Jersey.

Strader Nelson, (col.,) porter, H. C. Chandler & Co., bds, 144 n. Douglas.

Straight Charles, cabinet-maker, res. 169 n. Mississippi.

Strand George C., dry goods clerk, res. 26 Fayette.

Strange Chapel M. E. Church, e. s. Tennessee, bet. Indiana av. and Vermont.

Strange L. G., shoe-maker, res. 186 Harrison.

Strange Mrs. Louisa, (wid. William R.,) res. 322 Winston.

Strange S. L., master of shoe-shop Deaf and Dumb Asylum.

Strangmeier Frederick, porter, 49 s. Meridian, res. 412 s. Delaware.

Strap Patrick, works Junction R. R., bds. Wiles House.

Strassner Frederick, tailor, res. 479 n. Alabama.

Stratton Henry, (col.,) servant at 252 n. Meridian.

Stratton William, (col ,) lab., res. 350 w. North.

Straub Elizabeth, (wid. Albert,) res. 247 w. Maryland.

Straub Vinzenz, shoe-maker, 10 Bates House blk., res. same.

STRAUSS & ELLENBOGEN, (Solomon S. & E. M. E.,) merchant tailors and clothiers, 19 w. Washington.

Straus Isaac A., clothier, and dealer in gents' furnishing goods, 38 w. Washton, res. 178 Virginia av.

Straus Leopold, clerk, 19 w. Washington, bds. Circle Restaurant.

Strauss Solomon, (S. & Ellenbogen,) bds. Bates House.

Strawbridge Mrs. Hannah, (wid. Benjamin,) res. 350 Winston.

Strawbridge William T., student, commercial college, bds. 350 Winston.

Street Charles, cabinet-maker, res. 166 n. Mississippi.

Street George G., inmate Deaf and Dumb Asylum.

Street John A., occupant Deaf and Dumb Asylum.

Street Nathaniel, carpenter, res. 41 Peru.

Street W. R., inmate Deaf and Dumb Asylum.

Streeter Noble, salesman, Wilkison & Co., bds. 268 e. St. Clair.

Streicher Barbary, (wid.,) res. 171 Fort Wayne av.

Streight A. D., subscription book publisher, Yohn's blk., cor. Meridian and Washington, res. two and one-half miles e. on National rd.

Streight C. F., lumber-dealer, office Yohn's blk., bds. Littles hotel.

Stretch Edward, inmate Deaf and Dumb Asylum.

Stretcher Miss Ella F., res. 421 n. Tennessee.

Stribling Mary, (wid. Cornelius,) res. 506 n. Delaware.

Strickland David, foreman, Sheets' Paper Mill, bds. 254 w. Washington.

Strickland Joseph, book-binder, W. & J. Braden, res. 128 w. Market.

STRICKLAND R. J., editor and publisher Odd Fellows' Talisman, cor. Meridian and Circle, bds. Spencer House.

Strickler Eli, brick-mason, res. e. Washington.

Striebeck Charles, bakery, 319 n. West.
Stringfellow Rev. Horace, minister, St. Paul's Church, cor. New York and Illinois, res. 333 n. Illinois.
Strip Frank, porter, J. M. Lunt, bds. 15 Fletcher av.
Strip Mary, (wid. Peter,) res. 15 Fletcher av.
Strobel John, bar-tender, 154 w. Washington, bds. 23 Kentucky av.
Straele Frederick, works Cabinet-Makers' Union, bds. 518 e. Washington.
Stroh John, hostler, bds. 82 Indiana av.
Strong Melville, (S. & Smith,) res. 231 n. East.
Strong & Smith, (M. S. & E. S.,) Vinton's blk.
Strothman William, (Grosch & S.,) 37 s. Delaware, bds. William Dell.
Strothers Nathan, (col.,) messenger, U. S. Arsenal, res. on Arsenal grounds.
Stropel John, shoe-maker, 554 e. Washington, res. same.
Strouse Miss Sarah, student, Indiana Female College, 146 n. Meridian, bds. same.
Strow John, hostler, 10 e. Pearl, bds. 124 s. Meridian.
Struble Miss Emma, seamstress, works 182 e. Washington, res. 112 n. Noble.
Struble John, fireman, Peru & Indianapolis R. R., bds. 325 e. Ohio.
Struble John, bar-tender, 154 w. Washington, res. 112 n. Noble.
Struble Miss Mary, dress-maker, res. 112 n. Noble.
Struble Michael, engineer, Peru & Indianapolis R. R., bds. 325 e. Ohio.
Struble Philip, carpenter, res. 112 n. Noble.
Struckman Fred., lab., res. 173 Union.
Struckman William, tailor, 335 Virginia av., bds. same.
Stuart Francis, lab., bds. 72 Wilkens.
Stuart George, res. e. side Douglas, bet. Washington and New York.
Stuart Jacob, well-digger, res. 72 Wilkens.
Stuart James A., (col.,) lab., res. w. Center.
Stuber John, res. 384 s. Missouri.
Stuck John W., teamster, res. Shelbyville pike, three-fourths of a mile s. corporation.
Stuck John, brick-mason, res. 348 Virginia av.
Stuck Nathan, boiler-maker, res. 161 Huron.
Stuck William, lab., res. 68 Eddy.
Stuckmier Augustus, butcher, 362 Virginia av., bds. 358 Virginia av.
Stuckmier John H., grocer, 362 Virginia av., res. 358 Virginia av.
Stukey Charles, cooper, rear of 111 Spring, res. 111 Spring.

Stulting Charles, engineer, Terre Haute shops, res. 86 Railroad.
Stulting Fred., teamster, bds. 238 Bluff rd.
Stultz John, lab., res. 4 Rockwood.
Stump Conrad, cigar-maker, bds. 21 s. John.
Stump John, contractor, res. 317 n. Alabama.
Stumph Mrs. Anna, (wid. George,) res. 171 n. Noble.
Stumph George H., brick-mason, res. 171 n. Noble.
Stumph Henry, tinner, 169 w. Washington, bds. 268 Bluff rd.
Stumph John B., wholesale liquor dealer, cor. Alabama and Washington, res. 459 e. Market.
Stumph Henry, brewer, res. Morris, bet. East and Madison rd.
Stumph John J., stone-mason, res. 21 John.
Stumph John J., carpenter, res. 91 Buchanan.
Stunden John, hod-carrier, res. 22 Buchanan.
Stunden Mrs. Mary, (wid. Daniel,) res. 360 s. Delaware.
Stunden Patrick, expressman, res. 360 s. Delaware.
Stunden Thomas, freight agt., C., C. C. & I. R. R., res. 235 e. Louisiana.
Sturch George, res. 209 Buchanan.
Sturgeon Alfred, real estate agt., bds. Court, bet. East and New Jersey.
Sturms Frederick, gardener, res. near Arsenal av.
Sturm Fredrica, servant, 152 e. Washington.
Sturm George, tailor, bds. 23 Kentucky av.
Stylaur J. H., student, Bryant & Stratton's Commercial College.
Styles James, shoe-maker, bds. 103 w. South.
Styner Jacob O., conductor, I., C. & L. R. R., bds. 47 Bates.
Suart John, hub-turner, res. 55 e. McCarty.
Suart John B., grocer, 219 Massachusetts av., res. same.
Suart Miles, moulder, bds. 55 McCarty.
Suats Andrew, res. 19 Lord.
Sudbrock Frank, lab., res. 227 Davidson.
Sudbrock Henry, carpenter, res. 318 n. Noble.
Suddith George, (Haynes & S.,) 107 s. Illinois, res. 139 e. Louisiana.
Suddith Miss Maggie, res. 239 Louisiana.
Suddrink Mrs. Minnie, weaver, res. 117 n. West.
Suess Charles A., tailor, 21 s Meridian, res. same.
Suess Godfrey, shoe-maker, works 218 e. Washington, res. 320 e. Ohio.
Suher Lewis, saw grinder, res. 23 Wyoming.
Suhr John, lab., bds. Union.

Suhr Albert, watchman, T. H. & I. freight depot, res. 231 Bluff rd.
Suhr Fred., lab., 172 Union.
Suhre Frederick, (Voight & S,) 26½ n. Pennsylvania, res. 178 Winston.
Suhre Henry, lab., res. 170 Union
Suhre John H., lab., 178 Winston.
Suing Mrs. Nancy, (wid.,) res. 301 w. Market.
Suitt James B., foreman, Eagle Machine Works, bds. 247 s. Meridian.
Sulgrove Berry R., retired journalist, res. 125 w. South.
Sulgrove Eli L, harness-maker, 20 w. Washington, res. 16 w. First.
Sulgrove George W., salesman, 20 w. Washington, bds. Palmer House.
Sulgrove Henry J., harness-maker, 20 w. Washington, bds. 16 w. First.
Sulgrove James, (J. S. & Son,) 20 w. Washington, res. Bluff rd., five miles s.
Sulgrove James W., (J. S. & Son,) 20 w. Washington, res. 137 w. New York.
SULGROVE JAMES & SON, (James & James W. S.,) saddlery, hardware, coach and harness trimmings, 20 w. Washington.
Sulgrove Jerome B., salesman, 20 w. Washington, res. n. Mississippi.
Sulgrove John M., harness-maker, 20 w. Washington, res. Bluff rd., five miles s.
Sulgrove John, harness-maker, res. 190 n. Mississippi.
Sulgrove Joseph, harness-maker, 20 w Washington, res. 235 w. Vermont.
Sulgrove Milton M., 20 w. Washington, res. n. w. cor. Illinois and Ohio.
Sulgrove William, engineer, res. 75 Mc-Carty.
Sullivan Arthur, lab., res. cor. Union and Phipps.
Sullivan Anna, servant, J. B. McChesney, 454 n. Tennessee.
Sullivan Beverly W., dentist student, 76½ e. Market.
Sullivan C. T., inmate Deaf and Dumb Asylum.
Sullivan Miss Catharine, bds. 5 Bates.
Sullivan Cornelius C., lab., res 142 Meek.
Sullivan Cornelius, lab., res. 335 Winston.
Sullivan Daniel, lab., 191 Meek.
Sullivan Daniel, lab., res. 276 s. Delaware.
SULLIVAN & DREW, (John B. S. & John A. D.,) livery and sale stables, 10 e. Pearl.
Sullivan Enos, inmate Deaf and Dumb Asylum.
Sullivan George, dentist, bds 152 n. Meridian.
Sullivan George T., clerk, C., C., C. & I. R. R., 321 s Alabama.
Sullivan Hannah, (wid. John,) res. 191 Meek.
Sullivan John, lab., res. 5 Bates.

Sullivan James, lab., rolling mill, res. cor. Merrill and Missouri.
Sullivan John, lab., res. 56 s. Noble.
Sullivan John, moulder, bds. 38 s. Tennessee.
Sullivan John, lab., bds. 191 Meek.
Sullivan John, (S. & Drew,) 10 e. Pearl, res. 83 e. Pratt.
Sullivan Julia, waiter, dining room, Commercial Hotel.
Sullivan Miss Julia A., bds. 29 w. Michigan.
Sullivan Margaret, kitchen-girl, Bates House.
Sullivan Michael D., railroader, res. Cady, cor. Meek.
Sullivan Oliver H., student, Racine College, res. 75 w. Ohio.
Sullivan Patrick, lab., res. near Arsenal av.
Sullivan Patrick, lab., res. 258 s. Delaware.
Sullivan Thomas L., student, Racine College, res. w. Ohio.
Sullivan Timothy, lab., res. 335 Winston.
Sullivan Timothy, lab., res. 578 Maple.
Sullivan Timothy, plasterer, res. 19 Buchanan.
Sullivan William, lawyer, over Fletcher & Sharpe's Bank, res. 410 n. Meridian.
Sullivan William, Sr., carpenter, res. 427 n. Tennessee.
Sullivan William H., groceries, provisions, fruits and game, 76 w. Washington, res. 60 n. California.
Sullivan William J., brakesman, Cincinnati R. R., res. 216 Winston.
Sullivan William, lab., res. 456 s. East.
Sumerland Fred., varnisher, res. 315 s. Delaware.
Sumner William, (Wm. S. & Co.,) 10 w. Washington, res. Cincinnati, O.
SUMNER WM. & CO., (William S., John R. Wright & Alva S. Walker,) State agts. Wheeler & Wilson's sewing machines, 10 w. Washington.
Summers August, drayman, res. Union, bet. McCarty and Phipps.
Summers Albert B., carpenter, res. 83 California.
Summers George (col.,) lab., res. Sixth, bet. Tennessee and Mississippi.
Summers Martin, (col.,) lab., res. 144 Douglas.
Summers Mena, servant, Robinson's, 381 s. Alabama.
Summerville Thomas, conductor, I., C. & L. R. R., bds. Ray House.
Summens Martin, (col.,) works H. C. Chandler & Co.'s, res. 144 n. Douglas.
Summitt Benjamin, (col.,) lab., res. 154 Douglas alley.
Surbey J. S., (Baker & S.,) res. South, near Noble.

Surface Goodwin, student, N. W. Christian University, bds. 40 Christian av.

Surface John W., carpenter, res. near rolling mill.

Surface John W., watchman, Speigel, Thoms & Co., res. 177 Bluff rd.

Surface Lyida, (wid. John,) res. 40 Christian av.

Sup Willie, tender, Mozart Hall, bds. same.

Suter James A., salesman, Tyler's Bee Hive, res. 9 Cherry.

Sutherland Levi, wheel-wright, res. 59 e. McCarty.

Sueter Frederick, physician, 15 Virginia av., res. 290 Virginia av.

Sutter George, gardener, res. cor. Sixth and Michigan rd.

Sutter James, res. 9 Cherry.

Sutton Joseph M., plasterer, res. 82 Massachusetts av.

Sutton Salathiel L., engineer, Bellefontaine R. R., res. 311 Davidson.

Swarles John S., stone-cutter, res. 42 Henry.

Swain D. F., book-keeper, 38 s. Meridian, bds. 67 Madison av.

Swain Morley William, fireman, I., C. & L. R. R., bds. 129 Bates.

Swain James, printer, res. 41 n. Illinois.

Swain Jane S., ocupant Deaf and Dumb Asylum.

Swain Mrs. Mary J., (wid. Rufus,) res. 41 Fletcher av.

Swain Miss Sallie, clerk, 68 n. Illinois, bds. 210 e. Ohio.

Swan Miss Elizabeth, lady boarder, 27 n. New Jersey.

Swan French, (col.,) lab., res. over 221 Massachusetts av.

Swaney L. J., assistant toll-gate keeper, w. end Washington.

Swank Miss Angie, milliner, over 8 w. Washington, bds. 44 s. Tennessee.

Swank M., cancer-doctor, 76 n. Pennsylvania.

Swartz F. W., painter, res. 339 n. Noble.

Swartz Huldah, inmate Home for the Friendless, w. s. n. Pennsylvania, beyond city limits.

Swartz Henry, peddler, bds. 261 Massachusetts av.

Swartz John, gardener, cor. Michigan and Patterson.

Swartz Peter, teamster, res. 206 Winston.

Swartz Samuel, peddler, bds. 261 Massachusetts av.

Sweeney Eugene, lab., res. 347 Winston.

Sweeney Fanny, servant at 182 n. Meridian.

Sweeney Charles, soldier, U. S. Arsenal, res. Arsenal.

Sweeney Hugh, saloon, 116 s. Illinois, res. same.

Sweeney Jeremiah, lab., Scott & Nicholson's stone-yard.

Sweeney John, cigar-maker, John Heidlinger, res. 17 s. Mississippi.

Sweeney John, conductor, J., M. & I. R. R., bds. Ray House.

Sweeny Thomas, machinist, res. 39 Maple.

Sweetser George M., dis. clerk, p. o., res. Pennsylvania, north of city limits.

Sweetser James N., lawyer, over 21 e. Washington, res. 650 n. Pennsylvania.

SWEETZER JOHN, wholesale dealer in brandies, rum, whiskies, &c., 30 s. Meridian, res. 242 n. Meridian.

Sweetser Mrs. Reuben, res. n. Pennsylvania.

Sweetsman Christian, machinist, bds. cor. Georgia and Liberty.

Sweigel Daniel, collar-maker, res. 261 s. Pennsylvania.

Sweinhart A., teamster, res. 134 e. St. Mary.

Sweinhart Andrew, carriage painter, works S. W. Drew & Co., s. e. cor. North and East.

Sweinhart Charles E., clerk, 21 s. Meridian, bds. 379 n. Alabama.

SWEINHART WILLIAM, merchant tailor, 21 s. Meridian, res. 379 n. Alabama. See card, page 2, adv. dept.

Sweir Mrs. Mary, (wid. Charles,) res. 576 e. St. Clair.

Swemle John, baker, 262 s. Delaware, res. same.

Swett C. A., works rolling mill, res 326 w. Maryland.

Swick Caroline, servant, 202 e. Ohio.

Swindler Benjamin F., clerk, 44 n. Pennsylvania, res. 232 n. Noble.

Swindler John H., boarding house, 232 n. Noble.

Swing Edward, lab., res. n. s. National rd., half-mile from river bridge.

Swing Henry, clerk, 7 Odd Fellows' Hall, bds. Patterson House.

Swinge Edward, clerk, H. H. Lee, tea-store, bds. Patterson House.

Swishart Christopher, gardener, res. Tinker, near Pennsylvania.

Swisher Alexandria, brakesman, Bellefontaine R. R., bds. 276 Railroad.

SWISHER JOHN, conductor, C., C., C. & I. R. R., bds. Palmer House.

Swofard Edward, wood-hauler, res. 321 w. Market.

Swope Mrs. Elizabeth, res. 654 w. Third.

Sylvester David, railroad contractor, Vincennes R. R., res. 27 Lockerbie.

Sylvia Marion, lab., works John F. Hill, bds. same.

Syms James, machinist, Sinker & Co., res. 346 s. Alabama.

Syrup Henry, shoe-store, 195 Massachusetts av, res. 191 Massachusetts av.

TAFFE GEORGE, lieutenant of police, res. 175 Spring.

Taffe Hannibal, policeman, third ward, res. 69 w. Market.

Taggart Daniel, carriage-maker, bds. 24 w. Georgia

Taggart Samuel, mill-wright and mill furnisher, 132 s. Pennsylvania, res. 118 n. Mississippi.

Tague Johnson, lab., bds. 397 Massachusetts av.

Talbott Miss Bettie M., bds. 94 n. Meridian.

Talbott Rev. Bishop, res. Tinker, cor. Pennsylvania.

Talbott Charles H., (Rickard & T.,) 78 s. Meridian, res. 28 n. Mississippi.

Talbott Miss Ella, bds. 114 n. Tennessee.

Talbott Gabriel, cooper, res. w. side Douglas, bet. Washington and New York.

Talbott George, (col.,) lab., res. 60 Arch.

Talbott John M., res. 114 n. Tennessee.

Talbott M., works Junction R. R., bds. Wiles House.

Talbott Miss Mattie, bds. 114 n. Tennessee.

Talbott Richard L., (Alford, T. & Co.,) 2 Morrison's Opera blk., res. 136 e. North.

Talbott W. H., prest. Ind. & Illinois R. R. Co., office e. Washington, res. 94 n. Meridian.

Talbott William, (Gabrael & T.,) cooper, bds. Douglas, bet. New York and Washington.

Talley Nancy, servant at 67 w. Michigan.

Tallon John, lab., bds. 232 s. Tennessee.

Tandy John, (col.,) lab., res. 223 e. Michigan.

Tangly Mrs. Mary, (wid. Dennis,) res. 151 s. Alabama.

Tanner Mrs. Emily, (wid.,) seamstress, res. 388 Indiana av.

Tannes Isaac, (col.,) lab., res. near City Hospital.

Tanner James, hackman, res. 218 n. Missouri.

Tanner John A., works Speigel & Thoms, res. 81 n. Missouri.

Tanner James A., lab., res. 388 Indiana av.

Tanner Richard S., lab., res. 388 Indiana av.

Tanner Samuel, (col.,) servant, P. P. Haughey, 242 n. Pennsylvania.

Tanzey A. L., brick-mason, bds. Ray House.

Tapking John, carpenter, works Cabinet-Makers' Union, res. 123 n. New Jersey.

Tapking Mrs. Minna, (wid. Frederick H.,) res. 189 s. Alabama.

Tarkington John S., (Morton, Martindale & T.,) over 2 w. Washington, res. 272 n. Meridian.

Tarkington Robert, brick-mason, res. 240 e. Louisiana.

Tarkington William C., (Hibben, T. & Co.,) 112 s. Meridian, res. 118 w. Vermont.

Tarkington William W., clerk, p. o., bds. 118 w. Vermont.

Tarkington W. S., bds. Bates House.

Tarlton John, grocer, 47 n. Illinois, res. 492 n. Tennessee.

Tarmy Martin, machinist, bds. 82 Huron.

Tate James, porter, John Woodbridge, bds. Concordia House.

Tate Robert, blacksmith, bds. 177 Massachusetts av.

TATE WARREN, door, sash and blind manfr., 38 s. New Jersey, bds. Emenegger's Hotel. See card, page 54.

Tate William, bds. 410 n. Tennessee.

Taten Eugene, stone-mason, res. 66 s. West.

Tatham Curtis W., carpenter, bds. 255 n. Mississippi.

Tatham George W., bar-keeper, Clipper Saloon, 33 n. Illinois.

Tattersall Joseph, stone-cutter, res. 186 Virginia av.

Taucit A. H., works Phœnix Foundry, res. 370 w. Washington.

Taylor Aaron, (col.,) teamster, res. 344 w. North.

Taylor Benjamin, (col.,) lab., res. Lenox, bet. Eighth and Ninth.

Taylor Charles, (col.,) bell-boy, Oriental House.

Taylor Charles C., (col.,) Rockwell's dining room, bds. same.

Taylor Charles, (col.,) lab., res. 300 e. Michigan.

Taylor Clinton, horse-broker, res. 211 e. Ohio.

TAYLOR & CRAIN,
(Samuel T. & William N. C.,) merchant tailors, drapers and clothiers, 3 Bates House blk., w. Washington.

Taylor David, (col.,) steamboatman, res. 300 e. Michigan.

Taylor David M., cashier Indiana National Bank, and Indianapolis branch Bank of the State, 2 e. Washington, cor. Meridian, res. 680 n. Illinois.

Taylor Dorsey, (col.,) lab., res. cor. Sixth and Lafayette R. R.

Taylor Emma, servant, 286 e. Ohio.

Taylor Edwin, student, bds. 251 n. Alabama.

Taylor Edmund, (col.,) teamster, bds. 435 n. East.

Taylor Franklin, (Chandler & T.,) res. 290 w. Vermont.

Taylor George, (col.,) waiter, Dr. Wright, res. n. Missouri.

Taylor George, (col.,) lab., res. Howard, bet. Second and Third.

Taylor George, (col.,) waiter, Bates House.

Taylor Howard, bridge builder, res. near e. end Market.

Taylor Isaac, architect, res. 124 n. Liberty.

Taylor I. J., (T. & Sherwood,) attorney at law, bds. Pattison House.

Taylor Israel, book-keeper, Harrisons' Bank, 15 e. Washington, res. 397 n. Pennsylvania, cor. St. Clair.

Taylor Isaac H., traveling agt., H. Dailey & Co., bds. Oriental House.

Taylor Jane, servant, 184 n. Meridian.

Taylor Jesse D. B., bds. Oriental House.

Taylor John, sawyer, Osgood, Smith & Co., bds. 59 Eddy.

Taylor John, (col.,) dining-room boy, Oriental House.

TAYLOR J. F.,
ornamental plaster supplies, 80 Massachusetts av., res. 61 n. New Jersey.

Taylor Miss Julia A., matron, Deaf and Dumb Asylum.

Taylor Mrs. L. M., (wid. Richard E.,) res. 397 Virginia av.

Taylor Miss Mary, teacher, public school, bds. 168 N. Illinois.

Taylor Mrs. Mary C., (wid. Joseph,) res. 45 Huron.

Taylor Mrs. Mary E., (wid. Selyn,) res. 76 Ft. Wayne av.

Taylor Miss Mary E., 138 n. Mississippi.

Taylor Miss Mary L., music-teacher, res. 61 n. New Jersey.

Taylor Mrs. M. J., milliner and millinery goods, over 6 w. Washington, bds. Palmer House.

TAYLOR NAPOLEON B.,
lawyer, room 4 Brown's blk., n. Pennsylvania, res. 251 n. Alabama.

Taylor Patsey, (col.,) res. 145 n. Bright.

Taylor Samuel, groceries and produce dealer, 42 w. Washington, res. cor. New York and Tennessee.

Taylor Samuel, (T. & Crain,) 3 Bates House blk., res. n. w. cor. New York and Delaware.

TAYLOR & SHERWOOD,
(I. J. T. & A. W. O. S.,) real estate brokers and gen. collecting agts., cor. Virginia av. and Washington.

Taylor Simon, inmate Deaf and Dumb Asylum.

Taylor Stephens, (col.,) farmer, res. w. Center.

Taylor William, clerk, Mooney, res. 266 s. New Jersey.

Taylor William, clerk, Willard & Stowell, bds. 273 e. Market.

Taylor William, lawyer, bds. Pattison House.

Taylor William A., salesman, 147 s. Meridian, res. 266 s. New Jersey.

Taylor William M., clerk, Union Depot, bds. 168 n. Illinois.

Teague John, inmate Deaf and Dumb Asylum.

Teal N., physician, office room 5, 2d floor Blake's row, res. 80 s. Tennessee.

Teasing Josephine, servant, Court, bet. East and New Jersey.

Teckenbrock Christian, blacksmith, T. H. & I. R. R. engine house, res. 26 Henry.

Teckenbrock William, car-inspector, T. H. & I. R. R., res. 26 Henry.

Tedrow David F., carpenter, res. 333 Davidson.

Teepe Harmon, blacksmith, res. 330 Virginia av.

Teerhern John, machinist, res. cor. Georgia and Liberty.

Tehan Michael, (T. & Shea,) res. 296 e. Washington.

Tehan & Shea, (Michael T. & Thomas S.,) saloon, 294 e. Washington.

Telfelt Mayer, clothing, 34 w. Louisiana, res. 225 s. Delaware.

Tellkamp John, blacksmith, res. 232 s. New Jersey.

Temple Benjamin, brakesman, J., M. & I. R. R., bds. Ray House.

Temple William, brakesman, J., M. & I. R. R., res. 144 e. McCarty.

Templer J., carpenter, res. 2 Dougherty.

Templin G. W., salesman, Donaldson & Co., bds. 62 s. Pennsylvania.

Teney Mrs. Margaret, (wid. Abraham,) res. 169 Winston.

Teneyck J. A. & R. F., boots and shoes, 340 w. Washington.

Teneyck Jeremiah A., (J. A. & R. F. T.,) 340 w. Washington, res. same.

Teneyeck John, shoe-maker, res. 120 Indiana av.

Tenneyeck Richard F., (J. A. &,R. F. T.,) res. 157 w. South.

Tenneycke Sarah, (wid.,) res. 181 s. Tennesee.

Tenth Ward School, cor. Seventh and Tennessee, J. W. Myers, principal.

Terre Haute R. R. Freight Depot, cor. Tennessee and Louisiana.

Terrell Mrs. Eliza B., (wid. Henry,) res. 175 n. New Jersey.

Terrell James, (col.,) servant, T. A. Lewis, n. w. cor. Meridian and First.

Terrell Laura, servant, Ovid Butler.

Terrell Lynch M., clerk, Adjutant General's office, new State bldg., bds. Bates House.

TERRELL WILLIAM H. H., Adjutant General of Indiana, office new State bldg., bds. Bates House.

Terry William H., (col.,) lab., res. 156 Douglas alley.

Tessler Michael M., res. 384 w. North.

Tetez H. L., hucksterer, res. 323 n. Alabama.

Terrell Ezra Y., clerk, Willard & Stowell, res. 69 n. East.

Teures Henry, cooper, res. 353 n. Noble.

Thalman Isaac, (Geisendorff & Co.,) res. 171 w. New York.

THALMAN JOHN, baker, 75 n. Alabama, res. same.

Tharlman Isaac, piano-maker, res. 324 e. Ohio.

Tharner Gerhard, gardener, res. e. city limits.

Thacher Rebecca, (wid.,) res. Meek, near city limits.

Thayer & Frauer, (George T. & Albert F.,) groceries and produce, 248 e. Washington.

Thayer Mrs. Mary, (wid. Daniel,) res. 309 e. Market.

Thayer George, (T. & Frauer,) 248 e. Washington, res. 309 e. Market.

Thayer Selden, salesman, 32 w. Washington, res. 309 e. Market.

Theaver Michael, lab., res. Bluff rd.

THE CLIPPER, 33 n. Illinois, under Exchange Theater, C. S. Butterfield & Co., proprs., agt. for Lills' Chicago Brewery Co., sample rooms 10 w. Washington.

Theder Alexander, plasterer, res. 255 c. Washington.

Theobold Frederick, queensware, glass and lamps, 94 e. Washington, bds. 113 o. Washington.

Thicks John, servant, 477 n. Tennessee.

Thicke J. H., machinist, I. & C. shops, res. 103 Forest av.

Third Street M. E. Church, Third, bet. Illinois and Tennessee.

Third Presbyterian Church, n. e. cor. Illinois and Ohio.

Third Ward Free School, Miss Eliza T. Ford, principal.

Thistlethwaite J. P., (Roach & T.,) publisher, res. 24 w. New York.

Thomaun John, confectioner, 319 Virginia av., res. same.

Thomas Albert, blacksmith, bds. 192 Virginia av.

Thomas Albert, (Charles Thomas & Bros.,) res. 115 n. Noble.

Thomas Benjamin, dyer, res. 26 Dunlap.

Thomas Charles, (Charles Thomas & Bros.,) n. w. cor. East and Ohio, res. 115 n. Noble.

THOMAS CHARLES & BROS., (Charles, Conrad & Albert T.,) groceries and produce dealers, 250 e. Ohio, cor. East.

Thomas Conrad, (Charles Thomas & Bros.,) res. 115 n. Noble.

Thomas Daniel L., student, N. W. C. University, res. 76 Ash.

Thomas Eddie, grocer, cor. New Jersey and St. Clair, res. 69 n. Liberty.

Thomas Elizabeth, (col.,) servant, at 546 n. Meridian.

Thomas Frederick, shoe-maker, works 223 w. Washington.

Thomas George, Sr., res. 115 n. Noble.

Thomas George, Jr., night policeman, ninth ward, res. 115 n. Noble.

Thomas Mrs. Helen, (wid.,) bds. 24 w. New York.

Thomas Henry P., Merchants' Police, bds. 37½ n. Pennsylvania.

Thomas J. Q., student, N. W. C. University, res. 76 Ash.

Thomas James, brick-layer, res. 301 Indiana av.

Thomas James E, book-keeper, Western Union Telegraph office, res. e. Georgia, near cor. Georgia.

Thomas John, manager, Indianapolis Rolling Mill, res. 319 s. Meridian.

Thomas John P., lab., res. Pearl, below w. end canal.

Thomas John S., brick-layer, res. e. s. Blake, bet. Washington and New York.

Thomas K., teamster, Hoosier Mills, bds. 391 w. Washington.

Thomas L. L., res. 176 Virginia av.

Thomas Miss L., res. 176 Virginia av.

Thomas Lewis, shoe-maker, 223 w. Washington, bds. 222 w. Maryland.

Thomas Lewis A., clerk, E. L. Hutton & Co, bds. 176 Virginia av.

Thomas Mrs. M. A., milliner, over 8 w. Washington, res. 704 n. Tennessee.

Thomas Lizzie, (col.,) res. 86 n. Missouri.

Thomas Miss Maggie, bds. 36 s. New Jersey.

Thomas Miss Mary J., dress-maker, bds. 176 Virginia av.

Thomas Mrs. Martha E., (wid.,) res. 725 n. Illinois.

Thomas Oscar, res. 192 Virginia av.

Thomas O. E , (Richards & T.,) 399 n. New Jersey, res. 69 n. Liberty.

Thomas Olive P., (wid.,) res. 192 Virginia av.

Thomas Mrs. Rebecca W., (wid. David,) res. 354 s. Delaware.

Thomas Richard, carpenter, res. 319 s. Meridian.

Thomas Robert, tile-maker, res. 177 Fort Wayne av.

Thomas R. & Co., produce and commission, 155 w. Washington.

Thomas Simon, stone-mason, res. 135 n. Noble.

Thomas Theodore, brick-layer, res. 285 n. East.

Thomas W. H., carpenter, res. 195 w. Maryland.

Thomas William H., car repairer, J., M. & I. R. R., res. 236 s. Alabama.

Thomas Wyatt, brick-layer, res. 83 Beaton.

Thompson Mrs. Anna, (wid. Thomas,) news-dealer, 13 n. Pennsylvania, res. 131 n. Alabama.

Thompson A. B., clerk, Bates House, n. w. cor. Washington and Illinois, bds. same.

THOMPSON D. I.,
fish, oysters and game, 31 s. Meridian, res. 86 e. South.

THOMPSON EDWARD P.,
asst. post-master, res. 430 n. Tennessee.

Thompson Ellen, (col.,) servant at 262 n. Meridian.

Thompson Eli, (Emerson, T. & Beam,) res. 125 n. West.

Thompson Florella, servant, Ovid Butler.

Thompson George C., carpenter, res. 190 Davidson.

Thompson George, lab., res. 272 s. Missouri.

Thompson Gideon B., printer, Journal office, res. 224 e. Michigan.

Thompson Harrison, (col.,) works Philagelphia Dye House, bds. Blackford alley, bet. New York and Vermont.

Thompson Henry, soldier, U. S. Arsenal, res. same.

Thompson J. F., (C. S. Butterfield & Co.,) 72 w. Washington, res. over 24 s. Meridian.

Thompson J. O., student commercial college, bds. 452 s. New Jersey.

Thompson James B., moulder, res. 310 e. Georgia.

Thompson James L., clerk, bds. 84 Massachussetts av.

Thompson John, painter, res. 173 Stevens.

Thompson John, saloon, 302 s. West, res. same.

Thompson John C., pump-maker, res. 226 s. East.

Thompson John G., res. 467 s. Illinois.

Thompson John H., bds. 430 n. Tennessee.

Thompson John M., carpenter, works Vincent & Thompson, bds. 190 Davidson.

Thompson Joseph, stove-moulder, Root's foundry, res. 54 Greer.

Thompson Joseph, stone-sawyer, res. 37 s. West.

Thompson Julia, (wid.,) res. 35 Henry.

Thompson Lewis, (col.,) white-washer, res. 94 s Meridian.

Thompson Robert, stoves, tin-ware, 19 w. Washington, bds. Ohio, bet. Mississippi and Canal.

Thompson Philip, clerk, 24 e. Washington, bds. 356 n. Illinois.

Thompson Samuel, blacksmith, Greenleaf, bds. Ray House.

Thompson Samuel, lab., works near e. end Market.

Thompson Samuel, carpenter, res. 485 s. Illinois.

THOMPSON WM. H. A.,
canvassing and collecting agt., H. C. Chandler & Co., bds. 35 w. Georgia.

Thompson W. J., stone-cutter, res. 223 Buchanan.

Thompson W. Clinton, (T. & Woodburn,) 90 n. Illinois, res. 248 n. Pennsylvania, cor. Michigan.

Thompson Washington, (col.,) lab., res. 145 n. Bright.

Thompson William, (col.,) dining-room boy, Oriental House.

THOMPSON & WOODBURN,
(W. Clinton T. & James K. W.,) physicians and surgeons, 90 n. Illinois.

Thoms Frederick, (Speigle, T. & Co.,) res. 76 n. East.

Thomson Henry, (col.,) lab., res. 235 w. Ohio.

Thomson Milton, carpenter, res. 138 Elm.

THOMSON WILLIAM,
physician and surgeon, and specialist in the treatment of chronic and venereal diseases, 29 s. Delaware, res. same.
See card, page 9, adv. dept.

Thomson Quinton, bakery, 12 s. Meridian, res. same.

Thoussen B. E., (L. Ludorff & Co.,) 42 s. Meridian, bds. Bates House.

Thorn John, butcher, res. 133 Harrison.

Thorn William, lab., res. 83 Jackson.

Thorne David, upholsterer, Hume, Adams & Co., bds. Pyle House.

Thorne Kate, (wid.,) servant, Mrs. Ferguson, 60 w. Market.

Thorn William F., lab., res. 13 n. Blake.

Thornbrough Allen, policeman, third ward, res. 240 n. Mississippi.

Thornbrough Mrs. Clarico, (wid. R.,) res. second floor, w. Washington.

Thornbrough John M., hat and bonnet bleacher, res. n. Blake.

Thornbrough Miss Mary E., res. second floor, w. Washington.

Thornbury Joseph, clerk, E. T. Miller, bds. 30 Indiana av.

Thornley Jasper, machinist, bds. 86 Forest av.

Thornley Orien, machine shop, 28 e. Louisiana, res. 86 Forest av.

Thorpe Ann, servant, 163 n. Alabama.

Thorpe C. P., real estate agt., res. 103 Fort Wayne av.

Thorpe Thomas, salesman, 16 w. Washington.

Thorpe Thomas D., book-keeper, bds. 427 n. Tennessee.

Thornton Benjamin, (col.,) lab., bds. 79 s. Missouri.

Thornton Gardner P., agt. New York Life Insurance Co., bds. 27 w. Ohio.

Thornton Margaret, servant, 274 n. Liberty.

Thornton Maggie, servant, works 345 n. Noble.

Thoriz John, (J. F. & Co.,) 351 s. Pennsylvania.

Thum Charles, engraver, W. & J. Braden, res. Cherry, near Plum.

Thumlert William, clerk, 49 and 53 w. Washington.

Thurston William B., (Maxwell, Fry & T.,) 34 s. Meridian, res. 79 w. North.

Thurston W. B., Jr., clerk, Snyder & Hays, 17 n. Meridian, res. 79 w. North.

Thurston E. R., messenger, American Express Co., 34 e. Washington, bds. Spencer House.

Tichtner Miss Mary, hair-worker, 50 s. Illinois, bds. 273 s. West.

Tichtner Rachel, (wid.,) res. 273 s. West.

Tickembrock Christopher, blacksmith, res. 36 Henry.

Ticknor George P., printer, Journal bldg, bds. 30 n. Pennsylvania.

Tidd George, cooper, res. 289 s. East.

Tiffany George E., book-keeper and salesman, 74 w. Washington.

TILFORD J. M., office, Tilford's bldg., cor. Meridian and Circle, res. 79 e. Ohio.

Tilford Samuel E., route agt., L. & I. R. R., res. 85 e. Pratt.

Tillberry Matthew, teamster, res. Ninth, near Lafayette R. R.

Tillman Elizabeth, (col.,) servant at 528 n. Tennessee.

Tillson Emmzeta, occupant Deaf and Dumb Asylum.

Tilly Joseph, res. 143 Union.

Tilt Thomas C., salesman, New York Store, bds. 50 w. New York.

Tinman William, varnisher, 56 and 58 e. Washington, res. 452 n. New Jersey.

Timmons Martha, bds. 255 e. Washington.

Timmons Patrick, driver Frank Wright's ale wagon, res. 65 s. California.

Tinsley Miss Jennie, teacher drawing, in ward schools, bds. 146 n. Meridian.

Titcomb Daniel, agt. Rolling Mill Coal Co., res. 107 w. South.

Tirick Philip, tinner, res. 15 s. Alabama.

Toal Charles H., salesman, New York Store, bds. 58 s. Pennsylvania.

Tobin Thomas, boiler-maker, Eagle Machine Works, res. 1 Ann.

TODD, CARMICHAEL & WILLIAMS, (Charles N. T., Jesse D. C. & Daniel G. W.,) book-sellers, stationers and religious and Sunday-school book depository, 33 e. Washington, Glenns' blk.

Todd Charles N., (T., Carmichael & Williams,) 33 e. Washington, res. 228 n. Tennessee.

Todd John M., real estate agt., res. 312 Indiana av.

TODD R. N., physician, office on Kentucky av. res. 78 w. Market.

Tolbert Henry, (col.,) porter, G. G. Holman, bds. Wabash, bet. New Jersey and East.

Tomb Charley, lithographer, res. 107 Cherry.

TOMLINSON & COX,
(J. M. T. & William C. C.,) drugs and medicines, 18 e. Washington.

Tomlinson I. G., res. 17 Cherry.

Tompkins J. H. F., book-keeper, 26 e. Georgia, res. 241 n. Meridian.

Tomlinson J. M., (T. & Cox,) 18 e. Washington, res. n. w. cor. St. Clair and Meridian.

Tool John H., turner, bds. 445 s. Illinois.

Tool Martin, lab., res. 281 s. East.

Toon Mrs. Mariah, (wid. Josiah,) res. 191 s. New Jersey.

Topp Mrs. Frederica, (wid. Charles,) res. 247 n. Liberty.

Tarpay Thomas, brick-layer, bds. 84 s. Mississippi.

TOUSEY GEORGE,
prest. Ind. National Bank, 2 e. Washington, cor. Meridian, res. 415 n. Meridian.

Tousey Oliver, prest. Branch Bank of State, res. 182 n. Meridian.

Tousey Omer, salesman, 108 s. Meridian, res. n. Illinois, near cor. Tinker.

Tousey Ralph, secretary Y. M. C. Association, res. n. e. cor. Tennessee and Third.

Tousey Wood G., (Lesh, T. & Co.,) 43 s. Delaware, res. 545 n. Illinois.

Tousley Joseph H., switchman, C., C. & I. C. R. R., bds. 75 Kentucky av.

Tout Harry F., brick-mason, res. 15 Vine.

Tout Joseph H., butcher, res. 210 e. St. Clair.

Tout Isaac W., brick-mason, res. 555 n. Illinois.

Tout W. M., brick-layer, res. 625 n. Meridian.

Townley George E., clerk, F. P. Rush, bds. Bates House.

Tounson William, physician, res. 142 s. East.

Toushan Michael, shoe-maker, bds. 267 e. Washington.

Tox Francis, cash boy, New York Store, res. 70 Hosbrook.

Traub Charles, painter, res. Jackson, outside city limits.

Traub Conrad, brick-mason, res. 111 Ft. Wayne av.

Traub Israel, grocer and produce dealer, 500 n. Alabama, res. same.

Traub Jacob, painter, res. 500 n. Alabama.

Traub Jacob, gardener, res. n. s. National rd., w. White river bridge.

Troub Nancy, (wid. Henry,) res. n. s. National rd., w. White river bridge.

Tracy John, farmer, res. 83 Indiana av.

Tracy Kate, cook, Oriental House, bds. same.

Trail Miss Louisa, seamstress, res. National rd., w. White river bridge.

Trail R. A., tobacconist, bds. Ray House.

Tranbarger John W., soldier, U. S. Arsenal, res. same.

Trask George R., messenger, American Express Co., res. 33 e. Pratt.

Trask John, merchants' police, res. 25 Greer.

Traver George M., (L. H. Tyler & Co.,) 2. w. Washington, res. n. w. cor. Meridian and Circle.

Travelers' Ins. Co., of Hartford, Conn., Davis & Greene, agts., 27 s. Meridian.

Travis Albert, machinist, Emmerson & Thomson's planing mill, res. over 167 w. Washington.

TRAYSER GEORGE,
piano manfr., factory cor. New York and Davidson. See card, page 4, adv. dept.

Trayser F. L., piano manfr. and tuner, 84 e. Market, res. same.

Trayser Powell, piano-maker, works Robinson & Co., res. 278 e. Washington.

Treat A. A., bds. 38 w. Market.

Treat Atwater J., (T. & Claflin,) 30 n. Pennsylvania, bds. 172 w. Ohio.

TREAT & CLAFLIN,
(Atwater J. T. & Charles C. C.,) merchant tailors and drapers, 30 n. Pennsylvania.

Treep Henry, turner, Colp's, res. 213 s. Alabama.

Trembly James C., (col.,) res. near cor. Blake and Michigan.

Trendelmann Frederick, lab., res. 326 e. Vermont.

Treon Miss Kate, ladies' boarding house, 316 w. Washington.

Treter John, stone-mason, res. s. side Lockerbie, bet. Liberty and Noble.

Trigg Doc, miller, bds. 346 w. Washington.

Trinmous Pat, drives ale wagon, res. Minerva, near brewery.

Trindle Samuel, conductor, I. & Terre Haute R. R., res. 419 w. New York.

Trinity Methodist Episcopal Church, n. w. cor. North and Alabama.

Triplett James, (col.,) lab., bds. rear 343 Massachusetts av.

Troth Finley, salesman, Cottrell & Knight, bds. 486 n. Pennsylvania.

Trotter John, lab., res. 65 n. East.

Trontman James B., messenger, American Express, res. 551 n. Illinois.

Troy James, works Junction R. R., bds. Wiles House.

Troy John, works Junction R. R., bds. Wiles House.

Trucksess Frederick, teamster, bds. 76 Kentucky av.

Truax Henry, expressman, bds. 132 Maple.

Trucksess John, blacksmith, 76 Kentucky av., res. same.

Trucksess John, trader, s. Illinois, near cor. South.

Trueblood James, res. 347 n. Delaware.

Trueblood Newton A., res. 323 n. Illinois.

Truman Alexander, butcher, res. s. Tennessee.

Trusel Elizabeth, teacher, bds. 76 Benton.

Trusel William, blacksmith, bds. 76 Benton.

TRUSLER NELSON,
(N. & J. Trusler,) Secretary of State, office new State bldg, cor. Tennessee and Washington, res. 162 n. Tennessee.

Trusler Thomas J., lawyer, res. Western av., near city limits.

Tucker D. H., traveling agt., Stoneman & Tuttle, res. 58 s. Pennsylvania.

Tucker H. S., Trade Palace, bds. Macy House.

Tucker Joshua, traveling agt., T. F. Ryan, res. 104 w. Vermont.

TUCKER MISS MARGARET,
ladies' boarding house, 6 Pearl.

Tucker T. H., clerk, Stoneman & Tuttle.

Tuell E. Y., tuner, Willard & Stowell, res. n. East.

Tull John H., painter, res. 388 Indiana av.

Tully Mrs. Eliza N., boarding house, 58 s. Pennsylvania.

Turbyville Johanna, boarding house, National rd., near White river bridge.

Turbyville Robert, res. National rd., near White river bridge.

Turmyer Henry, clerk, res. 134 n. Mississippi.

Turner Augustus, (col.,) barber, shop s. w. cor. Meridian and Washington, res. 99 w. Georgia.

Turner A. H. (Johnson & T.,) 7 Blackford's blk., s. e. cor. Washington and Meridian, res. over 6 w. Washington.

Turner Andrew, (col.,) servant, at cor. Meridian and Vermont.

Turner Miss Belle, bds. 296 w. New York.

Turner Burten, (col.,) carpenter, res. Douglas alley.

Turner Edward, lab., bds. 227 s. Missouri.

Turner Grace, (col.,) servant at cor. Meridian and Vermont.

Turner Halle, Maryland, bet. Delaware and Alabama.

Turner James H., (Burk, Earnshaw & Co.,) res. beyond city limits.

Turner Joseph, lab., 16 Chadwick

Turner Robert, (col.,) lab., res. Second, bet. Howard and Lafayette R. R.

Turner William, cook, bds. 122 s. Benton.

Turner William, brick-mason, res. 416 n. New Jersey.

Turpen Miss Josephine, student Indiana Female College, 146 n. Meridian, bds. same.

Turpin James, brick-layer, res. 161 High.

Turquin Martin, res. 304 e. New York.

TUTEWILER BROS.,
(John W., Henry W. & Charles W. T.,) stoves, tin-ware and house-furnishing goods, 74 e. Washington, Tousey & Byram' s old stand. See card, page 8, adv. dept.

Tutewiler Charles, (T. Bros) bds. 85 Massachusetts av.

Tutewiler Henry, plasterer, res. 85 Massachusetts av.

Tutewiler Henry W., (T. Bros.,) res. 166 n. Alabama.

Tutewiler John, (T. Bros.,) bds. 85 Massachusetts av.

Tuttle Benjamin F., (Stoneman & T. and T. & Co.,) res. 496 n. Meridian.

Tuttle Gaylord P., clerk, 44 n. Pennsylvania, res. 326 n. Meridian.

Tuttle Orion, driver hose-reel, engine No. 1, res. 302 w. Washington.

Twilliger William, lab., res. 66 n. Noble.

Tyer George W., conductor, I., C. & L. R. R., res. 189 s. East.

Tyer Madison, fireman, res. 139 s. East.

Tyler J. D., saloon, Capital Garden, bds. 269 n. West.

Tyler Miss Anna M., principal A., Intermediate, high school, bds. 216 n. West.

Tyler Charles D., (L. H. T. & Co.,) 2 w. Washington, bds. Pyle House, n. Meridian.

Tyler Charles M., book-keeper, res. 239 n. Illinois.

Tyler George W., (col.,) lab., res. Athon, near city limits.

TYLER L. H. & CO.,
(Lewis H. T., George M. Traver & Charley D. T.,) Tyler's Bee-Hive, dry goods, notions, 2 w. Washington.

Tyler Lewis H., (L. H. T. & Co.,) 2 w. Washington, res. New York city.

Tyner Mrs. Amelia, (wid. Charles,) bds. 428 e. St. Clair.

Tyner Christian, works Hill's nursery, res. 553 e. St. Clair.

Tyner Mrs. Elizabeth, (wid. Henry,) res. 55 Peru.

Tyner Frederick, lab., res. 803 n. Tennessee.

Tyner Gotleib, lab., res. 563 e. St. Clair.

Tyner Henry, nurseryman, bds. N. M. Davidson, Highland Home av.

Tyner John, blacksmith, bds. 144 Virginia av.

UDOLPH THOMAS, engineer, I., C. & L. R. R., bds. 37 Bates.

Uhl John, clerk, 97 e. Washington, bds 252 s. Delaware.

Uhl Matthew, physician, office 63 w. Georgia, res. same.

Uhl Peter, clerk, 11 e Washington, res. 139 Fort Wayne av.

Umphreys W. W., assistant deputy clerk, United States District Court, bds. 126 n. Tennessee,

Union Depot, Louisiana, bet. Meridian and Illinois.

Union Fire Company, No. 3, South, bet. Delaware and Alabama.

Union House, by George Ilg, 202 s. Illinois.

Union Mission Chapel, (col..) e. s. Blackford, bet. Michigan and Vermont.

UNION RAILROAD CO., office in Union Passenger Depot, Louisiana, bet. Meridian and Illinois, E. J. Peck, prect., Wm. N. Jackson, secy., W. H. Robinson, supt.

UNION STARCH FACTORY, e. end New York.

United Brethren Church, s. e. cor. Ohio and New Jersey, Amos Hanaway, pastor.

United Presbyterian Church, Ohio, bet. Delaware and Pennsyvania, A. W. Clokey, pastor.

United States District Attorney, office 15 p. o. bldg.

United States Express office, 34 e. Washington.

Unversaw Andrew, carpenter, res. 125 e. Merrill.

Unversaw John, city marshal, res. 345 s. Alabama.

Updike John, plasterer, res. 154 s. noble.

Updike Samuel, plasterer, res. 40 Lord.

Upfold George, bishop Diocese of Indiana, res. 83 n. Tennessee.

Uphaus Henry, shoe-maker, 266 s. Delaware, res. same.

United States District and Circuit Court rooms, p. o. bldg., third floor.

United States Pension Office, cor. Pennsylvania and Virginia av., J. P. Wiggins, agt.

Utz Frederick, retired tobacconist, res. 187 Davidson.

VAHLE HENRY, teamster, 329 n. Noble.

Vajen J. H., (J. II. V. & Co.,) 21 w. Washinton, res. 128 n. Meridian.

VAJEN J. H. & CO., (J. H. V., J. S. Hilderbrand & J. L. Fugate,) wholesale hardware merchants, 21 w. Washington. See card, adv. dept., page 132.

Vail Sidney J., teacher, Deaf and Dumb Asylum, res. same.

VALENTINE WILLIAM H., hoop-skirt manfr., and corset and hosiery house, 34 w Washington, res. 115 n. Illinois.

Vanantwerp George W., blacksmith, Washington, bet. East and Liberty, s. s., res. 175 n. East.

Van Benthuysen H. J., confectionery, 145 Virginia av., bds. same.

Van Benthuysen J. H., fish stand, 149 Virginia av., res. 147 Virginia av.

Vanbergen ———, carpenter, res. 75 w. Michigan.

Vanblaricum Jesse M., wagon-maker, 231 w. Washington, res. 233 w. Washington.

Vanblaricum Michael, saloon, White river bridge, res. same.

Van Buren Fred. A., book-keeper, Grover & Baker Sewing Machine Co., res. 22 n. Noble.

Van Buskirk Elias, (Eldridge & Van B.,) over 30 w. Washington, res. 128 e. Maryland.

Vancamp Miss Frank, servant girl, at 195 Meek.

Van Camp G. C, (V., Jackson & Co.,) res. 222 w. Ohio.

Van Camp, Jackson & Co., (G. C. V. & T. B. J.,) grocers and produce dealers, 223 w. Ohio.

Vance Harrison, (col.,) lab., res. Howard, bet. Second and Third.

Vance John J., watch-maker, 36 e. Washington, res. 327 e. Vermont.

Vance Mrs. L. M., res. cor. Washington and Cady.

Vance L. M., (Porter, V. & Beck.,) res. cor. Washington and Cady.

Vance Noah N., physician, bds. 383 Massachusetts av.

Vance Samuel C., (Indiana Banking Co.,) 28 e. Washington, res. at terminus e. end Market.

Vance Thomas P., clerk, E. L. & E. B. Noel, res. 64 Oak.

Vancles Benjamin, carpenter, res. 178 n. Mississippi.

Vancles J. B., carpenter and box manfr., 195 e. Washington, res. 178 n. Mississippi.

Vandegriff Harry, mail agt., Union Depot, res. 502 n. Tennessee.

Vandegrift W. H., telegraph operator, 11 s. Meridian, res. 502 n. Tennessee.

Vandgrift Millard, printer, bds. 128 w. First.

Vandervort J. O. P., starch-maker, res. 120 Massachusetts av.

Vanduzan Chauncey, road-master, I., C. & L. R. R., res. 248 s. Alabama.

Vandyke W. W., shipping clerk, Stoneman & Tuttle, res. 58 s. Pennsylvania.

Vanhorn Nicholas, (Harvey & V.,) 101 e. Washington, res. 87 Ash.

Vanhouten Cornelius W., formerly grocer, cor. Market and Illinois, res. 217 Massachusetts av.

Vanhouten Isaac, res. 217 Massachusetts av.

Vanhouten Mrs. Joanna, (wid. Alamus,) res. 217 Massachusetts av.

Vanida Philip, lab., res. Kansas, s. city limits.

Vankemin Edward, builder, res. cor. Michigan and California.

Vanlaningham A. M., student, commercial college, bds. 77½ e. Market.

Vanlaningham Columbus, student, commercial college, bds. 77½ e. Market.

VANLANINGHAM LEMUEL, secy. Indianapolis Gas Light and Coke Co., cor. Maryland and Pennsylvania, res. 274 n. Alabama.

Vanlandingham Mrs. Jane, bds. 316 n. Illinois.

Vanlandingham L., lab., res. s. New Jersey, near city limits.

Vanlandingham Sarah, (wid.,) res. 408 n. New Jersey.

Vannattan Mrs. Martha J., (wid. William,) res. 127 n. Liberty.

Vannibal Willis, (col.,) white-washer, res. 97 Buchanan.

Vanpelt Lewis, auctioneer, res. 18 Fletcher av.

Vanplake Alexander, soldier, United States Arsenal, res. same.

Vansicklen Alexander, book-keeper, Hume, Adams & Co., bds. R. B. Duncan.

Vanstan John, shoe-maker, 239 s. Alabama, res. same.

Vantaye Abram, machinist, res. 328 e. Georgia.

Vantilburgh John B, conductor, Bellefontaine R. R., res. 272 Railroad.

Vanvleck Henry, cook, Palmer House, res. 391 n. New Jersey.

Vanvleck Mrs. Susan, cook, Pattison House, 63 n. Alabama.

Varney Mrs. Caroline, (wid. Thaddeus,) res. 291 e. Ohio.

Vater Thomas J., contractor, res. 330 n. Tennessee.

Vaughan Dennis, car inspector, I., C. & L. R. R., res. 75 w. Louisiana.

Vaughan Jacob M., carpenter, res. 548 n. Mississippi.

Vaughan Margaret, inmate Deaf and Dumb Asylum.

Vawter James A., huckster, res. 275 Bluff rd.

Veach Joseph, street car driver, bds. 132 n. Liberty.

Veach Samuel P., lab., res. 132 n. Liberty.

Veast Christopher, gardener, res. 474 c. Washington.

Veertler John, lab., res. 211 s. Pennsylvania.

Vehling Frederick, tailor, 182 c. Washington, res. 191 s. New Jersey.

Vehling Henry, lab., bds. 293 c. Washington.

Veilt Christopher J., (V. & Clark,) 19, 21 and 23 n. Tennessee, res. 128 Duncan.

VEITH & CLARK, (Charles V. & William C.,) props. Capitol Tobacco Works, 19, 21 and 23. n. Tennessee. See card, page v, front fly leaf.

Velosee Thomas, master mechanic, C., C. & I. C. shop, res. 326 e. Georgia.

Venable Edward, (col.,) servant, Pattison House.

Verrill Samuel K., student, commercial college, bds. 62 s. Pennsylvania.

Verity Stephen, piano-finisher, 159 and 161 c. Washington, res. 42 Huron.

Verity Stephen, Jr., piano key-board-maker, 159 and 161 e. Washington, res. 42 Huron.

Vernickel Joseph, bakery, 269 e. Washington, res. same.

Vernon Miss Ida, lady boarder, 281 c. New York.

Vert Elizabeth, (wid.,) res. 282 w. Merrill.

Vert William, driver, City R. R., res. 228 w. Maryland.

Vestal J. N., printer, Journal office, res. 140 n. Blackford.

Vick Mrs. Abby, (col.,) res. 248 w. Ohio.

Vick Alonzo, (col.,) barber, W. II. Franklin.

Vickers W. B., printer, cor. Meridian and Circle, res. 87 Benton.

Victor Mrs. Catharine E., seamstress, res. 166 n. Mississippi.

Victor Julius A., soldier, United States Arsenal, res. same.

Vielhaber Augustus, shoe-maker, bds. East, bet. Washington and Market.

Vielhaber Daniel, boot and shoe-maker, 204 c. Washington, res. same.

Vigo Agnes, lady boarder, 6 Pearl alley.

Vinyard Thomas W., railroader, res. 9 Graper.

Vincent Ann B., (wid. Henry,) res. 254 s. Tennessee.

Vincent Miss Catharine, dress-maker, 8 n. Pennsylvania, res. 73 n. Liberty.

Vincent Mrs. Catharine, (wid. Samuel,) res. 73 n. Liberty.

Vincent James M., conductor J., M. & I. R. R., bds. Ray House.

Vincent J. R., bds. Palmer House.

Vincent & Thompson, (William II. V. & John M. T.,) carpenters and builders, c. s. Railroad, bet. New York and Vermont.

Vincent William A., conductor, C., C. & I. C. R. R., res. 73 n. Liberty.

Vincent William II., (V. & Thompson,) res. 178 Davidson.

Vinnedge George W., (Hill & V.,) 3 w. Washington, res. cor. Walnut and Illinois.

Vinnedge John A., res. 704 n. Illinois.

Vinnedge Joseph D., (V., Jones & Co.,) 66 s. Meridian.

Vinnedge, Jones & Co., (Joseph D. V., Aquilla J. Jr., & William S. Armstrong.) wholesale boots and shoes, 66 s. Meridian.

Vinton A. E., (Kiefer & V.,) 68 s. Meridian, res. n. Meridian, outside city limits.

Vinyard Linnis, hoop skirt-maker, 34 w. Washington, res. 9 w. Draper.

Vinzing Herman, tailor, 307 s. Pennsylvania, res. same.

Violland Eugene L. hopper clerk, p. o., res. 421 n. Tennessee.

Virt John W., saddler, res. over 357 e. Market.

Virt William P., works Terre Haute depot, res. over 351 e. Market.

Virgil Isaac H., works American Express Company, res. 164 n. Alabama.

VOEGTLE JACOB,
dealer in stoves and house-furnishing goods, agt. Deibold, Bahmaun & Co.'s safes, 103 e. Washington, res. 473 n. Delaware.

Vogle Frederick, lab., res. 446 s. West.

Vogle Henry, carpenter, res. 523 e. Market.

Vogt Prof. B. J., leader Metropolitan Theater band, res. 244 e. Ohio.

Vogt Clara, servant, 283 e. Market.

Vogt Elizabeth, servant, 229 e. Ohio.

Vogt Frederick, (Langenberg, V. & Rozier,) res. 246 w. Washington.

Vogt Henry, clerk, res. 217 w. Michigan.

Voidy Lewis, lab., res. 68 Indiana av.

Voigt David, belt-maker, 125 s. Meridian, res. 235 s. Meridian.

Voight Frederick, (V. & Suhre,) 26½ n. Pennsylvania, res. 111 n. Noble.

Voight & Suhre, (Frederick V. & Frederick S.,) city express, 26½ n. Pennsylvania.

Voker John, lab., res. 315 s. Pennsylvania.

Vollman John, stone-mason, res. 50 s. West.

Vollmer Charles, lab., bds. 227 s. Missouri.

Vollmer Miss Louisa, tailoress, 168 e. Washington, res. 45 s. West.

Voltman Herod, lab., res. 406 s. Delaware.

Vondergotten Henry, (V. & Klein,) 37 s. Illinois, res. 279 n. Liberty.

VONDERGOTTEN & KLEIN,
barbers and hair-dressers, 37 s. Illinois.

VONNEGUT CLEMENS,
hardware and cutlery, 178 and 180 e. Washington, res. e. Market, near corporation line.

Voorhees Benjamin, mechanic, bds. Elm, bet. Georgia and Maryland.

Voorhees Jacob, plasterer, res. 140 e. St. Clair.

Voorhees Mrs. Mary J., (wid. Abram,) res. 135 n. Illinois.

Voorhees William, blacksmith, res. 232 s. Missouri.

Voorhees William, blacksmith, s. s. National rd., near Insane Asylum.

Voss Hermann, salesman, 37 e. Washington, bds. 204 n. Illinois.

WAAR WILKINS, lab., bds. Court, bet. East and New Jersey.

Waber Adam, lab., res. 340 s. Delaware.

Wachtstetter Charles, bar-keeper, 14 w. Louisiana, bds. 33 Madison av.

Wachtstetter Gotleib, saloon, 14 w. Louisiana, res. 23 Madison av.

Wachtstetter Jacob, saloon, 154 w. Washington, res. same.

Wachtstetter John, saloon, 180 s. Meridian, res. same.

Wade Mrs. Margaret, (wid. Henry,) res. Court, bet. East and New Jersey.

Waerner Philip F., bar-tender, House of Lords, 68 w. Washington.

Waginer Fred., works freight depot, res. 204 Union.

WAGNER S. W.,
banker, broker and loan-office, room 11, third floor Yohn's blk, n. Meridian, res. same.

Wagner George W., car-repairer, res. 123 e. Merrill.

Wagner Henry, brick-moulder, res. e. Washington, beyond city limits.

Wagner Henry, miller, res. 315 e. New York.

Wagner John, lab., 7 Willard.

Wagner John, cabinet-maker, bds. 65 s. East.

Wagner Joseph, teamster, res. 315 e. New York.

Wagner Lewis, (col.,) cooper, res. bet. Meek and Georgia.

Wagner Mary, servant, 477 n. Tennessee.

Wagner Mrs., res. 261 Bluff rd.

Wagner William, farmer, res. 562 Indiana av.

Wailing William, cooper, res. Fourth, bet. Railroad and Canal.

Wainwright Samuel, tin-ware and job shop, 18 w. Maryland, res. 278 s. Mississippi.

Wainwright William H., dealer in patent rights, bds. 96 w. First.

Wakeland A. A., porter p. o., bds. 92 e. Washington.

Waldon William, (col.,) white-washer, res. 223 n. West.

Waldo George W., tinner, res. 78 Benton.

Waldo Mrs. Mary T. M., (wid.,) res. 258 n. Mississippi.

Waldo William, lab., U. S. Arsenal, res. cor. Benton and Georgia.

Walden Mrs. Nancy, (col., wid.,) res. 553 n. Mississippi.

Waldy James M., miller, res. 309 Indiana av.

Walk Emile, shoe-maker, over 336 c. Market, res. same.

Walk Julius C., watch-maker, 50 e. Washington, res. s. c. cor. Washington and West.

Walk Lewis, boarding-house, 28 w. Georgia.

Walker Addison A., inmate Deaf and Dumb Asylum.

Walker Andrew, engineer, J., M. & I. R. R., res. 128 e. St. Mary.

WALKER ALVA S., (William Sumner & Co.,) Wheeler & Wilson's sewing machine, 10 w. Washington, res. 81 w. Vermont.

Walker Edward, stencil brand cutter, 45 s. Illinois, res. same.

Walker Miss Ellen, milliner, bds. 309 s. Meridian.

Walker Elwood L., inmate Deaf and Dumb Asylum.

Walker Frank, (col,) lab., res. Camp Carrington.

Walker George W., works G. A. Branson & Co, bds. under First National Bank.

Walker H. T., engineer, I., P. & C. R. R., bds. 142 s. East.

Walker Henry, lab., res. 41 Elm.

Walker Henry, (col.,) lab., res. w. Center.

Walker Henry H., special agt., resident adjuster Home Insurance Campany of New York, office over Bee Hive, 2 w. Washington, res. 555 n. Illinois.

Walker J. J., carpenter, res. 29 Chatham.

Walker John W., carpenter, bds. 124 n. Tennessee.

Walker Martha, inmate Deaf and Dumb Asylum.

Walker N. A., corresponding secretary Christian Association, res. 48 Cherry.

Walker Reuben, porter, Macy House, bds. same.

Walker S. W., engineer, I., C. & L. R. R., bds. Ray House.

Walker Thomas, brick-maker, bds. Shelbyville pike, ¾ mile s. corporation line.

Walker Thomas R., salesman, Mayhew & Branham, bds. Spencer House.

Walker Webster, spoke-turner, bds. 211 s. Illinois.

Walker William, yard-man, California House, bds. same.

Wall Arthur, carpenter, res. 199 cor. Missouri and Ohio.

Wall Charles A., physician and surgeon, res. 167 n. Tennessee.

Wall Charles E., oculist and aurist, 21½ w. Maryland, bds. Palmer House.

Wall George, lab., res. 23 bet. Liberty and East.

Wall John, printer, bds. 54 Stevens.

Wall Mrs. Lottie E., bds. 199 cor. Missouri and Ohio.

Wall Thomas, flagman, I. & C. R. R., res. 154 Stevens.

Wallace A. G., justice of the peace, office 74 e. Washington, res. n. e. cor. Ash and Cherry.·

Wallace Andrew, stone-cutter, bds. 258 s. Missouri.

WALLACE ANDREW, wholesale grocer and commission rooms, cor. Delaware and Maryland, res. 86 n. Delaware.

Wallace Henry, stone-cutter, res. 167 s. Alabama.

Wallace J. Andy, book-keeper, res. 38 Forest av.

Wallace James, res. 370 s. Delaware.

Wallace James, stone-cutter, bds. 167 s. Alabama.

Wallace John W., clerk, 322 c. Washington, res. 329 e. Market.

Wallace Johnston, stone-cutter, bds. 258 s. Missouri.

Wallace Joseph A., clerk, 74 e. Washington, bds. cor. Ash and Cherry.

Wallace Matthew, blacksmith, res. 73 s. Liberty.

Wallace Oliver, brick-mason, res. 370 s. Delaware.

Wallace Robert, moulder, bds. Ray House.

Wallace Samuel, brick-mason, bds. cor. Morrison and Alabama.

Wallace Wm., machinist, res. 258 s. Missouri.

Wallace William, lab., Sinker's foundry, res. Coburn, bet. Wright and East.

Wallace William J., grocer, 322 e. Washington, res. 329 e. Market.

WALLACE WILLIAM P., wholesale and retail manfr. and dealer in cigars and tobacco, 28 w. Louisiana, res. 160 e. Market.

Wallace William P., lawyer, res 285 n. Delaware.

Wallace Will W., notary public, with A. Metzger, 6 Odd Fellows' Hall, n. e. cor. Pennsylvania and Washington, res. 29 w. Michigan.

Wallace William W., lumber business, res. 284 n. Tennessee.

Wallace Zerelda, (wid.,) res. 273 n. New Jersey.

Walle John, (Wehling & W.,) res. 244 s. Delaware.

Waller Bernhard, shoe-shop, 151 Indiana av., res. same.

Wallick J. P., district supt. W. U. Telegraph Co., res. 36 w. Michigan.

Wallingford Catharine, (wid. Estes,) res. 456 n. Delaware.

Walls John, (col.,) regular army, res. Eighth, w. Lafayette R. R.

Walls William, brakesman, C., C. & I. C. R. R., bds. 424 on Central R. R.

Walls Henry, res. 21 e. North.

Walls W. L., printer, bds. 113 s. New Jersey.

Walpole Mrs. Esther, (wid. Thomas D.,) res. 410 n. Illinois.

Walpole Luke, bds. 410 n. Illinois.

Walpole Miss Susan B., res. 236 n. Meridian.

Walsman Frederick C., pastry-cook, Union Depot Hall, res. 178 e. Vermont.

Walsman Jacob, lab., res. 178 c. Vermont.

Walsh John, boiler, White River Iron Works, bds. California House.

Walsh Margaret, (wid. Thomas,) res. 334 s. Alabama.

Walsom Charles, hostler, 16 n. Pennsylvania.

Walter Charles, cabinet-maker, res. 200 n. Mississippi.

Walter George, cook, Palmer House, res. 249 w. South.

Walter Victor, brush-maker, works Schmedel & Fricker, bds. Morris, bet. East and New Jersey.

Walter William boot-maker, 51 w. Washington, bds. 23 Kentucky av.

Walters L. M., minister, res. 162 w. South.

Walton Houston F., merchant, bds. 89 n. Delaware.

Walton Wm., heater, rolling mill, res. 424 s. Tennessee.

Walts Frank, lab., res. Geisendorff, near Geisondorff's woolen factory.

Wampler David, boarding house, 99 s. Bentoon, n. e. cor. Georgia.

Wamsley Harvey, carpenter, res. 354 n. West.

Wan John, shoe-maker, res. 37 Fletcher av.

Wanderly Henry, brick-mason, res. 146 Davidson.

Wanderly Mrs. Mary, milliner and dressmaker, 146 Davidson, res. same.

Wands Alex., boot-maker, bds. 65 Greer.

Wands Alexander, (W. & Ruschaup,) 81 e. Washington, res. n. Pennsylvania.

Wands John, shoe-maker, res. 55 Greer.

Wands John, shoe-maker, res. 65 e. McCarty.

Wands John, Jr., shoe-maker, bds. cor. Noble and Huron.

Wands & Ruschaup, saloon, 81 e. Washington.

Wands William, physician and surgeon, office 66 e. Market, bds. 330 e. Vermont.

Wann H. L., mill-wright, res. 256 s. Pennsylvania.

Ward B., druggist and physician, 397 n. New Jersey, res. 357 n. New Jersey.

Ward Daniel, peddler, res. 9 Peru.

Ward Daniel, carpenter, res. Geisendorff, near Geisendorff's woolen factory.

Ward E. S., bds. 85 Circle.

Ward Gabriel, res. 348 Indiana av.

Ward Hannah, servant at 213 n. Illinois.

Ward C., railroader, bds. 161 High.

Ward Kate, servant, kitchen, 165 c. Merrill.

Ward Michael S., salesman, New York Store, res. 165 St. Joseph.

Ward Michael, lab., res. 311 s. Missouri.

Ward Mrs. ——, (wid.,) charge ladies' room, Union Depot, bds Commercial Hotel.

WARD PETER H., attorney at law, room 4 Talbott & New's blk., bds. n. w. cor. Illinois and New York.

Ward Thomas, salesman, New York Store, bds. Macy House.

Ward Thomas M., painter, 128 e. Washington, bds. Union Hall.

Ward Thoms, lab., bds. Ray House.

Warden William, lab., bds. 140 cor. Elm and Grove.

Ware Catharine, (wid. Robert,) res. 157 w. South.

Warfield Charles, (col.,) lab., res. 112 Ash.

Warford A., occupant Deaf and Dumb Asylum.

Warne James P., bill-clerk, I. & C. R. R., res. 41 Huron.

Waring Isaac, clerk, Indiana Fire Ins. Co., 5 Odd Fellows' Hall, res. 140 n. Alabama.

Warman Charles, clerk, Haskit & Co., bds. 139 n. Tennessee.

Warne Joseph B., salesman, Ray, Mayhew & Co., bds. 59 w. Maryland.

Warner C. H., student, commercial college, bds. cor. Jackson and Cherry.

Warner Charles G., printer, res. 35 Ellsworth.

Warner Edward, printer, bds. 35 Ellsworth.

Warner George S., (J. H. Baldwin & Co.,) 6 e. Washington, bds. Spencer House, s. Illinois.

Warner Marcus, speculator, res. 408 n. Illinois.

Warner Marcus, lab., res. Michigan rd., e. city limits.

Warner Miram, res. Michigan rd.

Warner Miss Susie, milliner, over 8 w. Washington, bds. w. Washington.

Warner Thomas, printer, res. 226 w. New York.

Warner Wallace, brick-mason, res. n. e. cor. East and Vermont.

Warren Joseph, carpenter, res. 156 High.

Warrenberg John, teamster, res. rear 26 Lockerbie.

Warrenberg William, lab., res. s. e. cor. Noble and New York.

Warriner Mrs. M. A., (wid.,) res. 89 Indiana av.

Washburn Calvin, carpenter, Bellefontaine shops, res. 346 Winston.

Washburn Dewitt C., claim broker, n. c. cor. Washington and Illinois, bds. Palmer House.

Washington Miss Allice, ladies' boarding house, 131 and 133 n. East.

Washington Ferris, (col.,) lab., res. cor. Howard and Second.

Washington George, (col.,) lab., res. Lafayette R. R., bet. First and Second.

Washington Henry, (col.,) teamster, res. Second, bet. Howard and Lafayette R. R.

Washington Henry, lab., res. 223 e. Michigan.

Washington House, 181 s. Meridian, Henry Weiglein, propr.

Washington Lucy, (col.,) washing and ironing, bds. 224 Huron.

Wason Alexander W., veterinary surgeon, office 40 e. Washington, res. 85 s. Pennsylvania.

Wason William, machinist, res. 225 s. Tennessee.

Wason W. G., machinist, bds. 175 s. Tennessee.

WASON W. P., boot and shoe maker, 175 s. Tennessee, res. same.

Wate Miss A. S., teacher, German school, res. 497 n. Alabama.

Water Charles, telegraph operator, J., M. & I. R. R., bds. 361 s. Delaware.

Waterman Christian, (H. Berg & Co.,) 193 s. Tennessee, res. same.

Waterman L. D., physician, 68 n. Pennsylvania, res. 377 n. Delaware.

Waters John G., deputy city clerk, office Glenns' blk., e. Washington, res. 86 n. Mississippi.

Waters Miss Lucy, dress-maker, 120 n. Tennessee, res. same.

Waters Morris, lab., T. H. & I. R. R. freight depot, res. 27 Row.

Waters Samuel D., lab., res. 168 Buchanan.

Watkins Edward, works Junnction R. R., bds. Wiles House.

Watkins James, engineer, I., C. & L. R. R., res. 92 Bates.

Watkins Mrs. Maria, (col.,) washer-woman, res. Second, bet. Howard and Lafayette R. R.

WATKINS W. W., bds. Palmer House.

Wats William, grate-setter, res. 458 e. Georgia.

Watson Elmer W., (Watson & Bro.,) painters, 194 Indiana av., res. 607 c Washington.

Watson J. C., lab., res. 27 s. Liberty.

Watson Morris, (Watson & Bro.,) painters, 193 Indiana av., res. 425 w. New York.

Watson J. M., machinist, Sinker's, res. 607 e. Washington.

Watsou Joseph S., printer, W. Sheets, res. 207 w. Maryland.

Watson Mrs. Nancy, (wid. Joseph,) bds. s. w. cor. Meridian and Vermont.

Watson R. J., brakesman, C., C. & I. C. R. R., bds. 607 e. Washington.

Watson Robert H., machinist, works I. & C. R. R, bds. 320 e. Washington.

Watson Samuel W., book-keeper, Harrisons' Bank, 15 e. Washington, res. 119 w. Maryland.

Watson William P., book-keeper, First National Bank, res. 421 n. Illinois.

Walter Byron, Jr., lab., res. 317 w. Washington.

Walters Warren, lab., res. 27 Rose.

Walti Rudolph, butcher, National rd., w. White river bridge.

Waugh Daniel, machinist, res. 49 Ellen.

Waugh Harrison, lab., res. Blackford alley.

Way Miss Amanda M., editress, Western Independant, office and res. 35 n. East.

Way Miss Lou., manuf. of Good Templars' regalias, 35 n. East. res. same.

Way Robert, boarding house, 35 n. East.

Way Truman, railroader, res. 296 s. Alabama.

Way William W., baggage-master, I., C. & L. R. R., bds. 294 s. Alabama.

Wayne Christopher, currier, 78 e. Washington, res. 451 s. New Jersey.

Weakley Gorman A., foreman, foundry, res. 179 w. New York,

Wearner John, (Geis & W.,) 99 e. Washington, res. 262 s. East.

Weathers John, railroader, res. s. Noble, near South.

Weaver Edward, painter, bds. 69 w. Market.

Weaver Frank W., book-binder, bds. 233 n. Illinois.

Weaver Frederick, works Union Factory, res. 336 n. Noble.

Weaver George, brick-mason, bds. 201 Davidson.

Weaver John, salesman, s. w. cor. Washington and Delaware.

Weaver Wesley, lab., res. 142 Elm.

WEAVER WILLIAM W., undertaker, 39 n. Illinois, res. 233 n. Illinois.

Webb A. L., gen. agt. Massilon excelsior reaping and mowing machines, 81 w. Washington, bds. 69 w. Market.

Webb Charles, (col.,) driver, N. S. Baker, res. 161 Elm.

Webb Coy, (col.,) waiter, Bates House.

Webb Ira C., (Clancy & W.,) 18 s. Meridian, res. 69 w. Market.

Webb John W., carpenter, res. 150 Winston.

Webb Mrs. Laura, boarding-house, 69 W. Market.
Webb Leonidas, blacksmith, s. s. National rd., near Insane Asylum.
Webb Sidnor, res. 91 s. Pennsylvania.
Webb William, blacksmith, s. s. National rd., near Insane Asylum.
Webb William, miller, res. 230 Bluff rd.
Webber John, (col.,) res. 237 Michigan.
Weber David, iron-moulder, works D. Root & Co., res. 278 Winston.
Weber Erhard, porter, Crossland, Maguire & Co., res. 53 s. California.
Weber Frederick, carpenter, res. over 277 Massachusetts av.
Weber George H., lab., res. 130 Bluff rd.
Weber Henry, moulder, Root's foundry, res. w. Seventh, bet. Lenox and Michigan rd.
Weber John, blacksmith, res. 791 n. Illinois.
Weber John A., (J. A. W. & Brother,) res. over 210 Massachusetts av.
Weber J. A. & Brother, dealers in Madison and North Vernon XXX ale, 211 Massachusetts av.
Weber J. Fred., salesman, 4 w. Washington, res. 366 n. Noble.
Weber Lewis, barber, 94 e. South, res. same.
Weber Peter F., (J. A. Weber & Bro.,) bds. over 211 Massachusetts av.
Weber William, blacksmith, res. 372 Virginia av.
Webster Abner, res. 706 n Illinois, s. w. cor. Fifth.
Webster G. C., (Daggett & Co.,) 28 s. Meridian, res. 314 n. East.
Webster George S., machinist, res. 88 California.
Webster Harvy, candy-maker, bds. 314 n. East.
Webster E. Harvey, driver, Hook and Ladder Co., res. 17 old number n. New Jersey.
Weckerly W. H., stave-factory, bds. Bates House.
Wegman Herman, music-teacher, res. 259 e. New York.
Weeks Richard, works Munson & Johnson, bet. Liberty and East.
Weeks George, machinist, works Spiegle, Thoms & Co., res. over 174 e. Washington.

WEGHORST HENRY,
gardener and fruit-grower, s. East, beyond city limits, res. same. See card, page 98.
Weghorst Hermann, gardener, s. East, near corporation line.
Wegman Gustave, clerk, Union depot eating saloon.
Wegmouth Amos, blacksmith, w. White river bridge.

Wehent Michael, boot-maker, 6 s. Delaware, res. n. Tennessee.
Wehle Lucius, boots and shoes, 235 e. Washington, res. same.
Wehling Charles H., (W. & Walle,) wagonmakers, 234 s. Delaware.
Wehn Christian, tanner, res. 451 s. New Jersey.
Wehn Mary, milliner, res 451 s. New Jersey
Wehrle George, shoe-maker, works 350 s. Delaware, res. same.
Weibel John E., barber, 33½ w. Washington, res. 376 e. Ohio.
Weidle Jacob, book-keeper, White River Rolling Mill Co., bds. 27 w. Ohio.
Weigart Joseph, carpenter, res. 127 Duncan.
Weigle Gottlieb, currier, 125 s. Meridian, res. 85 n. Noble.
Weigler Gustavus A., Swiss Dairy, s. s. National rd., 1 mile w. White river bridge.
Weiglein H. F., propr. Washington House, 181 s. Meridian.
Weikert Alonzo, clerk, 14 w. Washington, res. 27 Duncan.
Weiland August, tailor, res. 158 Maple.
Weiland Christian, switchman, res. 134 Union.
Weiland William C., clerk, 397 s. Meridian, bds. 558 s. Illinois.
Weiland William, baggage-porter, Union Depot, bds. California House.
Weilleman Jacob, lab., res. 17 John.

WEINBERGER & CO.,
(Ernest W. & Herman W.,) eating-stand and restaurant, 10 w. Louisiana.
Weinberger Ernest, (W. & Co.,) 10 w. Louisiana, res. 279 n. East.
Weinberger Herman, (W. & Co.,) 10 w. Louisiana, res., 138 s. Meridian.
Weingarten Christiana, servant, 171 s. New Jersey.
Weier I. L., salesman, New York Store, bds. Oriental House.
Weis John, brick-layer, res. 343 n. Delaware.
Weis Peter, (Stiegman & W.,) res. 150 Madison av.
Weismeyer John, lab., rolling-mill, res. 345 e. McCarty.
Weisz S., hoop-skirt manfr. and ladies' furnishing goods, 26 n. Pennsylvania, res. same.
Weiss John L., saloon, 401 e. Washington, res. same.
Weitchman Charles, painter, res. 53 n. Alabama.
Weithaup Frederick, pastor, German Evangelical Church, res. Wabash, rear of church.
Welburn Mrs. Ann., (col.,) washer-woman, res. Camp Carrington.

Welsh A. J., brakesman, T. H. & I. R. R., res. 83 w. Louisiana.

Welch Mrs. Catharine, (wid. Christian,) res. 235 Davidson.

Welch Miss Margaret, bds. 355 s. Meridian.

Welch Maurice, saloon, 79 e. Washington, res. 355 s. Meridian.

Welch Patrick, saloon, 23 w. Washington, res. 355 s. Meridian.

Welch Patrick, engineer, C., C. & I. C. R. R., res 58 Benton.

Welken Henry, works Cabinet-Makers' Union, res. 110 n. Noble.

Weller James, night-watchman, Sinker's foundry, res. cor. Blake and New York.

Weller Levi, mail-carrier, res. 651 n. Tennessee.

Weller William, blacksmith, Sinker & Co., res. 281 n. Tennessee.

Wellerdin Mrs. Alice, (wid. Anthony,) dress-maker, n. Delaware, bds. 159 s. Alabama.

Wellman Hiram B., res. 447 n. Mississippi.

Wells Anna, servant, 130 n. Alabama.

Wells Andrew J., policeman, second ward, res. 240 n. Illinois.

Wells Carrie, lady boarder, 36 s. New Jersey.

Wells Charles, (col.,) lab., res. Minerva, near City Hospital.

Wells Edward, shoe-maker, res. 191 s. New Jersey.

WELLS GRAHAM A.,
dentist, over 15 e. Washington, res. 181 n. New Jersey.

Wells Haden, contractor, Vincennes & Indianapolis R. R., res. 156 Huron.

Wells James, engineer, spice mills, res. 77 s. East.

Wells John H., carpenter, res. w. s. Tennessee, bet. Sixth and Seventh.

Wells Joseph, clerk, 96 e. Washington, bds. 38 Cherry.

WELLS MERIT,
dentist, room 2 Yohn's blk., over 11 n. Meridian, res. 285 n. East

Wells Peter, (col.,) lab., res. 201 n. Meridian.

Wells Thomas L., boot and shoe-maker, room 9, Miller's blk., up-stairs.

Wells W. F., carpenter, res. 38 Cherry.

Welsh B. D., painter, bds. 71 Indiana av.

Welsh Catharine, servant, res. 97 n. Delaware.

Welsh D. S., picture-dealer, e. Washington, bds. Pattison House.

Welsh Daniel, lab., res. 70 Railroad.

Welsh Eliza, servant at 284 n. Meridian.

Welsh Miss Emma, bds. 265 n. Illinois.

Welsh James, lab., res. 70 Railroad.

Welsh John, works on Junction R. R., res. 109 Railroad.

Welsh John, watchman, Bellefontaine depot, res. 374 s. Delaware.

Welsh Mary, servant, E. Benham, 240 n. Tennessee.

Welsh Michael, porter, 38 s. Meridian, res. 167 e. St. Joseph.

Welsh Thomas, lab., res. 30 Helen.

Wempner Henry, lab., res. 59 Harrison.

Wenger George M., saloon and beer garden, n. w. cor. Noble and Market, res. same.

Wenger Miss Lizzie, milliner, bds. 50 n. Noble.

Wenken August, cabinet-maker, res. 178 n. Noble.

Wenken E., (Back & W.,) 209 e. Washington, bds. same.

Wenken William, cabinet-maker, res. 178 n. Noble.

Wentling L. L., salesman, New York Store, bds. Macy House.

Wentz Morris, farmer, res. 562 Indiana av.

Wentz William W., conductor, I. & C. R. R., res. 165 s. Alabama.

Werbe Charles, (Charles W. & Co.,) 81 e. Market, res. 300 e. Market.

WERBE CHARLES & CO.,
(Charles W. & C. E. McDonald,) solicitors of patents and meddle builders, 81 e. Market. See card, page 52.

Werbe Christopher G., lawyer, over 75 e. Washington, res. near Madison tollgate.

Werber George A., porter, 34 s. Meridian, res. 30 Bluff rd.

Werbe Emil, lithographic printer, W. & J. Braden, bds. California House.

Werbe Francis L., grocery, 249 w. Washington, res. same.

Werbe Henry V., porter, Jefferson House.

Werbe L. & Co., (L. W. & J. M. Cooper,) drugs and medicines, 253 n. Illinois.

Werb J. W., book-keeper, 76 e. Washington, bds. 127 n. Alabama.

Wert Joseph, boot and shoe manuf., 10 s. Pennsylvania, res. 127 n. Alabama.

Wery W. B., carpenter, res. 3 Thomas.

Wosly E., cooper, res. 324 w. Maryland.

Wesly William, res. 324 w. Maryland.

Wesley Chapel, s. w. cor. Meridian and Circle, Rev. C. N. Sims, pastor.

Wesley Mary, servant, 266 e. Market.

Wesling Conrad, drayman, res. 330 n. Noble.

Wesser John, lab., res. 213 n. Noble.

West Charles M., traveling agt., Stewart & Morgan, bds. Bates House.

West George H., (H. F. W. & Co.,) 37 s. Meridian, res. 483 n. Tennessee.

WEST H. F. & CO.,
(H. F. & George H. W., John I. Morris & A. W. Gorrell,) china, glass and queensware and silver-plated goods, 37 s. Meridian.

West Henry F., (H. F. W. & Co.,) 37 s. Meridian, r**e**. Cincinnati, O.

West J. C., (Scott, W. & Co.,) 127 s. Meridian, res. Richmond, Ind.

West William, (col.,) lab., res. 130 n. East.

Westonheimer Louis, cabinet-maker, bds. 45 cor. Fletcher av. and Huron.

Western Fire Co., No. 1, 277 w. Washington.

WESTERN FURNITURE CO., 105 e. Washington, I. Wust, prest. See card, page iv.

WEST. UNION TELEGRAPH OFFICE, 11 s. Meridian, Charles C. Whitney, manager,

Westfall Theodore, works Bellefontaine depot, res. 150 Union.

Westfall Thomas, lab., res. 150 Union.

West J. M., moulder, Root's, res. 124 e. Merrill.

Wethers Ermsted, (col.,) barber, works 50 e. Washington, bds. 212 Vermont.

Wetzel Henry, clerk, 29 w. Washington, bds. cor. North and Illinois.

Wetzel Peter, gardener, res. s. West, near city limits.

Whalen Catharine, servant, Palmer House.

WHEAT, FLETCHER & CO., (William C. W., L. W. F., Samuel Cutsinger & D. Coffin, provision dealers and pork-packers, room 1, Vinton's blk., n. Pennsylvania.

Wheat William C., (W., Fletcher & Co.,) room 1, Vinton's blk., n. Pennsylvania, res. Franklin, Ind.

Wheatly Henry H., box factory, cor. South and Delaware, res. 311 s. East.

Wheatley John M., book-keeper, McCord & Wheatley, res. 309 s. East.

Wheatley Julia, (col.,) servant, 309 e. Market.

Wheatley William M., (McCord & W.,) 19 s. Alabama, res. 202 e. Ohio.

Wheden A., conductor, J., M. & I. R. R., bds. Bates House.

Wheeler Albert, tinner, bds. Pattison House.

Wheeler Anna, (col.,) washer-woman, res. 259 n. West.

Wheeler D. Y., clerk, bds. Pyle House.

Wheeler Ephraim, barber shop, cor. Indiana av. and Michigan, res. same.

Wheeler John, brakesman, C., C. & I. C. R. R., res. 58 Benton.

Wheeler M., bds. 556 n. Illinois.

Wheeler W., tinner, Tutewiler Bros., res. 63 n. Alabama.

Wheeler W. V., driver, M. U. Ex. Co., 42 and 44 e. Washington, bds. 79 n. Alabama.

Wheeling Edward, railroader, res. 245 w. South.

Whiney Charles C., manager, Western Union Telegraph, res. 94 s. Noble.

Whipke Henry, drayman, res. 293 Davidson.

Whipple Charles W., machinist, Root's, res. 315 s. East.

Whitaker John, (col.,) lab., res. bet. Meek and Georgia.

Whitaker L. L., clerk, 55 w. Washington, res. 157 n. Mississippi.

Whitcomb Jerome G., freight agt., Jeffersonville R. R., res. 162 e. Market.

White Alonzo M., agt., Berkshire Life Ins. Co., res. 377 n. East.

White Allen C., paper-hanger, res. 102 Bates.

White Alfred, (col.,) lab., res. 450 s. Tennessee.

White Mrs. Catharine, (wid. John,) res. 578 e. St. Clair.

White Charles H., (Coulter & W.,) 77 e. Market, res. 365 e. New York.

White Charles H., carpenter, works Warren Tate's factory, res. Court, bet. East and New Jersey.

White Mrs. E., actress, Metropolitan Theater, res. 224 Huron.

WHITE F. G., comic actor, Metropolitan Theater, res. 224 Huron.

White George W., traveling agt., 42 s. Meridian, bds 33 w. Maryland.

WHITE H. W., merchant tailor, over 11 s. Meridian, res. 212 e. Market.

White Miss Harriet, res. 49 cor. Huron and School.

White Hiram, lab., res. 4 Harris.

White J. B., baggage-master, C. & I. C. R. R., res. 388 s. Missouri.

WHITE MRS. JANE, (wid. David,) boarding-house, 75 s. Pennsylvania, res. same.

White Miss Jane, bds. 85 Indiana av.

White James M., machinist, bds. 233 n. Noble.

White James W., lab., res. 793 n. Tennessee.

White Joel M., soldier, U. S. Arsenal, res. Arsenal.

White Joseph, lumber dealer, res. 49 cor. Huron and School.

White Joseph E., salesman, 22 w. Washington, res. 72 Maple.

White Line Freight Office, cor. Alabama and Union R. R. track.

White Martha J., (col.,) res. 194 Douglas alley.

White Miss Mary, res. E. L. Hasting's, n. Illinois, bet. First and Second.

White Miss Mary, lady boarder, 201 e. Market.

White Michael, lab., bds. 578 e. St. Clair.

White Nineveh, dealer in fruit, shade and ornamental trees, cor. Delaware and Market, res. e. city limits.

White Norah, (col.,) servant, M. J. Oatman, 712 n. Tennessee.

White Philip, (col.,) servant at 284 n. Meridian.
White Pompey, (col., laborer, bds. Howard, bet. Third and Fourth.
White R. B., farmer, res. 869 n. East.
White Rhoda, (wid.,) res. 53 e. Maryland.
White Richard, lab., res. Michigan rd., beyond city limits.
WHITE RIVER IRON CO., office 244 Kentucky av. See card, page 222.
White Mrs. Sarah, (wid. Samuel E.,) res. 117 n. Mississippi.
White Mrs. Susan, (wid. Milton,) res. 494 Virginia av.
White Miss Susan A., res. 494 Virginia av.
White Thomas, lab., bds. 378 e. St. Clair.
White Thomas, lab., res. 340 s. Alabama.
White William, carpenter, bds. 20 s. Pennsylvania.
White William H., carpenter, res. 72 Maple.
White William M., bds. 57 Eddy.
Whiteford M. M., teacher, Institute of the Blind, res. same.
Whitehead Thomas, carpenter, res. 160 Ft. Wayne av.
Whitehead Thomas, miller, res. 420 w. Washington.
Whitehead William, clerk, 405 w. Washington, res. same.
Whiteman Peter, lab., res. 326 Railroad.
Whiteside John, engineer, C., C. & I. C. R. R., res. 43 Bates.
WHITING T. M., bleachieg manufactory, 31 Kentucky av., res. same.
Whitlow Eli, soldier at Arsenal, res. 576 e. St. Clair.
Whitman B. F., clerk, B. & I. office, bds. 380 Massachusetts av.
Whitman J. M., res. 493 n. East.
Whitmore Elizabeth C., res. 58 Benton.
Whitmore Oliver, compositor, Downey, Brouse, Butler & Co., bds. Mrs. Reed's n. Pennsylvania.
Whitney C. W., bds. Macy House.

WHITNEY CHARLES C., manager W. U. Telegraph Co., office 11 s. Meridian, res. 94 s. Noble.
Whitney Jonathan, blacksmith, res. 306 e. Georgia.
Whitney Phineas W., clerk, T. H. & I. R. R., bds. Bates House.
Whitney William, res. 426 n. Mississippi.
Whitney William, shoe-maker, 119 s. Illinois, bds. 124 s. Meridian.
Whitridge James, student, bds. 363 n. New Jersey.
Whitridge Samuel, painter, res. s. s. Second, bet. Meridian and Illinois.
Whitridge William, painter, res. 363 n. New Jersey.
Whitsit Benjamin F., brick-layer, res. 291 Virginia av.
WHITSIT C. E., builder and contractor, also, manfr. of brick, office s. w. cor. Meridian and Washington, res. 291 Virginia av.
Whitsit James, (col.,) lab., bds. Huron, bet. Ceder and Elm.
Whitsit Jesse S., brick-layer, res. 296 Virginia av.
Whitsit John, brick-maker, res. 291 Virginia av.
Whitsit John (col.,) lab., bds. Huron, bet. Cedar and Elm.
Whitson John M., engineer, J. M. & L. R. R., bds. Ray House.
Whitton Robert L., clerk, 40 e. Washington, res. 198 s. Illinois.
Whitton Rev. Elijah, minister, Methodist Church, res. 124 n. Tennessee.
Whittenberger Mrs. Cordelia, bds. 316 n. Illinois.
Wichen John, lab., bds. 351 Massachusetts av.
Wick Isabella, clerk, p. o., res. n. Meridian, near Tinker.
Wick Miss Ina D., res. n. Meridian.
Wick William, judge, res. w. s. n. Meridian, beyond city limits.
Wickens Thomas, works Junction R. R., bds. Wiles House.

Wickerley Robert J., cooper, bds. Bates House.

Wickliff Henry, lab., res. 32 Ann.

Wickliff Peter, res. 452 s. Tennessee.

Wickliff Peter, (col.,) waiter, Bates House,

Wicks Richards, porter, 62 e. Washington. res. Wabash.

Wiegand John, works Union Depot, res. 147 Bluff rd.

Wiegant Anthony, propr. City Garden, res same.

Wierer Chas., brush-maker, works Schmedel & Fricker, res. e. Washington, near Michigan rd.

Wiese Anthony F., lab., res. 327 e. Michigan.

Wiese Andy, carpenter, works Miller & Paule, res. 283 e. Ohio.

Wiese Charles, carpenter, works Bellefontaine R. R. shop, res. 283 e. Ohio.

Wiese Christian, lab., Spiegle, Thoms & Co., res. 84 s. Liberty.

Weisman Simon, teamster, res. 355 w. Washington.

Weiseman William, res. 391 w. Washington.

Wiggins George W., tinner, res. 36 s. Alabama.

Wiggins Henry D., machinist, Root's foundry, res. 507 n. Mississippi.

WIGGINS JOSEPH P.,
(Foster W. & Co.,) and United States Pension office, cor Virginia av., res. 325 n. Pennsylvania.

Wiggins Lizzie, seamstress, 124 Duncan.

Wiggins Miss Mary, tailoress, works White's shop, Blackford's blk, res. 237 n. Noble.

Wiggins Percival E., clerk, pension office, bds. 381 n. Illinois.

Wiggins W. W., res. 222 s. East.

Wiland Wm. D., clerk, res. 558 s. Illinois.

Wilcox Charles D., agt. St. Louis Mutual Life Insurance Co., room 4 Yohn blk., res. 64 Fletcher av.

Wilcox David H., lab., res 285 n. Blake.

Wilcox George H., printer, bds. 9 Vine.

Wilcox John, street-car driver, res. 293 w. Blake.

Wilcox Thomas, plasterer, res. 62 Fletcher av.

Wilcox Wm. B., cabinet-maker, res. 9 Vine.

Wilcox Wm. H., new rolling mill, res. 154 cor. New York and West.

Wilcus Jacob, lab., res. 70 s. Illinois.

Wilde John H., saw-maker, res. 274 Bluff rd.

WILDER C. P.,
books, stationery, wall-paper, &c., 26 e. Washington, res. 26 n. Mississippi. See card, page 76.

Wilding William, shoe-maker, 46 Indiana av., res. same.

Wilding William, shoe-maker, res. 370 w. Vermont.

Wildrick William, chair-manfr., 476 Virginia av., res. same.

Wiland Minnie, servant, 190 n. East.

Wiles Charles, clk, 32 s. New Jersey, res. 282 s. Mississippi.

Wiles Daniel H., (Connely, W. & Co.,) 149 s. Meridian, res. 53 Fort Wayne av.

WILES & REYNOLDS,
(William M. W. & Thomas E. R.,) drugs, medicines and toilet goods, 48 n. Pennsylvania.

Wiles Theodore, propr. Wiles House, 41 w. Maryland.

Wiles Thomas S., Jr., 32 s. New Jersey, res. 182 s. New Jersey.

Wiles Thomas, stone-ware house 32 s. New Jersey, res. 182 s. Mississippi.

Wiles William D., (Connely, W. & Co.,) 149 s. Meridian, res. 394 n. New Jersey.

Wiles William M., (W. & Reynolds.) 48 n. Pennsylvania, res. 346 n. Meridian.

Wiley Andrew, clerk, 13 n. Pennsylvania, res. 131 n. Alabama.

Wiley Charles, clerk, 13 n. Pennsylvania, res. 131 n. Alabama.

Wiley Delaney, physician, 116 e. New York, res. 79 e. Michigan.

Wiley Miss Elizabeth, res. 67 w. Michigan.

Wiley James G., salesman, New York Store, res. Macy House.

Wiley Joseph, salesman, New York Store, bds. Macy House.

Wiley W. M., paper-maker, res. 126 n. Blackford.

Wiley William Y., captain and O. S. R., United States Arsenal, res. Arsenal grounds.

Wilgus Jacob, engineer, res. 370 s. Illinois.

Wilheim Christ, lab., Central Depot, res. 265 s. Alabama.

Wilkens C. L, foreman, Mooney & Co., bds. Macy House.

WILKENS & HALL,
(John A. W. & Thomas Q. H,) dealers and manfs. of furniture, 38 e. Washington.

Wilken John, res. 80 e. Market.

Wilkens John A., (W. & Hall,) 38 e. Washington, res. e. New York.

Wilkes T. A., harness-maker, res. cor. West and Maryland.

Wilkes Thomas, saddler, e. Washington, res. 39 s. West.

Wilkining Charles, expressman, res. 283 Davidson.

Wilkins Charles H., res.117 s. Noble.

Wilkins Frank C., res. 117 s. Noble.

Wilkins Peter, carpenter, res. 117 s. Noble.

Wilkinson F. M., book-keeper, J. S. Dunlop & Co., bds. 258 s. Meridian.

Wilkinson Henry, (col.,) teamster, res. cor. Oak and Vine.

Wilkinson John, clerk, Bee-Hive, bds. 73 n. Illinois.
Wilkinson William, retired, livery business, res. 85 n. Delaware.
Will Frederick, works Speigle, Thoms & Co., res. 99 n. Noble.
Will John, butcher, res. s. Kansas, beyond city limits.
Will J. F., (Frenzel, W. & Co.,) 104 s. Illinois, res. 96 n. Noble.
Willard A. E., salesman, 4 and 5 Bates House blk., res. n. w. cor. Alabama and New York.
Willard A. G., (W. & Stowell,) 4 and 5 Bates House blk., res. 92 Massachusetts av.
Willard H., cabinet-maker, 83 e. Market, res. n. Mississippi.
Willard William, retired teacher of deaf mutes, res. near Deaf and Dumb Asylum.
Willard W. F., (wid. William,) res. 264 s. Tennessee.
Willard Nicholas, printer, Journal office, res. 73 e. St. Clair.
Willard & Stowell, (A. G. W. & M. A. S.,) 4 and 5 Bates House blk., w. Washington.
Wildrick Mrs. Nancy, (wid.,) cook, 131 n. East.
Willhoff George, drives beer wagon, res. 64 e. McCarty.
Willhoff Martin, carpenter, bds. 152 Madison av.
William Hillman, grocery, 401 Virginia av., res. 42 Water.
William Hubbard, house painter, res. 259 Virginia av.
Williams H. F., grocery, res. 192 w. Ohio.
Williams Aaron F., cashier Indianapolis National Bank, bds. 181 e. Ohio.
Williams August, moulder, res. 172 w. New York.
Williams Benjamin H., traveling agt. Cotton Express Co., res. 298 e. Market.
Williams Benjamin, (col.,) lab., res. back of I. & C. shops.
Williams Bruno, clerk, 30 w. Washington, res. 171 w. New York.
Williams Champion, bds. 20 w. Michigan.
WILLIAMS CHARLES, undertaker, over 10 Bates House blk., w. Washington, res. 20 w. Michigan.
Williams Charles C., res. 748 n. Illinois.
Williams Charles, cabinet-maker, res. 163 e. St. Joseph.
Williams Daniel, plasterer, res. 277 e. New York.
Williams Daniel, student, North-Western Christian University, bds. 402 n. New Jersey.
Williams Daniel G., (Todd, Carmichael & W.,) 33 e. Washington, res. 164 e. St. Clair.

Williams David, lab., res. 237 w. Merrill.
Williams E. H., traveling agt., bds. 84 Massachusetts av.
Williams E. L., clerk, 7 and 9 e. Washington, bds. 226 n. Illinois.
Williams Alexander, (col.,) lab., cor. Blake and Center.
Williams Hart, (col.,) hod-carrier, res. 191 Huron.
Williams J. H., lab., res. 225 w. Merrill.
Williams James, hostler, bds. 198 s. Illinois.
Williams James D., carpenter, res. 418 Indiana av.
Williams James T., machinist, bds. 88 n. California.
Williams Mrs. Jane, (wid. John,) ladies' boarding house, 289 e. New York.
Williams Jefferson, life insurance agt., bds. 184 n. Tennessee.
Williams Joshua, res. 249 s. New Jersey.
Williams John C., (col.,) white-washer and paper-hanger, res. 85 w. Georgia.
Williams John, heater, rolling mill, res. 260 s. Missouri.
Williams John R., lab., res. 363 s. Missouri.
Williams Minerva, (wid.,) res. 192 w. Ohio.
Williams Owen, (W. & Maston,) s. s. Maryland, bet. Illinois and Meridian, res. 226 n. Illinois.
Williams R. R., lab., res. 250 s. Tennessee.
Williams Rachel, (wid.,) seamstress, res. 655 n. Tennessee.
Williams Robert, hostler, W. Hinesley, bds. Pyle House.
Williams Rufus, (col.,) res. n. s. Elizabeth, bet. Blake and Harris.
Williams Sarah C., occupant Deaf and Dumb Asylum.
Williams Sandy, (col.,) works Crown Hill Cemetery, res. cor. Seventh and Lafayette R. R. track.
Williams, Scott & Co., manfs. and wholesale dealers in smoker's articles, 4 w. Louisiana.
WILLIAMS MISS SUSAN, ladies' boarding house, 281 e. New York.
Williams Thomas H., teamster, res. 131 Huron.
Williams Wallace, lab., res. Camp Carrington.
Williams William, (W., Scott & Co.,) 4 w. Louisiana, res. 168 n. East.
Williams William, policeman, seventh ward, res. 299 s. East.
Williams William B., freight agt. Atlantic & Great Western R. R., office 80 Virginia av., res. 119 Massachusetts av.
Williams W. D., Trade Palace, bds. Palmer House.
Williams William G., blacksmith, res. 70 Meek.

Williams Williams R., receiver, Citizen's Street R. R., res. 11 n. West.

Williamson Hiram, farmer, res. n. s. National rd., w. White river bridge.

Williamson John W., salesman, Tyler's Bee Hive, bds. 73 n. Illinois.

Williams n Levi B., lab., Root's foundry, res. 31 Coburn.

Willis & Co., (Jonathan W. & John Moffit,) tin shop, 166 Indiana av.

Willis George, messenger, American Express Co., res. 376 e. New York.

Willis Jonathan, (W. & Co.,) 166 Indiana av., res. 78 Minerva.

Willis Lemuel, cook, Union Depot Dining Hall, res. same.

Willits James, baggage-master, C., C. & I. C. R. R., res. 117 s. Noble.

WILLMAN HIRAM B., inventor and patentee in kerosene lamps, oil-cans and illuminating fluid, office, room 7 Vinton's blk., n. Pennsylvania, res. Vine, bet. Broadway and Plum.

Wilmington Edward M., deputy auditor, res. 122 e. St. Mary.

Wilmington Levi F., night-policeman, res. 65 Arch.

Wilmot Mrs. Caroline, (wid. James,) res. 276 s. Delaware.

Wilmot Horace Q., book-binder, Meikel's, bds. 89 n. Delaware.

Wilson Andrew, paper-maker, McLene, McIntire & Hays, bds. 327 w. Washington.

Wilson Ann, (wid.,) notion store, 88 e. South, res. same.

Wilson Miss Anna, student, Indiana Female College, 146 n. Meridian, res. same.

Wilson Benjamin A., dry goods and groceries, 160 Indiana av., res. 686 n. Illinois.

Wilson Benjamin F., works Street Railway Co., res. 18 n. Noble.

Wilson C. F., general agt. New Jersey Mutual Life ¦Insurance Co., office 19 w. Washington.

Wilson C. P., book-keeper, Willard & Stowell, res. 181 s. Tennessee.

Wilson Mrs. Cassia M., (wid.,) res. Eighth, bet. Lenox and Knox.

Wilson Charles, clerk, 7 Odd Fellows' Hall, bds. 178 s. New Jersey.

Wilson Charles, lab., res. 188 Winston.

Wilson Charles, (col.,) lab., res. 67 Hosbrook.

Wilson Charles, book-binder, bds. 20 s. Pennsylvania.

Wilson Charles G., Sr., carriage-painter, res. 266 s. Mississippi.

Wilson Charles G., Jr., book-binder, Journal office, res. 266 s. Mississippi.

Wilson Mrs. E. G., bds. 236 n. Illinois.

Wilson E. I., telegraph operator, 11 n. Meridian, bds. Pattison House.

Wilson Eliza, (col.,) servant, 268 w. Vermont.

Wilson Elizabeth, servant at 296 n. Meridian.

Wilson Emily, (col.,) servant at 21 Indiana av.

Wilson Frank, compositor, Sentinel news room, res. cor. Ohio and Mississippi.

Wilson Fred., moulder, bds. 267 e. Washington.

Wilson Miss J. L., teacher, bds. 37 Maryland.

Wilson George, clerk, p. o., res. 400 n. New Jersey.

Wilson George W., revenue inspector, room 13 p. o. bldg.

Wilson Guy, salesman, New York Store, bds. Macy House.

Wilson Harry, lab., res. 507 s. Tennessee.

Wilson J. B., stoves and tin-ware, 169 and 171 w. Washington, res.476 n. Illinois.

Wilson J. C., supt. W. Union Telegraph, office Union Depot, res. 236 n. Illinois.

Wilson J. T., stable-boss, Citizens' Street Ry., bds. Globe House.

Wilson J. W., tailor, 32½ s. Meridian, res. 40 Fletcher av.

Wilson James, brakesman, I., P. & C. R. R., res. 179 s. Illinois.

Wilson James, stone-cutter, res. 322 s. West.

Wilson James, carpenter, res. 477 w. Michigan.

Wilson James H., works Street R. R. Co., res. 18 n. Noble.

Wilson James H., assistant book-keeper, A. Jones & Co., 74 and 76 s. Meridian, res. 20 w. Georgia.

Wilson James W., lumber-dealer, res. n. w. cor. Liberty and North.

Wilson Mrs. Johanna, (wid. William,) res. 360 s. Delaware.

Wilson John, lab., res. 188 w. Georgia.

Wilson John, chair-maker, res. 159 w. Elizabeth.

Wilson John, painter, bds. Wiles House.

Wilson John, carpenter, res. 29 Jones.

Wilson John, salesman, Dorsey & Layman, bds. 268 e. St. Clair.

Wilson John, marble-cutter, works Emmons & Wilson, bds. 168 Winston.

Wilson John C., baker, res. 264 s. Mississippi.

Wilson John L., trader, res. 117 Indiana av.

Wilson John S., carpenter, res. 68 n. East.

Wilson John T., plasterer, res. 117 Benton.

Wilson John W., tailor, res. 226 s. Noble.

Wilson L. B., clerk, Union Line office, res. 97 w. Maryland.

Wilson Laura, servant, Palmer House.

Wilson M. W., piano case-maker, 159 and 161 e. Washington, bds. Jager Halle.

For Grover & Baker Sewing Machines, card opposite letter A.

Wilson Lizzie, bds. 22 Fletcher av.
Wilson Mrs. Mattie, (wid.,) dress-maker, bds. Ballard House, e. Market.
Wilson Martin B., res. 253 Bluff rd.
Wilson Mrs. Margaret, (wid. Patrick,) res. 276 s. Delaware.
Wilson O. M., lawyer, office Aetna bldg., res. 73 s. Tennessee.
Wilson Olney F., student, Purdy's Commercial College, bds. 73 n. Liberty.
Wilson Ransom (col.,) porter, 14 Bates House, res. Benton.
Wilson Richard, (col.,) brick-moulder, res. Lafayette R. R., bet. First and Second.
Wilson Sanford B., res. e. National rd.
Wilson Miss Sarah A., bds. 440 n. Meridian.
Wilson Stephen B., traveling agt., Connelly, Wiles & Co., res. 126 e. Walnut.
Wilson Stephen B., plasterer, res. 325 s. Alabama.
Wilson Stephen C., chair-maker, res. 159 w. Elizabeth.
Wilson Thomas E., clerk, 76 w. Washington, res. 20 w. Georgia.
Wilson Thomas S., chief of police, res. 178 s. New Jersey.
Wilson William, book-keeper, 123 s. Meridian, res. 20 w. Georgia.
Wilson William, painter, bds. 267 e. Washington.
Wilson William E., carpenter, res. e. National rd.
Wimer Frank, teamster, res. 18 Arch.
Winch Fred., stone-cutter, res. 139 Stevens.
Winchell Mrs., seamstress, res. 198 n. Mississippi.
Windall Charles, works Junction R. R., bds. Wiles House.
Winder Alfred, telegraph operator, res. 339 n. Illinois.
Winder Joseph, express driver, bds. on alley in rear 140 Winston.
Wineburg William, lab., res. 309 e. New York.
Winengs Miss Jennie, res. 115 n. Missouri.
Wing Thomas R., conductor, C., C. & I C. Ry., bds. Bates House.
Wingate E. H., grocer and produce dealer, 82 e. Washington, res. 141 s. New Jersey.
Wingate Joseph F., groceries and provisions, 42 n. Pennsylvania, res. 306 n. Delaware.
WINGATE T. H., actuary, Great Western Horse Ins. Co., room 7 Vinton's blk., bds. 52 n. Pennsylvania.
Wingate William D., (Hill & W.,) res. 122 Virginia av.
Wink Miss Isabella, millinery store, 152 e. Washington, res. same.
Winken August, piano-top-maker, 159 and 161 e. Washington, res. 178 n. Noble.

Winkel William F., clerk, James Blake's flour and feed store, s. Delaware, res. 194 Davidson.
Winken William, piano-case-maker, 159 and 161 e. Washington, res. 178 n. Noble.
Winkles Caroline, servant at 383 n. Illinois.
Winn Cynthia, (wid.,) res. 186 e. St. Joseph.
WINNESHEIK FIRE INS. CO., J. F. Smith, prest., W. Prembor, sec'y, Jones & Child, State agts., Ind., 25 w. Washington. See card, page 42.
Winslow A. B., book-keeper, J. D. Conditt, Blackford's blk., bds. 54 Circle.
Winslow Annie, (col.,) res. 219 n. West.
Winslow Isaac, (col.,) waiter, Bates House.
Winslow Jacob, (col.,) lab., res. 104 Ash.
Winslow Mrs Mary, (col.,) res. 558 n. Mississippi.
Winsor John, cabinet-maker, res. 101 Bates.
Winter D. E., painter, res. 68 Gregg.
Winter Frederick W., lab., res. 335 w. Maryland.
Winter Fritz, lab., bds. Nagle House.
Winter John A., painter, res. 317 s. East.
Winters George, cash boy, New York Store, res. 371 e. St. Mary.
Winters Henry, works stave factory, bds. 172 w. Maryland.
Winters Michael, lab., res. 19 Willard.
Winters Philip, machinist, bds. Ray House.
Winton Jack, (col.,) porter, 38 s. Illinois, bds. w. Washington.
Wirt Joseph, shoe-maker, res. 127 n. Alabama.
Wirtz Jacob, horse doctor, res. 503 s. East.
Wise August, helper, B. F. Hay, bds. 573 e. St. Clair.
Wise George, tailor, bds. 73 n. Illinois.
Wise Thomas, railroader, bds. 58 Benton.
Wise William T., (col.,) barber shop, 223 Massachusetts av., res. same.
Wiseman Anna, (wid. John,) res. 199 n. Pennsylvania.
Wiseman William W., watchman, C. & I. C. shops, res. 114 Meek.
Wishmeyer Henry, works starch factory, res. 194 n. Noble.
Wishmeyer Michael, clerk, Hay & Co., 48 w. Washington, res. 345 e. McCarty.
Wishmire Anthony, Sr., lab., res. 274 e. Ohio.
Wishmire Anthony, Jr., clerk, Seventh Ward Grocery, res. 274 e. Ohio.
Wishmire Charles F., works Union Starch Factory, res. 292 Winston.
Wishmier Christian F., saw-mill, w. side Davidson, bet. Michigan and North, res. 258 Davidson.
Wister Miss Annie E., ladies' boarding house, 97 w. South.
Withers George T., lab., bds. 342 Railroad.

Witman Henry L., carpenter, Vermont, near Delaware, res. 243 n. New Jersey.

Witner Frederick, lab., bds. s. s. National rd., w. White river bridge.

Witt Bennett F., gen'l agt. Franklin Life Ins. Co., res. 364 n. New Jersey.

Witte & Boerner, groceries and produce, 249 w. McCarty.

Witte Edward, grocery, res. 249 w. McCarty.

Witte & Arbuckle, (B. F. W. & Matthew A.,) real estate agts., s. w. cor. Washington and Meridian.

Wittenberg Charles, (W. & Ruschaupt,) 37 e. Washington, res. 217 e. Ohio.

Wittenberg Robert, salesman, 37 e. Washington, res. 217 e. Ohio.

WITTENBERG & RUSCHAUPT, (Charles W. & Frederick R.,) dry goods, notions, fancy goods and trimmings, 37 e. Washington.

Wittenbring Henry, cigar-maker, works 266 e. Washington, bds. same.

Witthoft Frederick, groceries and provisions, 1 Buchanan, res. same.

Witthoft Henry, cabinet-maker, res. 82 s. East.

Wittinger Jacob, grocery, 100 s. Noble, res. same.

Witzmann John, teamster, res. 162 Winston.

Wocher John, stone-cutter, res. 21 Meek.

Woelz Charles A., wholesale and retail confectionery, s. e. cor. New York and Delaware, res. same.

Woert Jacob, lab., res. n. s. National rd., w. river bridge.

Woert John, lab., bds. Gardner's Saloon, National rd.

Wolcott Oliver, traveling agt., res. over 248 e. Washington.

Wolf Adam, clerk, 131 w. Washington, res. same.

Wolf Catharine, (wid.,) boarding house, 176 s. Delaware, res. same.

Wolf Charles, saddler, res. 147½ e. Washington.

Wolf E. M., painter, 44 w. Pearl, res. 255 s. Mississippi.

Wolf Elihue, carpenter, res. 99 Maple.

Wolf George, cigar-dealer, Franklin, Ind., res. 176 s. Delaware.

Wolf Henry, shoe-maker, bds. 117 s. Illinois.

Wolf Isaac, cooper, n. side New York, bet. Blake and Minerva.

Wolf John, moulder, res. 144 Union.

Wolf Joseph, moulder, bds. n. East.

Wolf Michael, conductor, Jeffersonville R. R., res. 229 e. South.

Wolf Moses, with Hays & Rosenthal, res. 250 e. Vermont.

Wolf Philip, cigar-maker, bds. 176 s. Delaware.

Wolf Mrs. Sophia, (wid.,) bds. 65 n. Bright.

Wolf W. W., painter, 123 e. Washington, bds. Union Hall.

Wolfenden A., carpenter, res. 399 s. West.

Wolfrom Albert, (Wolfrom & Bros.,) res. 201 n. New Jersey.

Wolfrom & Bros., dealers in stoves, tin and sheet-iron ware, 197 e. Washington.

Wolfrom Charles A., printer, works Journal office, res. 201 n. New Jersey.

Wolfrom Christian A., (Wolfrom & Bros.,) cor. New Jersey and Washington, res. 201 n. New Jersey.

Wolfrom Ernest E., clerk, Fletcher & Sharpe's Bank, res. 201 n. New Jersey.

Wolfrom Mrs. Sarah, (wid. Charles,) res. 201 n. New Jersey.

Wonder Miss Sophia, res. 60 Hosbrook.

Wonnell Charles, blacksmith, works 60 e. Maryland.

Wood A. D., capitalist, res. 201 n. Delaware.

Wood Alexander, rodman for city engineer, res. Vermont, bet. Meridian and Illinois.

WOOD & BOYD, (Levi W. & Frank A. B.,) burning and lubricating oils, paints and varnishes, 22 s. Meridian.

Wood Mrs. Cynthia A., (wid. Stephen,) res. 74 n. Liberty.

Wood D. L., (Nutting & W.,) 17½ w. Washington, res. 417 n. Pennsylvania.

Wood David A., book-keeper, 60 s. Meridian, res. e. city limits.

Wood Edmondson, carpenter, res. 124 Bates.

Wood Frank, with Nutting & Wood, bds. 417 n. Pennsylvania.

Wood Frank M., carriage blacksmith, bds. 35 Circle.

Wood & Foudray, (John M. W. & John E. F.,) livery, sale and boarding stable, 16 n. Pennsylvania.

Wood George P., foreman, J. S. Carey & Co., res. cor Georgia and Helen.

Wood Herman, (Hinsely & W.,) 21 w. Pearl, res. 123 n. East.

Wood James W., carpenter, res. 124 Bates.

Wood Jacob P., pump-maker, res. 428 e. St. Clair.

Wood John B., bds. 35 Circle.

Wood John C., carpenter, res. 124 Bates.

Wood Jacob S., (Jordon & W.,) res. 378 Indiana av.

Wood John M., (W. & Foudray,) res. 4 Massachusetts av.

Wood John F., secy. Republican State Central Committee, res. 185 e. New York.

Wood Mrs. L. J., boarding house, 62 s. Pennsylvania.

Wood L. J., lab., res. 205 w. McCarty.
Wood Levi, (W. & Boyd,) 22 s. Meridian, res. n. Mississippi, beyond city limits.
Wood Mrs. Mollie, (wid. James,) res. 174 Virginia av.
Wood N. H., conductor, C., C. & I. C. R. R., bds. Bates House.
Woods N. M., book-keeper, S. Kaufman, 116 s. Meridian, res. 168 n. Noble.
Wood Nicholas, pump-maker, bds. 428 e. St. Clair.
Wood Sarah E. A., (wid. Ely,) res. e. Washington, beyond city limits.
Wood William E., horse-dealer, res. 442 n. Pennsylvania.
Woodbridge Charles A., (John Woodbridge & Co.,) 16 w. Washington, res. 160 n. Meridian.
Woodbridge John (J. W. & Co.,) 16 w. Washington, bds. 160 n. Meridian.
WOODBRIDGE JOHN & CO., china, glass and queensware, plated ware and table cutlery, 16 w. Washington, wholesale house, 36 s. Meridian.
Woodbridge Wesley, (col.,) waiter, Bates House.
Woodburn James H., (Thompson & W.,) physician and surgeon, 90 n. Illinois, res. 264 n. Illinois.
Woodbury Uriah T., dentist, rooms 39½ w. Washington, res. 44 n. Mississippi.
Woodby George W., (col.,) lab., bds. Eighth, bet Lenox and Knox.
Woodfill George, groceries, 323 s. Delaware, res. same.
Woodford James E., book-keeper, Frank Wright's brewery, bds. 160 w. Washington.
Woodford Mrs. Nancy, (col., wid.,) washerwoman, res. 157 Indiana av.
Woodruff Ada, (wid.,) res. 83½ e. Washington.
WOODS MISS ALICE, ladies' boarding house, 27 n. New Jersey.
Woods Miss Annie, knitter, res. 70 w. Elizabeth.
Woods Benjamin F., supt. wood-yard, res. 234 Huron.
Woods Daniel, razor sharpener, res. 209 e. Market.
Woods F. M., blacksmith, bds. 25 Circle.
Woods John, blacksmith, bds. 35 Circle.
Woods L. E., salesman, New York Store, bds. Oriental House.
Woods Mary, servant, H. D. Carlisle, 77 w. Ohio.
Woods Mrs. seamstress, res. 70 w. Elizabeth.
Woods Neander M., book-keeper, S. Kaufman, 116 s. Meridian, res. 168 n. Noble.
Woods Thomas, res. 469 s. Illinois.

Woods William, stock-trader, res. 303 e. Market.
Woodsides Alexander, butcher, res. s. s. National rd., w. White river.
Woodson John S., painter, res. s. Second, bet. Meridian and Illinois.
Woodson Mrs. Millie, (col., wid.,) washerwoman, res. Railroad, bet. Fifth and Sixth.
Woodward John, book-binder, Journal office, bds. 25 Harris.
Woollen Miss Anna, bds. cor. West and Michigan.
WOOLLEN, BAAR & CO., (W. J. W., G. L. B. & ———,) furniture manfs. and dealers, 75 w. Washton.
Woollen Kesiah, (wid.,) boarding house, 83 n. Pennsylvania.
Woollen Greenly V., physician, 35 e. Washington, res. City Hospital, cor. Locke and Margaret.
Woollen Milton A., constable, office over e. Washington, res 248 n. w. cor. Michigan.
Woollen William J., 74 w. Washington, res. 279 w. Vermont.
Woollen William M., groceries and provisions, 101 Indiana av., res. 288 n. Tennessee.
Woollen William W., Jr., attorney at law and district prosecutor, over 353 e. Washington, res. 405 n. Pennsylvania.
Woollen William W., cashier Indiana Banking Co., 28 e. Washington, res. 167 n. Tennessee.
Woolley William B., brakesman, Bee Line R. R., bds. 103 s. New Jersey.
Worley John, res. n. s. National rd., half mile from bridge.
Worley Lina, res. n. s. National rd., half mile from bridge.
Worton Benjamin, pump-repairer, res. 47 Rose.
Worman Charles R., clerk, 14 w. Washington, bds. Pyle House.
Worrell J. R., driver, J. R. Marot, res. 186 n. Davidson.
Worson Hiram P., salesman, Tyler's Bee-Hive, bds. 175 s. Tennessee.
Worthington W. H., trunk-maker, res. 266 n. West.
Wose Julius L., (Williams, Scott & Co.,) 4 w. Louisiana, res. McGill.
Wren Mrs. Eve, (wid.,) res. 269 n. Blake.
Wren Miss Ellen, seamstress, bds. 160 s. Noble.
Wren Edward, wagon-maker, res. 99 s. New Jersey.
Wren Miss Jennie, room second floor, 186 w. Washington.
Wren Thomas, contractor, res. cor. Norwood and Tennessee.
Wren Mike, lab., res. 123 w. McCarty.

WRIEDT CHARLES,
saloon, and bowling and shooting alley, 34 w. Georgia, res. same.

Wright Aaron, gardener, res. n. s. National rd., one mile w. White river.

Wright Mrs. Anna, boarding house, 366 w. Washington.

Wright Asa, lab., res. over 212 e. Washington.

WRIGHT ARTHUR L.,
county treasurer, Marion county, res. 426 n. New Jersey.

Wright Benjamin, book-keeper, Davis & Wright, 88 e. Washington, bds. 228 n. East.

Wright Charles, (Davis & W.,) auctioneers, 88 e. Washington, res. 228 n. East.

Wright Charles A., bds. Bates House.

Wright Charles E., (Parvin, Fletcher & Wright,) physician and surgeon, bds. 236 e. Vermont.

Wright D. B., currier, 49 s. Delaware, res. Michigan rd.

Wright Edward B., book-keeper, bds. 228 n. East.

Wright Miss Elizabeth, seamstress, res. 212 e. Washington.

Wright Elizabeth, (wid. Alonzo,) res. 182 w. Georgia.

Wright Francis, salesman, Bee-Hive Store, res. 228 n. East.

Wright Frank, clerk, 3 Odd Fellows' Hall, 189 e. Ohio.

Wright Frank, ale brewery, foot w. New York, res. 160 n. West.

Wright Henry, minister, res. 88 e. Pratt.

Wright Hiram N., boarding house, 366 w. Washington.

Wright J. J., engineer, I., C. & L. R. R., bds. 99 Benton.

Wright J. J., physician Insane Hospital, res. 498 n. Pennsylvania.

Wright I. T., secy. and treas. White River Iron Co., 275 n. Delaware.

Wright John, (col.,) lab., res. 30 Ann.

WRIGHT JACOB T.,
clerk, county auditor's office, res. 275 n. Delaware.

Wright Jeremiah, farmer, res. n. s. National rd., w. White river bridge.

Wright John, salesman, New York Store, bds. 185 e. Washington.

Wright John R., (Wm. Summer & Co.,) 10 w. Washington, res. Cincinnati, O.

Wright John S., clerk, street R. R. office, res. 795 n. Tennessee.

Wright Levi, grocery-dealer, 323 n. Alabama, res. 314 n. Alabama.

Wright Mansur H., physician, res. 103 n. Meridian.

Wright R. M., res. Orient, e. city limits.

Wright Theodore F., foreman, Downey, Brouse, Butler & Co., res. 361 w. Vermont.

Wright Thomas, lab., res. 135 n. Bright.

Wright W. G., pump-maker, res. 271 Virginia av.

Wright W. H., salesman, 52 s. Meridian, res. 83 e. Michigan.

Wright Wesley, res. 15 Kentucky av.

Wright William, salesman and collector, Crossland, Maguire & Co., bds. 204 n. Illinois.

Wrighter G. W., student, commercial college, bds. 147 n. Meridian.

WUEST & CO.,
manfrs. and dealers in furniture, 105 e. Washington. See card, page iv.

Wuest Christopher, tinner, 103 e. Washington.

Wuest John, (W. & C.,) res. 143 Ft. Wayne av.

Wuest Louis, cigar-maker, bds. 452 .c Washington.

Wundrum William, tailor, res. 383 s. Delaware.

Wundran Louis, shoe-maker, res. 83 s. Illinois.

Wvser Mrs. Elizabeth, (wid. Frederick,) dress-maker, Wabash, bet. New Jersey and East, res. same.

Wvser Frederick, works Gates, Pray & Co., res. Wabash, bet. New Jersey and East.

Wyatt William D., plasterer, bds. 83 Benton.

Wycoff Samuel, lab., Central depot, res. 179 c. South.

Wylend Ellen, servant, 242 n. Meridian.

Wynn Miss Annie, teacher, German-English school, res. 38 e. St. Joseph.

Wynn Willber S., salesman, Bowen, Stewart & Co., res. 138 e. St. Joseph.

Wyre Michael, res. Kansas, out city limits.

Wyrick Michael, engineer, J., M. & I. R. R., bds. Oriental House.

WYSONG CHRISTOPHER,
brick-layer, res. 281 n. Noble.

Wysong George, brick-layer, bds. 281 n. Noble.

Wysong Jesse, brick-layer, res. 337 n. Noble.

Wysong John, brick-layer, res. 329 n. Noble.

YACHMAN HARMAR, tailor, bds. 110 Virginia av.

Yagan Henry, foundryman, bds. 46 Hosbrook.

Yagan Matthew, wood-peddler, bds. 46 Hosbrook.

Yager Michael, lab., res. 432 e. Georgia.

Yaer Christian, res. 293 e. Washington, up-stairs.

Yaer William, res. 293 e. Washington.

Yambelle Andrew, blacksmith, bds. 479 e. Georgia.

Yandes Daniel, (Sinker & Co.,) s. Pennsylvania, bds. 84 w. Vermont.

Yandes Daniel, Jr., wholesale dealer in leather, hides, oil, &c., 76 e. Washington, res. 179 e. New York.

Yandes George B., leather and shoe-findings, 76 e. Washington, bds. Bates House.

Yandes & Kemper, (G. B. Y. & William K.,) last and boot-tree factory, 262 s. Illinois.

Yarbrough Peter, engineer, C., C. & I. C. R. R., res. 76 Benton.

Yarper Herman, brick-maker, res. 493 s. New Jersey.

Yeager William, grocer, 246 n. Noble, res. same.

Yeakle Henry R., clerk, U. S. paymaster's department, room 14 Talbott & New's blk., n. Pennsylvania, res. cor. Virginia av. and Alabama.

Yeaton L. B., superintendent, Fire Alarm Telegraph, res. 167 n. Delaware.

Yewell Solomon, book-keeper, res. 320 Madison av.

Yewell Solomon, Jr., bds. 326 Madison av.

Yeiser Jacob, conductor, C., C. & I. C. R. R., bds. Spencer House.

Yohn's Block, n. e. cor. Meridian and Washington.

Yohn Charles G., student, bds. 206 n. Delaware.

Yohn James C., capitalist, res. 206 n. Delaware.

Yorger & Bro., (J. Y. & N. Y.) meat-market, 245 e. Washington.

Yorger Charles, wood-sawyer, res. s. Pennsylvania.

Yorger Clemens, butcher, res. 137 n. Noble.

Yorger John, (Y. & Bros.,) 245 e. Washington, res. e. city limits.

Yorger Matz, (Y. & Bros.,) res. Vermont, near Noble.

York Andrew J., steward, Ray House, bds. same.

York E. D., messenger, American and U. S. Express Cos., 34 e. Washington, res. 216 e. South.

Yost Henry, stone-mason, bds. 271 w. Washington.

Yost Taylor, stone-mason, res. 378 s. West.

Yost Thomas, stone-mason, res. 271 w. Washington.

Youart John M., surgeon, 130 n. Pennsylvania, res. 128 n. Pennsylvania.

Young ———, res. 121 Duncan.

Young Mrs. Ann, (wid. John,) bds. 210 e. Ohio.

Young Christopher, pattern-maker, White River Iron Works, res. 121 Duncan.

Young George, (col.,) lab., res. 171 Indiana av.

Young Granville, tailor, bds. 340 n. Meridian.

Young Isaac, (col.,) servant, 139 w. New York.

Young Jacob, res. 290 e. St. Clair.

Young John, lawyer, room 5 Hereth's blk., res. 103 Jackson.

Young Junius, tailor, works over 11 s. Meridian, bds. 212 e. Market.

Young Levi, (col.,) lab., res. 224 Huron.

Young Louis, tobacco and cigars, and barber shop, 77 s. Illinois, res. same.

Young Men's Christian Association Sunday School, No. 2, 300 e. St. Clair.

Young Men's Library Association, s. w. cor. Washington and Meridian, upstairs.

Young Millege, (col.,) barber, Dr. Franklin.

Young Richard, lab., res. 109 Huron.

Young Richard, (col.,) gardener, res. 224 Huron.

Young Miss Sarah, res. 213 w. Market.

Young Squire, (col.,) lab., res. 259 n. West.

Young Thomas J., (col.,) lab., res. 122 n. Pennsylvania.

Young Taylor, (col.,) teamster, res. 224 Huron.

Young Thornton, (col.,) lab., res. 228 n. Noble.

Young William, carpenter, res. Athon, near City Hospital.

Youngerman Mary P., (wid. Conrad,) res. 120 Massachusetts av.

Younk John, teamster, bds. 59 Eddy.

Youts Peter, wagon-maker, works 231 w. Washington, bds. 272 w. Washington.

Youtsay Thomas, sawyer, res. 57 Eddy.

Youtsey William, res. 43 Eddy.

ZAGG FERDINAND, cabinet-maker, bds. 267 e. Washington.

Zahn Bernhard, engineer, res. 113 Benton.

Zeeber S. S., Trade Palace, bds. Macy House.

Zehringer Frank, porter, 6 e. Washington, bds. 164 n. Davidson.

Zehringer Landolin, cabinet-maker, res. 164 Davidson.

Zeigler George H., claim agent, res. 202 n. West.

Zeigler Miss Mary, res. 202 n. West.

Zelath Russell, pay-master, Bellefontaine R. R., res. 38 w. St. Clair.

Zellers Henry, matrass-maker, Spiegel, Thoms & Co., bds. Macy House.

Ziegelmueller Herman, shoe-maker, 270 s. Delaware, res. same.

ZIEGLER GEORGE H., military claim-attorney and notary public, room 6 Talbott & New's blk., n. Pennsylvania, res. 202 n. West.

Ziep Anna, servant, 82 n. East.

Zimmer Ferdinand, saloon, 110 s. Illinois, res. same.

Zimmerman Christopher, slate-roofer, res. e. Washington, near corporation line.

Zimmerman George, drayman, res. 284 n. Noble.

Zimmerman Gothlep, butcher, res. 211 w. Michigan.

Zimmerman H. C., slate-roofer, res. 130 n. Spring.

Zimmerman James, slate-roofer, res. 72 n. Liberty.

Zimmerman John R., slate-roofer, bds. 130 n. Spring.

Zimmerman Mrs. Mary, (wid. William,) res. 130 spring.

Zink Henry, (Braham & Z.,) Sherman House barber-shop, res. 328 s. Delaware.

Zion's Church, (German Lutheran,) n. s. Ohio, bet. Illinois and Meridian.

Zscheck Frederick, carpenter, res. 90 Union.

Zscheck Gustavus, Eagle Machine Works, res. s. Meridian.

Zulmer Charles, machinist,C., C. & I. C. R. R. shop, res. 399 e. Georgia.

Zumbusch Theodore, watch-maker, 93 e. Washington, res. 61 w. Maryland.

Zwick William, tailor. works over 182 c. Washington, res. 111 n. Noble.

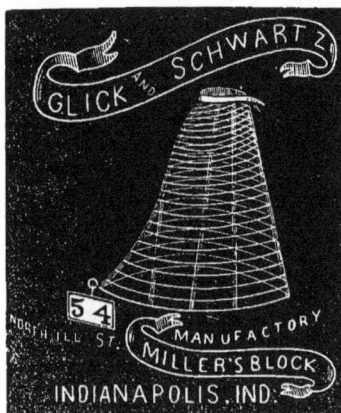

ALPHABETICAL DIRECTORY

— OF —

STREETS, AVENUES AND ALLEYS

IN INDIANAPOLIS.

The principal streets crossing Washington Street are divided into North and South; those crossing Meridian Street into East and West. The four principal Avenues extend in four diagonal directions, from near the center to the extreme limits of the city.

AGNES, north and south, from New York to North, twelve blocks west of Meridian.

Alabama, north and south, three blocks east of Meridian.

Alleghaney Alley, east and west from Tennessee, bet. Vermont and Michigan.

Ann, from Macauley to Catharine, bet. Tennessee and Mississippi.

Arch, east and west, bet. Jackson and Noble, nine blocks north of Washington

Archer, from Michigan to St. Clair, four blocks east of corpration.

Arsenal, from east National road to Michigan, one-half mile east of corporation.

Ash, from Massachusetts av. to Home av., bet. Bellefontaine and Oak.

Athon, north and south, from Rhode Island to Indiana av., ten blocks west of Meridian.

BARNHILL, north and south from Eliz abeth to Coe, sixteen blocks west of Meridian.

Bates, east and west, from Noble to corporation east, four blocks south of Washington.

Beaty, from Buchanan to McCarty, bet. Noble and Greer.

Bellefontaine, from corporation to Home av., bet. Peru and Ash.

Benton, north and south, from Harrison to Market, bet. Noble and Cady.

Bicking, east and west, from Delaware to East, two blocks south of McCarty,

Biddle, east and west, bet. Winston and corporation east, seven blocks north of Washington.

Blackford, north and south, from National road to North, seven blocks west of Meridian.

Blake, north and south, from National road to Indiana av., ten blocks west of Meridian.

Bluff Road, terminus south Meridian.

Bradshaw, east and west, from Beaty to Virginia av., bet. Buchanan and McCarty.

Brett, east and west, beyond corporation, west of Michigan road.

Bright, north and south, from Ohio to North, eight blocks west of Meridian.

Broadway, from St. Clair to Home av., bet. Plum and Jackson.

Brooks, north and south, from First to Drake, bet. Michigan road and Fall creek.

Buchanan, east and west, from East to Virginia av., bet. Dougherty and McCarty.

Butler, east and west, from Ft. Wayne av. to College av., twelve blocks north of Washington.

CADY, north and south, from Harrison to Market, one block east of Benton.

California, north and south, from Washington to St. Clair, six blocks west of Meridian.

Campbell, east and west, east of corporation, six blocks north of Washington.

Catharine, east and west, from Mississippi to West, bet. Merrill and McCarty.

Cedar, north-east and south-west, from Dillon to Virginia av., bet Grove and Pine.

Center, east and west, from Douglas to Ellen, bet. North and Elizabeth.

Chadwick, from McCarty to city limits south, bet. Missouri and West.

Chatham, from Massachusetts av. to St. Clair, bet. East and Noble.

Cherry, east and west, bet. Ft. Wayne av. and Charles, ten blocks north of Washington.

Chestnut, from Georgia to Morris, bet. Delaware and Pennsylvania.

Chesapeake Alley, east and west, from Mississippi to West, bet. Maryland and Georgia.

Choptank Alley, from Washington to St. Clair, bet. New Jersey and East.

Christian Avenue, east and west, from Ft. Wayne av. to Peru R. R., eleven blocks north of Washington.

Circle, crossing of Meridian and Market, one block north of Washington.

Coburn, east and west, from East to Short, bet. Dougherty and corporation south.

Coe, east and west, west of corporation line, ten blocks north of Washington.

College Avenue, from Christian av. to Home av., bet. Ash and Broadway.

Columbia Alley, north and south, from Georgia to Michigan, bet. West and Missouri.

Cottrell, from Louisiana to Georgia, bet. Missouri and West.

Court, east and west, bet. Washington and Market, from Pennsylvania to Delaware.

Crane, east and west, from Arsenal to Seymour, two blocks north of Washington.

Cross, east and west, bet. Peru and Bellefontaine R. R., eleven blocks north of Washington.

DACOTA, from Rockwood to city limits south, bet. West and White river.

Davis, north-east and south-west, from Indiana av. to Fall creek, twelve blocks north of Washington.

Delaware, north and south, two blocks east of Meridian.

Dillon, north and south, from Harrison to corporation south, on corporation line east.

Dorman, from Michigan to St. Clair, one block east of corporation.

Dougherty, east and west, from East to Virginia av., bet. Buchanan and Coburn.

Douglas, north and south, from Ohio to Indiana av., nine blocks west of Meridian.

Downey, east and west, from Bluff road to Japan, fourteen blocks south of Washington.

Drake, east and west, beyond corporation, west of Michigan road.

Duncan, east and west, from Delaware to New Jersey, bet. South and Merrill.

Dunlop, east and west, from Bluff road to Japan, fifteen blocks south of Washington.

EAST, north and south, five blocks east of Meridian.

East Cumberland, east and west, from Delaware to East, one-half block south of Washington.

East National Road, terminus e. Washington.

Eckert, from Kentucky av. to Merrill, bet. West and Kentucky av.

Eddy, from Merrill to South, bet. Illinois and Tennessee.

Eighth, east and west, eighteen blocks north of Washington.

Elizabeth, east and west, from Blake to Ellen, eight blocks north of Washington.

Elk, north-east and south-west, from Dillon to Virginia av., bet. Dillon and Virginia av.

Ellen, north and south, from North to Indiana av., eight blocks west of Meridian.

Ellis, from Georgia to Maryland, bet. West and Helen.

Ellsworth, north and south, from New York to Vermont, bet. Missouri and Mississippi.

Elm, north-west and south-east, from Noble to Dillon, bet. Virginia av. and Huron.

Erie Alley, from Washington to St. Clair, bet. Alabama and New Jersey.

FAYETTE, north and south, from North to St. Clair, bet. Missouri and West.

Fifth, east and west, fifteen blocks north of Washington.

First, east and west, west of Meridian, eleven blocks north of Washington.

Fletcher Avenue, north-west and south-east, from Noble to Dillon, bet. Forest av. and Huron.

Forest Avenue, north-west and south-east, from Harrison to Dillon, bet. Harrison and Fletcher av.

Fort Wayne Avenue, north-east and south-west, from Pennsylvania and North to city limits north-east.

Fort Wayne Road, terminus Ft. Wayne av.

Fourth, east and west, fourteen blocks north of Washington.

Franklin, from Morris to city limits south, bet. Wallace and Japan.

GARDEN, east and west, from Mississippi to Pennsylvania, bet. South and Merrill.

Geisendorff, north and south, from National road to New York, nine blocks west of Meridian.

Georgia, east and west, two blocks south of Washington.

Grant, bet. West and Kentucky av., one block south of Merrill.

Greer, from Buchanan to Stevens, bet. East and Beaty.

Gregg, east and west, bet. New Jersey and Jackson, nine blocks n. of Washington.

Grove, north-east and south-west, from Dillon to Virginia av., bet. Elk and Cedar.

HARRISON, east and west, from Noble to corporation east, four blocks south of Washington.

Helen, from Maryland to Louisiana, bet. Ellis and White river.

Henderson, north and south, terminus of north Illinois.

Henry, east and west, from Missouri to Mississtppi, bet. south and Merrill.

High, from McCarty to corporation south, bet. New Jersey and Alabama.

Home Avenue, east and west, from Ft. Wayne av. to Peru R. R., thirteen blocks north of Washington.

Hosbrook, north-west and south-east, from Cedar to Dillon, bet. Virginia av. and Elm.

Howard, north and south, from First to Seventh, bet. Lafayette and Mill.

Hudson Alley, from Ohio to Walnut, bet. Delaware and Alabama.

Huron, east and west, from Virginia av. to Noble, one block south of South.

Huron, north-west and south-east, from Noble to Dillon, bet. Fletcher av. and Elm.

ILLINOIS, north and south, one block west of Meridian.

Indiana Avenue, north-west and south-east, from corner Ohio and Illinois to city limits north-west.

JACKSON, from St. Clair to Home av., bet. Broadway and East.

Japan, north and south, extension of south East.

John, east and west, bet. Peru and Bellefontaine R. R., ten blocks north of Washington.

Jones, east and west, from West to Dacota, six blocks south of McCarty.

KANKOKEE ALLEY, from Michigan to North, bet. Illinois and Tennessee.

Kansas, east and west, from Meridian to Minnesota, thirteen blocks south of Washington.

Kentucky Avenue, north-east and south-west, from corner Washington and Illinois to city limits south-west.

Kingan, east and west from West to White river, two blocks south of McCarty.

LAFAYETTE, north and south from First to city limits, bet. Mississippi and Howard.

Lafayette Road, terminus Indiana av.

Lenox, north and south, from Seventh to Ninth, bet. Lafayette and Mill.

Liberty, north and south, six blocks east of Meridian.

Lockerbie, east and west, from East to Liberty, bet. New York and Vermont.

Locust, from McCarty to Morris, bet. Meridian and Union.

Lord, east and west, from Noble to corporation east, bet. Louisiana and Harrison.

Louisiana, east and west, three blocks south of Washington.

MACAULEY, east and west, from Ann to Missouri, one block south of McCarty.

Madison Avenue, north-west and south-east, from corner South and Meridian to city limits.

Madison Road, terminus Madison av.

Maple, from Ray to Morris, bet. Tennessee and Illinois.

Margaret, east and west, south of City Hospital.

Maria, east and west, east of City Hospital.

Market, east and west, one block north of Washington.

Maryland, east and west, one block south of Washington.

Massachusetts Avenue, north-east and south-west, from corner of Ohio and Pennsylvania, to city limits north-east.

Maxwell, north and south, from Elizabeth to Davis, fourteen blocks west of Meridian.

Mayhew, east and west, beyond corporation, west of Michigan rd.

Meek, east and west, from Noble to corporation east, two blocks south of Washington.

Meikle, from McCarty to city limits south, bet. Mississippi and Missouri.

MERIDIAN, north and south, through Governor's Circle, bet. Pennsylvania and Illinois.

Merrill, east and west, six blocks south of Washington.

Miami Alley, east and west, bet. Ohio and New York.

Michigan, east and west, five blocks north of Washington.

Michigan Road, terminus north-west.

Michigan Road, (east,) east terminus, Washington, ten blocks east of Meridian.

Mill, north and south, from Fifth to city limits, bet. Howard and Michigan road.

Minerva, north and south, from Ohio to North, eleven blocks west of Meridian.

Minnesota, from Morris to city limits south, bet. Tennessee and West.

Mississippi, north and south, three blocks west of Meridian.

Missouri, north and south, four blocks west of Meridian.

Mobile Alley, east and west from Meridian to Mississippi, bet. Georgia and Louisiana.

Morris, east and west, twelve blocks south of Washington.

Morrison, east and west, bet. Delaware and Alabama, twelve blocks north of Washington.

Mulberry, from McCarty to Morris, bet. Union and Chestnut.

Muskingum Alley, from Louisiana to First, bet. Tennessee and Illinois.

McCarty, east and west, eight blocks south of Washington.

McGill, from Louisiana to South, bet. Mississippi and Missouri.

McGinnis, from McCarty to Ray, bet. Tennessee and Mississippi.

McIntire, east and west, beyond corporation, west of Michigan road.

McKernan, from Buchanan to corporation south, bet. Short and Wright.

McNabb, east and west, from Illinois to Meridian, bet. Louisiana and South.

NEW JERSEY, north and south, four blocks east of Meridian.

New York, east and west, three blocks north of Washington.

Ninth, east and west, fourteen blocks north of Washington.

North, east and west, six blocks north of Washington.

Noble, north and south, seven blocks east of Meridian.

OAK, from Massachusetts av. to Christian av., bet. Ash and Plum.

Ohio, east and west, two blocks north of Washington.

Oregon, north and south, from First to Pratt, bet. Brooks and Michigan road.

Osage Alley, north and south, from Georgia to Pratt, bet. Missouri and Mississippi.

Oxford, east and west, bet. Charles and corporation east, nine blocks north of Washington.

PATTERSON, north and south, from Vermont to Elizabeth, thirteen blocks west of Meridian.

Pearl, east and west, from Illinois to Pennsylvania, half block south of Washington.

Peck, bet. old and new cemetery, terminus Kentucky av.

Pendleton Pike, terminus Massachusetts av.

Pennsylvania, north and south, one block east of Meridian.

Peru, from North to Home av., nine blocks east of Meridian.

Phipps, east and west, from Meridian to Pennsylvania, bet. Merrill and McCarty.

Pine, north-east and south-west, from Harrison to Virginia av., one block east of Noble.

Plum, from St. Clair to Christian av., bet. Oak and Broadway.

Poplar, east and west, from Union to Chestnut, two blocks south of McCarty.

Potomac Alley, east and west, bet. Washington and Market.

Pratt, east and west, nine blocks north of Washington.

RAILROAD, from Market to Massachusetts av., bet. Spring and Davidson.

Ray, east and west, from McGinnis to Chestnut, two blocks south of McCarty.

Rhode Island, east and west, eight blocks north of Washington.

River, south of old cemetery.

Roanoke Alley, north and south, from Ohio to First, bet. Tennessee and Mississippi.

Rockwood, east and west, from West to Dacota, three blocks south of McCarty.

Root, east and west, from West to White river, one block south of McCarty.

Rose, between West and White river, two blocks south of Merrill.

Russell, north and south, from Meridian to Illinois, bet. McCarty and Merrill.

SAND, south-east, from Kentucky av. to White river, one block west of West.

Sanders, east and west, from Shelbyville road to terminus of Wright, terminus Virginia av.

School, north and south, from South to Huron, bet. Noble and Virginia av.

Scioto Alley, from Washington to New York, bet. Meridian and Pennsylvania.

Second, east and west, twelve blocks north of Washington.

Seventh, east and west, seventeen blocks north of Washington.

Severn Alley, north and South, from Louisiana to Second, bet. Meridian and Illinois.

Seymour, from east National road to Crane, one-half mile east of corporation.

Sharpe, east and west, from Eckert to Missouri, bet. South and Merrill.

Shelbyville Road, terminus Virginia av.

Short, from Dougherty to city limits south, bet. McKernan and Virginia av.

Sinker, east and west, from Alabama to East, one block north of McCarty.

Sixth, east and west, sixteen blocks north of Washington.

Smith, north and south, from Rhode Island to Indiana av., eleven blocks west of Meridian.

South, east and west, four blocks south of Washington.

Spring, from Market to St. Clair, bet. Noble and Railroad.

Stevens, east and west, from East to Virginia av., one block north of McCarty.

Susquehanna Alley, from Washington to North, bet. Pennsylvania and Delaware.

St. Clair, east and west, eight blocks north of Washington.

St. Joseph, east and west, ten blocks north of Washington.

TENNESSEE, north and south, two blocks west of Meridian.

Tenth, east and west, twenty blocks north of Washington.

Third, east and west, thirteen blocks north of Washington.

Thomas, east and west, from West to Dacota, five blocks south of McCarty.

Tinker, east and west, seventeen blocks north of Washington.

Tippecanoe Alley, east and west, from Tennessee to Illinois, bet. New York and Vermont.

Torbet, east and west, from Fall Creek to Michigan road, beyond corporation.

UNION, from Merrill to Morris, bet. Meridian and Chestnut.

VERMONT, east and west, four blocks north of Washington.

Vine, east and west, bet. Jackson and Charles, nine blocks north of Washington.

Vinton, east and west, from West to Dacota, four blocks south of McCarty.

Virginia Avenue, north-west and south-east from corner Washington and Pennsylvania, to city limits south-east.

WABASH ALLEY, east and west, bet. Market and Ohio.

Wallace, from Morris to city limits south, bet. Madison road and Franklin.

Walnut, east and west, seven blocks north of Washington.

WASHINGTON, east and west, length of city, first street south of Governor's Circle.

Waters, from Stevens to McCarty, bet. Greer and Virginia av.

Wesson, east and west, from Arsenal to Seymour, one block north of Washington.

West, north and south, five blocks west of Meridian.

West Cumberland, east and west, from Tennessee to White river, one-half block south of Washington.

West National Road, east and west, west White river bridge.

Westfield Pike, terminus north Illinois.

Wilkins, east and west, from Tennessee to Chestnut, three blocks south of McCarty.

Willard, from Merrill to Garden, bet. Tennessee and Mississippi.

Willard, north and south, south side east National road, one-half mile east of corporation.

Wilson, north and south, from Elizabeth to Davis, fifteen blocks west of Meridian.

Winston, from Ohio to Walnut, ten blocks east of Meridian.

Wisconsin, east and west, from West to Meridian, fourteen blocks south of Washington.

Wood, north and south, from Michigan to North, bet. Missouri and Mississippi.

Wright, from Buchanan to corporation south, one block west of McKernan.

Wyoming, east and west, from Delaware to East, one block south of McCarty.

YEISER, east and west, from Bluff road to Japan, thirteen blocks south of Washington.

PUBLIC HALLS,
BLOCKS AND BUILDINGS,
INDIANAPOLIS.

ALVORD'S Block, south-west corner Meridian and Georgia.

Ætna Building, east side Pennsylvania, bet. Washington and Market.

Academy of Music, south-east corner Illinois and Ohio.

BATES HOUSE Block, north-west corner Illinois and Washington.

Blackford Block, south-east corner, Washington and Meridian.

Bismark Hall, Virginia avenue, near McCarty.

Brown's Block, north-west corner Washington and Pennsylvania.

COLLEGE Hall, south-west corner Washington and Pennsylvania.

Commercial Building, corner Meridian and Circle.

Court House and County Offices, full square, bet. Washington and Market and Delaware and Alabama.

EDEN'S Block, south side Market, bet. Pennsylvania and Delaware.

Emmenegger Halle, south side Washington, bet. Delaware and Alabama.

FATOUT Block, south side Washington, bet. Mississippi and Canal.

GLENNS' Block, south side Washington, bet. Meridian and Pennsylvania.

Good Templar's Hall, south-west corner Meridian and Washington.

Gymnasium Hall, north-west corner Meridian and Maryland.

HERETH'S Block, north Delaware, opposite court house.

Hubbard's Block, south-west corner Washington and Meridian.

JOURNAL Building, (new,) corner east Market and Circle.

MARMONT'S Hall, south Illinois, corner Georgia.

Masonic Hall, south-east corner Washington and Tennessee.

Metropolitan Theater Hall, north-east corner Washington and Tennessee.

Miller's Hall, corner Delaware and Pearl.

Miller's Block, north-west corner Illinois and Market.

Morrison's Opera Block, north-east corner Meridian and Maryland.

Mozart Hall, east side south Delaware, bet. Washington and Maryland.

Music Hall, north side Court, bet. Delaware and Pennsylvania.

ODD FELLOWS Hall, north-east corner Pennsylvania and Washington.

PALMER HOUSE Block, north-east corner Illinois and Washington.

Post-Office Building, south-east corner Pennsylvania and Market.

SCHNULL'S Block, south-west corner Meridian and Maryland.

Seidensticker's Block, opposite south side Union Depot.

State House, full square, bet. Washington and Market and Tennessee and Mississippi.

Supreme Court and State Office Building, south-west corner Washington and Tennessee.

TALBOTT & NEW'S Block, east side north Pennsylvania, bet. Washington and Market.

Temperance Hall, north side west Washington, bet. Illinois and Meridian.

UNION DEPOT, Louisiana, bet. Illinois and Meridian.

Union Hall, south side east Washington, bet. Delaware and Alabama.

United States Offices and Court Room, in Post Office Building, south-east corner Pennsylvania and Market.

VINTON'S Block, south-west corner of Pennsylvania and Market.

WILEY'S Block, west side north Pennsylvania, near corner Washington.

YOHN'S Block, north-east corner Washington and Meridian.

ALTERATIONS, CORRECTIONS AND REMOVALS.

ALLEN JAMES, pressman, H. C. Chandler & Co., res. 31 w. Georgia.

Alvord Mrs. Mary H., (wid. E. B.,) res. 334 n. Illinois.

BALLARD T. M., retired merchant, res. 356 n. Alabama.

Barker W. H., bds. 17 w. Maryland.

BEAULIEN CHARLES S., physician, office 63 e. McCarty. See card, adv. dept., page 6.

CARPENTER B. O., marble dealer, 36 e. Market, res. 246 n. Illinois. See card, page 6, adv. dept.

Casey Michael, harness-maker, res. 114 w. Georgia.

Chapman Mrs. C. M., (wid.,) dress-maker, res. cor. East and Washington.

Clay H., (A. Jones & Co.,) 74 and 77 s. Meridian, res. 240 n. Meridian.

Colclazer J. H., at W. P. Bingham & Co., bds. 17 w. Maryland.

Couse Riley, (col.,) lab., res. 751 n. Mississippi.

Craft J., bds. 17 w. Maryland.

Cruze Mary, servant, 381 n. Illinois.

Curtis T. M., engineer, Geisendorff's res. 122 e. Merrill.

DEWIRE JOHN, carpenter, bds. w. s. Mississippi, bet. First and Second.

ENOS T. H. K., book-keeper, Browning & Sloan, 7 and 9 e. Washington, res. 350 n. Illinois.

FLETCHER STOUGHTON A., Jr., pres. Indianapolis Gas-Light, Coal and Coke Co., office cor. s. Pennsylvania and Maryland, res. cor. Virginia av. and South.

Fuller James C., lab., Blind Asylum, res. 27 s. Alabama.

Fuller Lorenzo D., painter, res. 27 s. Alabama.

Fuller Sylvester R., lab., res. 27 s. Alabama.

GORDON JAMES, A., speculator, bds. 83 Indiana av.

GAS OFFICE, n. e. cor. Pennsylvania and Maryland, Stoughton A. Fletcher, Jr., pres., L. Vanlaningham, sec.

GEBHARD AUGUST, upholsterer and spring-bottom mattrass, 14 s. Delaware. See card, page 122.

German Methodist Episcopal School, Ohio, bet. New York and East, J. F. Miller, teacher.

Graves George H., brakesman, I., C. & L. R. R., bds. Ray House.

Gregg Joshua, conductor sleeping-car, C., C. & I. C. R. R., bds. 248 n. Alabama.

Gregg Sarah, (wid.,) res. 248 Alabama.

GLICK & SCHWARTZ, (Herman G. & Joseph S.,) manfr. and dealer in hoop-skirts and fancy goods, 54 n. Illino is. See card, page 231.

HACKET WILLIAM, lab., res. 64 s Liberty.

Hogan Israel, machinist, res. 268 w. Vermont.

Holliday John H., journalist, res. 242 n. Alabama.

Hoskins John, fireman, J., M. & I. R. R., bds. 361 s. Delaware.

JONES WILLIAM J., yard-master, T. H. & I. R. R., res. 132 w. First.

Judson & Dodd, (William J. & J. W. D.,) steam coffee and spice mills, s. e. cor. Washington and East.

KAHLER REV. SAMUEL J., pastor Third Street M. E. Church, res. e. s. n. Illinois, bet. Third and Fourth.

Keely William, carpenter, res. 158 e. Michigan

Keith Mrs. P. H., (wid. William,) seamstress, res. 47 cor. Huron and Noble.

Koller William H., grocer, e. Washington, res. near Arsenal av.

Kunkel Benhart, cigar-maker, 61 e. Washington, res. 253 s. Union.

MARONE & BERINGER, (T. M. & J. B. B.,) saloon, 145 w. Washington.

Martindale Mrs. Julia, (wid. Alston,) seamstress, 194 w. Georgia, res. same.

Mikels Philip, machinist, res. 449 s. Missouri.

SINKS JAMS M., carpenter and builder, contractor and jobber, 240 n. Mississippi. See card, page 80.

Stelzel John, (S., Jordan & Co.,) barber, 33½ w. Washington, res. 376 e. Ohio.

MUNICIPAL RECORD

OF INDIANAPOLIS.

MAYOR:

DANIEL MACAULEY.

TERM EXPIRES MAY, 1869.

CITY COUNCILMEN.

First Ward—Sims A. Colley, P. H. Jameson.

Second Ward—H. Coburn, J. H. Kappes.

Third Ward—J. W. Davis, J. H. Woodburn.

Fourth Ward,—J. B. McArthur, A. P. Stanton.

Fifth Ward—Samuel Goddard, George A. Foster.

Sixth Ward—A. H. Brown, James Burgess.

Seventh Ward—Thomas Cottrell, C. F. Schmidt.

Eighth Ward—W. H. Loomis, W. H. Henchen.

Ninth Ward—A. Seidensticker, Henry Geisel.

CITY OFFICERS.

OFFICE, GLENNS' BLOCK, EAST WASHINGTON STREET.

City Clerk—Daniel Ransdell.
Deputy Clerk—John G. Waters.
Deputy Clerk—John R. Clinton.
Treasurer—Robert S. Foster.
Deputy Treasurer—John W. Coone.
City Judge—John N. Scott.
City Attorney—B. K. Elliott.
Civil Engineer—R. M. Patterson.
Assessor—William Hadley.

Marshal—John Unversaw.
Deputy Marshal—M. R. Scudder.
Street Commissioner—August Richter.
Chief Fire Engineer—Charles Richmond.
Market Master—Gideon B. Thompson.
Sealer—S. B. Morris.
Sexton---G. W. Alred.
Printer—James G. Douglass.

Standing Committees of City Council.

Accounts—Henry Coburn, J. H. Woodburn, J. H. Kappes.
Benevolence—J. H. Kappes, W. H. Loomis, Henry Geisel.
Bridges—J. W. Davis, James Burgess, Henry Geisel.
Finances—P. H. Jameson, C. F. Schmidt, Thomas Cottrell.
Fire Department—J. W. Davis, Henry Coburn, J. H. Kappes.
Gas Light—C. F. Schmidt, Samuel Goddard, James Burgess.
Judiciary—Sims A. Colley, A. Seidensticker, A. P. Stanton.
Market—J. B. McArthur, Samuel Goddard, W. H. Henchen.
Police—A. Seidensttcker, W. H. Loomis, A. P. Stanton.
Printing and Stationery—J. H. Kappes, A. H. Brown, A. P. Stanton.
Public Buildings—J. H. Woodburn, W. H. Henchen, A. P. Stanton.
Public Schools—W. H. Loomis, A. H. Brown, J. H. Woodburn.
Revision of Ordinances—A. Seidensticker, S. A. Colley, Thomas Cottrell.
Streets and Alleys—A. H. Brown, Henry Coburn, J. W. Davis.

Board of City Government.

CITY COMMISSIONERS.

President—S. M. Seibert.
Secretary—J. N. Russell.
J. C. Yohn, W. Braden, Thomas Schooley.

DIRECTORS CITY HOSPITAL.

Dr. John M. Kitchen, W. W. Smith, J. C. Geisendorff, W. Braden, George Merritt, Dr. F. S. Newcomer, Charles Glazier, E. J. Holiday, Dr. J. M. Phipps.

HEALTH.

President—Dr. G. M. Mears.
Dr. John P. Avery, Dr. R. M. Todd.

SCHOOL TRUSTEES.

President—Thomas B. Elliott.
Secretary and Treasurer—W. H. L. Noble, Clemens Vonnegut.

POLICE COMMISSIONERS.

A. Seidensticker, W. H. Loomis, A. P. Stanton.

PUBLIC IMPROVEMENTS.

J. W. Davis, Samuel Goddard, Henry Coburn.
Clerk of the Board—D. M. Ransdell.

Police.

Police Judge—John N. Scott.
Chief of Police—Thomas S. Wilson.
Lieutenants—Henry Paul, George Taffe.

DAY PATROLMEN.

First Ward—Geo. W. Bennett.
Second Ward—James N. Stevens.
Third Ward—Hannibal Taffe.
Fourth Ward—William B. Bolen.
Fifth Ward—Samuel Buser.
Sixth Ward—J. P. Duval.
Seventh Ward—William Williams.
Eighth Ward—L. M. Russell.
Ninth Ward—J. T. Murphy.

NIGHT PATROLMEN.

First Ward—Robert Barbee, Thomas Horniday.
Second Ward—E. P. Hoppe, A. J. Wells.
Third Ward—John Cahill, Allen Thornbrough.
Fourth Ward—Wm. F. Brunnemer, Michael Murphy.
Fifth Ward—Frederick Scheigert, John L. Brown.
Sixth Ward—Hiram Minick, O. B. Boardman.
Seventh Ward—George Buser, Francis Otwell.
Eighth Ward—A. H. Catterson, August Reick.
Ninth Ward—Pauline Landormi, George Thomas.

Ward Boundaries.

First Ward—North of Washington, bet. Alabama and Liberty, to corporation north.
Second Ward—North of Washington, bet. Alabama and Meridian, to corporation north.
Third Ward—North of Washington, bet. Meridian and Mississippi, to corporation north.
Fourth Ward—All that part lying north of Washington and west of Mississippi, to corporation.
Fifth Ward—All that part lying south of Washington and west of Illinois, to corporation.
Sixth Ward—South of Washington, bet. Illinois and Delaware, to corporation south.
Seventh Ward—South of Washington, bet. Delaware and East, to corporation south.
Eighth Ward—All that part lying south of Washington and east of East, to corporation.
Ninth Ward—All that part lying north of Washington and east of Liberty, to corporation line.

Wood Measurers.

East Market—L. H. Jameson.
West Market—A. W. Jenkins.

Fire Department.

Chief Engineer—Charles Richmond.
Watchmen City Tower—Charles Rhoads, Thomas Burnitt.

STEAM ENGINE, NO. 1.

South side Washington, bet. West and California.
Engineer—Frank Glazier.

STEAM ENGINE, NO. 2.

South-west corner Massachusetts av. and New York.
Engineer—C. E. Curtis.

STEAM ENGINE, NO. 3.

South s. South, bet. Delaware and Alabama.
Engineer—Daniel Glazier.

STEAM ENGINE, NO. 4.

Company not yet organized.

HOOK AND LADDER COMPANY.

East side New Jersey, bet. Market and Washington.
Driver—E. H. Webster.

PUBLIC FREE SCHOOLS.

The city free schools are under the general management of a Board of three Trustees, elected by the Common Council, consisting at present of Thomas B. Elliott, president, W. H. L. Noble, secretary and treasurer, and Clemens Vonnegut; A. C. Shortridge being clerk of the Board and Superintendent of the Public Schools. Office of the Board and Superintendent, in High School building, corner West Market street and the Circle.

The Board of Visitors,

Are appointed by the Board of Trustees, and have special supervision over the educational interests of the schools in the different wards, during the terms, and at the semi-annual and annual examinations.

High School—Hon. John Caven and I. W. Monfort.
First Ward—L. G. Hay and W. W. Leathers.
Second Ward—Hon. J. I. Morrison.
Third Ward—Rev. E. T. Fletcher and D. V. Culley.
Fourth Ward—J. B. McArthur and H. A. Edson.
Fifth Ward—Rev. L. H. Jameson and Simon Yandes.
Sixth Ward—Rev. C. H. Marshal and A. H. Brown.

Seventh Ward—Col. Sam Merrill and Granville Ballard.
Eighth Ward—Rev. N. A. Hyde and W. H. Loomis.
Ninth Ward—Rev. J. Stuckenberg and J. H. Kappes.

There are twelve School Buildings and sixty-two teachers. The Schools are divided into three departments: Primary, Intermediate and High School, with four grades in each department. A new building for the use of the High School is being completed, and will be occupied after September 1st, 186 . Its location is on the corner of West Market and the Circle, which, for accommodation and convenience, owing to its central location, will be equal to the increasing demand of this school. A large School House is just completed in the southern part of the city, corner of Union street, bet. Merrill and McCarty, which will accommodate 800 pupils. A new School Building is contemplated, and will be erected in the extreme northern part of the city, in some eligible location, which, with the present large number of School Buildings now completed, will afford accommodations equal to any city in the west, compared to the population of the city.

LOCATION OF SCHOOL BUILDINGS.

First Ward—South-west corner New Jersey and Vermont.
Second Ward—North Delaware, bet. Vermont and Michigan.

Third Ward—New York, bet. Illinois and Tennessee.
Fourth Ward—(Old house,) Market, west of West.

(16)

Fourth Ward—(New house,) north-east corner Michigan and Blackford.
Fifth Ward—Maryland, bet. Mississippi and Missouri.
Sixth Ward—(Old house,) Pennsylvania, south of South.
Sixth Ward—(New house,) Union, bet. Merrill & McCarty.

Seventh Ward—East, bet. Georgia and Louisiana.
Eighth Ward—Virginia avenue, bet. School and Noble.
Ninth Ward—Vermont, bet. Railroad and Davidson.
High School—North-west corner Market and Circle.

INSTITUTIONS, COLLEGES, &C.

Indiana Agricultural College.

President, Hon. Conrad Baker; *Secretary*, J. J. Hayden; *Treasurer*, E. B. Martindale; *Board of Trustees*, Smith Vawter, Lewis Burke, of Richmond, Henry Taylor, of Lafayette, Isaac Jenkinson, of Fort Wayne.

Indiana Female College.

South-west corner Meridian and New York. The building affords accommodations for fifty boarding, and one hundred and fifty day pupils.

BOARD OF TRUSTEES.

President, Rev. F. C. Holliday; *Vice-President*, Oliver Tousey; *Secretary*, John W. Ray; *Treasurer*, T. P. Haughey; Ingram Fletcher, John W. Holland, W. Hannaman, James C. Ferguson and Jesse Jones.

Indianapolis Female Institute.

North-east corner Pennsylvania and Michigan. The building affords accommodations for one hundred and fifty boarding, and three hundred day pupils.

OFFICERS.

President of the Institute, Rev. C. W. Hewes; *President of the Board of Trustees*, Rev. Henry Day; *Secretary*, E. C. Atkins; *Treasurer*, J. R. Osgood.

Indianapolis Law College.

President, John T. Elliott; *Secretary*, S. E. Perkins, Jr.; *Treasurer*, David McDonald; *Trustees*, J. E. McDonald, M. Finch, M. B. Taylor, T. A. Hendricks, A. G. Porter and R. B. Duncan; *Professors*, Hon. Samuel E. Perkins, Hon. Lucien Barber.

N. W. C. University.

Located near corporate limits, north-east part of the city. The charter of this Institution authorizes its Board of Directors to organize Colleges for Literature, and Science, Law, Medicine, and a Normal School. The College, proper, was opened in November, 1855; the preparatory department was taught a year before. The sessions for 1868–69, opens September, 1868.

FACULTY.

President and Professor of Ethics and Greek, Rev. O. A. Burgess, A. M.; *Secretary of Faculty*, W. M. Thrasher, A. M.; *Professor of Latin and Modern Languages*, S. K. Hoshour; *Professor of Natural Science*, R. T. Brown; *Professor of Mathematics*, W. M. Thrasher; *Professor in Preparatory and English Department*, A. Fairhurst, A. B.

Purdy's Commercial College.

Eden's Block, east Market.

OFFICERS.

President, William Purdy.

St. John's (R. C.) Academy for Young Ladies.

Georgia, corner Tennessee. *Superioress*, Sister Antoinette, assisted by eight Sisters of Providence.

St. John's (R. C.) Academy for Boys.

West Georgia, near Illinois, under the charge of Rev. A. Bessonies.

LIBRARIES.

State Library.

Located in the State House. The Library consists of twenty-four thousand volumes of historical, law and miscellaneous works. Librarian, Rev. R. F. Foster.

County Library.

Located in the court house, up-stairs. The Library consists of two thousand volumes. Open and accessable to all responsible parties. Librarian, James A. Hamilton.

Township Library.

Located in rooms 4 and 6 Langsdale's Block, 16 north Delaware. The Library consists of fifteen hundred volumes.

Young Men's Library Association.

Located in Hubbard's block, corner Washington and Meridian. Open to strangers day and evening, except Sundays. *President,* John Caven; *Vice-President,* D. E. Snyder; *Treasurer,* D. M. Taylor; *Secretary,* D. W. Grubbs; *Librarian,* C. P. Taylor; *Directors,* C. Dickson, D. W. Grubbs, V. T. Malott, G. B. Yandes, L. R. Martin, G. W. Sloan and C. A. Ray.

CHURCHES.

Baptist.

FIRST BAPTIST CHURCH.

North-east corner New York and Pennsylnia. Pastor, Rev. Henry C. Day.

MISSION CHAPEL.

In charge of the First Baptist Church, corner Noble and South. Sabbath School at 9 o'clock A. M. Superintendent, E. J. Foster.

AFRICAN BAPTIST CHURCH.

Mississippi, bet. Ohio and New York. Pastor, Rev. Moses Broyles, res. 227 n. Minerva.

Catholic.

ST. MARY'S CHURCH.

South side Maryland, bet. Pennsylvania and Delaware. Pastor, Rev. S. Seigrist, res. near church.

ST. JOHN'S CHURCH.

Georgia, bet. Tennessee and Illinois. Pastor, Rev. Augustus Bessonies.

ST. PETER'S CHURCH.

Dougherty, near Fletcher avenue. Pastor, Rev. Joseph Petit.

Christian.

CHRISTIAN CHAPEL.

South-west corner Ohio and Delaware. Pastor, Rev. O. A. Burgess, res. 324 n. Delaware.

MISSION CHURCH, (COLORED.)

Corner Lafayette R. R. and Second. Pastor, Rev. Conrad.

Congregational.

PLYMOUTH CONGREGATIONAL CHURCH.

North-west corner Meridian and Circle. Pastor, Rev. E. P. Ingersal, res. 383 n. Pennsylvania.

Episcopal.

CHRIST'S CHURCH.

North-east corner Meridian and Circle. Organized August, 1837. Pastor, Rev. J. P. T. Ingraham, res. 65 Circle.

GRACE CHURCH.

South-east corner St. Joseph and Pennsylvania. Rector, Rev. M. V. Averill, res. north Tennessee, bet. Second and Third.

ST. PAUL'S CHURCH.

South-east corner Illinois and New York. Rector. Rev. Horace N. Stringfellow.

German Evangelical.

ZION'S CHURCH.

North side Ohio, bet. Meridian and Illinois. Pastor, Rev. Herman Quinius.

GERMAN EVANGELICAL.

East side New Jersey, bet. Ohio and Market. Pastor, Rev. John Fuchs.

Friends.

FRIENDS' CHURCH.

South-east corner Delaware and St. Clair. Erected 1856. Minister, Rev. Enos G. Pray, res. north-west corner Christian avenue and Broadway.

German Reformed.

East side Alabama, bet. Washington and Market. Pastor, Rev. Henry Eschmeier, res. 41 n. Alabama.

Jewish Synagogue.

South side Market, bet. East and New Jersey. Minister, Rev. M. Messing.

Lutheran.

FIRST ENGLISH LUTHERAN.

South-west corner Alabama and New York. Pastor, Rev. J. Stuckenberg.

ST. PAUL'S GERMAN LUTHERAN.

North-east corner East and Georgia; erected in 1861. Pastor, Rev. ⸺ ⸺, residence ⸺ ⸺.

Methodist.

ASBURY CHAPEL.

West side New Jersey, between Louisiana and South; erected 1850. Pastor, Rev. John H. Lozier, residence, East city limits.

ROBERTS CHAPEL.

Meets at Morrison's Opera Hall; new church in process of erection. Pastor, Rev. D. Mendenhall.

STRANGE CHAPEL.

East side Tennessee, between New York and Vermont; erected in 1852. Pastor, Rev. C. S. Burgner.

TRINITY CHURCH.

North-west corner Alabama and North; erected 1865. Pastor, Rev. R. D. Robinson.

THIRD STREET CHURCH.

Third, between Illinois and Tennessee; erected 1867. Pastor, Rev. S. J. Kahler.

WESLEY CHAPEL.

South-west corner Meridian and Circle; erected 1827. Pastor, C. M. Sims.

GERMAN CHURCH.

North side Ohio, between East and New Jersey; erected 1850. Pastor, Rev. H. G. Lich.

AFRICAN CHURCH.

North side Georgia, between Mississippi and Canal. Pastor, Rev. E. McIntosh.

Presbyterian.

FIRST CHURCH.

South-west corner Pennsylvania and New York; erected 1865. Pastor, Rev. J. H. Nixon, residence 75 e. Michigan.

SECOND CHURCH.

North-west corner Pennsylvania and Vermont; erected 1867. Pastor, Rev. H. H. Edson, residence 157 n. Tennessee.

THIRD CHURCH.

North-east corner Illinois and Ohio; erected 1859. Pastor, Rev. ⸺ ⸺, residence ⸺ ⸺.

FOURTH CHURCH.

South-west corner Delaware and Market; erected 1858. Pastor, Rev. C. H. Marshall, residence 80 Christian avenue.

FIFTH CHURCH.

(German,) East side New Jersey, between Washington and Maryland. Pastor, Rev. Charles Steinbach.

REFORMED CHURCH OF COVENANTERS.

North side South, bet. East and Noble. Pastor, Rev. John Crozier.

SEVENTH PRESBYTERIAN.

North-east corner Elm and Cedar; erected 1867. Pastor, Rev. J. Howard.

UNITED PRESBYTERIAN.

North side Ohio, between Pennsylvania and Delaware. Pastor, Rev. A. W. Clokey.

EIGHTH PRESBYTERIAN.

North side McCarty, between Union and Pennsylvania; erected 1867. Pastor, Rev. J. D. Brandt.

United Brethren.

South-east corner New Jersey and Ohio; members, 400. Pastor, Amos Haunaway.

Universalist.

FIRST CHURCH.

Meets in Wallace's Hall, south-west corner Delaware and Maryland; organized 1863. Pastor, Rev. B. F. Foster.

SECOND CHURCH.

Michigan, between Illinois and Tennessee; organized 1867. Pastor, ⸺.

Mission.

ILLINOIS STREET CHURCH.

Corner Illinois and Phipps. Pastor, Rev. J. Tarkington.

UNION MISSION CHAPEL.

South-west corner Union and Madison avenue; Sunday-school, 9 A. M. Superintendent F. W. Davis.

Young Men's Christian Association.

Meets at rooms in Vinton's blk., opp. p. o. *Pres.*, W. H. Hay; *Treas.*, J. C. Hays; *Rec. Sec.*, E., P. Ingersoll; *Sec.*, C. P. Wilson.

SOCIETIES AND ASSOCIATIONS.

PUBLIC.

Butcher's Association.

OFFICERS.

President, H. Kramer; *Treasurer*, Frederick Beck; *Secretary*, Michael Mayer.

Eclectic Medical Association.

OFFICERS.

President, D. II. Prunk; *First Vice-President*, J. F. Ridgeway; *Second Vice-President*, N. S. Pendry; *Secretary*, G. W. Pickerill, *Treasurer*, L. Abbott.

Indianapolis Academy of Medicine.

OFFICERS.

President, R. N. Todd; *Vice-President*, F. S. Newcomer; *Secretary*, William Wands, *Treasurer*, J. M. Kitchen.

Indianapolis Female Bible Society.

OFFICERS.

President, Mrs. M. Given; *Vice-President*, Mrs. J. M. Graydon; *Treasurer*, Mrs. S. P. Ray; *Secretary*, Miss J. A. Bassett; *Depository*, Todd, Carmichael & Williams; *Managers*, Mrs. E. Wilkinson, Mrs. F. C. Holliday, Eliza Newman.

Indianapolis Mannærchor Society.

Meets at Miller's Hall, corner Delaware and Pearl.

OFFICERS.

President, G. Recker; *Vice-President*, A. Dennescheek; *Secretary*, L. Klemm; *Treasurer*, F. Theobald; *Librarian*, L. Haller; *Musical Director*, —— Weegman.

Indianapolis Typographical Union.

OFFICERS.

President, John G. Doughty; *Vice-President*, William Meredith; *Corresponding Secretary*, Harry Cassill; *Recording Secretary*, D. L. Payne; *Financial Secretary*, John Hargin; *Treasurer*, Francis A.

Ratti; *Guardian*, Edward Guthrie; *Executive Committee*, John Fray, A. D. Stevens, John A Rankin, S. J. Pearce, P. Griffin, R. Moffit, D. M. Cantrell.

SECRET.

Masonic.

OFFICERS.

GRAND LODGE.

M. W. G. M., Martin L. Rice; R. W. D. G. M., A. G. Porter; R. W. S. G. W., L. A. Smith; R. W. J. G. W., A. J. Holmes; R. W. G. T., Charles Fisher; R. W. G. S., J. M. Bramwell; G. C., Geo. B. Ingle; G. L., William Blinks; G. M., L. A. Foot; G. S. D., W. E. Hollingsworth; G. J. D., W. H. Smith; G. Tyler, Fred. Haueisen.

GRAND COMMANDERY OF KNIGHTS TEMPLARS.

M. E. G. C., Thomas Newby; R. E. D. G. C., D. P. Whedon; G. G., Thomas Pattison; G. C. G., E. G. Hamilton; G. T., Charles Fisher; G. R., John Bramwell; G. P., T. H. Linch; G. S. W., L. B. Stockton; G. J. W., Christian Fetta; G. S. B., H. W. Daniels; G. S. B., G. H. Fish; G. W., Erie Locke; G. C. G., W. M. Black.

GRAND CHAPTER.

M. E. G. H. P., Thomas Newby; D. G. H. P., R. J. Chestnutwood; R. E. G. K., Hugh Hannah; R. E. G. S., George V. Howk; E. G. T., Charles Fisher; E. G. S., William Hacker; G. Chap., John Leach; G. Captain, Joseph Hale; G. R. A. C., Alex. Thomas; G. Guard, William M. Black.

GRAND COUNCIL OF ROYAL AND SELECT MASTERS.

M. P. G. M., Thomas Newby; D. P. G. M., Thomas Pattison; T. I. G. M., William W. Austin; G. P. C., M. H. Rice; G. C. Guards, A. H. Thomas; G. Treas.,

Charles Fisher; G· Recorder, William Hacker; G. Chaplain. John Leach; G. Steward and Sentinel, A. A. Wilson.

INDIANA CONSISTORY S. P. R. S.

J. C. C., E. A. Davis; J. L. C., C. J. Dobbs; J. L. C., P. G. C. Hunt; J. G. O., John Love; J. G. C., Nathan Kimball; J. G. S., Geo. II. Fleming; J. G. T., L. R. Martin; J. G. E., William Glenn; J. G. H., N. G. Burnham; J. G. M., N. R. Ruckle; J. G. S., J. W. Smith; J. G. C., S. T. Scott; J. G. S., J. F. Haueisen.

INDIANAPOLIS CHAPTER OF ROSE CROIX.

M. W. and P. M., J. Barnard; M. X. and P. K., Sen., N. R. Ruckle, M. X. and P. K., Jun., J. W. Smith; Res. P. K. Treas., L. R. Martin; Res. P. K. Secy., Geo. K. Fleming; Res. P. K. Mr. Cer., W. H. Valentine; Res. P. K. Capt., A. M. Benham; Asst. P. K. Capt., Fred. Haueisen.

SARAITT COUNCIL PRINCES OF JERUSALEM.

M. E. G. M., W. C. Stone; G. H. P. S. B., P. G. C. Hunt; M. E. S. G. W., N. R. Ruckle; M. E. J. G. W., John Caven; G. T., L. R. Martin; G. M. C., J. W. Smith; G. M. of E., F. M. Heron; G. Tyler, Fred. Haueisen.

ADONIROM LODGE OF PERFECTION.

T. P. G. M., John Caven; H. T. P. G. M., John Love; S. G. W., W. H. Valentine; J. G. W., Wm. Glenn; G. K. S., C. W. Dobbs; G. Sec., George Fleming; G. Treas., L. R. Martin; G. Orator, F. S. Newcomer; G. Master, J. W. Smith; G. Captain, M. T. Scott; G. Tyler, Fred. Haueisen.

RAPER COMMANDERY, No. 1.

E. C., E. Colestock; C. G., Erie Locke; Prelate, John Caven; S. W., E. S. Dow; J. W., J. Ebert; Treas., H. Daumont; Recorder, C. Fisher; Warden, Geo. H. Fleming, Sentinel, W. M. Black.

INDIANAPOLIS CHAPTER NO. 5.

II. P., J. M. Bramwell: R., Roger Perry; S., E. Colestock; C. H., B. C. Darrow; P. S., G. B. Ingle, Jr.; R. A. C., N. R. Ruckle; 1st V. G. M., John B. Kelley; 2d V. G. M., L. Seibold; 3d V. G. M., J. McKibben; Treas., J. Reynolds; Secy., C. Fisher; Guard, W. M. Black.

CITY LODGES.

ANCIENT LANDMARKS LODGE No. 319.

W. M., George S. Warren; S. W., J. C. Walke; J. W., W. H. Valentine; Treas., D. P. Jones; Secy., E. Harmell; S. D., W. O. Stone; J. D., C. A. Bates; Tyler, Fred. Haueisen.

CAPITAL CITY NO. 312.

M. W., W. M. Davis; S. M., W. H. Ireland; J. M., Jeff. Harper; Treas., Fred. Baggs; Sec., A. F. Coorse; S. D., John Sullivan; J. D., A. Bavington; Tyler, J. J. Merritt.

CENTRE LODGE NO. 23.

W. M., B. C. Darow; S. W., Joseph Solomon; J. W., John Cavin; Treas., H. Daumont; Secy., Charles Fisher; S. D., N. R. Ruckle; J. D., C. E. Wright; Stewarts, H. White and A. B. Prather; Tyler, J. H. Kappes.

INDIANAPOLIS COUNCIL NO. 2, OF ROYAL AND SELECT MASTERS.

Gr. Master, ———; Dept., Roger Parry; P. C. W., George B. Ingle, Jr; C. G., Frank Farmer; Treas., H. Daumont; Recorder, C. Fisher; Sentinel, W. M. Black.

MARION LODGE NO. 35.

W. M., John Ebert; S. W., Jackson Saylor; J. W., G. B. Ingle; Treas., H. S. Bighorn; Secy., W. S. Cone; S. D., E. J. Hardesty; J. D., T. C. Rout.

TEUTONIA LODGE.

M. W., J. C. Brinkmeyer; S. W., G. H. Brinkmeyer; J. W., C. Dehne; Secy., Louis Helle; Treas., Adam Spreng; S. D., Christian Karle; J. D., Fred. Meyer; Tyler, ——— Bernauer.

Odd Fellows.

THE GRAND LODGE OF INDIANA.

I. O. O. F.,

Holds its semi-annual communication at Odd Fellows Hall, in the city of Indianapolis, on the Third Tuesdays of May and November of each year.

OFFICERS.

M. W. G. M, J. T. Sanders; R. W. D. G. M., S. L. Adams; R. W. G. W., J. A. Wildman; R. W. G. S., E. H. Barry; R. W. G. T., T. P. Haughey; G. Chap.,

Rev. S. Bowers; G. M., F. A. Jeter; G. Con., F. W. Kizer; G. H., William Bellis; G. G., G. W. Rose; G. Rep., T. B. McCarty; G. Rep., J. A. Funk.

GRAND ENCAMPMENT INDIANA.

OFFICERS.

M. W. G. P., C. P. Tally; M. E. G. H. P., T. G. Beharrele; G. S. W., G. H. Brink-meyer; G. J. W., G. W. Gordon; G. Treas., T. P. Haughey; G. Sec., E. H. Barry; G. Sent., Chris. Toler; D. G. S., J. S. Watson; S. Rep., F. J. Blair.

CAPITAL LODGE NO. 12.

W. G., A. McLane; V. G., J. H. Hedges; Secretary, J. B. Kelly; Per. Secretary, J. F. Walleck; Treas., C. Hamlin.

CENTRE LODGE NO. 18.

N. G., J. A. Buchanan; V. G., S. W. Cochrane; Secretary, E. M. Byrkit; Per. Secretary, G. P. Anderson; Treasurer, John G. Waters.

GERMANIA LODGE NO. 129.

N. G., Charles Schmidt; V. G., M. Ginz; Secretary, Charles Lauer; Per. Sec., Tob Bender; Treasurer, J. Schneider.

PHILOXENIAN LODGE NO. 44.

N. G., W. S. Cone; V. G., H. M. Mounts; Secretary, A. B. Howard; Per. Sec., Geo. G. Staats; Treasurer, Jo. S. Watson.

MARION EMCAMPMENT NO. 35.

C. P., Carlin Hamlin; H. P., A. McLane; S. W., A. J. Buckhart; J. W., ——; Scribe, J. A. Ringer; Per. Scribe, W. W. Weeks; Treasurer, J. F. Wallick.

METROPOLITAN ENCAMPMENT NO. 5.

G. P., W. S. Cone; H. P., J. W. Jones; S. W., Chas. Buck; J. W., A. J. Corey; Scribe, J. W. Byrkit; Treasurer, John Reynolds.

TEUTONIA ENCAMPMENT NO. 57.

C. P., M. Ginz; H. P., H. Wilking; S. W., P. Heddrick; J. W., ——; Scribe, Fred. Smith; Per. Scribe, J. Scribner; Treasurer, T. Bender.

Sons of Temperance.

GRAND DIVISION OF INDIANA.

G. W. P., William W. H. McCurdy, Indianapolis; G. W. A., C. E. Scarlett; G. S., L. Abbett, Indianapolis; G. T., J.

B. Abbett; G. Chap., R. T. Brown; G. C., J. W. Vance; G. Sent., J. S. Vanarsdel. Next session at Indianapolis, the first Tuesday in November, 1868.

CITY DIVISIONS.

WASHINGTON DIVISION NO. 10.

Meets every Friday night in Temperance Hall, 30 west Washington street.

Cadets of Temperance.

GRAND SECTION OF INDIANA.

Grand Patron, W. R. Ellis, Lafayette; Vice-Grand Patron, J. L. Harris, Attica; Grand Secretary, L. Abbett, Indianapolis; Grand Treasurer, John E. Taylor, Evansville; Grand Guide, Joseph McLain, Kent Station; Grand Watchman, J. S. Vanarsdel, Thorntown; Grand Chaplain, J. E. Ferrill, Indianapolis. Next session at Indianapolis, first Tuesday in November.

CITY SECTION.

MORRIS SECTION NO. 2.

Meets every Saturday night in Temperance Hall, 30 west Washington street.

Independent Order of Good Templars.

GRAND LODGE OF INDIANA.

OFFICERS.

G. W. C. T., Amanda M. Way, Indianapolis; G. W. C., S. Montgomery, Kokomo; G. W. V. T., J. W. Hasket; G. W. S., J. W. Husper, Terre Haute, and D. R. Pershing; G. W. T., J. Jenkins, Fort Wayne; G. W. Chap., H. J. Lacy; G. W. M., J. M. Merwin, Cloverdale; G. W. D. M., Miss Cynthia A. Gard; G. W. I. G., Mrs. C. A. P. Smith, Delphi; Representatives to R. W. G. L., Amanda M. Way, William Copp and S. T. Montgomery; Alternates, M. F. Thomas, Cynthia A. Gard and N. Simmons. Next session at Terre Haute, commencing on the third Tuesday of October, 1868, at 2 o'clock P. M.,

CITY LODGES.

FOREST LODGE NO. 381.

Meets on Friday evening, at Wood's Hall.

CENTER LODGE NO. 322.

Meets every Tuesday night in Wood's Hall, over Dorsey, Layman & Fletcher's Hardware Store.

JULIAN LODGE NO. 74.

Meets every Wednesday evening in Temperance Hall, 30 west Washington street.

GOUGH LODGE NO. 178, I. O. G. T.

Meets in Wood's Hall, 64 east Washington street, every Monday evening. Tom. E. Null, W. C. T.; H. Clay Sculors, W. S.

Independent Order of Knights Templar of Temperance.

SUPREME COUNCIL.

G. W. C., Sir Harry Cassil, Indianapolis; R. L. C., Lady Peep Cassil, Indianapolis; R. W., Sir Thos. S. Walterhouse, Muncie; E. C., Sir Samuel O. Budd, Muncie; E. H., Sir Andrew A. Kaufman, Anderson; E. S., Sir Joshua E. Knight, Anderson; E. T., Sir John W. Westerfield, Anderson.

COEUR DE LION COUNCIL NO. 2.

Meets every Saturday, in Wood's Hall.

Druids.

WASHINGTON GRAND GROVE NO. 3.

Meets 27½ s. Meridian, on the last Thursday of every month. H. E. E., A. Haffner; Secretary, I. Kern.

Haragarie Society.

Meets every Tuesday evening, at the Hall, 14 and 16 south Delaware. D. G. B., A. Naltner; E. B., Charles Heiser; C. B., Edward Muller; W. B., H. Tilly; Secretary, H. Roy; Treasurer, W. Richter.

Helvetia Bund.

Meets at 61 east Washington, every other Wednesday. President, C. M. Meyer; Secretary, R. Hoefler; Treasurer, C. Fisher; Doorkeeper, N. Pfaender.

HUMBOLDT GROVE NO. 8.

E. E., P. Richwein; W. E., Henry Piell; Secretary, J. Verenickel; Treaurer, Geo. Fahrion.

I. O. B. B.

President, Joseph Myer; Vice-President, Sol. Straus; Secretary, J. G. Joseph; Treasurer, Samuel Kahn; Monitor, Leo. Kahn; Assistant Monitors, Lyon Kahn; Warden, A. Kahn; C. G., H. Rosenthal.

Grand Army of the Republic.

Head-Quarters Department of Indiana Grand Army of the Republic, Adjutant General's office, 2 Ætna Building. Grand Commander, Major General R. S. Foster; S. V. G. C., Charles Craft; J. V. G. C., George Humphreys; J. G., T. W. Bennett; Q. G., Samuel Merrill; L. C., L. D. Waterman; G. C., L. H. Jameson; A. G., O. M. Wilson.

Merchants and Manufacturers Exchange.

Meets every Saturday 3 P. M., at 27 south Meridian. This society, being recently organized, comprises the Merchants and Manufacturers, in general, of the city of Indianapolis. President, W. E. Tarkington; First Vice-President, Robert Connely; Second Vice-President, Samuel Merrill; Secretary, James Green; Treasurer, John W. Murphy. Executive Committee, E. T. Sinker, Chairman; J. M. Caldwell, R. S. Foster, E. C. Mayhew, J. D. Vinnedge. Railroad Committee, George Merritt, J. E. Mooney, Frank Landers, H. Daily, A. Wallace.

Chamber of Commerce.

Vinton's Block, north Pennsylvania, opposite post-office. President, James C. Ferguson; First Vice-President, S. V. B. Noel; Second Vice-President, Thomas Kingan; Third Vice-President, A. Jones; Secretary, J. Bernard; Board of Directors, John Carlisle, J. D. D. Pattison, J. W. Murphy, Lucien Hill, F. P. Rush, G. W. Smith, L. W. Hasselman, D. Gibson, Fielding Beeler, B. Coffin.

MARION CO. COURTS AND OFFICERS.

County Officers.

Clerk, William C. Smock. *Deputies*, C. F. Rooker, R. M. Smock, L. L. Harvey, D. C. Granfield.

Sheriff, George W. Parker. *Deputies*, J. T. Elliott, H. C. Adams, John L. Hanna. *Auditor*, George F. McGinnis.

Deputies, Frank Hamilton, E. M. Wilmington
Treasurer, Frank Eldermeyer.
Deputy Treasurers, A. L. Wright, B. F. Riley.
Surveyor, Oliver W. Voorhies.
Commissioners, Aaron McCreery, L. Vausyoe, J. K. English.

Common Pleas Court.

Meets first Mondays in February, June and October. Length of term, six weeks. Judge, S. T. Blair.

Marion Civil Circuit Court.

Meets first Mondays in November and May. Length of term, nine weeks. Judge, Cyrus C. Hines.

Criminal Court.

Meets first Mondays in January and July. Length of term, six months. Judge George H. Chapman.

INDIANA COURTS.

Supreme Court.

Meets at the Supreme Court Rooms, southwest corner Washington and Tennessee, in Indianapolis, on the fourth Monday in May and November.
Judges, Hon. James S. Frazer, Hon. Charles A. Ray, Hon. John T. Elliott, Hon. Robert O. Gregory.
Reporter, Gen. Benjamin Harrison.
Attorney General, D. E. Williamson.
Clerk, General Laz Noble.
Sheriff, Samuel Lamb.
Deputy Sheriff, Samuel R. Judah.

U. S. Circuit Court,

FOR THE DISTRICT OF INDIANA.

Meets first Tuesdays in May and November. Circuit Court held by Hon. David Davis, Assistant Justice of the United States Supreme Court, and Hon. D. McDonald, District Judge.
Clerk, John D. Howland.

U. S. District Court.

Meets first Tuesdays in May and November.
Judge, Hon. David McDonald.
Clerk, John D. Howland.
Deputy Clerk, William V. Humphreys.
District Attorney, Alfred Kilgore.
United States Marshal, General Benjamin J. Spooner.
United States Deputy Marshals, J. L. Bigelow, C. E. McDonald, J. C. Spooner.
Land Office Register, Edmund Browning
U. S. Commissioners, Edwin A. Davis, J. W. Raymond, Eben W. Kimball, O. M. Wilson and Fred. Knefler.

INDIANA STATE GOVERNMENT.

Lieutenant Governor—Conrad Baker, acting Governor.
Governor's Private Secretary—J. M. Commons.
Secretary of State—Nelson Trusler.
Auditor of State—T. B. McCarty.
Treasurer of State—Nathan Kimball.
Superintendent of Public Instruction—Prof. George W. Hoss.
State Librarian—Rev. B. F. Foster.
Attorney General—D. E. Williamson.

Adjutant General—W. H. H. Terrell.
Quarter-Master General—Peter Schmock.

Indiana Military Agency.

Office, cor. Tennessee and Market, opposite State House.
General Agent—William Hannaman.
Notary Public—James. Turner.
Cashier—Lina J. G. Greenwalt.
Clerk—J. H. Turner.

AGRICULTURE.

Indiana State Board of Agriculture.

OFFICERS.

President—Hon. A. D. Hamrick, Hamrick's Station, Putnam Co.

Vice-President—Dr. John C. Helm, Muncie, Delaware Co.
Treasurer—Carlos Dickson, Indianapolis.
General Superintendent—John B. Sullivan, Indianapolis.

Secretary—A. J. Holmes, Rochester, Fulton Co.
OFFICE—State House, Indianapolis.

MEMBERS.

1st *District*—E. T. Cox.
2d *District*—Hon. J. D. Williams.
3d *District*—John C. Shoemaker.
4th *District*—John McCrea.
5th *District*—Benjamin North.
6th *District*—D. E. Rees.
7th *District*—Jacob Mutz.
8th *District*—Hon. W. C. Danaldson.
9th *District*—Hon. A. D. Hamrick.
10th *District*—Alexander Heron.
11th *District*—Dr. John C. Helm.

12th *District*—Joseph Poole.
13th *District*—Hezekiah Caldwell.
14th *District*—A. J. Holmes.
15th *District*—John Sutherland.
16th *District*—Dr. George W. McConnell.
The Sixteenth Annual Fair will be held at Indianapolis Sept. 28th to Oct. 3d.

Marion County Agricultural and Horticultural Society.

Office, Hubbard's block, s. w. cor. Washington and Meridian.
President—John S. Dunlop.
Vice-President—D. Mears.
Secretary—John T. Francis.
Treasurer—W. S. Hubbard.

U. S. OFFICES IN THIS CITY.

United States Arsenal.

Located one-half mile from city corporation east. The grounds consist of about seventy-five acres. There is already completed a main store-house, one building for storing artillery, one magazine for storing powder, one set of officers' quarters and one office. Other buildings, for manufacturing and storing ammunition and for other purposes, will be put up from year to year, as fast as it is possible to do so. Brevet Lieutenant Colonel William H. Harris, Colonel commanding.

United States Internal Revenue, Sixth District, Indiana.

Assessor—David Braden.
Deputy—L. M. Phipps.
Office room 14, post-office building.
Collector—Austin H. Brown.
Deputy—Thomas Madden.
Office room 15, post-office building.
Register—Edmund Browning.
Office room 8, post-office building.

United States Marshal's Office.

(Room 6 post-office building.)

U. S. Marshal—Benjamin Spooner.

Deputies—J. S. Bigelow, C. E. McDonald, W. C. David, John C. Spooner, H. N. Bigelow.

Indianapolis Post-Office.

POST-OFFICE BUILDING.

Located south-east corner Pennsylvania and Market. Open, from the first of October to the first of April, from 7½ A. M. to 6½ P. M., and from April 1st to October 1st, from 7 A. M. to 7 P. M., on Sundays from 9 A. M. to 10 A. M.
Post-Master—D. G. Rose.
Assistant Post-Master—E. P. Thompson.
Money Order Clerk—T. B. Messick.
Special Mail Agent—W. R. Bowen.
Local Mail Agent—H. Vaudegriff.

MAILS.

Going East, over Bellefontaine and Central Railways.
Going West, over Terre Haute & Indianapolis and St. Louis Railroads.
Going North, over Peru and Lafayette Railroads.
Going South, over Cincinnati, Madison and Jeffersonville Railroads.
Going South-west, over Vincennes Railroad.
Going North-west, over Indianapolis, Crawfordsville & Danville Railroad.

BANKS AND BANKING HOUSES.

Bank of the State, incorporated 1857; closing business. James M. Ray, prest., Joseph Moore, cashier.

Branch of the Bank of the State, n. e. cor. Washington and Meridian, Oliver Tousey, prest., D. M. Taylor, cashier.

Citizens' National Bank, 4 e. Washington; organized 1864, capital $300,000. Isaiah Mansur, pres., Joseph R. Haugh, cashier.

FIRST NATIONAL BANK, s. e. cor. Washington and Meridian; organized 1863, capital $500,000. William H. English, prest., John C. New, cashier.

FLETCHER'S BANK, 30 e. Washington; organized 1830, capital $200,000. S. A. Fletcher & Co., props. Deposits received, discounts made, exchange and government securities bought and sold. Banking hours from 8 A. M. to 4 P. M.

HARRISON'S BANK, 15 c. Washington; established in 1855, capital $100,000. Alfred & John C. S. Harrison, proprietors. Deposits received, discounts made, gold, silver, bought and sold. Banking hours from 8 A. M. to 4 P. M.

INDIANA BANKING CO., 28 e. Washington; organized 1865, capital $100,000. F. A. W. Davis, prest., W. W. Woolen, cashier, Samuel C. Vance, asst. cashier, John P. Lord, book-keeper, Oliver Bonz, messenger. Deposits received, discounts made, exchange and government securities bought and sold. Banking hours from 8 A. M. to 4 P. M., daily.

INDIANA NATIONAL BANK, 2 e. Washington, cor. Meridian; organized 1865, capital $400,000. George

Tousey, prest., D. M. Taylor, cashier, Morris R. Eddy, book-keeper, James Nichol, teller. George Tousey, Oliver Tousey, George Merritt, Wm. Coughlin, Daniel Stewart, Jacob P. Dunn, directors. Banking hours from 8 A. M. to 4 P. M. daily.

Indianapolis Branch Banking Co., Fletcher & Sharpe, props., 49 e. Washington, cor. Pennsylvania, capital $200,000; have been engaged in banking business for 35 years. Deposits received and discounts made daily from 8 A. M. to 4 P. M.

INDIANAPOLIS NATIONAL BANK, under Odd Fellows' Hall, n. e. cor. Washington and Pennsylvania, chartered 1864, capital $500,000, surplus fund, $80,800. Theodore P. Haughey, prest., A. F. Williams, cashier, Henry Latham, asst. cashier. S. A. Fletcher, Sr., F. M. Churchman, Ingram Fletcher, E. Sharpe and Theodore P. Haughey, directors. Deposits received, discounts made, gold, silver, exchange and government securities bought and sold. Banking hours from 8 A. M. to 4 P. M.

Merchant's National Bank, 48 East Washington; organized 1865, capital, $100,000. John S. Newman, prest., V. T. Malott, cashier.

Locke Erie, banker and broker, 19 n. Meridian.

SAVINGS BANK, J. B. Ritzinger, propr., 38 e. Washington, capital $50,000; gold, silver and exchange, bought and sold. Deposits received and discounts made daily, from 8 A. M. to 4 P. M.

Wagner S. W., banker, broker and loan office, room 11 Yohn's blk., n. Meridian.

INSURANCE COMPANIES.

FIRE.
(Home Companies.)

EQUITABLE,
a mutual company, incorporated 1861, now closing business. Wm. Manlove, receiver; office, room 4, Langsdale's blk., n. Delaware.

GERMAN MUTUAL,
a mutual company, incorporated 1864, A. Seidinsticker & Co., agts., 14 s. Delaware.

HOME,
A mutual company, organized in 1864, now closing business, under the management of a receiver. Charles W. Smith, Jr., room 5, Yohn's blk., n. Meridian.

INDIANA FIRE,
originally a mutual company, organized 1862, now doing business on the stock system, with a capital of about $200,000. J. T. Harvey, prest., W. T. Gibson, secy., office, room 5 Odd Fellows' Hall, over Indianapolis National Bank, cor. Washington aed Pennsylvania.

INDIANAPOLIS,
a stock company, chartered 1836, authorized capital, $500,000; office in old bank bldg., cor. Virginia av. and s. Pennsylvania. Wm. Henderson, prest., Alexander C. Jamison, secy.
Sinnissippi, a mutual company, organized in ——, now closing business under the management of a receiver, R. J. Thompson, over 87 e. Market.

UNION,
a stock company, organized 1865, with a cash capital of $200,000, has lately retired from business by reinsuring her risks in the Home Insurance Co., of New York.

(Insurance Companies having Agencies in this City.)

ÆTNA,
of Hartford, Conn., cash capital $4,375,830.55, incorporated 1819, charter perpetual, do a Fire and Marine Insurance, L. I. Hendee, pres't; J. Goodnow, secy.; J. B. Bennett, manager, Cincinnati; A. Abromet, agt., office Ætna bldg., n. Pennsyvania, bet. Washington and Meridian.
Baltic, of New York, cash capital $200,000, T. A. Goodwin, agt., office 35 e. Market.

BUCKEYE,
of Cleveland, O., J. S., Dunlop & Co., agts., office 16 n. Meridian.

CHARTER OAK,
of Hartford, Conn., Davis & Greene, agts., 27½ s. Meridian.

CITY FIRE,
of Hartford, Conn., cash capital $465,965.00, Martin, Hopkins & Follett, agts., office in Journal bldg.

CONTINENTAL,
of New York, cash assets $2,000,266.00, Martin, Hopkins & Follett, agts., office in new Journal bldg.

CORN EXCHANGE,
of New York, capital $400,000, invested in Government bonds, bank stock and mortgages on real estate, R. F. Mason, prest.; George A. Dresser, secy.; C. A. Beidenmeister, agt., 96 e. Washington.

ENTERPRISE,
of Cincinnati, cash capital $1,304,328.00, Martin, Hopkins & Follett, agts., office Journal bldg.

FIREMANS,
of Chicago, Ills., J. S. Dunlop, agt., office 16 n. Meridian.

HARMONY.
of New York, J. S. Dunlop, agt., office 16 n. Meridian.

HARTFORD,
of Hartford, Conn., cash assets $2,026,220.79, Snyder & Hays, agts., office 17 n. Meridian.

HOME,
of New Haven, Conn., capital $2,000,000, invested in Government bonds, bank stock and mortgages, D. R. Satterlee, prest.; Charles Wilson, vice-prest.; W. A. Goodell, secy.; C. A. Beidenmeister, agt., office 96 e. Washington.

HOME,
of New York, assets $3,623,876.78, H. H. Walker, adjusting agt.; E. B. Martindale, agt., 2 w. Washington.

INSURANCE COMPANY,
of North America, cash assets $2,000,000, Martin, Hopkins & Follett, agts., office new Journal bldg.

LIVERPOOL, LONDON AND GLOBE, fire and marine, J. S. Spann & Co., agts., Brown's block, n. Pennsylvania.

LORILLARD,
of New York, cash capital and assets

1,600,000, J. S. Dunlop & Co., agts., office over Bee Hive Store, entrance on Meridian, over 16.

LUMBERMANS,
of Chicago, Ill., Snyder & Hays, agts., 17 n. Meridian.

MANHATTAN,
of New York, Davis & Greene, agts., office 27½ s. Meridian.

MARKET,
of New York, J. S. Dunlop & Co., agts., 16 n. Meridian.

MERCHANTS,
of Hartford, Conn., Davis & Greene, agts., office 27½ s. Meridian.

MERCHANTS,
of Chicago, Ill., Martin, Hopkins & Follett, agts., office new Journal bldg.

NEW ENGLAND,
of Hartford, Conn., J. S. Dunlop & Co., agts., 16 n. Meridian.

North American, of New York, D. E. Snyder, agt., 17 n. Meridian.

PHŒNIX,
of Hartford, Conn., Snyder & Hays, agts., office 17 n. Meridian.

REPUBLIC,
of Chicago, Ill., capital and assets $1,330,468.67, central office 82 La Salle street, Chicago, Ill., John V. Farwell, pres't; J. R. Payson, secy.; J. S. Dunlop & Co., agts., 16 n. Meridian.

SANGAMO,
of Springfield, Ill., capital $200,000, F. M. Blair, agt., Vinton's block, opp. p. o.

SECURITY,
of New York, J. S. Dunlop & Co., agts., 16 n. Meridian.

SPRINGFIELD,
of Mass., cash assets $808,892.33, W. T. Gibson, agt., room 5 Odd Fellows Hall.

Sun, of Cleveland, O., Davis & Greene, agts., office 27½ s. Meridian.

TEUTONIA,
of Cleveland, O., capital $200,000, H. W. Luetkemoyer, pres't; I. Stopple, vice-pres't; E. Hessenmueler, secy.; C. A. Biedenmiester, agt., 96 e. Washington.

UNDERWRITER'S AGENCY,
of New York, is composed of the German, Hanover, Niagara and Republic Ins. Co.'s, of New York, capital nearly $4,000,000, invested in government bonds, bank stock and mortgages on real estate, Alexander Stoddard, gen'l agt.; W. F. Collier, special agent for Indiana; C. A. Beidenmeister, local agt., 96 e. Washington.

Winnesheik, of Decatur, Ill., capital $500,000.00, Jones & Childs, State agts., 25 w. Washington.

YONKERS & NEW YORK,
Martin, Hopkins & Follett, agts., new Journal bldg., e. Market.

HORSE.

AMERICAN,
of Indianapolis, E. J. Burkert, secy., room 13 Vinton blk., n. Pennsylvania.

(Foreign Companies having Agencies in this City.)

GREAT WESTERN,
of Decatur, Ill., T. H. Wingate, actuary, Vinton blk, n. Pennsylvania, opp. p. o.

LIFE.

(Home Companies.)

FRANKLIN,
of Indianapolis, Ind., chartered 1866, James M. Ray, pres't; Edward P. Howe, secy.; B. F. Witt, supervising agt., office in Company's bldg., cor. Kentucky av. and Illinois.

(Foreign Companies having Agencies in this City.)

ÆTNA,
of Hartford, Conn., Snyder & Hays, agts, 17 n. Meridian.

AMERICAN LIFE,
home office s. e. cor. Fourth and Walnut sts., Philadelphia; Indiana branch office 35½ e. Washington; Alexander Whilldin, pres't; Geo. Nugent, vice-pres't; John C. Sims, actuary; John S. Wilson, secy.; George M. Bowen, gen'l agt. for Indiana; incorporated April 1850, charter perpetual, amount of capital stock, all paid in, $500,000; present value of said stock at least $700,000; assets, Jan. 1, 1868, $1,- 901,234.90; amount necessary to re- insure all outstanding risks, Jan. 1, 1868, $723,337.80; ratio of assets to liabilities 2,62; policies issued on both joint stock and mutual plans; dividends declared and paid annually, averaging 50 per cent. for several years past. All policies non-forfeiting, and payable when the insured attains his eightieth year, or on previous decease. The Company has one hundred thousand dollars deposited in the State treasury of Pennsylvania for the security of its insured, and it makes annual sworn statements to the auditor gen'l of that State, showing its condition, etc.; copies of which sworn statements are deposited with the State auditor of Indiana.

ATLANTIC MUTUAL,
of New York, J. B. Barnard, agt., office Vinton blk., opp. p. o.

Atlas Mutual, of St. Louis, Mo., Akin & Reynolds, gen'l agts. for Indiana, office 39½ w. Washington.

BERKSHIRE,
Pittsfield, Mass., cash assets $100,000, J. W. Greene, agt., 25 w. Washington.

BROOKLYN LIFE,
of New York, 141 Broadway, New York, and 159 Montage, Brooklyn, chartered 1853, assets $1,000,000, C. W. Bouck, pres't; William M. Cole, secy.; Daniel Ayers, M. D., medical examiner; dividends paid annually in cash, no restriction on travel or residence; one-third of the premiums loaned annually; note will not constitute a claim against policy after two annual payments, F. M. Blair, gen'l agt., Indianapolis, office Vinton blk.

CHARTER OAK,
of Hartford, Conn., organized A. D., 1850, James C. Walkley, pres't; U. S. Palmer, vice-pres't; Samuel H. White, secy.; S. J. Beston, asst. secy.; L. W. Meech, mathematician; Henry M. Palmer, supt. of agencies; W. H. Hay, gen'l agt. for Indiana; cash assets $4,500,000, dividends declared and paid annually, a dividend of twenty-five per cent. on note plan, and thirty per cent. on all cash plan, is guaranteed, and in each triennial year the entire surplus earnings returned to policy holders; the triennial dividend for 1867 amounted to seventy per cent. Office, room 6 Blackford's blk.

CINCINNATI MUT'L HEALTH
ASSURANCE, capital $101,600, Geo. W. Bishop, Pres't; N. Roff, secy.; M. Rosenstock, gen'l agt.; Alexander Metzger, State agt. for Indiana, office Odd Fellows Hall.

CONNECTICUT MUTUAL,
of Hartford, Conn., assetts $20,000.00, H. R. Dutton, agt., 77½ e. Market.

CONTINENTAL,
of New York, chartered March, 1866, assets $1,500,000, Justus Lawrence, pres't; G. H. Scribner, vice-pres't; J. P. Rogers, secy.; R. C. Frost, actuary; E. D. Wheeler, M. D., medical examiner; thirty days grace allowed in payment of premiums after three annual payments have been made, a loan of four-fifths of the amount paid in, will be loaned to the policy holder for the advantage of subsequent payments; Johnson & Turner, agts. for Indiana, room 7 Blackford's blk.
Continental, of Hartford, Conn., T. D. Douglas, agt., s. w. cor. Washington and Meridian.
Great Western, of New York, Haehl & Menns, agts., 20 s. Delaware.
Guardian Mutual, of New York, incorporated 1859, capital $1,500,000, E. Gilbert, agt., room 4 Blackford's block.

HANNEMAN,
of Cleveland, O., cash assets $288,- 678.04, H. M. Chapin, pres't; J. P. Dake, vice-pres't; J. F. Crank, secy.; D. H. Beckwith, M. D., medical examiner; W. J. Copeland, gen'l agt. for Indianapolis.
Manhatten, of New York, Davis & Greene, agts., 27½ s. Meridian.
Mutual Benefit, of Newark, N. J., assets $15,000,000, Nutting & Wood, agts., 21 w. Washington.
New England Mutual of Boston, assets, $6,082,400.41, Snyder & Hays, agts., 17 n. Meridian.
North Western Mutual, of Milwaukee, Wis., assets $3,145,126, Martin, Hopkins & Follett, agts., Journal bldg.
New Jersey Mutual of Newark, N. J., C. F. Wilson, agt., 19 w. Washington.

NEW YORK LIFE,
established in 1845, principal office, 112 and 114 Broadway, New York, assets July 1, 1868, $12,000,000, Morris Franklin, prest., Wm. H. Beers, actuary; Theodore M. Banta, cashier; Cornelius R. Bogart, M. D., and George Wilkes, M. D., medical examiners; Charles Wright, M. D., asst. medical examiner; W. W. Byington, general agts. for Indiana, No. 11 s. Meridian.

PHŒNIX MUTUAL,
of Hartford, Conn., cash capital, over $3,000,000. This company is purely mutual; charter perpetual. Edson Fessenden, James T. Brown, secy.; E. S. Folsom, general agt. for Indiana. Office, room 3, Tallbott & New's blk.

SECURITY LIFE INSURANCE
AND ANNUITY, of New York; assets $1,500,000, Robert L. Case, prest.; Theodore R. Wetmore, vice-prest.; Isaac H. Allen, secy., W. W. Northrop, general agent for Indiana and southern Illinois, office, room 2, Blake's row, Indianapolis, Ind. No restriction on travel or residence. No extra rates on female risks. Dividends on Life and Ten Year Life rates have always been 50 per cent.

STANDARD LIFE,
of New York, guarantee fund, $125,- 000; Henry H. Elliott, prest.; James L. Dawes, secy.; Charles White, superintendent agces.; A. C. Metzger, gen. agt. for Ind., room 6 Odd Fellows' Hall.
St. Louis Mutual, Charles D. Wilcox, agt., office, Yohn's blk.
Travelers' of Hartford, Martin, Hopkins & Follett, agts., new Journal bldg.
Universal, of New York, W. T. Gibson, agt., room 5 Odd Fellows's Hall.
Western Life, of Cininnati, Martin & Gibson, gen'l agts. for Indiana.

ADVERTISING DEPARTMENT,

——CONTAINING——

ILLUSTRATED AND DISPLAYED CARDS

——OF——

Principal Merchants, Manufacturers, Bankers, Lawyers, Physicians, Insurance Companies, Colleges, Educational Insti-
tutions, &c., &c.

The remaining cards of prominent individual dealers and business firms, will be found on fly-leaves
in front and back of book, and at bottom of pages among
names of citizens.

BATES HOUSE,

North-West Corner Washington and Illinois Streets,

INDIANAPOLIS, IND.,

N. D. KENEASTER, - - - PROPIETOR.

This old and popularly established Hotel, the largest in this city or State, more complete in its appointments, having lost none of its original glory, is adding to its already accumulated patronage as it justly deserves.

The location of the "Bates" being on one of the principal corners and two of the great thoroughfares of the city, near the principal jobbing and most extensive retail business houses, public halls, churches, theatres and places of amusement; and containing large sample rooms, spacious parlors and convenient office, well arranged sleeping apartments, largest dining hall in the city, fine saloon affording the best wines, liquors and cigars, added to other conveniences, combine to make the "Bates" the most desirable Hotel in the city.

Business men, travelers, tourists and all others, will find it pleasant and profitable to stop at this Hotel on visiting Indianapolis.

Capt. E. HARTWELL, Chief Clerk.

PALMER HOUSE,

SOUTH EAST COR. WASHINGTON & ILLINOIS STS.,

(THREE SQUARES NORTH OF UNION DEPOT,)

INDIANAPOLIS, IND.

Alonzo Black,   -   -   -   -   -   **Proprietor.**

Jeff. K. Scott,   -   -   -   -   -   **Chief Clerk.**

The Palmer House is one of the oldest and most favorably known hotels in the State of Indiana, owing to its having been conducted by enterprising men for years; and it has gained a popularity that any number one hotel is justly entitled to. Its location being on one of the greatest thoroughfares of the city and on one of the principal corners, where the street cars pass running to any part of the city, near the centre of business, places of amusement, public halls, theatres, churches, county and State offices, renders it especially convenient for business men from neighboring towns and villages, politicians, commercial travelers, tourists, pleasure seekers and others, who may have occasion to visit this city. They will have a guarantee of a quiet and comfortable home during their stay, as the "Palmer" contains fine accommodations, a bountiful table, comfortable sleeping apartments (the office and dining hall being on the ground floor,) and all the conveniences that are to be found in any western hotel. The proprietor is an affable gentleman, and the attaches are courteous and obliging. All will do well to give the Palmer House a trial, and be satisfied of the truth of the above statement.

RAY HOUSE,

INDIANAPOLIS, IND.

South-East Corner South and Delaware Streets.

James M. Lambert, - - Prop'r.

This house is one of medium size, pleasantly located near the Union Passenger Depot and the different Railroad Freight Depots, yet far enough away from the rush of business to be a pleasant hotel and public boarding house, affording fair accommodations to either strangers or business men from neighboring cities and towns, commercial travelers, railroad men and others.

The proprietor, Mr. Lambert, being a gentleman of large experience, a practical hotel keeper, burthens his table with everything the country affords or the market produces.

Persons visiting Indianapolis or traveling through the western country should try the Ray House.

GIBSON HOUSE.

DAVIDSON & SINKS, PROPRIETORS.

WALNUT STREET, BETWEEN FOURTH AND FIFTH, OPPOSITE MERCHANTS' EXCHANGE,

CINCINNATI, OHIO.

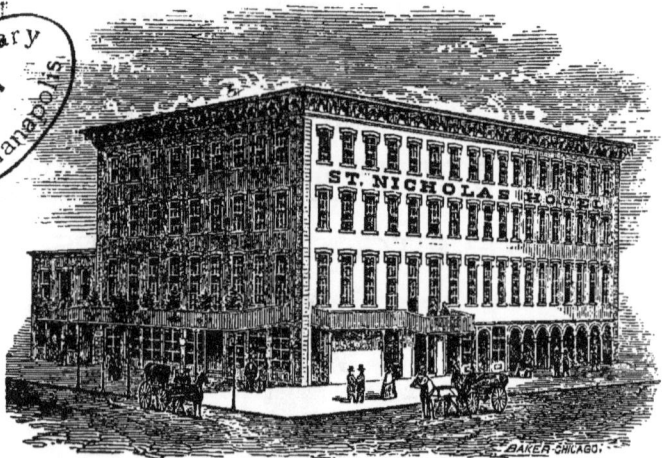

LOGAN'S
HISTORY OF INDIANAPOLIS
FROM 1818.

GIVING A CAREFULLY COMPILED RECORD OF EVENTS OF THE CITY FROM THE ORGA-
NIZATION OF THE STATE GOVERNMENT; ITS MERCANTILE, MANUFACTURING,
POLITICAL AND SOCIAL PROGRESS, COURSE OF DEVELOPMENT, PRES-
ENT IMPORTANCE AND FUTURE PROSPERITY; AS SEEN BY
A NATIVE BORN RESIDENT AND WORTHY CITIZEN.

Indianapolis, the political and commercial capital of Indiana, is situated on the west fork of white river, latitude 39° 55′, longitude 86° 5′, and about 527 feet above the sea. It is two miles north-west of the centre of the State, and one mile south-west of the centre of Marion county. It occupies the midst of a shallow basin, the ground rising gradually for miles in all directions. The soil is a clayey loam, sub-soil clay, on thick beds of drift gravel and sand, resting on silurian clays, limestones and shales. The gravel beds are great natural filters, producing thorough drainage and holding ample supplies of the purest water. The whole country was once densely covered with large hard wood trees, and in many places on the city site were extensive thickets of prickly ash and spicewood. The thick undergrowth afforded safe covert for all kinds of game, and for a number of years after the settlement bears and deer were readily found in the neighborhood. Hunters seldom returned unsuccessful from the chase, and, as late as 1842, saddles of venison sold at from 25 to 50 cents, turkeys at 10 and 12 cents, and a bushel of pigeons for 25 cents. The river was so fully stocked with fish that an old settler declared "a stone thrown in it anywhere, from the grave yard ford to the mouth of Fall creek, would strike a shoal of fish." The Indians reluctantly yielded the country on account of the abundance of fish and game, and many of them lingered in the vicinity long after the treaty. Though they had no permanent village here, their hunting and fishing camps were numerous on and north of the city site, and a traveller who passed up the river several years before the settlement, says the banks were then dotted with wigwams and the river often parted by their canoes. The scene was very striking at night when the savages were fire hunting or fishing. The Shawnees and Delawares had moved to this section sometime between

1790 and 1795, and had built several villages along the river, the nearest being about twelve miles above this point. An old white woman, the wife of a French trader, lived there after the rest of the tribe had left. She had been taken prisoner, when nine years old, at Martin's Station in Kentucky, had married an Indian and raised a half breed family, and after the death of her Indian husband married the Frenchman.

1818 By treaty at St. Marys, Ohio, October 2, between the Delaware Indians and Lewis Cass, Johnathan Jennings and Benjamin Parke, United States commissioners, the former ceded all their lands in central Indiana, agreeing to give possession in 1821. The reported fertility and beauty of "the new purchase," as it was afterward called, excited the frontiersmen, and, without waiting for possession to be given under the treaty, they entered it at various points. William Conner, an Indian trader, had settled at a Delaware village on White river, four miles this side of Noblesville, several years before this date. His location drew the attention of others to that stream, and several persons from Fayette and Wayne counties, visited this section just before and after the treaty. In the Spring of 1819, two brothers, named Jacob and Cyrus Whitzel, having got permission of the old Delaware chief, blazed a trace from the Whitewater river to the bluffs of White river. They remained and raised a crop there during the Summer, and moved their families out in October. (Jacob Whitzel died there July 2, 1827.) Lewis Whitzel, the noted Indian scout, celebrated in border annals, was a brother of these men and visited them there shortly after, while on his way to Louisiana. Late in the Fall of 1818, Dr. Douglas had ascended the river from the lower settlements, stopping awhile at the bluffs; and James Paxton descended it from the headwaters, reaching this point in January, 1820. These exploring trips were attended with some risk, for the Indians were in full possession and not well disposed toward the intruders.

1819 According to most authorities, the honor due to the first settler belongs to George Pogue, a blacksmith from Whitewater, who reached this point from that section March 2, 1819. After reaching the river he turned back and built his cabin on the high ground east of the creek which now bears his name, close to a large spring, and near the present eastern end of Michigan street. The ruins of this cabin were

(George Pogue's Residence, the First Cabin Built on the Donation.)

visible for many years afterward. Pogue was killed by Indians about daybreak one morning in April, 1821. His horses had been disturbed during the night, he declared the Indians were stealing them, and taking his rifle set out in pursuit. When last seen he was near their camp, gunshots were heard, and as his horses and clothes were afterward seen in their possession little doubt remained as to his fate. His death greatly excited the settlers, but their numerical weakness prevented any effort to avenge it. The creek on which he settled, which then pursued a very winding course through the south-east part of the plat, alarming the inhabitants by its floods, received his name and remains a lasting memorial of the first inhabitant of the present city.

Pogue's claim as the first settler has been contested, and in a published article by Dr. S. G. Mitchell, in the Indianapolis *Gazette*, in the Summer of 1822, it is stated that the McCormicks were the first emigrants in February, 1820, and that Pogue arrived with others in March, 1820, a month later. It is singular that this statement, if ill-founded, should not have been contradicted publicly in the paper at the time, but the weight of tradition is against it and concurs in fixing Pogue's arrival in 1819.

1820 Pogue seems to have been the only inhabitant from March, 1819, to February 27, 1820, when John and James McCormick arrived and built their cabins on the river bank, just below the mouth of Fall creek and near the present bridge. John Maxwell and John Cowan followed shortly after, building cabins early in March, in the north-west corner of the donation on the Fall creek, near the present Crawfordsville road bridge. In March, April and May, other families arrived following the trace left by Cowan and Maxwell, and by the first of June there were perhaps fifteen families on the present donation. Among them were those of Henry and Samuel Davis, Corbaley, Barnhill, VanBlaricum, Harding and Wilson. The first cabin on the old town plat was built in May, by Isaac Wilson, near the north-west corner of the state house square. Other emigrants arrived during the Summer and Fall, and the settlement grew slowly for a year afterward. The government surveys in this section were made in 1819 and 1820.

The congressional act of April 19, 1816, authorizing a state government for Indiana, had donated (with the privilege of selection,) four sections of unsold lands for a permanent capital. The assembly, on January 11, 1820, appointed George Hunt, John Conner, John Gilliland, Stephen Ludlow, Joseph Bartholomew, John Tipton, Jesse B. Durham, Frederick Rapp, William Prince and Thomas Emerson, commissioners to make the selection, directing them to meet at Conner's house, on White river, early in the Spring. A part of them only served. Ascending the valley on horseback and making examinations, they met as directed at Conner's, where, after very serious disputes between them as to sites at the bluffs, at the mouth of Fall creek and at Conner's, the present location was chosen by three votes against two for the bluffs. On the 7th of June, 1820, they reported the choice of sections one and twelve, east fractional section two and eleven, and enough of west fractional section three, in township fifteen, range three east, to make the four sections granted. The location gave the place instant reputation, and assisted in bringing emigrants to it during the Summer and Fall of 1820, and Spring of 1821. Among those who then came were Morris Morris, Dr. S. G. Mitchell, John and James Given, Matthias Nowland, James M. Ray, Nathaniel Cox, Thomas Anderson, John Hawkins, Dr. Livingston Dunlap, David Wood, Daniel Yandes, Alexander Ralston, Dr. Isaac Coe, Douglas Maguire and others, and the cabins clustered closely along the river bank, on and near which almost the whole settlement was located. Most of the above named parties came in the Spring of 1821. In the north-west part of the donation, and west of the present blind asylum, a tract of one hundred and fifty or two hundred acres was found where the heavy timber had been killed years before by locusts or worms. The undergrowth was cut off, brush fences enclosed portions of the "caterpillar deadning," and during this and following years it was cultivated in corn and vegetables by the settlers as a common field. Its existence was a great benefit, for it saved much heavy labor in cutting off dense timber and was immediately available for cultivation. It yielded abundantly, game was readily procured, and though considerable sickness occurred during the Summer and Fall, the people got along with comparative comfort during the Fall and Winter of 1820.

1821 The legislature confirmed the choice of site January 6, 1821, named the town Indianapolis, and appointed Christopher Harrison, James Jones and Samuel P. Booker, commissioners to lay it off, directing them to meet on the site first Monday in April, appoint surveyors and clerk, make a survey, prepare two maps, and advertise and sell the alternate lots as soon as possible, the money received from the sales to be set apart as a public building fund. At the appointed time Judge Harrison was the only commissioner here and the only one who acted. Elias P. Fordham and Alexander Ralston had been selected as the surveyors, and Benjamin I. Blythe clerk. Mr. Blyth became a resident of the town and was subsequently the agent. Of Fordham little is known. Ralston was an old bachelor, a talented Scotchman, and when young had assisted in surveying Washington city. He was afterward connected with Burr's expedition and on its failure remained in the West. We are indebted to him for the regular plan, large squares, wide streets and diagonal avenues of the old plat. He afterward settled here, highly esteemed for his virtues and mental powers, and dying January 5, 1827, lies somewhere in the old cemetery in an unmarked grave.

The surveying party having been organized in April, the plan was determined on, the plat made and the survey begun. The lines and corners of the four sections were traced out, with a fraction on the west bank to complete the 2,560 acres granted. A town plat one mile square was marked out near the middle of the donation. A circle lot of nearly four acres in extent surrounded by a street eighty feet wide occupied the centre, and from the outside corners of the blocks next to it avenues ninety feet wide were drawn to the corners of the plat. The other streets ran north and south and east and west, and were ninety feet wide except Washington which was one hundred and twenty. There were eighty-nine squares of four acres in extent, each four hundred and twenty feet front, divided by two alleys fifteen and thirty feet wide crossing at right angles. There were also six fractional squares and three large irregular tracts in the valley of Pogue's run. The present North, South, East and West streets, were not included in the original design, the plat abutting directly against the undivided donation lands, but were added afterward by Judge Harrison at the suggestion of James Blake, who said that fifty years afterward they would afford a fine four mile drive around the town and a half mile from its centre. The donation outside the plat was not laid off or divided, for no one supposed the town would ever extend beyond the plat, and no provision was made for it. It was afterward divided by the agent, under direction of the assembly, into large outblocks, with few and narrow roads or streets, and sold for farms. The "sub-divisions" are properly in the squares of the old plan and in these out-blocks, and the "additions" are properly outside of the donation limits. Unfortunately no rule has ever been adopted by the legislature or city council requiring sub-divisions, and especially additions, to conform generally to the city plat. Each owner has been left free to regulate the size and shape of blocks and lots, and the width and direction of streets and alleys, to suit his own interest or convenience, and as a natural consequence the newest portions of our city are the most irregular and unsightly portions shown in its map. A rule on this subject should be at once adopted for the future, and large sums will have to be expended some day on account of the failure to adopt it in the past. The city long since covered the donation, and its suburbs extend in most directions from a half mile to a mile beyond, but the municipal government and revenues are still restricted to the original donation limits. The old town plat was not located in the center of the donation. The joint corner of the four sections is in the alley ten feet west and five feet south of the southeast corner of the Palmer House lot. The surveyors found that if the centre of the plat was fixed there too much of the plat would be thrown in Pogue's run valley, then a most unpromising locality. In searching for a better point the natural elevation in the present circle was found and at once chosen. It was then covered with a fine grove of tall, straight sugar trees, which should have been preserved. The surveyors were much embarrassed in their work by the bayous which then crossed the donation in a north-cast and south-west direction, and by the dense thickets through which they had to cut their way. In some places these bayou channels are not yet entirely obliterated, and portions of the old thickets were found in protected spots till 1850.

The surveys and maps being completed, the lot sale was duly advertised and held by Gen. John Carr, (the first State agent, who had reached here shortly before,) on the 10th of October, at a cabin on Washington street just west of the pressnt canal. The sale lasted nearly a week. The first day was cold and raw with a high wind, and a man at the sale came near being killed by a falling limb. There were many buyers present both citizens and strangers, and Carter's, Hawkins' and Nowland's taverns, as well as many of the private houses, were thronged with guests; competition was brisk and high prices were obtained. The main settlement was near the river, but lots to the cast and north sold best, for the unusual sickness during the Summer and Fall (hereafter mentioned) had convinced the people they must leave the river neighborhood. Each four acre block was divided into 12 lots 67½ by 195 feet, and the alternate lots were reserved beginning with number one. Three hundred and fourteen lots in the central and northern parts of the old plat were sold for $35,596,25, one-fifth or $7,119,25 down and the balance in four equal annual installments. The lot west of court square on Washington street sold highest, $560, and the similar lot west of state square brought $500. Intervening lots on the street sold from $100 to $300. One hundred and sixty-nine lots sold at this time were afterward forfeited or exchanged by the buyers for others. The reserved and forfeited lots were repeatedly offered at subsequent periods, both at public and private sale; but money was scarce, the town improved slowly, prices declined and for several years few sales were made. Nineteen hundred acres of lots and lands remained unsold as late as 1831, but were mostly disposed of in that year by order of the legislature, the minimum price being ten dollars per acre. The amount received up to 1842, when the sales were ended and closed, was about $125,000, and from this fund the state house, court house, Governor's circle, clerk's office and treasurer's house and office were built. General Carr received the money and made the deeds at the first sale. His cabin stood on Delaware street where Hereth's block now stands, and the elections were held and the courts began there till the court house was built. He was appointed in 1821 at a salary of $600, but it was reduced next year to $300, and he resigned

in September, 1822. The people were dissatisfied with him and with his successor, James Milroy, (who held the office a few months and then resigned,) because they did not become permanent residents of the town. Bethuel F. Morris was appointed December 24, 1822; Benjamin I. Blythe Fcburary 1, 1825; Ebenezor Sharpe April 8, 1828, dying September, 1838; John G. Brown then held it a few months, being succeeded January or February, 1835, by Thomas H. Sharpe; John Cook, state librarian, held it a short time in 1843-4, and the office was then transferred to the auditor of State January, 1844, and the business closed up by him.

Until 1821 the centre and north part of the State was included in Delaware county yet unorganized but attached, for judicial purposes, to Fayette and Wayne counties, whose courts had concurrent jurisdiction. The people in the new purchase were sued and indicted in the courts at Connersville and other points on Whitewater, and the costs often exceeded the debt, damages or fines. Conflicts of jurisdiction also occurred, ill-feeling was aroused, and the people here finally rebelled against it. To prevent trouble the assembly, January 9, 1821, authorized the appointment of two justices of the peace for the new settlements, appeals lying from them to the Bartholomew circuit court. In April Governor Jennings appointed John Maxwell, of this place, a justice of the peace, the first judicial officer in the new purchase, but he resigned in June, and the citizens elected James McIlvain, who was duly commissioned in October. His twelve foot cabin stood on the north-west corner of Pennsylvania and Michigan streets, where he held court, pipe in mouth, in his cabin door, the jury ranged in front on a fallen tree, and the first constable, Corbaley, standing guard over the culprits, who nevertheless often escaped through the woods. Calvin Fletcher was then the only lawyer, and the last judge in all the knotty cases, the justice privately taking his advice as to their disposal. There was no jail nearer than Connersville, and it being expensive and troublesome to send culprits there in charge of the constable and posse, the plan was adopted of frightening them away. A case of this kind occurred on Christmas, 1821. Four Kentucky boatmen, who had "whipped their weight in wild cats" on the Kanawha and elsewhere, came from the bluffs to "Naplis" to have a Christmas spree. It began early, for the citizens were roused before dawn by a great uproar at Daniel Larkins clapboard grocery, which contained a barrel of whisky. The four heroes were discovered busily employed in tearing it down. A request to desist produced a volley of oaths, a display of big knives, and an advance on the citizens, most of whom immediately found pressing business elsewhere. They were interested, however, in the existence of the grocery, and furthermore such defiance of law and order could not be tolerated. A consultation was held, resulting in the determination to take the rioters at all hazards. James Blake volunteered to grapple the leader, a man of great size and strength, if the rest would take the three others. The attack was made, the party captured and marched under guard through the woods to justice McIlvaine's cabin, where they were at once tried, heavily fined and ordered to jail at Connersville in default of payment of bail. Payment was out of the question, and they could not be taken to Connersville at that season of the year. Ostentatious preparations were made, however, for the trip, the posse was selected for the journey next day, a guard was placed over them with secret instructions, and during the night the doughty heroes fled to more congenial climes.

But the Fayette and Wayne county courts still claimed jurisdiction, and the annoyance therefrom continued. Doubts existed as to the legality of Maxwell and McIlvain's appointments, and a meeting was held at Hawkins' log tavern, late in the Fall, to devise some remedy for the difficulty. It was resolved to demand the organization of a new county, and James Blake and Dr. S. G. Mitchell were selected as lobby members to attend at Corydon and secure it.

The Summer of 1821 was noted for continuous and heavy rains. There is little doubt that much more water fell forty years ago than now. Storms of wind, rain and thunder, were more frequent and violent; streams rose higher and remained full longer; sections now dry were then very swampy; and bayous ran bank full that are now unknown. To travel even a few miles was sometimes a desperate undertaking, and teams were often stopped for weeks by high water. The whole country was wooded and wet; the air was damper, modifying the Winter cold and Summer heat; the wind generally came from the south and west, and the climate was milder and more uniform than now. As the timber and swamps disappeared the air grew dryer, fogs were less frequent, winds had more sweep and came oftener from the north, variations of heat and cold increased, till at present the cultivation of peaches,—formerly a certain crop,—has been abandoned; and if the change continues with the deforesting of the country, it is questionable whether other crops besides peaches will not be lost.

In consequence of the wet condition of the country and the want of roads the settlement was almost entirely isolated. The national road had been designed to run fifteen miles south of this point before the site was chosen, but the assembly, January 8, 1821, memorialized congress, stating the location of the capital, and asking that it be made a point on the line. This was afterward conceded, to the great joy of the people, but the road was not commenced in this State till 1830, and was abandoned in 1839 before its completion, leaving the town still in the mud. It is impossible, at present, with our railroads and good common roads, to realize the situation of the early settlers after a Spring thaw or a long wet spell, when the road was a "stage" often consisted of the four wheels and axles, on which balanced a crate containing one or two wet, muddy, half-frozen passengers, dragged wearily into town by four or six horses looking like animated masses of mud.

The Summer of 1821 was distinguished by the general sickness resulting, it was thought, from the heavy fall of rain. It is said that storms occurred every day in June, July and August. Clouds would suddenly gather and send a deluge of water, then as quickly break away, while the sun's rays fairly scorched the drenched herbage, generating miasmatic vapors with no wind to carry them off. Sickness began in July but did not become general till after the 10th of August, on which day Matthias Nowland had a raising, all the men in the settlement assisting. Remittant and intermittent fevers, of a peculiar type, then began, and in three weeks the community was prostrated. Thomas Chinn, Enoch Banks and Nancey Hendricks, were the only persons who escaped. Though so general the disease was not deadly, about twenty-five only, mostly children who had been too much exposed, dying out of several hundred cases. The few who could go about devoted their time to the sick, and many instances of generous devoted friendship occurred. Their mutual suffering at this time bound the early settlers together in after life, and none recur to this period without emotion. New comers were disheartened at the prospect, and some left the country circulating extravagant reports about the health of the town, greatly retarding its subsequent growth. Disease that year was general in the West. It was little greater here than elsewhere, and the relative mortality was scarcely so great. It abated here by the end of October, the general health was soon after entirely restored, and the people busily engaged in preparations for the winter.

The sickness having prevented proper cultivation of the common field, and the throng of strangers at the lot sale having consumed all surplus food, absolute starvation impended over the settlement. No roads or mills whatever existed, and all provisions and goods had to be packed on horses sixty miles through the wilderness from Whitewater. Regular expeditions were organized for procuring food. Flour and meal were brought on horseback from Goodlander's mill on Whitewater, then the nearest one, and corn was bought and boated down in canoes and rafts from the Indian villages up the river. The arrival of supplies from either of these points excited general joy among the half sick and half starved people. They aided each other in this new distress as in the former one, and many pecks of meal, pounds of flour, bacon, fish and other articles of food, were given more destitute neighbors.

Emigrants were constantly arriving during the year ending August 1, 1821, by which time there were fifty or sixty resident families. The October sales attracted others and by the end of the year the population was estimated at four or five hundred. Many, however, were only waiting till their cabins were built in the country to move out. Obed Foote, Calvin Fletcher, James Blake, Alexander W. Russel, Caleb Scudder, Nicholas McCarty, George Smith, Nathaniel Bolton, Wilkes Reagan and others, arrived during the Summer and Fall of 1821. The wet and sickly Summer was succeeded in October by a long and beautiful Indian Summer. The sick recovered health and spirits, business improved, new and better cabins were built further from the river, for the settlement left the river after the sickness, though it was still mainly west of the canal, where a cluster of cabins was dignified with the title of Wilmot's row, Wilmot keeping a little store there. During the Fall the timber on the streets was offered to any one who would cut it, and as it was largely composed of splendid ash, walnut and oak trees, Lismund Basye accepted the grant as a chance for fortune, and labored zealously in felling the trees on Washington street. After cutting a large part of the timber down the question arose "What will he do with it?" and as there were no mills to cut it into lumber, Basye was unequal to the answer. He had drawn the elephant and having done so abandoned it. The street was so blocked with standing and felled timber and undergrowth that it was impossible to get through it, and the citizens burned it where it lay during the

Winter and Spring. John Hawkins had built a log tavern early in the Fall, where the *Sentinel* office now stands, using logs cut from the site and the street, and so dense was the timber and undergrowth that a person at that tavern could not see Isaac Lynch's house and shoe shop where 5 and 7 west Washington now are, and it took nearly a half mile travel to go from one point to the other. The work of clearing and burning steadily progressed, and by the close of the Spring of 1822 the people rejoiced at being able to take a wagon along a zig zag path on and near the street for a considerable part of its length.

The first marriage, first birth and first death, occurred during the Summer of 1821. The first marriage was that of Jeremiah Johnson to Miss Jane Reagan. He walked to Connersville and back, one hundred and twenty miles, for the license, and had to wait several weeks for a preacher to come along and marry them. He died at his residence near the city April 5, 1857. Mordecai Harding (still living,) was the first person born on the donation, and James Morrow, the first in the old town plat. The first death was that of Daniel Shaffer, the first merchant of the place, who had come in January, 1821, and kept a few goods and groceries at his cabin on the high ground south of Pogue's run, near Pennsylvania street. He died in May or June and was buried in Pogue's run valley, near Pennsylvania street, but was taken up and reburied in the old graveyard August 25th. The first woman who died was Mrs. Maxwell, wife of John Maxwell, dying July 3d, and buried on the 4th on the high ground near the Crawfordsville road bridge over Fall creek. Eight persons were buried there during the Summer and Fall. No cemetery had been set apart in the original survey, but Judge Harrison, at the request of the people, assigned the lot on the river afterward known as the old burying ground, and on December 31, 1822, the assembly confirmed the grant. In the meantime twenty-five or thirty persons had been buried there. It was covered with heavy timber and undergrowth, but at a citizens' meeting March 10, 1824, it was resolved to clear and enclose it. Nearly fifty persons had then been laid in it.

It may be interesting to give here the names and dates of arrival of the pioneers in the different trades and professions. John McClung, a new light minister, came in the Spring of 1821, and preached the first sermon here shortly after, in the grove on the circle, the audience sitting around him on the grass and logs in Indian style. Services continued there during the Summer and Fall whenever the weather permitted. He died north of town August 18, 1823. Other authorities say the first sermon was preached during the Summer, at the state house square, by Rev. Resin Hammond. James Scott, first Methodist preacher, was sent by the St. Louis conference, and reached here October, 1821, after much difficulty in finding the place. O. P. Gaines, first Presbyterian minister, came August, 1821. John Waters, first Baptist preacher, came October, 1823. Isaac Coe, physician, May, 1820. Calvin Fletcher, lawyer, September, 1821. Daniel Shaffer, merchant, January, 1821, died May, 1821. James B. Hall, carpenter, Winter of 1820. Matthias Nowland, brick-maker and mason, November, 1820, died November 11, 1822. Andrew Byrne, tailor, November, 1820. Isaac Lynch, shoemaker, Fall of 1821. William Holmes, tinner, Spring of 1822. Michael Ingals, teamster, Fall of 1820. Kenneth A. Scudder, Summer of 1820, died March 5, 1829, opened first drug store in 1823. Wilkes Reagan, butcher and auctioneer, Summer of 1821. John Shunk, hatter, October, 1821, died September 2, 1824. Amos Hanway, cooper, came up the river in a keelboat, June, 1821. Conrad Brussel, baker, Fall of 1820. Milo R. Davis, plasterer, Winter of 1820. George Norwood, wagon maker, Spring of 1822. John McCormack, tavern keeper, February 27, 1820, died August 27, 1825. George Myers, potter, Fall of 1821. Caleb Scudder, cabinet maker, October, 1821. Henry and Samuel Davis, chair makers, April or May, 1820. Isaac Wilson, miller, March, 1820. He built the first cabin on the old plat, on the north-west corner of the state house square, in March, 1820, and the first grist mill on Fall creek, north-west of Blackford's addition, in the Summer of 1821, and died November 4, 1823. George Pogue, first settler and blacksmith, March 2, 1819, killed by Indians April, 1821. James Linton, sawyer and mill-wright, Summer of 1821, built the first saw mill on Fall creek, near the Crawfordsville road bridge, in September and October, 1821. Nathaniel Bolton, editor and printer, September, 1821. George Smith, printer and book-binder, August, 1821, began book-binding March, 1823. Joseph C. Reed, teacher and county recorder, Spring of 1821. Samuel Walton, spinning wheel maker, October, 1826. R. A. McPherson, first foundry, July, 1832. Samuel S. Rooker, house and sign painter, Fall of 1821. Daniel Yandes, tanner, January, 1821. John Ambrozene, watch and clock maker, February, 1825. James Paxton, militia colonel, October, 1821, died April 5, 1829. Samuel Morrow, lieut. colonel, Spring or Summer of 1820. Alexander W. Russell, major, Spring of 1821.

John Maxwell, justice of the peace, March, 1820. William W. Wick, circuit judge, February, 1822. Harvey Bates, sheriff, February, 1822. James J. McIlvain and Eliakim Harding, associate judges, Summer of 1820. James M. Ray, county clerk, Spring of 1821. Joseph C. Reed, county recorder, Spring of 1821. John McCormack, county commissioner, February 27, 1820. John T. Osborn, county commissioner, Spring of 1821. Samuel Henderson, postmaster, Fall of 1821. William P. Murphy, dentist, November, 1829. Elizabeth Nowland, first boarding house, November, 1820, began 1823. Samuel Beck began gunsmithing July, 1833, (still at it, 1868,). Hubbard, Edmunds & Co., book-store, began May, 1833. David Mallory, colored barber, in Spring of 1821.

Daniel Shaffer had opened the first store in February or March, 1821, at his cabin on the high ground south of Pogue's run; but dying in May or June, stores were shortly afterward opened by John and James Given and John T. Osborn, near the river bank, and by Wilmot, at Wilmot's row, near the present site of the old Carlisle house, Luke Walpole began in the Fall or Winter, on the south-west corner of the state house square, and Jacob Landis on the south-east corner. Jeremiah Johnson also began on the north-west corner of Market and Pennsylvania streets. The first log school house, Joseph C. Reed teacher, was built in 1821, near a large pond just west of the Palmer house. Reed taught a short time being succeeded temporarily by two or three others, but no permanent school existed till after June 20, 1822, when trustees were chosen, and Mr. and Mrs. Lawrence selected as teachers by a meeting held for the purpose at the school house. After the school opened there, Mr. and Mrs. Lawrance taught there for several years. The first frame and also the first plastered house was built in the Fall of 1821, by James Blake, on the lot east of Masonic hall. It stood till 1852, and was occupied as the *Sentinel* office from 1841 to 1844. During the same Winter Thomas Carter built a two story ceiled frame tavern, (the first two story house,) eighteen by twenty feet, at 40 west Washington street. It was long known as the Rosebush tavern from its sign. It was afterward moved to the vicinity of the canal, and again to a point near the soldier's home, where it is yet standing. James Linton built the first saw mill in September and October, 1821, on Fall creek, above the Crawfordsville bridge; and about the same time he built the first grist mill, for Isaac Wilson, on Fall creek bayou north-west of Blackford's addition. Until this mill was

finished the people sent sixty miles to
Goodlander's for flour and meal, or hulled
hominy in a stump mortar. The mills afterward built here had no bolting cloths,
and fine flour was not made here until the
steam mill was built in 1832. Linton also
built the first two story frame dwelling in
the Spring of 1822, at 76 west Washington
street. It was burned during the Winter of
1847. The first market house was built in
the maple grove on the circle, in May,
1822, and Wilkes Reagan first sold meat
there in June. The first brick house was

(The First Brick House.)

built for John Johnson, begun in 1822 and
finished in the Fall of 1823, on the lot east
of Robert's chapel and is yet standing.

Doubts having arisen as to the validity
of the survey and sales, Harrison only having acted, the assembly confirmed them
November 28th, and on the 31st of December passed an act organizing Marion county.
The organization to be complete April 1,
1822. Square fifty-eight,—court square,—
was made the permanent seat of justice.
Eight thousand dollars was appropriated to
build a two story brick court house, fifty
feet square, to be completed in three years,
and used by the State, federal and county
courts forever, and by the assembly for fifty
years or till a State house was built. Two
per cent. of the lot fund was devoted to
county library. The sessions of the courts
were to be held at Carr's house. Johnson,
Hamilton, and most of Boone, Madison
and Hancock counties, were attached to
Marion for judicial purposes. Marion,
Lawrence, Monroe, Morgan, Greene, Owen,
Hendricks, Rush, Decatur, Bartholomew,
Shelby and Jennings counties, constituted
the fifth judicial circuit. William W.
Wick was elected judge and Harvey Bates
was commissioned sheriff by Governor Jennings. Both gentlemen were from Whitewater, and arrived here in February or
March, 1822.

During the Winter, the people being

healthier and better housed and acquainted,
became sociable and merry. Dances, quilt-
ings and weddings were frequent. Candidates were numerous and busily canvassing
for the county offices. Christmas brought
its round of festivities, and the Winter passed pleasantly in spite of past sickness,
threatened famine and cold, which was both
severe and protracted. The snow was deep
and large logs were hauled on the ice in
the river, but fuel at least was plenty, and
with large chimneys, great back-logs and
roaring fires, the inmates of the rude cabins
bid defiance to the weather.

1822. The assembly, on the 3d of January, ordered the unsold lots to be leased,
the lessees to clear them in four months.
Two acres were to be sold for a brick-yard,
and a three year lease given of the ferry.
Lands in west Indianapolis were leased in
lots of five to twenty acres. Improvements
on unsold lots could be removed in forty
days after sale. One hundred thousand
dollars were soon after appropriated to cut
roads through the wilderness.

The Indianapolis *Gazette*, the first journal in the new purchase, edited printed and
published by George Smith and Nathaniel
Bolton, was first issued January 28th, from
a cabin south-west of the intersection of the
canal and Maryland street. The office was
moved to the present theatre corner the
next year, and a few years afterward to east
Washington street near Glenn's block. The
ink used on the first numbers was a tar
composition. The paper appeared irregularly, the mails being so infrequent that
news matter could not be obtained to fill
the columns, but several mail routes were
opened in April and May and that difficulty was measurably obviated. The second
number appeared February 11th, third the
25th, fourth March 6th, fifth the 18th, sixth
April 3d, seventh, May 4th, after which
date it appeared weekly till discontinued in
1831. Heavy rains fell in April flooding
the country, and as the editors happened to
be absent when the flood came, they were
stopped by high water for a month, sus-
pending publication from April 3d to May
4th. B. F. Morris became editor May 3,
1821. Smith & Bolton dissolved April 27,
1823, Bolton continued the paper about a
year, when they rejoined and published
together till July 23, 1829, when they again
dissolved. Bolton continued it till after
the *Indiana Democrat* was issued, when the
list of subscribers was transferred to that
paper.

The *Gazette* of February 25, 1822, stated
that much improvement was going on.
Forty dwellings and several workshops had
been built, a grist and two saw mills were
running and others being built near town.

There were thirteen carpenters, four cabinet makers, eight blacksmiths, four shoemakers, two tailors, one hatter, two tanners, one saddler, one cooper, four brick-layers, two merchants, three grocers, four physicians, three lawyers, one preacher, one teacher, and seven tavern keepers. This list gives, perhaps, half the adult population of the place.

Harvey Bates, sheriff, by proclamation February 22, directed an election on April 1st, for two associate judges, a clerk, recorder, and three county commissioners. The voting precincts were at Carr's house, John Finch's, near Conner's station, John Page's, Strawtown, John Berry's, Andersontown, and William McCartney's on Fall creek near Pendleton. Returns were to be forwarded by the 3d of April. James Page, Robert Patterson, James McIlvain, Eliakin Harding, John Smock and Rev. John McClung were candidates for associate judges. James M. Ray, Milo R. Davis, Morris Morris, Thomas Anderson and John W. Redding for clerk. Alexander Ralston, James Linton, Joseph C. Reed, Aaron Drake, John Givans, John Hawkins, William Vandegrift and William Townsend, for recorder, and twelve or fifteen candidates for county commissioners. Nearly half the population were candidates for some office, and all were busily canvassing. Nominating conventions were unknown and each ran on his personal merit. The Whitewater and Kentucky emigrants had brought their local prejudices and candidates with them. James M. Ray represented the first, and Morris Morris the last party. The canvass was thorough and the excitement culminated at the election.— Whisky flowed freely. Persons usually sober, excited by victory or grieved at defeat, joined in the spree and the whole community got drunk. Many Kentuckians had lived here less than a year and had no vote, and the Whitewater party being ably managed defeated them. The Kentuckians however, afterward outvoted and outgeneralled their opponents. James McIlvain and Eliakin Harding were chosen associate judges; James M. Ray, clerk; Joseph C. Reed, recorder; and John T. Osborn, John McCormack and William McCartney, county commissioners. Two hundred and twenty-four votes were cast here, nearly half being from residents on the donation, and 336 votes were east in the county, which then included most of the present adjoining counties. James M. Ray got 217 votes, the highest for any candidate. The county board organized and held their first session April 15, at the corner of Ohio and Meridian streets, and divided the county into Fall creek, Anderson, White river, Dela-

ware, Lawrence, Washington, Pike, Warren, Centre, Wayne, Franklin, Perry and Decatur townships, but several of these were united for township purposes for want of population.

No post routes or office was opened here till March, 1822. The mails had been brought, until that date, from Connersville at different intervals, by private hands. A citizens' meeting was held at Hawkins' tavern, January 30, to take measures for a regular private mail. Aaron Drake was chosen postmaster. He issued a circular to postmasters stating the fact and asking that letters for this point be sent to Connersville. He returned from the first trip after nightfall, his horn sounding far through the woods, arousing the people who turned out in the bright moonlight to greet him and learn the news. This effort aroused the government, and in February President Monroe appointed Samuel Henderson postmaster. He opened the office March 7th or 8th, and on the 3d of April published the first letter list of five letters to old residents. Henderson continued in office till removed by Jackson in February, 1831, being succeeded by John Cain, who resigned in 1841. Joseph M. Moore then held it till 1845. John Cain again held it until 1849. Alexander W. Russell succeeded in 1849, dying in office, and his son, James N. Russell, was appointed for the balance of his term. William W. Wick held it from 1853 to 1857; John M. Talbott till 1861; Alexander H. Conner till 1866; and D. G. Rose till the present time. The office was first kept near the canal, then at Henderson's tavern, then on the north side of Washington west of Meridian street, then in the present Hubbard's block on south Meridian street, then in Blackford's old building opposite, from which it was moved in 1861 to the government building on north Pennsylvania street.

Plans for a court house were called for by the commissioners May 22. That of John E. Baker and James Paxton was chosen, and the contract given them in September. The house was begun the next Summer and finished in the Fall of 1824 at a cost of $14,000. Wilkes Reagan, Obed Foote, and Lismund Basye, were elected justices May 23. The sheriff was directed in May to obtain proposals for building a jail and clearing the court house square, both to be completed by the first of August. James Blake induced the board to save two hundred of the young maples growing on the square, but no specific instructions being given the contractor left two hundred of the largest trees on the square, and when the surrounding forest was cut away the storms so damaged them that all had to be cut down. The jail was a two story hewed log house, built in July and August, in the north-west corner of the square, and was used till 1833 when it was burned by a negro prisoner, who was nearly suffocated before being rescued. Its foundations were visible till filled over in 1852. After its

(The First Jail.)

destruction the old brick jail was built east of the court house and used till 1845, when a hewed log jail was added just north of it. These were torn away on the completion of the present stone jail begun in 1852, finished in 1854, and since enlarged at a total cost of $60,000.

Arrangements for the first Fourth of July celebration were made at a meeting June 17th, at Hawkins' tavern. The celebration occurred at the corner of West and Washington streets. The Rev. John McClung preached from Proverbs XIV, 34. Judge Wick read the declaration, prefacing it with remarks on revolutionary events and men. Obed Foote read Washington's inaugural address, with remarks on sectional issues and parties. John Hawkins read Washington's farewell address, with appropriate remarks. Rev. Robert Brenton closed with prayer and benediction. A barbecue then succeeded. A deer killed on the north part of the donation the preceding evening by Robert Harding, was roasted in a pit under a large elm tree close by. An ample supper was served on long tables under the trees. Speeches were made by Dr. S. G. Mitchell and Major John W. Redding, toasts were offered and the festivities closed with a ball at Jacob R. Crumbaugh's house near the canal.

William Hendricks received 315 out of 317 votes cast here at the August election for Governor. Harvey Bates was elected sheriff and George Smith coroner, the first elected incumbents. The first militia election was held September 7. James Paxton was chosen colonel of the fortieth regiment, Samuel Morrow lieutenant colonel, and Alexander W. Russell major.

The first session of the circuit court began September 26, 1822, at Carr's cabin, William W. Wick presiding judge, James McIlvain and Eliakim Harding associates, James M. Ray, clerk, Harvey Bates Sheriff. After organizing the court adjourned to Crumbaugh's house west of the canal. Calvin Fletcher was appointed prosecuting attorney for the first three terms, being succeeded by Harvey Gregg, Hiram Brown, William Quarles and others. There were thirteen civil causes on the docket at the first term. The first case tried was Daniel Bowman vs. Meridy Edwards, action on the case. The grand jury, Joseph C. Reed foreman, returned twenty-two indictments, six of which were non prossed. The first criminal case tried was the State vs. John Wyant for selling whisky without license, and nearly all the rest were like unto it. The term lasted three days and eleven attorneys were present, five of them being residents. Richard Good, an Irishman, was naturalized on the first day. John Hawkins was licensed to keep tavern and sell whisky. "Prison bounds," beyond which no debtor under arrest could go, were established along certain streets the first day. The first divorce case was brought at the May term, 1823, Elias Stallcup vs. Ruth Stallcup. The second session of court began at Carr's May 5, 1823, and adjourned to Henderson's tavern where Glenn's block now is. The third session began at Carr's November 3, 1823, and adjourned Harvey Gregg's, lot 11, square 46. The fourth began at Carr's April 12, 1824, adjourned to John Johnson's, lot 8, square 44; the fifth began at Carr's Oct. 11, 1824, and adjourned to the court house, then nearly finished. The first sessions were attended by several prominent lawyers from abroad, who talked of locating here; but the sickness, isolation of the place and dullness, deterred them. The early local bar comprised a number of talented men, including William W. Wick, James Morrison, Hiram Brown, Calvin Fletcher, Philip Sweetser, William Quarles, Harvey Gregg and others, and held a high rank in the State. Many amusing anecdotes are related showing the peculiarities of the bench and bar at that period.

A meeting held at Crumbaugh's September 26, petitioned the assembly for representation therein, for the improvement of White river, and for opening roads. A committee made and published a long report on the improvement of the river. Several roads to Whitewater and the South were located and partly opened in September and October, by commissioners who directed the work and expenditures; but years elapsed before the roads were really passable, and not until a recent period, when gravelled or planked, have they been firm in wet or thawing weather.

A westward migration of gray squirrells was noticed in the Fall, these animals crossing the river at several places in almost countless numbers. These movements have occurred several times since, and in one in 1845 they came into the town. The first camp meeting began September 12, east of town, lasting three days, under charge of Rev. James Scott, the first Methodist Minister, but no facts can now be given regarding it. A meeting was held December 1st, at Carter's tavern, to get a weekly mail to and from Vernon during the session. The first tax sale occurred December 7th, the long delinquent list and the amounts due generally ranging from twenty-five cents to one dollar, the highest being $2,87½, showed the existence of hard times. A petition was sent to the assembly in December to incorporate the town, but the project was strongly opposed and abandoned. No municipal government existed till 1832. The year closed with better prospects than the last. The adjacent country was being settled, the sickness had not been so general as in 1821. People were becoming acclimated and were better fixed, and Christmas was greeted with the usual festivities.

1823. The people had clamored for a year for representation in the Assembly, and that body yielded it January 7th. Candidates were numerous and busy till the August election, and their merits were duly set forth in the papers; for, in addition to the *Gazette*, a second journal, *The Western Censor and Emigrants' Guide*, was now published. The first number appeared March 7th, 1823, from an office opposite Henderson's tavern, edited and printed by Harvey Gregg and Douglass Maguire. The second number appeared March 19, third, March 26, fourth, April 2, fifth, April 19, sixth, April 23, after which it appeared regularly. Much difficulty was experienced in getting the press and material over the bad roads from Cincinnati, and for ten years afterward all the papers frequently passed a publication day on account of failure in the arrival of their paper. The *Censor* started with the motto, "He is a freeman whom the truth makes free." Mr. Gregg was chief editor, but retired from the paper October 29, 1824, and was succeeded November 16 by John Douglass, Mr. Maguire acting as editor. January 11, 1825, the paper was enlarged to super-royal size and called the *Indiana Journal*. It was enlarged to imperial size October 29, 1831. Mr. Maguire left the paper November 7, 1826, S. Merrill taking his place as editor; but in the fall of 1829 Douglass and Maguire resumed their partnership and continued till October 17.

1835, when Maguire sold his interest to S. V. B. Noel. Douglass & Noel (Mr. Noel editor,) continued till February, 1842, when Douglass became sole proprietor, and T. J. Barnett editor. Mr. Noel bought the establishment in March, 1843, Barnett remaining editor. Kent succeeded him, and in March, 1845, John D. Defrees became editor. He also became proprietor in February, 1846, and edited and published it till October 20, 1854, when the *Journal Co.* was formed (he being a large stockholder), by which it was published till 1863, John D. Defrees and B. R. Sulgrove being editors for part of the time, and B. R. Sulgrove and Barton D. Jones for the remainder. Wm. R. Holloway & Co. then purchased the establishment, Holloway becoming chief manager and editor. Shortly afterward James G. Douglass and Alexander H. Conner became partners, and in 1865 Samuel M. Douglass purchased Holloway's share, and the paper has since been published by Douglass & Conner, with H. C. Newcomb and W. R. Holloway as editors. During its existence the *Journal* has been published from several different offices on Washington street, being located for long periods opposite Washington Hall, and also over the present Gem billiard room, and in the three-story brick just opposite. From 1853 to 1860 it was located in Sharpe's building on Pennsylvania street, opposite the old Branch Bank. It was then removed to the Journal building, erected for it by the company on the corner of Circle and Meridian streets, and issued there till January, 1867, when it was transferred to the present five-story building on Market and Circle streets, erected in 1866 by the company. The weekly edition of the paper has borne the same name ever since January 11, 1825. Semi-weekly editions were published for many years during the sessions, the first appearing December 10, 1828; the first Tri-Weekly December 12, 1838. Daily editions were at first only issued during the sessions, the first appearing December 12, 1842, and ending February 15, 1843. The present daily began October 7, 1850, and with successive changes in size, shape and in name, October 20, 1854, to *Indianapolis Daily Journal*, has regularly appeared to the present time. Since January, 1866, it has appeared as an eight-page sheet. The *Journal* earnestly supported the Whig party during its existence, and aided the organization of the Republican party, to which it has since devoted its energies. It has always been the State organ of its party, is the leading journal of the State, and holds high rank among western newspapers.

There was no church edifice except the Methodist, no regular minister till 1823. A

Methodist camp-meeting was held east of town in September, 1822, and union meetings were occasionally held at the circle grove and in private houses. The Presbyterians met February 23d and March 6th at the schoolhouse, to organize and build a church. Subscription and building committees were appointed, and March 22 trustees appointed. The church was formally constituted in July. A lot was bought on Pennsylvania street, and the building raised in the summer and finished in 1824, at a cost for house and lot of $1200. It was used till 1842 or 3, then used as a carriage shop, and finally torn down in 1859. A

(The First Presbyterian Church.)

new brick church was built in 1841-2, on Market and Circle streets, at a cost of $8,000, and used till 1866, when sold to the Journal Co. and torn away. The present edifice on New York and Pennsylvania streets was built in 1865-6-7, at a cost of $75,000, and occupied in December, 1867. Rev. O. P. Gaines was the first Presbyterian minister, acting as a missionary in 1821-2, but David C. Proctor, a missionary here in 1822, was first pastor of the church from 1823 to August, 1824. George Bush—widely known afterward as a theologian—was pastor from September, 1824, to June, 1828, and left here March 20, 1829. Differences had arisen betwen him and the church on church government, and after severing his relation with them he preached for some time in the Court House. The average attendance during his ministry was seventy-five to one hundred persons. John Moreley was called May or June, 1829, remaining until 1832. Wm. A. Holliday was called in the fall of 1832. James W. McKennon was called February, 1835, remaining till 1840. Phineas D. Gurley was called November, 1840, and remained till the fall of 1849. The church was without a pastor till October, 1851, when John A. McClung was called. T. L. Cunningham was called October, 1855, leaving in 1858.

Then ensued two years without a pastor, and in 1860 J. H. Nixon was called and still remains with the society. After the division in the church on the slavery question a portion of the members left, forming the Second church in the summer of 1838, and in September, 1851, a further division formed the Third church. These in turn have colonized until at present seven or eight prosperous bodies look to the First church as a common mother. It would be interesting to mention their history in detail, but the limits allowed in this sketch forbid it. Beside these, other branches of the great Presbyterian family exist here, and movements have lately been made to unite them as one common body.

The first Sabbath School was organized April 6, 1823, in Caleb Scudder's cabinet shop, on the south side of the State House square. It was a union school, very successful for the time, seventy scholars being in attendance the third Sunday, but was discontinued in the fall. It was revived on its anniversary, and continued steadily from that time, the First Presbyterian being its present representative. After the Presbyterian church was finished the school met there. The average attendance at the union school was forty the first year, fifty the second, seventy-five the third, one hundred and six the fourth, one hundred and fifty the fifth. 150 volumes were in the library bought in 1827. Successive colonies formed schools for other churches, the first forming the Methodist school April 24, 1829, and the third the Baptist in 1832. Want of space forbids fuller mention of this important enterprise, but it may be stated here that Dr. Isaac Coe was the founder and most active supporter of the movement. Nearly every church now has a school, and a number of mission schools originated by associations or individuals also exist.— Thousands of scholars and teachers are enrolled, and thousands of books and papers are circulated each week from the libraries. A Sabbath School Union was started shortly after the first school, with visiting committees to solicit the attendance of scholars and keep up the interest of parents in the enterprise.

Israel Mitchell, Stephen Howard, and Martin Smith, three resident young men, left March 21st for Russian America via the Pembina settlement. They reached Fort Armstrong on the Mississippi May 4th, and Fever river August 15th, having seen no white men for twenty-three days after leaving the Vermillion salt works, and being robbed by the Indians and nearly starved for food. Their ultimate fate was unknown. The Indiana Central Medical Society was formed in the spring, with Dr. S. G. Mitchell, President, and Livingston Dunlop, Secretary. It licensed physicians to practice under the law at that time, and continued in existence for years, being the forerunner of the present medical society of the city.

The first woolen machinery in the county was started at Wilson's mill June 20, by Wm. Townsend and Earl Pierce.

The celebration of the 4th of July occurred at Wilkes Reagan's cabin on Pogue's run and Market street. D. C. Proctor was chaplain, Daniel B. Wick reader, Morris Morris orator, and Rev. Isaac Reed closed with benediction. Reagan gave the barbecue and fed the crowd and Capt. Curry's rifle company, closing with toasts and speeches. Political feeling grew warm as the August election approached. Two hundred and seventy votes were cast in the county, James Gregory, of Shelby, being elected first senator, and James Paxton first representative. The population was estimated at six hundred in September by the *Censor*, and the health was better than had been reported. The paper denounced the jealousy manifested toward the capital by other towns — a jealousy which lasted through subsequent years, and until the growth and superiority of the city rendered such a feeling ludicrous. Instead of aiding to build a city here of which the State could be proud, every town long labored to prevent its growth and build up cities in other States.

During this summer Thomas Carter built a frame tavern on Washington street opposite the court house, and opened it October 6th, and on the 26th the first sermon by a Baptist preacher was delivered there. This house was burned January 17, 1825, during the first session of the Assembly; and between the fire and the efforts of excited citizens to save property, Carter lost nearly all he had. Several persons desirous of saving the new sign on a tall post in front of the house chopped it down, and were much astonished when the fall crushed it into splinters. James Blake and Samuel Henderson had also built a tavern during the summer and fall, the Washington Hall, a two-story frame, where Glenn's block now is, and opened it with a ball January 12, 1824. Henderson had kept there before in a log house. Blake & Henderson dissolved in March, 1826, and for a few months after November, 1832, Town & Pullian succeeded Henderson, but he resumed in March, 1833, and kept it till June, 1836, when the house was removed to the lot east of its former site, and the new Washington Hall built in its stead. A part of the old frame house was standing, occupied as a clothing store, till February, 1866, when it was torn down and Gramling's block afterward built on its

site. The clearing of lots along Washington and the cross streets progressed during this year, and scattered farms on the plot and donation were opened, connected by foot-paths winding through the dense thickets, in which it was easy to miss the way and get lost.

The *Gazette* in December surprised the citizens by stating that Mr. and Mrs. Smith, late of the New York theatre, would appear at Carter's tavern, Wednesday night, December 31st, in the "Doctor's Courtship, or the Indulgent Father," to be followed by the "Jealous Lovers;" tickets 37½ cents. The town was excited and considerable opposition aroused. Carter insisted that the orchestra — one poor fiddle — should only play solemn music. A curtain was drawn across one end of the room for the players. The orchestra occupied a stool at one side, and the audience were seated at the other end of the room. Several performances were given. Such was the origin of the drama here. Mr. and Mrs. Smith returned in June, 1824, and gave several performances, the first on the 21st, but the experiment was not repeated for many years. The editor of the *Censor* in announcing the show in 1824, said he did not oppose the representation of tragedies and comedies as many did, but he thought that company would not do. In the next issue he announced that they had absconded without taking any of his money.

1824. The first military school here was opened January 13, by Major Sullinger, for the instruction of militia officers and soldiers. The first real estate agency was opened early in the same month by Wm. C. McDougal.

The Assembly had hitherto declined to move to the new Capital, and the southern counties delayed action as long as possible, but the new purchase members having taken their seats the subject was pressed, and on the 25th of January an act passed making Indianapolis the permanent seat of government, directing the State offices and archives to be moved here by January 10, 1825, and the Assembly to meet in our court house on that day. Samuel Merrill, State Treasurer, was charged with the removal, and effected it in the following November, twenty-five miles over the rough roads then existing. After the Assembly adjourned, Messrs. Gregory and Paxton returned from Corydon, and received a complimentary supper February 21st, at Washington Hall, in approval of their services. The toasts and speeches evinced great joy at the removal of the government to this point.

Many Indians still lingered in this country, and an event occurred March 22d which caused much fear of a border war. Two men, three women, two girls and two boys of the Shawnee tribe were murdered at their camp, eight miles above Pendleton, by four white men and two boys. The whites were Bridges and his son, Sawyer and his son, Hudson and Harper. The Indians had hunted and trapped on Fall Creek during the winter, obtaining so many furs that Harper determined to secure them. He got his party drunk, told them the Shawnees were horse-thieves, and proposed to kill them. They went to the camp, asked the three men, Logan, Stephen Ludlow and another to help hunt cattle, and after going a short distance fired on them, killing the first two, but the third escaped. Returning to camp the women and children were killed, the children's brains knocked out against trees, and the bodies mutilated as if Indians had killed them, and the bodies thrown in a pond where they were found next day, one of the women still breathing. The wretches divided the property between them, and its possession betrayed them. They were arrested, confessed the crime, but being assisted by friends soon after escaped. All were retaken but Harper, the leader, who traveled on foot to Ohio, eighty miles through the woods, in twenty-four hours, and escaped. They again escaped in July, but were recaptured. Hudson was tried at Anderson in November before Judge Wick, was convicted, and hung in the winter. The rest were tried in May, 1825. Young Sawyer was convicted of manslaughter, the rest of murder. Old Bridges and old Sawyer were hung June 3d. Young Bridges was brought under the rope where his father had just died, his coffin by his side, when Governor Ray mounted the platform and announced his pardon in a speech to the people. These executions quieted the Indians and no retaliatory measures were taken; but at first the settlers in the vicinity were much alarmed and fled to the Pendleton mills for protection, and there was a general uneasiness here.

A census taken by Sunday school visitors in April showed one hundred families on the donation, comprising one hundred and seventy-two voters, forty-five single women between fifteen and forty-five; number of children not stated. There had been but little increase since November, 1821, but many persons then here had moved to the country. For a number of years the town increased very slowly. The want of roads, and of a market for surplus products cut off travel or trade, and prevented any rapid progress. Improvements, however, were made. The court house, school house, Presbyterian church, and State offices were being erected, the trees on the streets felled and the plat gradually cleared. A series of great storms in April and May deluged the country with water, bayous, ponds and creeks everywhere overflowed, and White river attained a height never equaled, unless by the floods of 1828 and 1847. The boats took advantage of the high water, and the keel-boat "Dandy," twenty-eight tons, arrived May 22d with the new purchase staples, salt and whisky.

The Methodist quarterly meeting began May 15th in the Presbyterian church, then nearly finished. James Scott was the first minister here, sent by the St. Louis conference, and arriving October, 1821, after much difficulty in finding the town. Services had been held at private houses, and camp meetings held, the first September 12th, 1822, on James Givens' farm east of town, and the second began there May 23d of this year, lasting one week. These meetings were held in or near the town for ten or fifteen years, not only by the Methodists, but other denominations; but as church accommodations increased they were abandoned, and none have been held in the immediate vicinity for nearly twenty years. The Methodists had no church edifice till the summer of 1825, when they bought a lot and hewed log house for $300, on the south side of Maryland street east of Meridian, which was used till 1829, when a brick church, built in 1828-9, at a cost (with lot) of $3000, was opened on Circle and Meridian streets. This was used till 1846, when the walls becoming cracked and unsafe, it was torn down and Wesley Chapel built on its site at a cost of $10,000. This chapel has been used till the present time, but preparations are now on foot for its sale, and the erection elsewhere of a new and more expensive edifice. In 1842 the church was divided into the eastern and western charges, but in 1843-4 Roberts Chapel was built at a cost of $10,000, on Market and Pennsylvania streets, by the eastern charge. This church also will soon be sold and a new and more expensive edifice erected for the

(First Methodist Church.)

congregation. By the division of conferences and charges, Strange, Asbury and Trinity, with several Mission, German and African Methodist churches have since been built, and the denomination is perhaps the strongest in the city unless the Catholics outnumber it. Further mention of the church or of the many talented ministers who have been stationed here is prevented by limited space.

The 4th of July being Sunday, the celebration took place at Wilkes Reagan's on the 3d. Gabriel J. Johnson addressed the citizens and Major J. W. Reding the militia. Obed Foote was reader, and Reagan furnished the barbecue, the affair ending with the usual toasts and speeches. The August election was hotly contested, the contest being on sheriff, Morris Morris and A. W. Russell being candidates. Four hundred and thirty votes were cast, one hundred and sixty more than in 1823, Russell having two hundred and sixty-five and Morris one hundred and forty-eight votes. At the November election Clay received two hundred and thirteen, Jackson ninety-nine, Adams sixteen. Clay always received a heavy vote here afterward, and his supporters had held the first meeting and organized July 17th, James Paxton, President, and Hiram Brown, Secretary.

A large number of emigrants passed through the town during the fall on their way to the Wabash country.

The Indianapolis Legislature was organized during the fall by the lawyers and leading citizens, and sessions were held during the winter for ten or fifteen successive years. Its rules, and the pending measures and subjects for debate, were similar to those in the body it copied. Talented men were assigned as members from the several counties, and the mock representative often had far more ability than the real one. The Governor's messages were often witty and able documents, and sometimes published. The Governor was elected whenever the members wanted a new message or inaugural. After the General Assembly met here, its leading members joined the Indianapolis organization, and the debates and proceedings in the last frequently guided and controlled legislation in the first-named body.

1825. The State officers having arrived with the archives in November, 1824, the State government was formally and permanently located here January 10th, 1825. The Assembly met in the court house (still unfinished)—the Senate in the upper, the House in the lower room—and the sessions continued there till December, 1835, when the State house was finished, and the Legislature met there for the first time. The members at that time fully earned their mileage over the terrible roads. They arrived on horseback, singly or in groups, muddy and weary, at the different taverns, for several days before the session. The influx of strangers, with new topics of thought and conversation, excited the quiet villagers; and after the session opened crowds of gaping natives witnessed the proceedings with unsated curiosity. For years afterward the annual session was anxiously awaited. The money then disbursed was an important item; trade then revived, and business of all kinds improved. Property which had formerly declined was held more firmly, though no marked advance took place in it till 1835, when it suddenly reached extravagant figures, only to fall back and leave the people poorer than before.

On the 23d of January, 1824, the Assembly ordered the agent to lay off twenty out-lots of four acres each on the north and south sides of the old plat, and sell them by auction January 24th, 1825. The lots had been laid off during the following summer, and were sold as directed, the highest bringing $155, the lowest $63, the average being about $100 for each four-acre block. After this sale, the Assembly on the 12th of February ordered the agent to lay off and sell, on the 2d of May, twenty additional lots on the north and south of those already sold; also the reserved lots on Washington street and elsewhere; to have Pogue's run valley cleared if the expense did not exceed $50; and to lease the ferry for five years. Mr. Blythe complied with these directions, except clearing the valley, part of which was heavily timbered till 1845. Two of the old trees are still standing south of the Central depot; others south of the old Bellefontaine depot were cut down in April of this year,. He held the sale of reserved and other lots on the 2d of May; $360 was the highest price obtained for reserved lots on Washington street, and $134 the lowest. Seventeen lots on Washington street, equivalent to a frontage of nearly three squares, sold for $3,328. The twenty additional out-lots sold for $1,467, averaging a little over $18 per acre.

This year was distinguished for the formation of various societies. The Indianapolis Bible Society was formed on the 18th of April, and has continued in active operation ever since. Mrs. George Bush was among the most earnest supporters of the society, and for many years past Mrs. Margaret Givan has been the President of the society. The Marion County Bible Society, an auxiliary of the American Bible Society, was organized November 13th, 1825, B. F. Morris, President, J. M. Ray, Secretary. The Indianapolis Tract Society was formed in the spring of this year and continued its operations for many years. In July and August meetings were held at the court house to organize an agricultural society, and it was completed September 3d, Calvin Fletcher, Henry Bradley, Henry Burton, and others being leaders in it, but no permanent effect resulted from the effort, and it is notable only as the first· attempt in that direction.

In September the land office was removed from Brookville to this point, and in September and October an unusual number of emigrants passed through the town on their way to the Wabash and the Illinois prairies.

1826. On the 13th of January the Assembly directed the agent to contract with Ashael Dunning to build a two-story brick ferry house 18 x 30 feet, on the river bank. It was built the following summer, and though partially burned November 27th, 1855, was repaired, and is standing in good repair near the mill-race on Washington street. Sickness, and lack of trade and money, had prevented many lot buyers from meeting deferred payments on their lots, and they were liable to forfeiture at any time. The Assembly, January 20th, allowed further time, and permitted buyers of several lots to surrender part, and transfer the cash payments on the lots surrendered to meet deferred payments on others. This act was followed by similar ones at subsequent dates, greatly relieving embarrassed buyers. Western lots were surrendered and the settlement went still further east. The centre of population and business has shifted considerably at different periods. At first the town was on the river. The sickness in 1821 drove it eastward, and the lot-relief act carried it still further to the east. Till 1836 the town was on and near Washington street, between West and New Jersey streets. It then tended westward to the canal, under the internal improvement excitement. After the abandonment of the public works it moved eastward to the square on which the Palmer House stands, and for a long time was nearly stationary, for there was little change in the size and business of the place. In 1848 it moved southward, tending to the Madison depot; the construction of other lines arrested it and it moved north-east, till the war suddenly scattered business and population in every direction. At present it is probable the centre of population is not far from the east market house, and the centre of business near the north-west corner of Pennsylvania and Washington streets.

A census in February showed seven hundred and sixty inhabitants, two hundred and nine of them being children of school age, and one hundred and sixty-one of them in the Sabbath school. In March the influ-

enza prevailed here as an epidemic, attacking nearly every person in the town. Great rains fell for two weeks in March and April, four inches of water falling in one night. The streams rose very high, and all mails were stopped.

A cannon having been sent here an artillery company was formed under Captain James Blake, and thereafter at 4th of July and other celebrations, the artillery squad became an important though dangerous adjunct, for several men were afterward maimed for life by that gun, On the 20th of June the Indianapolis Fire Company was formed, John Hawkins, President, J. M. Ray, Secretary. The company used buckets and ladders, and turned out at the call of the church bell. It maintained its organization (being incorporated January, 1830,) till February, 1835, when it was merged in the Marion fire engine company.

The usual military and civic parade occurred on the 4th of July, with exercises at the court house. Rev. George Bush was chaplain, L. Dunlap, reader, C. Fletcher, orator, and John Hays furnished the dinner. On the 12th of August public funeral services were held for Adams and Jefferson. A military and civic procession marched to the court house, where B. F. Morris and D. Maguire delivered eulogies on the illustrious dead.

There was the usual great westward emigration in the fall. The town was unusually healthy, although the summer was hot and dry. Lorenzo Dow, the noted revivalist, visited the town in June and preached to the people in a grove near the present Madison depot, and the next evening at the Indian depot, and the next evening at the court house steps. He attracted large audiences, more by eccentricities of speech and dress than by eloquence.

A treaty was concluded with the Indians at Fort Wayne in the fall, by which more territory was ceded, and the government agreed to deliver certain cattle, hogs, wagons, &c., the next spring. In January, 1827, John Tipton, Indian agent, advertised for proposals for the delivery of two hundred hogs, two hundred cattle, ten wagons, and the building of eight brick houses in the Indian country under the treaty. The heavy rains the following spring prevented the delivery of the wagons and stock, and the savages were somewhat dissatisfied thereat.

1827. The Assembly, on the 26th of January, directed the agent to survey and sell seven acres near the river for a steam mill site, and on the 28th of January, 1828, incorporated the Steam Mill Company with $20,000 capital, in $50 shares. The company—the first one incorporated here—organized shortly after, Nicholas McCarty,

James Blake and J. M. Ray being the lead-ers in it. Subscriptions were slowly ob-tained during 1829–30, materials were col-lected in 1830–1, the building raised in Sep-tember and finished in December, 1831. The saw mill had been finished before. The grist mill began work in January, 1832, and was the first in this section that had

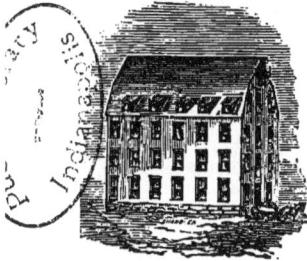

(Old Steam Mill.)

bolting cloths or made fine flour. The wool-carding apparatus was put in motion in June, 1832. The mill ran irregularly, for there was difficulty in getting good wood at seventy-five cents per cord ; the de-mand for flour was not equal to the supply, and shipments were out of the question. The mill stood north-east of the present bridge, and was the largest building in the place, being a heavily framed structure of three full stories with a high gambrel roof, allowing two additional stories. The boil-ers and engines—the first ones ever used here—were to have been brought up on a steamboat, but were wagoned out from Cin-cinnati with great difficulty in 1831. The mill was unprofitable, and was abandoned and the machinery offered for sale in 1835. It remained vacant till 1847, when it was refitted and used till 1852 by Geisendorffs as a woolen mill. It again became vacant, and was fired and totally destroyed with the neighboring toll house, on the night of November 16, 1853, endangering the White river bridge, which was only saved by great exertions on the part of the firemen. One hundred men worked two days in rais-ing its heavy frame, and no liquor was used, a fact which excited much comment at the time, for serious doubts had been enter-tained whether so large a building could be raised without the aid of whisky.

The Assembly appropriated five hundred dollars January 26th, to build a Supreme Court clerk's office, eighteen by thirty-six feet, on the west side of court square. It was built by S. and J. Patterson during

the summer, and stood there till 1855.

(Clerk's Office.)

Four thousand dollars were also appropri-ated for a two-story brick house on the Circle for the Governor, and the Circle was to be enclosed by a rail fence by the first of May. The house contract was signed March 17th, and it was built at a cost of six thous-and five hundred dollars during the sum-mer by Smith, Culbertson, Bishop and Speaks. It was a solidly-built, square, two-story, hipped-roofed brick house, with look-out, large windows, doors and chimneys, two cross halls, and four large rooms on each floor, and dark, damp basement under the whole structure. These vaults were a

(Governor's House.)

source of terror to all small boys, for they fully credited the legend that they were tenanted by a headless ghost whose appetite for youngsters was insatiable. The house was totally unfit for a residence and was never occupied as such. At the session of 1829 it was proposed to add wings to the east and west ends and use it as a State house, but the proposition failed. The rooms were successively occupied by the State officers, State library, State Bank, State engineers, Supreme Judges, old bach-elors, debating societies, and Supreme Court clerk. At the session of 1856–7 it was or-dered to be sold, and was disposed of by auction April 16th, 1857, for six hundred and sixty-five dollars, and torn down April 25–30. Its material was partly used in the Macy house and the dwelling adjoining it. The Circle has since been used for political and other open air meetings. In the fall of 1867 the city council ordered it graded, planted, fenced, and surrounded with a decent sidewalk, for the first time in its history.

The Assembly, January 26th, directed the agent to offer at public sale, with certain exceptions, all reserved, forfeited and unsold lots. Several alleys and squares were vacated. Square 22 was reserved for a State Hospital and square 25 for a State University. This square has since been claimed by the Bloomington College, which was then a "State Seminary," so designated in the act creating it, and with funds and lands specially set apart for it; and though afterward made a college, no act ever recognized it as the "University" for which square 25 was reserved as a site, nor has the Assembly ever at any time in any manner given it any claim on that square. The Assembly, January 26th, 1832, authorized the agent to lease square 25 for thirty years to the trustees of the Marion County Seminary, who might build on the south-east or south-west corner thereof, and if the square was needed for a university before the lease expired, a half-acre where the seminary stood was to be sold or deeded to the trustees. The trustees took possession under the lease, and in 1833–4 built on the

(Marion County Seminary.)

south-west corner and opened the school September 1st, 1834, with E. Dumont as principal. W. J. Hill succeeded January, 1835; Thomas D. Gregg, May, 1836; Wm. Sullivan, December, 1836; Wm. A. Holliday, August, 1837; James S. Kemper, October, 1838; J. P. Safford, 1843; Benjamin L. Lang, 1844. The seminary was long the leading school in Central Indiana, and under Kemper, Safford and Lang had a high reputation. Many of the present business men of the city were wholly or partially educated in it. After the city free

school system was adopted the building was used from Sept., 1853, to 1859, as a high school, but was torn down in August and September, 1860. After the lease to the seminary trustees, the Assembly directed the agent, February 6th, 1837, to lease the north-west corner for twenty years to the Lutheran church, the lease to be given up if the square was needed for a University. The church, however, was built elsewhere. On the 17th of February, 1838, the agent was directed to lease the north-west corner for twenty years to the trustees of the Indianapolis Female Institute, first getting a release from the Lutheran church, but the institute also was afterward built elsewhere. On the 21st of January, 1850, the Governor and State officers were directed to sell one acre of the square at its appraised value, to the Indiana Asbury University for the use of its medical department, the Central Medical College. The acre was accordingly selected, and appraised at $3,566, but the appraisement being thought too high, and opposition arising to the sale, it was never completed, and the college was discontinued. In 1865–6 the city took possession of the square, fenced, graded and planted it at an expense of over $2,000, and in future it will probably be used as a park. Hitherto it has been used as a pasture, as a lumber and stone yard, and as a parade and play ground. In June, 1860, a large part of it was covered with a frame structure called a "Coliseum," built by Mr. Perine, and intended for shows and monster meetings. The edifice was about three hundred feet square, consisted of a board wall twenty-five feet high, with battlemented towers at the entrances and corners. The interior contained a large pit or open space at the south side, with a tall flag-staff, from which seats ranging from four feet at the front to twenty feet high near the walls, were arranged on the east, west and north sides, making an amphitheatre capable of seating fifteen or twenty thousand persons. Wide aisles led to the several tiers of seats. By great efforts it was got ready and opened July 4th with a military parade, band concert, and balloon ascension by J. C. Bellman, closing at night with the finest display of fireworks ever seen here. The enterprise was not pecuniarily successful, but deserved to be so, if only for its magnitude and boldness. No auditorium as large has ever been built elsewhere in the West, and perhaps not in the country. After standing some weeks it was torn away. The vacant square was subsequently used for military parades, especially during the Morgan raid, when the City Regiment, twelve hundred strong, was daily and nightly mustered there at stroke of bell, to go through agonizing partings with mothers, wives and sweethearts, while their twelve hundred martial bosoms throbbed, doubtless, with strong desires to meet the foe.

The *Journal* in February, 1827, said the town then contained a court house, a Presbyterian church with thirty members; a Baptist church with thirty-six members, worshiping in a small cabin; a Methodist church with ninety-three members, worshiping in a small cabin, but building a new brick church, the walls of which were completed and enclosed during the fall. A Sabbath school had also existed for five years, and now contained twenty teachers and one hundred and fifty scholars. There were twenty-five brick, sixty frame, and eighty hewed and rough log houses in the town. In the fall it stated that rents were high and houses in demand. The Governor's Circle was being built. Six two-story and five one-story brick houses, with a large number of frame houses, had been built. It called for the introduction of steam engines and home manufacturing, and said nearly $10,000 worth of goods and provisions had been brought to the town and sold during the past year. Among the articles were seventy-six kegs tobacco, two hundred barrels flour, one hundred kegs powder, four thousand five hundred pounds spun yarn, and two hundred and thirteen barrels of whisky. Seventy-one additional barrels of whisky had also been made here and sold. A Sunday school census taken November 25th showed five hundred and twenty-nine white, and thirty-four colored males; four hundred and seventy-nine white, and twenty four colored females; total, one thousand and sixty-six inhabitants in the town. Two hundred and eighty-four barrels of whisky seems a large allowance for this number of people, but the water then was doubtless very impure, from the vast quantity of decaying vegetable matter.

A tornado passed a few miles south of town on the 5th of April, destroying the timber but injuring no person.

The sale of lots ordered by the Assembly took place May 7th and 8th. One hundred and fifty-three lots (twenty-four of them on Washington street,) and thirty or forty squares of four acres each, were offered. One hundred and six lots sold at $180 per acre, and thirty-eight outlots and squares at $23 per acre. Mr. Knight, commissioner in charge of the National road survey, located the line to this point July 8th, and went on westward next day. The Fourth of July was ushered in with twenty-four rounds by the new artillery company. The procession included citizens and the rifle and artillery companies, and marched to the court house. Ebenezer Sharpe was reader, N. Bolton orator. John Hays provided the dinner, which closed with the usual toasts and speeches. The first public school examination and exhibition took place at the court house October 5th. During the fall squirrels and other animals were migrating in great numbers, and several bears were killed close to town. Hitherto the ladies of the place had been compelled to make their own bonnets and clothes in backwoods fashion, but in October the first millinery establishment was opened by Mrs. Matilda Sharpe, and thereafter style began to be assumed in the new town.

The town improved but slowly from this date to 1834. The settlement was mainly on Washington street and one or two squares north and south, with detached dwellings on other parts of the plat. The timber had been cut from the greater portion of the plat, but the outlots were still in the woods. Large trees stood in places within two squares of Washington street, and the greater part of the ninth ward was a forest till 1846. All the territory south of Maryland and east of Meridian streets was unimproved except as farms till 1845, and most of it till 1855. A fine walnut grove existed in the first and second wards north of North street, and Drake's addition was a good hunting ground till 1848. Squirrels, rabbits and turkeys were killed in sections now thickly peopled. No grading whatever had been done, and few sidewalks existed, even on Washington street. Ponds along the bayous afforded skating in winter, and in summer were covered by green scum and tenanted by countless frogs. The streets were semi-fluid in thawing weather, but the drainage in many places was better than since the engineers changed it. The town was a dull country village, with no excitement beyond the annual sessions, when a little animation was given to society and to trade. It seemed to have attained its growth. Few expected a brighter future, nor was there any prospect of it till the internal improvement scheme was originated.

1828. The spring was very wet with heavy rains, and in May a flood occurred in White river, rivaling that of 1824, and those of 1847 and 1858. Less damage was done then than since, there being fewer settlements along the bottoms. There is no doubt that White river then had a greater average depth of water than now, and was better fitted for navigation. Repeated attempts were made to navigate it, and boats of good size used. In May, 1822, the keelboat Eagle, fifteen tons, with salt and whisky, arrived from the Kanawha, and the Boxer, thirty-three tons, with merchandise, from Zanesville; and the Dandy, twenty-eight tons, in May, 1824, with salt and whisky, and many other boats arrived from the lower river, and departed loaded with produce. Large flatboats also were built and ran to the southern market, and the trade was kept up till the dams on the river interfered with its navigation. The Assembly and the people regarded White river as a very important channel for heavy freights. Alexander Ralston was appointed commissioner February 12th, 1825, to survey and report the expense of removing obstructions in it from drift, snags and leaning trees. He made the survey during the summer, and reported that from Sample's Mills in Randolph county to Indianapolis was one hundred and thirty miles, from here to the forks two hundred and eighty-five miles, and from thence to the Wabash forty miles; total four hundred and fifteen miles; and that for that distance the river might be made navigable for three months in the year by expending $1,500. There were two falls, one of eighteen inches, eight miles above Martinsville, and one of nine feet in one hundred yards, ten miles above the forks. There was also a great drift at the Daviess and Greene county line. After this report the Assembly repeatedly memorialized Congress, asking for the improvement of the river, and considerable sums were appropriated from the State treasury for that object, the county commissioners along the river governing the expenditure. In 1830–35, John Matthews and others proposed slackwater navigation, building levees, dams and locks, and using steamboats and tugboats for barges, to carry passengers and freight from this point to the lower river. Mills would be built at the dams, and serve as feeders to the trade, and the stone, timber, iron ore, coal and produce of the river valley, could be brought more cheaply to our town than by any other mode. Matthews pressed this plan for years, and the Assembly in February, 1851, chartered the White River Navigation Company for twenty years, but nothing was done, not even a survey, to test the practicability of the plan. If at all feasible it certainly deserves attention and a survey at least to test its practicability, for our manufacturers and builders would derive advantages from it they can never get from any other work. In 1828 or 9, Governor Noble becoming convinced that steamboats of a small size could be used on the river, endeavored to get some captain to bring a boat to this point, and offered $200 reward to the first one who succeeded, and to sell the cargo free of charge. In April, 1830, Captain Saunders with the "Traveller" reached Spencer, and the "Victory" came within fifty-five miles of this point, but the

river falling rapidly they returned. In 1829–30 General Hanna and others took contracts on the National road, and resolved to bring up a boat to haul stone and timber from the bluffs for the abutments and bridges. A medium-sized boat, the "Robert Hanna," was bought, and after some trouble arrived here loaded and towing a loaded barge, on the 11th of April, 1831. She was greeted by the entire community, and by Captain Blythe's artillery squad firing a National salute. A meeting was called on the 12th, Isaac Blackford, president, and James Morrison, secretary, which passed resolutions of welcome, asked for the improvement of the river, and extended an invitation to the boat owners and officers for a public dinner. Two excursion trips were made up the river on the 12th with a great crowd of passengers. During the second one she ran into the trees on the bank, knocking down her pilot-house and chimneys, and injuring the wheel-house. The passengers were terribly frightened, and slid off in great numbers. The boat was too high and large for so narrow a river with overhanging trees, and unfit for the purpose for which she was designed. She started down on the 13th, grounded for six weeks on a bar at Hog Island, where the captain's child was drowned, and did not get out of the river till the fall. No subsequent effort at steam navigation was made till 1865, when the Indianapolis and Waverly packet, Governor Morton, built by a company at a cost of $11,000, ran a few trips several miles up and down the river during the summer and fall, and following spring. From want of water, leakiness, defective construction, and distrust by the community, she failed to realize the hopes of her builders, and was wrecked just below the bridge in the summer of 1866, after a brief but glorious career.

The first stage line from Indianapolis was started to Madison by Mr. Johnson, in June or July, 1828. In July the Indianapolis Library Society was formed, the members donating the books, and continued its existence for six or eight years. The Fourth of July was celebrated with more display than usual. The artillery and rifle companies, the citizens, and the Sabbath school, which now participated for the first time, formed in procession and marched to the court house. Hiram Brown acted as president, Henry Brenton vice president. Rev. Geo. Bush was chaplain, A. Ingram reader, B. F. Morris orator. The Handelian Society (formed in the spring) furnished music. After the exercises closed the Sabbath school returned to the school house, and the military and citizens marched to Bates' grove, east of town, where a dinner was eaten, with the usual toasts and speeches. A military ball at Vigus' tavern, opposite the court house, closed the festivities.

Nine hundred and thirteen votes were cast at the August election, and nine hundred and sixty-one at the November election, Adams receiving five hundred and eighty-two, Jackson three hundred and seventy-nine. The first cavalry company, David Buchanan, captain, was organized in August. A heavy emigration westward occurred this fall, and also during several following years, fifty teams per day often passing through town. A similar movement occurred in 1839–40. In December, twenty-eight blocks and seventy-two lots in the old plat were yet unsold, and nearly all the donation land outside the plat. The winter was colder than usual, with much snow in February.

1 8 2 9. The Methodist Sabbath school, the second one in the town, was organized April 24th with eleven teachers and forty-six scholars, and at the end of the year had twenty-seven teachers and one hundred and forty-six scholars. Wesley Chapel school is its present representative, but eight or nine colonies have left it since its origin. The Fourth of July hitherto had been celebrated by the civic and military procession, the schools participating for the first time in 1828, but this year the school display was the only one. The two town, with five country schools, formed on the Circle, and accompanied by eight hundred adults, marched to Bates' woods, on East, between Ohio and Market streets, where the children were seated, a hymn sung, and bread and water distributed. Reverend Jamison Hawkins prayed, Ebenezer Sharpe was reader, James Morrison, orator, and Rev. Henry Brenton closed with benediction, and the procession returned to town. James Blake acted as marshal, and continued, with but few exceptions, to act in that capacity for nearly thirty years afterward. The Sabbath school celebration continued a leading feature till 1858, but the number of schools and scholars became so great that the general celebration was abandoned. The exercises were always of the same character. During the war the military displays were the chief attraction. Since that date the firemen's processions and picnics have been the chief features of the day.

There was much sickness during the summer and fall, and many deaths, an unusual proportion being young married people. The Indiana Colonization Society, Isaac Blackford, president, was organized in November, and continued its operations for many years afterward. In September and October contracts were let on the National road. The people were much rejoiced, for it promised a direct route to the East, and its early completion was confidently expected. It was begun in 1830, but from deficient appropriations, and the fact that work was carried on simultaneously across the whole State, it progressed slowly, and was abandoned in 1839 before its completion. The bridge here was contracted for July 26th, 1831, by Wm. H. Wernweg and Walter Blake, at $18,000, and finished in the spring of 1834.

1 8 3 0. The winter was very severe, the thermometer marking five or six deg. being zero, and much snow fell. The Legislature celebrated the 8th of January, A. F. Morrison delivering an address. For eight or ten years afterward this celebration continued regularly. A theological debate—the first one here—on the future punishment of the wicked, began January 21st, between Jonathan Kidwell, Universalist, and Rev. Edwin Ray, Methodist. Like all such discussions it settled nothing and roused bad feelings.

The Indiana Democrat, an administration paper, was first issued by A. F. Morrison in the spring. The Gazette, which had been published since January, 1822, was discontinued in the fall, and the Democrat furnished to its subscribers. The paper was published till 1841, the office being most of the time in a one-story brick building at 32 West Washington street, and was owned successively by Morrison, Morrison & Bolton, Bolton & Livingston, and John Livingston. It was sold to the Chapmans July 21st, 1841, who moved the office to a frame house where Blake's Commercial Row now stands, and changed the name to Indiana Sentinel. The second number of the Sentinel was issued August 4th, 1841, and weekly afterward. In November, 1844, the office was moved to a brick built for it on North Illinois street. In November, 1846, John S. Spann became a partner. Chapman & Spann dissolved May 20th, 1850, and June 1st W. J. Brown bought the paper and moved it to 8 West Washington street, Ellis & Spann retaining the old job office. In August, 1852, the office was moved to Tomlinson's new building, and published by A. H. Brown (Wm. J. Brown, editor,) till March 2d, 1855, when Walker & Cottam became proprietors, Walker & Holcombe editors. Spann & Norman bought it December 4th, 1855, and sold to Larrabee & Cottam January 24th, 1856, A. F. Morrison and W. C. Larrabee being editors. Larrabee, Bingham & Co. became proprietors August 25th, 1856. Bingham & Doughty bought it January 13th, 1857, and moved the office to the old Capital House. On the 7th of April, 1857, the office was nearly destroyed by a boiler explosion, which killed a boy and badly injured one or two others, and the paper was suspended till April 21st. The office had just been completed and the engine put in motion for the first time, and the explosion entailed a heavy loss. The paper was then published by the *Sentinel Company* till July 31st, 1861, when it was moved to the old *Locomotive* office in Hubbard's block, the *Locomotive* discontinued and merged with the *Sentinel*, which was then published by Elder, Harkness & Bingham. A new three-story brick office was built for it in 1863, on Pearl and Meridian streets, where it was issued till 1865, when the paper was bought by C. W. Hall and moved to the old office, 16 East Washington street, where it has since been located. The name was changed to the *Indianapolis Herald*, and published by Hall & Hutchinson till October, 1866, when it passed into a receiver's hands and was bought by Lafe Develin in January, 1867, and published by him till April, 1868, when R. J. Bright became the owner and changed the name to *Indianapolis Sentinel*. Joseph J. Bingham has been the chief editor for over ten years.

The Chapmans issued the first daily paper in the place, the *Daily Sentinel* first appearing December 6th, 1841, and continuing during the session. The second volume began December 6th, 1842, for the session, and the third began December 6th, 1843. Semi-weekly editions had been issued during the sessions before and after these dates. The present daily began April 28th, 1851, and appeared regularly till April 7th, 1857, when the boiler explosion destroyed the office and suspended the paper till April 21st. It has since appeared regularly, under the names of the *Sentinel* and *Herald*.

The Fourth of July was separately celebrated by the schools and citizens. Considerable rivalry existed. Demas McFarland and James Blake, the respective marshals, addressed the crowds on the street corners, calling for adherents. Rain being threatened the schools went to the Methodist church, where the usual exercises took place. The citizens went to a grove near the present central engine house. Isaac Blackford was president, W. W. Wick, orator, and A. St. Clair reader. A dinner was spread and the usual toasts given. The cannon was taken to fire salutes, but the artillery officers being with the schools, inexperienced men were handling the gun, and at the third fire Andrew Smith lost his arm. The accident put an end to the exercises and threw a damper on such celebrations for several years afterward.

McComber & Co.'s menagerie, the first show here, exhibited at Henderson's tavern July 26-7th, and on the 23d-4th of August another exhibited at the same place.—

Among its animals was a "Rompo," doubtless a relative of the "Guyascutas." The summer was hot and dry, with considerable sickness and many deaths. The Indiana Historical Society, Benjamin Parke, president, B. F. Morris, secretary, was organized December 11th, at the court house, and continued its existence for many years. The first gift enterprize was started in the fall by T. J. Langdon, who offered the Indianapolis Hotel, opposite the court house, as the first prize, to be drawn December 30th.

The winter of 1830-1 was steadily and severely cold. The snow fell twelve to eighteen inches deep in February, and the thermometer fell to 18 and 20° below zero, by far the coldest weather since the settlement.

1831. M. G. Rogers, the first portrait painter here, announced his arrival in February for a few weeks' stay, at Henderson's tavern. In the same month, Samuel Henderson, who had been postmaster since February, 1822, was removed and John Cain appointed.

Several railways had been projected in 1830, and the Assembly on the 2d and 3d of February chartered the Madison & Indianapolis, Lawrenceburgh & Indianapolis, Harrison & Indianapolis, Lafayette & Indianapolis, New Albany, Salem & Indianapolis, and Ohio & Indianapolis railways. Surveys were made on them in following years, being completed on the Madison, Lawrenceburgh, Jeffersonville and Lafayette roads in 1835. Several were rechartered in 1834-5, and some work done on them. They were revived in 1835-6, and State aid given them, but stopped with the State work and were not built until 1849-53.

The agent was directed, February 9th, to divide the donation into outlots, fix a minimum price, and sell them publicly in May. The subdivision was accordingly made, and nearly nineteen hundred acres in and out of the plat offered in lots of two to fifty acres at a minimum price of ten dollars per acre, but a part only was sold.

The Assembly on the 10th of February resolved to build a State house. A committee had reported in its favor at the last session, estimating the cost at $56,000, and estimating the value of the unsold donation at $58,000. James Blake was appointed commissioner to superintend it and procure materials, and $3,000 was appropriated therefor. He was to offer $150 for a plan (to be reported at the next session) comprising a Senate hall for fifty members, Representatives' hall for one hundred members, Supreme Court and Library rooms, twelve committee rooms, &c. The building was not to cost over $45,000. Blake bought some stone and other materials, and received a plan from Ithiel Town and I. J. Davis, of New York City, which was adopted by the Assembly January 20th, 1832, Noah Noble, Morris Morris and Samuel Merrill were appointed commissioners Feb. ruary 2d, 1832, to superintend the building according to the plan, to employ an architect, and use the material already bought. The house was to be completed by November, 1838, and examined and approved by a committee of five from each House before being accepted. They contracted February 19th with Ithiel Town for its erection, at $58,000. It was begun in the spring of 1832, and by great exertion finished in December, 1835, in time for the annual session beginning on the 7th. It is generally Doric in style, but contains a large rotunda and dome, surmounted by a cap ornament modeled after the tomb of Lycidas. The brick work was well done, but the stone used in the foundation was not durable. The house was stuccoed inside and out in imitation of sandstone, and though well done such work is not durable in this climate, and always looks ragged. The building cost about $60,000, and was regarded with great pride as the finest in the West. The feeling has since diminished. The roof has several times been partly stripped off by winds, and in December, 1867, the ceiling of Representatives' Hall was thrown down in a storm, crushing the desks and injuring the building. A new structure is needed, one in which the materials and construction will defy time and bad usage. The square was filled to a depth of nine feet in 1834, and the trees now growing on it were planted in 1835-6.

On the 11th of April the steamboat Robert Hanna arrived and was greeted as heretofore stated. On the 17th of May Sophia Overall, a colored woman, was declared by all the physicians as having the small pox, the first case here. A panic ensued, and a citizens' meeting was called. Dr. S. G. Mitchell, Isaac Coe, L. Dunlap, J. E. McClure, C. McDougal, J. L. Mothershead, Wm. Ticknor, and John H. Sanders, were appointed the first board of health, and authorized to take all necessary measures to prevent the spread of the disease. No other cases occurred, however, and the panic subsided.

The first soda fountain in the place was put up July 2d in Dunlap & McDougal's drug store, and largely patronized. The Fourth of July was celebrated in the usual way by the schools and young men. Nine hundred and fifty votes were cast in the township at the August election. A full-grown elephant and calf elephant, the first here, were shown as "natural curiosities," at Henderson's tavern August 12th. The first three-story brick house in town was erected at 4 and 6 West Washington street, during the summer, and is still standing. The Methodist conference held its first session here October 4th, with a full attendance. The summer and fall were the healthiest since the settlement of the place. The Indianapolis Lyceum or Athenæum was organized in the fall, giving lectures and scientific discussions, and continued its existence for several years. The winter was cold and snowy.

1832. News of the Indian outbreak under Black Hawk was received June 3d, and one hundred and fifty mounted volunteers from the fortieth regiment were called for on the 4th, by Colonel A. W. Russell, and the same number from adjoining counties. They rendezvoused here June 9th, armed with rifles, tomahawks, knives, a pound of powder each, and balls in proportion, and were organized in three companies, under Captains J. P. Drake, J. W. Redding and Henry Brenton, and marched for Chicago the same day under Colonel Russell. The cannon was fired on the day of rendezvous, and by a premature explosion William Warren, an Irishman, lost both arms, shedding the only blood here during that war. After reaching Chicago the battalion marched round the south end of the lake to St. Joseph, and returned home without accident July 3d, participating in the celebration and dinner of the 4th as veterans. They were paid off by Major Larned, January, 1833. Wm. Conner, a merchant here, and formerly an old Indian trader and scout, piloted the expedition.

Meetings had been held and subscriptions made in August and September, 1832, to build a market house, C. J. Hand, John Givans and others being prominent in the movement, and after some difficulty as to location, it was contracted for in May, 1833, and finished in August, on the square north of the court house, and regulations agreed on for holding the markets. Josiah Davis, Thomas McOuatt and John Walton were the committee in charge of the work. L. Dunlap, J. S. Hall and D. McFarland were elected the first seminary trustees in August. The Indianapolis Foundry, the first in the place, was started in August west of the river, by R. A. McPherson & Co., and continued several years. The cholera swept many places in the West this year, being diffused by the troops from the Indian war. The people here held meetings, organized a board of health, and adopted sanitary measures, but no cases occurred and the panic passed off.

Until this time no municipal government had existed, the township and county officers enforcing the State laws; but at a meeting held September 3d, at the court house, it was resolved to incorporate the town under the general law. The election of five trustees was held in September, and the board organized shortly after, electing Samuel Henderson, president, I. P. Griffith, clerk, Samuel Jenison, marshal and collector. The town was divided into five wards, inside the old plat: all east of Alabama, 1st; thence west to Pennsylvania, 2d; thence to Meridian, 3d; thence to Tennessee, 4th; thence west, 5th. A general "ordinance" No. 1, in thirty-seven sections, "established by the board of trustees of the town of Indianapolis for their own government and for the regulation of the town," was probably adopted in November, and published December 1st, signed by S. Henderson as president. At the same time a market ordinance in seventeen sections was adopted and published. The general ordinance or charter provided for the election by the board of a clerk to keep records, issue warrants, &c.; a treasurer, who was to report annually in December; an assessor, who was to make an annual assessment in January; a marshal, who also acted as collector, and enforced ordinances, abated nuisances, &c., reporting taxes in June to the treasurer. All these officers were to give bond. The firing of guns, flying kites, leaving open cellar doors, racing horses, driving over foot-paths, leaving unhitched teams, letting hogs run at large, keeping stallions on Washington street, &c., was prohibited under penalties. Wood piles were not to remain on Washington street over twelve hours, or shavings in any place over two days. Shows and tippling houses were required to take out license. Offences against the ordinances were to be sued within twenty days, in the name of the trustees before a justice. Regular meetings were held the first Friday in each month, but meetings could be called at any time. The markets were held for two hours after daylight, Wednesdays and Saturdays, by a market master, who governed the markets, tested weights, &c. Huckstering was prohibited. The elections were held annually in September, and the town continued under this ordinance, or charter, until April, 1836. The officers so far as known with those elected at subsequent dates, are given in the table hereafter inserted.

On the 5th of February, 1836, the Assembly incorporated the town and legalized the acts of the first trustees. The wards were left as before, all east of Alabama being the first; thence to Pennsylvania, second; thence to Meridian, third; thence to Tennessee, fourth; thence west, fifth. One trustee to each ward was to be elected April 4th, and the board was to elect one of their number

president, and a clerk, marshal, lister, collector, trustees and other officers, whose duties were prescribed. They could pass all necessary ordinances, levy taxes and improve the streets and sidewalks at the expense of property holders. Taxation was not to exceed one-half of one per cent. and was limited to the old plat, though the incorporation covered the donation. The board elected under this act re-enacted, with but few changes, the ordinances formerly in force. The officers of the old board settled to the first of April, 1836. The treasurers' report showed $1,610 receipts for the year; $1,150 of this was paid for the Marion engine, five public wells, and other fire department expenses, and a balance of $124 was turned over to the new board.

On the 17th of February, 1838, the place was re-incorporated, the corporation covering the donation, but taxation being still limited to the plat, and not to exceed one-half of one per cent on real property. The town was divided into six wards, as follows: All east of Alabama, the first; thence west to Pennsylvania, second; thence to Meridian, third; thence to Illinois, fourth; thence to Mississippi, fifth; thence west, sixth. An election was to be held March 27th for a president, by the general vote, and one trustee for each ward, by the voters thereof, to hold office one year, and to constitute the "common council," four being a quorum. The president had justice's jurisdiction, and was to sign all ordinances, keep a docket, &c. The council met regularly once each month, but called meetings might be held. The trustees received twelve dollars each per year. They could pass all necessary ordinances for the improvement and government of the town, levy taxes, borrow money, regulate and license shows, groceries, saloons, fire companies, &c. They were to elect a clerk, marshal, collector, lister, treasurer, supervisor, clerk of markets, and other officers, and prescribe their duties. The marshal had a constable's authority, and was to enforce all ordinances. The officers were to give bond and receive such compensation as the council allowed. Tax sales on the municipal assessment were authorized and rules prescribed therefor.— Several sales were made under this authority, the first being held October 25th, 1839, at Washington Hall, but the records being all destroyed by fire in 1851, but few traces remain of them. North, South, East and West streets were declared public highways and ordered to be opened. The new board was elected in March under this act, and shortly after enacted ordinances regulating markets, prescribing the duties of the corporation officers, fire department, police, street improvement, licensing tippling houses, groceries, shows, &c.

This charter, with some subsequent changes, continued in force till the city charter was granted in February, 1847. The changes were as follows: On the 15th of February, 1839, the Assembly ordered the council to expend the revenue collected in West Indianapolis in that part of the town, and to open the alleys in the donation. In February, 1840, the charter was amended so that councilmen were elected for two years, and received twenty-four dollars annually, householders only being eligible. In February, 1841, the office of marshal was made elective by the people, and West Indianapolis was detached from the corporate limits; and on January 15th, 1844, all the officers were made elective by the people.

The first trustees made no effort to improve the streets, and no engineer was employed till 1836. The first street improvement was made that year in filling a pond near Wesley Chapel. No street grading was done, and few sidewalks existed, even on Washington street, till 1839-40. James Wood was employed March, 1841, to make a street profile, which was adopted in April, 1842, and thereafter followed in the street grades. The corporation officers and councilmen from 1832 to 1847 are given, as far as known, in the following table. The destruction of the records by fire in 1851 left no trace of them, and the table has been made from the contemporary journals and tradition:

TRUSTEES AND COUNCILMEN FROM EACH WARD, FROM 1832 TO 1846.

YEARS.	1st WARD.	2d WARD.	3d WARD.	4th WARD.	5th WARD.	6th WARD.
1832.	John Wilkens....	H. P. Coburn....	John G. Brown......	S. Henderson	Sam. Merrill	
1833.	John Wilkens....	H. P. Coburn....	S. Henderson........	John Cain.....	Sam. Merrill	
1834.	Alex. Morrison...	L. Dunlap.........	Jos. Lefevre........	J V" Blarleum	Nat. Cox....	
1835.	Jas. M. Smith.....	Jos. Lefevre......	Charles Campbell..	H. Griffith......	N B Palmer	
1836.	Geo. Lockerbie.	John Foster......	S. Merrill.............	H. Griffith.....	J. L. Young	
1837.	....	Joshua Soule....	....	....		
1838.	....	....	....	....	C. Scudder..	Nat. Cox.....
1839.	Geo. Lockerbie.	Wm. Sullivan....	John E. McClure..	P. W. Seibert.	G. Norwood	S.S. Rooker
1840.	Mathew Little...	S. Goldsberry...	Jacob Cox............	P. W. Seibert.	G. Norwood	A.A.Louden
1841.	M. Little..........	S. Goldsberry...	Jacob Cox............	A. A. Louden.	G. Norwood	C H Beatri't
1842.	Joshua Black.....	S. Goldsberry...	Jas. R. Nowland...	P. W. Seibert.	T. Rickards	A.A.Louden
1843.	Joshua Black ...	S. Goldsberry...	Jas. R. Nowland...	A. A. Louden..	T. Rickards	S.S. Rooker.
1844.	Wm. Montague.	S. Goldsberry...	Jas. R. Nowland...	A. A. Louden..	H. Griffith.	S.S.Rooker.
1845.	Wm. Montague.	S. Goldsberry...	Jas. R. Nowland...	A. A. Louden..	H. Griffith.	Wm. C. Van Blaricum.
1846.	Wm. Montague.	S. Goldsberry...	A. W. Harrison....	A. A. Louden..	C. W. Cady.	Wm. C. Van Blaricum.

NOTE. The first incorporation in September, 1832, was by vote of the people under the general law, the town being divided into five wards, and the councilmen chosen by general vote. The Assembly incorporated the place in 1836, making five wards, the trustees to be elected by general vote. On the 17th of February, 1838, the town was reincorporated and the trustees made councilmen, to be chosen by the voters of the several wards, with a president by the general vote. The wards were increased to six in number.

(3)

TOWN CORPORATION OFFICERS FROM 1832 TO 1847.

The following persons were the Corporation Officers, as far as can now be ascertained, from 1832 to 1847, when the City Government was organized. The records of the old Corporation up to 1839 were all destroyed by fire in the year 1851, and the list has been culled from the public prints and other sources.

Year.	Pres't of Council.	Clerk.	Marshal.	Collector.	Treasurer.	Assessor.	Engineer.	Clk. of Markets.	Supervisor of Sts.
1832.	Sam'l Henderson	I. P. Griffith	Samuel Jenison	Samuel Jenison		Glidden True			F. T. Luse
1833.	Sam'l Henderson	I. P. Griffith	Samuel Jenison	Samuel Jenison		Geo. Lockerbie			F. T. Luse. (?)
1834.	Alex. F. Morrison	Jas. Morrison	John C. Busle	John C. Busle		Geo. Lockerbie			F. T. Luse. (?)
1835.	N. B. Palmer	Joshua Soule	R'd D. Mattingly	R'd D. Mattingly	Thos. H. Sharpe	Geo. Lockerbie			F. T. Luse
1836.	Geo. Lockerbie	Joshua Soule	Wm. Campbell	Wm. Campbell	Thos. H. Sharpe	John Elder	Wm. Sullivan	J. Wornnagen	Wm. Ballenger.
1837.	Joshua Soule	Hugh O'Neal	Wm. Smith	Wm. Smith	Thos. H. Sharpe		Wm. Sullivan	J. Wornnagen	Thos. Lupton (?)
1838.	Jas. Morrison	J. Soule	Wm. Campbell.(?)	W. Campbell	Thos. H. Sharpe	A. G. Willard	Luke Munsell	J. Wornnagen / W. Campbell	Thos. Lupton.
1839.	N. B. Palmer	Hervey Brown	Jas.VanBlaricum	Jas.VanBlaricum	Chas. B. Davis	A. G. Willard	R. B. Hanna / Luke Munsell	J. Wornnagen	J. Van Blaricum
1840.	Henry P. Coburn	Hervey Brown	J. Van Blaricum	J. Van Blaricum	Humph. Griffith	Henry Bradley	Luke Munsell	J. Wornnagen	J. Van Blaricum
1841.	Wm. Sullivan* / D. V. Culley	Hervey Brown	J. Van Blaricum	J. Van Blaricum	Chas. B. Davis	Thos. Donnellan	James Wood	J. Wornnagen	J. Van Blaricum
1842.	David V. Culley	Hervey Brown	Rob't C. Allison	Rob't C. Allison.	C. B. Davis	Jas. H. Kennedy	James Wood	J. Wornnagen	Rob't C. Allison.
1843.	David V. Culley	Wm. J. Wingate	Benjamin Roan	Benjamin Roan.	C. B. Davis.	Thos. Donnellan.	Luke Munsell	J. Wornnagen	Thos.M.Weaver
1844.	Laz. B. Wilson	Wm. L. Wingate	J. Van Blaricum	Henry Ohr.	John L. Welshans	Thos. Donnellan.	James Wood	J. Wornnagen	
1845.	Joseph A. Levy	James G. Jordan	N. N. Norwood.	Henry Ohr.	John L. Welshans	Thos. Donnellan.	James Wood	J. Wornnagen, F.	Wm. Wilkinson
1846.	Joseph A. Levy	James G. Jordan	Jacob B. Fitler.	Henry?Ohr.	George Norwood.	John Coen	James Wood	Jacob Miller, W. / Jacob B. Fitler, E / Jacob Miller, W	Jacob B. Fitler.

*Wm. Sullivan resigned November 12th, and D. V. Culley was elected by the Council.

NOTE.—In addition to the above-named officers, James Morrison was the Corporation Attorney in 1834 and 1837; Hugh O'Neal in 1833, and John L. Ketcham in 1846. John F. Ramsey was Weighmaster in 1836, and Adam Haugh from 1840 to 1846 inclusive. John Musgrove was Sexton in 1843, '45 and '46, and John O'Connor in 1844. David Cox was Messenger of the Marion Fire Company from 1843 to 1846 inclusive, and Jacob B. Fitler of the Good Intent in 1845-6. Thomas M. Smith was elected Chief Fire Engineer for 1846, the office being created that year.

1833. William Henry Harrison, the former Governor of the Territory, visited the town for the first time January 11th. He was received by the Assembly and tendered a public dinner at Washington Hall, January 17th, at which he made a Union speech. He visited the town again January 13th, 1835.

The first homicide here occurred on the 8th of May, Michael Van Blaricum drowning William McPherson by upsetting a boat in the river. The murder created great excitement at the time. He was tried and sent to the penitentiary in October, 1834. The first wholesale grocery was opened in June by Beard & Patterson.

The cholera had been prevailing elsewhere this year, and on the 18th of June one or two cases of supposed cholera—not fatal—occurred here. The churches assigned and kept the 26th as a special fast day. No other cases happened then, but in July it became very fatal at Salem, Indiana, and the trustees of the town called a meeting on the 17th at three court house. One thousand dollars were subscribed by the citizens, resolutions passed, a board of health consisting of five physicians and five citizens appointed, visiting committees were assigned to each ward, sanitary measures were adopted and medicines procured. The trustees were also requested to open a hospital. The Governor's Circle was accordingly secured for the purpose, and Dr. John E. McClure assigned as physician. There were no cases here however, and the building was not used.

The first circus, (combined with a menagerie, Brown & Bailey's,) exhibited at Henderson's tavern August 13th and 14th. A new graveyard was laid out east of the old one, and lots sold in October by Isaac Coe. The great meteor shower on the 13th of November, from 2 A. M. to daylight, was witnessed with awe by the people, many of whom thought the end of the world was close at hand and they unprepared for the event.

1834. The State Bank of Indiana was chartered January 28th, 1834, for twenty-five years, with a capital of $1,600,000 in fifty dollar shares, one-half of the stock to be held by the State. Its charter was amended with its consent in several particulars at subsequent dates. Samuel Merrill was elected president by the Legislature, with Calvin Fletcher, Seton W. Norris, R. Morrison and T. H. Scott State directors. J. M. Ray was chosen cashier, a position he held till the charter expired. The bank was organized February 13th, with ten branches, (ultimately increased to sixteen,) and books opened for stock subscriptions for thirty days from the 7th of April. Samuel

Merrill served as president till 1840, James Morrison till 1850, Ebenezer Dumont till 1855, H. McCullough till 1859. Additional time was given to wind up the business. The bank was first located in the Governor's Circle in 1834, then on Washington street till 1840, when the banking house on Illinois street and Kentucky avenue being completed, it was removed to and remained there till 1859, being succeeded in its occupancy by the Bank of the State. The old State Bank was a safe and very lucrative enterprize for its stockholders, and made good and steady dividends. All the branches suspended specie payments under its direction May 18th, 1837, during the financial panic and bank run of that period, and did not resume payment till June 15th, 1842, when directed to do so by act of the General Assembly.

The Branch of the State Bank at this point was organized November 11th, 1834, with Harvey Bates, president, B. F. Morris, cashier. These officers served for two or three years, and were succeeded by Calvin Fletcher as president and Thos. H. Sharpe cashier, who served till the charter expired. The State and Branch Banks began business November 20th, 1834. The Branch banking house, on Pennsylvania street and Virginia avenue, was built in 1839, and occupied from 1840 to 1859, when it was sold for nearly $16,000 to the Sinking Fund, and by the Fund in 1867 for $30,000 to the Indianapolis Insurance Company, who now occupy it. For many years the rule of the bank was to loan but $200 to any one person, unless a greater sum was needed for stock or grain enterprizes, which were made special exceptions.

The old State Bank charter being about to expire, the General Assembly, on the 3d of March, 1855, chartered "The Bank of the State of Indiana," with seventeen branches, (three additional branches being afterward authorized,) and it was organized November 1st, 1855, Hugh McCullough being elected president, and J. M. Ray cashier, with seventeen directors—one from each Branch. It began business January 2d, 1857, with a capital of $1,836,000, and reported $132,216 profits over all expenses in the first six months. It continued an extremely lucrative business, rapidly extending its capital, until after the adoption of the National Bank system and the taxation of free and State bank paper. In January, 1865, the Assembly authorized it to reduce its capital, redeem its stock, distribute surplus funds, &c., to stockholders, and close up its branches and business, and at present it is about completed, the branches having nearly all been merged in National Banks. It was located in the building of the old

State Bank on Illinois street and Kentucky avenue, which was sold in May, 1868, to the Franklin Life Insurance Company, and now occupied by that corporation. Hugh McCullough, George W. Rathbone and J. M. Ray have been the presidents, J. M. Ray and Joseph A. Moore cashiers of the institution.

The Branch at this point of the Bank of the State was organized July 25th, 1855, with a capital of $100,000, afterward increased to over $200,000, W. H. Talbott being elected president. The stock was afterward sold at an advance to other parties, and the bank began business in January, 1857, at the north-west corner of Washington and Illinois streets, with George Tousey, president, C. S. Stevenson, cashier. Stevenson resigned to enter the pay department in June, 1861, and D. E. Snyder was cashier till November, 1866, being succeeded by D. M. Taylor, present cashier. Oliver Tousey was elected president in June, 1866, succeeding George Tousey, who had resigned to become president of the Indiana National Bank. The bank was removed in March, 1860, to the corner room of Yohn's block, where it remained till 1867, when it was removed to the back room in the same building and its affairs wound up.

A general bank law was adopted by the Assembly in May, 1852, and shortly afterward applications were filed by different parties for a number of banks at this point, some of which were afterward organized under other names, and others were never completed. Among these applications were the City Bank, nominal capital $500,000, in December, 1852, A. Defrees, proprietor ; Bank of Indianapolis, J. Woolley & Co., proprietors, capital $400,000, January, 1853; State Bank of Indiana, $500,000, January, 1853 ; Agricultural Bank, $200,000, February, 1853 ; Traders' Bank, Woolley & Wilson proprietors, $300,000, May, 1853.

The banks actually organized here under the law were the Bank of the Capitol, J. Woolley & Co., proprietors, nominal capital $400,000, W. S. Pierce and J. H. Bradley successive presidents, J. Woolley, cashier. It began business in 1853 in a little frame house where Blackford's block now stands, then removed to Dunlop's building, then lately built on North Meridian street, and then to No. 6 East Washington street, which had just been finished. The concern carried more sail than ballast, and capsized September 15th, 1857, in the financial storm of that date, with liabilities to over $80,000, nominal assets $56,000.

The Farmers' and Mechanics' Bank, Allen May and G. Lee successive presidents, William F. May and O. Williams successive cashiers, began business February, 1854,

in the basement of Masonic Hall. The cashier, W. F. May, absconded in May, 1855, taking about $10,000 with him, eripnow pling the bank so badly that it collapsed shortly afterward.

The Central Bank, Ozias Bowen and J. D. Defrees, successive presidents, Sidney Moore and W. H. McDonald, successive cashiers, with a nominal capital of $500,000, began business in July, 1855, at No. 23 West Washington street. The Traders' Bank, Woolley & Wilson, proprietors, began in 1854 at the office of Ellis & Spann on Illinois street ; and the Metropolitan Bank, A. F. Morrisrn & Co., proprietors, J. D. Dunn, president, Jerry Skeen, cashier, in 1855 in Blake's Commercial Row, but neither of them did much business, and suspended payment soon after getting their notes in circulation, and were shortly after closed up by their owners or by the Auditor of State. The free bank system entailed great loss on the community from the depreciation of the circulation, the owners finding it much more profitable to buy in at a heavy discount than to redeem it or attempt to do a legitimate business.

The State and free bank systems have been superceded in the last five years by the National banking system. The First National Bank was organized August 1st, 1863, with $150,000 capital, under the National law. W. H. English was president, and W. R. Nofsinger, cashier. John C. New was chosen cashier January 11th, 1865. The bank was reorganized September 22d, 1864, and the capital increased to $500,000.— There are at present sixty stockholders. The bank was first located just north of Odd Fellows Hall, then in the north room of the hall, and removed thence October 1st, 1865, to the corner room of Blackford's block. It has been a government depository from its origin, and has done a very extended and lucrative business. Its circulation during the first quarter of 1868 was $450,000, deposits $700,000, discounts $600,000, surplus $75,000, profit and loss $125,000 ; exchange sales in 1867, $4,620,000.

The Indianapolis National Bank was organized December 15th, 1864, with $500,000 capital, Theodore P. Haughey being elected president, and Ingram Fletcher, cashier. He resigned in January, 1866, being succeeded by A. F. Williams, present cashier. The bank rented the corner room of Odd Fellows Hall, where it has since been located. It has been a government depository from its origin, and has done a large and lucrative business. The circulation during the first quarter of 1868 was $450,000, surplus fund $78,000, deposits $432,900, discounts $416,000 ; commercial exchange sales in 1867, $3,606,650.

The Indiana National Bank was organized, with $250,000 capital, March 14th, 1865, Oliver Tousey being elected president, David M. Taylor, cashier. The capital was increased June 6th, 1865, to $400,000, and on the 27th of July George Tousey was elected president, D. E. Snyder, cashier. D. M. Taylor was chosen cashier November 26th, 1866. The bank was opened at 19 North Meridian street in July, 1865, but the location being an unfavorable one, it was removed November 26th, 1866, to the corner room of Yohn's block, the Branch of the Bank of the State removing to the back room, and its business being transferred to the Indiana National Bank. The bank is a government depository, and since its removal to the present location has rapidly increased in business. The circulation during June, 1868, was $350,000, deposits $354,235, discounts $292,800 ; exchange sales in 1867, $2,787,370.

The Merchants' National Bank was organized January 17th, 1865, with $100,000 capital, Henry Schnull, president, V. T. Mulott, cashier, and began business at 23 North Meridian street, but finding that location unfavorable it was removed in January, 1867, to 48 East Washington street, where it has since been located, and has done much more business. John S. Newman became president September 1st, 1866, The circulation for the first quarter of 1868 was $90,000, discounts $132,000, surplus funds $6,000, profit and loss $13,500 ; exchange sales for 1867-8, $950,000. The bank has nine stockholders.

The Citizens' National Bank was organized November 28th, 1864, with $200,000 capital, Isaiah Mansur, president, Asa G. Pettibone, cashier, and began business shortly after at No. 3 West Washington street. It was consolidated December 1st, 1865, with the Fourth National Bank, Isaiah Mansur being elected president, and Joseph R. Haugh, assistant cashier of the combined corporation, which retained the name of Citizens' National Bank, and the capital increased to $300,000. It was removed to No. 2 East Washington street November 20th, 1866. Joseph R. Haugh was elected cashier in January, 1866. Circulation June, 1868, $270,000, deposits $206,000, discounts $338,- 000, profit and loss $24,000, surplus fund $35,000 ; exchange sales in 1867, $1,067,- 000.

The Fourth National Bank was organized January 23d, 1865, with a capital of $100,000, Timothy R. Fletcher, president, Joseph R. Haugh, cashier, and began business at No. 11 North Meridian street. It was merged and consolidated in December, 1865, with the Citizens' National Bank, as above stated, losing its separate existence.

It is difficult to give with certainty the history of the different private banking enterprises of the city, some of which now vie in business and importance with the public organizations. So far as is known, the first private banking enterprise (though an incorporated company its banking privileges were at first taken advantage of only by the secretary, Mr. Gregg,) was the Indianapolis Insurance Company, chartered February 8th, 1836, with $200,000 capital, and with insurance and favorable banking powers. It began operations in April, and for some years did considerable business in insurance and banking, but gradually declined, and suspended active operations about 1840. It was reorganized by Defrees, Morris and others in 1852 or 3, and continued till 1858 or 9, when it again suspended. In 1865 the stock was purchased, a new company organized, business resumed, and the capital increased to $500,000. The old Branch Bank building was bought in 1867. It now does an insurance and banking business. Its discounts in the bank department for the first quarter of 1868 were $99,220, deposits $159,647 ; exchange sales for fractional quarter in 1868, $67,884 ; average amount of discounted paper held during fractional quarter of 1868, $216,519.

John Wood, exchange broker and banker, began business in 1838 and continued till September, 1841, when he failed, causing considerable loss to the community from the shinplaster notes which he had issued, together with those of other equally responsible parties, that he had circulated. He soon after left this section.

E. S. Alvord & Co. did a banking business from January, 1839, to 1843, but nothing can now be stated as to its extent or character.

S. A. Fletcher, Sen., opened an exchange office in 1839 in a one-story frame shed next to Wolfram & Rommel's saddle shop, at the present No. 8 East Washington street, continuing there till 1850, when he moved to the room now occupied by Raschig's cigar store, and from thence in December, 1852, to the present bank, 30 East Washington street, then just built. Timothy R. Fletcher was a partner from 1839 to 1858, when he retired. On the 1st of June, 1864, S. A. Fletcher, Jr., and F. M. Churchman, became partners, S. A. Fletcher, Sen., retiring from the firm. On the 1st of January, 1868, F. M. Churchman and S. A. Fletcher, Jr., dissolved, S. A. Fletcher, Jr., retiring from, and S. A. Fletcher, Sen., re-entering the firm. The bank has done a very lucrative business since its origin, increasing its capital from $3,000 in 1839 to $200,000 in 1868, and is now the leading private bank, doing the heaviest banking business in the city. The deposits for the first quarter of 1868 were $635,000, discounts $560,000 ; exchange sales in 1867, $13,228,000.

Before the expiration of the old State Bank charter, Calvin Fletcher, Sen., and Thomas H. Sharpe, who had long been the president and cashier of the Branch at this point, started the Indianapols Branch Banking Company on the 1st of January, 1857, at the south-west corner of Washington and Pennsylvania streets, where the bank has ever since been located. As the capital of the old Branch was diminished and its business closed, the capital of the Banking Company was increased, and it has done a large and lucrative business, second only if not equal to S. A. Fletcher & Co. Calvin Fletcher, Sen., died May 26th, 1866, and his interest in the bank descended to his sons, Ingram and Albert Fletcher. The capital of the bank is $200,000. The discounts for the first quarter of 1868 were $500,000, deposits $500,000 ; exchange sales in 1867, $3,147,280.

Alfred and John C. S. Harrison started an exchange office in May, 1854, in the second-story room of the Johnson building, remaining there till August, 1855, when the adjoining bank building was completed and the bank removed there, where it has since remained. No changes have occurred in its ownership since its origin. S. W. Watson is cashier. For the first quarter of 1868 the capital was $100,000, discounts $188,000, deposits $227,347 ; exchange sales in 1867, $2,140,000.

The Indiana Banking Company, with seven partners, F. A. W. Davis, president, W. W. Woollen, cashier, was organized March 1st, 1865, with a capital of $100,000, and began business in Vance's building, corner Washington street and Virginia avenue, March 14th, 1865, where the bank remained till May 16th, 1867, when removed to 28 East Washington street. No changes in organization or amount of capital have since been made. The discounts for the first quarter of 1868 were $394,540, deposits $380,274 ; exchange sales in 1867, $3,000,000.

J. B. Ritzinger opened a savings bank the 26th of March, 1868, at 38 East Washington street, J. B. Ritzinger, proprietor, A. W. Ritzinger, cashier ; capital $50,000.

Dunlevy, Haire & Co., brokers, began business in Blake's Commercial Row in February, 1856, and continued here for a year or two. They were agents of the Cincinnati banks, and bankers, to run our State and free banks for gold, and within three months afterward had returned $2,000,000 currency for redemption. This action on their part made them and their principals at Cincinnati very unpopular, and produced the commercial convention of 1856.

But few failures of banks or bankers have occurred here, the following list comprising about all that have happened :

John Wood's bank, established in 1839, failed in 1841, as before stated.

In the spring of 1852 John Woolley & Co. began a private bank in a one-story frame, where No. 4 Blackford's block is now, remaining there till the establishment was merged in the Bank of the Capitol in May, 1853, and moved to Dunlop's building, and subsequently to No. 8 East Washington street. The failure of that bank has already been mentioned. It produced a run on the other banks, resulting two days after in the failure of the savings bank.

William Robson, A. L. Voorhees and others started a savings bank in 1854 in the corner room of Odd Fellows Hall, Robson and Voorhees being successively the presidents, and Joseph R. Robinson cashier. Robinson became proprietor in 1857, and in the panic following the failure of the Bank of the Capitol was compelled to suspend payment September 17th, 1857, owing his depositors $15,000. The most if not all of this was paid by the receiver in April, 1858.

In the fall of 1862 Kilby Ferguson started the Merchants' Bank at No. 2 North Pennsylvania street, K. Ferguson, proprietor, G. R. Gosney, cashier, and continued business there till August, 1863, when by reason of unfortunate gold speculations he was compelled to suspend payment. The liabilities have lately been settled.

In the spring of 1856 G. S. Hamer started an exchange office in the basement of the American House, where shaving was closely done and shinplaster notes circulated, but the enterprising financier was arrested in November for passing counterfeit money, and shortly after disappeared.

No effort has hitherto been made to ascertain the extent of the dry goods and grocery trade here. The exchange sales by the banks in 1867, amounting to $34,614,180, may give an approximate measurement for that year, but a large additional sum should be added for currency transmitted by express. It may be safe to estimate this sum at $2,884,515, one-twelfth of the total, and by adding this we get $37,498,695 as the approximate importations of groceries and dry goods in 1867, and the trade has rapidly increased in 1868.

A number of railways were chartered and re-chartered in 1833–4–5, and efforts made to build them. Government surveyors ran the lines from Lawrenceburgh, Madison and Lafayette to this point, and from Columbus to Jeffersonville, in August, 1835. The first railroad meeting ever held here was on March 24th, 1834, to secure subscriptions on the Lawrenceburgh line, from individuals and from the county commissioners.

The first meeting of the Whig party by that name, was held at the court house May 17th, Robert Brenton, president. John Hobart, Hiram Brown, Wm. Quarles, and John H. Scott were the speakers.

A meeting was held at the court house June 9th to devise means for the suppression of gambling. Resolutions were adopted, and prosecutions threatened unless the gamblers left. Meetings of a similar character were held in subsequent years, and an association formed to suppress the vice. Another raid was made in August, 1835, on the gamblers.

The Indianapolis Brewery, the first one in the place, was started this year near the canal, on Maryland street, by Wernwag. A ropewalk was started on Market street, east of the market house.

The pension agency was removed here from Corydon in January.

1835. The State House being nearly completed, the Assembly, February 7th, directed the State treasurer to insure it, and to buy twenty fire-buckets, and ladders to reach the roof, and if the citizens subscribed half the cost of an engine, to subscribe the balance for the State. A citizens' meeting was held on February 12th. The old fire-bucket company reorganized as the Marion Fire and Hose and Protection Company. The trustees were called on by resolution to subscribe the money for the engine, and levy a fire and public well tax. Caleb Scudder was chosen captain of the company. The trustees levied the tax, and subscriptions were also made by individuals; the State furnished her quota, and in the summer of 1835 the old Marion, a box, hand-brake engine, was bought in Philadelphia for about $1,800, and duly received here in September. A one-story frame house was first built for it by the State in 1836, but on the 6th of February, 1837, a two-story frame house was ordered to be built on the north side of the Circle, and was erected during the summer. It was occupied as an engine house and council chamber till the summer of 1851, when it was burned and the records of the town were destroyed with the house. On the 20th of February, 1838, the Marion Fire Company was incorporated. In the spring of 1840, the Good Intent, a box, hand-brake engine, was bought in Philadelphia, and used for a time by the Marion company with the old Marion, but in 1841 the company was divided, and the Independent Relief Company was formed and took the Good Intent. After the burning of the Marion house on the circle, a brick house was built in 1855-6, at the corner of Massachusetts avenue and New York street, and the Marion was located there.

The company disbanded in October, 1859, during the trouble preceding the introduction of the paid department, but re-entered the service in November, and was finally disbanded February, 1860. The old engine was used by the company till July, 1858, when a new, powerful side hand-brake engine was purchased by the council and givsen to the company. This machine was sold in April, 1860, to the town of Peru for $2,130.

The Independent Relief Fire and Hose Company was formed and incorporated with peculiar privileges in 1841, taking the Good Intent and using it till November, 1849, when it was given to the Western Liberties Company and a row-boat engine was bought by subscription and money realized from fairs, and used till August, 1858. The company became dissatisfied with it, and bought (aided by the city,) a powerful hand-brake engine at that time, which they used till they disbanded in November, 1859. Difficulty ensued between the company and the city authorities as to the ownership of the engines and other property, but in February, 1860, they surrendered everything to the city except the old row-boat engine, which was broken up and the materials sold in April, 1860, and the company finally dissolved. Their engine house during the greater portion of their existence was in Hubbard's block, on Meridian street.

The Western Liberties Company was formed in November, 1849, taking the old Good Intent, and occupying an old frame house at the fork of Washington street and the National road, near the race, using a large iron triangle for a bell, but they moved in 1857 to the house now used by the steam engine No. 1, west of the canal. In April, 1857, a new hand-brake engine, the Indiana, was bought for them, and used till November, 1859, when the company was disbanded, and the steam engine No. 1 afterward stationed in their house. The Indiana was afterward sold.

The Invincibles, a company mostly composed of Germans, was formed in May, 1852, in the first ward, and the Victory, a small hand-brake engine, procured shortly afterward, and used by them till March, 1857, when the Conqueror, a fine hand-brake engine, was bought and used by them till August, 1859, when the company disbanded and surrendered its property to the city. The house of this company, built in 1854-5, just north of Washington on New Jersey street, is now occupied by the hook and ladder company. The company was large, prompt and effective, and during its existence made several trips to other cities. After the new engine was bought the Victory was used by a company of boys. After the first paid department was organized, the Invincible company was re-organized as a part of it, and the Conqueror continued in use till the summer of 1860, when the company was finally disbanded, and the engine sold shortly after to the town of Ft. Wayne.

The Union Company, No. 5, was organized in 1855, and a house built on South street for it in 1856, and in April of that year the "Spirit of 7 & 6," a Jeffers hand-brake engine was bought and used by the company till November, 1859, when the company was disbanded and surrendered its apparatus to the city. Some effort was afterward made to re-organize the company under the paid department, but without success. The engine was sold at $600 in October, 1860, as part pay for the steam engine No. 3, which was subsequently stationed in the Union house.

The Rover Fire Company was formed in the third and fourth wards in March, 1858. A house was secured for them, one of the old engines assigned to them, and steps taken to purchase an engine, but before anything was done the approaching change of system became evident, and the company was disbanded in June, 1859, and the house sold in 1860. Hose companies were simultaneously formed for each of the foregoing fire companies, and the necessary hose, reels and other apparatus furnished to them.

A hook and ladder company was formed in 1843, as a part of the old volunteer department, and the necessary wagon, ladders, ropes, hooks, axes and buckets procured. The company continued its organization till disbanded with the rest of the department November 14th, 1859, but was re-organized as a part of the paid department, and still continues in service, occupying the old Invincible house on North New Jersey street.

The Young America Hook and Ladder Company was formed in May, 1858, and got their wagon and apparatus in June, remaining in service till disbanded in November, 1859. In December, 1849, a number of boys formed the "O K Bucket Company," and procured a wagon and the old ladders and leather fire-buckets which belonged to the State and private citizens, and to the Indianapolis Fire Company in the earliest organization of the department. The council subsequently gave them a new wagon and buckets, and provided a house for them. They were effective—generally getting the first water on fires—until they disbanded in 1854. The company was revived in 1855, but disbanded finally in 1856, the boys taking the Victory formerly used by the Invincibles.

Under the volunteer system each company was independent, having its president, sec-

retary and messenger for ordinary business, and its chief and assistant engine directors, pipemen, hosemen and brakemen for serva ice. The corporate authorities exercised little control over the firemen until after the city charter in 1847, and not much then till 1853, when the office of chief fire engineer was created and rules prescribed for the government of the department. Joseph Little was chosen first chief May 6th, 1853. His successors since that date have been Jacob B. Fitler, elected 1854; Chas.W. Purcell, 1855; Andrew Wallace, 1856; Joseph W. Davis, 1858; John E. Foudray, 1859; and under the paid department, Joseph W. Davis, 1859; Charles Richmann, 1863; Geo. W. Buchanan, 1867; Charles Richmann, May, 1868.

The volunteer system worked well till 1857. The rivalry between the companies produced good results; but the organization of the fire association in 1856, while rendering the department more efficient, also made it a political machine and increased the demands on the treasury. Conflicts and jealousies gradually arose between the companies, and on the choice of J. W. Davis as chief engineer in May, 1858, disputes arose as to the fairness of his election and management. The dissension impaired the effieiency of the organization, and the trouble was not entirely healed the next year under Foudray. It broke out afresh in August, 1859, on the proposition to substitute a paid department, which was earnestly advocated by Davis. The Invincibles disbanded in August, 1859, the Marions and Westerns in October, the Relief, Rover and Union in November, and the city was left for a short time without a fire organization. The Marions re-entered the service in November, but finally disbanded in February, 1860. The volunteer department in the spring of 1859 included six engine and six hose companies, with about four hundred and eighty men; two hook and ladder companies, with about one hundred men; one chief and two assistant engineers; seven houses, and about seven thousand feet of hose.

It was evident that a change would have to be made in consequence of the dissension arising over the election of engineer in May, 1858, and on account of the rapidly-increasing expense of the system. Fire alarms were very frequent, and the companies were charged with their origin. The council, in August, 1859, declared it inexpedient to re-organize the volunteer department. The fire committee reported, September 4th, in favor of a paid system, and the purchase of a third-class steam engine, and selling the old Relief and Good Intent engines. A Latta steam engine was exhibited here September 23d–4th at the county fair, and tried

stern before the com-
ned engine was also
:d October 15th and
t was determined to
,arned machines, and
1860, it was received
Vestern engine house.
mber, 1859, the old
vas disbanded by or-
:partment, consisting
hand engines, and a
iany, was authorized,
e chief engineer at a
limann and W. Sher-
ins of the two hand
, W. Darnell of the
iany, and Frank Gla-
iteamer. Some diffi-
in forming the hand
of the general oppo-
gineer, but the force
January, 1860. The
to sell the old and
ie Marion engine was
Peru; the Union in
Falls Company; the
y, 1861, and the re-
riod, the last one be-
t year.
third-class Latta en-
ring here in October,
he old Marion house.
was exhibited at the
)ctober 22d before a
uncil in competition
, the result being that
l it at $3,500, giving
in part pay, and sta-
house on South street.
ppointed engineer of
rtis of the No. 2, and
No. 3. Hosemen and
pointed, and but few
en made in the force.
l of the three engines,
rchased an additional
, No. 4, which was re-
ice in December, and
: for repairs. These
he engine returned in
hole cost of the new
s on the old one being
Latta engine was then
for repairs, and the
: repaired in its turn.
w in an efficient state.
reels and other appar-
ided by the council.
:he organization of the
central alarm existed,
1863 an alarm tower
in the rear of Glenns'
by wires and pulleys
station on the tower of

the building. Two watchmen have since
been employed, giving the locality of the
fire by striking the number of the ward. In
February, 1868, a fire-alarm telegraph was
adopted, and the wires, boxes and fixtures
completed and put in operation by the end
of April, at a cost of about $6,000.

During the existence of the first bucket
fire company the dependence for water was
wholly on private wells. After the Marion
and Good Intent engines were bought a few
large public wells were dug in the central
part of town. The first cisterns (two in
number, holding three hundred barrels
each,) were built by the trustee government
in the spring of 1840, but it was not till October, 1852, when a cistern tax was ordered
by special election, that any number of cisterns were built. Sixteen were constructed
by the close of 1853, and since that date fifty
two, ranging from three hundred to eighteen
hundred barrels, have been built in various
quarters of the city, and though the supply
is still inadequate, the protection is ample
against all ordinary fires. In the spring of
1868 $300 were appropriated to bore an ar-
tesian well to test the project for supplying
cisterns from underneath the surface. At
present they are filled from wells, and the
creek and canal by the engines, or by a
steam pump, built for the purpose in 1864,
at a cost of about $1,000.

Though so largely built of wood, this
city has been remarkably fortunate in regard to fires. The streets are so wide, and
the department has been so prompt, that
fires rarely go beyond the houses in which
they originate. As the present buildings
are replaced by brick, stone or iron structures, with fire-proof walls and roofs, the
immunity from destructive conflagrations
will be still greater. The ordinary rates of
insurance are too high for this city, and our
people are now helping to insure property
in cities like Chicago, where more loss is
frequently suffered in a single fire than oc-
curs here in a year.

The State Board of Agriculture was chartered in February, 1835, Jas. Blake, Larkin
Simms, John Owen and M. M. Henkle, directors; James Blake, president, M. M.
Henkle, secretary. Premiums were offered
April 28th for essays on specified subjects,
and rules adopted for organizing county societies. The first State agricultural convention met December 14th, 1835, in Representatives' Hall, and several annual meetings
were afterwards held, but the enterprise
died in a few years. Meetings were held at
the court house June 6th and 27th, to form
a county agricultural society under the
State Board rules. N. B. Palmer was president, D. Maguire, secretary. Subscriptions
were made for premiums, and the Board of

Justices also appropriated fifty dollars. The first fair was held October 30-1 in the court house yard. One hundred and eighty-four dollars were awarded in premiums. Much interest was manifested. Four hundred dollars were subscribed for the next fair. Annual fairs were held by the society for two or three years.

In the fall the papers said much improvement was going on. Property had doubled in value in two years, and business lots on Washington street were selling at fifty, sixty-two and seventy-five dollars per front foot.

The Benevolent Society was formed November, 1835, with a president, secretary, treasurer, depository and visitors, and has been active and efficient to the present date. Its system has always been the same, and prevents street begging. Funds and clothing are collected in specified districts in the fall by visitors, who deposit the same with the officers, and who also ascertain and report all cases needing aid. Written orders for money, clothes or provisions are given to applicants, and transient cases are cared for by a special committee. The society has been sustained by private contributions, the city and township authorities furnishing wood only when needed. Mr. James Blake has been the president for many years, and much of the good effected by the enterprize has been due to his zeal and energy.

The Young Men's Literary Society, designed for debate, composition and general mental improvement, was formed in 1835, and continued its meetings for twelve or fifteen years. It was incorporated in April, 1847, under the general law, collected a considerable library, and from 1843 to 1848 gave each winter a series of lectures by its members, and others from abroad. It was the successor here of the Indianapolis Athenum, and the precursor of the lecture societies of the present day.

The winter of 1834-5 had been cold and protracted. The spring was backward. More rain fell in May and June than in any season before for ten years, and at Fort Wayne ten inches of water fell in two hours, the storm being limited to a small space. This statement was made by Jesse L. Williams, State engineer on the Wabash canal. There was a hard frost on the morning of July 1st, followed by a hot and dry season, closing on the night of August 18th in a tornado of wind and rain, unroofing houses, destroying fences, timber and crops, and killing horses, cattle and hogs. The following winter lasted till April.

1836. The want of natural channels for trade had prompted many improvement schemes in past years, and at an early day

the Legislature had given $100,000 for opening roads, had often asked aid to improve the rivers, and had chartered many railways. From various causes these expenditures and efforts had effected little. With increasing resources the demand for greater facilities increased. The National road gave an impetus to other projects of more doubtful utility. A pressure from all sides was brought to bear on the Assembly, and on the 26th of January, 1836, the internal improvement bill was passed. The State not only undertook several great works, but extended aid to others under private companies. The act was greeted with rejoicing. Bonfires and illuminations marked the spread of the news. Our citizens were especially elated, for several of the works terminated or crossed at this point, and more than one outlet would exist to the world. A general illumination took place here on the night of January 16th, after the passage of the bill had become a certainty. The bill at once improved the prospects of the town. Property rose in price rapidly, new houses were built, the settled limits extended westward, mechanics were busy, merchants sold large stocks, money was plenty, and every one prosperous. This continued nearly three years, when funds gave out, public works stopped, trade ceased, property declined, laborers went elsewhere, and ruin stared every one in the face. The hard times of 1839-42 were sorely felt. The leading business men were most involved, and for years their lives were struggles to save something from the wreck. The forbearance of creditors alone saved them from utter poverty. The bankrupt act of 1841 afforded relief to the whole country, easing the general distress, and enabling many to get another start. From this time till 1847 the town remained a dull country village, with so unfavorable an experience of internal improvements that our capitalists subsequently kept out of them or aided them but little.

Under the internal improvement system the central canal, from the Wabash to Evansville, together with railroads from various points, had been intended to centre here. All were abandoned in 1839, after much work had been done. The Madison railroad had been completed nearly to Vernon and graded to Columbus. It was operated by the State till 1843, then surrendered to a company, and finally finished in October, 1847. Before competing lines reduced its traffic it made more money than any road in the country. The State was cheated out of her interest in the road, and the road itself, after losing business and importance, was finally bought and operated by the Jeffersonville line.

The canal was nearly done when abandoned; $1,600,000 had been expended, and a comparatively small sum would have completed it from Noblesville to Martinsville. It was begun in October, 1836, work being prosecuted simultaneously along its line by gangs of Irishmen, whose disputes with spade and shillelah gave animation to their encampments. A great debate of this kind occurred in 1838 near town, between the Corkonians and fardowners, several hundred disputants being engaged, and the discussion occupying the greater part of the day. The sections to Noblesville and Martinsville were nearly ready, and that to Broad Ripple was finished late in November, 1838, and opened for use June 27th, 1839, with an excursion by boats to Broad Ripple in July. Considerable preparations were made for traffic on it. Several freight and passenger boats were built, and flour, timber, grain, &c., were brought from Broad Ripple and above. The mill sites here were leased June 11th, 1838, and one woolen, one cotton, two paper, one oil, two grist and two saw mills built shortly afterward. The power proved less than was promised, the canal not having fall enough to cause a free flow of water, but the mills went to work, and with others since built have greatly benefitted the place. The millers were always complaining of seant water and much moss; the people grumbled when the water was drawn off to clean the bed; and the Assembly, wearied by the incessant complaint, January 19th, 1850, ordered the canal to be sold. It was soon after sold to persons who were chartered as a company in February, 1851. In April the company sold to Gould & Jackson, who sold in October, 1851, to "The Central Canal, Hydraulic Waterworks and Manufacturing Company." This company sold to another company in 1859, who now rent out the power. For years after the first sale it was regarded as a nuisance, and propositions to fill it up were seriously considered in the council, both in 1855 and 1858, but having lately been kept in better order the opposition has measurably abated. It was dry for months in 1847, from the breaking of the banks and acqueduct, and in 1866-7 from the breaking of the feeder dam at Broad Ripple. It now furnishes mill power and transportation for wood and logs. The company owning it lately sued for the possession of a part of the military park, on the ground that it passed at the sale as an appurtenance of the canal.

The town having been specially incorporated in February by the Assembly, the new board of trustees was elected under the new act in April, and the officers of the old board settled to April 1st, 1836. The treasurer's report showed $1,610 receipts for the year, and $1,150 of this sum had been expended for the Marion engine and in digging five public wells, and other fire deville. A balance of $124 was turned over to the new government. The new board passed ordinances regulating markets, ordering the streets to be opened, and prohibiting riots, drunkenness, horseracing and indecent language on the streets.

The work on the National road in the last few years had attracted many men of bad character and habits to this point. These, banded together under a leader of great size and strength, were long known as "the chain gang," and kept the town in a half subjugated state. Assaults were often committed, citizens threatened and insulted, and petty outrages perpetrated, until at last a meeting was called March 9th at the court house to take the matter under advisement. Harrod Newland, a revolutionary soldier, was chosen president and made a radical speech against the gang. Resolutions were adopted to abate the nuisance. The citizens resolved to elect trustees and officers who would see the ordinances enforced, and pledged themselves to assist them. The determined stand taken somewhat awed the gang, and they became less bold in their demonstrations. At the camp-meeting in August on the military grounds, the leader made some disturbance and was knocked down and subjugated by Rev. James Havens, the preacher in charge, and shortly afterward was also soundly whipped by Samuel Merrill. These defeats broke his prestige, the gang was demoralized, and most of them left the town or ceased their lawless conduct.

The second homicide here occurred April 27th, Zachariah Collins being killed by Arnold Lashly. The county agricultural society held its second fair at the court house October 7th and 8th. C. Fletcher delivered an address, stating that 1,300,000 bushels of corn had been raised this year on the thirteen hundred farms in the county. Luke Munsell copyrighted a map of the town May 30th, and Wm. Sullivan published a map of the town in October. A great camp meeting was held on the military ground August 25-30, under James Havens and John C. Smith. One hundred and thirty experienced religion. Professor C. P. Bronson [died in New York, April, 1868,] gave the first lecture here on elocution, August 30th. Hiram Devinny began the manufacture of mattresses, cushions and carpets here in October.

The new Washington Hall, a three-story brick hotel, built by a company in 1836-7, on the site of the old frame Washington Hall, at a cost of $30,000, was opened by E.

Browning November 16th, and kept by him till March 15th, 1851. It was then one of the largest and best western hotels, had a high reputation, and was the Whig head-quarters for its entire existence. It was damaged by fire $3,000 in February, 1843, and came near burning up. Several attempts were made to burn it in May and June, 1848. It was sold to F. Wright in March, 1851, was subsequently known as the Wright House, was successively kept by Henry Achey, Robert Browning, Burgess & Townley, W. J. Elliott, Louis Eppinger and others, and was bought in March and remodeled in the summer of 1859 by the Glenns, and is now known as Glenns' block, the lower story being used as business rooms, and the upper by the council, city officers and police, with the fire tower and alarm on the roof. A very brief mention may be given here of the other leading hotels at various dates in the history of the town and city.

John McCormick was the first tavern and boarding-house keeper, beginning in the spring of 1820 on the river bank, in a little cabin with small pens around it as sleeping apartments for his guests. In 1821 Hawkins, Carter and Nowland each opened "taverns,"—Nowland in a cabin on Washington street west of the canal. He shortly after died, and his widow, Elizabeth Nowland, in 1823 opened a boarding-house where Browning's drug store is now, continuing there for many years. Carter's "Rosebush Tavern," a two-story ceiled frame, eighteen by twenty feet, built in 1821-2, at 40 West Washington street, was occupied by him till 1823. It was afterward moved near the canal, and then near the soldiers' home, where it yet stands. Carter in 1823 built a two-story frame tavern opposite the court house, which was burned in 1825. Hawkins' "Eagle Tavern," a double log house, was built in the fall of 1821, where the Sentinel office is now, the logs-being cut from the lot and street. It stood there till 1826 or 7, when it was replaced with a small two-story brick. Bazel Brown took it in 1829, and was succeeded by John Hare, John Cain and others. It was torn down in 1849 and replaced by the Capital House, which was opened by John Cain July 14th, 1850, and subsequently succeeded by D. D. Sloan and others, till March, 1857, when it was occupied by the Sentinel as a printing office. It has since been used as a printing office and bindery, and for business rooms and offices. It was the first four-story house built here. The successive hotels on this site were the Democratic headquarters; and it was at the Capital House, as the most stylish in the city, that Kossuth was lodged during his visit here in February, 1852.

The Palmer House, a two-and-a-half-story brick, was built in 1840-1 by N. B. Palmer, on Washington and Illinois streets, and opened by John C. Parker in the summer of 1841. It was enlarged and raised to four stories in 1856 by Dr. Barbour, the lessee. Parker, Barbour, J. D. Carmichael, D. Tuttle, C. W. Hall, B. Mason, and others have been its lessees. It has always kept the same name, was for some time the leading house, and has had a fair share of patronage. Little's Hotel, first built in 1834 or 5, on New Jersey and Washington streets, by John Little, and known then as Little's Sun Tavern, (from the sign, a blazing sun,) was originally a small two-story frame house. A three-story ell was added by M. and I. Little in 1847, and in 1851 the old frame was moved to East and Washington streets, and a three-story brick front building put in its place. It also has frequently changed lessees but has retained its old name. The Duncan House, a three-story brick, subsequently the Barker and the Ray House, was built in 1847 on South and Delaware streets, by R. B. Duncan. It did a good business for some years, but has long been mostly devoted to boarders. D. J. Barker, M. M. Ray and others have been lessees. The Carlisle House, a three-story frame, built by Dan Carlisle in 1848, on Washington street, west of the canal, has so often changed names and lessees that they are unknown. From its position it never did as good a business as other houses, and is now used as a brewery. The Morris House, a two-and-a-half-story brick, subsequently much enlarged and raised to four stories, and known as the "American," "Mason," and "Sherman House," was built by Thos. A. Morris in 1852-3, north of the Union depot, and has done a good business. It has often changed its lessees. The Bates House, a four-story brick, which has retained its name though often changing lessees, was built on the corner of Washington and Illinois streets in 1852-3, by Harvey Bates, and has since been much enlarged, being the largest and leading hotel of the city, and doing perhaps the heaviest business. The Oriental, a four-story brick built in 1856-7, and opened in June by Francis Costigan, has retained its name though often changing lessees, and has done a fair business. The Tremont, afterward the Spencer House, a four-story brick, was built on the corner of Louisiana and Illinois streets, near the Union depot, in 1857, and has done a good business under J. W. Canan and others, its lessees. The Farmers', now the Commercial Hotel, was built in 1856 by Henry Buchig, as a three-story brick, and enlarged and raised to four stories by F. A. Reitz in 1864. It has often changed lessees.

The Macy House, a three-story brick, was built by David Macy, on Illinois and Market streets, in 1857, and has since been occupied mostly by boarders. A large number of other less important houses exist, mostly built in the last ten years, but want of space forbids further mention of them.

The Indianapolis Insurance Company was chartered for fifty years February 8th, 1836, with a capital of $200,000, in fifty dollar shares, and with very favorable banking privileges. It was organized March 16th with nine directors, D. Maguire being president and C. Scudder, secretary, and began operations in April. It did a limited business for many years, but finally suspended operations in 1859 or '60. In 1865 the old stock was purchased and a new company organized, with Wm. Henderson as president and A. C. Jameson, secretary. The charter was amended December 20th, 1865, increasing the capital to $500,000 by vote of the stockholders, and making the company perpetual. The old Branch Bank building was purchased for about $30,000 from the Sinking Fund, in April, 1867, and the office has since been located there. It is now doing a prosperous insurance and banking business, and ranks high among the home enterprises of the city.

The other insurance companies since started may be briefly mentioned here. The Indiana Mutual Fire Insurance Company was chartered January 30th, 1837, and amendments made to the act at several subsequent dates. It was organized in February with James Blake, president, Charles W. Cady, secretary, and began business in March in an office opposite the Washington Hall. It was prosperous and did a good business for two or three years, but from inherent defects in the plan, heavy losses and mismanagement, became involved, insolvent, and finally suspended operations about fifteen years ago.

The Indiana Fire Insurance Company was chartered in February, 1851, with a nominal capital of $300,000, and was organized May 1st, 1851, ———————— being president, ——————— secretary. It did a limited business, and suspended operations after a few years.

The German Mutual Fire Insurance Company was organized under the general law January 21st, 1854, and has successfully conducted its business to the present date. Its office was first located at 81 East Washington street, removed in 1859 to Judah's block, and in March, 1866, to 16 South Delaware street. Henry Busher, Julius Boetticher and A. Seidensticker have been the presidents, and A. Seidensticker, Valentine Butsch, Charles Volmar, Charles Balke, Adolph Miller and F. Ritzinger secretaries

of the company. The risks assumed during the first year amounted to $136,000; its present risks to $3,146,000; cash and premium notes on hand in April, 1868, $284,ber of losses in last year, $10,606; no unadjusted liabilities.

The Indiana Fire Insurance Company— a mutual company—was organized May 9th, 1862, under the general law of 1852, and the office has since been located in Odd Fellows Hall. Jonathan S. Harvey was chosen president, and W. T. Gibson, secretary, at the time of the organization, and have served till the present time. The amount of risks assumed by the company during the first fiscal year was about $600,000, and the amount now incurred is between eight and nine millions.

The Sinnissippi Mutual Insurance Company was organized November 18th, 1863, under the general law, with Elijah Goodwin, president, John R. Berry, secretary, and continued its operations till 1866. It advertised extensively, did a large business, incurred risks (many of dangerous character) to the amount of millions of dollars, paid good salaries and commissions, and incurred heavy expenses and losses. Assessments were rapidly made on the premium notes, and the company broke in 1866, passing into a receiver's hands, and its affairs are now being closed up. The office of the company was at 35 East Market street.

The Equitable Fire Insurance Company was organized on the mutual plan in September, 1863, under the general law, W. A. Pellee, president, E. D. Olin, secretary, and its office opened in Odd Fellows Hall. The company was authorized by law in 1865 to change the character of its business substantially to the stock system, dispensing with premium notes and receiving premiums in cash. Its operations were limited mostly to the centre and north of the State, but its expenses and losses compelled its suspension in January or February, 1868, and its affairs are being adjusted by a receiver. The office was in Odd Fellows Hall.

The Home Mutual Insurance Company was organized in April, 1864, under the general law, with J. C. Geisendorff, president, J. B. Follett, secretary. Its business was conducted substantially on the same plan as that of the Equitable Company, but was mostly confined to risks in the city and vicinity. Not being very remunerative, and some losses having occurred, the company voluntarily suspended operations in June, 1868, and its business is being closed by a receiver appointed by the court. The office was most of the time at 64 East Washington street.

The Farmers' and Merchants' Insurance Company was organized on the same general plan and under the same law as the two foregoing companies, on the 1st of April, 1864, with Ryland T. Brown as president, and A. J. Davis, secretary, and the office located in Blackford's block. It continued its operations, doing a moderate business in the central portion of the State, till the summer of 1867, when it suspended, and its affairs are now in process of settlement.

The Union Insurance Company was organized on the stock plan under the general law, in the spring of 1865, with a capital of $200,000, James M. Ray being president, and D. W. Grubbs, secretary. The office was first opened in Talbott & New's building on Pennsylvania street, but removed in 1867 to Dunlop's building. E. B. Martindale was elected president, and George W. Dunn, secretary. The company continued its operations, doing a good business but meeting with considerable losses, till April, 1868, when it was determined to close its affairs and dissolve the company. Its risks were accordingly re-insured in the Home Fire Insurance Company of New York, and the Union Company discontinued.

The American Horse Insurance Company, (for security against loss by death, &c., of horses and other animals,) was organized under the general law in August, 1865, with a nominal capital of $100,000, Thomas B. McCarty being elected president, J. F. Payne, secretary, and has continued its business to the present date, at the office in Vinton's block on Pennsylvania street.

The Franklin Mutual Life Insurance Company was organized under the general law in July, 1866, James M. Ray being elected president, and D. W. Grubbs, secretary, (since succeeded by E. P. Howe,) and has been very successful, as all life companies are that are carefully managed. It has done a good business and met with few losses, standing well among such enterprises. The office was first opened at 19 North Meridian street, but in April, 1868, the company purchased the old State Bank building, at the corner of Illinois street and Kentucky avenue, and removed to that point.

Beside the foregoing home organizations, agencies, general and special, exist here for forty or fifty foreign life, accident and fire insurance companies. Most prominent among these is the Ætna, of Hartford, which, under William Henderson and A. Abromet as agents, has done a very lucrative business at this point, its net receipts here during the continuance of the agency, in excess of all expenses, amounting to nearly if not quite $200,000. The company in 1858-9 erected a four-story brick building on North Pennsylvania street as an office and for business purposes.

1837. At a meeting held February 22d it was determined by the young men to form a military company, and at subsequent meetings a constitution, by-laws and uniform were adopted, members enrolled, and officers elected, Alexander W. Russell being captain, and serving till August, 1838, when Thomas A. Morris succeeded and commanded the company for years afterward. The uniform was gray with black velvet facings, and tall leather caps with pompons and brass mountings. The company was armed with muskets and drilled by Scott's tactics. It was the best organization in the State, attracted much admiration on parade, and existed till 1845. The "Graybacks" were the first independent company, and were specially incorporated February 14th, 1838. Their fine discipline and soldierly bearing aroused the long dormant military feeling, and other companies were shortly afterward formed in the town and vicinity. Prominent among these were the "Arabs," or Marion Riflemen, under Captain Tom. McBaker, uniformed in fringed hunting shirts, and armed with breech-loading rifles. In August, 1842, the independent companies formed a battalion and elected Hervey Brown Lieutenant-Colonel, and George W. Drum, Major. Frequent parades and several encampments were held by the companies, and the military feeling was active till near the time of the Mexican war. Three companies of volunteers were raised here during that war, under Captains J. P. Drake, E. Lander and John McDougall. For two or three years after that war no organization existed. In 1852 the City Guards were formed under command of Governor Wallace, and in May, 1853, the Mechanic Rifles, but neither of these lived long.

The Saint Louis National Guards passed through here in February, 1856, and the effect produced was such that a similar organization was effected here on the 12th of March. The National Guards were uniformed in blue, with caps and white plumes, and were successively under the command of W. J. Elliott, Thomas A. Morris, George F. McGinnis, Irwin Harrison, J. M. Lord, and W. P. Noble. When the war occurred the company entered the eleventh regiment, and closed its existence with the end of the war. An unsuccessful effort was afterward made to revive it. It was a well-drilled and officered organization, held frequent parades and a number of encampments, and supplied many competent officers to the army during the war. It revived the military spirit here when it was at the lowest ebb, and aided in keeping it alive until the war demonstrated the absolute necessity of such organizations in time of peace. George F. McGinnis, W. W. Darnell, J. H. Livsey and others commanded the company through the war. Shortly after it was first formed the National Guards Band was organized, and under different names and with some changes, still exists, holding a high rank among the musical organizations of the State.

The City Greys and the City Greys Band were organized August 12th, 1857, and under the successive command of W. J. Elliott, E. Hartwell attained a high state of discipline. It was uniformed in gray, wore bearskin shakos, and was armed like the Guards with muskets. It entered the eleventh regiment and closed its existence with the war, being commanded by R. S. Foster, S. W. Butler and Henry Kemper. The Greys Band, in March, 1859, during the Pike's Peak fever, started for that locality, but turned off toward Santa Fe, and thence down through Mexico to Matamoras, and through Texas to New Orleans and home, receiving a public welcome here June 7th, 1860, after their fifteen months of wandering and hardship. The band entered the service, though not as the old organization.

The City Greys Artillery was organized in 1859 as an adjunct to that organization, under J. A. Colestock as captain, but the commander lost his arm not long after by a premature explosion of the gun, and the company was suspended.

In July, 1858, the Marion Dragoons, Captain John Love, were organized, and for a year or two kept up their organization and occasional parades, but the difficulty of properly drilling and keeping up a cavalry company prevented their continued existence.

The Montgomery Guards visited the city on the 21st of February, 1860, and with our city companies paraded on the 22d. In the afternoon they gave a fancy drill by drum-beat, in Zouave dress, near the Bates House, in presence of an immense crowd, and excited great admiration. It was at once determined to form a Zouave company here, and on the 1st of March the Independent Zouaves, Captain F. A. Shoup, were organized, uniformed as Zouaves, armed with sabre-bayonet rifles, and persistently drilled. Shoup resigned in January, 1861, went south and joined the rebel army, in which he afterward became a brigadier general, and was noted as the first one on that side to propose using the negroes as soldiers in the rebel cause. The Independent Zouaves entered the eleventh regiment and terminated

their existence with the end of the war, being commanded by W. J. H. Robinson, F. Kneffer and others.

A military convention was held here June 27th, 1860, under the leadership of Captain Lewis Wallace, eleven companies being represented, and an encampment was determined on, to be held September 19th on the State military grounds. It was accordingly held September 19th–24th, the Greys, Guards, Zouaves, Montgomery Guards, Fort Harrison Guards, and Vigo Guards participating, General Love commanding, Captain Shoup Adjutant. The unfavorable weather prevented a large attendance.

The Zouave Cadets were organized in August, 1860, and the Zouave Guards, Captain John Fahnestock, in October. This company also entered the eleventh regiment, and terminated its existence at the end of the war. The Cadets were in existence for a year or two after the war began under Captain George H. Marshall, and most of them entered the service singly as officers in various regiments subsequently organized.

The news of the attack on Sumter was received April 12th, and the next day recruiting began. The Guards, Greys, Zouaves, and Zouave Guards at once filled up, and were all in camp by the 17th. Two reserve companies of National Guards were formed. Two companies of the Greys entered the service, leaving one reserve company at home. Two companies of the Independent Zouaves were in the eleventh regiment. The Zouave Guards left no reserve company. Besides these organizations an artillery company was formed, and Home Guard companies in every ward. Several thousands of men were raised here for the service during the war, without counting the gallant City Regiment, twelve hundred strong, with its artillery and cavalry wings, raised here during the Morgan raid, or the one thousand "hundred daysers" at a later date in the struggle. The military record of the city during the war was a proud one, and her quotas were always filled, although by the remissness of the authorities in securing the proper credits, a draft was ordered early in 1865, and a debt of several hundred thousand dollars incurred for bounties to volunteers to fill requisitions that should never have been made.

On the 4th of February, 1837, Calvin Fletcher and Thomas Johnson were appointed commissioners by the Assembly to receive subscriptions and drain the swamp north-east of town, which discharged its waters by two bayous through the place. They proceeded to execute the work by cutting a ditch west to Fall creek, south of and through the present fair grounds. During the flood of 1847 the banks of the drain broke and the water again came down the old channels, flooding the houses and alarming new comers. These bayou channels are now nearly obliterated by the street grades and filling of lots. On the 6th of February the Assembly authorized the Internal Improvement Board to use the half of square 50, which had been given to the town for market purposes in 1821, and in lieu there-of to set off the north half of square 48 to the town, the town and the State to exchange deeds on the transfer. On the 4th of February the first carpenters' association was incorporated, and it shortly after limited a day's work to ten hours.

The Episcopalians had met occasionally in 1835 for worship at the court house, as the services of a minister of that church could be secured, but in the winter of 1836 the meetings had been more frequent, and in March or April, 1837, a church was organized and Rev. James B. Britton chosen rector, preaching at the court house and seminary. Preparations were made for building in November, and on the 7th of May, 1838, the corner-stone of Christ Church was laid, a plain wooden Gothic structure, on the north-east corner of Circle and Meridian streets. The house was opened for services November 18th, 1838. This building was used till 1857, when it was sold to the African Methodist church and removed to West Georgia street. A new stone church (the first in the city) was begun in May, 1857, and completed in 1859. The spire yet remains unfinished. A peal of bells was placed in it in May, 1860, and taken out and replaced with a better one in September, 1860. A tasteful brick parsonage was built near the church in 1857. Rev. J. B. Britton, S. R. Johnson, M. M. Hunter, N. W. Camp, J. C. Talbott, II. Stringfellow, T. P. Holcomb, J. T. P. Ingraham have been rectors of this church.

In 1865 the church divided, a part of the members forming St. Paul's church, and in the spring of 1867 the corner-stone of a large brick edifice was laid at the corner of New York and Illinois streets, with appropriate services. Rev. II. Stringfellow has been the rector to this date. This church has recently been completed and dedicated as the cathedral church of the diocese. Grace church, on Pennsylvania and St. Joseph streets, was built in 1863–4, M. V. Averill, rector. Several mission chapels of this denomination have since been built in different quarters of the city.

The Evangelical Lutheran church was formed in the spring of 1837, and the first communion held May 14th, Rev. A. Reck being pastor. It was at first proposed to build the church on the north-west corner of University Square, and a lease was obtained from the Assembly ; but the house, a small, plain brick, was commenced in the fall on the south side of Ohio street, between Pennsylvania and Meridian, and was torn down in 1852 and a new church built in 1853–4 on the south-west corner of New York and Alabama streets. The German Lutheran church was built in 1860–1 on East and Georgia streets, Rev. Charles Freke, pastor.

The Indianapolis Female Institute was chartered at the session of 1836–7, and opened June 14th by Misses Mary J. and Harriet Axtell, in Sanders' building. It was subsequently removed to the upper rooms of the house opposite Washington Hall, and finally to a frame school-house on Pennsylvania street next the old Presbyterian church. The first examinations were held April 30th, 1838, and the school subsequently attained a high reputation, attracting scholars from abroad. Miss Axtell was a faithful and competent teacher, held in grateful remembrance by her pupils, but her health failing the school was discontinued in the fall of 1849, and she died at sea shortly after on her way to the West Indies.

The Indianapolis High School, afterwards called the Franklin Institute, was opened on Washington street, opposite Washington Hall, October 25th, 1837, by G. Marston and Eliza Richmond. A frame school-house was built in the spring of 1838 on Circle street next the present high school building, and occupied by the school for four or five years. Marston left in 1839, being succeeded by Orlando Chester, who died in October, 1840, and was succeeded by John Wheeler, who taught until the school was discontinued. In December, 1837, it was proposed to establish a State Female Seminary as the counterpart of the Bloomington College for males, and use the Governor's Circle as the college building, but the project was not executed. The Indianapolis Academy, under Josephus Cicero Worral, had been in existence from 1836, and continued for several years after this date. Worral was a man of considerable education but peculiar idiosyncracies, and his addresses to his scholars (often published) excited much amusement on account of the flights of fancy, classical allusions, and stilted style in which he indulged.

The first editorial convention in the State met May 29th in the town council chamber, twenty editors and publishers being present. John Douglass acted as president and John Dowling secretary. Fifty-two papers were then published in the State. An association was formed, constitution adopted, and advertising rates agreed on.

As the National Government was McAdamizing the centre of Washington street, it was proposed in June that the trustees improve the sidewalks, and steps were accordingly taken to do so. The sidewalks as originally designed were fifteen feet wide on Washington and ten feet on other streets. At a subsequent date they were made twenty feet on Washington and twelve feet on other streets; and within the last ten years fifteen feet has been adopted as the standard width on the ninety-feet streets. The increased width of the pavement on Washington street was bitterly opposed by the property-holders on account of the increased expense entailed in their improvement. The first street improvements were begun in 1836-7.

A great hail storm occurred on the 6th of June, many of the stones weighing three and four ounces, and measuring three inches in length. Nearly all the windows in town were broken. The usual military and school celebration occurred on the Fourth of July, the exercises closing with a military reception, and ball at night in the Governor's Circle building. The Ladies' Missionary Society held the first fair here on the 31st of December, realizing $230 for the cause. Such fairs were afterward very frequently held by various societies and for various objects.

1838. The Assembly re-incorporated the town on the 17th of February, including the whole of the donation, but limiting taxation for municipal purposes to the old plat. The town was divided into six wards, all east of Alabama street constituting the first; thence west to Pennsylvania the second; thence to Meridian the third; thence to Illinois the fourth; thence to Mississippi the fifth; thence west the sixth. One trustee was to be elected by each ward, and a president by the whole town. They were to be freeholders, hold office one year, and constitute the common council, the president and four members being a quorum. The president had a justice's jurisdiction, was to enforce all ordinances, and keep a docket. The marshal had a constable's authority and was to keep the peace. The council met monthly, the members each receiving twelve dollars per annum. They had all necessary powers, to pass ordinances, levy taxes, (not over one-half per cent. on real property) improve streets, borrow money, tax shows, saloons and groceries, regulate markets, guard against fires, &c. The assessment was to be made annually by June 1st, and collected by September 1st. The council was to elect a secretary, treasurer, collector, marshal, supervisor, market master, lister and assessor. The election under this act was held the last Saturday in

March, and resulted in the election of Jas. Morrison as president. In April and May the council passed ordinances governing the markets, regulating cases before the president, licensing groceries, and improving sidewalks and streets.

The summer and fall of 1838 was very sickly and many deaths took place. The first "steam foundry" in the town was started in January by Wood & Underhill, on Pennsylvania street, where the Second Presbyterian church now stands. The old steam mill was finally closed in February of this year and the machinery offered for sale, though not disposed of finally until a year or two afterward. Benjamin Orr opened the first ready-made clothing store here during this year.

1839. On the 13th of February the Assembly directed the State officers to buy a residence for the Governor, and early in the spring Dr. Sanders' two-story brick dwelling, erected in the summer of 1836 on the north-west corner of Market and Illinois streets, was purchased and used as the official residence till 1864. It was sold by order of the Assembly in 1865, and a row of business rooms built along the Illinois street front of the lot.

Three hundred and twenty-four votes were cast at the corporation election in March, N. B. Palmer being elected president. At the meeting in April the public wells were ordered to be repaired, by-laws adopted for the government of the town officers, and the streets which were still fenced up ordered to be opened. The corporation receipts for the year ending March 27th were $7,012, the expenditures $6,874; $3,850 of this sum was paid Elder, Colestock & Co., for building the west market house and adding to the east one; $443 were paid M. Shea, sexton, for clearing and fencing the old graveyard; $58 for printing, and $145 for street improvements and gravel,

The first revision of the town ordinances was made and published in July. In November $300 were appropriated to buy a new engine; a committee was appointed to see if it could be bought for $600, and donations solicited for the purpose.

An accurate survey of the donation this year showed a mistake in the original survey by which the title to eight acres, which had been laid off in lots and sold in 1831, was still in the general government. The Assembly memorialized Congress in February, 1840, stating the mistake and asking a donation of the eight acres. This was granted and the title quieted.

The first municipal tax sale took place October 25th at Washington Hall, by James Van Blaricum marshal and collector. A considerable number of sales were subse-

5

quently made, but the records have since been lost.

In November Mrs. Britton opened a female seminary near the foundry. This school—afterward known when under the care of Mrs. Johnson as the "St. Marys Seminary"—was subsequently removed to a building adjoining the Episcopal church, and for many years was quite prosperous.

The first Thanksgiving proclamation was issued on the 4th of November by Governor Wallace, the day fixed on being the 28th.

The Presbyterian church having divided in May, 1838, on the slavery and other questions, the church here was also divided, fifteen of the members forming the Second church November 19th, 1838, under Rev. J. H. Johnson. One or two calls were extended to pastors but declined, and in May, 1839, Rev. H. W. Beecher, then of Lawrenceburgh, was called, and began his ministrations July 31st. The congregation worshiped in the seminary. In 1839–40 a frame church (the present high school building,) was erected at the north-west corner of Market and Circle streets, and occupied by the congregation October 4th, 1840. Mr. Beecher remained till September 19th, 1847, and was succeeded by Rev. Clement E. Babb in July, 1848, who remained till January 1st, 1853. Rev. T. A. Mills was called as pastor January 1st, 1854, remaining till February 9th, 1857. Rev. G. P. Tindall became pastor in August, 1857, and Rev. H. A. Edson in November, 1863. In November, 1851, twenty-four of the members formed the Fourth Presbyterian Church, and erected a brick church in 1853–4 on Delaware and Market streets. In the spring of 1864 a new stone church, not yet fully completed, was begun on Vermont and Pennsylvania streets, and is now nearly completed at a cost of about $100,-000. It is the finest church building in the city. The chapel was occupied December 2d, 1867. The Fifth Presbyterian church is a colony from the Second, and their church was dedicated May 15th, 1864. The Olivet church is also a colony, dedicating their church October 20th, 1867. The old frame church was sold to the city for a high school building in the spring of 1867, and was last used as a church July 16th, 1867.

1840. Much political excitement occurred this year, and the Whigs carried the municipal election in March for the first time, electing the trustees and town officers. The corporation receipts for the year 1839 amounted to $5,975, the expenditures to $4,753; $1,984 of this sum were spent on the market houses, $1,350 on streets and bridges, $197 on the fire department, $974 for salaries, and $244 for incidentals.

The first cisterns, two in number, of three hundred barrels each, were ordered to be constructed in the spring of this year.

The political excitement increased in intensity as the elections approached, both parties holding monster conventions. A very large convention was held at Tippecanoe about the last of May, many persons attending from this place. A great Whig convention was also held here on the 5th of October, and on the 14th of October the Democrats held a great meeting in the walnut grove north of the Blind Asylum to welcome Richard M. Johnson, Vice President and reputed slayer of Tecumseh. He was received with due honors and addressed the convention. Colonel Johnson visited the town once or twice afterward on private business. One thousand three hundred and eighty-seven votes cast in the township at the November election, Harrison receiving eight hundred and seventy-two, Van Buren five hundred and fifteen.

The Indiana Horticultural Society was formed August 22d and continued active operations for several years, Henry Ward Beecher and James Blake being among its most prominent supporters.

The annual Methodist conference met here October 21st, Bishop Soule presiding.

1841. In March, James Wood, civil engineer, made a profile of the streets by direction of the council to establish a uniform system of grades, to be followed in their future improvement. The profile was filed with the authorities, adopted by the council April 8th, 1842, and has been followed in nearly all the subsequent improvements. The survey and profile cost $303.

On the 10th of April a meeting was held to make arrangements for funeral services for President Harrison. The exercises took place on the 17th, Governor Bigger and Henry Ward Beecher delivering addresses. Business was suspended during the day, and the funeral procession was imposing. The 14th of May was observed throughout the country as a fast day for the death of the President.

1842. By the treasurer's report in March the corporation receipts for the past year amounted to $3,197, expenditures $2,-957; $1,138 had been expended for street improvements and $767 for salaries. The county receipts from March 1st, 1841, to June 1st, 1842, were $9,942, expenditures $8,194. The salaries of the town officers for 1842 were as follows : Secretary $200, treasurer $100, marshal $100, supervisor $200, collector $200, assessor $75, market master $140, messenger of fire company $100. An effort was made in the fall to repeal the act of incorporation on account of the expenses attending the municipal government.

On the 25th of April at two o'clock A. M., the town was startled by a heavy explosion, and on examination it was found that the grocery of Frederick Smith, a one-story frame house, where 93 East Washington street now is, had been blown up with powder, and further search revealed the body of Smith badly burned and wounded. He had attempted suicide during temporary insanity, sitting on the keg of powder and applying the match.

The first daguerreotype saloon here was opened by T. W. Whitridge in July or August. During the fall James Blake erected a mill and furnaces and attempted the manufacture of syrup and sugar from cornstalks.

This year was distinguished by the visits of two Presidential candidates, Van Buren and Clay. Mr. Van Buren arrived by stage on Saturday, the 11th of June, being received east of town by a procession composed of citizens, firemen, and four military companies, and was escorted with due honors to the Palmer House, where he made a speech in reply to the welcoming address. He visited Governor Bigger at the State house, and held a reception in the evening. On Sunday he attended the Methodist and Second Presbyterian churches, and left on Monday by stage for Terre Haute, being upset near Plainfield while en route. Henry Clay arrived October 5th, attending a Whig convention in response to an invitation of the party. The crowd on that occasion was generally estimated at thirty thousand, and considering the facilities for travel, then and since, it has never since been equaled. The procession included many bands, many military companies, representatives of all trades and professions, and was nearly two hours passing a given point. It proceeded to a grove north of Governor Noble's house, where a great barbecue was spread for the assembled thousands. Mr. Clay spoke for two hours after dinner, and was followed by Governor Crittenden, Governor Metcalf and other Whig leaders. The festivities lasted three days, and included a grand military parade, and review by the Governor, a fine exhibition of fireworks and an agricultural fair.

During this and several following years an excitement about mesmerism spread through the West. Lecturers went from point to point explaining the new science to the natives and giving experiments in illustration. Many amusing scenes occurred in the trials made on the "subjects" by committees appointed by the audiences.

1843. Physicians and philanthropists had repeatedly called the attention of the Legislature to the condition of the insane, blind, and deaf and dumb persons in the State, suggesting steps for their education and maintenance; and as early as January, 1839, the Assembly had memorialized Congress asking a grant for that object, and on the 13th of February, 1839, the assessors were directed to ascertain and report the number of deaf mutes in each county. The Governor was directed, January 31st, 1842, to correspond with the Governors of other States concerning the cost, construction and management of Insane Hospitals. Dr. John Evans delivered a lecture December 25th, 1842, before the Assembly on the treatment of insanity, and on the 13th of February, 1843, the Governor was directed to correspond with superintendents of hospitals and procure plans to be submitted with his suggestions at the next session. This was done, and a tax of one cent on the hundred dollars was levied January 15th, 1844, for hospital buildings. On the 13th of Jan., 1845, John Evans, Livingston Dunlap and James Blake were appointed commissioners to select a site of not more than two hundred acres. They chose the present site in the spring of 1845, and reported it, with a plan of the building, at the following session. On the 19th of January, 1846, they were ordered to begin the hospital according to the plan on the site, and sell hospital square 22, its proceeds, with $15,000 in addition, being appropriated to the building. The central portion of the hospital was begun in the summer of 1846 and finished in 1847, at a cost of about $75,000. The south wing was built in 1853–4, and the north wing several years afterward. Various additions, changes and repairs have also been made, and the house as finally completed has cost nearly if not quite $500,000, and is among the largest buildings in the West. It is situated on a quarter-section of land two miles west of the city, is from three to five stories in hight, with a basement, and is about five hundred feet in length. It was first opened for the reception of patients in 1847, and has ever since been fully occupied. Dr. John Evans was its originator and first superintendent. He resigned July 1st, 1848. R. J. Patterson, J. S. Athon, J. H. Woodburn and W. J. Lockhart have since been the successive superintendents of the institution.

The first steps having been taken to provide for the insane, the Assembly, on the 13th of February, 1843, levied a two-mill tax to support the deaf mutes and build them an asylum. William Willard, a mute teacher from Ohio, arrived here in the spring of 1843 and opened a private school for mutes on the 1st of October, having sixteen pupils during the first year. This school was adopted by the State on the 15th of January, 1844, and the Governor, Treasurer and Secretary of State, with Henry Ward Beecher, Phineas D. Gurley, P. H. Jamison, L. Dunlap, James Morrison and Matthew Simpson appointed trustees, with instructions to rent a room and employ teachers. They rented the house on the south-west corner of Illinois and Maryland streets, and opened the school there October 1st, 1844. The Governor was also to receive proposals for site, &c. The Governor was authorized on the 15th of January, 1845, to appoint five trustees in place of the former board. He did so, and in the fall of 1846 the new board rented the Kinder building on East Washington street and removed the school there, where it remained until the completion of the Asylum in October, 1850. The institution was permanently located here January 9th, 1846, the trustees being directed to buy thirty acres near the city, $3,000 being appropriated therefor. They were subsequently directed to buy one hundred acres in addition to instruct the pupils in agriculture. The site was bought east of the city in the summer of 1846 and the building begun in 1849 and finished by October, 1850, at a cost of about $30,000. It was rough-casted and completed in 1853. On its completion the school was removed there and has been prosperously managed ever since. Many mutes have received their entire education there and been fitted for active business pursuits. Prior to 1848 pupils who were able were required to pay tuition and board, but since then the education and maintenance of all have been free. William Willard was the originator and first teacher of the school. James S. Brown was the first superintendent from 1845 to October, 1852, and since that date Dr. Thomas McIntyre has been in charge of the institution.

The insane and the deaf mutes being thus provided for, the blind were still neglected; but during the session of 1844–5 pupils from the Kentucky Institution gave an exhibition before the Assembly with such success that a two-mill tax was at once ordered for the support and education of the blind. James M. Ray, George W. Mears, and the Secretary, Treasurer and Auditor of State were appointed commissioners at the next session to expend the fund thus created in starting a school or maintaining pupils at the Ohio or Kentucky institutions. They appointed William H. Churchman as lecturer to present the case to the people and to ascertain the number of blind in the State. On the 27th of January, 1847, G. W. Mears, J. M. Ray and Calvin Fletcher, were appointed commissioners to erect asylum buildings and arrange for a school,

$5,000 being appropriated for a site, furniture, &c. Mr. Fletcher declining to serve, Seton W. Norris was appointed trustee. Two blocks on North street were purchased for a site, a plan selected and the building commenced. The school was opened October 1st, 1847, in the building on the south-west corner of Illinois and Maryland streets by Mr. W. H. Churchman, who had been appointed superintendent. Nine pupils were in attendance on the 4th, and thirty during the session. In September, 1848, the school was removed to a three-story brick building erected on the grounds and afterward used as a workshop. The asylum was commenced the same year and finished, with some changes of plan and details, in 1851, at a cost of $60,000, and the pupils and school at once removed to it. The surrounding grounds have since been tastefully laid out and planted with trees and shrubbery. W. H. Churchman, G. W. Ames, W. C. Larrabee and James McWorkman have been superintendents of the institution.

The asylums are creditable to the city and State, not only for extent, management and arrangement, but also that they were built when the State was heavily in debt and the people unprepared for the extra taxation necessary for their support.

In February, 1843, a fire damaged the Washington Hall to the extent of $3,000, and seriously threatened its entire destruction. The weather was excessively cold, the water freezing as it fell, and the house was saved after several hours' hard work by the engine companies, aided by hundreds of citizens in passing buckets.

The Millerite delusion, which had some of the citizens among its adherents, created some excitement during the winter and spring. The belief in the approaching end of all things was strengthened by an earthquake on the 4th of January between eight and nine o'clock, lasting nearly a minute and sensibly shaking the buildings. It was also encouraged by the great comet which nightly flamed in the south-west during February and March, its train reaching across the sky like a destroying sword. The weather however was adverse, being cold and stormy during March and April, with deep and drifting snows, followed in May by heavy rains, filling the streams, sweeping off bridges, breaking the canals, and raising White river over the bottoms.

The 22d of February and the 4th of July were celebrated by the military, four companies participating, and the last anniversary by the schools in the usual style. In the month of June R. Parmlee began making pianos here, and continued the business two or three years. In November "The New York Company of Comedians" gave a series of concerts in Gaston's carriage shop on Washington west of Illinois street, each concert being succeeded by a theatrical representation. John and Mary Powell, Sam. Lathrop, Mr. Wallace, Tom. Townley and others were the actors. The company had considerable merit and attracted good audiences. During the season, which lasted for ten weeks, the noted tragedian, Augustus A. Adams, Mrs. Alexander Drake and Mr. Morris were the stars. This company was the third which performed here, Lindsay's company having performed several years before, and Mr. and Mrs. Smith in 1823-4.

The Indianapolis Female Collegiate Institute, Miss Lesuer, principal, began in September in the Franklin Institute on Circle street, and continued two or three years. The Roberts Chapel Methodist church was built during this and the following year at a cost of eight or ten thousand dollars, on the corner of Market and Pennsylvania streets, under J. S. Bayless, the first pastor. The congregation worshiped in the court house until the completion of the church. The present lot and building were sold in June, 1868, and steps are being taken to erect a larger and finer edifice at a cost of about $80,000, on the north-west corner of Vermont and Delaware streets.

1844. The Union Cemetery was laid out in April adjoining the old burying ground. In 1852 Messrs. Ray, Peck and Blake, laid out the ground north and east of this cemetery for burial purposes, and in 1860 the Greenlawn Cemetery, west of the last-named ground and next the river and Terre Haute railroad, was added.

A meeting was held on the 5th of August to make arrangements for the contemplated visit of Lewis Cass. He came on the 25th and was received with due honors and conducted to the State military grounds, where a welcoming address was made by Governor Whitcomb, and a long speech made by General Cass in response. He was followed by Senator Hannegan and others. The procession and audience was large and enthusiastic. A reception was held for several hours at the Palmer House, and he left at six in the evening for Dayton.

1845. The Thespian Society, composed of young men of the town, gave a series of dramatic performances during July, August and September. They also performed during September and October of the following year. Several of the performers evinced decided talent for the stage, and their efforts attracted good audiences.

The usual celebrations occurred on the Fourth of July, but the day was signalized by a riot, resulting in the murder of John Tucker, a negro, on Illinois street opposite the present site of the Bates House. Balon Washington west of Illinois street, each lenger, the principal in the affray, made his escape. Nick Woods was sent to the penitentiary, and the others were acquitted.

Washington street was graded and graveled in July. In August and September Seton W. Norris built the present Hubbard block, then the best business house in the place.

On the 16th of August John H. Ohr, Daniel B. Culley and David R. Elder, apprentices in the *Journal* office, issued the first number of the *Locomotive*, and continued its publication weekly for three months. It was revived by them April 3d, 1847, and again issued for three months. Its size was seven by ten inches, and each three months' issue formed a volume. Douglass & Elder revived it January 1st, 1848, and issued it weekly from an office on South Meridian street in Hubbard's block, till July, 1861, when its publication was suspended and its subscription list transferred to the *Sentinel*. Its size when first issued by them was eight by thirteen inches, and after several enlargements it was finally published on a sheet twenty-three by thirty-one inches. Elder & Harkness became proprietors March 30th, 1850, and continued such till its suspension. For a number of years it had the greatest circulation in the county, and published the letter-list. It was neutral in politics, and devoted to literary and news matters.

The old Methodist church, erected in 1828-9 on Meridian and Circle streets, having become unsafe from the cracking of the walls, was torn down and Wesley Chapel erected in this and the following year on its site. It has since been in constant use by Wesley Chapel charge, but will probably be sold this year and a finer and larger edifice will be built on the south-west corner of Meridian and New York streets.

1846. The corporation receipts for the year ending March 31, amounted to $2,636. This had all been expended and a debt of $370 contracted. This debt caused some uneasiness to the citizens.

The Mexican war began early in April, and the news was received here early in May. The Governor's proclamation calling for volunteers appeared May 23d. Recruiting at once began and a company was formed in June under captain J. P. Drake, and lieutenants John A. McDougall and Lewis Wallace, and marched to the rendezvous at New Albany. This company was attached to the first Indiana regiment under colonel Drake, and spent the year of its enlistment guarding stores in Matamoras. Two additional companies, under captains Edward Lander and John A. McDougall, were raised in May and September, 1847, and attached to the fourth and fifth regiments. A number of recruits were also secured here for the regular army. But little excitement existed here in regard to this war, and it was generally viewed from a party stand point.

The Madison railroad depot was located this summer on the high ground south of Pogue's run, nearly half a mile from the settled portion of the town. The location caused much dissatisfaction, and the company was strongly urged to build its depot on Maryland street; but, the location having been finally determined on, the council ordered the improvement of Pennsylvania and Delaware streets across the low valley of the run, and the creek bed was straightened from Virginia avenue to Meridian street by the property holders.

The citizens became provoked during the summer at the bold operations of the gamblers. Meetings were held, a committee of fifteen appointed, resolutions to abate the nuisance adopted, and Hiram Brown, the oldest member of the bar, retained to prosecute the offenders. Vigorous measures were taken, and repeated in December, 1847, and the gamblers compelled to leave the town. Much feeling was aroused by these measures and the fifteen were denounced as a vigilance committee, but the desired object was attained and the town rid of the presence of many bad characters.

1847. Heavy and continued rains, amounting to twelve inches in forty-eight hours, had fallen over the State during the last days of December, 1846, producing by the first of January the greatest flood in White river and its tributaries since 1824. The whole valley was flooded, washing off soil, cattle, hogs, fences, hay, and causing in various ways so much damage that the Assembly authorized a deduction of taxes for the year to parties residing on the streams. The swamp north-east of town becoming full, the banks of the drain broke flooding the two bayous, and causing loss and inconvenience to parties who had built along them. West Indianapolis was covered, and the National road and canal badly injured. The aqueduct by which the canal crossed Fall creek was broken, and not repaired till late in the fall, the mills meanwhile lying idle. This flood was almost equalled by another in November.

The 22d of February was celebrated by the mechanics with a procession, speeches, dinner, &c. A meeting was held on the 26th of February to take measures for the relief of the starving poor in Ireland. An organization was effected, committees appointed, subscriptions of money and grain procured and forwarded, and for several

weeks the work was actively and effectively prosecuted.

The Assembly on the 13th of February, 1847, granted the town a city charter, its acceptance or rejection to be decided by a vote of the citizens on the 27th of March, and in case of its acceptance the Governor was to proclaim the fact and that it had become a law. The donation east of the river was included in the corporation, and was divided in seven wards. Washington street was the boundary between the north and south wards. All east of Alabama and north of Washington was the first; thence west to Meridian the second; thence to Mississippi the third; thence west, fourth; all west of Illinois and south of Washington, fifth; thence east to Delaware, sixth; thence all east the seventh. The first city election was to take place April 24th. The Mayor was to serve two years, had a justice's jurisdiction and the veto power. One councilman was to be elected from each ward at $24 annual salary and serve one year. The council was to elect one of their number president, hold monthly meetings, two-thirds being a quorum. They had full power to pass ordinances, levy taxes, establish district schools and levy taxes therefor, grade streets, suppress nuisances, &c., and were to elect a secretary, treasurer, assessor, marshal, (who was to have a constable's authority,) street commissioner, attorney, and such other officers as might be needed. Taxation for general purposes was limited to fifteen cents on the $100, but could be increased if specially authorized by vote of the people. At the election for city officers in April a vote was also to be taken on the question of tax for free schools.

Joseph A. Levy, the last president of the old town council, issued a proclamation directing an election to be held in the six wards of the town on the 27th of March, to determine the acceptance or rejection of the new charter. The election resulted in 449 votes for to 19 against it. This vote was certified to Governor Whitcomb on the 29th, and on the 30th he proclaimed the adoption of the charter and that it had become a law. Joseph A. Levy, president of the old council, then issued a proclamation directing an election, on the 24th of April, in the seven wards of the city, for mayor and councilmen, and also to decide whether a tax should be levied for free schools. The election was held and the tax almost unanimously authorized. Samuel Henderson was elected the first mayor, and the following persons from the several wards the first city councilmen: Uriah Gates from the first, Henry Tutewiler from the second, Cornelius King the third, Samuel S. Rooker the fourth, Charles W. Cady the

LIST OF PRINCIPAL CITY OFFICERS FROM 1847 TO 1868.

Year.	Mayor.	Prest. of Council.	Clerk.	Treasurer.	Marshal.	Engineer.	Attorney.	Assessor.
1847.	S. Henderson	S. S. Rooker / C. W. Cady	James G. Jordan	N. Lister / H. Ohr	Wm. Campbell	James Wood	A. M. Camalian / N. B. Taylor	Joshua Black
1848.	S Henderson	Geo A Chapman	James G Jordan	James Greer	John Bishop	James Wood	Wm B Greer	Chas I Haul
1849.	H C Newcomb	Wm Eckert	Jos T Roberts	J H Kennedy	S A Colley	James Word	Ed Coburn	H Ohr
1850.	H C Newcomb		Jos T Roberts	John S Spann	B Pillean	James Wood	Wm Wallace	S P Ienniels
1851.	C Scudder	A A Louden	D B Culley	A F Shortridge	S A Colley	James Wood	A G Porter	I Vanlandingh'm
1852.	C Scudder	D V Culley	D B Culley	A F Shortridge	E McNeely	James Wood	A G Porter	Jacob S Allen
1853.	C Scudder	D V Culley	D B Culley	A F Shortridge	B Pillean	James Wood	N B Taylor	M Little
1854.	Jas McCready		Jas N Sweetser	A F Shortridge	B Pillean	James Wood	N B Taylor	John G Waters
1855.	Jas McCready		Alf Stevens	H Vaudegrift	G W Pitts	A B Condit	N B Taylor	J H Kennedy
1856.	Henry F West		Fred Stein	Francis King	Jeff Springsteen	D B Hosbrook	John T Morrison	John B Stumph
1857.	Wm J Wallace		Geo H West	Francis King	Jeff Springsteen	D B Hosbrook	B Harrison	John B Stumph
1858.	Wm J Wallace		John G Waters	J M Jamison	A D Rose	James Wood	S V Morris	D L Merriman
1859-60	Sam D Maxwell		John G Waters	J M Jamison	Jeff Springsteen	James Wood	B K Elliott	R W Robinson
1861-2	Sam D Maxwell		John G Waters	Jos K English	D W Lowcks	James Wood	J N Sweetser	John B Stumph
1863-4	John Caven		C S Butterfield	Jos K English	John Unversaw	James Wood, Jr.	R J Ryan	John B Stumph
1865-6	John Caven		C S Butterfield	W H Craft	John Unversaw	James Wood, Jr.	B K Elliott	Wm Hadley
1867-8	Dan McCauley		Daniel Ransdell	Robert S Foster	John Unversaw	James Wood, Jr. / Joshua Staples / R M Patterson	B K Elliott	Wm Hadley

LIST OF PRINCIPAL CITY OFFICERS FROM 1847 TO 1868—CONTINUED.

Year.	Street Com'r.	Market Master.	Weighmaster.	Sexton.	Ch'f Fire Eng'r.	Sealer Weits & Meas.	Printers.	Chief Police.
1847.	Jacob B Fitler	Sampson Barlee	John Patton	B F Lolaugh				
1848.	John Bishop	Jacob Miller	A Haugh	J I Strecher				
1849.	George W Pitts	Jacob Miller	A Haugh	J I Strecher				
1850.	Geo Youngerman	Jacob Miller	A Haugh	Phil Socks				
1851.	Jos Butsch	Jacob Miller	A Haugh	Phil Socks			Statesman and Locomotive	
1852.	Hugh Slaven	Jacob Miller	A Haugh	Phil Socks			Sentinel and Locomotive	
1853.	Wm Hughey	H Ohr	A Haugh	Phil Socks	Joseph Little	J W Davis	Locomotive	Jeff Springsteen
1854.	Wm Hughey	Jacob Miller	A Haugh	Geo Bishing	Jacob B Fitler	J T Williams	Elder & Harkness	Jeff Springsteen
1855.	J B Fitler	Richard Weeks	A Haugh	John Moffitt	Chas W Purcell	J T Williams	Chas G Berry	Jeff Springsteen
1856.	J B Fitler	Geo W Harlan		A Lingenfelter	Samuel Keeley	H J Kelley	Larrabee & Cottam	J M Van Blaricum / Chas W Warner
1857.	H Colestock	R Weeks	None	John Moffitt	Andrew Wallace	J M Jamison	Ind'p's Journal Co	A D Rose
1858.	H Colestock	Chas John		John Moffitt	Jos W Davis	J G Flemming	Ind'p's Journal Co	Samuel Lefevre
1859-60	H Colestock	Chas John		G W Allred	John F Foudray / Jos W Davis	C S Butterfield	Ind'p's Journal Co	A D Rose
1861-2	Jno A Colestock	Thos J Foos		G W Allred	Jos W Davis	Jas Loucks	Ind'p's Journal Co	A D Rose
1863-4	John M Kemper	J J Wenner		G W Allred	Chas Richmann	Jas Loucks	Ellis Barnes	Thos A Ramsey / Thos D Amos
1865-6	August Richter	Chas John		G W Allred	Chas Richmann	Jas Loucks / Joseph Bishop	James G Douglass	David Powell / J Van Blaricum
1867-8	August Richter	Sampson Barlee	Sampson Barlee	G W Allred	Geo W Buchanan / Chas Richmann	Aug Bruner	James G Douglass	Thos S Wilson

NOTE.—The city was incorporated by the Assembly February 13th, 1847, the act being accepted by the people at a general election held March 27th. A mayor was to be elected in April for two years, one councilman from each of the seven wards for one year, and the council were to elect the city officers, who also served one year. This government continued till March 7th, 1852, when the council accepted the general law of June 18th, 1852, as the city charter. By this act the mayor became president of the council, and all the officers and councilmen were to be elected by the people and serve one year. Two councilmen were to be elected from each ward by the voters thereof. This charter was amended in 1857, extending the term of mayor and councilmen to two years, and on the 1st of March, 1859, it was amended so that the city officers elected by the people were to hold office two years and the councilmen four years. This act was superseded by the act of December 20th, 1865, under which the officers and councilmen were elected for two years, the auditor, assessor, attorney and engineer being elected by the council. This act was superseded by the act of March 14th, 1867, under which the city is now governed. This act provides for a police judge, John N. Scott being elected the first incumbent May, 1867. The mayor, clerk, assessor, judge, marshal, treasurer and councilmen are elected by the people, and hold their offices for two years; the other officers are elected by the council, and hold office for one year.

fifth, Abram W. Harrison the sixth, William L. Wingate the seventh. The new council was organized May 1st, and elected Samuel S. Rooker president, and James G. Jordan sec'ry, at a salary of $100; Nathan Lister, treasurer, at $50; James Wood, engineer, at $300; William Campbell, collector, with per cent. compensation; William Campbell, marshall, at $150 and fees; A. M. Carnahan, attorney, with fees; Jacob B. Fitler, street commissioner, at $100; David Cox and Jacob B. Fitler, messengers of the fire companies, at $4; Sampson Barbee and Jacob Miller, clerks of the markets, at $50; Joshua Black, assessor; and Benjamin F. Lobaugh, sexton. [The city officers, from 1847 to the present time, are named on pages 47 and 48.] The tax duplicate for 1846-7 amounted to $4,226, and $865 of this sum were delinquencies from former years. Though there was little money in the treasury the council at once began to improve the streets, and it was waggishly suggested that they employ a squad to tramp down the dog-fennel and thus give the place a business appearance.

Little had been done by the old trustees and councilmen in the way of street improvements, beyond filling mud holes, cutting drains or grubbing stumps, and though James Wood had been employed to make a street profile in March, 1841, which had been adopted in April, 1842, and followed in the subsequent improvements, and considerable sums expended, no permanent results had been achieved. The street profile was re-adopted by the new city council June 21, 1847, and a new system commenced, beginning at the centre of the city and extending gradually outward. Property holders were required to bear the expense of grading and gravelling in front of their lots, and the city finished the crossings. The first bouldering was done in May, 1859, by Looker and Lefevre, on Washington between Illinois and Meridian streets, and by the summer of 1860 it was completed from Mississippi to Alabama streets, and from thence it has been extended east and west and north and south. Nearly all the present street improvements, culverts and bridges, have been completed in the last twelve years.

The free school tax having been authorized by a large majority, at the election held April 24, 1847, the council levied it and made arrangements for the schools. Each ward was made a district under the supervision of a trustee. Houses were rented and teachers employed, the schools being free only for one quarter each year under the State law. Donations of lots and money were asked, and the thanks of the council extended, in December, 1847, to Thomas

D. Gregg, for a gift of $100. Lots were purchased at from $300 to $500 in the seven wards in 1848-9, and in 1851-2 plain, cheap, one story brick structures, so planned that additional stories could afterward be added, were built in five of the wards. Those in the second, fourth and sixth wards, had two rooms each, and in the others but one room each. A second story was added to the first, second and fifth ward houses in 1854-6, and all except the old seventh ward house have since been enlarged or raised. A good two story house was built in the eastern part of the seventh (now in the eighth,) ward in 1857, and it was raised an additional story in 1865. Lots were bought in view of the future extension of the city beyond the donation it would be good policy to secure sites for future houses on or beyond the present boundaries of the city. In 1867-8 a large, four story building, with basement, was erected in the south part of the sixth ward and will cost, when fully completed, about $43,000. It is at present the largest and finest school building in the city. The houses recently built are well designed, well finished, and have far more architectural pretensions than the earlier ones. Additional buildings are still needed as the schools from the start have been much cramped for room.

The first tax levy, in 1847, produced $1,981; that of 1848, $2,385; that of 1849, $2,851. In 1850 the fund amounted to $6,160, $5,938 of which sum was spent that year and the beginning of the next for lots and buildings. The tax produced a larger sum each year with the increased growth of the city, and in 1857 yielded $20,329. At first the entire amount was expended for buildings, the teachers being paid by tuition fees, but after the first houses were finished the annual return was mostly expended in salaries, the schools being kept open longer, more teachers employed and better salaries paid.

In 1847 the several wards were constituted independent districts, each under the supervision of a trustee, and schools were opened in the fall of that year or spring of 1848, in rented houses. This continued till January, 1853, when the council elected Henry P. Coburn, Calvin Fletcher and Henry F. West, a board of trustees under the new law, giving them the sole control and management of the city schools. A code of rules was drawn up by Calvin Fletcher, arrangements made, and on the 25th of April the free schools were opened for the first time, two male and twelve female teachers being employed. Until that date the number of pupils had averaged only 340, but by the first of May the attendance rose to 700, and over 1,000 out of the 2,600 children in the city were enrolled. Until the election of this board of trustees the schools had been conducted independently, without a common system, text books or course of study. At the request of the trustees the principals of the leading private schools prepared a list of text books and a course of instruction which was adopted and subsequently followed. In August the graded system was adopted, and the high school, for more advanced pupils, was opened September 1st, by E. P. Cole, with one assistant, in the old county seminary, which had been repaired and refitted for the purpose. From this date to February, 1855, the system was under the sole supervision of the trustees, who served without compensation and almost without thanks, to the detriment of their private interests, but they persevered in the work, overcame all obstacles, and at last interested the people in the enterprise. The work, however, proved too great, and at their request the council in February, 1855, elected Silas T. Bowen superintendent, at a salary of $400 per annum, (which he earned twice over,) requiring him to give a large share of his time to the duties of the office. He effected a marked improvement, but it was soon evident that the duties required more labor and time than he could bestow, and the council, in March, 1856, appointed George B. Stone (who had succeeded E. P. Cole as principal of the high school,) superintendent at a salary of $1,000 a year, requiring him to give all his time to the schools. He at once perfected the system, adopted improved methods of teaching, held meetings of the teachers and examined and drilled them for their work, inspired them with his own zeal and energy, and made the system so thorough and popular that the prejudice which had existed against it died out. The school tax was willingly paid, and the private schools sank into the back ground or languished for want of their former support. With the increasing revenue better salaries (ranging from $300 to $600,) were paid, the terms were lengthened, more teachers engaged, 35, mostly females, being employed in 1857. The average attendance of pupils had risen from 340 in April, 1853, to 1,400 in 1856, and 1,800 in 1857. The total number enrolled at that date was about 2,800. Ten houses were occupied, seating comfortably only 1,200, but crowded with 1,800 pupils. Forty-four per cent. of the children in the city were enrolled, and 73 per cent. of those enrolled were in average

daily attendance. The schools were graded as primary, secondary, intermediate, grammar and high schools. The system was working prosperously and a bright career seemed certainly before it when the supreme court decision on the tax question in January, 1858, struck a fatal blow at the whole fabric. The city council was immediately convened to consider the question. It called meetings of citizens in the several wards to devise measures by which the schools could be continued. The meetings were held January 29th, and 1,100 scholarships were subscribed amounting to $3,000, and it was resolved to sustain the free system for the current quarter, and as a pay system afterward. The schools were closed, however, at the end of the quarter, the superintendent and teachers left for other points, and the houses remained vacant or used occasionally for private schools for a year or two afterward.

No free schools were opened in 1859. A small tax was levied for the repairs of houses and furniture, and from the State fund free terms of eighteen weeks each were held in 1860 and 1861. The system was reorganized under the law of 1862, and a term of twenty-two weeks held that year and since that date it has been gradually regaining the ground occupied in 1858. Prof. George W. Hoss acted as superintendent in 1862-3, having 29 teachers employed and 2,374 pupils enrolled. In September, 1863, the system was again reorganised, A. C. Shortridge being elected superintendent, and since that date full terms of thirty-nine weeks have been held each year. The schools are graded as primary, intermediate and high, with four subordinate grades (A. B. C. and D.) in each. Common text books are used in the similar grades, and all the children in any given subordinate grade of all the schools are simultaneously pursuing the same course of study, graduating from the lower to the higher subordinate grades, and from the primary to the intermediate and thence to the high school, the whole course requiring twelve years, (ten months in each year,) and giving the pupils a thorough English education. Daily registers are kept showing the conduct, attendance and scholarship of each pupil, and a given average must be attained before promotion to a higher grade is granted. The registers thus kept show a great improvement in attendance and scholarship in the last three years.

The school buildings and the whole system are controlled by three trustees elected by the city council, but accountable for their acts and expenditures to the county commissioners and the superintendent of public instruction. They have charge of the expenditures for buildings, tuition, employment of teachers, &c; the expenditures being made from two separate funds, one being for buildings and repairs, the other for tuition, and derived partly from the State school fund and partly from a special city tax. The immediate management of the schools devolves on a superintendent, who devotes his whole time to them and receives a salary of $2000. The teachers (sixty-two of whom are now employed, three male and fifty-nine female,) receive salaries ranging from $400 to $700, and are only employed after a thorough examination of their qualifications for the position. I m p r o v e d methods of instruction have been promptly adopted, object teaching, gymnastics, music, penmanship and other branches, are taught by special instructors, who visit the schools in turn for that purpose.

The following table shows the number of houses, teachers, children enrolled in the schools, average number enrolled, daily average attendance and per cent. of attendance from 1863 to the present time. No reliable returns exist as to the total number of children of school age (6 to 21,) in the city for the several years, and no records exist as to above items for the years 1853-8. When the new sixth ward building is opened, 4,200 children can be accommodated with seats, and 75 or 80 teachers can be employed.

Years.	School Houses.	Teachers	Children Enrolled.	Average No. Pupils	Per Cent. Attendance
1863-4	30		2,374	1,260	86
1864-5	28		2,533	1,428	92
1865-6	9	34	3,242	1,600	91.1
1866-7	11	58	4,399	2,505	94.2
1867-8	12	62	4,949	3,137	95.3

In September, 1853, when the graded system was adopted, the schools were rated as primary, intermediate, grammar and high school, the last being opened in the old seminary building, on the first of September, by E. P. Cole, with one assistant. It was held there till the downfall of the schools in 1858. It was re-established in 1864, and held at the first ward house, and from the spring of 1867 in the old Second Presbyterian Church on Circle street, which was then purchased for $13,500. This building is now undergoing alterations and being better fitted for school uses at an expense of about $4,500. The principals of this school from 1853 to 1858 were E. P. Cole, George B. Stone and W. B. Henkle. Since 1864 W. A. Bell, Pleasant Bond, W. J. Squier and W. A. Bell. The present salary is $1,600.

From 1847 to January, 1853, the schools were conducted independently in the seven wards, under the supervision of seven trustees, one to each district or ward. A board of three trustees was then elected by the council to take charge of the entire system, and retained the control of it till April 12, 1861, when (under the new law) an ordinance was passed making the wards districts, and requiring the voters of each of the seven wards to elect a school trustee for their ward. They were elected in May of that year for two years. This system continued till April, 1865, when, under the law of that year, the council elected three trustees, W. H. L. Noble, T. B. Elliott and C. Vonnegut, who have since been continued in office and had the entire management of our city school system. The city is greatly indebted to the early trustees (prominent among whom were Henry F. West, Henry P. Coburn, Calvin Fletcher, sr., Silas T. Bowen, David V. Culley, David S. Beatty and Jno. B. Dillon,) for their zeal, energy and perseverance under very discouraging circumstances, and to the present board, Messrs. Noble, Elliott and Vonnegut, for reviving and carrying forward the system. Silas T. Bowen, George B. Stone, George W. Hoss and A. C. Shortridge, have been the superintendents. To Mr. Stone belongs the credit for perfecting the system and demonstrating its usefulness, and to Mr. Shortridge its revival and present efficiency. The city may well be proud of the system, and of the thoroughly drilled corps of instructors now employed, and with continued careful management the free schools will be among the first of her future glories.

In May, 1847, the Grand Masonic Lodge bought a lot at the south-east corner of Washington and Tennessee streets and formed a stock company to build a hall. A plan drawn by J. Willis, architect, having been accepted, the corner-stone was laid with appropriate ceremonies October 25th, 1848, and the hall built in 1849-50 at a cost of about $20,000. It was opened in the spring, but not finished till the fall of 1850, and was finally dedicated by the Grand Lodge May 27th, 1851. The concert room in the second story was the first large hall opened here for public meetings, and was in almost constant use from the time of its opening till the erection of Morrison's Opera Hall on Meridian street in 1865, since which time it has been comparatively little used. The constitutional convention of 1850 was held in Masonic Hall, and nearly all the conventions, concerts, lectures, panoramas, and exhibitions, dramatic and otherwise, for fifteen years, were given in it. Almost all the leading speakers, lecturers and singers of the country have appeared on its stage. The stock in the building was long since purchased by the Grand Lodge, and it is now proposed to change and improve the building.

A meeting was held in May to make arrangements for a formal welcome to the First Indiana Regiment of Volunteers expected soon to return from Mexico. The welcome proved a failure, as the volunteers returned in small squads in wagons and stages at different periods, and it was impossible to divide the "enthusiasm" accordingly.

The first instalment of female teachers sent by Governor Slade from New England arrived here in June and were sent to various parts of the country. They were soon married, and others were afterward sent in their stead. In July, the remains of Captain T. B. Kinder, brought from Buena Vista by his company, were buried with military honors in the old cemetery.

The near completion of the Madison railroad awakened the interest of the community in such enterprises, and frequent meetings were held during the summer and fall to advocate roads to different points and organize companies. A new impetus was given to business, street improvements were begun, new buildings and workshops erected, and new residents were met daily on the streets.

Arrangements were made September 25th at a citizens' meeting to celebrate the completion of the railroad on the 1st of October. The last rail was laid at about nine o'clock that morning, just as two crowded excursion trains arrived from below, greeted by a great crowd of rejoicing natives, many of whom then first saw a locomotive and train, and who joyously filled an excursion train to Franklin and back. The great even was celebrated by the firing of cannon, and by a procession which included Spalding's entire circus outfit, Ned Kendall's band and a country cavalry company. An address was also delivered by Governor Whitcomb from the top of a car at the depot, and an illumination and fireworks exhibition closed the festivities at night. The excursionists were hauled across the low and muddy valley of Pogue's run in carriages and wood wagons, and the few hotels were crowded with hungry guests. The depot had been located on the high ground south of the creek, a quarter of a mile from the town, during the preceding summer, its location there being opposed by many persons who urged that it should front on Maryland street, which was then the southern settled limit. A cluster of warehouses was built around it, and for several years it formed a separate settlement until the expansion of the city included it in the body of the place. The depot was built in 1846-7, the engine house and shops in 1850, and the road had

a flat bar track till 1850-2, when it was taken up and a T rail substituted.

The Madison road had been begun in 1838 by the State, the cost being estimated at $2,240,000, of which sum the inclined plane was to cost $272,000. Twenty-eight miles were finished in 1841 at a cost of $1,500,000. Branham & Co. leased the road in April, 1839, for sixty per cent. of the receipts, the State keeping up repairs and supplying motive power. The work was surrendered to a company in 1842, and completed October 1st, 1847. N. B. Palmer, S. Merrill, John Brough, E. W. H. Ellis, F. O. J. Smith and others were presidents till the line was sold. In January, 1854, it was consolidated with and operated together with the Peru road, but the arrangement was severed after a few months. It was sold by the United States Marshal March 27th, 1862, for $325,000, and a new company organized, and was bought a year or two afterward by the Jeffersonville Company, and has since been operated by that organization. For some time after its completion the road paid better than any other in the country. In 1852 its stock sold at $1.60, and in January, 1856, had fallen to two and one-half cents on the dollar. The State held stock in the road valued at $1,230,000, but was ultimately cheated out of it, receiving scarcely anything for it.

The isolation of the town ended with the completion of this road. An outlet for travel and surplus products at last existed, and the town became a centre of traffic for a considerable region around it. Wheat, which had been selling at forty cents per bushel, rose in a few weeks to ninety cents. Other farm products advanced in proportion, and goods and groceries declined. Trade improved, building increased, workshops were started, property advanced in price, and city airs were timidly assumed.

The Madison road exacted such high rates for fares and freights, and for several years made such heavy profits that opposition was aroused; other routes were demanded, and roads to Bellefontaine, Terre Haute, Peru, Lafayette, Lawrenceburg and Jeffersonville, were advocated. The old companies were resuscitated, or new charters obtained; the projects were energetically pushed in 1848-9, meetings were held, stock subscribed, surveys made and contracts let. In 1849-50 a railroad fever prevailed in the community, and did not subside until eight lines were completed, and the city became widely known as the "railroad city" of the west. From under estimates as to cost and over estimates as to immediate business, the lines failed to realize the hopes of stockholders, but while not at once remunerative to them, the gain to the State and city was very great. The construction, in a few years, of many depots, shops and warehouses, disbursed much money, attracted many workmen, and stimulated manufacturing enterprises. The population of 4,000 in 1847, increased to 8,100 in 1850. 10,800 in 1852, 15,000, in 1857, and 18,000 in 1860.

For sometime each road used its own depot; passengers and freights being transferred from one to the other by hacks and drays, but a connection by rail was soon proposed, and an agreement having been made in August, 1849, between the companies, and the right of way having been granted December 20, 1848 by the council, the Union Railroad Co., was organized, the Union track located and laid in 1850, (relaid in 1853,) the ground bought and a Union passenger depot, 120 by 420 feet, built in 1852-3, on Meridian, Illinois and Louisiana streets. It was opened September 28, 1853, William N. Jackson being appointed general ticket agent, a post ever since held by him. It has since been used by eight separate lines, and was enlarged, improved and an eating house added in 1866. In December, 1867, the Junction Railroad Co., and the Crawfordsville and Vincennes lines unsuccessfully applied for admission to the depot, and it is possible that a Union passenger station will yet be erected in the western part of the city. Such a depot will ultimately be erected, for the present one can not accommodate all the business of the future.

A brief statement of the history of the several roads projected and built since the Madison road, may be given here. Prominent among these was the Bellefontaine road to Union City on the State line, which was energetically pushed by the first President, Oliver H. Smith, its construction being largely due to his efforts. It was chartered in 1848, meetings held, stock subscribed and right-of-way secured in 1848-9; contracts were let in the fall of 1849, track-laying began April, 1850, cars ran to Pendleton, twenty-eight miles, December. 1850, and the road was finished, eighty-four miles, to the State line, December 1852, at a cost of $21,550 per mile. The brick depot and shops were built in 1851, in the north-east part of the city and used till the Union depot and track were finished, when a frame freight depot and brick engine house and shops were built in November, 1853, at the corner of Virginia avenue and Pogue's run. These were used till 1864 when the large frame freight depot and brick shops and engine house were completed and occupied in the eastern part of the city. The engine house and shops on Virginia avenue were then torn away,

but the frame depot is still used for way freights. The first depot and shops, with 1,100 feet of track and five acres of ground were sold in July, 1853, for $17,500 to Mr. Farnsworth, and were used by Farnsworth & Barnard as a car factory from November 1853 till 1859. It then remained vacant till after the war began and was occupied as a Government stable from 1862 to 1865, when it was burned down. The Bellefontaine road was consolidated in 1855 with the connecting Ohio line to Galion. The stock was "watered" and the name changed to the Indianapolis, Pittsburg & Cleveland Railroad. In the spring of 1868 a further consolidation was effected with the Cleveland, Columbus & Cincinnati road, and the new road is known as the Cleveland, Columbus, Cincinnati & Indianapolis Railroad. O. H. Smith, Alfred Harrison, Calvin Fletcher, John Brough, S. Witt, and others, have been Presidents of this corporation since its charter. It has been one of the best freight and passenger roads leading to this point.

The Lawrenceburg and upper Mississippi road was originally begun in sections, or several short roads, in 1850, a through road being bitterly and successfully opposed by the Madison Co., but was finally chartered in 1851 and finished to Lawrenceburg. 90 miles, in October 1853, under Geo. H. Dunn, the first president. The name was changed December 1853 to the Indianapolis and Cincinnati road. The Ohio and Mississippi road having been finished from Cincinnati to Lawrenceburg in April 1854, a third rail was laid and the cars run to that city, 110 miles, under a lease. In 1854-5 the old White-water canal was bought, and a separate track laid in its bed, and a fine passenger and freight depot built. The shops of the company were built south-east of the city in 1853, but were burned in 1855, and soon afterward rebuilt. They were removed to Cincinnati in 1865 and are now located there. The brick freight depot was built on Louisiana and Delaware streets in 1853, and is now used by the consolidated roads. In 1866, after an effort to build a rival line via Crawfordsville to Lafayette, a consolidation was effected with the Lafayette road and the name adopted for the united corporation is Indianapolis, Cincinnati and Lafayette road. Branch roads have been built up the Whitewater valley on the canal bank, and from Fairland to Martinsville, and in March 1868 a consolidation was effected with the Vincennes road.— Much opposition was aroused by this last movement, but Mr. Lord, in a speech to our business men, in April 1868, greatly allayed the feeling, and promised that his policy should not prove detrimental to the interests of this city. Geo. H. Dunn, Thos. A. Morris and Henry C. Lord have been presidents of this corporation.

The Jeffersonville road was begun in 1848 and finished to Edinburgh, 78 miles, in 1852, at a cost of $1,185,000. It had been designed to extend to this point, but in August 1853 a lease was obtained from the Madison road, by which the use of that road with its shops, depots and houses was perpetually secured, and in 1863 the Jeffersonville company bought the entire road and equipment and now operate both lines. A branch road was built in 1852 from Edinburgh to Shelbyville and Rushville, 26 miles, at a cost of $525,000, but was afterward abandoned. The war traffic and travel was immense over the Jeffersonville road, it being the only direct southern line leading to the seat of war. John Zulauf, Dillard Ricketts and others, have been its presidents.

The Terre Haute and Richmond road was projected in 1846, surveyed December 1847, contracts let in 1848-9, commenced in 1850, and finished to Terre Haute, 73 miles, in May 1852, at a cost of $1,415,000, under Chauncy Rose, its first president. The eastern section was abandoned and its construction undertaken by the Indiana Central Railway Co. in 1851. The brick freight depot (remodeled in 1857,) was built on Louisiana and Tennessee streets in 1850-1. Its roof was partly blown off in 1865 by the explosion of the pony engine of the Central company, inside the building. The engine house and the frame bridge over White river were built in 1851-2, and the bridge was replaced by a handsome iron structure in 1866, without interrupting traffic on the line. The road has been prosperous, well managed, has met with few accidents, and is the main line for western trade and travel. It is also the only coal road yet built. The company have no shops here, the repairs being made at Terre Haute. Chauncy Rose, S. Crawford, E. J. Peck and others, have been its Presidents.

The Peru and Indianapolis road was chartered at the session of 1845-6, the company organized July 1847, road surveyed October 1847, located July 1848, commenced 1849, cars were run to Noblesville, 21 miles, March 1851, and the road completed to Peru, 73 miles, April 3, 1854, at a cost of about $760,000. It was consolidated June 1, 1854, with, and operated for several months by the Madison road. The road traversed a new country, encountered many obstacles, and has not been as successful as other lines. It has been the main source of supply for lumber and tim-

ber, and since its northern connections were finished has had a fair share of the north-western trade and travel. It passed into a receiver's hands in 1857, and has since been operated for the bondholders.— Its shops are at Peru, and its buildings here have never been of much value. It was originally laid with flat bar, taken up from the Madison road, but T rail was substituted in 1855-6. The first frame depot was commenced in August, 1856, on New Jersey street and Pogue's run, but was blown down during a storm, September 17, burying about a dozen men in the ruins, and badly injuring several of them. Another was built in November following.— W. J. Holman, Jno. Burk. E. W. H. Ellis, J. D. Defrees and David Macy, have been presidents.

The Lafayette and Indianapolis road was begun in 1849 and finished to Lafayette, 65 miles, in December 1852, at a cost of about $1,000,000, under Albert S. White, the first president. The stock subscription was small, the road being mostly built by loans which were subsequently paid off from the earnings of the road, making its stock very valuable. Until the completion of the northern connections of the Peru road it was the main route to the north-west, and did a very lucrative business during the war. In 1866 Henry C. Lord having failed to buy the road or effect a consolidation with it, began the construction of a rival route to Danville on the north-west via Crawfordsville, and after doing considerable work achieved his object, and obtained a perpetual lease of the line, and it is now controlled and operated by the Cincinnati company. The Lafayette freight depot was built in 1852-3, on North street and the canal, but was burned in 1864, and rebuilt in 1865. Since the consolidation it has been but little used, the business of both roads being done at the Delaware street depot. The company never had any shops at this point, the construction and repairs being done at Lafayette. A. S. White and Wm. F. Reynolds, were the presidents of the company.

The Indiana Central Railway Company was organized in the spring, surveys made in the summer, and contracts let in the fall of 1851. Track-laying began November, 1852, and the road was completed to the State line, seventy-two miles, December 8, 1853, at a cost of $1,223,000, under John S. Newman, the first President. It divides eastern trade and travel with the Bellefontaine road, and was consolidated with the Ohio connecting road in 1863, and afterwards known as the Indianapolis & Columbus road. A further consolidation was effected in 1867, with the Chicago and Great Eastern road, and the offices and shops are to be removed elsewhere. The brick freight depot was built on Delaware street and Pogue's run in 1852, and its shops just east of the city, in the same year.

At and since the date of completion of the foregoing roads, several others were projected, or in course of construction; among them was the Junction road, ninety-eight miles long, from Hamilton, Ohio, via Rushville and Connersville, to this city. It was begun in separate sections, in 1850, by the Ohio and Indianapolis, and the Junction Companies, which were consolidated, April, 1853, with $1,800,000 stock subscriptions. Several hundred thousand dollars were expended on the line, the depot grounds here were purchased, and the road half finished, when the hard times of 1855-6 caused its suspension and the sale of its lands at a nominal price. The company was re-organized in 1866, work was resumed, a subsidy of $45,000 voted to it by our city, depot grounds bought, and the road finished to this point in May, 1868. The freight depot will be built on Virginia avenue, south of Pogue's run, and the shops and offices are to be located here by contract with the city. Caleb B. Smith, Jno. Ridenour and others have been Presidents of the Company.

The Vincennes road was first projected in 1851, and a company organized in 1853, with John H. Bradley, President; but only a preliminary survey was made, and the enterprise was abandoned during the subsequent monetary revulsion. A new company was organized under General Burnside, in 1865, the contracts let, and a subsidy of $60,000 granted by the city in 1866, and right of way secured; work is now being rapidly prosecuted along the line, and the road will be finished from Gosport to this city during the present year. The shops and offices, by agreement with the city, are to be located here. The road traverses the best iron, coal, stone, timber and grain region of the State, and will be second to none in importance, and it is all important that its management should not be adverse to our interests. On the 3d of April, 1868, it was consolidated with the Cincinnati road.

A direct road to Evansville, one hundred and fifty miles long, had been projected in 1849, but nothing was done till April, 1853, when Oliver H. Smith and Willard Carpenter organized a company under the general law, and held meetings, subscribed stock, surveyed the line, let contracts, and pushed the work rapidly forward till 1856, when the monetary pressure stopped the enterprise, and caused the loss of nearly

everything invested in it. It is still dormant, but its importance, and the rich agricultural and mineral region it traversed, the amount expended on it, and the heavy south-western trade, certainly demand a renewal of the enterprise, and its favorable consideration by our people, especially since the management of the Vincennes road will probably be adverse to our interests.

The Cincinnati & Indianapolis Short-line Railroad Company, from this point via Rushville, Laurel and Brookville to Cincinnati, was organized in January, 1853; subscriptions were obtained, surveys made, contracts let, and other steps taken, but the enterprise was suspended by hard times in 1854-5, before any tangible results were obtained, and has not since been revived.

The Toledo & Indianapolis Railroad Company, via Muncie to Toledo, one hundred and eighty-five miles, was organized February, 1854, under the general law. Seventy-five miles of road, only, were to be built to make connections with existing roads, and secure a short and direct route for grain to the lake. Surveys were made, and efforts to obtain subscriptions, but the financial pressure of 1855 put an end temporarily to the scheme.

The Indiana & Illinois Central Railroad, one hundred and sixty miles long on an air line, to Decatur, Illinois, was proposed in December, 1852, and organized February 15, 1853. Surveys were made, and subscriptions obtained, and contracts let in July, 1853, for the whole line, at $22,000 per mile, to be done in 1855, and $500,000 of work was done. The hard times intervened, the work stopped, and the company lands were sold to pay the contractors. The line is almost straight, traverses a beautiful and rich country, opens up coal and iron regions, and gives a direct western line to the Pacific road. Its importance merits renewed effort, and the company—which was re-organized in 1866—should attempt its construction.

In 1866, before the Cincinnati road had succeeded in forcing the sale of the Lafayette line, H. C. Lord, as the final effort, determined to build a rival line via Crawfordsville. The city voted a subsidy of $45,000, right of way was secured, surveys made, contracts let, and considerable work done at this end of the line, when the Lafayette road consented to sell, and the new line was at once abandoned. This summary disposal of the matter displeased the residents along the line; the company was soon re-organized, contracts relet, and the work is now in progress. It is to be hoped that a new outlet to the north-west will be speedily found through the rich region traversed by this line.

In 1867 an effort was made by the eastern roads to force a sale or consolidation of the Terre Haute road, which having failed, it was announced that a straight-line road to St. Louis would be built from this point. Surveys were made, right of way secured, subscriptions voted, and the contracts, it is said, will be let this year. The road should be built, as it will give an additional and competing route to the coal and iron beds of the western part of the State, and the city can well afford to aid the enterprise, first providing that no consolidation shall be made with competing roads. The Terre Haute company is also engaged in building a straight line from that city to St. Louis, as a continuation of their own route.

It will be seen from the foregoing brief statement of facts connected with the several roads, that only one of the completed lines, (the Bellefontaine,) ever located its principal shops at this point, and even that road, since its consolidation, has its main shops in Ohio. The excuse advanced for this general action has been that work could be done cheaper elsewhere; but this, even if true in one or two cases, can scarcely be true of every little town in this or other States, and the solution of the problem is to be found partly in the jealousy of other cities toward this, and mostly in the want of enterprise on the part of our own people. They have not deemed it necessary, either for their own interests or those of the city, to hold a controlling interest in the highways leading here, and the consequence has been that as little as possible has been done by the railways toward building up our manufacturing interests. In many respects this city is better situated for manufacturing than any other in this or the adjoining States, and its advantages increase with the opening of every additional line; and, if it fails to achieve a high rank in this respect, the fault will lie solely with our own capitalists, and the blame should lie where it belongs. It has been too much the fashion here to wait for others to increase the value of property which is held by the few, and the money on hand, instead of creating wealth by producing manufactured articles from comparatively valueless raw material, is doled out sparingly at one and two per cent. per month, taxing the life out of those who do attempt to create such articles. It seems singular that, while the railway companies combined and successfully operated a union track and depot, that they never entered into a union company for the manufacture of locomotives, cars, and all other articles needed in the equipment of their roads. One great establishment, under competent management, could combine the iron and brass foundries, rolling mills, machine shops, saw and planing mills, forges, upholstery, paint and other shops, needed in the fabrication of every item used by them. Such an establishment, with the capital it could employ, the thorough subdivision and supervision of labor, the extent and variety of articles manufactured, the steady demand therefor by the stockholding roads and outside lines, located here where the influx and efflux of materials and articles would be so ready and certain, and skilled laborers, so readily brought, could defy private competition, furnish all articles to its stockholders at cost, and pay all expenses and a profit from outside work.

But few mills or manufactories existed here till after the completion of the Madison road, for the local demand was very limited, and shipments to other points almost impossible. Underhill's foundry, on Pennsylvania street, started by Grover in 1836, was the only one here. The grist mills of West and of Carlisle, West's cotton and woolen mill, Hannaman's woolen and oil mill, and Sheet's paper mill, were on the canal, and had been built since 1838. Patterson's grist mill was on Fall creek, and the old steam (grist, woolen and saw) mills, on the river, had been repaired by Geisendorffs in 1847, and used as a woolen mill till 1852, when they built a mill (subsequently enlarged,) on the west branch of the canal. Of mills and manufactories, built since 1847, the more prominent may be briefly mentioned here. The principal grist mills were Carlisle's, (his old mill was burnt January 18, '56,) now Sohl & Gibson, on the canal, built 1863; Underhill's, south of the city, 1851; Skillen's, 1863; Capital mills, 1856; Morris' mills, south Pennsylvania street, 1848, burnt 1851; Bates' mills, Pogue's run, 1859. Of saw mills, Kortpeter's, south Pennsylvania street, 1849; Fletcher & Wells, Massachusetts avenue, 1857; Gay & Stevens, Madison depot, 1857; Hill's, East street, 1858, burned and rebuilt October, 1859; Off & Wishmire's, Railroad street, 1858; Helwig & Blake's, canal, 1858; Marsee's, New Jersey street, 1859; McKernan & Pierce, Kentucky avenue, 1865. Of planing mills, Shellaberger's, east Market, 1852; Blake & Geutle's, (the first one here,) Vermont street, 1849; Kreglo & Blake, canal, 1855, burned and rebuilt in Aug., 1860; Byrket's, Tennessee street, 1857; McCord & Wheatley's, Alabama street, 1865; Tate's, New Jersey street, 1864; Hill & Wingate's, East street, 1858, burned in October and rebuilt November, 1859; Builders & Manufacturers' Association, Delaware street, 1866; Carpenters' Association, South and Meridian streets, 1866; Emerson's, near the canal, 1863; Beam's, west Washington street, 1865; Behymer's, east Market street, 1864.

Shingle mills, Evarts', south Pennsylvania, 1857; Smock's, east Washington, 1858.

Of furniture and chair factories, John Ott, west Washington, 1855; Sloan & Ingersoll, 1850; Espy & Sloan, 1848; John Vetter, Madison depot, 1857, burned 1866; Philip Dohn, south Meridian, 1865, burned and rebuilt, 1867; Spiegel and Thoms, east Washington, 1855, and East street, 1863, enlarged to double size, 1866, and the first five-story house built in the city; Helwig & Roberts, canal, 1857, burned and rebuilt 1860; M. S. Huey, west Washington, 1855; Field & Day, Vermont street, 1850; Wilkens & Hall, west Washington, 1864; C. J. Meyer, east Washington, 1860; Cabinetmakers' Union, east Market, 1859.

Of coopering establishments, there have been Defrees, on the canal, Murphey's and May's on East street; Careys and Brennon's, near Soldiers' Home; McNeeleys, near Lafayette depot; Kingans and others.

Of peg and last factories, Crawford & Osgood, south Pennsylvania street, 1848, and burned 1851; Osgood & Smith, south Illinois, 1852, burned and rebuilt once or twice afterward; Yandes & Kemper, south Illinois, 1867.

Of wagon or carriage manufactories, Hiram Gaston, Kentucky avenue, 1853; Lowes, east Market, 1863; Drews, east Market, 1852; Shaws, Georgia street, 1866.

Of spokes and felloes, Osgood Smith & Co., south Illinois, 1852.

Of woolen mills, Geisendorffs, on the canal, 1852; Merritt & Coughlen, in Hannaman's old mill, on the river, 1849 or '50, were burned out in January, 1851, and rebuilt in May, 1851; West's, 1839; Younts, 1849, on the canal.

Of paper mills, Sheets, on canal, 1839; Gay & Bradens, canal, 1862; McLean & Co., river, 1861.

Of cotton mills, West, canal, 1839, and the Cotton Mill Co., on the river, 1867.

Of agricultural and farm implements and machinery, W. M. Gause, 1856; Beard & Sinex, and Beard & Forsha, Tennessee street, 1857; Hasselman & Vinton, south Meridian, 1852; Chandler & Taylor, west Washington, 1859, burned and rebuilt 1863(?); Binkley & Co., south Tennessee, 1860; Beard & Starr, north Tennessee, 1860; Agricultural Works Co., south Tennessee, 1864.

Of oil mills, J. P. Evans & Co., south Delaware, 1862.

Iron manufactures have taken the leading rank at this point, and promise still more rapid growth in future. The interest has risen in the last fifteen years from a very small beginning. The first steam engine ever built here, a small affair of three or four horse power, was completed in June, 1848, by Mr. Sergeant, at Bardwell's shop, in the basement of Crawford & Osgood's factory, on south Pennsylvania street. The first foundry in the place was started in July, 1832, by R. A. McPherson & Co., near the bridge, west of the river. Joshua Glover had been doing some iron work on a small scale in 1831. Underhill, Wood & Co. started a foundry in July, 1835, on north Pennsylvania street, and in 1838, Underhill applied steam power in it, being the first to use it in a foundry here. He manufactured plow points, skillets, and other small castings, remaining there till 1852, when he built a large foundry on south Pennsylvania street, and failing in business the building was applied to other purposes, and burned up in November, 1858. Taylor, Watson & Co., in 1848 built a small foundry in the low ground south of Pogue's run, and first began to make steam engines here in 1849. This establishment subsequently passed into Hasselman & Vinton's hands, who built the present foundry, boiler and machine shops in 1852. The firm suffered heavy losses in May, and also in July, 1853, from fires. In 1865 the establishment passed into the control of the Eagle Machine Works Co., who now carry on a heavy business in the manufacture of castings, boilers and agricultural implements, their trade extending over a large territory, and employing a heavy capital. In March, 1854, Wright, Barnes & Co., afterward Ira Davis & Co., built a foundry on Delaware street and Pogue's run, which burned down in 1857. Curtis & Dumont began the manufacture of boilers on south Pennsylvania street in 1852, next north of Underhill's foundry, and Kelshaw & Sinker began the same business at about the same time, just south of the same foundry. Their shop was burned in December, 1853, and rebuilt in 1854. Dumont & Sinker became partners, continuing the business, and adding a foundry. In 1863, Dumont left, and the establishment, now greatly enlarged, is carried on as a foundry, machine shop and boiler factory, on the site of Underhill's old City Foundry, by Sinker, Allen & Yandes. In 1851, Deloss Root & Co., built a small frame stove foundry, south of the Gas Works on Pennsylvania street. It was burned up in January, 1860, but soon rebuilt of brick on a much more extended scale, and stoves, heavy castings and boilers, are now largely manufactured by the establishment. Wiggins & Chandler, in June, 1859, built a small foundry and machine shop on the Canal and west Washington street. It was burned in 1863, (?) but soon after rebuilt on a more extended scale by Chandler & Taylor, and has since done a large business. In 1858, Redstone, Bros. & Co., started a foundry and machine shop on Delaware street south of the Union track, making small castings and sawing machines. Spotts & Thompson started a foundry near the same place in 1859, but both establishments were shortly afterward burned. The Hoosier Stove Foundry was built in 1861, by Cox, Lord & Peck, on Delaware street and Pogue's run, and was operated by them for two or three years and then discontinued. It passed into the hands of A. D. Wood in 1867, and is now carried on by him. Ruschaupt & Co. built a large foundry and machine shop on South Meridian street in 1865, but as they soon afterward became interested in the Eagle Machine Works, the establishment was vacated, and is now used by the Carpenter's Association. Frink & Moore started the Novelty Works in 1860, for the manufacture of small castings, and have done a good business. A foundry was started in 1863, on East Market street, by some one, (unknown to the writer,) and has since mainly been doing railroad work. B. F. Hetherington & Co. started a foundry and machine shop on south Delaware street in 1866 or '67 and are still located there.

Jos. W. Davis & Co., started a brass foundry in 1855, on south Delaware street, and has since added steam and gas-fitting, building up a good business. Garrett & Co., in 1858, started a brass and bell foundry, on the railroad between Meridian and Pennsylvania streets, but failed a year or two afterward.

In 1856, Williamson & Haugh began the manufacture of iron railings, and jail work, on Delaware street opposite the Court House, and at a subsequent date B. F. Haugh & Co. removed to south Pennsylvania street, erecting new buildings and continuing the business on an enlarged scale.

In 1857, E. C. Atkins began the manufacture of mill and other saws, in the old City Foundry building on south Pennsylvania street, but being burned out in 1858, he built a small shop near by, which was also burned in June, 1859. A new shop was then built on south Illinois street, a company formed in 1863 or '64, and the business and buildings have since been greatly enlarged, and a heavy trade carried on. In 1867 Farley & Sinker built a shop and began the manufacture of saws on south

Pennsylvania street, and are doing a good business.

Cottrell & Knight, in 1855 or '56, began the copper-smithing business on south Delaware street, and have since built up a large trade.

In addition to the foregoing, other establishments exist or have existed, and the different railroads have nearly all had repair shops of greater or less extent at this point.

The Indianapolis Rolling Mill was built by R. A. Douglass & Co., and a railroad track down Tennessee street constructed to it, in the summer of 1857, and work began October 29. The owners became involved in the spring of 1858, and for some time it was doubtful whether the works would be continued, but the mill was purchased shortly after by a new company, with John M. Lord as president, and has since been much enlarged and profitably operated. The company have purchased coal and iron mines in Clay county, have erected a furnace to supply their mill with iron, and have also supplied coal for the use of the citizens. The success of the company stimulated other parties, and during the summer of 1867, the White River Iron Company was formed, and a rolling mill was erected on White river, at the foot of Kentucky avenue, and put in operation in April of the present year, for the manufacture of bar iron, about $100,000 of capital being invested in the enterprise.

Several pork and beef packing establishments have been built since 1847.— Blythe & Hedderly began the first one, on Fall creek race in the fall of 1847. It was afterward carried on by Blythe & McNeely. Mansur & Ferguson built one west of White river in 1850. It was burned and rebuilt in 1858. Their packing establishment was located at the Madison depot.— Macy & McTaggart built one near Terre Haute railroad bridge in 1852. Gulick & Tweeds was built just north of it in 1854-5. Allen May's was built north-west of the city in 1855, and burned in 1858. Kingen & Co., built in 1864, on the river bank, the largest and best packing establishment in the country. It was of brick, five stories high, slate roofed, and finished in the best style. They were putting mill machinery in it in the spring of 1865, intending to use it as a mill in summer and packing house in winter. It was filled at the time with lard and pork, on storage, when it was fired by an incendiary and utterly destroyed, involving a loss of $250,000 to the insurance companies, and being by far the largest and most destructive fire that ever occurred here. It was rebuilt in 1866, but not so large or expensively as before. Want of space prevents further mention of the different manufactories of the city. They are almost wholly the growth of the past fifteen years, and with proper encourage- ment and enterprize could be easily doubled in the next ten years.

The first wholesale dry goods house in the place was started in 1847 by J. Little & Co., at 28 west Washington street. It was burned May 14, 1848, when owned by Little, Drum & Andersons.

1 8 4 8. It was announced about the middle of December, 1847, that Andrew Kennedy, an ex-member of Congress from Indiana, was ill of small-pox at the Palmer House, and he died in January, 1848. Many members of the legislature having visited him before the disease was known, a panic ensued and the assembly adjourn- ed. This act excited much ridicule at the time, b t as a number of other cases occur- red in January and February, the mirth soon ceased, and panic seized the citizens. The council ordered a general vaccination, estab- lished a board of health, and authorized the construction of a hospital. A lot was accordingly bought, material collected and a contract made with Seth Bardwell for a frame house, but before its erection the disease and panic subsided, and a citizens' meeting protested against further taxes for hospital purposes. The council in April gave the contractor $225 with the mate- rial, to give up the contract; the lots were sold, and Bardwell built the Indiana House, on west Market street out of the material. A citizens' meeting in the summer of 1847, had recommended the building of a hospi- tal, and parties had then offered to advance the necessary funds. In July, 1849, anoth- er case of small-pox ocurred, and as the cholera was prevailing severely on the river, another first class panic ensued. A citizens' meeting recommended the cutting of the dog fennel in the streets, and ap- pointed a committee to quarantine the cars, several miles south of town, and remove the cholera and small-pox patients who might be on board. The plan was very brilliant, but failed for the want of a suf- ficiently self-sacrificing committee. The board of health also recommended dog fen- nel mowing, general sanitary precautions, and the erection of a hospital. The mow- ing was accordingly done, but the dog fen- nel was found to be worse when cut than when standing. This recommendation hav- ing failed, no hospital was erected, and but few sanitary measures taken. Many German emigrants were arriving at that time, and the first fatal case of cholera hap- pened among them, July 18, 1849, and sev- eral of them subsequently died. The Pres- ident appointed the first Friday of August,

1849, as a fast day, on account of the cholera. It was generally observed as such throughout the country.

On the 14th of February, 1848, the as- sembly passed an act chartering telegraph companies, and on the 26th, Henry O'Reilly advertised for subscriptions to build a line from here to Dayton. It was constructed immediately afterward, and the first dis- patches sent to Richmond, May 12th. The first published dispatches appeared in the *Sentinel* May twenty-fourth. The of- fice in the second story of Norris', now Hubbard's block, was crowded by excited natives, who doubted the genuineness of the invention; and the first operator, Isaac H. Kiersted, was greatly worried in ex- plaining it. In 1850, Wade & Co. built a second line, which was consolidated with the first in April, 1853, and since that date other lines have been built by companies and railways, till twenty-nine wires now centre at the office in the third story of Blackford's block, all under one corpora- tion, with Jno. F. Wallack as superintend- ent. Isaac H. Kiersted, J. W. Chapin, An- ton Schneider, Sidney B. Morris, J. F. Wil- son and J. F. Wallack, have been chief op- erators and superintendents at this point.

A merchants' exchange was formed in June, for the reception of dispatches and the transaction of business. C. W. Cady being secretary, K. Homburgh, treasurer. It failed in a few weeks for lack of money. A citizens' meeting was called at College Hall in August, 1853, to revive it, and af- ter discussion it was resolved to form a board of trade. N. McCarty, J. D. Defrees, Ignatius Brown, R. J. Gatling, A. H. Brown and J. T. Cox, were appointed to prepare a constitution, circular and map, and solicit funds. D. Maguire was elected president, J. L. Ketcham, secretary. R. B. Duncan, treasurer. Funds were subscribed and a circular and map, prepared by Mr. Brown, were published and sent over the country, calling attention to the advanta- ges held by the city for manufacturing and wholesaling. Active efforts continued for about two years, and did much good, but the interest died out, and the effort was suspended. The board was again revived in 1856, and for two years actively dissem- inated information concerning the city.— The establishment of the rolling mill here was owing to its efforts. It again sus- pended for want of funds. In 1864, the chamber of commerce was formed. T. B. Elliott, (succeeded in 1865 by W. S. Pierce,) president, Jehiel Barnard, secretary, and has since continued operations at its office in Vinton's block; though not supported as it should be. The merchants and manu- facturers' association was formed in the spring of 1868, with objects substantially similar to the old board of trade, and opened an office at 16 south Meridian street.

A new engine was demanded by the Relief Company, and subscriptions being scanty, the Council ordered an election in June, for a special tax to buy one. The decision was against it, as also at another election in July, ordered for the same object. The first foreign paper published here, the Indiana *Volksblatt*, a democratic weekly journal, edited and published by Julius Bœtticher, appeared from an office at Temperance Hall, in September, and has since been regularly issued under the control of Mr. Bœtticher. It is now published at 166 east Washington street.

The companies commanded by Captains Lander and McDougall having returned from Mexico, a procession and barbecue in their honor took place, October 4th, in the woods where the Soldiers' Home was afterwards located. Senator Hannegan, Thomas J. Henley and others, were the speakers.

The Central Plank Road Company was formed in November, contracts let May, 1849, and the road finished from Plainfield to Greenfield, in April, 1851, on the old National road, which, with its bridges, was taken by the company. Gates were located at the east and west ends of Washington street, and tolls charged on the bridge. Citizens' meetings were held, denouncing this action on the part of the Company, and the Council finally procured the removal of the eastern gate, by releasing the Company from all liability for improving Washington street.

The railroads being desirous to connect their several depots by rail, the Council, on the 20th of December, prescribed by ordinance the conditions on which they might lay the present Union track, and in the following August the Companies formed the Union Railroad Company, and laid the track in 1850.

1 8 4 9. The street improvement ordered in 1847–8, had caused a debt of about $6,000, and William Eckert, President of the Council, ordered an election June 9th, to authorize a special tax of ten cents to pay it. Two hundred and fifty-eight votes were cast, and the tax carried by eleven majority. The people grumbled greatly that the tax was now forty-five cents on the one hundred dollars. H. C. Newcomb was elected Mayor at the April election, succeeding Samuel Henderson, the first incumbent of that office. The population this year was found to be 6,500.

Much improvement was taking place, three hundred houses were supposed to have been built, shops and factories were started, and steam engines were at last made here.

The Central Medical College, a department of the Indiana Asbury University, was organized during the summer, with J. S. Bobbs, Richard Curran, J. S. Harrison, George W. Mears, C. G. Downey, L. Dunlap, A. H. Baker and D. Funkhouser as Professors, and began its first session, November 1st, (lasting four months,) in Matthew Little's two-story brick dwelling, south-east corner East and Washington streets, which had been fitted up as the College Buildings. Twenty or thirty students were in attendance the first session, and several were graduated in March, 1850, President Simpson delivering the diplomas. Annual sessions were held for two or three years, when the institution was discontinued. The Assembly, January 21, 1850, authorized the sale of one acre of University Square, at its appraised price, to Asbury University, for the buildings of the Central Medical College, but the selected acre being appraised in April at $3,566, the price was thought to be too high, and opposition arising to the sale, it was abandoned.

The Court of Common Pleas of Marion county was organized, and began its first session, on the second Monday of July, 1849, under a special act of the preceding session, Abram A. Hammond being judge and ex-officio clerk. He was afterwards succeeded by Edward Lander, who served till the Court was abolished, in 1851–2. About fifty cases were on the docket at the first term. The present Court of Common Pleas was established by the revised laws of 1852, Levi L. Todd being elected by the people first Judge, in August, 1852. His successors since have been Sam'l Corey, David Wallace, Jno. Coburn, Charles A. Ray and Solomon Blair.

The Widows and Orphans Society was organized early in December, 1849. The receipts for the first year were $113.16, expenses $98.30. It has been mainly sustained by private contributions, aided by fairs and exhibitions held for its benefit, and has steadily grown in usefulness and importance. Two lots in Drake's addition were donated to the Society by Allen May, and a third bought in 1852. A neat brick building was erected on the property in 1855, at a cost of about $3,000, and the affairs of the society have been successfully administered to the present date. The thanks of the community are due to the noble women who struggled against every disadvantage in the inception of this great charity, and direct and sufficient aid should be annually given them by the city government. For the last two or three years small appropriations have been annually voted to the Society by the City Council.

1850. An earthquake, which was felt all through the west and south, occurred at 8 o'clock A. M. on the 4th of April, shaking the buildings.

The City Treasury receipts for the year ending April 25th, were $9,327, expenditures $7,554. The total taxables for 1850 amounted to $2,326,185. The school fund was slowly accumulating, amounting to $3,205, the receipts for the year being $2,385. Polls, 1,243, an increase of 400 over last year. The population, as shown by the census in October, was 8,097, an increase of 1,530 over 1849. The wealth had increased about $800,000. There were twenty-five physicians, thirty lawyers, and one hundred and twenty industrial establishments.

Governor Crittenden and suite arrived May 28th, on invitation of Gov. Wright, and a Union meeting was held in the State House yard on the 29th, when resolutions were passed, and speeches made by the Governors and others.

A union funeral service was held July 27th, by all denominations and parties, for President Taylor, Rev. E. R. Ames delivering an able eulogy on the deceased President.

Many German emigrants were arriving this year, and brought the cholera with them, nine or ten of them dying during the summer. There was no panic, however. And the disease did not spread.

The Christian Church was built during this and the next year, on the south-west corner of Delaware and Ohio streets.

The Indiana *Statesman*, a weekly, democratic paper, was first issued September 4th, by Ellis & Spann, from the old Sentinel office, on Illinois street. It was merged with the *Sentinel* in September, 1852.

The Indiana Female College was organized, and the house and lot on the south-east corner of Ohio and Meridian streets purchased during the summer, and the school opened there in the fall by Rev. T. A. Lynch. His successors in the Presidency of the institution have been Rev. Charles Adams, G. W. Hoss, B. H. Hoyt, O. M. Spencer and W. H. Demotte. The college was suspended in 1859, but in 1865 the old lot and buildings were sold, and the lot and buildings of the former McLean Female Seminary bought and used from that date by the institution. The school was well conducted and prosperous, but was closed with the June term, 1868, and in that month the house and lot was purchased by the trustees of Wesley

Chapel, for about $16,000, and a church will shortly be erected there by that congregation, at a cost of seventy-five or eighty thousand dollars.

1851. The Toledo Theatrical Company, under Mr. Shires as manager, with H. A. Perry, Robert Buxton, Mrs. Coleman Pope and other good actors, gave a series of dramatic performances, January 7–26, in Masonic Hall, and though sadly embarrassed by lack of scenery and stage room, did themselves credit, and drew large and enthusiastic audiences.

The Indianapolis Gas Light and Coke Co., (originated by John J. Lockwood,) was incorporated by the assembly in February 1851, for thirty years, with $20,000 capital. Stock books were opened March 6th, and on the 26th the Company organized with D. V. Culley, President; W. W. Wright, Secretary and H. V. Barringer, Superintendent. The City Council, by ordinance, March 3d, gave the Company the exclusive right, for fifteen years, of supplying the city and its inhabitants with gas, prescribing the conditions on which pipes might be laid in the streets, and stipulating that gas should be furnished for the street lamps at the price then prevailing in Cincinnati. In July the Company bought a lot on Pennsylvania street, south of Pogue's run, and built a retort house and gas-holder during the fall. Mains were also laid on Pennsylvania and Washington streets. The works were finished in December, and gas was first furnished for consumption on the 10th of January, 1852. In the following April 7,700 feet of pipe had been laid. Thirty bushels of coal were daily consumed, 675 burners employed and 116 consumers using gas. Before the construction of the gas works, the only building in the city lighted by gas was the Masonic Hall, which was furnished with a gas-making apparatus, and the first street lamps in the city were the two in front of the hall, supplied from its apparatus. For two or three years the Company was unsuccessful, the machinery and works being defective in construction and the Superintendent inexperienced in the business. An additional sum was then expended in modifying the works. Christopher Brown was appointed Superintendent, an increased pressure was put on the mains, more gas was consumed, and the Company began to prosper. The mains were extended on additional streets, and further improvements were made in the works. But little gas was used by the city until within the last ten years. The first lamps were put up on Washington street, between Meridian and Pennsylvania streets, in the fall of 1853, and were supplied with gas at the expense of the property-holders on that square, the tax for gas lighting having been defeated at the elections in 1851-2. The first contract for supplying street lamps was made by the Council and Company in December, 1854, and portions of Washington and some of the adjacent streets were lit in 1855. In 1858-9, a large increase was made in the length of streets lighted and number of lamps, and the increase has been steady since that date. In May, 1860, there were eight and one-half miles of street lit, two hundred and sixty-five lamps were used and eighty-five more were being erected. At present twenty-one miles of streets are lit and nearly nine hundred lamps have been erected, only seven hundred and fifty of which are used, the Council having recently decided to light only those at the street corners. The lamp posts and lamps are put up at the expense of the property-holders and kept in repair by the city. Twenty-three miles of mains and nearly seventy-five miles of service pipe are now in use. There are one thousand five hundred and fifty consumers. Extensive changes, additions and repairs have been made to the works, and they have also been largely extended. In 1863, the Company built, on Delaware street, a new receiving reservoir, or gas-holder, of about 300,000 cubic feet capacity, at a cost of about $120,000. The retort house, which originally held six retorts, now has fifty-five. The average daily production of gas at present is about 175,000 feet.

No rule was at first adopted as to the number and position of street lamps on each square, and some trouble and irregularity resulted from it, but on the 12th of February, 1859, the Council fixed the number at four to each square, placed at equal diagonal distances, and so arranged that the opposite street corners should be lit.

As the charter granted, March 3, 1851, for fifteen years, by the city, would expire March 4, 1866, the Council, in May, 1865, ordered the clerk to advertise for proposals to light the city for twenty years with gas. It was done, and on the 4th of September the Gas Company submitted the only proposition that was received. They had been charging private consumers $4.50 per 1,000 feet, and the city $20.00 per lamp, with $8.44 per annum for lighting and cleaning. They now offered to supply the city and citizens, for the ensuing twenty years, at $3.48 per thousand feet, light and clean the lamps at $5.40 each per annum, all payments to be in currency at par, free of Government tax,

which was to be paid by consumers. They also claimed the exclusive right, under Legislative charter, to supply the citizens for five years longer with gas. The committee on gas made long reports in July and October on the subject, setting forth that eighteen miles of mains had been laid, five hundred and thirty three lamp posts erected and one hundred more being erected: that the gas used by private parties in 1864 amounted to about 17,000,000 feet, and by the city to 4,500,000: that one thousand two hundred meters were in use, and 90,000 bushels of coal consumed. They considered the question of cost and price here and elsewhere, and submitted a proposition that the Company be given the contract for fifteen years at $3.00 per one thousand feet, and the lamps at $28.80 per year, consumers to pay tax, and the city to light and clean the lamps—a gas inspector was recommended. They also denied the Company's asserted right to continue for five years longer than the period fixed by the original contract with the city. It was afterward proposed to capitalize the property of the Company at $350,000, the city to divide profits above 15 per cent., and on the 22d of January, 1866, a gas ordinance was passed granting the company the right for twenty years on a capital of $350,000. The Company, on the 31st of January, declined to accept it, and said they would continue to furnish gas to all consumers at $3.75 per thousand by actual measurement, consumers to pay tax. Matters remained in this state till the 5th of March, when R. B. Catherwood & Co., offered to take the charter for thirty years, with the exclusive privilege, and furnish gas at $3.00 per thousand feet, the city to contest the claim of the old Company. In response to this offer the Gas Committee, on the 12th of March, reported an ordinance giving Catherwood & Co., or "the Citizens' Gas Light and Coke Co.," the exclusive right for twenty years, reserving the right of the city to buy the works after ten years, and all profits over 15 per cent. on the capital were to be divided equally between the Company and city. The new Company was to test the claim of the old Company by suit. The capital was to be appraised every five years, and the Company was to fix the rate on the first of March annually for gas, at not over $3.00 per thousand feet. They were to extend mains whenever fifteen burners were promised to the square, and lay them and repair streets at their own cost. The company were to insure the works against fire, and forfeit their charter if the conditions were not fulfilled. While this ordinance was pending, the old company got alarmed, and came forward with another proposition, offering to furnish gas for twenty years at $3 per 1,000 feet, to make no charge for meters, to charge only actual cost of pipe connections, to extend mains whenever fifteen burners to the square were promised, &c. This offer was accepted, and on the 19th of March the council passed an ordinance rechartering the old company for twenty years from March 4, 1866. Good gas was to be furnished at $3 per 1,000 feet, with no charge for meters, the company to lay mains when fifteen burners to the square were promised, and make all pipe connections at actual cost. The price of gas was to be reduced if improvements in its manufacture were adopted; all streets to be repaired when torn up to lay pipes, and damages paid by the company in case of injury to any party. The city was to light and clean the lamps, and have the quantity and quality of the gas tested. The company accepted this charter on the 21st of March, and has since been acting under it.

It was found, shortly after the new contract was made, that the city gas bills were rapidly increasing under the meter-measurment system; and on investigation, in the spring and summer of 1867, it was discovered that the city had been paying for sixteen or twenty lamps beyond the actual number, and for all of them whether lighted or not, and that by defective burners and too heavy pressure, more gas was consumed than was necessary — nearly 6,000,000 feet having been burned in eleven months in 1866-7. The committee recommended the election of a gas inspector, and George H. Fleming was chosen to that office in the spring of 1868, and furnished with a set of instruments at a cost of $800. Rules were adopted for testing quantity, quality and pressure of the gas, and the number of hours the lamps were to be lighted. It was also resolved to light the lamps only on the street corners, and to shut off the gas at midnight. By this action the cost to the city has been reduced from nearly $40,000 to little over $20,000 annually.

The original capital of the gas company was $20,000; but the works and mains, as first built, cost $27,000. They were rebuilt in 1856, at an additional expense of $30,-000—making the total outlay, before the works proved profitable, about $57,000. From that time the enterprise has been successful. Few or no dividends have been declared, the profits all being devoted to the additions, repairs and extensions of the property; the works being again entirely rebuilt in 1860, and an additional

gas-holder of 75,000 feet capacity built. Three reservoirs, one of 20,000, one of 75,-000 and one of 300,000 cubic feet capacity are now in use; 700 bushels of coal are daily used in making gas, the average product being 175,000 feet. In the spring of 1868 the company built a three-story brick office on the north-east corner of Pennsylvania and Maryland streets, at a cost of about $12,000. The present value of the property and franchise of the company is over $500,000. D. V. Culley, D. S. Beatty, E. J. Peck and S. A. Fletcher, Jr., have been the presidents, and H. V. Barringer, Christopher Brown, E. Bailey and H. E. Stacey superintendents.

The State Board of Agriculture was chartered by the Assembly, February 14th, 1851, and was organized May 27 with a board of directors, Gov. Wright being chosen president, John B. Dillon, secretary, and R. Mayhew, treasurer. The first fair was held here on the military grounds October 19–25, 1852—1,365 entries were made, a large crowd of visitors attended, many of whom experienced difficulty in procuring food and lodging, but the railways enabled most of them to come and return the same day. The citizens were then first astonished with the numberless side-shows, since so common, at such gatherings. The fair of 1853 was held October 11–13, at Lafayette; that of 1854 in October, at Madison. Those of 1855, '6, '7 and '8 at Indianapolis. Receipts, respectively,'$11,-000, $13,000, $14,600 and $11,000; that of 1859 at New Albany, receipts $8,000. Those of 1860, '2, '3 and '4, were held at Indianapolis, receipts $11,000, $4,200, $8,-000, $10,000. That of 1865 at Ft. Wayne, receipts $10,500. That of 1866 at Indianapolis, and of 1867 at Terre Haute. No fair was held in 1861. It will be seen that the most successful fairs have been held at this point, and the fact would be still more marked by the comparison of the entries made at each. The most successful fair was that of 1857, both in receipts and in number of entries. The fairs here until 1860, and during the war, were held on the military grounds, which were fitted up by the Board and citizens for the purpose. Those held elsewhere were on grounds furnished and fitted up by the citizens of the respective cities. In 1859 the Board determined to locate the fair permanently at this point and procure larger grounds. Proposals were invited, and during the winter and following spring much competition arose between the partizans of different sites adjoining the city, and some ill feeling was caused. The Otis grove, north of the city, was bought by the board and railway companies in 1860, and expensively fitted up during the summer, and the first fair held there in October. It was not very successful pecuniarily; many of the premiums were left unpaid, and for a number of years the board was much embarrassed financially, being relieved at last by State appropriations and damages received from the general government. The fair of 1861 was announced, but the war intervening, it was abandoned.

With the first rush of troops to this point, the fair ground was occupied, called Camp Morton, and used at intervals afterward until the capture of Fort Donalson, when it was selected as a prison camp, and used as such till after the close of the war—having, often, 5,000 inmates. Its use as a camp and prison injured the grounds exceedingly and destroyed nearly all the trees. It is now being improved, the city having voted $3,000 for that object; and when the improvements are completed will again be used by the board. The State fairs have all been alike in their essential features, and are now what they were at the beginning. Gov. Wright, Jos. Orr, A. C. Stevenson, G. D. Wagner, D. P. Holloway, J. D. Williams, Stearns Fisher and A. D. Hamrick have been the presidents of the society; and J. B. Dillon, W. T. Dennis, Ignatius Brown, W. H. Loomis and A J. Holmes the secretaries.

Nine hundred and fifty-five votes were cast at the city election, April 26th. H. C. Newcomb was elected mayor, but resigned November 7th, and the council elected Caleb Scudder for the balance of the term. A tax of five cents was authorized at the April election for the fire department and purchase of engines.

John B. Gough made his first visit to this city in May, and gave a series of temperance lectures in Masonic Hall. He has lectured here many times since before different societies, but never equalled the impression he then made, when he was in his prime, and before his English trip injured his voice and manner.

A violent storm of wind and rain occurred on the 16th of May, blowing down fences and trees, and prostrating the M. & I. R. R. car house, and on the 22d a heavy hail-storm broke thousands of panes of glass. On the 28th of May Gov. Reuben Wood, of Ohio, visited the city and was suitably received by the authorities.

The papers in May stated that there were then two foundries, three machine shops, and a boiler factory in operation; fifty steam engines had been built, and the manufacture of threshers had been commenced at the Washington foundry. Charles Mayer was also building a three-story bu-

siness house with an iron front, the first one in the city. An "old resident," in a communication, asserts that "nobody is crazy enough to think the city will have 30,000 inhabitants during this century." The receipts of the city treasury for the year ending May 1st, 1851, were $10,515; expenditures the same; debt $5,407; school fund from last year $3,308, amount collected $2,851, expended $5,935 on building; balance $221. The number of children in the city was stated to be 2,126.

W. McK. Scott started the first commercial college here in March, 1851, continuing it for several years, and in October 1851, he originated a library and reading room association. Rev. N. W. Camp, president, A. M. Hunt, secretary, and W. McK. Scott, treasurer and librarian; but the enterprise lived only about a year. He also started the first real estate agency that had existed here for many years. Commercial colleges have been founded since that date by Bryant, Hayden, Gregory, Purdy, and others, graduating many young men for active business pursuits.

It being proposed to light Washington street with gas, and to buy a town clock, a vote was taken September 13, to authorize a gas tax of eight cents, and clock tax of one cent. The first was heavily defeated, and the last authorized. It was levied, and a sufficient fund having accumulated, Jno. Moffatt was employed in April, 1853, to build the clock for $1,200, and after much dissension as to where it should be placed, it was located in Roberts' Chapel steeple in 1854, and remained there till July 1868, when it was removed and put in charge of the chief fire engineer.

The first express office here was opened September 15, by the Adams Express Co., the line being over the Madison road, and Blythe & Holland, agents, till December, when Charles Woodward was appointed. He was succeeded a year or two after by John H. Ohr, who held the office till it was discontinued in March, 1868. Offices of Wells, Fargo & Co.'s Express, of the United States Express, of the American and Merchants' Union have been established here at different dates. Since the consolidation of the companies in March, 1868, the Merchants' Union and American have been the only offices open here.

The county agricultural society was formed in August, and held its first fair in October. Fairs have been held nearly every year since with moderate success, doing well when the State fairs were held elsewhere.

On the 23d of September, twenty-two members of the First Presbyterian church formed the third church. Rev. David Stevenson was called to the pastorate Nov. 17. He has been succeeded by Rev. Geo. Heckman, and Rev. Robt. Sloss. The church building on the corner of Illinois and Ohio street, was begun in 1852, and partly completed in May, 1859, at a cost of about $25,000 for house and lot. The towers have not yet been built. The congregation occupied College and Temperance Halls till January, 1854, when they went into the basement of the church, using it till 1859. The United Brethren Church was built during 1851-2, on the corner of Ohio and New Jersey streets.

Washington street had formerly been planted along portions of its sidewalks with trees, but they had gradually been cut away, and on the first of October the old locust trees in front of the present Dunlop corner, the last ones in the center of the city, were cut down.

Madame Anna Bishop and Bochsa, the first noted musicians who visited the place, gave a concert at Masonic Hall, on the 24th of November.

In November the experiment was tried of having markets at noon instead of at daylight, but it was abandoned after a short period. The weather in December and January was excessively cold.

1852. On the 10th of January a fire broke out in the old frame and brick houses extending east of the Capital House to the alley, utterly consuming them, and burning up nearly all the records in the City Treasurer's office. The present buildings were erected there during the summer and occupied in the fall.

P. J. Ash opened a theatre with a small company at Masonic Hall, in February, but failed and discontinued shortly afterwards.

The Assembly, on the 20th December, 1851, had invited Kossuth to visit the city, and at a subsequent public meeting, fifty citizens had been appointed a committee of reception. They met him February 26th, at Cincinnati, and on Friday, the 27th, he arrived here via Madison, and was escorted by a procession across the muddy valley of Pogue's run to the State House, where he was welcomed as the guest of the State by Governor Wright, and replied in an address of some length, to the vast crowd assembled in the yard. The party was quartered at the Capital House, (now the *Sentinel* office,) then the best and largest hotel in the city. A reception was held at the Governor's residence at night. On Saturday he was received by the two houses of Assembly, and received delegations, and contributions for Hungary. Sunday he attended

Roberts Chapel and the Sunday schools. On Monday he received delegations and contributions, and at night delivered a long and elaborate address, at Masonic Hall, before the society of "The Friends of Hungary." On Tuesday he left for Louisville, after collecting about $1,000.

Dr. C. G. McLean built, during this summer, a three-story brick building, on the corner of New York and Meridian streets, and opened the first session of the McLean Female Seminary at that place in September; one hundred and fifty pupils were in attendance during the first year, and the school soon took high rank. Dr. McLean died in 1860, and the school was continued until 1865, under Professor C. N. Todd, Professor Sturdevant, and others. It was then discontinued, and the property bought by the Indiana Female College, which was located there till June, 1868, when it was discontinued, and the property sold to the Wesley Chapel congregation for about $16,000, as the site for their new Church.

The North Western Christian University was chartered by the Assembly, Feb., 1852. A meeting of the commissioners was held June 22, and stock subscriptions reported, amounting to $75,000. Twenty-one directors, with Ovid Butler as President, were elected July 14th. A site of twenty acres of fine woodland was donated to the institution by Ovid Butler. Plans by Wm. Tinsley, architect, were adopted, and the contracts were let in July, 1853, for the west wing of the building. It was erected in 1854-5, at a cost of $27,000, and dedicated November 1st, 1855, by Horace Mann, who delivered an able address on the occasion. John Young, J. R. Challen and A. R. Benton were the first Professors. John Young, S. K. Hoshour and A. R. Benton have been the Presidents. The institution has been prosperous under an able corps of instructors. Three societies, Pythonean, Mathesian and Threskomathian, are sustained by the students. Pupils of both sexes are in attendance at the institution. The College buildings are still incomplete.

The City Assessor returned the population of the city in July, at 10,812. The fourth of July was celebrated with more display than usual. The Sabbath School procession, embracing about two thousand children and teachers, marched to the State House square. The firemen and military, comprising the City Guards, the Marion, Western, Independent Relief and Invincible fire companies, and the O. K. bucket company, headed by Downie's band, (which had been formed in August, 1850,) also paraded the streets, with the

fire engines and hose reels fancifully decorated.

The first balloon ascension here, was
made at 4 o'clock p. m., July 29th, at the
State House square, (which had been enclosed for the purpose,) by Wm. Paullin.
The balloon rose to a great height, remaining above the clouds for an hour, and
lighting in the evening near Greenfield.
At night, Diehl of Cincinnati, gave a fine
exhibition of fire-works inside the en-
closure. The show was gotten up by Jas.
H. McKernan, and the ascension was witnessed by over 15,000 persons, nearly all
of whom held curb-stone tickets. Since
that time balloon ascensions have been
made here by Pusey, Bannister, Bellman,
and a number of others.

Much improvement was made in the
place this year, and many buildings
erected or begun; among these were the
Bates House, Morris (now the Sherman)
House, McLean's Seminary, three brick
school houses, Lafayette and Union depots,
Terre Haute shops, Washington foundry,
Sinker's boiler factory, Osgood & Smith's
peg and last factory, Geisendorff's woollen
factory, Drew's carriage factory, Shella-
barger's planing mill, Macy's pork-house,
Blake's Commercial Row, Blackford's
building on Meridian street, and others.
The railroads were being actively constructed, streets improved, and cisterns
built for the fire department, as voted for
in October by a small majority. The first
State and county fairs were held by the
present societies, drawing large crowds;
great conventions were also held during
the summer, by the political parties.

1 8 5 3 . Among the side shows in attendance at the State fair, in October, 1852, had
been Yankee Robinson's atheneum, or tent
theater, placed where Gallup's building now
is, east of the State House. He returned
here during the winter, and on the 21st of
January opened in the Washington Hall,
(which had been fitted with stage and raised seats,) with the Alphonso troupe of vo-
calists, the concert being a blind for the
theatrical performance which followed. After ten days or two weeks, he announced
himself as manager, and continued the
performances till March 7th, drawing very
good houses, and employing a good company; among them were Henry W. Waugh,
J. F. Lytton, D. W. Waugh, Robinson and
his wife, Mr. and Mrs. Sidney Wilkens,
and others.   After Robinson left, H. W.
Brown opened the hall as a theater, with
Sidney Wilkens and wife, Meehen, and
others, forming a good stock company. The
season lasted from July 1st to the 26th, and
Uncle Tom's Cabin was first represented
here to crowded houses.   Sidney Wilkens

again opened it as manager, on the 10th of
August, and continued for a short time with
nearly the same company.   Wilkens was
an actor of considerable merit.

The first old settlers' meeting was held
at the State house, January 31st. Speeches
were made, anecdotes of the early settlement related, and an organization effected
with arrangements for annual meetings.
These were subsequently held till 1860, at
Calvin Fletcher's and James Blake's, and
at the fair grounds, but were abandoned
during the war, and have not since been
revived.

The Odd Fellows had determined to build
a grand lodge hall here, and during the
winter had organized a stock company.—
Subscriptions to about $45,000 were taken
by the grand and subordinate lodges and
encampments, and by individuals, and in
February the lot at the corner of Pennsylvania and Washington was bought for
$17,000.   A plan was adopted, afterward
modified by F. Costigan, architect, and during 1854-5 the present building was erected on the site of the two-story brick and
frame houses which had formerly occupied
the lot. It cost about $30,000, and was oc-
cupied in the summer of 1855, the city council room and city offices being on the second floor, where they remained till the
present offices were occupied in Glenns'
block, in May, 1862. The style of the hall
is peculiar, probably unlike any other on
earth. The lower floor is occupied as business rooms, the second as offices, and on
the third are two large halls and ante-
rooms, used by the lodges and encampments, who occupy them each secular night
of the week. The house is stuccoed inside
and out, and is surmounted by a dome, designed by D. A. Bohlen architect. The
hall was dedicated, with appropriate ceremonies, May 21, 1856.

The dates of organization of the several
lodges and encampments, and the names of
their first officers are as follows:

Lodges—Centre No. 18, December 25,
1844, Wm. Sullivan, N. G., E. B. Hoyt, secretary, J. B. McChesney, treasurer; Phi-
loxenian, No. 44, July 8, 1847, Hervey
Brown, N. G., W. W. Wright, secretary,
John J. Owsley, treasurer; Capital No.
124, January 20, 1853, John Dunn, N. G.,
Wm. Wallace secretary, Geo. F. McGinnis,
treasurer; Germania No. 129, January 24,
1853, Chas. Coulon. N. G., Julius Boetticher, secretary, B. H. Mueller, treasurer;
Encampments—Metropolitan No. 5, July
20, 1846, J. P. Chapman, C. P., Edwin Hedderly, H. P., B. B. Taylor, secretary, A. C.
Chrisfield, treasurer; Marion No. 35, March
24, 1853, Obed Foote, C. P., J. K. English,
H. P., A. Dercis, secretary, Geo. G. Holman,

treasurer; Teutonia No. 57, August 13, 1855, Geo. F. Meyer, C. P., Chas. Coulon, H. P., F. H. Tapking, secretary, Alex. Metzger, treasurer.

A State convention of brass bands was held at Masonic Hall, February 22, under George B. Downie, as leader. Twelve or thirteen bands were present, and engaged in a contest for a prize banner, which was taken by the New Albany band. A similar convention, eight or nine bands being in attendance, was held at the same place, November 29, 1853, under C. W. Cottam, as leader.

The taxing power of the council being restricted under the charter of 1847, it was proposed in December, 1852, to adopt the general incorporation act of 1852, but much opposition arising, the project was not pressed at that time. In March, 1853, however, the council adopted the general act, and the city was governed under it till March, 1857. The elections were changed from April to May, and all the officers and councilmen were elected annually. 1450 votes were cast at the election, May 3d, under the new law. Caleb Scudder being chosen mayor, Daniel B. Culley, clerk, A. F. Shortridge, treasurer, Matthew Little, assessor, Benj. Pilbean, marshal, N. B. Taylor, attorney, Wm. Hughey, street commissioner, and James Wood, engineer. The new officers and council assumed their duties May 6th, and Joseph Little was elected first chief fire engineer. The receipts of the city for the year ending May 1, 1853, were $10,905, expenditures $7,030.

The fire tax amounted to $2,093, expenses, $2,018; clock tax, $1,005, expenses, $18; school fund, $6,745, expenses, $6,458, in building houses, etc. $895 had been expended for cisterns, five of which were finished, five in progress, and six others located. The council chamber was removed in June, from Hubbard's block to Dunlop's building, then lately finished, and in 1855, to Odd Fellows' Hall, then completed. The new city assessment in July, gave of personal property, $1,239,507; real, $3,891,875; total, $5,131,082, and 1,460 polls. 35 persons paid tax on over $20,000 of property, and 59 on from 10 to $20,000. Until July, the marshal was the only police officer in the city, but in that month he was authorized to appoint a deputy. The council fixed the salaries of the officers in September; that of the mayor being $600; clerk, $600; marshal, $500; engineer, $800; street commissioner, $400; clerk 'of markets, $350; sexton, $80; deputy marshal, $400; councilman, each meeting, $2.

The fourth Presbyterian church on Delaware and Market streets, was contracted for in May, and built during this and next year, though not finally finished till within a few years past. The third Presbyterian church, on Illinois and Ohio streets, was also begun this year, but not completed for several years after. The towers are now being built. The tower of the fourth Presbyterian church, about one hundred and forty feet in height, is entirely of brick, the only one so built, and is the tallest brick structure in the city. The outside of the church is stuccoed. These were the finest and most expensive church edifices in the city when erected, but have since been surpassed by the first and second churches.

John Freeman, an old and respectable colored citizen, was arrested, May 21st, as the fugitive slave of Pleasant Ellington, and taken before William Sullivan, U. S. Commissioner. The case caused great excitement. Crowds thronged the court room, writs of habeas corpus were issued, and successful efforts made to delay the case to get evidence. Freeman, in the mean time, had to lay three months in jail, guarded by special marshals, while his attorney went south to get witnesses. Several planters came on from Georgia, proved his freedom, and on the 27th of August he was released. This case had no small influence on political matters afterward, and made many earnest opponents of slavery among those who had been formerly indifferent on the subject.

The fourth of July was celebrated in the forenoon in the usual manner, by sixteen Sabbath schools, at the State House; by four fire and hose companies, with the Franklin band, in the afternoon, and by the Turners in the evening, south of the city.

A temperance excitement arose during the summer, and out-door meetings were held on the corners, and in front of the saloons, during July, August and September. A committee was appointed in the last month, to wait on the sellers, and reported forty-four then engaged in the business, most of whom had agreed to quit it. The meetings were kept up at intervals for a year or two.

All the omnibuses in the city having been bought by Garner & Plant, an omnibus company was formed on the 1st of August, and lines established from the depot, and along Washington street, but the enterprise was abandoned as unremunerative, after two or three months trial.

A great fire, on the evening of the 10th of August, consumed the extensive stables on Maryland and Pearl streets, back of the Wright House, and other buildings were repeatedly on fire, but by great exertions on the part of citizens and firemen, the fire was confined to the stables alone.

The Indianapolis Coal Co. was formed in the spring, working mines in Clay county, and the first loads of coal were sent to our market during the summer and fall. Hitherto wood had been the only fuel used here, being cheap and plentiful. The first horse-power wood-sawing machine was used on street during the fall, creating much excitement among the boys.

The first number of the *Frie Press*, a German independent weekly paper, appeared September 3d, and has been regularly issued to the present time. It is owned by a stock company, and has generally supported the republican party. The company is also publishing the *Daily Telegraph*, the only German daily paper in the city.

An auction stock exchange was started by William Y. Wiley, in October, weekly sales and meetings being held, but the city was too small to support such an enterprise, and it was abandoned after several weeks trial. No subsequent effort has been made to revive it.

The famous dissenting Priest Gavazzi delivered two eloquent lectures on the papacy, at Masonic Hall, October 28–9, to crowded houses. Lucy Stone, at the same place, on the 24th, 25th and 26th of November, and 3d of December, delivered addresses on woman's rights and wrongs. Ole Bull gave his first concert here, in the same hall, on the 6th of December, in company with Maurice Strakosch and the now world-renowned Adalini Patti, then a child of twelve or thirteen years of age. Ole Bull, since that time, has given several concerts here, the last being in February, 1868. During Christmas week, W. H. Howard gave several theatrical performances, which he terminated by running off and leaving his company unpaid.

Much improvement had taken place in the city during the summer and fall, and it was supposed that $500,000 had been expended in the erection of houses.

1854. The Young Men's Christian Association was organized on the 21st of March, and has since steadily and successfully pressed forward in a useful work. It made efforts to collect a library, and from 1855 to the present time, has given, each winter, a series of lectures by distinguished persons. Rooms have been rented, an agency office opened, a city missionary appointed, and sabbath schools organized under its direction.

2012 votes were cast at the city election on the 1st of May. The officers elected

will be found in the table heretofore published. A great storm occurred May 13, blowing down trees, fences and Robinson's atheneum tent, injuring several persons in the audience. Robinson, during the summer and fall, fitted up the third story of Elliott's building, on the corner of Maryland and Meridian streets, and commenced the theatrical season in the fall, ending April 14, 1855. The company was unusually good, comprising R. J. Miller, Yankee Beirce, Yankee Robinson, F. A. Tannyhill, McWilliams, J. F. Lytton, H. W. and D. W. Waugh, Mrs. Robinson, Mrs. Beirce, Miss Mary McWilliams, and others. He introduced Miss Susan Denin to an Indianapolis audience. She had two engagements during the season, and aroused great interest among the drama-loving part of the community. She was succeeded by Maggie Mitchell and J. P. Addams.

The marshal was the only police officer until July, 1853, when he was authorized to appoint a deputy, but on the 14th of September of this year, the council established a police force of fourteen men, with a captain; Jefferson Springsteen being chosen the first chief. This force was continued till December 17, 1855, when the ordinance was repealed, and the whole squad and the deputy marshal discharged: the marshal again being left the only police officer in the city. The repeal arose from the general discontent at the expense attending the maintenance of the police, and at the conduct of the police in enforcing the liquor law. Conflicts had occurred immediately after the law took effect, between the Germans and the police, and on the 1st of August, an attempt to make an arrest on east Washington street resulted in a riot, in which several of the Germans were shot. A citizens' meeting, held immediately afterward, at the court house, sustained the police, proffered the aid of one hundred special policemen in each ward, and determined on the enforcement of the law, and preservation of the peace. The council also commended the act of the police. The ill feeling gradually subsided, but the general discontent over the matter resulted at last in the discharge of the force. For a month or two afterward, the streets were much disturbed by noisy rioters, among whom (as it was charged at the time,) were a number of ex-policemen, who thus evinced their desire for re-employment, and demonstrated its necessity. The papers soon asked for another force, and the council, on the 21st of January, 1856, created one of ten men, one to each ward and three at large, with a captain ; Jesse M. VanBlaricum being chosen chief. This force continued till after the May election, when the new democratic council discharged it, and by ordinance allowed the city marshal to appoint one policeman to each ward, with a captain; Charles G. Warner being selected for the post. The republicans repealed this ordinance, May 18, 1857, and passed another, by which the council elected seven policemen and a captain; A. D. Rose being chosen. Two additional policemen at large were appointed in 1858, and Samuel Lefever elected captain. A. D. Rose succeeded in 1859. The force was increased May 11, 1861, to two men from each ward, and on the 2d of July, 1861, was fixed by new ordinance at fourteen men and a captain; A. D. Rose retaining the post. He held it till October, and then entered the army, being succeeded by Thos. A. Ramsey. The two day policemen were discharged in November. John R. Cotton was chosen chief in May, 1862. Two day patrolmen were again added, and the men first uniformed at the expense of the city. Thos. D. Amos was chosen chief, May 19, 1863, and the force increased to one lieutenant, seven day and eighteen night patrolmen. D. M. Powell succeeded as chief, May 25, 1863. During the fall much trouble was experienced in preserving the peace, in consequence of the great number of rowdies in the city, and on the 4th of December a new ordinance was passed reorganizing the force. On the 4th the mayor was authorized to appoint detectives, and on the 21st the military authorities were asked to detail guards to assist the police. The request was granted, and until after the war a strong guard materially aided in preserving order in and around the city; the guard headquarters being at the police office. A new ordinance fixing police districts, was passed March 21, 1864, and amended May 9th, and Samuel A. Cramer elected chief. On the third of October, twenty-six special policemen were added, during the State fair. Complaints being made of the insufficiency of the force, the council, on the 5th of December, 1864, authorized an addition of sixteen men until the second Tuesday in May, 1865, and raised the chief's salary to $1,-500. The pay of the men was also increased once or twice during 1863 and 1864, being finally fixed at $2.50 and $3.00 per day. Jesse VanBlaricum was chosen chief in the spring of 1865, with two lieutenants, nine day and eighteen night patrolmen, two detectives, and sixteen special men under his command. He served till April, 1866, when Thos. S. Wilson was elected chief, and still holds the office. The force has been maintained for the last three or four years at an annual cost of

$25,000 or $30,000, and now consists of about thirty men.

In September, 1865, Mr. A. Coquillard organized a merchants' police force for the patrol of the business squares along Washington street, and on the 16th of October the council recognized the force, granting it police powers. A. D. Rose took the control of it in September, 1866, and is now at its head. It is composed of twelve men, paid by the parties whose property it guards. In addition to the regular and merchants' police, there is a force of three or four men at the Union Depot, appointed by the company, and confirmed by the council, and invested with police powers.

1855. A financial panic had occurred in the West during the fall of 1854. The Free state-stock banks had very generally stopped payment, and their notes, which formed the great bulk of the circulation, were passing at a heavy discount. Railway and other pending enterprises, were greatly embarrassed, and nearly all those in progress suspended operations. Traders and manufacturers were much cramped, and general distrust prevailed among business men. A bankers' convention was held here on the 7th of January to classify the notes of the suspended banks and fix discount rates according to the value of their securities. The rates were accordingly fixed, but not adhered to even by those who made them, and the discounts were raised or lowered at the caprice of brokers, entailing great losses on the community, and making large sums for the operators in the business.

The mayors of the several cities of the State met in convention at this point on the 22d of January, for consultation and mutual improvement, but without any visible result.

A colored lithographic engraving of the city, as seen from the top of the Blind Asylum, was published in January by J. T. Palmatary.

A deep and lasting snow fell in February, affording fine sleighing.

A number of cases of small pox occurred in January, and as the disease began to spread during February, the council, on the 10th of March, ordered the erection of a hospital. Several lots were bought in the north-west corner of the plat, plans adopted, and the house begun; but the disease and panic soon subsided, funds ran low, and the house was suspended or prosecuted at intervals for years, and was not finished till the spring of 1859, requiring a new roof and other repairs in the meantime. Its erection was due to Dr. Livingston Dunlap, councilman from the Sixth

ward, who persevered against all obstacles till his object was achieved. It cost
about $30,000, and remained unused, ex-
cept as a rendesvous for bad characters,
till April, 1861. It was proposed in February, 1860, to sell it, but the council
committee reported in favor of renting it.
During the summer it was proposed to use
it as a city prison or a house of refuge, or
a home for friendless women; but each of
these projects was successively defeated.
The Sisters of Chartiy, on the 21st of June,
asked its use, under their control, as a
hospital, but other christian denominations
opposed the plan, and the application was
withdrawn. The council finally, on the
21st of July, granted it to a society of ladies as a home for friendless women. It
was not occupied, however, for that purpose, and was given rent free to a keeper,
who was to take care of it. After the war
began and the sudden concentration of
men at this point, the sick were taken
there, and the council, on the 18th of May,
granted its use to the government for a
hospital, and it was occupied as such till
July, 1865, and as a soldiers' home till November, 1865, when, with the additions
and improvements, it was surrendered
again to the city. These improvements
consisted of two large three-story ells, several outbuildings, fences, trees, gardens,
&c. They had been offered for sale by
the government authorities, but were finally surrendered to the city with the building in lieu of rent. After the government
vacated it, Rev. August Bessonies, January 2d, 1866, submitted a proposition to
the council to give the house to the Sisters
of the Good Shepherd, as a city prison for
females, and also asked that the unfinished
house of refuge be deeded to them, to be
finished and used as a reformatory school
for abandoned females. These propositions were opposed by the citizens, and a
subscription of $6,000 made to finish the
house of refuge, and Mr. Bessonies' proposition was defeated. The house remained
vacant till the spring of 1866, when about
$2,000 were spent in buying hospital fur-
niture and supplies at the government
sales at Jeffersonville. A board of directors was elected, Dr. G. V. Woollen chosen
superintendent, a corps of consulting physicians and surgeons appointed, and the
hospital opened for patients July 1st, 1866.
It has since been conducted at an expense
of six or seven thousand dollars per year.
Two thousand, six hundred and ninety
votes were cast at the May election. The
revenue for general purposes, for 1854
amounted to $20,500; school fund $10,800.
The general expenditures exhausted the receipts and left a debt of $567—the bal-

ance left in the school fund was $6,880.
The street improvements requiring considerable labor in the engineer department,
the council, in July, first authorized the
office of assistant engineer, at $300 salary.
A wood-measurer was also appointed for
the newly-established wood markets. A
market house was built this year on South
street, between Delaware and Alabama
streets. But few markets were held there,
and the house was torn down in 1858.
The first city directory was issued this
year by Grooms & Smith. Directories have
since been issued by A. C. Howard, Henry
E. McEvoy, J. T. Talbott, Sutherland &
McEvoy, J. C. Sutherland, H. H. Dodd &
Co., Richard Edwards, A. L. Logan and
others.
The liquor law took effect June 12th,
and the county agency was started.
The law was generally observed for a few
weeks, and unusual order and quiet reigned on the streets, but on the 2d of July
R. Beebee was arrested for selling liquor,
fined and imprisoned; the case went to the
Supreme Court, and the impression gain-
ing ground that the law would be declared
unconstitutional, it was soon generally
disregarded and the traffic reopened.
Blake's, Drake's, Fletcher's, Drake &
Mayhew's, Blackford's and other additions
to the city were made in 1854–5, and the
lots mostly disposed of and their improvement begun. Between sixty and eighty
additions and sub-divisions have been
made to the city since the first one was
made by John Wood, in June, 1836.
The fourth of July was celebrated by
the Sabbath Schools at the State House
yard, in the usual manner. Nineteen
schools, comprising 2,100 children, participated. The firemen paraded in the
afternoon, making a fine display. The
Hope company, of Louisville, then visiting here, was in the line.
The Indianapolis Building, Loan Fund
and Savings Association was organized
in October, and continued its existence
for several years, its object being to make
loans to its members at ostensibly low
rates of interest, to aid in building houses.
The Marion Loan Fund and Savings Association, a similar organization, was started
in March, 1856. These organizations
when wound up, failed to realize the
hopes of their projectors. The Indianapolis Fuel Association was formed on the
31st October, and supplied its members
during the winter, with wood and coal at
but little over one-half the rates charged
in the open markets.
A women's rights convention was held
at Masonic Hall, October 22d and 23d,
Mrs. Rebecca Swank, President. Mrs.

Lucretia Mott, Ernestine L. Rose, Frances D. Gage, Adaline Swift, Harriet L. Cutler, and Joseph Barker, of Pittsburg, and other speakers addressed the convention. But few persons attended, and the movement excited no remark.

The city was well supplied with amusements this year. The Black Swan, with the African Mario, sang at Masonic Hall on the 2d of May, (she again visited the place in the spring of 1868.) Du Bufe's paintings of Adam and Eve were shown May 22–6, at Washington Hall. Powers's Greek Slave, October 19–25, at College Hall; Parodi, with Maurice and Madam Strakosch and others, sang, Dec. 10th, at Masonic Hall. Brown and Commons opened the Atheneum, May 14, ending the season June 25, with C. J. Fyffe, manager, and J. F. Lytton, Beaver, and others, in the company; Harry Chapman and his wife, Mrs. A. Drake, William Powers and James E. Murdoch were the stars. Murdoch left in disgust before the close of his engagement. Commons re-opened the Atheneum, September 15th, ending the season December 8th, with Thos Duff, manager, and about the same company; Eliza Logan, Joseph Proctor, Susan and Kate Denin, Peter and Caroline Richings, and Mr. and Mrs. Florence were the stars. Yankee Robinson had returned during the fall, and wintered here with his circus company. An amphitheatre was fitted up in Delzell's stable, on east Pearl street, and horse opera given during the winter.

The first effort at numbering the houses on Washington street, was made during the fall, but no settled system was adopted and the numbering was partial and faulty. The Council, in July, 1858, authorized A. C. Howard to number all the streets of the city, and the work was completed during the fall, but the system was defective in numbering only the houses then built, and the work was badly done, resulting in confusion as new buildings were erected. The Council, in June, 1864, adopted a system authorizing fifty numbers to the square. The work of renumbering was done by A. C. Howard, and the plan has since been followed in the numbering of new buildings.

The Young Men's Christian Association gave their first course of lectures during the fall and winter, Park Benjamin, Rev. Mr. Butler, David Paul Brown, Edwin P. Whipple, Henry B. Staunton, H. W. Ellsworth, Bishop Simpson, and Edward P. Thompson being the lecturers.

1856.' The General Conference of the Methodist Episcopal Church met on the 1st of May, in the hall of the house of representatives, and continued in session for about a month, attended by the full board of Bishops, and the leading men of that denomination. The delegates were the guests of citizens of all the churches, and the pulpits of the churches were filled each Sabbath by preachers in attendance at the conference. The session was important and interesting, and drew the attention of the whole country to this city. It was the first national body meeting here.

The city election took place May 6th, 2,776 votes being cast, the democrats electing the whole city ticket, with ten out of fourteen councilmen.

The assessment for this year amounted to $7,146,670, $1,892,152 being personal property. The receipts in the general fund for the past year were $27,889, expenditures $46,105. The debt on the 1st of May, 1854, was $567; May 1st, 1855, $11,000; May 1st, 1856, $15,295. It was proposed to fund the debt by a loan, and Jeremiah D. Skeen was chosen in August, by the Council, as financial agent, to sell city bonds in the New York market. He accordingly went there, and not succeeding in negotiating a loan for the city, hypothecated the bonds for $5,000, which he applied to his own use. The defalcation was discovered in the spring of 1857, and unsuccessful efforts made to recover the bonds. The money was finally paid by the city to the parties who had advanced the money to Skeen. Suit was brought against Skeen and his sureties, and judgment finally recovered in January, 1868, for the principal and interest of the defalcation.

Alfred Stevens, the City Clerk, died October 26th, and George H. West was appointed Clerk pro tempore, to fill the vacancy. Henry F. West, Mayor of the City, died November 8th, and was followed to the grave by an immense concourse of citizens. He was the only incumbent of that office who has died during the term. He had been an earnest and active promoter of the public schools, and their success had been largely due to his efforts as trustee. The Council ordered a special election to be held, November 22d, to supply vacancies in the offices of Clerk and Mayor. It was held, and for the first time in several years the democrats were beaten. Two thousand nine hundred and thirty-one votes were cast; William J. Wallace was chosen Mayor, and Frederick Stein, city Clerk. The republicans indulged in wild demonstrations of delight when the result became known.

Early in February, Dunlevy, Haire & Co. began business as brokers and runners of the State and free banks, in the interest of Cincinnati bankers. In two months $2,000,000 of the circulation was returned for redemption, causing such financial stringency that a State commercial convention was held here, in April, to protest against the course of the Cincinnati and Indianapolis brokers in crippling the trade and resources of the State, by contracting the circulating medium. Delegates from Cleveland, St. Louis, Toledo and Louisville, were in attendance. Bitter resolutions were adopted in regard to the conduct of Cincinnati business men and bankers, and efforts were made to divert the trade of Indianapolis to other points. The meeting had the effect to seriously diminish the war on Indiana banks, and open other markets to our people.

Clinton Watson opened an exchange and reading room in August, in the room over Harrison's bank, but the enterprise failed in a few weeks from want of patrons.

Professor Pusey made a balloon ascension on the 28th June, and attempted another on the 4th of July, but failed for want of sufficient gas. The usual celebration of schools and firemen occurred, and in the afternoon the first fantastic parade attracted great crowds.

The political canvass this year was unusually animated and bitter, both parties putting forth their full strength, and holding frequent great conventions. The largest republican demonstration was held on the 15th of July, attended by many thousands of persons from all parts of the State. A great procession took place, and an almost equally great torchlight procession at night, closing with fireworks and balloon ascensions. During the afternoon, a border ruffian demonstration and dramatic representation of the designs of the slave interest, and life in Kansas, was given by a club of young men in fantastic dress, and with proper accessories. It created great amusement at the expense of the opposite party, and was repeated with effect by the club at several other points during the canvass. The largest democratic convention followed on the 17th, closing also with a torchlight procession at night, and in numbers and enthusiasm vied with that of their opponents.

A great storm of wind and rain took place November 21st, doing considerable damage, not only here, but all over the western States.

The Indianapolis Art Society was formed during this or the next year, and held annual drawings for several years, under the direction of a committee, at Herman Lei-

ber's print and picture store, where the pictures (mostly by Indianapolis or Indiana artists,) were placed on exhibition.— Messrs. Jacob Cox, P. Fishe Reed, Jas. F. Gookins and others, being contributors.— The paintings were purchased by an association, at their value, each member contributing a stipulated sum, and the pictures were divided by lot. Many good paintings were thus distributed at small cost among the citizens.

The Young Mens' Literary, and the Young Mens' Christian Associations each gave a course of lectures during the winter. Charles Sumner, J. B. Gough, T. A. Mills, S. S. Cox, Elihu Burritt and others, appearing before our people. Judson, John and Asa Hutchinson sang, January 22, at Masonic Hall. Ole Bull appeared February 27, Signor Blitz, (the elder,) in April, Tom Thumb in July, Miss Richings October 10th, and 30th; Strakosch, Parodi, Tiberini, Morini, and Paul Julien, November 24th; and a State musical convention under George F. Root, was held there November 20-1. W. L. Woods opened the atheneum in March, for one month; W. Davidge being the only noted star. It was reopened by Vance & Lytton, May 16, closing June 3; Eliza Logan, Miss Richings, and Mrs. Coleman Pope, being the stars.— It was opened by Maddocks & Wilson several times in June and July, for a day or two at a time. Wilson, Pratt & Co. appeared there during the State fair; Yankee Bierce and the Maddern sisters early in December, and on the 16th of December it was opened by Lytton & Co. for the season, closing March 9, 1857. The company included Mr. and Mrs. R. J. Miller, Mr. and Mrs. Lacey, Taunyhill, Lytton, and others. Sue Denin, Dora Shaw, John Drew, Charlotte Crampton, Mrs. Drake and Miss Duval, appeared as stars. It was reopened for a few days, afterward, for benefits, and in March 1857, for a week or two, under C. J. Smith, as manager.

1857. The Germans, during the fall of 1856, had requested that a portion of the city free school fund should be set apart for the support of German schools, and the council in December had requested the trustees to report whether the project was feasible and proper. They reported against it in January, 1857, stating that the fund and school accommodations were insufficient for the schools then in operation. There were nine houses (two of them rented,) and the old seminary, in use, properly accommodating twelve hundred pupils, while eighteen hundred were in attendance. The fund for 1856 had amounted to $27,050, the expenses to $19,428; balance $7,616. There were thirty-five teachers employed in June, and 2,730 children enrolled, being about forty-four per cent. of the children in the city, and but seventy-three per cent. of those enrolled were in daily attendance. The first ward house had been raised to two stories, in 1854, and the fifth ward house in 1856. The eighth ward house was built this year. D. V. Culley, John Love and N. B. Taylor, were elected trustees in January. In August there were twenty-nine sabbath schools, with two thousand nine hundred and fifty scholars.

The city council on the 16th of March adopted the new incorporation law as the city charter, under which the city officers and councilmen were elected for two years. Three thousand three hundred votes were cast at the May election, each party electing part of its ticket. The council organized and drew for short and long terms, and elected Andrew Wallace chief fire engineer. The receipts in the general fund for the past year were $32,697; expenditures $31,003; balance $1,232; debt $23,740; school fund $20,329; expenses $15,384; balance $4,945. The assessment was $9,874,700, and a tax levy for general purposes of sixty cents on each $100. The salaries of the city officers were fixed as follows: Mayor $800, clerk $600, marshal $500, deputy $400, attorney $400, street commissioner $450, engineer $600, clerk of markets $300, sexton $80, chief fire engineer $175, treasurer four per cent. on current and six per cent. on delinquent receipts, and councilmen $2 each meeting.

On the 22d of May the German Turners had a celebration, procession, address and gymnastic exercises on the military grounds.

The spring had been backward and wet, and on the 10th, 12th and 16th of June there were tremendous thunder storms, resulting in a sudden and high freshet in White river and other streams in the State. A brilliant comet appeared in the western sky in the latter part of June.

The Fourth of July was celebrated by the Sabbath-schools only, the firemen not parading, and the Guards were at Lexington attending the Clay monument dedication. This celebration was notable only as the last general one held by the schools.

Meetings were held in July by the business men to encourage the establishment of exclusively wholesale dry goods and notion houses. A committee appointed by the meeting reported that though there were seventy-five establishments and thirty-two manufactories which did a wholesale business to a greater or less extent, there was but one exclusively wholesale dry goods house in the place. Blake,

Wright & Co., started a dry goods house in response to the demand of the meeting; but the enterprise was short lived.

There were two riots in July in which the firemen were prominent actors, attacking houses of ill fame in the western part of the city, destroying the furniture and injuring the buildings. Several affairs of this kind occurred afterward in this and the following years, the firemen being principal actors in all of them.

The county fair this year was a failure on account of unfavorable weather, but the State fair was the most successful ever held here, there being over three thousand seven hundred entries of articles for exhibition, and the gate receipts amounting to nearly $14,600. A vast crowd was in attendance during the three leading days. A grand parade of our fire department, with visiting companies from New Albany and Dayton, was held during the fair.

A negro was arrested here in December under the fugitive slave law. The arrest caused much excitement, and being favored by the crowd, he escaped, but was recaptured after a long chase in the north part of the city, and remanded to his master in Kentucky, being convoyed thither by a large squad of heavily armed deputy marshals.

Dodworth's New York band, ninety in number, gave a concert on the 30th of June on the military grounds, under contract with H. Stone, of Cleveland, in his gift concert enterprise. They also gave a concert at night, in Masonic hall, for their own benefit; but neither of the performances was largely patronized.

Edward Everett delivered his Mt. Vernon lecture on the 4th of May at Masonic hall. Thalberg, Parodi and Mollenhauer gave a concert May 7th at the hall. Dudley Tyng, Horace Greeley, Ex-Gov. Boutwell and others lectured during the fall and winter for the Young Men's Christian Association. Mr. Kunz and his daughters gave a series of German theatrical performances, during June and July, at the Apollo Gardens. Stetson & Wood opened the Atheneum September 5th, with Mr. and Mrs. Harry Chapman and an indifferent company, closing November 2d.

The Indianapolis Daily Citizen was started May 14th, 1857, by Cameron & McNeely, at their office, 10 east Pearl street. It was regularly issued by them till June, 1858, when it was discontinued. It was republican in politics, and well conducted. The Western Presage, a literary and political weekly paper, was first issued by Bidwell Bros. at 84 east Washington street, January 3d, 1857. It was the exponent of advanced republican ideas, was issued in expensive style, resulting in the failure of the firm and the discontinuance of the paper in April. It deserved a longer life and better fate.

Much building was done in 1857. The block opposite the court-house, the Episcopal, and Third and Fourth Presbyterian churches, the United States post-office, Metropolitan Theatre and many other prominent buildings being in progress.

1 8 5 8. The question as to the constitutionality of the free school tax was decided in January by the Supreme Court, against the tax. The citizens of each ward were requested by the city council to meet and, if possible, devise means by which the system could be maintained. The meetings were held January 29th. It was resolved to continue the schools, and one thousand one hundred scholarships, amounting to $3,000, were subscribed to keep them going for the current quarter. At the end of that time they stopped, the teachers left, the system was broken up, and the houses were closed. Some effort was made to re-establish private schools, and the free schools were opened each year for a short time under the State law.

Three thousand, three hundred and forty-three votes were polled at the May election, the republicans electing the entire ticket and a majority of the councilmen. The council elected Samuel Lefever chief of police, and the fire association having presented the name of Jos. W. Davis for chief fire engineer, he was elected to that office on the 22d of May. Much dissatisfaction arose among the firemen at his election, and from this date, till November, 1859, when it was disbanded, the efficiency of the department was much impaired. The opposition to Mr. Davis was mainly owing to his imperious manner, for otherwise he was a good executive officer. The assessment of city property for the current year showed a total of $10,475,000, and the increase in buildings over last year was $600,000.

The spring of 1857 had been unusually wet, and the spring and early summer of this year were still more so. Constant and heavy rains fell from early in April to the middle of June. Great storms occurred on the 11th of April, the 11th and 12th of May and about the 10th of June. Pogue's run completely flooded its valley on the 12th of April. Several street bridges were swept off; the Central railroad bridge giving way as a locomotive was passing over, throwing it into the creek. The culvert under the canal was also carried off. White river was over the bottoms repeatedly during the spring, and on the 14th of June reached a point but little below the flood-mark of 1847, causing great loss in fencing to the farmers along the valley. The wet season was succeeded by very hot, dry weather, and on the 26th of June eight cases of sun-stroke occurred, five of them being fatal. Several cases happened the next day, and for two or three days afterward all persons kept in the shade as much as possible.

A brilliant comet, which passed very near the earth in its course, was visible in the western heavens in September and October, its train bending like a bow.

A Bible investigating class was originated during the summer or fall, holding meetings every Sunday at the court house, for investigation of the authenticity of the Scriptures, or the meaning of disputed passages. Atheists, Deists and members of all orthodox churches participated in the discussions, which were often keen and searching, sometimes acrimonious. The meetings were kept up during this and the next year, were well attended, excited much interest, and if they did no other good, at least caused more study of the Bible by some persons than they otherwise ever would have given it.

Four or five miles of mains were laid by the Gas Company during the summer and fall, and several miles of streets were lighted. Much building and street improvement also were undertaken. Blackford's block, the Ætna building, Metropolitan Theater and the Washington street culvert over Pogue's run were built.

The 4th of July happening on Sunday, no general celebration took place. The 3d and 5th were devoted to pic-nics by the schools, firemen and Turners, the military companies going to Richmond.

A Jewish church, Rev. T. Weschler, was organized in August, worshipping in Judahs' block till 1866, when the Synagogue on east Market street, built in 1865-6, was completed at a cost of $25,000, and occupied by the congregation.

There was great rejoicing and an extemporised illumination on the night of the 7th of August, over the completion of the Atlantic Cable, and on the 17th a formal celebration of that event took place in the Circle, with a display of fire-works and an oration by Governor Wallace. The National Guards held a three days encampment, in October, on White river, north-west of the city.

The Indianapolis Academy of Science was organized during the summer, R. T. Brown, J. W. Barnitz, and others, being prominent in the matter. A room in Judahs' block was rented, meetings and discussions held, papers read on scientific subjects, and a considerable cabinet of geological specimens accumulated, but the community not taking sufficient interest in it, the society was suspended in July 1860, and its collections scattered.

Lectures and amusements were not lacking this year. Thomas F. Meagher lectured, February 17th, at Masonic Hall. Ormsby M. Mitchell began a series of astronomical lectures there, October 27th, B. F. Taylor, M. F. Maury, E. L. Youmans, Bayard Taylor, Dr. Holland, and others, lectured during the season before the Young Men's Christian Association. Andrew Jackson Davis, the "Pokepsie seer," gave a series of spiritual lectures there, beginning December 16th. The German singing societies of the State held a convention, June 10th–13th, with a procession and grand concert. A German theatrical troupe appeared at the Atheneum in August, and in January and February there were two German theaters at Washington and Union halls. Sam. and Kate Denin Ryan had appeared with a small company at Washington Hall in April. Harry Chapman during the State Fair, opened the Atheneum, Mrs. Drake and J. K. Mortimer appearing on the boards. It had also been opened for a few nights by strolling companies, several times during the summer.

The dramatic event of the year, however, was the opening of the Metropolitan Theater, the first building specially devoted to amusements here. It was erected by Valentine Butsch in 1857–8, on the northeast corner of Washington and Tennessee streets. The corner stone was laid in August 1857, and the house opened September 27, 1858. The building was eighty-two by one hundred and twenty-five feet, three stories high, of brick stuccoed in imitation of sandstone, and, with the lot, cost when completely fitted up, about $58,-000. The cellars and ground floor are used for business purposes. The dress circle and parquet are well arranged, but the gallery was not well designed for a proper view of the stage. The building will comfortably seat about twelve hundred persons. The interior was neatly frescoed and gilded by artists from Cincinnati, and the scenery was mostly painted by S. W. Gulick.

E. T. Sherlock was the first manager and lessee, opening September 27th, 1858, with a rather indifferent company, and closing Feb'y 29th, 1859. Harry Chapman continued it as manager till March 13, 1859. The Keller troupe, H. W. Gossin, Sallie St.Clair, Hacket, Dora Shaw, the Florences, J. B. Roberts, Mrs. J. W. Wallack, Mrs. Howard, Adah Isaacs Menken, the Cooper opera troupe, Eliza Logan, Mr.

and Mrs. Waller, Mrs. Edwin Forrest, Mr. Sedley and Miss Matilda Heron appeared as stars during the season. George Wood & Co. opened it again for a short time in April. John A. Ellsler opened it in April, 1859, for a two months season; Miss Kimberly, Collins, and Kate and Sam Ryan appearing as stars. He again opened it, October 1st, the season closing March 2d, 1861. The Webb sisters, Miss Ince, Sallie St. Clair, Marion McCarthy, F. A. Vincent, Barras, J. B. Roberts, the Richings and others being the stars. The war having begun, and thousands of men thronging here, the theatre was re-opened by Mr Butsch, as proprietor and manager, on the 25th of April, F. A. Vincent being stage manager, and Miss McCarthy leading lady. A good company was also secured, and from this date until after the close of the war, the enterprise was well supported and profitable. Most of the leading members of the stock company continued here for several successive seasons, and some of them, as Mr. and Mrs. Hodges, and F. C. White, until the theatre was finally closed in the spring of 1868. Vincent continued as stage manager until 1863. William H. Riley then succeeded, holding that position till the spring of 1867. He then removed to the St. Charles theatre, New Orleans, dying shortly after his arrival there. M. V. Lingham became manager for the season of 1867–8, and in the spring of 1868 Charles R. Pope became the last manager, with a good company, and giving the people the most brilliant season ever witnessed there. Edwin Forrest played an engagement of five nights, beginning March 16th, to crowded houses, at double the usual rates of admission. Since April, 1861, nearly all the leading actors and actresses in the country have appeared on the boards of the Metropolitan, and among others, Adelaide Ristori appeared there with her company, under Graus' management, on the 25th March, 1867.

The theatre has not been so well supported since the close of the war. Its position was against it, being too far west. The proprietor, Mr. Butsch, early in 1868, purchased Miller's Hall, (then nearly completed,) on the corner of Illinois and Ohio streets, for about $50,000, and has fitted it up in tasteful style for a theatre and music hall, to be opened in the fall of this year. The building is much larger than the old theatre, and the auditorium will comfortably accommodate a much larger audience. The old theatre will hereafter be used for concerts, lectures, meetings, &c.

1859. Some efforts were made in January, to organize a corporation for a University at this point, and in February an application was made to the Assembly for a lease of University Square for a term of ninety-nine years, as a site for the contemplated buildings, the property to be surrendered to the State at the end of the term. As there was some doubt as to the ownership of the square, between the city and the State, the application was not granted, and the project was dropped. The city terminated the dispute as to ownership in 1860, by taking possession of the square and the military grounds. The old seminary was torn down in August and September, 1860, and the square improved as a park. In 1867-8 the military grounds were fenced, and also improved as a park, at the expense of the city. The ownership and possession of the city will probably be uncontested hereafter.

The gas company had laid a number of miles of mains during 1858, and during this year were still further extending the pipes. Many applications for street lamps had been granted, and others were pending, and as no uniformity existed in the position of the lamps, or their number to the square, and no regulations had yet been adopted on the subject, the Council, on the 12th of February, passed an ordinance prescribing a general plan for lighting the city, fixing the number of lamps at four for each square, and their position, and distance from each other. Under this ordinance several additional miles of streets were lit for the first time, in the fall and winter of this year, Washington street, from Pennsylvania to New Jersey, and Illinois from Washington to North street, being in the number.

Early in 1854 a number of young men had formed a gymnastic association, adopted by-laws, fixed admission fees, dues, &c., and elected officers. The third story of Blake's commercial row was rented, and fitted up with a complete set of apparatus. The gymnasium was popular, and well patronized for two or three months, but as the novelty wore off and the hard work began, the interest rapidly lessened, and but few steadily availed themselves of its advantages for exercise and health. The association declined for want of members, and died in a year or two, after spasmodic efforts to continue it. No further effort was made till March, or April, 1859, when the Indianapolis Gymnastic Association was formed, with Simon Yandes, President, and Thomas H. Bowles, Secretary. A code of rules was adopted, and the third story of the Athe-

neum building rented, and fitted up with gymnastic apparatus, bowling alleys, &c., at a cost of about $1,200, and the room opened for use in June. The older men were also invited to share in the enterprise, and with their aid it did very well for two or three years, the bowling alleys and chess tables largely adding to its attractiveness. The interest gradually diminished, however, and though the ladies were asked to share its advantages, the organization became defunct at the breaking out of the war.

A grand procession and celebration by the Odd Fellows took place on the 29th of April.

In April, Rev. Gibbon Williams bought the house and one and a half acres of ground at the north-west corner of Pennsylvania and Michigan streets, and shortly afterward opened the Indianapolis Female Institute, a school which has increased in importance and prosperity to the present time. The building, (at first small and ill arranged) was greatly enlarged and improved at several subsequent periods, and at present is one of the largest educational structures in the city, having a capacity for nearly two hundred boarding, and three hundred day pupils. Rev. Mr. Williams left in 1863, and was succeeded in the presidency of the institution, by C. W. Hewes. A full corps of able professors are connected with the college, and the number of pupils has steadily increased since its origin.

The city election took place May 3d, the city officers being elected for two years, and the councilmen for four years, under the amended charter adopted by the assembly March 1, 1859. At the same time a proposition was submitted to the general vote of the people to divide the first and seventh wards, so that two new wards should be created, forming the eighth and ninth wards, but the result of the vote was largely against it. The proposition was again submitted to vote in May 1861 and carried by six hundred and twenty-one majority. Councilmen were elected from the new wards, but were refused their seats, and the wards were unrepresented for a year or two afterward.

The city clerk reported the receipts from May 8, 1858 to May 30, 1859, at $71,211, expenditures the same, with a debt of $9,-317. The total city assessment for the year was $7,146,677. The treasurer reported the receipts from May 8, 1858 to May 1, 1859 at $59,168. Expenditures $56,442, the leading items being $10,232 for the fire department; gas $4,771; watchman $4,882. The salaries of the city officers were raised in May and June. The bouldering of Washington street, between Illinois and Meridian streets, (the first done here,) had been ordered in April and was done in May, and further street improvements were designed. The council, in view of the probable expenditures, fixed the tax levy at sixty cents, which so aroused the tax-payers that they held a public meeting June 22d, to protest against it. They little knew what was in store for them in the future.

A proposition was entertained by the council, during the spring, to build a City Hall on the lot south of the Journal office on Meridian street, but no final action was taken. The city offices and council room were located in the Odd Fellows Hall where they remained till May, 1862, when a lease, for ten years, was secured of the upper stories of Glenns' block. Efforts have often been made to secure the erection of a City Hall and prison, but without success.

The General Assembly of the Old School Presbyterian church met in the basement room of the Third Presbyterian church, May 18th, continuing in session till the 2d of June. The eminent men of the church were in attendance, and the debates between Dr. McMasters and N. L. Rice, and others, on the establishment of theological schools and the policy of the church on the slavery question, excited great interest and attracted crowded audiences.

The national anniversary was celebrated with unusual display. The City Council appropriated $500 for the purpose, and large subscriptions were made by individuals. The procession comprised the artillery, cavalry and infantry companies, three bands, Turners, Butchers, Fenians, Catholic societies, Madison firemen and our own fire department, seven companies with eight engines, reels, hook and ladder wagons and a long line of carriages. The engines were beautifully decorated. The procession, which was nearly two miles in length, marched through the principal streets to the old fair ground, where the usual exercises occurred, Caleb B. Smith delivering the address. A great pic-nic dinner was spread, after which the military were reviewed by Governor Hammond. A grand fantastic parade took place in the evening, and a fine display of fire-works at night. Over twenty thousand persons were present at the celebration. It was rumored in the evening that the "Sons of Malta," a mysterious organization, which had rapidly increased in number during the spring, would parade at midnight; their rigid rules preventing public demonstrations at any other hour. The report

caused much excitement, especially among country visitors and the ladies, thousands of whom impatiently awaited the strange display. It proved to be all that fancy painted it, and the procession was accompanied through its midnight march by a multitude of half crazy spectators, though the gravity of the puissant Knights and reverend prelates was sadly disturbed by the noisy advice of the street boys, "go faster old tin-head," "step up brass mounted man."

On the 23d of August, Adam Deitz drank eight gallons of lager beer together with a bottle of brandy, inside of twelve hours, attaining a wide notoriety thereby and winning a wager.

Much improvement took place during the summer and fall, and a number of good business houses were erected. Yohns', Rays' and Glenns' blocks being among them.

The Daily Atlas was first issued by John D. Defrees as editor and publisher, in July, from an office in Van Blaricum's block, on south Meridian street. The presses were run by a small Ericsson hot air engine, (the only one ever used here,) which attracted many visitors. The paper was regularly issued till about the end of March 1861, and then discontinued, the material and subscription list being sold to the Journal office. Several other newspaper enterprises have been started here before and since the Citizen and Atlas were established. The Brookville American was transferred to this point by the editor and proprietor, Thomas A. Goodwin, in 1857. It was afterward sold to Downey & Co., who issued it as a daily for a short period, and then sold the establishment to Jordan & Burnet. They changed the name to the Evening Gazette. Dr. Jordan afterward issued it till the spring of 1865, when he sold it to Smith & Co. They afterward sold it to Macauley, Shurtleff & Co., and they sold the office and list, in May or June 1867, to the Journal Co. The Gazette was issued most of the time from an office in Hubbard's block, and latterly from the Sentinel office on Pearl and Meridian streets. It was well conducted during a part of its existence, and attained a considerable circulation during the war.

The Daily Telegraph, the only German daily in the city, was issued by the Free Press Co., in 1866, and has continued to the present time. The office is on west Maryland street.

The Evening Commercial was established in 1867 by Dynes & Co., and issued from Downey & Brouse's Publishing House in the Sentinel building on Pearl street. It was subsequently moved with their office to the old Journal building, on Circle and Meridian streets, and is now published by M. G. Lee.

The year 1859 was dull so far as lectures, concerts and amusements were concerned. Geo. D. Prentice lectured at the hall on the 6th of February, and Henry S. Foote, of Mississippi, at Roberts' chapel, December 2d. Dr. Boynton delivered a series of geological lectures, at the hall, in December and January, 1860. Miss Laura Melrose sang there March 24, and the Cooper opera troupe April 1st.

The coming political contest began to excite attention. Gov. Corwin addressed a large serenading party at the American House, on the 6th of July. Abraham Lincoln visited the city for the first time, and addressed a large audience at Masonic Hall, on the 19th of September. He was personally unknown to the great mass of the citizens, and considerable curiosity was manifested to hear the man who had so gallantly struggled with Senator Douglass, then at the zenith of his power.

Richard Cobden, of England, then on a visit to this country, reached the city on the 5th of May, but remained a few hours only, passing on to the north-west. The year closed with excessively cold weather.

1860. The military grounds being thought too small to properly accommodate the visitors and exhibitors, at the State fairs, the agricultural board determined in 1859 to secure a large tract for the purpose, and locate the fair permanently at this point. Proposals were invited in the fall of 1859, and an unsuccessful effort was shortly after made here to form an association to buy the grounds for the board. An appropriation of $5,000 was then asked from the city, and the proposition being submitted in February to a vote of the people, it was authorized. A question arising, however, as to the legality of such an appropriation, it was not made. The railways and the board finally made an arrangement for the purchase of the grounds, and after much competition between the advocates of various sites, the Otis grove, of forty acres, north of the city, was bought in the spring of 1860. Extensive and costly improvements were made during the summer, and the fair held there, October 15th to 21st. It was not as successful as had been desired. $11,900 only were realized, and a part only of the awarded premiums were paid. The board was seriously embarrassed for several years afterward, but is now getting out of debt.

In April a Mr. Bell, of Rochester, New York, submitted a plan for water works to the council. The project was discussed at a number of meetings. Estimates were made, but no definite action was finally taken. It was again broached by the central canal company in July, 1864. They proposed to furnish water from their ditch. This project was also considered, and committees appointed who reported on it, but the subject was finally dropped without definite results. In October, 1865, the Mayor again brought up the subject by a message, urging the building of such works, and recommending Crown Hill as the point for a reservoir The council passed a resolution declaring it expedient that such works be built, and that it was inexpedient for the city to undertake them. This action was intended to invite proposals from private companies, but had no immediate effect. In May, 1866, the Mayor again brought the subject before the council, introducing questions propounded by him to James B. Cunningham, civil engineer, and the answers and estimates made by that gentleman in reply. The subject was again brought up October 15, 1866, on a proposition by R. B. Catherwood and associates to build water-works if a liberal charter was granted them. The council thereupon by resolution declared it expedient that water works be built, and inexpedient for the city to build them. A committee on the subject was appointed.— It reported an ordinance on the 22d of October, authorizing R. B. Catherwood & Co. as the Indianapolis water works company, to build such works, and furnish the city and people with water for fifty years. The ordinance, after various amendments, was finally passed, November 3, 1866. It gave the company the right, for fifty years, to furnish the people and city with pure water, to be taken from White river or its tributaries, several miles above the city.— To use the streets and alleys for pipes, the company to repair the streets when torn up. The city reserved the right to buy the works after twenty-five years; required operations to be commenced within one year, and a given sum to be expended within two years. Hydrants and fire-plugs were to be located where desired, and the city was to pay from $40 down to $25, according to the number ultimately erected. The amount of capital was specified, and the amount of profit on it limited to fifteen per cent., water rates to be placed as low, from time to time, as practicable. The company was organized under the charter, with R. B. Catherwood, president, Jno. S. Tarkington, secretary, and accepted the ordinance, November 5, 1866, filing it with the mayor, who, on the 6th of November, issued his proclamation, stating that fact, and publishing the ordinance. The company, within the year, and to save their charter, nominally began operations by laying about fifty feet of pipe on North street. Nothing has since been done with the work.

So far as a convenient and plentiful supply of water is concerned, the works will doubtless be of great benefit, but no surface water will ever equal in purity and healthfulness the water now drawn from wells sunk in the great gravel and sandbeds underneath the city, and if surface drainage was carefully prevented, no deterioration in its purity will occur for scores of years. No artificial filters can equal those nature has given us, and the phosphates and carbonates dissolved by the water in its passage through the sand are those most needed in the human system.

By the treasurer's report in May, the receipts for the past year were $87,262, expenditures $80,172, balance $7,090, debt $11,553. The leading items were for fire department $11,353, bridges $13,915, street improvements $14,875, police $5,980, gas $6,445. The city duplicate showed an assessment amounting to $10,700,000.

Street railroads in the city were first proposed in November of this year, and an unsuccessful attempt was made to form a company to build them. No further action was taken in regard to them until June 5th, 1863, when a number of our citizens formed a company under the general law, electing Thomas A Morris president, Wm. Y. Wiley, secretary, and Wm. O. Rockwood, treasurer. They filed an application with the council on the 24th of August, setting forth their organization, and asking a charter from the city. The application was referred to a committee, who prepared an ordinance and submitted it for the consideration of the council. Amendments were proposed, and while the ordinance was still pending, R. B. Catherwood, of New York, associated with several of our own citizens, formed the Citizens' Street Railroad Company, with John A. Bridgland as president, and proposed more favorable terms to the council, agreeing to begin the construction of the lines at once, and finish a greater number of miles in a given time. The competition between the two companies grew warm. It was charged that the Citizens' company was not responsible or able to fulfill their offers. They responded to this by paying down nearly $30,000 of their capital, and offering bond of $200,000 to fulfill all their agreements. The council finally decided the contest in favor of the Indianapolis company, granting them a charter on the 11th of December, 1863. They declined to accept it on the 28th of December; and the mayor having telegraphed that fact to

Mr. Catherwood, at Brooklyn, New York, he immediately answered that he would accept the charter, re-organize the company, and begin the work. On the 18th of January, 1864, the council passed an ordinance giving the Citizens' Street Railroad Company, (which had re-organized, with R. B. Catherwood, president, E. C. Catherwood, secretary, and H. H. Catherwood, superintendent,) the right to lay single or double tracks of railway on all the streets and alleys of the city, or its future extensions. Horse-cars were to be used only for transportation of passengers and baggage. The council retained the right to govern speed and time. The tracks were to conform to the street grades, and the company were to boulder between the tracks and two feet each side. The tracks were to be laid in the center of the street, or, if double, on each side of the center, and not nearer the side-walks than twelve feet. Fares on any route were not to exceed five cents. The company to repair all damage to the streets, relay tracks when the street grades are changed, and be liable to private parties for all damages they might sustain. They were to return annually, on the first of January, a full statement of all property for taxation; but each separate line was to be exempt from taxation for two years from its completion. Rules were prescribed for the running and management of the cars, and the cars were given right of way against all other vehicles. The charter was given for thirty years, subject to the following conditions: Three miles were to be built and fully equipped by October 1, 1864, two additional miles by October 1, 1865, two additional miles by December 25th, 1866, unless a further extension of time was granted by the council, otherwise all rights, &c., under the charter were to be forfeited. The council reserved the right to order additional lines constructed after the first seven miles were finished; and in case of failure, the company was to forfeit the right to that particular street or route. If, after ten years, the company had not built and fully equipped ten miles of track in the best style, the council might order an appraisement and pay the company therefor, or transfer the property and franchise to another company. The ordinance was to be in force after two weeks publication in the weekly Journal.

The company accepted the charter, and immediately began preparations for building lines. Materials were collected during the spring, cars ordered, and property secured for stables and car-houses. Their operations were somewhat delayed, and the iron and cars detained by the use of

the railways by government. But on application, the council, on tne 27th of August, 1864, extended the time for sixty
days, and no forfeiture of their franchise
occurred. Track-laying began on Illinois
street at the Union depot, and the line was
finished on that street to North street within the year. Tracks were also laid on
Washington from Pennsylvania to West
streets, and thence to the military ground,
in time for the State fair in October. The
line on Illinois street had been opened for
travel in June, 1864—the mayor driving
the first car on the first trip, accompanied
by the council, city officers and officers of
the company. In the fall of 1864 the citizens along Virginia avenue, having subscribed from $25,000 to $30,000 for a bonus, the company built a single-track
road from Washington street to the end of
the avenue, making the route along the
avenue and Washington street (which had
a double track from Illinois to Pennsylvania street,) to West street. The route was
afterward limited to the avenue alone,
causing much dissatisfaction, and the company subsequently changed to the old
route, limiting it to the avenue and Tennessee street. In March, April and May,
1865 the Massachusetts avenue line,
(which had a double track,) was laid from
Washington street up Pennsylvania, Mas-
sachuscets avenue and New Jersey street
to St. Clair street. In June, 1867, one of
one of the tracks on New Jersey street was
taken up and used to extend the line on Ft-
Wayne avenue, and thence east on Christian avenue to College street. In October,
1865, the Washington street line was extended on Washington street and the National road, (which had been adopted by
the council, September 18th, as one of the
city streets,) to the White river bridge—
the line to military ground having been
taken up in 1864 after the fair. The council also gave the company the right to lay
tracks on all new streets. In the spring
and summer of 1866 the Washington street
line was extended east by single track to
the culvert over Pogue's run. The Illinois
street line was extended to Tinker street
in June and July, 1866, and the line to
Crown Hill, (built by a separate company,)
was begun in the fall of 1866, and opened
for travel in Aprii or May, 1866.

In the spring of 1868, a new line was laid
from Washington street down Kentucky
avenue and Tennessee street, and east on
Louisiana to Illinois street, being opened
for travel in April. The first stables and
car house were built on Tennessee and
Louisiana streets, in October, 1864, and
extended and improved in the summer of
1867. After the first lines were built and

opened, the company placed about thirty
two horse cars upon them, and continued
using them with drivers and conductors
till April, 1868. At one time an effort was
made to dispense with conductors, but after
trial for some days, the company resolved to
adopt a different car. Thirty or thirty-
two one-horse cars, requiring a driver only,
were procured during the spring of 1868,
and placed on the different lines on the
3rd of April. The driver now merely fur-
nishes change, the passengers themselves
place the fare in safety boxes. The cars
are turned on turn-tables at each end of
the route, and trips are made at greater
speed than under the old system. The old
cars are used only on the Crown Hill route,
or in case of pic-nics, or unusual demands
on the rolling stock of the company. A
portion of them have been sold, eighteen
or twenty only being left at the present
time. Mules are now almost exclusively
used by the company. No bouldering has
been done by the company on their tracks,
except where they run along bouldered
streets, as it is claimed that bouldered
streets injured and crippled the animals.

Five hundred and fifty round trips are
run, and four thousand passengers carried
over the lines daily.

At present, including the Crown Hill
line from Tinker street, and including side
and double tracks, the company have about
fifteen miles of finished and equipped road,
costing $468,000. They also own fifty cars,
employ sixty-four men, and one hundred
and fifty mules and horses. The enterprise
has not been as profitable as it was expected to be, but with the future increase of the
city, its success will be assured.

R. B. Catherwood in September or Octo-
ber 1865, sold the controlling interest in the
company to Messrs. English, Alvord and
others. A reorganization took place, E. S.
Alvord becoming President, R. F. Fletcher,
Secretary, W. H. English, Treasurer, and
H. H. Catherwood, Superintendent. J. S.
Alvord is the present Secretary, and R. F.
Fletcher, Superintendent.

A tornado swept across the State from
west to east in the afternoon of May 29th,
1860, passing just south-east of this city,
between 5 and 6 o'clock, p. m. It was a
rapidly moving, whirling cloud, of small
diameter, described by those who witnessed
it, as hanging from or cutting through the
clouds above and around it, swaying about
like an elephant's trunk, rising and falling
as it sped forward. Considerable damage
was done to houses, timber, gardens and
fences in its path. The residence of Gardner Goldsmith, at the end of Virginia
avenue, was thrown from its foundation
and partially destroyed, and Goldsmith was

seriously injured. It was much more destructive both east and west, however, than
near this city.

Great preparations were made for the
celebration of the fourth of July, the people feeling that it might perhaps be the last
under a united government. The procession included five bands, the entire fire department with beautifully decorated engines and reels, three military companies,
the butchers, gardeners, various societies,
and a long line of carriages. The usual
exercises took place at the fair grounds.
A very large frame building had just been
completed on University square, by Mr.
Perrine, and in the afternoon the military
companies drilled there for a prize of $100.
A balloon ascension by J. C. Bellman, took
place at 4 o'clock, p. m. He rose to a great
hight, and landed ten miles from the city.
The best display of fire works ever given
here took place at night in the enclo-
sure. The "Coliseum"—as it was termed—
could accommodate fifteen or twenty thousand persons, being, perhaps, the largest
structure of the kind ever built in this
country. It was torn down some weeks
after.

The political struggle of this year was
unprecedented in its interest and bitter-
ness, each party holding repeated monster
conventions and torch-light processions;
every effort being made by each to surpass
the last display by the opposite party. The
democrats held a great meeting at the State
house yard on the 8th of July, George E.
Pugh and C. L. Vallandigham being the
leading speakers. The republicans far
surpassed this demonstration on the 29th
of August, at the old fair ground, Corwin,
Blair, Stanton, Lane, Morton and others
being the speakers. A great procession
marched thither in the day time, and at
night a torch-light procession, which included several thousand Wide Awakes,
formed on University square, and filed
through the principal streets, saluted along
its line of march with a constant blaze of
fire works and illuminations. This demonstration was equalled if not surpassed by
the democrats on the 28th of September.
Much money had been spent by them in
tasteful arches and other decorations, and
the display was a very grand one. Douglass, H. V. Johnson, and other leaders of
the party were present, and delivered addresses at the fair ground. There was a
grand torch-light procession at night, and
the fire-works and illuminations equaled
if they did not surpass the display by the
republicans. The crowds in attendance
at these conventions were to be measured
only by the acre, and sufficiently demonstrated the perfection and extent of our

railway system. At no other place in the
country could such immense throngs have
been concentrated or dispersed so readily
as at this point.

The first rope-walking exhibition here
was given in September, by Theodore Price,
in the presence of an immense crowd, the
rope being stretched from the roof of the
Palmer house to that of the Bates house.
Several subsequent exhibitions have occurred, the most notable and dangerous
one occurring in the summer of 1865, on a
rope stretched from the roof of Blackford's
block to that of Yohn's block.

The Escott and Miranda Opera Troupe
sang at the theatre in January. A musical
convention was held at Masonic Hall in
September. Bayard Taylor and Henry J.
Raymond lectured there in February. Lola
Montez lectured there for several nights,
beginning February 23. In the fall and
winter, Bayard Taylor, Prof. Youmans, J.
B. Gough, Dr. Robt. J. Breckinridge, G. W.
Winship and others, lectured before the
Young Men's Christian Association. Sallie
St. Clair appeared at the Metropolitan for
a few nights in February.

In view of the threatening aspect assumed by the southern States, and the lack
of patriotism displayed by them, it was
deemed proper by the assembly to unfurl
the American flag from the State House
dome, and the ceremony was fixed for the
22d of January, 1861. A flag staff and
large flag were prepared. Extensive arrangements were made, the military, the
firemen, city and State authorities, and
citizens paraded. The preliminary exercises were concluded, and the flag was
started up in presence of a vast and ex-
pectant crowd, when the staff broke, and,
with the flag, tumbled down the dome to
the roof. The crowd dispersed silently,
deeming the event ominous of coming
trouble. A new staff however was afterward procured, and the flag successfully
raised, but with less display and enthusiasm.

1 8 6 1 – 8. The First Baptist church, on
the corner of Maryland and Meridian
streets, was burned during a great snow
storm, on the night of January 27th, 1861,
presenting a sad but magnificent spectacle
as the flames burst from the roof, and
wrapped round the spire, which soon top-
pled and plunged downward through the
roof. The fire was supposed to have caught
from a defective flue. The loss was a serious blow to the church. The first building occupied by the congregation was a
small one-story brick structure, on the
same site, built in 1829 or 1830, and holding two hundred and fifty or three hundred
persons. The small bell then used was

placed in a separate frame tower at one end of the house. This building was torn away, and the house which was now just destroyed was built there in 1851 or 1852. The first spire was built in the telescopic form usual in country towns, the upper portion being finished inside of the lower, and hoisted by tackle to its proper elevation. It had just been hoisted to its place during a hot summer afternoon, and the workmen were still on it, when a sudden thunder gust came up, and the spire being insufficiently stayed, the guy ropes parted and it turned a somersault, coming point down on the pavement in front of the building, narrowly missing a team and wagon, and shattering itself into splinters. The men at work on it had barely time enough to get off before it went over. Another spire was afterward built, but in a different way.

The congregation, after the destruction of the church, sold the lot (which is now occupied by Schnull's block,) and purchased the lot on the north-east corner of Pennsylvania and New York streets, and in 1862 erected the present large brick edifice upon it.

President Lincoln arrived here on the 12th of February, 1861, on his way to the national capital, and was received as the guest of the city and State, being met at the State line, and escorted thither by a committee. He left the Lafayette train at Washington street, and was escorted to the Bates House by the military companies, fire department, State authorities, and a vast crowd of citizens. In a short speech from the balcony of the Bates House, he outlined his future policy with regard to the rebellion, and held a reception during the evening, leaving for the east next morning.

Several meetings of conservative republicans were held at the court house in February and March, to urge a compromise of the existing political differences, and the settlement of the controversy by making concessions to the South. The sessions were stormy, in consequence of the attendance of the more radical men, who felt that the time for all compromise had passed, and before any definite action or course was decided on by the meetings, the acts of the rebels transferred the discussion from the forum to the field. There was then no further talk of compromise, and those who had urged it became earnest and active in the war.

It can scarcely be expected that a full history of the part taken by this city in the war can be given in the limits of an article like this. It could only be properly dealt with in a volume. But a brief out-

line at least may be presented of the leading events.

The news of the attack upon Fort Sumter reached the city April 12th, and at once produced the profoundest feeling.— Business was suspended, and every one eager for the latest intelligence. During the afternoon a handbill was posted calling a meeting at the court house, and at the appointed hour the room was thronged.— An adjournment at once voted to Masonic Hall, and the excited crowd, now momentarily augmenting, rolled down Washington street. The hall was at once filled, as well as the theatre and the intervening street. The American flag was produced, and greeted with deafening cheers. Speeches were made at the several meetings, bitter resolutions were adopted, and volunteering at once begun. The throng dispersed at a late hour, excited and enraged over the news that the Fort had been surrendered. On the following day the Greys, Guards, Independent Zouaves, Zouave Guards, and a light artillery company began recruiting. Flags were everywhere displayed, and the fife and drum heard at every corner. The president's proclamation for seventy-five thousand men appeared on the 15th, and the governor's call for six regiments from this State, on the 16th.

The State fair ground was chosen as the rendesvous. It was named Camp Morton, and on the 16th and 17th the city companies moved there, having meanwhile been quartered in the public halls of the city. Companies from abroad were also hourly arriving, greeted by cheers and the firing of cannon, and were sworn in at the State House and sent to camp. In a few days eight or ten thousand men had reported for duty. Had sixty, instead of six, regiments been demanded, the call would have been almost as readily filled. Our own companies were full and others forming. Home guards were organized for each ward. Every one was anxious to contribute, and blankets, food and clothing were collected by the wagon load for the men so suddenly collected with no provision for their comfort. The ladies formed societies and materially assisted in this work. The enthusiasm was wonderful: The zeal, faith and courage, sublime. The material and men were superabundant, and the excess made the labor of the authorities all the more difficult. Everything had to be learned by a people unacquainted with war, and for some time confusion reigned supreme. Order, however, was gradually restored, the six regiments were organized and brigaded, and the work of drilling and equipping them began.

On the 24th of April Stephen A. Douglass visited the city and made a speech. He went to Camp Morton, visiting the troops and arousing great enthusiasm among them.

Some feeling arising concerning the support of the families of soldiers during their absence, the City Council, on the 20th of April, voted an appropriation of $10,-000 for their maintenance.

Seven companies were formed here under this call, the most of them being in the eleventh regiment under Col. Lew Wallace. They were moved in a few days to the old Bellefontaine depot, uniformed soon after and persistently drilled. Stands of colors were presented to them at the State House on behalf of the ladies, and feeling like old troops they clamored for service. They were accordingly sent to Evansville, (ostensibly to guard the border,) on the 9th of May. The excess of troops reporting here, over the six regiments called for by the Government, were organized under State authority in six one year regiments for the State service, but were soon after re-enlisted, (except one regiment of one year men,) for three years and all transferred to the Federal service. The six regiments of troops under the first call were reviewed by General G. B. McClellan in the fields north-west of the military grounds, (then occupied by the State troops and known as Camp Sullivan,) on the 24th of May. He shortly after ordered them into active service in West Virginia, where they participated actively and effectively in the campaign. The eleventh regiment, meanwhile, was left at Evansville, but growing tired of their position, an order was obtained from Washington transferring them to Cumberland, Maryland. They afterward joined Patterson's army, participating in the movements of that force prior and subsequent to the battle of Bull run. The three months regiments were discharged, returned home, but shortly afterward were again rendesvoused here to re-enter the three years service. Their old organizations were maintained, although the regiments were mostly composed of new recruits. The State troops, meanwhile, had been transferred to the Federal service and sent to the field, and the additional regiments afterward called for by the Government were gathering here and elsewhere. The nineteenth Regular regiment, added with others to the army by President Lincoln, rendesvoused here and was gradually growing in strength. It remained here till the fall of 1862, when its head-quarters were transferred to Detroit.

After the first flurry arising from the sudden concentration of the three months volunteers and the State troops at this point was over, and they had gone to the field, the work progressed more quietly and methodically. The anxiety to enter to the service was greater than the demand for troops, and some trouble was experienced in securing permission to raise additional regiments. After the three months troops were re-organized as three years men, however, additional regiments were demanded, and recruits for the first organizations were constantly called for. They were very readily obtained without local bounties, for business had been very dull since the preceding winter, and hundreds of men were out of work. This stagnation in general business continued here until the winter of 1862 and spring of 1863, when, from the Government demand for various articles, and the scarcity of workmen, high wages began to be demanded, and volunteering decreased. Uniforms had been scarce on the streets after the first regiments left. They afterward began to multiply, and from the capture of Ft. Donelson till after the close of the war they constantly became more numerous, until the city at last was a heavily garrisoned post. During the late fall and winter of 1861, however, the skeleton nineteenth Regular regiment constituted the main force here, and their perfect discipline and fine dress parades, with the added attraction of their full regimental band, drew crowds of admiring spectators. The twentieth regiment and several batteries were rendesvoused here and camped on the commons north-west of Camp Sullivan. The twenty-sixth and thirty-third and other regiments subsequently occupied Camp Sullivan. The drafted men were also placed there in 1862-3. The fifty-seventh regiment occupied a camp on the canal west of the Lafayette depot, and later organizations, recruits and drafted men were sent to Camp Carrington. In August 1862 a further call for troops was made. Bragg and Kirby Smith were advancing on Louisville. Great efforts were made to fill the quota, and good bounties offered for recruits. A draft was ordered and the preparatory enrollment was made, but before it took place the requisition was filled. The seventieth and seventy-ninth regiments were raised at that time, mainly in this district, and hurried to Louisville. They served to the close of the war, participating in Sherman's campaign against Atlanta and the march to the sea. No unusual war excitement disturbed the city from this date until early in July 1863.

It was then announced by the papers that John Morgan had crossed the Ohio river, and later in the day news came that he was rapidly moving toward this city, to release the prisoners. The fire bells were rung, and a vast crowd collected at the Bates house. The governor announced the news, and recommended the immediate cessation of business, and the formation of military companies. It was resolved to form companies in each ward, and recruiting at once began. Dispatches were sent elsewhere calling for aid. The next morning martial law was declared, business ceased, the ward companies were sworn into the State legion, and a regiment twelve hundred strong organized under Colonel Rugg, armed, equipped and constantly drilled. It met that night on University square, to receive blankets, accoutrements and ammunition, and was ordered to march next day. During this and the two following days, companies and regiments were coming by rail from all parts of the State, and a considerable army was extemporized. The excitement and enthusiasm increased hourly, surpassing any thing seen during the war. Other regiments were organized and sent to meet the enemy, but the city regiment was persistently marched and drilled on University square and elsewhere, attaining very creditable proficiency in forty-eight hours. Signals were established by the fire bells, for the regiment to start on the campaign, and they were thus called together about twice a day. The warriors parted so frequently from their wives and sweethearts that they grew tired of it, and finally left for the seat of war on University square at each alarm, without a thought of those they left behind. The artillery and cavalry wings of the regiment meanwhile were executing various manœuvres not laid down in any system of tactics, sometimes putting the infantry in great bodily fear. Morgan soon turned eastward, but the regiment continued its martial exercises for several days afterward, and rapidly attained celerity and precision in marching and in the manual of arms. The organization was continued for two or three months, and in September an effort was made to uniform it and the police guards at the expense of the city, but it failed, and the force disbanded shortly afterward. Its services in the Morgan raid were afterward paid for by the State. The sudden organization of, and the immediate proficiency attained by this regiment conclusively proved that the people can be fully relied on in any emergency.

Recruiting went on steadily from this date, the city's quota always being supplied with reasonable promptness, but late in the fall another draft was expected, and

the citizens held a meeting on the 11th of December, asking the council to appropriate a sufficient sum to pay $50 of bounty to each recruit who might be credited to the township. On the 14th of December the council accordingly appropriated $25,-000 for that object, ordering the sale of bonds to that amount to raise the money. The bonds were prepared and sold in a few days, and recruiting went on with more activity. Committees were appointed, and funds raised in each ward to add to the bounty, and the required number of men was soon obtained.

During the winter of 1863-'64, and the following summer, the old veteran regiments were returning on thirty day furloughs for recreation and recruiting, before re-entering the service. One or more of them arrived every week, and were suitably received by the State and city authorities, the council having appropriated money for that purpose. Many recruits were obtained here for their ranks, and the Seventeenth Regiment re-enlisted and were credited, in a body, to this city. On learning that our quota had been filled, they confirmed their action regardless of bounty, but on the 8th of March Colonel Wilder asked the council to grant it to them. A committee reported against it, but the council, after further consideration of the subject, passed an ordinance on the 14th of March, appropriating $5,355 in bounties to the regiment. An attempt was afterward made to have this sum increased, but without success.

The campaign against Atlanta having begun, and the governors of Illinois, Indiana and Ohio having tendered a heavy force of one hundred day men to guard the lines of communication, a call was issued for troops for that term. The response not being very prompt, ward meetings were held, asking the council to appropriate bounties to those who might enlist under the call, and on the 9th of May $5,000 were appropriated for the maintenance of the families of one hundred day men, the sum to be disbursed by the Soldier's Aid Committee. Recruiting was actively prosecuted, and the city regiment was shortly raised, equipped and sent to Alabama under Colonel Vance, Lt.-Colonel Cramer and Major Bates. It was assigned to duty along the line of communication, and after the expiration of its term was sent home, discharged and paid off.

From this date recruiting became more difficult, and larger bounties were required. The demand for labor had increased the rates of wages, and few persons were out of work. Five hundred thousand more men were called for, and as the response was not satisfactory, preparations were made for a draft. The enrollment in June, 1864, showed seven thousand five hundred and seventy-three men subject to draft in the city, and the quota was fixed at one thousand two hundred and fifty-nine. Efforts to fill it by recruiting were made, and meetings were held in the wards and in the tabernacle on Court square, to secure subscriptions to pay bounties. Forty or fifty thousand dollars were subscribed and paid to recruits, but the required number was not obtained in time, and the draft took place September 25th, for about four hundred and fifty men. Drafted men's meetings were repeatedly held afterward, and great efforts made to raise money. Sixty or seventy thousand dollars more being subscribed by them, the council on the 28th of September, appropriated $92,000 to assist them, and on the 3d of October $40,000 more were appropriated. The city clerk was directed to collect the subscriptions of the citizens. Mayor Caven used every means to assist the work and by strenuous exertions the required number of volunteers were secured in October and November, and the drafted men relieved at a cost of nearly $180,000. Much complaint had been made prior and subsequent to the draft, of the incorrect enrollment on which it was made, and that the city and township were drafted together, compelling the city to expend $20,000 beyond its proportion, to relieve the township. The council on the 12th of December, appointed a committee to revise and correct the lists, and secure a correct enrollment.

The President, on the 20th of December, again called for three hundred thousand men, directing a draft if it was not filled by volunteers. Mayor Caven, on the 28th, recommended the Council to appropriate $90,000 for bounties, at $150 each, for recruits. The Council, after consideration of the subject, ordered the balance of the appropriation, $2,500, to be paid, and appropriated $20,000 in addition for the same purpose. On the 2d of January, 1865, the Mayor again urged an appropriation to pay $150 bounty for volunteers, and the appointment of ward committees to sell orders and raise funds. He also urged the correction of the enrollment lists, and that the city be drafted separately by wards. The Council at once responded, by appropriating $125,000, to be paid in $150 bounties and $10 premium for recruits. On the 5th of January they authorized the bounties to be increased to $200, and sent Hon. John Coburn to Washington to secure a draft by wards. He succeeded in his mission, and the draft was afterward so made. Committees were also appointed for each ward, to sell city orders, or warrants. On the 16th special committees were appointed to see if the bounties could be increased in amount, and to urge the Legislature to so amend the charter that loans might be made directly to pay bounties. On the 17th committees were appointed to superintend recruiting and assign the men pro rata to each ward. The time fixed for the draft was rapidly approaching, the quota was large and unfilled, the citizens grew excited, and many of them turned their attention to recruiting. In February the Council appropriated $400 to each man who might be drafted, provided he had purchased a $50 order before the draft. After the draft occurred they confirmed the grant, ordering the money to be paid at once to those who furnished substitutes, and in installments to those who were compelled to serve. The Council had furnished twelve hundred cords of wood to soldiers families in August, 1864, and now gave $3,500 more for the same purpose. On the 20th of February, three thousand six hundred citizens petitioned the Council to effect a loan sufficient to pay all orders, bounties, &c. The petition was deferred for more names, and on the 22d, seven hundred and seventy-two more were reported. A resolution offered by Mayor Caven was adopted, authorizing a loan of $400,000 in bonds of $50, $100, $500 and $1,000 each, signed by the Mayor and Clerk, at such rate of interest semi-annually, as might be lawful where the bonds were payable. A special tax levy was to be made to pay interest and form a sinking fund to meet the principal. Messrs. Brown, Coburn and Jamison were appointed a committee to prepare and negotiate the bonds. They did so. The bonds were sent to New York, where they remained unsold for several months, and were then recalled, cancelled, and the committee discharged.

The quota not being filled, the draft took place, by wards, on the 25th of February. The Council at once ordered the loan committee to borrow $100,000 from the banks, at one per cent., at four months, with privilege of renewal, depositing orders at sixty cents on the dollar as security, the orders to be sold by the banks on ten days notice, if the debt was not paid. On the 6th of March this was reconsidered, and the Treasurer ordered to borrow $100,000 from the banks, at one per cent., for four months, with privilege of renewal, depositing bonds and orders at seventy-five cents on the dollar, as security, giving the banks the privilege of selling at ten days notice, if the debt was not paid.

The loan was taken by Fletcher's, Harrisons', the Citizens' National, First National and Indianapolis National Banks, $20,000 from each, and the money thus realized was appropriated at once to bounties. The drafted men were now very active in securing recruits. Offices were opened in the Council chamber and elsewhere, $400 bounties were paid, a number of substitutes were furnished, and the quota was nearly filled, when it was announced that on a revisal of the lists of credits, the quota was entirely filled, and with several hundred to spare. Bounties at once fell from $400 to $100, but the work was stopped, and $25,000 to $30,000 of the fund saved. All felt, however, that the lists should have been revised before the draft was made, and a heavy expenditure thus avoided. The war ended four weeks afterward, and no further recruits were needed. The city and citizens had spent about $700,000 in the past ten months, in bounties for troops, and expenses connected with the war.

The government immediately began the reduction of the army. Sick and convalescent troops, new recruits, drafted men, Quarter-masters' employees and others were at once discharged. The rebel prisoners were released and sent home. The veteran regiments rapidly returned and were mustered out. The veteran reserve corps dwindled to a skeleton organization, and by the close of the year the ninth regiment of Hancock's corps constituted almost the entire force stationed in the city. The camps were abandoned and the property sold. The houses were removed elsewhere, and by the summer of 1866 a uniform was rarely seen on the streets. The return of the veteran troops kept up the excitement for some time, and caused great activity in trade, but as the great floating population of the past three years dwindled in number, and the government demand for supplies ceased, the difference in the throng on the streets was soon perceptible, and the town grew dull.

Extensive camps, hospitals, barracks, stables and other structures were built by the government during the war; the most prominent of these may be mentioned here.

Camps Morton and Sullivan had been occupied by the three-months men and State troops while organizing and preparing for the field, and the last named camp had afterward been sufficient for the regiments subsequently organized, Camp Morton being unused; but after the capture of Fort Donelson, when several thousand rebel prisoners were sent to this point, additional troops and camps were at once needed. Camp Morton was then fitted up as a prison camp. It was surrounded with a high, tight fence and sentry walk; additional buildings were added from time to time, and the defenses strengthened, until at last it was as complete in its appointments as any other in the country. More than five thousand prisoners were occasionally confined in it, and many thousands during the war. Among its inmates were the greater part of Morgan's men, captured after their celebrated raid through Indiana and Ohio. Toward the close of the war many of these men, becoming convinced that their cause was lost, enlisted in the Union army for service against the Indians; others took the oath of allegiance and were discharged, and several thousand were released and sent home after the war ended.

The prisoners were guarded at first by the Nineteenth regulars, but other troops were afterward detailed to that duty, and some regiments were raised for that special service. Temporary camps for the guards were at first established near the prison; but after the invalid corps (afterward the veteran reserve,) were detailed to guard duty, camps of a more permanent character were built, requiring many thousands of feet of lumber. Camp Burnside, just south of the prison, grew into a large, populous, well arranged and well built village by the end of the war. The veteran corps guarding the rebels occupied this camp—many of the officers and men having their families with them. Camp Carrington, formerly a temporary affair, and afterward one of the best arranged and constructed camps near the city, was mostly built in 1864. It was at a considerable distance to the west of the prison, near the Lafayette road, and was mostly occupied by recruits, new regiments and drafted men. Camp Sullivan, on the military grounds, was not so extensive, well built or arranged as the two former. It had been occupied by the State troops, and afterward by new regiments, transient troops and drafted men.

As the war progressed and this point became more important as a depot of supplies, troops and prisoners, all these camps, with others in and around the city, were constantly occupied. Among other important establishments the Soldiers' Home founded in 1862, for the accommodation of transient soldiers, soon became prominent, and was greatly enlarged before the war ended. It was in charge of the veteran reserve corps at first, and afterward in that of the Ninth regiment of Hancock's corps. Single soldiers, squads, detachments, and regiments of troops, passing through or temporarily stopping in the city, were accommodated with lodging and cooked food in this establishment, and it was of great service when the veteran regiments were returning on furlough during the war, and at its close, when they returned for discharge.

In addition to camps Carrington, Burnside, Sullivan and the Soldiers' Home, a cavalry camp was established near the city; and when the negro regiment was authorized late in the fall of 1863, Camp Fremont was temporarily established in Fletcher's woods, south-east of the city. The government, in 1864, took the old Bellefontaine depot, in the north part of the ninth ward, and fitted it up as an extensive stable to accommodate the thousands of artillery, cavalry and wagon horses, bought and brought to this point; and for the storage, also, of the necessary grain and forage. Barracks were also added for the many teamsters and quarter-masters' employees in service here.

It was proposed early in 1865 to abandon all the government camps, prisons, stables and hospitals then in use in and around the city, and construct new, more extensive and better arranged ones several miles out in the country. The site was selected, the plan approved by the authorities at Washington, and the order prepared, but before it was issued, the war terminated, and the new buildings were not needed.

When the war first began and the three-months troops collected here, but few arms and still less ammunition could be supplied. It was evident that ammunition would have to be fabricated, and Herman Sturm applied to the Governor for authority to manufacture it for the State. Permission was granted in May, and with one or two assistants, he immediately began making musket balls and cartridges at McLaughlin's gun-shop, on east Washington street. The demand soon extended the business, and a small frame structure was erected in July and occupied in August, north of the State-house. Additional buildings were soon erected and the number of workmen increased; but the facilities were not equal to the rapidly growing demand, and a removal took place to Ott's building, on Washington street, south of the State-house. It remained there some time, and was then removed to buildings specially designed for it east of the city. It had grown from a small beginning to great proportions; several hundreds of persons were employed, and vast amounts of artillery and small-arm ammunition were daily fabricated—the armies of the west being largely supplied by it. It filled

a pressing want early in the war; but the government having established an arsenal here, and ammunition being largely manufactured elsewhere, the State institution was discontinued in 1864,

The national government in 1861 determined to found a number of arsenals in the west, one of them being located here. Eighty acres of ground were bought north-east of and adjoining the city, plans adopted for the buildings and improvements, and Captain Jas. M. Whittemore, of the regular army, appointed commandant and superintendent. The improvements, consisting of buildings for the storage of small arms and accouterments, artillery and wagons, officers' quarters, magazines, barracks, fencing, grading, &c., were begun in 1862, and have been prosecuted to the present time, and are now nearly completed, at a cost of several hundred thousand dollars. The buildings are large, well planned and perfectly constructed. All the improvements are of the best design, materials, and finish. Large amounts of arms artillery, ammunition, and other government property, are now stored there. The Wallace building, on Delaware and Maryland streets, was used during the war as the U. S. Arsenal and storehouse. Wm. Y. Wiley was appointed military store-keeper. Capt. Whittemore served as commander and superintendent till the close of the war, being then relieved by brevet Col. W. H. Harris, the present commander. An arsenal guard of about thirty men was enlisted for that special duty in 1864, and is now stationed there.

The financial condition of the city was greatly influenced by the war, and it is best, perhaps, to consider it in connection with our war history; though, in doing so, many facts already given in the statement of the war movements will necessarily be repeated.

It is now impossible, from loss of records, to give a certain statement concerning the early financial condition of the corporation. The old books yet in existence are in such shape that no clear idea can be drawn from them. It is only within a few years that a system has been adopted showing the condition of the finances at any given time. Such facts for former years as were published at the time are given below.

The valuation of real and personal property in 1847 was about $1,000,000. In 1850 it had risen to $2,326,185; in 1853, to $5,131,582; in 1856, to $7,146,670; in 1858, to $10,475,000; in 1860, to $10,700,000; in 1862, to $10,250,000; in 1863, $10,750,000; in 1864, $13,250,000; in 1865, $20,144,447; in 1866, $24,231,750; in 1867, it sunk to

$21,943,605, and rose in 1868 to $23,593,-619. These figures show the steady growth of the place, as well as the temporary checks it has experienced. The listed polls in 1847 were about 400; in 1853, 1,460; in 1857, 1,862; in 1860, 2,200; in 1863, 3,200; in 1866, 5,160; in 1867, 5,800; in 1868, 5,780.

Taxation under the charter of 1847, for general purposes, was limited to 15 cents on the $100; but special taxes to any amount could be levied, if authorized by the general vote. Repeated efforts were made, from 1847 to 1853, to induce the citizens to vote special taxes for various objects; but with the exception of taxes for schools, clock, cisterns and to pay debts, the movements were generally defeated, and the entire levy did not exceed 45 cents on the $100. To avoid the trouble in regard to special taxes, the council, in 1853, adopted the general incorporation act as the city charter; and though the taxing power was thereby increased, they hesitated, in view of the general opposition of the taxpayers, to materially advance the rate, and it did not usually go beyond 60 or 80 cents before the war. After the war began, a different policy was necessarily adopted, and the people have since become acquainted with heavier rates on vastly increased valuations.

The receipts and expenditures for all purposes, (other than schools,) are given as published at the time, giving generally the actual current receipts without including balances. The levy for 1847, (including $865 of delinquencies from former years,) amounted to $4,226, nearly $4,000 being realized therefrom, and the expenditures considerably exceeded the receipts. In 1850 the receipts were $9,327, expenditures $7,554. In 1851, receipts $10,515; expenses over that sum. In 1853, receipts $10,906, expenses $7,030, $2,908 being devoted to cisterns and the fire department. In 1854 receipts .$20,500, expenses nearly the same. In 1856 receipts $27,889, expenses $46,105. In 1857 receipts $32,697, expenses $31,003. In 1859 receipts $59,-168, expenses 56, 442; $10,232, being spent on the fire department cisterns, $4,882 for police and $4,771 for gas. In 1860 the receipts were $87,262, expenses $80,172; leading items being for street improvements, repairs and bridges, $28,790; fire department and cisterns, $11,353; police, $5,986; gas expenditures, $6,445. The actual current receipts and expenditures, (not including balances from former years,) and the leading items of expenditure, as nearly as they can be obtained from the reports from 1861 to 1868, are given as follows:

	Receipts.	Expenses.	Street Improvements, repairs and Cleaning and Bridges.	Fire Department and Cisterns.	Police and Detectives.	Salaries, Fees & Per Centage.	Gas Expenditures, lighting tax, &c.	Jail Expenses.	Bounties and all War Expenses.
1861	$84,508	$84,508	15,653	16,249	$6,300	10,180	$7,648		
1862	79,132	79,132	2,744	12,510	9,693	10,662	8,066		
1863	97,119	99,487	18,809	12,668	10,687	11,524	10,988	$2,842	$5,010
1864	125,011	156,444	33,322	21,202	18,473	12,040	12,505	5,509	35,155
1865	597,891	854,391	20,240	21,612	27,990	14,618	15,220	7,086	718,179
1866	400,704	404,713	33,380	20,332	23,416	9,638	3,051	11,113	151,197
1867	445,253	331,525	52,186	27,207	37,511	17,452	38,164	8,116	70,575
1868	431,669	224,941	36,018	33,049	27,509	27,528	37,100	6,336	

The old corporation authorities had incurred a debt of a thousand or fifteen hundred dollars at the time the city charter was adopted. The street improvements then undertaken by the city government soon increased it to nearly $6,000, and in 1849 a tax of ten cents on the $100 was authorized by vote of the citizens to pay it. The proceeds of the levy almost extinguished it in 1850, but in 1851 it again swelled to $5,400. The increased receipts, however, enabled the treasury to meet current expenses and diminished the debt to $567 in 1854. The employment in that year of a police force, together with the increased current expenses, enlarged the debt to $11,000 in the spring of 1855, and to $15,300 in the spring of 1856. Orders were selling at a heavy discount, and the reputation of the city suffered. The Council determined to effect a loan of $25,000 to meet expenses and fund the debt, and having prepared the bonds, sent Jeremiah D. Skeen to New York City, in August 1856, as their agent to negotiate them. He succeeded in hypothecating them for $5,000, which he applied to his own use, and after much trouble and several years delay, they were recovered by the city on payment of that sum with interest. Skeen and his sureties were sued by the city, and judgment finally obtained in January

1868, for the principal and interest of the defalcation. This unfortunate effort to sell bonds still further injured the city credit, and the debt increased, in 1857, to $23,740. A change in the charter and city officers took place that year, and a general tax of sixty cents was levied to meet expenses and debts: until that date the entire tax had not exceeded forty-five or fifty cents on the $100. The debt was reduced to $9,300 in 1859, but swelled to $11,500 in 1860, and to nearly $25,000 when the war began. A considerable part of it was in short-time bonds issued to the makers of the three steam fire engines purchased in 1860, the bonds being the first that were negotiated and sold. The floating debt had not materially increased, but the growing expenditures for gas light and for the police department prevented any reduction in its amount. The salaries and fees of the city officers were also increased in May 1861, and the current expenses then enlarged.

Immediately after volunteering began for the three months service, a demand was made for municipal assistance for the families of soldiers, and on the 20th of April, $10,000 were appropriated to that object, and a committee appointed to supervise its distribution. From this time till the close of the war, many appropriations were made for this purpose, in buying wood and supplying money, and the aggregate sum thus expended was very large. Doubts existed whether bounties could be directly given by the city, and they were generally voted as appropriations to the soldier's families. The various war expenditures early in 1861, soon raised the floating and bonded debt to about $46,000, but the current receipts enabled the authorities to meet expenses, and make payments on outstanding liabilities, until they were reduced in May, 1862, to about $16,500. Recruiting becoming slack in the fall of 1862, bounties were first paid, a small appropriation being made therefor, and about $5,000 were spent in that way by May, 1863. Over $5,000 of the engine bonds had been paid in the meantime, and the debt reduced in May, 1863, to $11,250. This amount was practically paid off soon after, and a close calculation of the finances of the city would have shown her free of debt in the summer of 1863.

A rapid advance in the values of articles, and work, began in the spring of 1863. The officer's salaries, and the policemen and firemen's wages were raised; current expenses increased, large appropriations were made to the poor, and a house of refuge undertaken. To this increased expenditure was added the expense connected

with the city regiment in the Morgan raid, and on the 11th of December, in response to the request of the citizens, the council appropriated $25,000, to be paid in $50 bounties to the families of recruits credited to the several wards. The ordinance was amended and re-passed on the 14th of December, and six per cent city bonds to the amount of $25,000, due in fifteen months, were prepared and sold within a week, and the money expended. No further bounty appropriations were made till May 9th, 1864, when $5,000 were given to families of one hundred day men: the money to be paid out by the Soldier's Aid Committee. By these appropriations and the largely increased current expenses for street improvements, salaries, police, gas, &c., amounting to $116,000, the debt had risen in July, to about $80,000, the war expenses amounting to about $46,000. The tax levy for 1864-'65, was fixed at $1 for general purposes, 50 cents for specific objects, and 25 cents for soldier's families.

The President called for 500,000 men during the summer, ordering a draft if the call was not filled by volunteers. The response was not as prompt as had been expected, and the draft took place in September. The mayor in August had recommended appropriations be made for bounties to volunteers to fill the city quota, but no definite action was taken at the time in regard to it. On the 28th of September, however, the council appropriated $92,000 in aid of the drafted men; the sum to be added to that subscribed by the citizens prior to the draft, and to such sums as the drafted men might raise. Twelve hundred cords of wood were also purchased at an expense of $8,000 for the soldiers families. On the 3d of October, $40,000 were appropriated in addition to the former sums in aid of the drafted men, and the city clerk was directed to collect the citizens subscriptions. During October and November, four hundred volunteers were secured at an expense to the city and citizens of about $170,000, and the entire cost of relieving the city from the September draft amounted to about $180,000.

Another call for 300,000 men was made December 20th, 1864, and a draft ordered in sixty days, if the call was unfilled. The mayor on the 28th recommended an appropriation of $90,000, to be paid in $150 bounties. The council appropriated $20,-000, together with an unexpended balance of $2,500 of former appropriations.

The Mayor, on the 2d of January, 1865, again urged appropriations for $150 bounties, and suggested the correction of the enrollment lists, and the draft of the city by wards. The Council at once gave

$125,000, increased the bounty to $200, and sent John Coburn to Washington to secure a ward draft. In the meantime the competition for recruits forced bounties beyond $200, and the Council, on the 17th of January, increased them to $400. The Legislature was urged to amend the incorporation law so as to authorize bounty loans. Committees were appointed to sell war warrants, to oversee recruiting, and assign the men *pro rata* to the wards. Four hundred dollars were to be given each man who bought a $50 order and was subsequently drafted.

On the 20th of February the Council received a petition from three thousand seven hundred tax-payers, asking a loan to pay bounties and fund all orders, which were now selling at twenty to thirty cents discount. It was laid over for additional signatures, and seven hundred and seventy-two more being reported on the 22d, the Council authorized a loan of $400,000 on twenty year coupon bonds, signed by the Mayor and Clerk, with interest semi-annually, payable in New York, and pledged a tax levy to pay interest and sink the principal. The bonds were drawn, signed, sent to New York, where they remained unsold for several months, and were finally recalled and cancelled. The sale of war warrants and the work of recruiting actively went on in the meantime, but the draft took place, February 25th, for nearly five hundred men.

The Council then confirmed the gift of $400 to each drafted man who had bought $50 in war warrants, ordering it paid down to those who furnished substitutes, and in instalments to those who served. A loan of $100,000 was at once ordered from the banks, and on the 6th of March the Treasurer was directed to borrow $100,000, at one per cent., for four months, renewable if necessary, depositing orders and bonds at seventy-five cents as security, the banks having the right to sell them at ten days notice if the loan was not met. The loan was at once taken by the First National, Citizens National, Indianapolis National, and Fletcher's and Harrisons' banks, $20,000 each, and the money applied to bounties. A committee was appointed on the 6th of March to examine and report whether, under the new law, one-fourth of the amount of the war debt and bonds could be added as special tax upon the duplicate. The Mayor on the 3d of April, submitted an opinion by James Morrison, that the city could fund her debt by bonds under the existing law. The strictly war expenditures (except interest) of the city, in the way of bounties, ended with the February draft, the war

ceasing in less than four weeks after the quota was declared to be filled. Nearly $155,000 in war warrants were sold and in the hands of the people. The entire war expenses for the year, from May, 1864, to May, 1865, had reached $718,179.

The city war expenditure for the last three years of the rebellion approximated $1,000,000, and the municipal debt reached $368,000 at its close; $100,000 of this sum was in the shape of a bank loan, at 12 per cent., secured by deposit of warrants at seventy-five cents; the remainder consisted of six per cent. warrants, part of which were applicable on the payment of taxes for 1865, the rest in 1866-7. These orders were selling at twenty and thirty cents discount, and as the discount was added in all bills against the city, the depreciation was largely augmenting current expenses. The Council, therefore, levied a tax of $1 for general purposes, and fifty cents to pay the debt. The bank loan was renewed as it fell due, and in October an ordinance passed to renew it for a year. The unsold war bonds in New York were recalled and cancelled. The finance committee recommended the election of a city Auditor, and John G. Waters was accordingly chosen by the Council, in January, 1866, for two years; the office was discontinued at the expiration of his term. On the 11th of September, 1865, the Council authorized the funding of war orders in six per cent. three year bonds, and about $27,000 were so converted by May, 1866. The current redemption of orders in the mean time was large, amounting to $397,000 at the close of the fiscal year, and the debt had decreased from $368,000 to about $217,000, $151,000 being paid off. In May, 1866, a tax of $1.50 was levied for general purposes, and twenty-five cents for payment of debt, but in November, at the Mayor's suggestion, the outstanding six per cent. orders were funded to the extent of $82,000, in ten per cent. warrants running eighteen months, and the twenty-five cent tax was struck from the duplicate, materially lessening the burthen for that year. The actual current receipts (excluding former balance) for 1866-7, were $327,700. The expenditures (excluding bank loan,) $209,700. The total debt on three year bonds, ten per cent. warrants, and to the banks, amounted to $209,600, and $122,929 of a balance was left in the treasury. The debt had been reduced $108,787 during the year. The Council, in May, 1867, voted a general tax for the year, of $1.25, and the actual current receipts on it during the fiscal year, 1867-8, (not including the balance from 1867) were $231,669, the actual expenses, $225,000. The bank bond and warrant debt, in May, 1868, was estimated at $252,000, and the balance left in the treasury amounted to $210,657. The bond and warrant debt has since been paid at its maturity, and the debt now amounts to about $200,000. The levy for the current year was fixed at $1.10 for general purposes, and fifteen cents for sewerage.

The war brought many rowdies here, and in the summer of 1861 scarcely a day passed without affrays in which weapons were used. The police were kept busy in preserving order. Affairs grew still worse in the fall of 1863, and military aid was invoked. A strong guard was detailed, with its headquarters at the Police office, and until after the war the soldiery assisted in keeping the peace. The convenient position of the place, midway between the large western cities, made it a favorite rendezvous for rascals of all grades, and when large bounties were offered in 1864, hundreds of thieves and bounty-jumpers flocked here. They were soon arrested or scattered by the authorities, and three of them being tried by court martial, and shot, near Camp Morton, as deserters, the rest hurriedly left the place.

For some time after the war began little or no political excitement existed, but at the democratic county convention in Court Square, on the 2d of September, several of the speakers indulged in indiscreet expressions; equally indiscreet retorts were made by parties in the crowd; a personal difficulty occurred, weapons were drawn, and the convention was dispersed by soldiers and others. The leaders were pursued to their homes and compelled to take the oath of allegiance. For sometime a serious outbreak was threatened, and the Sentinel office was in danger. Order was finally restored by the military and police. The affair was discreditable to the city and to all engaged in it.

On the 8th of April 1862, Parson Brownlow, of Tennessee, having just been sent north by the rebels, reached this city, and in company with General Carey, of Cincinnati, appeared before our people at the Metropolitan Theater, where both made bitter speeches. Brownlow visited the city again just after the Philadelphia convention, and made one of his characteristic speeches to a large audience in the Circle.

In 1863 the democrats held a State mass convention in the State House yard, mustering in heavy force and generally armed. Anticipating an outbreak the authorities

had taken measures to prevent it. Guards were stationed on the streets, artillery was held in readiness, and the seventy-first regiment put under arms. No trouble occurred, further than the arrest and fining of many persons for carrying concealed weapons. As the delegates were leaving, however, they began random firing from the cars. The Lafayette train got off, but those on the Central, Cincinnati and other roads were alarmed by the military, the police and citizens. The trains were brought back, the passengers put under arrest and disarmed. They were permitted to leave after a detention of some hours and the confiscation of their revolvers, a large number of which were turned over to the military.

In August 1864, it was discovered that large quantities of arms and ammunition were being secretly imported into the State, and a seizure of four hundred navy revolvers and many boxes of fixed ammunition was made in H. H. Dodd's office in the old Sentinel building. Papers also were found disclosing the existence of a secret military organization opposed to the Government, and implicating prominent parties in the movement. Arrests of a number of them followed shortly afterward, and a military commission was convened here for their trial. After full investigation they were found guilty of treason and sentenced to be hung. The finding was approved and the day fixed for execution, but President Lincoln reprieved them. President Johnson afterward ordered their execution, but subsequently commuted the punishment to imprisonment in the Ohio Penitentiary, from which they were afterward discharged under a decision of the Supreme Court. During the pendency of the trial H. H. Dodd, one of the leaders in the scheme, made his escape from the third story of the post-office building and succeeded in reaching Canada.

The political canvass of 1864 was earnestly and enthusiastically conducted by the republicans, and the vote for Mr. Lincoln—about twelve thousand—was the heaviest ever cast in this township, probably over ten thousand five hundred voters being residents of the city and suburbs. The meetings were held in the tabernacle, a large frame structure erected on the Washington street front of Court Square, and capable of accommodating several thousand persons. This building remained there for a year or more, and was frequently used for meetings, concerts, lectures, etc. A similar tabernacle had been built for the campaign of 1860, in the south-west corner of the square, and used in the canvass of that year. It, also, remained standing about a year before its removal. Both buildings were used after the elections for shows and concerts.

The threatened political troubles had seriously contracted business enterprizes here for several months before the war began, and except the temporary activity imparted at intervals by the arrival and equipment of the different regiments, no general improvement took place until late in the winter of 1862-3. Until that time many men were out of work, and from that cause volunteering was steady and recruits easily obtained. After the city was made a prison depot and garrisoned post, the government demand for articles and labor steadily increased, and as operations in the south grew in magnitude, the advantageous position of the city as a supply depot became more evident. This fact attracted general attention and caused a rapid emigration hither, not only from all parts of the north, but thousands of southern refugees also made this their temporary home. The current constantly augmented during 1863-4. Houses could not be provided fast enough for the increasing throng, and cellars, garrets, and stables were crowded. Several families often shared the same tenement, and many persons who came here to settle were compelled to leave, for want of shelter for their families. Rents increased enormously for business houses and dwellings, prices being limited only by the landlord's conscience, or the bonus a former tenant would accept for his lease. House hunting became a serious business, and any tenement was gladly accepted. Many shanties paid fifty per cent. per annum on their prime cost, and the same remark could be truthfully made of some business rooms. Work was found however for all comers.—Business in all lines was brisk. Every one had money, and fortunes were made in two or three years, apparently without effort or skill. The influx of parties from abroad continued till the close of the war, and counting all persons, permanent residents, soldiers, prisoners, and the miscellaneous floating population in and around the city, it would be safe, perhaps, to estimate the population in March, 1865, at eighty thousand.

Building though vigorously prosecuted during 1863-4 and 5, was greatly limited by the scarcity and high price of materials, and the good wages asked and received by workmen. Little material was on hand when the war began, and the demand being very limited for the first two years, only a small amount of it was collected, and it was not till the early spring of 1863 that the manufacture and importation

of lumber and other materials began on a large scale. Prices then rapidly advanced, doubling within the year. The demand grew faster than the price. Heavy importations of pine lumber from the lakes to this point, were first made in 1863, and for nearly a year the stock was comparatively unsaleable, from the high price asked, and the ignorance of our people with regard to the lumber. It had never been used here to any extent before that year, except in doors and sash brought from Dayton. Brick, stone and lime, also quickly rose in price, and with the rapid increase in wages, contractors lost money on the houses they erected Many persons desirous of building were prevented from doing so by the fear that the improvement when finished would not be worth half what it cost; at least that was the excuse given by capitalists when urged to aid in the improvement of the city, and by building houses, afford homes, work, and business positions to those who were anxious to come here.

The settled limits of the city were largely extended in 1862-6, but the greatest improvement was effected in filling up vacant lots with houses, and crowding population more closely on the original plat. A rapid change also occurred in business localities. Washington street had thus far been the choice location for the heavier houses, the small retail groceries being thinly scattered elsewhere over the city, but with the rapid increase and concentration of population, came the concentration of this retail trade at subordinate centers, a half-mile from the street. Meat store, tin and shoe shops, drug stores, and doctors offices, collected in such centers, and the retail trade was so far diverted from Washington street that most of the grocery men left it. The wholesale trade also generally went to Meridian street, leaving Washington to the dry goods, boot and shoe and clothing houses, nearly a score of the latter being located along two or three squares.

The sudden and unexpected termination of the war closed many lines of business connected with it, and thousands were at once deprived of their usual employment. To these were soon added the discharged soldiers. Many of those thus left adrift were anxious to remain here, and would have done so had any chance been opened to them, but the general distrust regarding the future caused a rapid contraction in business, and the great mass were compelled to go elsewhere in search of employment. In a few months the unaccustomed sight of vacant dwellings greeted the eye, and shortly after, store rooms were to let. Rents grew less firm, then shaky, then had a downward tendency, and finally reached a living point; averaging at present about half the war rates.

All parties were inexpressibly shocked by the assassination of President Lincoln, the news being first made known at market on the morning of the 15th of April, and immediately afterward by the tolling of the central alarm bell, calling out the fire department and citizens. Business, which had begun for the day, at once ceased; manufactories closed, stores were shut, and without any concerted action, the people began draping their houses. Men with grief stricken faces gathered on the street, discussing the event. A notice calling a meeting at the State House was at once posted, and by nine o'clock thousands were assembled there. The troops stationed here were paraded, and marched with muffled drums and draped colors to the spot. The assassination and death of the President were officially made known, by the Governor, to the excited throng. Speeches were made in eulogy of the dead President by leaders of both parties, and resolutions adopted, pledging the support of the people to the government and incoming administration. The effect of the shock was so great that business did not recover its former tone and volume for several days afterward.

Toward the middle of April it was announced that the President's body would be brought through this city on its way to Springfield. Meetings were held, and arrangements made to give a suitable expression of the respect entertained by the people for his memory. The city Council endorsed the movement on the 17th of April, invited the authorities of Cincinnati and Louisville, and voted to defray the expenses. Many arches, beautifully decorated and draped, were thrown across the streets on the line of the contemplated procession. Festoons of black, bound with wreaths of evergreens and immortelles, were stretched at regular intervals across the streets, and from house to house. Many thousand yards of black and white fabrics, and car loads of evergreens, were thus used on the streets, and on the State House and other public buildings. All business houses and nearly all the dwellings in the city were more or less draped and ornamented, many of the decorations being very beautiful. Pictures and busts of the dead President, furled and draped flags, wreaths of evergreens, mottoes and shields, were displayed everywhere, until the appearance of the city was startlingly transformed, The State House, under the rotunda of

which the remains were to lie in state, was profusely and tastefully decorated, being wreathed with black and white, trimmed with evergreens and flowers, inside and out. The hall was lined with black, relieved by stars, flower wreaths, pictures, busts and flags. The gate entrance was occupied by a beautiful quadruple arch, profusely draped and covered with mottoes. The fence all round the square was covered with festoons of evergreens and flowers. It was said by parties accompanying the cortege, that the decorations here were more extensive and beautiful than those at any other place on the route.

The arrangements were completed late at night on the 29th of April, and the funeral cortege arrived by special train early on the 30th. A great civic and military funeral procession had been arranged, and extensive preparations made for the visitors from other parts of the State, who were to come by special trains. These arrangements were defeated, and the crowd greatly lessened, by a cold, heavy rain, beginning on the night of the 29th and lasting all the next day. The President's remains, removed from the train early in the morning, and placed on a large funeral car built for the purpose, were taken under military escort to the State House, where, during this and a part of the next day, they were visited by many thousand persons, who, regardless of the driving storm, patiently waited their turn for hours, in long lines before the building.

The decorations, though badly injured by the rain, were allowed to remain standing for nearly a month, when they were removed, and the materials sold by order of the Council.

The war having closed the people desired the great commanders who had become prominent in it to visit the place, and in response to their invitations Generals Sherman and Grant visited the city in 1865. General Sherman arrived on the 25th of July, and was conducted through the principal streets by a great civic and military procession to the State House yard, where he made an able speech to the people counselling peace, and earnest efforts to repair the damages caused by the war. He held a reception and attended a banquet at Military Hall given by the former officers and soldiers of his command. General Grant arrived in September, and was received by the State and city authorities and military forces with the honors accorded to the Commander-in-Chief of the American army. A great military and civic procession conducted him to the State House yard, where he was welcomed in fitting terms by the Governor, and bowed his acknowledgments with a few well chosen words to the public. He held a reception in the evening and attended the banquet at the Bates House at night.

Amusements were numerous and constant in the period intervening from 1861 to 1866. Nearly all the leading actors of the country appeared at the theater, which was open the greater part of each year, and constantly crowded by soldiers and strangers sojourning in the city. From 1864 to 1866 a museum was kept by Madame English in the Kinder building on east Washington street, and largely patronized by the rural population and soldiers. Shows and circuses appeared regularly each summer to reap a full harvest, and negro minstrel bands and panoramas drew crowded houses. Sleight of hand and ledgerdemain were illustrated at Masonic Hall, by Herman and Heller, the great masters in the art, exciting the wonder and adding to the enjoyment of their audiences. Concerts, operas and lectures had their full share of votaries, and fairs were revived for church and charitable purposes. A great fair was held in September, 1864, on the military grounds for the benefit of the Sanitary Commission, lasting one week, and realizing a large sum of money. Since the war ended amusements have been fewer and less well patronized, the hard times telling seriously upon them.

The leading event in the musical line since the war was the annual German Sœngerfest, held about the middle of September, 1867, lasting three or four days. The programme included processions, addresses, vocal and instrumental concerts, a ball, displays of fireworks, etc. The arrangements were made by a committee under direction of the Mannœrchor of this city. A two story frame building, ninety or one hundred feet wide and one hundred and eighty feet long, was erected on the south east corner of Court Square. The floor was closely seated and wide galleries ran round three sides of the house, the whole affording accommodations for three or four thousand spectators. The north end was occupied by a wide raised platform for the orchestra and singers, and the whole interior was profusely decorated with pictures, wreaths, flags, mottoes, gas jets, etc. The exterior was also fully decorated and the roof surmounted with the flags of all nations. Many buildings in the city were finely decorated with flags and evergreens. The expenses were met by individual subscriptions, and an appropriation of $1,500 from the city treasury.

The Fest was very successful pecuniarily and otherwise, a considerable sum being left on hand, and devoted afterward to charitable purposes. Thousands of visitors were in attendance.

It has been stated heretofore that the four acre tract on the river bank southwest of the town, set aside for burial purposes by Judge Harrison, in 1821, was for years the only cemetery, and that at subsequent periods two or three adjoining tracts were platted as cemeteries by different parties. These were rapidly filling up as the city increased in size, and it became evident that some further provision must be made for cemeteries at a greater distance from the city. With this object in view, a number of gentlemen held a preliminary meeting on the 12th of September, 1863, to consult regarding the matter, and on the 25th of September, an association was formed, with James M. Ray, President, Theodore P. Haughey, Secretary, S. A. Fletcher, Jr., Treasurer, and with seven directors. S. A. Fletcher, Sr., offered to loan the necessary funds to purchase grounds, and a committee being appointed to select a site, soon after reported in favor of purchasing the farm and nursery of Martin Williams, three miles north-west of the city, on the Michigan road, together with several smaller adjoining tracts. The report was accepted, and the purchases made in the fall of 1863, and January, 1864, at prices ranging from $125 to $300 per acre, two hundred and fifty acres in all being secured at a cost of about $51,500. The money was loaned to the association by Mr. Fletcher, with additional amounts to begin the improvements. A survey was ordered and plats made in October and November, and Mr. F. W. Chislett selected as Superintendent. He began the improvements in the spring of 1864. The large trees were cut into logs, which were sawed by a portable mill on the grounds, into lumber and fencing, with which the tract was enclosed. A gate lodge was built at the western entrance near the Michigan road, and in 1867, a large cottage residence for the Superintendent, was erected on the southern part of the grounds. The improvement of the carriage ways and footpaths began in the spring of 1864, lots, irregular in plan and of various sizes, ranging from a few square feet to half an acre or more, were laid out. The grounds were dedicated in May or June, 1864, Albert S. White, delivering the oration. The first lot sale took place June 8, by auction, the price of lots being fixed at twenty-five cents per square foot as a minimum. The price has been advanced several times at subsequent dates.

Rules and regulations were adopted for the government of the association and cemetery, June 4, 1864. Each lot-holder is interested in the capital of the association to the value of his lot. The lot-holders choose the officers. No profits or dividends are allowed, and after payment for the ground, (which has been fully made, the loan being repaid to Mr. Fletcher,) all receipts are expended in the care and improvement of the cemetery. No fences or enclosures of lots are permitted, and the erection of great monuments is very properly discouraged. Notwithstanding this rule, the cemetery already shows too much marble for a strictly pleasing effect.

The improvements, consisting of gate lodges, superintendent's cottage, enclosing fences, carriage and foot ways, grading, sodding, grubbing, &c., have been rapidly forwarded since the spring of 1864, covering forty or fifty acres near the hill, and already the cemetery compares well with older ones near other cities. The hill itself—formerly called Sand hill, and now known as Crown hill, giving name to the cemetery—covers a base of twelve or fifteen acres, and is over one hundred feet high. It is yet unimproved, and it is proposed to use it as the site for the receiving reservoir in the contemplated system of waterworks. Water is an excellent absorbent of gases arising from the decomposition of decaying bodies, and water consumers would be constantly reminded of their departed ancestors, by the taste and smell of their daily beverage.

A line of omnibuses was established to the grounds in 1864, but the facilities for reaching the spot were not thought sufficient, and in the spring of 1866, propositions were made to extend the street railroad from the terminus at the north end of Illinois street, to the cemetery. The residents in the neighborhood, the cemetery board of directors, and the street railroad company finally made the necessary arrangements, and the line was completed during the. fall of 1866 and spring of 1867, and opened for travel in April or May.

In May, 1866, the board dedicated a tract of ground to the government, for the interment of the Union soldiers buried in the vicinity of the city. The grant was accepted, and during the fall and following spring, the transfer of the bodies was effected under the direction of the government authorities, and the spot dedicated with appropriate ceremonies. On the 30th of May, 1868, under a general order issued by Gen. Logan, commander of the Grand Army of the Republic, a grand ovation was paid to the memory of the Union dead. Arrangements had been made by appro-priate committees. The ladies labored zealously in preparing the floral tributes. A procession marched to the grounds, which were thronged by several thousand spectators, and after an address, singing and other preliminary exercises, each grave was wreathed and strewed with flowers by young ladies, and orphans of deceased soldiers. The demonstration was a grand success, the only drawback being the difficulty experienced by many in reaching and returning from the grounds. Business was generally suspended, and the day observed as a holiday. It is probable that the ceremony will be continued annually hereafter.

This article may close with a rapid and brief mention of the more important acts of the city government from 1861 to 1867.

The mayor, in May 1862, called the attention of the Council to the number of abandoned women incarcerated in the jail, and the bad results arising from such a course toward them. He recommended the erection of a house of refuge to which they could be sent, and in which a reformatory treatment could be pursued. Nothing, however, was done at the time with the project. On the 27th of July, 1863, S. A. Fletcher, Sr., submitted a proposition to the Council, offering to give seven or eight acres of ground south of the city as a site, provided the city would agree to erect the buildings. Estimates, by D. A. Bohlen, architect, were also filed, fixing the cost of the house at $8,000, and a Citizens Committee, at the same time, asked that the proposed enterprise should be committed to the care of the Sisters of the Good Shepherd. The donation was accepted by the Council August 10th; $5,000 were appropriated toward the house, which was to be used partly as a house of refuge for abandoned and drunken women, and partly as a city prison for females. Plans were submitted and adopted on the 24th of August. The house was put in charge of the building committee, and a board of three trustees provided for. Contracts were let in the fall, and during the next year the basement story was finished in good style. The rapid advance in material and labor caused great loss to the contractor, and difficulty ensued between him and the city. The work stopped and has ever since been suspended. The entire cost thus far being about $8,000. Good faith to the generous donor of the site, and charity to the class provided for by the enterprise demand the speedy completion of the buildings.

A society for the amelioration of the condition of fallen women was formed in 1866, with a board of trustees and directors and a list of officers. Aid was also to be extended to worthy and friendless females. A house was rented in the north part of the second ward as a home for the friendless, and a home for those wishing to escape the life of infamy to which they seemed condemned. It was placed in charge of Mrs. Sarah Smith as matron, and has since sheltered many of this unfortunate class. Some have been entirely reclaimed, and the institution seems destined to effect much good. Material aid has recently been asked from the Council, and it is not improbable that to the society will be given the charge of the house of refuge when that building is completed.

The city ordinance required parties building houses to obtain special permission before obstructing the streets with materials. These applications consumed much time in the council, and to avoid further trouble from this source, an ordinance establishing a board of public improvements was introduced in the fall of 1863. It remained pending for several months, and on the 19th of April, 1864, another ordinance was substituted and passed, creating a board of public improvements, to be composed of three members annually selected from the council. They were to choose one of their number president, and the city clerk was to be their secretary. All projects connected with the public buildings, market houses, bridges, culverts, sewers, drains, cisterns, street improvements, parks, gas lighting, waterworks, &c., were to be referred to them for examination, and all work was to be executed under their direction. They were to report their action in all cases to the council. Persons intending to build, repair or remove houses, were to get permits from the board, giving the location, cost, &c., of the proposed work, and a register was to be kept and reported of the permits.

The board made no annual report for 1864, and the extent and value of the improvements for that year can not be given; but in 1865 they reported that one hundred and fifty houses costing $200,000, were built in the Additions, and one thousand four hundred and seventy-one permits issued for buildings and repairs in the city, costing $1,860,000. Nine miles of streets and eighteen of side-walks were graded and graveled; one mile of street was bouldered, and four miles of side-walk paved; three miles of streets were lighted. In 1866 permits for one thousand one hundred and twelve houses, costing $1,065,000, were issued; eight and one-half miles of streets and sixteen of side-walks graded and graveled; three and a half squares of streets bouldered, and two miles of side-

walks paved; three miles were lighted. In 1867 one hundred and ninety-five houses, costing $770,470, were built, and five hundred and fifty-two permits for repairs, costing $132,050 were issued; four and one-half miles of streets and nine of side-walks were graded and graveled; four squares were bouldered, and twenty-two squares of side-walks paved; four and one-half miles of streets were lighted. The members of the board receive pay for the time actually employed, and the clerk receives fees for the permits issued.

Under the provisions of the incorporation act, the council, on the 1st of October, 1864, nominated L. Vanlandingham, A. Naltner, James Sulgrove, D. S. Beatty and D. V. Culley as a board of city commissioners, to assess damages and benefits from the opening of new streets or alleys, or the cutting of sewers or new channels for streams. The nominations were confirmed soon after by the common pleas court, and applications of that nature have since been referred to that board.

The many troops and prisoners stationed here had caused uneasiness among medical men for fear of sudden epidemics. The prevalence of measles, small pox and cholera had been prevented by care and prompt attention—small pox cases being treated in a small building on the hospital grounds. In January, 1864, however, cases of small pox became quite numerous not only among the troops, but in different parts of the city; and in February, the government and city authorities rented ground and built a pest house on the river, two miles north-west of town. Further cases were promptly sent there, and the spread of the disease was soon checked. After the war the government turned the house over to the city, and the ground was afterward bought and deeded to the city, December 23d, 1865.

Repeated complaints of the inefficient drainage on Illinois street and elsewhere, and of the damage caused by Virginia river, Pogue's run and Lake McCarty, had been made to the council. Various plans for improving the drainage at small expense, had been proposed and considered at different times without result, and sewers had been advocated on particular streets. The council in July, 1865, selected James W. Brown, F· Stein and L. B. Wilson as a board of engineers to take levels on all the streets, and devise a general system of sewers for the city. Money was appropriated for the work, and the survey and profile was made during the fall. The expense involved had hitherto prevented the building of any regular sewers, but a tax of fifteen cents was levied in May, 1868, for a sewerage fund, and the council is now considering the propriety of building sewers to drain Lake McCarty and provide against floods in Virginia river. The residents in the seventh and eighth wards along the course of the last named bayou have been repeatedly drowned out. The trouble is increasing every year with the rapid settlement and improvement in that section, and large claims for damages are now pending against the city, with the prospect of many more in future. Some of them have already been decided against the city by the courts.

A large number of additions adjoining the corporation limits had been thickly settled, and the parties who lived in them were doing business in the city, and had the advantages of the city government and improvements without contributing by taxation to the city finances. It was proposed in 1865 to annex them to the city, under the provisions of the incorporation act, and an ordinance to include the additions on the north line of the city was introduced in the council, but while it was pending a remonstrance from the parties interested was presented against the measure, demanding that all the additions should be included. A new ordinance, therefore, was drawn up and introduced in December, 1865, providing for the annexation by name of forty-five separate additions adjoining the city on the north, east and south sides. The measure was resisted by the people of the additions, and the council, after consideration of the expense involved for police and other items for the new territory, let the matter drop for the time.

During 1865, several former railway enterprizes, suspended by hard times or by the war, were revived, and in May, 1866, petitions, largely signed by the citizens, were presented to the council, asking a subscription by the city to the Vincennes, Indiana & Illinois Central, and Crawfordsville lines, to enable them to construct their roads. The petitions being laid over for additional signatures, they were soon obtained by committees, and on the 21st of May, the council voted to issue $150,000 in twenty year bonds, in sums of $1,000 each, to be divided as follows: $60,000 to the Vincennes road, $45,000 to each of the other lines, and at a subsequent date the same amount was voted to the Junction road. The companies were first to finish forty miles of road inside of three years, favor the city in freights, and comply with other conditions. Work was afterward begun, and has been actively prosecuted on all except the Indiana and Illinois Central, the Junction road being completed, and

the Vincennes well advanced at the present time.

Several serious accidents having occurred by collisions between street cars and other vehicles, with trains on the Union track, the council on the 5th of February, 1866, ordered the employment of flagmen by the railroad company at each crossing: it being their duty to constantly watch the trains, and warn all parties of their approach. The company at once complied with the ordinance, and since that time few or no accidents have happened.

During the summer of 1866, to get rid of the heavy charges made for boarding city prisoners in the county jail, the council determined to build a station house, and after examining various sites, bought a lot in September, on Maryland, between Pennsylvania and Meridian, at $4,000. No subsequent effort has been made to build the house. Propositions were made at about the same time to rent buildings for the city offices, or sell lots for the site of a city hall. The Second Presbyterian church was offered at $15,000, in bonds. The Journal company offered to build a block next their office, and Andrew Wallace tendered his building. The council declined all these proposals, and resolved not to build a hall till the debt was paid.

On the 29th of October, 1866, the council passed the eight hour law. The question arose, (but was ignored,) whether it applied to the officers and police. It was applied by the street commissioner in his department, but as he reduced the wages in the same proportion, trouble ensued with the employees, who resisted the reduction in their pay. The commissioner applied to the council for instructions, but was advised to use his own discretion in the matter. The ten hour system has since been restored.

The names of the streets were ordered to be put on the lamps in November, 1866. In December, propositions for an alarm telegraph were received from several parties, but declined, and the arrangement was finally completed in 1867-'68, as stated in the history of the fire department. In February, 1867, the Vincennes railroad and Indianapolis Furnace company, were authorized to lay tracks on Kentucky avenue.

The corner stone of the Catholic Cathedral, on Tennessee street, was laid with appropriate ceremonies, on the 20th of July, 1867, in presence of a vast audience. The building will be of brick, with white stone facings, and is in the regular gothic style, with nave, transept, center and side aisles, high altar, and great eastern window. It is about 66 by 195 feet, will be very solidly built, and is to have the highest spire in the country. The walls are now being constructed, but several years will elapse before its completion. The estimated cost is over $300,000. It will be the largest religious edifice in the State.

The author regrets that he has failed to procure the facts connected with the organization of the several Catholic churches, schools, and societies in the city, and will therefore give generally such information as he has obtained.

St. John's Church, on west Georgia street, a small, plain, brick edifice, built about 1850, is the oldest one here. It has a large number of communicants, and is in charge of Rev. August Bessonies, who succeeded Rev. Daniel Maloney. St. Mary's Church, under Rev. Simon Seigrist, was built in 1858, on east Maryland street, near Delaware, and has many communicants, mostly Germans. St. Peter's Church, on Dougherty street, near Virginia avenue, was built about 1865, and is in charge of Rev. Joseph Petit. Flourishing Sabbath schools are attached to each of these churches, and a number of church and charitable societies are also directly or indirectly connected with them.

St. John's Academy for girls, in charge of the Sisters of Providence, is situated on Georgia and Tennessee streets, adjoining the Cathedral and St. John's Church. The buildings, (erected about 1860,) are well designed, and the school is large, well conducted and prosperous. St. John's Academy for boys, east of St. John's church, is in the care of Rev. August Bessonies. St. Mary's Academy for boys, on the alley south of St. Mary's church, is of brick, and three stories high. A school for young children in charge of Mrs Keating, is supported by the St. Peter's church congregation.

The writer neglected to state in its proper place, the fact that a very large and flourishing private German school has been conducted for ten or eleven years past, on east Maryland street, between Delaware and Alabama streets. The school-house, (originally small,) was much enlarged, and improved in its arrangements two or three years since. Several hundred pupils are in attendance.

The Saturday Evening Mirror, a literary weekly journal, was first issued December 22d, 1867, from an office in Schnull's building, by Harding & Henry: George C. Harding, the former noted war correspondent of the Cincinnati Commercial, and the local editor of the Journal and of the Sentinel, at subsequent periods, being editor. It was published on Sunday for a short time, but the Sentinel beginning the issue of a Sunday paper, the publication day of the Mirror was changed to Saturday. J. R. Morton subsequently bought Henry's interest, the office was removed to Tilford's building, on Circle street, and the paper is now issued by Harding & Morton, with G. C. Harding and W. B. Vicker, as editors. It has been much enlarged, is well conducted, and has steadily advanced in public favor.

The commissioners in the original survey made no provision for a public park, and with the exception of the squares or parts of squares, reserved for State, County, Hospital, University and Market purposes, no public square was designated. So long as the town was openly built, and the wide streets properly shaded, the want of public grounds was unfelt, but in recent years, with the crowding of population and the paving of the streets, the increased noise, dust and heat, drew attention to a want formerly unconsidered. The city took possession of the Circle, University square, and military grounds, in 1860, and since that date has expended considerable sums in the improvement and planting of each as public grounds, but the limited area afforded by these tracts will not supply the future demand for a properly constructed and ornamented park. To supply in some measure this public want, and as a memorial of Calvin Fletcher, Sr., the heirs of that gentleman, in the spring of 1868, offered to donate thirty acres in a triangular form, adjoining the Bellefontaine railway at the north-east corner of the city, for a public park; the city in case of acceptance, to expend the sum of $30,000 on it in improvements within a given period. The offer was at first favorably considered by the council, but unexpected opposition arose, partly on account of the location, partly on account of the expenditure to be incurred, and partly from the jealousy of the sections not thus favored. After long consideration, the city council coupled other conditions with the acceptance of the donation, and the offer was withdrawn. This result is to be regretted, for such tracts will ultimately be needed, not only in that neighborhood, but elsewhere, and they should be secured while the ground is comparatively cheap.

A brief statement of the facts connected with the formation of the leading libraries in the city may be given here. First in importance, both for the variety and number of volumes it contains, is the collection made by the State, now placed in the lower rooms of the State house. Its formation began shortly after the organization of the State government, though but little had been achieved until after the erection of the State house. The few books prior to that date had been kept in the Court house and Circle building. It has since gradually increased, by donations, exchanges and purchases, (a small appropriation being annually made for the purpose,) until it now numbers between twenty-five and thirty-thousand volumes. Many of these are in foreign languages, gifts from foreign governments. The library was at first used both for reference and circulation The State officers, legislators, judiciary, attorneys and professional men only being entitled to take books out, though any one could use them for reference at the library room The circulating feature was afterward abandoned, it being found that valuable sets were broken, and many books annually lost. The library is well supplied with works in the several departments, and contains some rare and valuable books. Though in better condition now than in former years, it has never been as well arranged and catalogued as it should be. The several rooms on the west side of the State house are now occupied by the library, and by the trophies and flags collected and returned by Indiana regiments in the Mexican war, and war of the rebellion. B. F. Foster, Gordon Tanner, S. D. Lyon. R. D. Brown, Nathaniel Bolton, John B. Dillon, John Cook and others, have been the librarians

The collection of books for the County library began shortly after the organization of the county, two per cent. of the lot-fund sales being set apart for that purpose, and though many of the original books have been lost or worn out, the library has slowly and constantly increased until it now numbers over two thousand volumes It has been located in the upper room of Court house for many years, and has been in charge of James A. Hamilton, John W. Hamilton, Calvin Taylor, John Caven and others, as librarians. Seventy-five cents fee per year is charged for the use of books, and the library, which is well selected and valuable, is largely patronized, but it deserves even more attention than it receives.

The township library, formerly kept in the upper rooms of the Court house, but more recently in the third story of Hereth's block, was formed under the law of 1852, providing for the formation of such collections, and levying taxes for their purchase and maintenance. It numbered about two thousand volumes of generally well selected works, but many of the volumes have since been lost and destroyed, and not over twelve or fourteen hundred are now retained. It is free to all readers, who can take out books if they choose, and is very well patronized.

The Indianapolis Library Society, the first private library association here, was formed in 1827, and collected by donation, subscription and purchase, a considerable number of good books, which were located the greater part of the time the organization existed, in the Circle building, and used by the members. Obed Foote, Sr., was the librarian. The greater part of the volumes were lost, and the rest divided, and the organization died after seven or eight years.

The next private library was collected by the Union Literary Society, formed in 1835, and existing till 1851. This collection consisted of several hundred books, for the use of the members, and after the death of the society, was handed over to the Young Men's Christian Association.

The Young Men's Christian Association formed in 1854, soon afterward began the collection of a library, receiving the books of the Union Literary Society, and adding thereto until about 1,500 volumes are now found in their rooms, under charge of Rev. Mr. Armstrong, librarian.

The Young Men's Library Association, formed in 1863, shortly thereafter established a reading room in the third story of Hubbard's block, gave annual courses of lectures, and began the formation of a library, which at present includes about two hundred volumes, mostly current magazine literature. The annual fee required of members is $5, entitling the holder to the use of the library and reading room, and attendance during the annual course of lectures. John Caven, has been president of the association since its origin.

The Ames Institute, a literary, lecture and library society, formed in 1860, has since accumulated a library of about five hundred volumes, now stored at the society room in Wesley Chapel. Carl Hamlin is president of the organization.

The writer has now briefly considered the leading events in the progress of the city from its first settlement to the present time. This consideration has shown that it has passed through four separate periods of development. The first began in the temporary reputation and prosperity enjoyed by the town when selected in 1820, as the seat of government. The location immediately drawing a relatively large population here, when the surrounding country was a complete wilderness. The slow development of a region so heavily timbered, the sickness among the early settlers, the delay in establishing the government here, and the want of communication with the outside world, put a stop to this speedy advance, and though the Capital was afterward removed here, very little improvement in the prospects of the town took place. The Internal Improvement scheme in 1836, began the second era, and for the time completely changed the aspect of affairs. Another sudden advance occurred. A marked increase in trade, in population, and in wealth, was visible, and the town was assuming an important rank, when the failure and suspension of the public works cut short its career. Its subsequent growth was very slow, being governed by the development of the surrounding territory, and it remained a country village of the better class, till October, 1847. The completion of the Madison railroad in that mouth and year, began the third era, giving the town an outlet, and making it a center for the surplus products of the surrounding region. From that time till the war of the rebellion, its growth was steady, rapid and solid, and the foundation gradually laid for its future trade, but it still remained subordinate to other business centers. The fourth period began with the war in 1861, the place being at first stopped in its development, but soon advancing with a rapidity astounding to those who had been educated only by their early experiences here, and who constantly predicted a downfall. The war growth, though so rapid, was a healthy one. It was the direct result of a large trade, and the fact that a greater scope of territory was made tributary to the city, and had manufacturing been largely commenced at the close of the war, no permanent cessation of the trade and growth of the place would have occurred. The four periods of development in the history of the city show that just as facilities for trade and travel have been increased, just so certain and constant has been its subsequent growth. Merchants and manufacturers should apply the lesson, and not only aid every effort to open new channels, but go before, and interest themselves in the trade and products of the region to be traversed by them. A great trading and manufacturing center may be created here by proper effort, and the destiny of the city rests directly in the hands now controlling its active business. On the merchants, bankers and manufacturers, rests the responsibility for its future growth or decadence and they can not escape it by waiting for

citizens of other sections to do that which so clearly devolves upon them.

This sketch is now ended. No apology is needed for the effort to write it, but one is due for the manner in which the task has been executed. When the writer consented to undertake it, he intended to give merely a general review of the progress of the city from its first settlement, (revising, correcting and extending an article he had prepared for the Directory of 1857,) and limiting the sketch to forty-eight pages. The material collected soon compelled an enlargement of the work, and finally much care was needed to prevent its expansion to a volume. All attempt at embellishment by personal sketches or anecdote, was abandoned, and the author's sole aim was to crowd the greatest number of facts, important or unimportant, into the fewest words, the object being to perpetuate matter that would soon be irrecoverably lost. To this cause must be ascribed the careless style, the paragraphic character of the contents, and the repetition of the same facts in different connections. Many of these repetitions were necessary, but others, especially in the last half of the work, arose from the fact that several compositors were constantly wanting "copy," and as fast as the manuscript was prepared, it went to the printer, and not being again seen by the writer, some repetitions unavoidably occurred. The collection of material and its preparation for the press, has been done at night, or in leisure moments, amid the press of other matters. It has involved much rapid and exhausting labor, and though errors have doubtless been committed, the author trusts he has recovered so much that was almost lost, that crudities in style and inaccuracies in statement will be forgiven.

The author would return his thanks to the old citizens who assisted him by their personal statement of facts, and especially to the heirs of the late Calvin Fletcher, for the use of the files of papers collected and left by that gentleman, from which, far more than from any other source, the facts were secured on which this article is founded.

IGNATIUS BROWN.

RAILWAY DEPARTMENT.

STATIONS AND DISTANCES FROM

INDIANAPOLIS, TO   MILES.

Moresville	16
Martinsville	31
Gosport	50
Spencer	—
Bloomfield	86
VINCENNES	131
EVANSVILLE	182

JEFFERSONVILLE, MADISON & INDIANAPOLIS R. R., offices east South, between Delaware and Pennsylvania, Passenger Depot at Union Depot. Horace Scott, General Superintendent; J. G. Whitcomb, General Agent.

STATIONS AND DISTANCES FROM

INDIANAPOLIS, TO   MILES.

Greenwood	10
Franklin	20
Edinburgh	30
Columbus Junction	40
Elizabethtown	48
Seymour	59
North Vernon	62
Crothersville	71
Vienna	82
MADISON	86
JEFFERSONVILLE	108
Louisville	110
Bowling Green	223
Nashville	294
Stevenson	417
CHATTANOOGA	445

TERRE HAUTE & INDIANAPOLIS R. R., offices south-west corner Louisiana and Tennessee, Passenger Depot at Union Depot. John E. Simpson, Asst. Superintendent.

STATIONS AND DISTANCES FROM

INDIANAPOLIS, TO   MILES.

Plainfield	13
Clayton	20
Greencastle	38
Brazil	56
Cleveland	62
TERRE HAUTE	73
Paris	92
Mattoon	129
Litchfield	207
Alton	247
ST. LOUIS	263

The Railroad interests of Indianapolis are equal to any other, this being, at present, one of the most important railroad centers in the Western States, compared with the population of its inhabitants, there being, as will be seen by a reference to the above and preceding and following pages, 9 distinct and separate railroads, and 3 more in process of completion, all leading in different directions to almost every conceivable point of the compass, from this city. There are also 14 lines of roads, either directly or indirectly leading to and from this city, by close and convenient connections, the cards of some of which may be found in the following pages, fully set forth, and it is designed to correct and increase this record from year to year. And all Railroad lines that desire to be identified or represented in these pages, can have space by sending the publishers copy, and conforming to our terms. See price list on first leaves of book; and any desiring to exchange, will notify the publishers of the fact, in advance of publication, each year. The following are a list of the through and fast freight lines and transportation companies having agencies in this city. The formation of these lines greatly facilitate the shipment of all classes of merchandise or produce of a heavy or sizable nature, as the majority of these lines own their own cars, which run through without reshipment.

FREIGHT LINES AND TRANSPORTATION COMPANIES.

ALLENTOWN LINE, Fast Freight, Samuel F. Gray, agent, office 85 Virginia avenue.

EMPIRE LINE, (Fast Freight,) W. S. Tarkington, agent, office 96 Virginia avenue.

ERIE TRANSPORTATION CO'S Fast Freight Line, ———, agent, office 94 Virginia avenue.

GREAT WESTERN DISPATCH, T. A. Lewis, agent, office 80 Virginia avenue.

MERCHANTS' DISPATCH, Fast Freight Line, office 19 Virginia avenue, D. Stevenson, agent.

PEOPLES' DISPATCH, Fast Freight Line, S. T. Scott, agent, office 44 east Washington.

STAR UNION LINE, Fast Freight, office 86 Virginia avenue, Samuel F. Gray, agent.

WHITE LINE FAST FREIGHT, office in Bellefontaine Depot, M. M. Landis, assistant superintendent.

GREAT WESTERN COTTON EXPRESS, Fast Freight Line, superintendent's office 80 Virginia avenue, T. A. Lewis, superintendent, W. B. Williams, agent.

NEW YORK CENTRAL

DOUBLE TRACK RAILROAD.

PASSENGERS CAN NOT BE DETAINED

By the New York Central Railroad, as there are

TEN DAILY EXPRESS TRAINS

LEAVING

BUFFALO AND NIAGARA FALLS

——FOR——

NEW YORK, BOSTON,

And all Points in New England.

Express Trains have New and Elegant "Red Line" Passenger Coaches and Luxurious Sleeping Cars, running over the New Hudson River Bridge at Albany,

WITHOUT TRANSFER OR FERRYING.

This is the only line running through and into the city of New York, landing passengers at Fourth and Ninth Avenues, Chambers Street, Canal Street, and Broadway Depots.

ASK FOR TICKETS VIA

NEW YORK CENTRAL RAILROAD,

And thereby secure the advantage of the Popular Passenger Route, its new and improved Equipments, its Smooth Track, Air Line and High Speed, passing through the Great Cities and Garden Districts of the Empire State, and in full view of Niagara Falls, the Great Suspension Bridge and Magnificent Scenery of the Mohawk and the Hudson, the River Rhine of America.

Passengers holding all Rail Tickets, can, at Albany, if they choose, take either the Night or Day line of Steamers on the Hudson, the accommodations and Splendor of which are not equaled in the old or new world.

THROUGH TICKETS AND BAGGAGE CHECKS

Can be had at all Principal Ticket offices and Depots in the West and South.

H. W. CHITTENDEN,
General Superintendent.   General Passenger Agent.

Cincinnati, Connersville

——AND——

INDIANAPOLIS JUNCTION

RAILROAD,

——VIA——

Rushville, Connersville, Oxford and Hamilton,

TO AND FROM CINCINNATI.

This Road will be COMPLETED FROM RUSHVILLE TO INDIANAPOLIS by the first of August, 1868, running

TWO PASSENGER TRAINS EACH WAY DAILY,

BETWEEN CINCINNATI AND INDIANAPOLIS,

Making all connections at both points, and also, via the Branch Road, from Connersville via Cambridge City to New Castle, Indiana, which will constitue it

THE GREAT CENTRAL ROUTE

From Cincinnati to the West and North-West,

Through the most desirable portion of Indiana, and on shorter time than any other route in the directions indicated.

J. H. SHELDON,	J. A. PERKINS,	J. M. RIDENOUR.
Superintendent, Hamilton, O.	Gen'l Freight and Passenger Agent.	Vice-President, Indianapolis.